Innovations and Developments of Swarm Intelligence Applications

Yuhui Shi
Xi'an Jiaotong-Liverpool University, China

Information Science
REFERENCE

Managing Director:	Lindsay Johnston
Senior Editorial Director:	Heather A. Probst
Book Production Manager:	Sean Woznicki
Development Manager:	Joel Gamon
Acquisitions Editor:	Erika Gallagher
Typesetter:	Nicole Sparano
Cover Design:	Nick Newcomer, Lisandro Gonzalez

Published in the United States of America by
Information Science Reference (an imprint of IGI Global)
701 E. Chocolate Avenue
Hershey PA 17033
Tel: 717-533-8845
Fax: 717-533-8661
E-mail: cust@igi-global.com
Web site: http://www.igi-global.com

Library of Congress Cataloging-in-Publication Data

Innovations and developments of swarm intelligence applications / Yuhui Shi, editor.
  p. cm.
 Includes bibliographical references and index.
  ISBN 978-1-4666-1592-2 (hardcover) -- ISBN 978-1-4666-1593-9 (ebook) -- ISBN 978-1-4666-1594-6 (print & perpetual access) 1. Swarm intelligence. I. Shi, Yuhui.
 Q337.3.I56 2012
 006.3--dc23
                    2012002108

British Cataloguing in Publication Data
A Cataloguing in Publication record for this book is available from the British Library.

The views expressed in this book are those of the authors, but not necessarily of the publisher.

Editorial Advisory Board

Table of Contents

Section 1
PSO Algorithms

Section 2
Other Algorithms

Detailed Table of Contents

Section 1
PSO Algorithms

Maurice Clerc, Independent Consultant, France

Currently, two very similar versions of PSO are available that could be called "standard". While it is easy to merge them, their common drawbacks still remain. Therefore, in this paper, the author goes beyond simple merging by suggesting simple yet robust changes and solving a few well-known, common problems, while retaining the classical structure. The results can be proposed to the "swarmer community" as a new standard.

William M. Spears, Swarmotics LLC, USA
Derek T. Green, University of Arizona, USA
Diana F. Spears, Swarmotics LLC, USA

The most common versions of particle swarm optimization (PSO) algorithms are rotationally variant. It has also been pointed out that PSO algorithms can concentrate particles along paths parallel to the coordinate axes. In this paper, the authors explicitly connect these two observations by showing that the rotational variance is related to the concentration along lines parallel to the coordinate axes. Based on this explicit connection, the authors create fitness functions that are easy or hard for PSO to solve, depending on the rotation of the function.

T. O. Ting, HKUSpace Global College, China

H. C. Ting, Tunku Abdul Rahman College, Malaysia

T. S. Lee, Multimedia University, Malaysia

In this work, a hybrid Taguchi-Particle Swarm Optimization (TPSO) is proposed to solve global numerical optimization problems with continuous and discrete variables. This hybrid algorithm combines the well-known Particle Swarm Optimization Algorithm with the established Taguchi method, which has been an important tool for robust design. This paper presents the improvements obtained despite the simplicity of the hybridization process. The Taguchi method is run only once in every PSO iteration and therefore does not give significant impact in terms of computational cost. The method creates a more diversified population, which also contributes to the success of avoiding premature convergence. The proposed method is effectively applied to solve 13 benchmark problems. This study's results show drastic improvements in comparison with the standard PSO algorithm involving continuous and discrete variables on high dimensional benchmark functions.

Wen Fung Leong, Oklahoma State University, USA

Gary G. Yen, Oklahoma State University, USA

In this article, the authors propose a particle swarm optimization (PSO) for constrained optimization. The proposed PSO adopts a multiobjective approach to constraint handling. Procedures to update the feasible and infeasible personal best are designed to encourage finding feasible regions and convergence toward the Pareto front. In addition, the infeasible nondominated solutions are stored in the global best archive to exploit the hidden information for guiding the particles toward feasible regions. Furthermore, the number of feasible personal best in the personal best memory and the scalar constraint violations of personal best and global best are used to adapt the acceleration constants in the PSO flight equations. The purpose is to find more feasible particles and search for better solutions during the process. The mutation procedure is applied to encourage global and fine-tune local searches. The simulation results indicate that the proposed constrained PSO is highly competitive, achieving promising performance.

Gomaa Zaki El-Far, Menoufia University, Egypt

This paper proposes a modified particle swarm optimization algorithm (MPSO) to design adaptive neuro-fuzzy controller parameters for controlling the behavior of non-linear dynamical systems. The modification of the proposed algorithm includes adding adaptive weights to the swarm optimization algorithm, which introduces a new update. The proposed MPSO algorithm uses a minimum velocity threshold to control the velocity of the particles, avoids clustering of the particles, and maintains the diversity of the population in the search space. The mechanism of MPSO has better potential to explore good solutions in new search spaces. The proposed MPSO algorithm is also used to tune and optimize the controller parameters like the scaling factors, the membership functions, and the rule base. To illustrate the adaptation process, the proposed neuro-fuzzy controller based on MPSO algorithm is applied successfully to control the behavior of both non-linear single machine power systems and non-linear inverted pendulum systems. Simulation results demonstrate that the adaptive neuro-fuzzy logic controller application based on MPSO can effectively and robustly enhance the damping of oscillations.

Xiangyin Zhang, Beijing University of Aeronautics and Astronautics, China
Haibin Duan, Beijing University of Aeronautics and Astronautics, China
Shan Shao, Shenyang Aircraft Design and Research Institute, China
Yunhui Wang, Shenyang Aircraft Design and Research Institute, China

Close formation flight is one of the most complicated problems on multiple Uninhabited Aerial Vehicles (UAVs) coordinated control. This paper proposes a new method to achieve close formation tracking control of multiple UAVs by applying Particle Swarm Optimization (PSO) based Proportional plus Integral (PI) controller. Due to its simple structure and effectiveness, multi-criteria PI control strategy is employed to design the controller for multiple UAVs formation, while PSO is used to optimize the controller parameters on-line. With the inclusion of overshoot, rise time, and system accumulated absolute error in the multi-criteria performance index, the overall performance of multi-criteria PI controller is optimized to be satisfactory. Simulation results show the feasibility and effectiveness of the proposed approach.

M. A. Abido, King Fahd University of Petroleum & Minerals, Saudi Arabia
Saleh M. Bamasak, Saudi Electricity Company, Saudi Arabia

This paper investigates the enhancement of power system stability via coordinated design of Power System Stabilizers (PSSs), Thyristor Controlled Series Capacitor (TCSC)-based stabilizer, and Static Var Compensator (SVC)-based stabilizer in a multi-machine power system. The design problem of the proposed stabilizers is formulated as an optimization problem. Using the developed linearized power system model, the particle swarm optimization (PSO) algorithm is employed to search for optimal stabilizer settings that maximize the minimum damping ratio of all system oscillating modes. The proposed stabilizers are evaluated on a two-area weakly-connected multi-machine power system with unstable interarea oscillation mode. The nonlinear simulation results and eigenvalue analysis show the effectiveness of the proposed coordinated stabilizers in damping low frequency power system oscillations and enhancing the system stability.

Anil Kumar Ramakuru, IIT MADRAS, India
Siva G. Kumar, IIT MADRAS, India
Kalyan B. Kumar, IIT MADRAS, India
Mahesh K. Mishra, IIT MADRAS, India

Dynamic Voltage Restorer (DVR) restores the distribution system load voltage to a nominal balanced sinusoidal voltage, when the source voltage has distortions, sag/swell and unbalances. DVR has to inject a required amount of Volt-Amperes (VA) into the system to maintain a nominal balanced sinusoidal voltage at the load. Keeping the cost effectiveness of DVR, it is desirable to have a minimum VA rating of the DVR, for a given system without compromising compensation capability. In this regard, a methodology has been proposed in this work to minimize VA rating of DVR. The optimal angle at which DVR voltage has to be injected in series to the line impedance so as to have minimum VA loading on DVR as well as the removal of phase jumps in the three-phases is computed by the Particle Swarm Optimization (PSO) technique. The proposed method is able to compensate voltage sags with phase jumps by keeping the DVR voltage and power ratings minimum, effectively. The proposed PSO methodology together with adaptive neuro–fuzzy inference system used to make the DVR work online with minimum VA loading. The proposed method has been validated through detailed simulation studies.

    P. K. Roy, National Institute of Technology
    S. P. Ghoshal, National Institute of Technology
    S. S. Thakur, National Institute of Technology

This paper presents two new Particle swarm optimization methods to solve optimal power flow (OPF) in power system incorporating flexible AC transmission systems (FACTS). Two types of FACTS devices, thyristor-controlled series capacitor (TCSC) and thyristor controlled phase shifting (TCPS), are considered. In this paper, the problems of OPF with FACTS are solved by using particle swarm optimization with the inertia weight approach (PSOIWA), real coded genetic algorithm (RGA), craziness based particle swarm optimization (CRPSO), and turbulent crazy particle swarm optimization (TRPSO). The proposed methods are implemented on modified IEEE 30-bus system for four different cases. The simulation results show better solution quality and computation efficiency of TRPSO and CRPSO algorithms over PSOIWA and RGA. The study also shows that FACTS devices are capable of providing an economically attractive solution to OPF problems.

    Sujatha Balaraman, Government College of Engineering, India
    N. Kamaraj, Thiagarajar College of Engineering, India

This paper proposes the Hybrid Particle Swarm Optimization (HPSO) method for solving congestion management problems in a pool based electricity market. Congestion may occur due to lack of coordination between generation and transmission utilities or as a result of unexpected contingencies. In the proposed method, the control strategies to limit line loading to the security limits are by means of minimum adjustments in generations from the initial market clearing values. Embedding Evolutionary Programming (EP) technique in Particle Swarm Optimization (PSO) algorithm improves the global searching capability of PSO and also prevents the premature convergence in local minima. A number of functional operating constraints, such as branch flow limits and load bus voltage magnitude limits are included as penalties in the fitness function. Numerical results on three test systems namely modified IEEE 14 Bus, IEEE 30 Bus and IEEE 118 Bus systems are presented and the results are compared with PSO and EP approaches in order to demonstrate its performance.

    Ying Tan, Peking University, China

Compared to conventional PSO algorithm, particle swarm optimization algorithms inspired by immunity-clonal strategies are presented for their rapid convergence, easy implementation and ability of optimization. A novel PSO algorithm, clonal particle swarm optimization (CPSO) algorithm, is proposed based on clonal principle in natural immune system. By cloning the best individual of successive generations, the CPSO enlarges the area near the promising candidate solution and accelerates the evolution of the swarm, leading to better optimization capability and faster convergence performance than conventional PSO. As a variant, an advance-and-retreat strategy is incorporated to find the nearby minima in an enlarged solution space for greatly accelerating the CPSO before the next clonal operation. A black hole model is also established for easy implementation and good performance. Detailed descriptions of the CPSO algorithm and its variants are elaborated. Extensive experiments on 15 benchmark test functions demonstrate that the proposed CPSO algorithms speedup the evolution procedure and improve the global optimization performance. Finally, an application of the proposed PSO algorithms to spam detection is provided in comparison with the other three methods.

Section 2
Other Algorithms

Chapter 12

K. Vaisakh, Andhra University, India

L. R. Srinivas, S.R.K.R. Engineering College, India

Ant Colony Optimization is more suitable for combinatorial optimization problems. ACO is successfully applied to the traveling salesman problem, and multistage decision making of ACO has an edge over other conventional methods. In this paper, the authors propose the Evolving Ant Colony Optimization (EACO) method for solving unit commitment (UC) problem. The EACO employs Genetic Algorithm (GA) for finding optimal set of ACO parameters, while ACO solves the UC problem. Problem formulation takes into consideration the minimum up and down time constraints, start up cost, spinning reserve, and generation limit constraints. The feasibility of the proposed approach is demonstrated on the systems with number of generating units in the range of 10 to 60. The test results are encouraging and compared with those obtained by other methods.

Chapter 13

Kevin M. Passino, The Ohio State University, USA

The bacterial foraging optimization (BFO) algorithm mimics how bacteria forage over a landscape of nutrients to perform parallel nongradient optimization. In this article, the author provides a tutorial on BFO, including an overview of the biology of bacterial foraging and the pseudo-code that models this process. The algorithms features are briefly compared to those in genetic algorithms, other bio-inspired methods, and nongradient optimization. The applications and future directions of BFO are also presented.

Chapter 14

Robert G. Reynolds, Wayne State University, USA

Leonard Kinniard-Heether, Wayne State University, USA

This article describes a socially motivated evolutionary algorithm, Cultural Algorithms, to design a controller for a 3D racing game for use in a competitive event held at the 2008 IEEE World Congress. The controller was modeled as a state machine and a set of utility functions were associated with actions performed in each state. Cultural Algorithms are used to optimize these functions. Cultural Algorithms consist of a Population Space, a collection of knowledge sources in the Belief Space, and a communication protocol connecting the components together. The knowledge sources in the belief space vie to control individuals in the population through the social fabric influence function. Here the population is a network of chromosomes connected by the LBest topology. This LBest configuration was employed to train the system on an example oval track prior to the contest, but it did not generalize to other tracks. The authors investigated how other topologies performed when learning on each of the contest tracks. The square network (a type of small world network) worked best at distributing the influence of the knowledge sources, and reduced the likelihood of premature convergence for complex tracks.

Chapter 15

A synthesis of findings from neuroscience, psychology, and behavioral biology has been recently used to show that several key features of cognition in neuron-based brains of vertebrates are also present in bee-based swarms of honey bees. Here, simulation tests are administered to the honey bee swarm cognition system to study its decision-making performance. First, tests are used to evaluate the ability of the swarm to discriminate between choice options and avoid picking inferior "distractor" options. Second, a "Treisman feature search test" from psychology, and tests of irrationality developed for humans, are administered to show that the swarm possesses some features of human decision-making performance. Evolutionary adaptation of swarm decision making is studied by administering swarm choice tests when there are variations on the parameters of the swarm's decision-making mechanisms. The key result is that in addition to trading off decision-making speed and accuracy, natural selection seems to have settled on parameters that result in individual bee-level assessment noise being effectively filtered out to not adversely affect swarm-level decision-making performance.

Chapter 16

This paper presents a novel theoretical framework for swarms of agents. Before deploying a swarm for a task, it is advantageous to predict whether a desired percentage of the swarm will succeed. The authors present a framework that uses a small group of expendable "scout" agents to predict the success probability of the entire swarm, thereby preventing many agent losses. The scouts apply one of two formulas to predict – the standard Bernoulli trials formula or the new Bayesian formula. For experimental evaluation, the framework is applied to simulated agents navigating around obstacles to reach a goal location. Extensive experimental results compare the mean-squared error of the predictions of both formulas with ground truth, under varying circumstances. Results indicate the accuracy and robustness of the Bayesian approach. The framework also yields an intriguing result, namely, that both formulas usually predict better in the presence of (Lennard-Jones) inter-agent forces than when their independence assumptions hold.

Chapter 17
Distributed Multi-Agent Systems for a Collective Construction Task based on
Virtual Swarm Intelligence 308

Yan Meng, Stevens Institute of Technology, USA
Yaochu Jin, University of Surrey, UK

In this paper, a virtual swarm intelligence (VSI)-based algorithm is proposed to coordinate a distributed multi-robot system for a collective construction task. Three phases are involved in a construction task: search, detect, and carry. Initially, robots are randomly located within a bounded area and start random search for building blocks. Once the building blocks are detected, agents need to share the information with their local neighbors. A distributed virtual pheromone-trail (DVP) based model is proposed for local communication among agents. If multiple building blocks are detected in a local area, agents need to make decisions on which agent(s) should carry which block(s). To this end, a virtual particle swarm optimization (V-PSO)-based model is developed for multi-agent behavior coordination. Furthermore, a quorum sensing (QS)-based model is employed to balance the tradeoff between exploitation and exploration, so that an optimal overall performance can be achieved. Extensive simulation results on a collective construction task have demonstrated the efficiency and robustness of the proposed VSI-based framework.

Preface

Swarm intelligence is a collection of nature-inspired optimization algorithms. Each swarm intelligence algorithm is a population-based stochastic optimization algorithm even though each has a different inspiration and/or motivation. Usually each individual in a population represents a potential solution, which may be a good or bad solution, to the problem to be solved. The purpose of a swarm intelligence algorithm is to iteratively update the population of individuals toward better and better solution areas iteration over iteration with high probability. Each different swarm intelligence algorithm has a different updating mechanism. For example, for the Particle Swarm Optimization (PSO) algorithm, the updating mechanism is to "fly" the individuals (called particles in PSO) toward better and better solution areas. Therefore its updating mechanism is to update particles' velocities dynamically according to each particle's historical flying experience and its companion's flying experience. There are many other swarm intelligence algorithms that have been reported in the literature, which include the ant colony optimization algorithm, artificial immune system, bacterial forging optimization algorithm, bee colony optimization algorithm, brain storm optimization algorithm, firefly optimization algorithm, firework optimization algorithm, fish school search optimization algorithm, intelligent water drops algorithm, and the shuffled frog-leaping algorithm, to name just a few. Compared with traditional search algorithms, swarm intelligence algorithms are less sensitive to the initial starting search points, have more capability to jump out of local minima, are suitable for wider range of optimization problems, and only require that any potential solution can be evaluated.

Even though most swarm intelligence algorithms are designed to solve unconstrained single objective optimization problems, swarm intelligence algorithms have been successfully modified and extended to solve all kind of optimization problems which include constrained single objective optimization problems, multi-objective optimization problems, constrained multi-objective optimization problems, combinatorial optimization problems, scheduling problems, etc. For the constrained optimization problems, there are several commonly used approaches to solve them using swarm intelligence algorithms such as penalty function approach which adds constraint violations into the objective function as a penalty, special encoding approach which generates only feasible solutions by designing special encoding method and/or special operators, repair approach which repairs each generated infeasible solution to be a feasible, separation of constraints and objective approach which evaluates objective function by taking consideration of constraints simultaneously, and multi-objective optimization approaches which convert a constrained optimization problem into a bi-objective or multi-objective optimization problem. For the multi-objective optimization problems, there are several commonly used approaches to solve them using swarm intelligence algorithms such as aggregating approaches which combine all objectives into a single objective, Lexicographic ordering approaches which rank the objectives in order of importance and optimize each objective independently, sub-population approaches which use a different sub-population to optimize a different objective, and Pareto-based approaches which use the concept of non-dominated solutions to find optimal solutions along the Pareto front. Among them, the Pareto-based approaches are the most commonly used approaches to solve multi-objective optimization problems using swarm intelligence algorithms.

For complicated nonlinear optimization problems to effectively and efficiently solve optimization problems, an optimization algorithm needs to possess the capability to either converge or diverge and whether to converge or diverge depends on the search state the search process is currently in. One way to solve optimization problems efficiently and effectively is to use a right algorithm with a right parameter set at the right search state. Each algorithm with a different set of parameters will perform differently and therefore will be better suitable for one kind of problem or for one search state among all different search states during the whole search process. For example, under some conditions, an optimization algorithm is preferred to have the global search capability or exploration capability, and under some other conditions, it is preferred to have the local search capability or exploitation capability. For the above purposes, studies on adaptation of swarm intelligence algorithms have been reported in the literature. For example, the adaptation of neighborhood structures or the adaptation of parameters of particle swarm optimization algorithms has kept being an active and hot research topic. Another research trend with this regard is to employ different optimization algorithms with different scales of learning capability. For example, one optimization algorithm is utilized for long-term learning, that is to learn the learning capability; another optimization algorithm is utilized for short-term learning, that is to learn the content that is required to be learnt in order to solve the optimization problem efficiently and effectively. One good example of researches on this kind of different scales of learning capability is the current research interests on memetic algorithms.

One of the challenging tasks for swarm intelligence algorithms is to solve large scale optimization problems, that is, the dimension of the problem is large, say larger than 1000. There are two kind of large scale problems. One is the kind of separable problems and the other is the kind of un-separable problems. For a separable large scale problem, its objective function value has contribution from each variable independently. Therefore, the large scale problem can be divided into several small or medium scale problems each of which will then be solved by a swarm intelligence algorithm independently. For an un-separable problem, each variable does not contribute to the problem's objective function independently, but as a whole, therefore, an un-separable problem in principle cannot be directly divided into several smaller problems as that do for separable problems. A simple and straightforward method to solve a large scale un-separable optimization problem using swarm intelligence algorithm is to transform the original un-separable optimization problem to be a new separable problem which then can be divided into several smaller problems for a swarm intelligence algorithm to solve. Certainly, such transformation may not always be possible, or even possible, it may not be easy to find the right transformation. These problems are considered as true large scale problems. For a true large scale problem, one way to solve it is to divide it into several smaller problems randomly or predeterminatively. For each smaller problem, a small number of variables will be optimized by a swarm intelligence algorithm while other remaining variables are kept to be constants which are previously determined by solving other smaller problems using swarm intelligence algorithms. All the smaller problems will be solved iteratively in the hope that the process will converge to one single solution that is good enough to the original large scale problem. There are usually overlaps of variables among all smaller problems. Another way to solve an un-separable problem is to treat the problem as a whole. In this way, the priority of the problem solving is to reduce computation cost, especially the number of function evaluations because it is the function evaluation that contributes the most to the computation cost and to the difficulty of solving a large scale problem. Therefore, it is critical to take advantage of existing knowledge such as the domain knowledge and knowledge that can be revealed by the search process itself at the risk of premature convergence. One kind of knowledge that can be revealed by the search process is the population diversity. For example, for particle swarm optimization algorithms, there are several definitions of population diversities which include position diversity, velocity diversity, and cognitive (*pbest*) diversity.

Swarm intelligence algorithms are good at solving complicated problems which can be represented as nonlinear, non-differentiable, and un-continuous functions. They have been successfully applied to solve a lot of real-world applications which cover almost all areas where there are things to be optimized. Actually, it is the successful real-world applications that are the sources of vitality for the swarm intelligence algorithms. Without good applications, the research on swarm intelligence algorithms will eventually lose its vitality. Therefore, one important and critical research direction on swarm intelligence is to find more and successful real-world applications.

WHAT IS THE BOOK ABOUT?

This book volume is about current researches on swarm intelligence algorithms and their applications. It does not intend to cover all aspects of researches on swarm intelligence algorithms. It actually is a collection of papers which were published in the 2010 issues of the *International Journal of Swarm Intelligence Research*. It can be looked as a snapshot of current research trend on swarm intelligence. This book is intended for researchers who have been working on or are interested in the research areas of swarm intelligence. It can also be used as a reference book for graduate students and senior undergraduate students who are interested in conducting their studies on swarm intelligence algorithms and/or their applications.

ORGANIZATION OF THE BOOK

This book volume consists of 17 chapters, which are organized into two sections for the convenience of reference. Section 1 includes 11 chapters, which are about current research works on particle swarm optimization algorithms and their application.

In the chapter, "*Beyond Standard Particle Swarm Optimization*," Clerc discussed Standard Particle Swarm Optimization (SPSO) algorithms. There are two versions of so-called standard particle swarm optimization algorithms, which are SPSO-2007 and SPSO-BK. The two versions are similar to each other. The similarities and differences of the two versions are discussed with regards to the following aspects: parameters settings, swarm size, initialization of the positions and velocities, confinement methods which are used to confine positions which are either too large or too small, and neighborhood topologies. Clerc further presented a formula to calculate the probabilities for a particle to be informed about the best particle's position for both SPSO-2007 and SPSO-BK, respectively. If the probability is low, the particle has more freedom to explore before it is impacted by the best particle's position. The probability may help to determine that a stagnation has occurred if the PSO has not improved its performance after a certain number of generations that any particle has been informed with probability one.

Furthermore, there are several common criticisms about SPSOs which are a PSO can easily get trapped into a local minimum, premature convergence may happen even with better topologies, the swarm size is constant, and it is sensitive to rotations of the landscape. The two versions of standard PSOs can be easily merged, but obviously with the same common drawbacks as those in the two SPSOs. Therefore, Clerc goes beyond a simple merging but suggests simple but robust changes to help PSO to escape from local minima, to have a global convergence, to have a variable swam size, and to rotate insensitively, which may be proposed to be a new flexible standard for particle swarm optimization algorithms.

In the chapter, "*Biases in Particle Swarm Optimization,*" Spears *et al.* discussed biases embedded in particle swarm optimization algorithms. According to the No Free Lunch Theorem, an algorithm cannot be the best for all optimization problems, but can be the best for the optimization algorithms which are aligned with the algorithm. By considering the problem and algorithm as two vectors, the problem is aligned with the algorithm when their dot product is zero, i.e. the algorithm is well matched to the problem. In the chapter, Spears *et al.* showed that PSOs with commonly used particles updating equations are rotationally variant and can concentrate particles along paths parallel to the coordinate axes. The rotational variance is closely related to the coordinate axes bias. Spears *et al.* showed that the connection between rotational variance and coordinate axes bias is not the effect of population size, problem dimension, and PSO parameters settings. Based on this explicit connection, Spears *et al.* further created fitness function landscapes that are easy or hard for PSO to solve, depending on the rotational angle of the function landscapes. The intention of the authors is to ask users of PSOs to be aware of the bias including its cause and its effect, but not to discourage users from using PSOs.

In the chapter, "*Taguchi-Particle Swarm Optimization for Numerical Optimization,*" Ting *et al.* applied Taguchi method to particle swarm optimization algorithms. The Taguchi method is an important tool for robust design. In the Chapter, Ting *et al.* proposed a hybrid Taguchi-Particle Swarm Optimization (TPSO) which combines the particle swarm optimization algorithm with the Taguchi method. The common drawback of hybrid algorithm is the extra algorithm complexity and therefore extra computational cost. To overcome this, in each generation of the proposed TPSO, the Taguchi method is run only once after conventional PSO particles' updates, therefore it does not add in too much algorithm complexity and computational cost. The Taguchi method utilizes the two-level orthogonal array and the Signal-to-Noise Ratio (SNR). With the Taguchi method and according to the two-level orthogonal array, a new particle is generated by selecting better dimensional values from two *bpest* particles which are randomly chosen. The effect of applying the Taguchi method is to create more diverse population to avoid premature convergence and to help particles to jump out of local minima, which are not good enough solutions.

In the chapter, "*Constraint Handling in Particle Swarm Optimization,*" Leong and Yen proposed to apply the multi-objective optimization method to handle constraints in optimization problems with constraints. Leong and Yen first transform constrained optimization problems into unconstrained bi-objective optimization problems, in which one objective is the original objective function and the other objective is the sum of all the constraint violations. The advantage of utilizing this strategy to solve constrained optimization problems is that it needs neither penalty function nor the selection proportion balance between feasible solutions and infeasible solutions. The transformed bi-objective optimization problems are then solved by applying Pareto-based Multi-Objective Particle Swarm Optimization algorithm (MOPSO). This differs from other Pareto-based optimization algorithms where a group of solutions (Pareto-front) are required to be obtained; here only the global optimum, which is feasible, is required to be obtained by the Pareto-based MOPSO. In the implementation of MOPSO, personal best particles are updated by giving preference to feasible solutions over infeasible solutions, to nondominated solutions over dominated solutions, so that the MOPSO can have higher possibility to find feasible solutions towards true Pareto front fast; the global best archive is updated to store only the best feasible solutions found so far and the infeasible non-dominated solutions with less constraint violation hidden information which can be exploited to guide search towards feasible solutions. Furthermore, mutation with nonlinear dynamic ranges is applied to personal and global best to facilitate the global search in early stage and local search in late stage.

In the chapter, "*Adaptive Neuro-Fuzzy Control Approach Based on Particle Swarm Optimization*," Ei-Far used a minimum velocity checking in addition to the maximum velocity checking in the velocity update in the proposed particle swarm optimization algorithm. The velocity is updated with specifically designed formula when it is below the predefined minimum velocity threshold. The purpose of the minimum velocity threshold is to keep particles to continue flying until the algorithm is terminated. Generally speaking, a large minimum velocity threshold facilitates a global search while a small minimum velocity threshold facilitates a local search. The balance between exploration and exploitation could be achieved if the minimum velocity threshold could be dynamically adjusted based on the search information revealed by the search process. When applying the proposed particle swarm optimization algorithm to solve constrained optimization problems, if a particle violates constraints, its velocity update is further modified by removing the contribution from the current velocity, that is, the velocity completely depends on only self-cognition part and social-cognition part. The proposed particle swarm optimization is applied to tune and optimize a neuro-fuzzy controller's parameters such as scaling factors, membership functions, and rule base. The designed neuro-fuzzy controller is applied to control a nonlinear single machine power system and a nonlinear inverted pendulum system, respectively.

In the chapter, "*Design of Multi-Criteria PI Controller Using Particle Swarm Optimization for Multiple UAVs Close Formation*," Zhang *et al.* discussed the issue of applying a particle swarm optimization algorithm to design a PI controller to control the close formation of multiple Uninhabited Aerial Vehicles (UAVs). The automatic cooperative control of a group of UAVs flying in close formation is a very active and hot research topic. Many researches have been conducted by utilizing many classic and modern control approaches such as Proportional plus Integral (PI) control, nonlinear adaptive control, robust control, *etc*. These approaches usually only consider one single performance index and can achieve good characteristic in frequency-domain, but not in time-domain. In this chapter, Zhang *et al.* employed a particle swarm optimization algorithm to design PI controller online. By taking consideration of overshoot, rise time, and system accumulated absolute error instead of a single performance index, the online designed PI controller can control the close formation flight of multiple UAVs with satisfaction.

In the chapter, "*Oscillation Damping Enhancement via Coordinated Design of PSS and FACTS-Based Stabilizers in a Multi-Machine Power System Using PSO*," Abido and Bamasak presented a method of applying the Particle Swarm Optimization (PSO) algorithm to design stabilizers in a multi-machine power system. Because disturbances may cause power systems to experience low frequency oscillations which may sustain and grow to cause system separation if no adequate damping is available, in this chapter Abido and Bamasak utilized the PSO algorithm to design a stabilizer to damp power system oscillation and increase system oscillation stability in a multi-machine power system. The stabilizer is designed by considering together the Power System Stabilizers (PSSs), Thyristor Controlled Series Capacitor (TCSC)-based stabilizer, and Static Var Compensator (SVC)-based stabilizer in the multi-machine power system. The design of the stabilizer is formulated as an optimization problem so that the PSO algorithm can be utilized to optimize the stabilizer parameter settings to maximize the minimum damping ratio under all system oscillating modes. The designed stabilizer is further tested on a two-area weakly-connected multi-machine power system with unstable inter-area oscillation mode to illustrate the effectiveness of the designed stabilizer.

In the chapter, "*Compensation of Voltage Sags with Phase-Jumps through DVR with Minimum VA rating Using PSO Based ANFIS Controller,*" Ramakuru *et al.* used Particle Swarm Optimization (PSO) algorithm based Adaptive Neuro–Fuzzy Inference System (ANFIS) to implement a Dynamic Voltage Restorer (DVR) with minimum Volt-Amperes (VA) rating. A DVR is a power electronic device, which protects loads from typical voltage problems such as phase-angle jump and load switching on and off in a distribution system. It is a series connected custom power device to mitigate the voltage sags with phase jumps. A DVR injects required amount of VA into the distribution system to compensate the voltage sag/swell with phase jumps. To be cost effective, a DVR requires to have a minimum VA rating for a given distribution system without compromising compensation capability. In this chapter, Ramakuru *et al.* utilized a PSO algorithm to obtain an optimal angle to inject DVR voltage in series to the line impedance to have minimum VA loading on DVR and to remove phase jumps in the three-phases. Furthermore, the designed DVR is implemented with an ANFIS to work online with minimum VA loading.

In the chapter, "*Optimal Power Flow with TCSC and TCPS Modeling using Craziness and Turbulent Crazy Particle Swarm Optimization,*" Roy *et al.* proposed two new versions of particle swarm optimization algorithms, i.e., Craziness Based Particle Swarm Optimization (CRPSO) and Turbulent Crazy Particle Swarm Optimization (TRPSO). In CRPSO, a predefined craziness probability is introduced to maintain the diversity of the directions of search to prevent premature convergence. In TRPSO, a minimum velocity threshold is utilized to control the velocity of particles to prevent premature convergence. The proposed two PSO algorithms are applied to solve Optimal Power Flow (OPF) in power system incorporating Flexible AC Transmission Systems (FACTS), which include Thyristor-Controlled Series Capacitor (TCSC) and Thyristor Controlled Phase Shifting (TCPS). The CRPSO and TRPSO are further compared with the Particle Swarm Optimization with Inertia Weight Approach (PSOIWA) and the Real Coded Genetic Algorithm (RGA) to illustrate their better performance.

In the chapter, "*Congestion Management Using Hybrid Particle Swarm Optimization Technique,*" Balaraman and Kamaraj proposed a Hybrid Particle Swarm Optimization (HPSO) algorithm. The HPSO combines an Evolutionary Programming (EP) algorithm and a Particle Swarm Optimization algorithm (PSO). In each generation of the HPSO, first, N individuals (particles) are generated according to the PSO updating equations where N is the population size; second, the EP is utilized to generate another N individuals; the 2N individuals are then sorted in ascending order according to their fitness values and the first half of the 2N individuals will survive and go through the PSO updating equation again to generate N individuals which will be copied into the next generation. The proposed HPSO is applied to solve congestion management problem in a pool based electricity market. Congestion in transmission lines is a challenging technical problem that has to be dealt with. The congestion management problem is modelled as a constrained optimization problem. The constraints are then added into the problem's objective function as a penalty function, which is based on the degrees of constraint violations, to form the fitness function for the HPSO.

In the chapter, "*Particle Swarm Optimization Algorithms Inspired by Immunity-Clonal Mechanism and Their Applications to Spam Detection,*" Tan proposed a Clonal Particle Swarm Optimization algorithm (CPSO) which combines the clonal principle in natural immune system and the Particle Swarm Optimization (PSO) algorithms. The cloning operator is employed to clone one particle into N copies in the solution space, then N new particles are generated via clonal mutation and selection processes. In CPSO, the cloning operator is applied to only the best individual in the population. To further improve the CPSO's performance, two strategies are introduced, which are the Advance-and-Retreat (AR) strategy and the Random Black Hole (RBH) strategy. With the AR strategy, the cloning operator is applied to the best individuals of several successive generations instead of only the best individual of the current generation which, as a consequence, can fine exploit the search area around promising candidate solutions, therefore improve the CPSO's search capability and convergence speed to perform better than the conventional PSO. In the RBH strategy, each dimension of a particle is considered independently. For each dimension in every generation, a particle is randomly generated to be close to the current best particle, which is regarded as a black hole for this dimension. Each dimension of each particle will be randomly assigned to be the black hole with small probability. The essence of the RBH strategy is to find other particles, which are close to the current best particle, which may happen to be the true best-fit position which has not been found by the algorithm so far. This mimics a black hole in physics, which has a huge quality (black hole). The proposed algorithm is further applied to spam detection. In this chapter, the Support Vector Machine (SVM) is utilized as a classifier for the purpose of spam detection. Basically, the SVM is to find an optimal hyper plane to have lowest classification errors. The software package LIBSVM is utilized for the implementation of the SVM for spam detection, in which there are four parameters that are required to be determined. The proposed algorithms are employed for the purpose of determining the four parameters.

Section 2 of the book includes 6 chapters, which cover various different swarm intelligence algorithms and their applications.

In the chapter, "*Unit Commitment by Evolving Ant Colony Optimization*," Vaisakh and Srinivas proposed an Evolving Ant Colony Optimization (EACO) algorithm for solving Unit Commitment (UC) problem. The objective of the Unit Commitment (UC) problem is to schedule generation units to minimize the overall cost of the power generation over the scheduled time while satisfying a set of constraints. UC problem is a nonlinear, combinatorial optimization problem which Ant Colony Optimization (ACO) algorithm is suitable for. The EACO combines Genetic Algorithm (GA) and ACO in which the ACO is utilized to solve UC problem and the GA is utilized to find an optimal set of parameters for the ACO algorithm.

In the chapter, "*Bacterial Foraging Optimization*," Passino described a parallel non-gradient optimization algorithm which is inspired by bacteria foraging process over a landscape of nutrients and which was introduced by him in 2002. He gave an insightful overview of biological foundation of bacteria foraging on which the Bacterial Foraging Optimization (BFO) algorithm was developed. In general, it is the flagella that makes bacteria swim. Bacteria swim toward high concentration of nutrients and swim away from high concentration of noxious substances. That is, bacteria will adapt to the environment that is beneficial to them and avoid the environment that is harmful to them. With the help of sensing and decision-making mechanisms, bacteria possess the capability of searching and avoidance in order to survive. With the operation of "conjugation," bacteria undergo mutation, but with very small probability. In a BFO, there are a population of bacteria or individuals x_i, ($i = 1, \dots n$), where n is the population size, x_i is the position of the ith bacterium (or individual). For a minimization problem f(x), the BFO finding the minimum is to find the position of the bacterium where its f(x) has minimum which corresponds to the place where the nutrient concentration is the highest. There are four operations in the BFO, which are chemotaxis, swarming, reproduction, and elimination/dispersal. The BFO has been further compared with Genetic Algorithm (GA). There are analogies between the BFO and GA. The bacteria reproduction in BFO is similar to the selection operation in GA; the bacteria elimination/dispersal in BFO is similar to the mutation in GA; the nutrient concentration function in BFO is similar to the fitness function in GA; the crossover operation in GA is similar to bacteria splitting which generally is ignored in BFO.

The chapter *"Networks Do Matter"* is an expansion of the authors' work which was submitted to a competitive event held at the 2008 IEEE World Congress. Reynolds and Kinnaird-Heether utilized cultural algorithms to design a controller which is modeled as a state machine. A cultural algorithm consists of a Population Space, a Belief Space, and a communication protocol. Population space is a network of components (population of chromosomes) each of which is evaluated based on the distance it travelled in each generation; Belief space consists of a collection of knowledge sources which are updated according to experience learned by the population of chromosomes; the communication protocol connects the components together with certain topology, e.g., LBest topology, GBest topology, or square topology, which is similar to the neighborhood concept in the particle swarm optimization algorithm. The state-of-the art open source TORCS system is utilized as the racing environment which supports multiple plug and play interfaces to controllers. The implemented controller is then plugged into the TORCS racing environment and is involved in a 3D racing game. During the race, the cultural algorithm is utilized to learn the social context to optimize the controller's state handler routines (or utility functions), which are used to handle the state which the controller is in or transfer the current state to another state when certain conditions are met. Simulation results illustrated that among the three topologies, the square topology worked the best.

In the chapter, *"Honey Bee Swarm Cognition: Decision-Making Performance and Adaptation,"* cognition in the honey bee swarm is discussed. Honey bee swarms possess several key features of cognition in neuron-based brains. In this chapter, Passino focused on analyzing honey bee swarm decision making performance and adaptation. He tested two basic properties of the swarm's choice process: discrimination and distraction. Discrimination is about the ability for honey bees to distinguish qualities of different nest sites; distraction is about the ability for honey bees to ignore nest sites with inferior quality. It was concluded that individual bee-level assessment noise could be effectively filtered out by natural selection and therefore does not adversely affect swarm-level decision-making performance. Simulation tests demonstrate that honey bee swarms do have a cognition process that possesses key features of neuron-based brains.

In the chapter, *"A Theoretical Framework for Estimating Swarm Success Probability Using Scouts,"* swarm risk assessment is discussed by using scout agents. It is natural for users to know with a certain level of confidence whether, at least, a portion of a swarm will successfully fulfill a task before the swarm is deployed to fulfill the task. If it can be known that the swarm will not be able to fulfill the task, the swarm should not be assigned to fulfill the task at the very beginning. Under the scenario that a swarm of agents needs to travel from an initial location to a goal location with the capability of avoiding obstacles, Rebguns *et al.* presented a novel theoretical framework for the swarm risk assessment, during which phase it can predict whether a desired percentage of the swarm will succeed in fulfilling the designated task before the swarm is deployed. With the risk information gained, it can then be decided to use which deployment strategy. For example, what is a good start location for the swarm, how to attain a desired success rate by deploying a swarm with a certain size, whether it is worth to take the risk to fulfill the task at hand or not. In the framework, among the swarm a relatively small group of agents is used as expendable "scout" agents to predict the success probability of the whole swarm during the risk assessment phase. The scouts apply the standard Bernoulli trials formula or a novel Bayesian formula proposed by the authors to predict. The experimental results demonstrated that both formulas usually predict better when there is the presence of (Lennard-Jones) inter-agent forces than when their independence assumptions hold.

In the chapter, "*Distributed Multi-Agent Systems for a Collective Construction Task based on Virtual Swarm Intelligence,*" a distributed multi-agent system is designed based on virtual swarm intelligence. Under dynamic environments, multi-agent systems should have the capability to create intelligent agents the behaviors of which should be able to adapt to changing environments and the skills of which should be able to improve over time. Meng and Jin proposed a Virtual Swarm Intelligence (VSI)-based algorithm to coordinate a distributed multi-robot system for a collective construction task. The Virtual Swarm Intelligence (VSI)-based algorithm consists of three parts, a Distributed Virtual Pheromone-trail (DVP) based model, a Virtual Particle Swarm Optimization (V-PSO)-based model, and a Quorum Sensing (QS)-based model. The DVP based model is developed for local communication to control the communication costs among the agents in a large-scale system to improve the efficiency of exploration; the Virtual Particle Swarm Optimization (V-PSO)-based model is developed to dynamically allocates agents to different blocks to improve the exploitation capability; the Quorum Sensing (QS)-based model is designed to allows the agents to achieve an optimal balance between exploration and exploitation.

Yuhui Shi
Xi'an Jiaotong-Liverpool University, China
December 30, 2011

Acknowledgment

I would like to thank the chapters' authors. It is them that make the book a reality. I would also like to take this opportunity to thank the National Natural Science Foundation of China and the Suzhou Science and Technology Bureau for their supports under Grant Number 60975080 and SYJG0919, respectively. Finally, I am grateful to the team at IGI Global Publishers who worked diligently with me throughout the process of editing and production. Working with Heather Probst, Jamie Wilson, and Jan Travers has been a pleasure and a learning experience.

Yuhui Shi
Xi'an Jiaotong-Liverpool University, China
December 30, 2011

Section 1
PSO Algorithms

Chapter 1
Beyond Standard Particle Swarm Optimisation

Maurice Clerc
Independent Consultant, France

ABSTRACT

Currently, two very similar versions of PSO are available that could be called "standard". While it is easy to merge them, their common drawbacks still remain. Therefore, in this paper, the author goes beyond simple merging by suggesting simple yet robust changes and solving a few well-known, common problems, while retaining the classical structure. The results can be proposed to the "swarmer community" as a new standard.

TWO FOR ONE

Standard Descriptions

A Standard PSO is now freely available on the Particle Swarm Central (PSC, 2010) since a few years. The current version is called Standard PSO 2007 (SPSO-2007 in short). The list of contributors is quite long as it also includes the "negative" contributions, i.e. work from people who have tested some possible variants, and found them to be not suitable for inclusion in a "standard" that should be both simple and robust.

The velocity update equation for one particle in SPSO-2007 is given by

$$v(t+1) = wv(t) + \tilde{c}_1\left(p(t) - x(t)\right) + \tilde{c}_2\left(g(t) - x(t)\right) \quad (1)$$

DOI: 10.4018/978-1-4666-1592-2.ch001

The notations in this equation are as usually found in papers about PSO, that is, t is the time step, v is the velocity vector (in fact the *displacement* vector), and x is the position. The positions and are respectively the best previous position of the particle, and the best previous position known by its neighbours (or *informants*) at time t. Also, this formula has to be applied independently for each dimension. $\tilde{c}_1$ (resp. $\tilde{c}_2$) is a random number drawn from the uniform distribution on $[0, c_1]$ (resp. $[0, c_2]$). The inertia weight is constant. The values of these three coefficients are derived analytically (Clerc, 2006b), and are

$$
\begin{cases}
\omega & = & \dfrac{1}{2\ln(2)} & \simeq & 0.72 \\
c_1 & = & \dfrac{1}{2} + \ln(2) & \simeq & 1.2 \\
c_2 & = & c_1
\end{cases}
\tag{2}
$$

These are slightly different from the ones used in SPSO 2006, which were derived using an older analysis (Clerc & Kennedy, 2002). The new position is given by

$$
x(t+1) = x(t) + v(t+1)
\tag{3}
$$

A typical example of a variant that is commonly used but is not included in this standard is the reduction of the weight w from w_{max} to w_{min} as a function (usually linear) of the time t (Shi & Eberhart, 1998). It does not mean that this method is bad. In fact, it is good for some problems, but is highly dependent on four parameters: w_{max}, w_{min}, the swarm size S, and the pre-defined maximum number of fitness evaluations FE_{max}. As the standard should be both simple and robust, and as this variant has too much dependence on too many parameters; it has not been retained in the standard.

Of course, SPSO-2007 also uses a swarm size, but it is not a parameter to be tuned. There, it is automatically computed by the formula

$$
S = 10 + 2\sqrt{D}
\tag{4}
$$

The initialisation of the positions is done at random (uniform distribution) inside the search space. The initialisation of the velocities is also done at random, by the "half-diff" method (see (Helwig & Wanka, 2008) for an analysis of various techniques). For each particle, it can be formulated as

$$
v(0) = 0.5\left(randomPosition - x(0)\right)
\tag{5}
$$

To control excessive movements of the particles, SPSO 2007 uses a confinement method: when a particle tends to leave the search space, the component of the position that is too big (resp. too small) is set to the maximum admissible value (resp. to the minimum acceptable value) and the corresponding velocity component is set to zero.

Finally, to complete the description of SPSO-2007, we have to define the communication network between the particles (the *topology*). It depends on a parameter K, set by default to 3. At the very beginning (initialisation), and after each unsuccessful iteration (i.e. if the current solution does not improve), each particle builds K information links at random, by using an uniform distribution over the whole swarm. Also, each particle informs itself. As a result, the number Y of informants of a given particle is given by a probability distribution

$$
prob(Y = n) = \binom{S-1}{n-1}\left(\frac{K}{S}\right)^{n-1}\left(1 - \frac{K}{S}\right)^{S-n}
\tag{6}
$$

Figure 1. Distribution of the number of informants in SPSO-2007 for a swarm size S=20. It may be any number between 1 and S, with a mean value slightly greater than K.

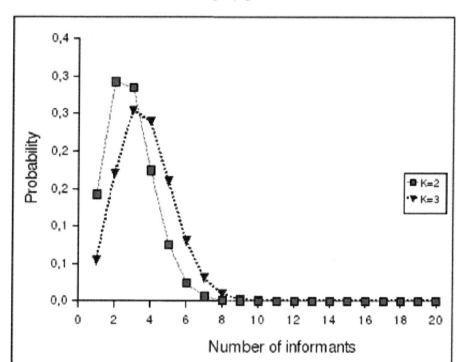

where $\begin{pmatrix} S-1 \\ n-1 \end{pmatrix}$ is the number of ways to choose $(S\text{-}1)$ elements amongst $(n\text{-}1)$. As we can see from Figure 1, the most probable number of informants is K, but any other value is possible.

Now, let us consider the proposed standard defined in (Bratton & Kennedy, 2007). We will call it SPSO-BK. What are the differences? Let us look at the coefficients first. The values are still the ones used in SPSO-2006, i.e. $w \simeq 0.73$, and $c_1 = c_2 = (\omega + 1)^2 / 2 \simeq 1.5$. So the difference for the coefficients is not significant.

Second, the swarm size is fixed at 50. However, this is just a compromise. In practice, for good performance, the swarm size is in fact a parameter that has to be tuned if the dimension of the problem is very different from the most commonly used in (Bratton & Kennedy, 2007), i.e. 30.

Third, there is no confinement. The approach taken here is to "let the particles fly", without re-evaluating the position of a particle that is outside the search space, for anyway it tends to get back sooner or later. This is indeed the simplest way, but the performance may be significantly worse than with a true confinement, particularly when the optimum lies near the search space boundary (Helwig & Wanka, 2007). Also, in some rare cases, the program may loop a very large number of times because the stopping criterion is the maximum number of fitness evaluations, which may be difficult to reach if there are too few re-evaluations.

Fourth, the initialisation method is different: it is done within a subspace of the entire feasible search space that does not contain the global optimum. However it is not really applicable in practice, for we are not supposed to know where the optimum is.

The fifth point, topology, is the most significant one. The authors propose the use of old classical fixed ring topology, in which each particle i (in $\{0,1,...,S\text{-}1\}$) is informed by the particles $(i+1)$ $mod\,S$ and $(i\text{-}1)\,mod\,S$ (and by itself). This method indeed often gives good results. However, it is less robust than a variable topology like the one used in SPSO-2007. Actually, it is interesting to compare the two topologies in terms of probability of being informed of the best position.

For simplicity, let us suppose that S is even and that the best known position is not modified over $S/2$ time steps. Now, let us choose a particle at random (uniform distribution). After t time steps it may or may not have been informed (directly or indirectly) about the best position. The probabilities of being informed are

$$\left[\begin{array}{l} \iota(S,t) = 1 - (1 - \dfrac{1}{S})^{Kt} \quad \text{for SPSO-2007} \\[2mm] \qquad\quad = \min(1, \dfrac{2t}{S}) \qquad \text{for SPSO-BK} \end{array}\right] \tag{7}$$

The lower the probability, the more "free" the particle is to explore without being too quickly attracted by the best position. Of course, the counterpart is that, for simple problems, the convergence, if any, can be slower. Note that formulae like (7) may help us to define a rule of thumb for detecting stagnation. We define a stagnation as follows: a stagnation occurs if there is still no improvement even though the probability of being informed about the best position is at least ι_0 for any particle. The corresponding number of iterations is then

$$\left[\begin{array}{l} t_{stag} = \dfrac{1}{K}\dfrac{\ln(1-\iota_0)}{\ln(1-\dfrac{1}{S})} \quad \text{for SPSO-2007} \\[4mm] \qquad\quad = \min(1, \iota_0\dfrac{S}{2}) \quad \text{for SPSO-BK} \end{array}\right] \tag{8}$$

Let us take an example from Figure 2. For $\iota_0 = 0.6$ we need to wait six or seven time steps for both SPSO-2007 ($K = 3$) and SPSO-BK, and nine time steps for SPSO-2007 ($K = 2$). Also, it can be derived from the formulae that the best similarity between the two curves is obtained for $S \simeq 30$, an empirical value that is often used.

From this point of view of information transmission, the ring topology is interesting, as after $S/2$ iterations, if there is still no improvement, stagnation is very probable. On the other hand, with this topology, the swarm may converge too quickly to a point that is not the optimum. So it is tempting to define a compromise between the two methods.

The Variable Ring Topology

The idea is very simple: we do use the ring topology, but after each unsuccessful iteration, the numbers that code the particle are randomly permuted[1]. In that case, the probability of being informed is at least[2]

$$i\left(S,t\right) = 1 - \left(1 - \frac{2}{S}\right)^t \tag{9}$$

We can compare this case with SPSO-2007 ($K = 2$). Writing the two formulae using their series expansions and comparing the first few terms, we see that the difference between them is of the order of $1/S^2$. In practice, it means that they are almost equivalent as soon as S is big enough (typically greater than 20). However, the difference is significant for $K = 3$, and also for small swarms. So it is probably worth applying this topology, at least for its robustness.

FOUR ISSUES ABOUT SPSO

As the two "standard PSO" discussed above are very similar, they exhibit more or less the same behaviours, and have similar weaknesses.

Figure 2. Probability of being informed about the best position, for S=20, assuming it does not change over 10 time steps

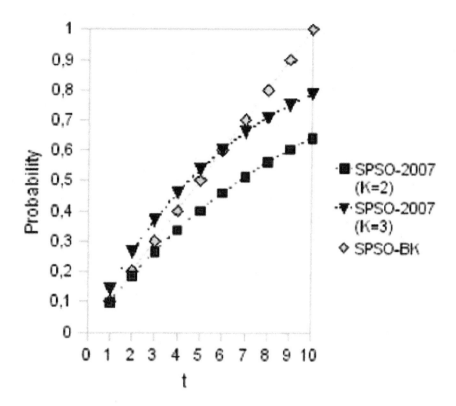

The most common criticism against SPSO is that it gets easily trapped into a local minimum. It is perfectly true for the so called "global best" version (gbest in short), which makes use of the "star" topology (each particle communicates with all the others). This topology is used in the old historical basic PSO, but as written by one of the inventors of the PSO method, James Kennedy (in 2006 on his Great Swarmy Speaks blog, unfortunately closed now):

and it might be time to mount a sword-swinging crusade against any use of the gbest topology. How did this happen? It is the worst way to do it, completely unnecessary. I will not tolerate anybody who uses that topology complaining about "premature convergence."

However, premature convergence may happen even with better topologies, like the ones we have seen above. It is due to the fact that SPSO[3] is not a globally convergent algorithm (Van den Bergh, 2002), which is the second known issue with SPSO. An iterative optimisation algorithm that has the global convergence property can find the optimum with probability 1,... provided you are patient enough. This is not true for SPSO. On the one hand, this is precisely why it is quick, but, on the other hand, it may converge to a point that is not even a local minimum, at least for some specifically designed problems (Langdon & Poli, 2005). As we will see, there are simple methods to solve this issue, but those are not robust enough to be included into a new "standard".

A third issue is that the swarm size is constant. In SPSO-2007, it is calculated as a function of the dimension by formula (4), but evidently it cannot be the "good" value for all problems. Moreover, being constant during the whole process is certainly just a compromise. Sometimes (for example at the beginning) it may be better to have a large number of particles, and sometimes (for example when the convergence becomes good) a small one.

Finally, we mention another point which is perhaps not as significant as the ones discussed above, but interesting nonetheless. SPSO is sensitive to rotations of the landscape (Hansen, Ros, Mauny, Schoenauer & Auger, 2008). This is usually not really an issue. Note that perfect insensitivity is not possible (and even often meaningless) except in very particular cases, but anyway this behaviour can also be easily modified. Actually, SPSO-2007 already includes an option to reduce this sensitivity.

DISCUSSIONS AND SOLUTIONS

Escaping Local Minima

The main difficulty when we want to design an algorithm that does not get trapped into a local minimum is defining precisely when it happens. More generally, how to guess when stagnation occurs? Some methods do not even try; instead, those just do something special from time to time, like a partial restart (Tindle, Tindle, Fletcher & Tann, 2002). Unfortunately, such "blind" approaches are not very effective, so the usual way is to use rules like "if there is still no improvement after k iterations...", or, "if the velocity becomes too small...". Such rules are more or less arbitrary, as they need at least one parameter to tune. However, because of equations like (8), it is not very difficult: we just have to define the probability.

A simple way is to re-initialise the current position of just one particle. Intuitively one feels that such a re-initialisation should be done on the worst particle, but in practice, which one is re-initialised is actually not important, for anyway the memory

of the best previous position is retained. So the particle could be chosen at random.

The re-initialisation itself can be done at random, or in a more clever way. The basic idea is to find the biggest "no-man's-land" area, and to put the particle on the middle of this area. There are sophisticated methods to find the largest unsearched area (for example by minimisation of a potential, like in Tribes (Clerc, 2003, 2006a; Cooren, Clerc & Siarry, 2009; Souad, Ruiz-Gazen & Tann, 2010), or by scatter search. However, we want something simple that might be added to a new standard PSO. Here is such a method[4], which is valid when the search space is a parallelepiped. Let $Z=(z_1,...,z_d,...,z_D)$ be the new position. The following process computes each z_d.

- For each dimension d, define the list of co-ordinates $(x_{min,d}, x_{1,d},...,x_{S,d}, x_{max,d})$
- Sort (in increasing order). The result is $(x_{min,d}, y_1,...,y_S, x_{max,d})$
- Find the biggest interval. It may be $[x_{min,d}, y_1]$ or $[y_S, x_{max,d}]$, or, for a given i, the interval $[y_{i,d}, y_{i+1,d}]$
- Choose z_d as the middle of this interval

As we can see from Figure 3, this method does not necessarily give the same result found by minimising a potential, but it is not too bad either, and has two advantages: it is simple, and consistent with the "spirit" of PSO, which considers each dimension independently.

After such a re-initialisation, the particle may maintain the same strategy (defined by the velocity update equation) or, may use a completely different one. This is a topic by its own right, and detailed discussion is out of scope of this paper.

Global Convergence

A simple way to transform SPSO into a globally convergent algorithm is to replace $\tilde{c}_1$ and/or $\tilde{c}_2$ in equation (1) by random numbers coming from

Figure 3. New position in an empty area by two methods: maximum intervals (described in the text), and minimisation of a potential

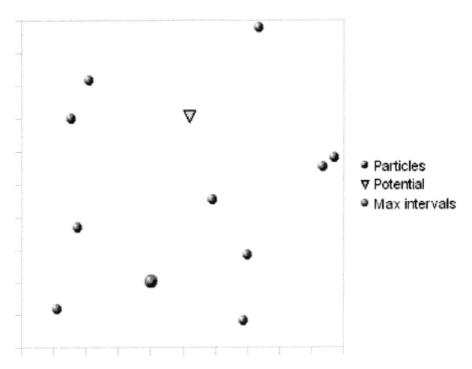

a distribution whose support is infinite, for example a Gaussian distribution $N(\mu,\sigma)$. Unfortunately, currently there is no theoretical analysis that defines "good" values for the mean μ and the standard deviation σ. So, by default, we may just keep the ones from the uniform distribution. Starting from equation (2), we then have

$$\left\{ \begin{array}{l} \mu = \dfrac{c_1}{2} \simeq 0.6 \\[2ex] \sigma = \dfrac{c_1}{\sqrt{12}} \simeq 0.34 \end{array} \right\} \qquad (10)$$

It is out of the scope of this paper to present and discuss long tables of results on a big benchmark, but a clear conclusion is that this variant is significantly worse than SPSO[5]. It is certainly possible to use some other distributions like Cauchy, or Lévy (Blackwell & Richer, 2006) and some other parameter values, but again, as

there are no well founded guidelines, it is not yet possible to recommend such approaches for a "standard" version.

Note that anyway the global convergence property alone is not very interesting, if nothing is said about how long it would take to find the optimum. After all, even pure random search is a globally convergent optimiser. It is in fact more useful to find ways to escape local minima.

Variable Swarm Size

In order to use a variable swarm size, or, more precisely, an adaptive one, we need to define three rules:

- How to compute the initial size
- When to add a particle (and where)
- When to remove a particle (and which one)

For the initial swarm size, a formula like (4) is not bad, but experimentally, it seems better to start from a bigger number of particles. Therefore we propose the following formula

$$S = 40 + 2\sqrt{(D)} \qquad (11)$$

To define when it is time to add a particle, the obvious idea is to define when stagnation occurs. As we have seen, an interesting method is to set the probability $i(S,t)$ to a fixed value, say $i_0 = 0.9$. If we use the variable ring topology, the number of iterations without improvement (of the global best) that defines "stagnation" can be derived from (9)

$$t_{stag} = \frac{\ln\left(1 - i_0\right)}{\ln\left(1 - \dfrac{2}{S}\right)} \qquad (12)$$

In practice, it appears that a simplified formula also gives good results (see Table 1)

$$t_{stag} = i_0 \frac{S}{2} \qquad (13)$$

In this last formula we can even set i_0 to 1 as a default value, and therefore we just have $t_{stag} = S/2$. It is important to propose such simple rules if we want to define a new standard.

Similar formulae can be derived for any kind of topology. Note that during the process this t_{stag} is not constant: it increases and decreases with the swarm size S. It appears that this method is significantly better than using a fixed value.

The new particle can be initialised by the method defined. In addition, the information links has to be redefined. An easy way is to re-initialise the whole variable ring. Another method is just to "insert" the new particle at random in the current

ring. Note that we do not set any upper bound for the swarm size. In practice, as some particles are removed, it rarely "explodes". Even if it tends to happen, the maximum number of fitness evaluations is quickly reached, and then the algorithm stops. Also, there is anyway a hard limit S_{max} imposed by the operating system and the hardware. So, the criteria for adding a particle are

- $S < S_{max}$
- Number of iterations without improvement $= t_{stag}$

Before removing a particle, we have to be almost sure that it is not useful. A reasonable way is to remove only the worst one (the one that has the worst previous best p), and only if majority of the particles have improved their own previous bests. Also, the remaining particles should be able to build a non-degenerate sub-space. Mathematically, this translates to the following two criteria for removing a particle:

- $S > D+1$
- Number of improved particles $> S/2$

Let us call this set of rules "Version A". It is indeed possible to define different rules. For example, another method (Version B) could be to check if several particles have improved the global best during the iteration, and, in that case, to remove the worst of them. It can also give good results (see Table 1, last column).

Here too, we note that whether we should remove a particle or not depends on the current swarm size. Also note the following fact. As we are starting from a quite big value (equation 4), in average, the swarm size usually tends to decrease. However, it may sometimes increase when it is "obviously" too small (no global improvement during t_{stag}). Some typical evolutions are given in Figure 8.

Rotation Insensitivity

Is it Really An Issue?

First of all, it is worth noting that perfect rotation insensitivity is usually impossible, except for particular landscapes. Here "perfect" means "for *any* values of the rotation angles". This is because the search space is almost never a (hyper)sphere. Usually it is a (hyper)parallelepiped[6], sometimes "cut" by some surfaces induced by constraints. In the following, we just consider cubes, for anyway it is always possible to apply an affine transformation before the optimisation process, and the inverse transformation on the solution after it has been found.

When rotating the landscape, some points that are inside the search space may fall out, and some points that were outside may come inside (note that it may be a problem if the fitness function is not defined everywhere). As a result the landscape (i.e. the problem to solve) does not remain exactly the same. In the worst case, as we can see from Figure 4 for the Alpine f3 function ($z = x\sin(x)\sin(y)$), the optimum may even be different, particularly when it lies near a corner of the search space.

Let us be more precise. Let O be the centre of rotation, and H the biggest hypersphere centred at O and entirely inside the search space. The only part of the landscape that is not geometrically modified by any rotation is H. To illustrate what happens, let us consider a classical optimisation problem, whose search space is a D-cube C. Then H is the interior tangent sphere. It means that the proportion of the landscape that is not modified by any rotation is given by

$$\left[\begin{aligned} rotInvar \quad &= \quad \frac{volume(H)}{volume(C)} \\ &= \quad \frac{\pi^{D/2}}{2^D \Gamma(D/2+1)} \end{aligned} \right] \quad (14)$$

As we know, the Γ function is an extension of the factorial, i.e. when $D = 2k$ we have $\Gamma(D/2+1) = k!$. So it is easy to see that *rotInvar* quickly tends to zero when D increases (see Figure 5).

Second, a great advantage of PSO is that it can handle heterogeneous problems, in which some variables are continuous and some discrete, or even without any order relation (e.g., say, colours), if a fitness function can be defined. This is because the different variables (i.e. dimensions) are never aggregated, but considered one at a time. In such cases, a rotation of the search space is meaningless.

Last, but not the least, being sensitive to rotation may be an advantage. If the performance is sometimes deteriorated when rotating the landscape, it necessarily means that it is also sometimes improved. Actually, this property suggests an interesting approach:

- Consider the smallest sphere that contains the cubical search space;
- Consider the smallest cube that contains this sphere, and take it as the new search space;
- If necessary, complete the fitness function by assigning arbitrarily high values outside the initial search space. A good way is to use an increasing function of the distance to the centre of this cube so that the particles leaving it tend to go back;
- Make use of an algorithm that *is* sensitive to rotation, and try different rotations. By construction the original search space is always inside the new one, and by definition the algorithm is better for at least one rotation.

Reducing the Sensitivity to Rotation

Having said that, it is anyway mathematically easy to reduce the rotation sensitivity of PSO: we just have to use a probability distribution of positions that are themselves insensitive to rota-

Figure 4. Rotating a landscape usually leads to a different optimisation problem, when the search space is not isometric

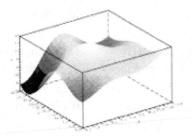

Alpine f3 on a small square search space

View from the top. The optimum is near the bottom left corner.

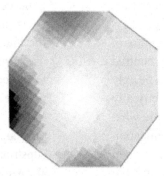

**Top view after rotation of the part of the initial landscape that is still inside the search space.
The optimum (on the left side) is not the same.**

Figure 5. Rotation insensitivity tends to be impossible when the dimension increases

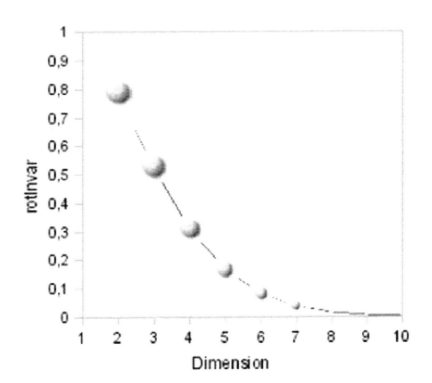

tion, i.e. isotropic (Clerc, 2006a). The simplest one is the sphere (but it could be, for example, a *D*-Gaussian distribution). Interested readers may want to try Tribes (Clerc, 2003, 2006a; Cooren, Clerc & Siarry, 2009; Souad, Ruiz-Gazen & Tann, 2010) where this is an option. In practice, it means that the standard velocity update equation, which is applied independently to each dimension, is replaced by a vectorial one, for example

$$v(t+1) = \omega v(t) + \left(H_1\left(o_1, r_1\right) - x(t)\right) + \left(H_2\left(o_2, r_2\right) - x(t)\right) \tag{15}$$

H_1 and H_2 are two positions generated by two isotropic distributions. The centres of these distributions are o_1 and $o2$, and their "radii" (which can in fact be other parameters, like standard deviations) are r_1 and r_2. If p is the best previous position of the particle, and g the best previous position known by its neighbours, in case of spheres, a good method is the following one:

- Define the radius r_1 (we see below how)
- Set $o_1 = x + r_1\left(p - x\right) / \|p - x\|$
- Do the same for o_2, with r_2 and g

Now, let us see how we can define the radii. In dimension one, we may want to be equivalent to SPSO. We should then have $r_1 = c_1/2$, and $r_2 = c_2/2$. However, what is important is not the radius itself, but the volume of the support of the distribution. For example, in dimension D, we want that the volume of the cube whose side is c_1 is equal to the volume of the sphere whose radius is r_1. Therefore, we derive from (14) a corrective coefficient

Figure 6. Corrective coefficient between sphere and cube for equivalent volumes

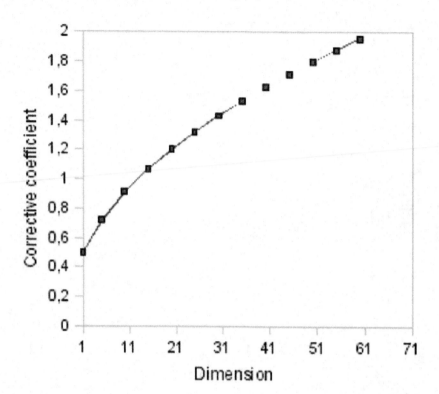

$$v(D) = \frac{"\left(D/2+1\right)^{1/D}}{\sqrt{(A)}} \qquad (16)$$

It means that for a good equivalence, we have to define $r_i = \nu(D)c_i$. As we can see from Figure 6 the value of the coefficient is never very big, but in practice, if we do not use it, the performance may be extremely bad because the spheres are too small.

TOWARDS A NEW FLEXIBLE STANDARD?

After this short discussion, let us summarise what could be the components of a new Standard PSO, more flexible than the previous one, i.e. with some options:

- Basically like SPSO-2007, except the topology;
- A variable ring topology. Let us call this version SPSO-vr;
- Option: variable swarm size. Let us call this version SPSO-vr-vs. Needs the additional parameter l_0. However, it can be set to 1 with good results;
- Option: probability distribution with an infinite support for $\tilde{c}_1$ and $\tilde{c}_2$, assuming that a theoretical analysis can suggest a robust one;
- Option: less rotation sensitivity (by using isometric distributions).

Whether such a new standard may indeed be defined will anyway depend on discussions inside the "swarmer community". To conclude, let us recall what was said during the presentation of the SPSO that was proposed on the Particle Swarm Central (PSC, 2010):

This PSO version does not intend to be the best one on the market [...]. It is simply very near to the original version (1995), with just a few improvements based on some recent works

REFERENCES

Blackwell, T., & Richer, T. J. (2006). The Lévy particle swarm. In *Proceedings of the IEEE Congress on Evolutionary Computation (CEC '06)*, Vancouver, BC, Canada (pp. 808-815). Washington, DC: IEEE Computer Society.

Bratton, D., & Kennedy, J. (2007). Defining a standard for particle swarm optimization. In *Proceedings of the IEEE Swarm Intelligence Symposium* (pp. 120-127). Washington, DC: IEEE Computer Society.

Clerc, M. (2003, October). *TRIBES - Un exemple d'optimisation par essaim particulaire sans paramètres de contrôle.* Paper presented at OEP'03 (Optimisation par Essaim Particulaire), Paris, France.

Clerc, M. (2006a). Particle Swarm Optimization. *ISTE.* International Scientific and Technical Encyclopedia. doi:10.1002/9780470612163

Clerc, M. (2006b). *Stagnation analysis in particle swarm optimization or what happens when nothing happens.* Retrieved July 25, 2010, from http://hal.archives-ouvertes.fr/hal-00122031

Clerc, M. (2010). *Balanced PSO, variable PSO.* Retrieved July 23, 2010, from http://clerc.maurice.free.fr/pso/

Clerc, M., & Kennedy, J. (2002). The Particle Swarm- Explosion, Stability, and Convergence in a Multidimensional Complex Space. *IEEE Transactions on Evolutionary Computation, 6*(1), 58–73. doi:10.1109/4235.985692

Cooren, Y., Clerc, M., & Siarry, P. (2009). Performance evaluation of TRIBES, an adaptive particle swarm optimization algorithm. *Swarm Intelligence, 3*, 149–178. doi:10.1007/s11721-009-0026-8

Gacôgne, L. (2002). Steady state evolutionary algorithm with an operator family. In *Proceedings of EISCI* (pp. 373-379), Kosice, Slovakia.

Hansen, N., Ros, R., Mauny, N., Schoenauer, M., & Auger, A. (2008, Februar). *PSO facing non-separable and ill conditioned problems* (Technical Rep. No. 6447). Paris: INRIA.

Helwig, S., & Wanka, R. (2007). Particle Swarm Optimization in High-Dimensional Bounded Search Spaces. In *Proceedings of the IEEE Swarm Intelligence Symposium* (pp.198-205). Washington, DC: IEEE Computer Society.

Helwig, S., & Wanka, R. (2008). Theoretical analysis of initial particle swarm behavior. In *Proceedings of the 10th International Conference on Parallel Problem Solving from Nature (PPSN 2008)*, Dortmund, Germany (pp. 889-898). Berlin: Springer.

Langdon, W., & Poli, R. (2005). Evolving problems to learn about particle swarm and other optimisers. In *Proceedings of the Congress on Evolutionary Computation* (pp. 81-88).

Onwubolu, G. C., & Babu, B. V. (2004). *New Optimization Techniques in Engineering.* Berlin: Springer.

PSC. (2010). *Particle Swarm Central.* Retrieved July 25, 2010, from http://www.particleswarm.info

Sandgren, E. (1990). Non linear integer and discrete programming in mechanical design optimization. *Journal of Mechanical Design, 112*, 223–229. doi:10.1115/1.2912596

Shang, Y.-W., & Qiu, Y.-H. (2006). A note on the extended Rosenbrock function. *Evolutionary Computation, 14*(1), 119–126. doi:10.1162/evco.2006.14.1.119

Shi, Y. H., & Eberhart, R. C. (1998, May 4-9). A Modified Particle Swarm Optimizer. In Proceedings of the *International Conference on Evolutionary Computation*, Anchorage, AK (pp. 69-73). Washington, DC: IEEE Computer Society.

Souad Larabi, M.-S., Ruiz-Gazen, A., & Berro, A. (2010). *Tribes: une méthode d'optimisation efficace pour révéler des optima locaux d'un indice de projection.* Paper presented at ROADEF, Toulouse, France.

Tindle, S., Tindle, J., Fletcher, I., & Tann, P. (2002). *Particle Swarm Optimization with Restart.* IEEE Journal of Evolutionary Computation.

Van den Bergh, F. (2002). *An Analysis of Particle Swarm Optimizers.* Unpublished doctoral dissertation, University of Pretoria, Pretoria, South Africa.

ENDNOTES

[1] For this variant, the interested user may "lay" with the programs called Balanced PSO and Variable PSO, whose C code are available on (Clerc, 2010). The first one includes a lot of options so that it can simulate many versions of PSO. The second makes use of just the variable ring and variable swarm options.

[2] The true probability is usually bigger, for the topology is in fact a fixed ring between two unsuccessful iterations.

[3] Unless stated otherwise, SPSO means here either SPSO-2007 or SPSO-BK.

[4] Again, the reader can try it (Clerc, 2010).

[5] Again, the reader may try Balanced PSO with this option (Clerc, 2010).

[6] To simplify, the "yper" prefix will be omitted from now on.

APPENDIX: A MINI-BENCHMARK

Just to illustrate the differences between some of the above variants, let us consider the results on a mini-benchmark of four problems.

Tripod

The function to be minimised is (Gacôgne, 2002) (Figure 7).

$$f \quad = \quad \frac{1 - sign(x_2)}{2}\left((x_1(+ (x_2 + 50()\right) \tag{17}$$

$$+ \frac{1 + sign(x_2)}{2}\frac{1 - sign(x_1)}{2}\left(1 + (x_1 + 50(+ (x_2 - 50()\right)$$

$$+ \frac{1 + sign(x_1)}{2}\left(2 + (x_1 - 50(+ (x_2 + 50()\right)$$

with

$$sign(x) \quad = \quad \begin{array}{ll} -1 & \text{if} x < 50 \\ 1 & \text{else} \end{array}$$

The search space is $[-100,100]^2$. The solution point is $(0,-50)$, where $f = 0$. Here, we allow 10^4 fitness evaluations and a run is said to be successful if it finds a fitness less than 0.0001.

Rosenbrock F6

$$f = 390 + \sum_{d=2}^{10}\left(100\left(z_{d-1}^2 - z_d\right)^2 + \left(z_{d-1} - 1\right)^2\right) \tag{18}$$

with $z_d = x_d - o_d + 1$. The search space is $[-100,100]^{10}$. The offset vector $O = (o_1,...,o_{10})$ is defined by its C code below. It is the solution point where $f = 390$. There is also a local minimum at $O = (o_1-2,...,o_{10})$, where $f = 394$ (the Rosenbrock function is indeed multimodal for dimension greater than three (see Shang & Qiu, 2006). Here, we allow fitness evaluations and a run is said to be successful if it finds a fitness less than 0.01. This problem is difficult for algorithms that prune the searched space too quickly, and particularly discriminant in terms of success rate.

Offset (C code)

static double offset_2[10] =

Figure 7. Tripod function

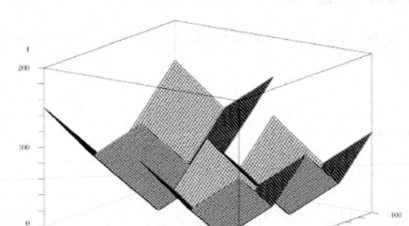

{ 8.1023200e+001, -4.8395000e+001, 1.9231600e+001, -2.5231000e+000, 7.0433800e+001, 4.7177400e+001, -7.8358000e+000, -8.6669300e+001, 5.7853200e+001};

Compression Spring

For more details, see (Sandgren, 1990; Onwubolu & Babu, 2004; Clerc, 2006a). There are three variables

$x_1 \quad \in \quad \{1,...,70\} \quad$ granularity $\quad 1$

$x_2 \quad \in \quad [0.6,3]$

$x_3 \quad \in \quad [0.207,0.5] \quad$ granularity $\quad 0.001$

and five constraints

$$g_1 \quad := \quad \frac{8 C_f F_{max} x_2}{\pi x_3^3} - S \leq 0$$

$$g_2 \quad := \quad l_f - l_{max} \leq 0$$

$$g_3 \quad := \quad \sigma_p - \sigma_{pm} \leq 0$$

$$g_4 \quad := \quad \sigma_p - \frac{F_p}{K} \leq 0$$

$$g_5 \quad := \quad \sigma_w - \frac{F_{max} - F_p}{K} \leq 0$$

with

$$C_f = 1 + 0.75 \frac{x_3}{x_2 - x_3} + 0.615 \frac{x_3}{x_2}$$

$$F_{max} = 1000$$

$$S = 189000$$

$$l_f = \frac{F_{max}}{K} + 1.05 (x_1 + 2) x_3$$

$$l_{max} = 14$$

$$\sigma_p = \frac{F_p}{K}$$

$$\sigma_{pm} = 6$$

$$F_p = 300$$

$$K = 11.5 \times 10^6 \frac{x_3^4}{8 \mathrm{x}_1 x_2^3}$$

$$\sigma_w = 1.25$$

wand the function to be minimised is

$$f = \dot{A}^2 \frac{x_2 x_3^2 (x_1 + 1)}{4} \tag{19}$$

The best known solution is $(7, 1.386599591, 0.292)$, which gives the fitness value $f* = 2.6254214578$. To take the constraints into account, a penalty method is used. Here, we allow fitness evaluations and a run is said to be successful if it finds a fitness f so that $(f - f(\leq 10^{-10}$. Because of the granularities this problem may be deceptive for some algorithms.

Gear Train

For more details, see (Sandgren, 1990; Onwubolu & Babu, 2004). The function to be minimised is

$$f = \left(\frac{1}{6.931} - \frac{x_1 x_2}{x_3 x_4} \right)^2 \tag{20}$$

The search space is $\{12,13,...,60\}^4$. There are several solutions, depending on the required precision. Here, we used 10^{-13}. So, a possible solution is $f* = f(19, 16, 43, 49) = 2.7 \times 10^{-12}$. We allow 2×10^4 fitness evaluations, and a run is then said to be successful if it finds a fitness f so that $(f - f(\leq 10^{-13}$. In this problem, only "integer" positions are acceptable. A lot of algorithms are not comfortable with such constraints.

Table 1. Success rates over 100 runs

			Simulated with Balanced PSO			*Variable PSO*	
			SPSO-2007	SPSO-vr		SPSO-vr-vs	
			re-init	(SPSO-2007		(SPSO-vr + variable swarm)	
			the worst particle	but	SPSO-vr	Version A	Version B
	SPSO-2007	SPSO-BK	with $l_0 = 0.9$	variable ring)	Gauss		
Tripod	50%	100%	84%	94%	90%	93%	85%
Rosenbrock F6	82%	3%	1%	2%	2%	75%	86%
Compression spring	35%	55%	62%	69%	67%	72%	73%
Gear train	6%	33%	19%	15%	14%	22%	20%
Mean	*43.25%*	*47.75%*	*41.5%*	*45%*	*43.25%*	*65.5%*	*66%*
Variance	*0.06*	*0.1*	*0.087*	*0.115*	*0106*	*0.056*	*0.073*

Results

We consider six variants, and the results are given in Table 1. Here "Gauss" means "using the Gaussian distribution defined by the equation (10)".

As we can see, compared to SPSO-2007, SPSO-BK is significantly better on some problems, but also sometimes much worse (Rosenbrock F6). In other words: not robust. SPSO-vr-vs, i.e. SPSO-2007 but with a variable ring topology and a variable swarm is the best on average, and also the most robust variant. Using a variable swarm size further improves the mean success rate significantly. It appears that re-initialisation and Gaussian distribution are not necessarily good ideas. Details are not given here, but the main reason is that both often induce too many useless fitness evaluations and thus waste time.

Figure 8. Four typical swarm size evolutions with Variable PSO. For Rosenbrock, finding the long "valley" is easy, so the swarm tends to the minimal value D+1. If it happens quickly enough, the run will be successful. For Gear train, the swarm size is stabilized after four or five time steps. Success or failure depends entirely on the final level. It suggests that a more sophisticated rule for removing a particle may be found.

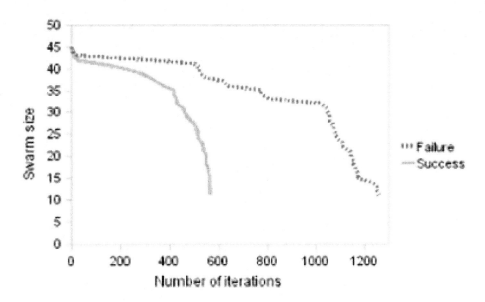

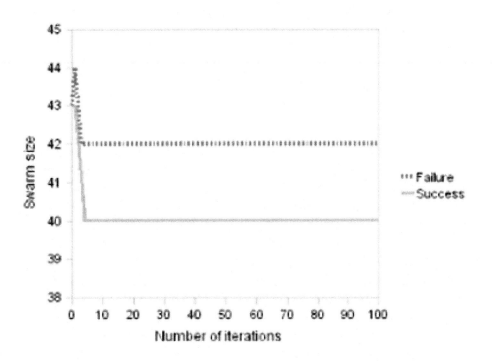

This work was previously published in International Journal of Swarm Intelligence Research, Volume 1, Issue 4, edited by Yuhui Shi, pp. 46-61, copyright 2010 by IGI Publishing (an imprint of IGI Global)

Chapter 2
Biases in Particle Swarm Optimization

William M. Spears
Swarmotics LLC, USA

Derek T. Green
University of Arizona, USA

Diana F. Spears
Swarmotics LLC, USA

ABSTRACT

The most common versions of particle swarm optimization (PSO) algorithms are rotationally variant. It has also been pointed out that PSO algorithms can concentrate particles along paths parallel to the coordinate axes. In this paper, the authors explicitly connect these two observations by showing that the rotational variance is related to the concentration along lines parallel to the coordinate axes. Based on this explicit connection, the authors create fitness functions that are easy or hard for PSO to solve, depending on the rotation of the function.

INTRODUCTION

The popularity and variety of Particle Swarm Optimization (PSO) algorithms have continued to grow at a rapid rate since the initial PSO algorithm was introduced in 1995 (Eberhart et al., 2001; Shi & Eberhart, 2008; Shi & Eberhart, 2009). Recently, great strides have been made in understanding the theoretical underpinnings of the basic PSO algorithm (Poli, 2009; Trelea, 2003; van den Bergh & Engelbrecht, 2006). However,

there are still some behaviors exhibited by PSO that require further examination. For example, although it has also been pointed out that when running the traditional PSO algorithm, "most movement steps occurred parallel to one of the coordinate axes" (Janson & Middendorf, 2007), this behavior is not well explained theoretically. In this paper, we examine this behavior and provide a theoretical explanation for why it occurs. Based on this explanation, we also show fitness landscapes in which the performance of PSO depends heavily on the rotation of the fitness

DOI: 10.4018/978-1-4666-1592-2.ch002

function. Through these observations we hope to help users of PSO-based algorithms to better understand the effects of the biases inherent in PSO on their own particular problems. In this paper, a "bias" is an implicit algorithmic preference; for a general discussion of biases, see Mitchell (1997).

The PSO Algorithm

The basic PSO algorithm (Kennedy & Eberhart, 1995) is usually described as follows. A swarm consists of N particles. Each particle i has a position at time t denoted by $\vec{X}_i(t) = (X_{i,1}(t),...,X_{i,D}(t))$ where $\vec{X}_i(t)$ is a D-dimensional vector. Each particle i has a velocity $\vec{V}_i(t) = (V_{i,1}(t),...,V_{i,D}(t))$, which is also a D-dimensional vector. The equations of motion are generally given as:

$$\vec{X}_i(t+1) = \vec{X}_i(t) + \vec{V}_i(t+1)$$

$$\vec{V}_i(t+1) = \omega\vec{V}_i(t) + c_1 r_1(\vec{P}_i - \vec{X}_i(t)) + c_2 r_2(\vec{G} - \vec{X}_i(t))$$

$\vec{P}_i$ is the "personal best" position, or the position of the best fitness ever encountered by particle i. $\vec{G}$ is the "global best" position ever found by all of the particles or, alternatively, the best position ever seen within a neighborhood of particles. In this paper, we will assume that all particles are neighbors. The best positions are updated when particles find positions with better fitness. The ω term, an "inertial coefficient" from 0 to 1, was introduced in (Shi & Eberhart, 1998). The "learning rates" c_1 and c_2 are non-negative constants. Very often these are both set to 2.0. Finally, r_1 and r_2 are random numbers generated in the range [0,1].

Looking again at the above equations, we point out an ambiguity that unfortunately continues to propagate throughout the literature. The ambiguity arises in the interpretation of the random numbers. In many papers, it is not made clear when the random numbers are calculated. The random variables r_1 and r_2 may be interpreted as scalars or vectors. Figure 1 shows the two most common implementations seen in the literature. In both versions, U(0,1) is a uniform random generator in the range of [0,1].

Version 1 is rotationally invariant, while Version 2 is not. James Kennedy, one of the creators of PSO, indicates that the second of the two versions is preferred -- because it is considered to be more explorative (Kennedy, 2007). Hence, the notation of Poli (2009) is preferred:

$$\vec{V}_i(t+1) = \omega\vec{V}_i(t) + c_1\vec{r}_1 \odot (\vec{P}_i - \vec{X}_i(t)) + c_2\vec{r}_2 \odot (\vec{G} - \vec{X}_i(t))$$

where $\odot$ represents component-wise multiplication.

In this paper, we will show that updating the random numbers in the preferred way is the cause of the biased behavior. In other words, the rotational variance and coordinate axes bias of Version 2 are related. It is not our intention to suggest that PSO should not be used due to the bias, but rather that users of PSO should be aware of the bias, its cause and how it might affect their particular needs.

The motivation for this view of bias stems from the original No Free Lunch Theorems, where "an algorithm's average performance is determined by how *aligned* it is with" the optimization problems being considered (Wolpert & Macready, 1997). The geometric interpretation is to consider both the algorithm and the problems as vectors. If they are aligned, the dot product is zero, and the algorithm is well matched to the problem. *In other words, the main objective of this paper is to assist the PSO practitioner in achieving an algorithm/problem alignment.* Here, the geometric interpretation of alignment is almost literal -- we show that the performance of PSO can depend to a very large degree on the rotation of fitness landscapes that contain linear features, such as troughs or ridges.

Figure 1. Two versions of PSO

```
void pso1_one_step ()
{
   for (i = 1; i <= N; i++) {
      r1 = U(0,1);
      r2 = U(0,1);
      for (j = 1; j <= D; j++) {
         V[i][j] = w * V[i][j] + c1 * r1 * (P[i][j] - X[i][j]) + c2 * r2 * (G[j] - X[i][j]);
} } }

void pso2_one_step ()
{
   for (i = 1; i <= N; i++) {
      for (j = 1; j <= D; j++) {
         r1 = U(0,1);
         r2 = U(0,1);
         V[i][j] = w * V[i][j] + c1 * r1 * (P[i][j] - X[i][j]) + c2 * r2 * (G[j] - X[i][j]);
} } }
```

Previous Analyses

In terms of rotational variance, Clerc (2001) noted the fact that PSO in its basic form, and hence many of its derivatives, is not rotationally invariant. The fact that PSO is rotationally variant was again noted by Wilke (2005), who also mentioned that both versions of PSO are translationally invariant. Wilke also presented a rotationally invariant modification of PSO. Furthermore, Hansen et al. (2008) noted that PSO is not rotationally invariant, and they investigated the effect this has on separable problems. They argued that invariance properties are desirable "because they increase the predictive power of performance results." Finally, Janson and Middendorf (2007) suggested that the rotational variance of PSO causes the bias towards directions parallel to the coordinate axes. It is this bias that we examine in this paper.

Most theoretical analyses of PSO make simplifying assumptions, including the lack of the stochastic component. For example, an early formal analysis of PSO was given by Ozcan and Mohan (1998). In this analysis, the system was simplified by setting $\vec{P}_i = \vec{G}$, using a one-dimensional search space, holding the random variables constant and examining a single particle. This one-dimensional, one-particle analysis was extended to multiple dimensions in Ozcan and Mohan (1999). Clerc and Kennedy (2002) also modeled a one-dimensional deterministic particle in one dimension. Brandstatter and Baumgartner (2002) used a damped spring model, but again the model was one-dimensional with one particle and no random component. Trelea (2003) also considered a deterministic version of PSO, in order to provide additional insight into the topic of parameter selection, and analyzed the model for convergence, harmonic oscillations and "zigzagging." Yasuda et al. (2003) also studied one one-dimensional particle without randomness, but included inertia. Blackwell (2005) included a constriction term, but did not model stochasticity. More recently, Campana et al. (2006) examined an extension of PSO but again restricted themselves by not including the random component. Similarly, van den Bergh (2001;2006) analyzed the convergence properties of the trajectory of a

Figure 2. PSO on the distance function in 2D (left), and in 3D (right). Note the concentration of particles on the coordinate axes.

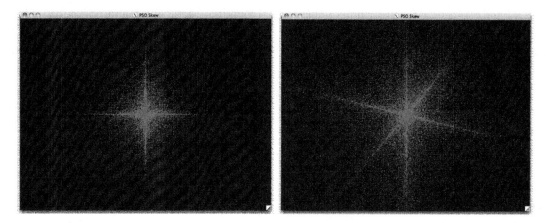

single particle. The model correctly predicts the trajectory of a single particle in the absence of a stochastic component. When the stochastic component is introduced, the model can no longer predict the exact trajectory, but can classify whether it is divergent or convergent.

Recently, PSO models that include their stochastic component have been derived. Kadirka-manathan and Fleming (2006) performed a Lyapunov stability analysis. The most relevant work, by Poli (2009), examined the expectation and standard deviation of the sampling distribution of the PSO. The key difference is that whereas Poli examined the position $\overrightarrow{X_i}(t)$, we focus primarily on $\Delta \overrightarrow{V_i}(t)$. It is this change in focus that allows us to explain the bias noted by Janson and Middendorf (2007).

Current Analysis

In this paper, we expand on the work by Janson and Middendorf (2007) and show that, for the standard PSO, the particular manner in which the random variables are applied causes both the rotational variance and the bias towards the coordinate axes. Finally, we create fitness landscapes that demonstrate some of the features that can cause

difficulties for PSO, depending on the rotational angle of the system.

Throughout the paper, our discussion will focus on the bearing of the velocity of the particles in the PSO as well as the change in velocity $\Delta \overrightarrow{V_i}(t) = c_1 \overrightarrow{r_1} \odot (\overrightarrow{P_i} - \overrightarrow{X_i}(t)) + c_2 \overrightarrow{r_2} \odot (\overrightarrow{G} - \overrightarrow{X_i}(t))$. The motivation for the latter focus stems from $\vec{F} = m\vec{a}$, where the acceleration of the particles is synonymous with calculating the force on the particles. Specifically, we will examine the expected bearing of $\Delta \overrightarrow{V_i}(t)$ to see if there is some angular bias that would explain the preference for the bearings associated with the coordinate axes.

BIAS PARALLEL TO THE COORDINATE AXES

In this section, we illustrate the behavior of PSO on a simple radially symmetric fitness function. The fitness is the distance of a particle from the origin. Throughout this paper, the PSO algorithm is minimizing. All of the fitness functions used in this paper are shown in Appendix B. Figure 2 shows snapshots for both the two-dimensional and three-dimensional distance functions. The particles are initially positioned using a Gaussian $\mathcal{N}(0, \sigma^2)$ with $\sigma = 1000.0$, which ensures a radially symmetric distribution. There are 100,000 particles and we used parameter settings $\omega = 1.0$, $c_1 = 2.0$, and $c_2 = 2.0$. PSO algorithms generally also include a maximum velocity V_{max}, which we set to 10.0.

What is interesting about the behavior on both problems is the concentration of particles along the axes, despite the radially symmetric fitness function and radially symmetric initial distribution of particles. There is no obvious reason for this concentration, and the PSO is behaving as if there are some additional structures in the functions that are aligned with the coordinate axes.

Naturally, a population size of 100,000 is unusually high for most PSO applications. In the next subsection, we quantify the behavior more precisely, and show that it is not simply a "large population" effect. We will also show that it is not a "small dimension" effect. Finally, we demonstrate that the settings of the PSO parameters have little effect on this axial concentration.

Analysis of Coordinate Axes Bias in PSO

In this subsection, we examine the coordinate axes bias of PSO, by monitoring the bearing of the velocity of each particle for a number of time steps. For the first experiment, we re-ran the PSO on the three-dimensional distance function, using the same Gaussian initialization of particles. However, the population size was lowered to a more standard size of 20. We allowed each PSO parameter to have one of two settings: $\omega \in \{0.729, 1.0\}$, $c_1 = c_2 \in \{1.49, 2.0\}$ and $V_{max} \in \{2.0, 10.0\}$. This yielded a total of eight different sets of parameters and experiments. The values of $\omega = 0.729$ and $c_1 = c_2 = 1.49$ are noted in Eberhart and Shi (2000).

The algorithm was run for 1000 steps. At each time step, we computed the bearing of the velocity for each particle in the XY and YZ planes. We maintained 360 bins for each plane, ranging from

$-180°$ to $180°$ degrees. Each bin maintained a count of how many times that bearing was observed (rounding real values appropriately). All eight experiments yielded very similar results. Each experiment was run over 10,000 independent trials, to provide good sampling for the bins.

Figure 3 presents the four graphs, where $V_{max} = 2.0$, in the XY plane. The horizontal axis is the bearing in degrees, while the vertical axis is the number of times that bearing occurred. We see a strong bias parallel to the coordinate axes. The values of the standard PSO parameters (c_1, c_2 and ω) have little effect on this bias, although some effect is noticeable. Throughout this paper the results are similar when $V_{max} = 10.0$, so we omit those graphs. Figure 4 shows the results for the YZ plane. Not surprisingly, Figure 3 and Figure 4 are identical, since there is no preference for any particular axis in PSO.

Finally, we tried the same experiment with the distance function in 20 dimensions. Each time we analyze the bearing of the velocity of a particle, we uniformly randomly choose two different axes (i.e., a random plane). Figure 5 shows the results. Again, PSO exhibits a strong preference for bearings aligned with the global coordinate axes despite the radial symmetry of the function and the initial conditions. With 20 dimensions the different parameter settings have almost no effect on the bias.

In summary, we have shown that in the presence of radial symmetry in both the fitness function and the initial conditions, the particles in PSO are drawn strongly towards bearings parallel to the coordinate axes. This result is consistent with that of Janson and Middendorf (2007). The behavior is similar regardless of the number of particles, the values of the standard PSO parameters and the number of dimensions. Hence, we can consider it to be a "core" behavior.

Figure 3. Angular bias with the 3D distance function in the XY plane. The x-axis represents the angle bins. The y-axis represents the frequency counts for the bins. On the upper left $c_1 = c_2 = 1.49$, and $\omega = 0.729$. On the upper right $c_1 = c_2 = 1.49$, and $\omega = 1.0$. On the lower left $c_1 = c_2 = 2.0$, and $\omega = 0.729$. On the lower right $c_1 = c_2 = 2.0$, and $\omega = 1.0$.

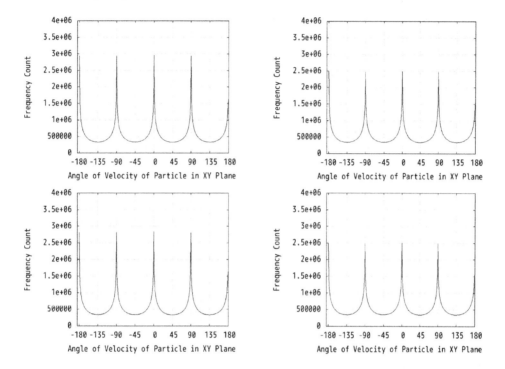

Analysis of Particle Trajectories

The previous subsection indicated that particles often travel along bearings parallel to the coordinate axes. But do they simply stay along one bearing, or do they switch bearings? In this subsection, we examine the trajectories of individual particles for the two-dimensional distance function. One trial is run, for 300 steps of the PSO algorithm. $V_{max} = 2.0$ and, as before, we examine the four combinations of values for $c_1 = c_2$ and ω The random seed for each of the four experiments is the same, so the initial location of the particles is the same for each experiment. Rather than follow the trajectory of only one particle (for all four experiments), we follow the trajectory of a different particle for each experiment, to demonstrate generality of the behavior.

Figure 6 shows the results. All four graphs show similar behavior. The velocity of a particle tends to remain parallel with a coordinate axis, although there is considerable noise. When there are changes, the velocity often switches to a direction approximately parallel to the other axis. In the upper right graph the particle switches (through a sequence of rather large changes) from an alignment parallel to the x-axis to an alignment parallel to the y-axis.

Again, there is no obvious reason for there to be *any* preferred alignments when using the distance function for fitness. To see if this behavior holds on other fitness functions, we chose the Ackley and Griewank functions. Neither of these functions has any obvious biases parallel to the coordinate axes. To avoid any potential "origin-

Figure 4. Angular bias with the 3D distance function in the YZ plane. The x-axis represents the angle bins. The y-axis represents the frequency counts for the bins. On the upper left $c_1 = c_2 = 1.49$, and $\omega = 0.729$. On the upper right $c_1 = c_2 = 1.49$, and $\omega = 1.0$. On the lower left $c_1 = c_2 = 2.0$, and $\omega = 0.729$. On the lower right $c_1 = c_2 = 2.0$, and $\omega = 1.0$.

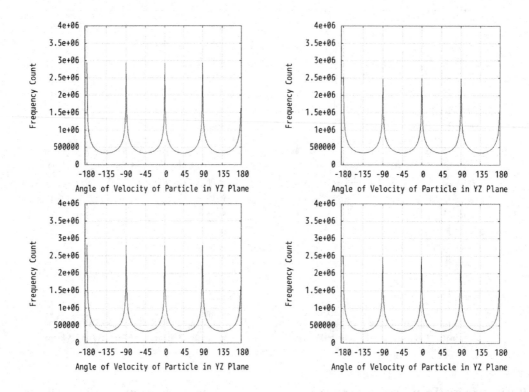

seeking bias" (Monson & Seppi, 2005), both functions have their optima at (500, 500).

Figure 7 and Figure 8 show the trajectories on the Ackley and Griewank functions. The graphs are qualitatively similar to those shown for the distance function. Again, the trajectories of particles tend to remain parallel with coordinate axes, although there is quite a bit of noise.

Given these results, and the fact that they appear even when the fitness function and initialization are both radially symmetric, there must be a core PSO bias that favors trajectories that are parallel to coordinate axes. We provide a theoretical explanation in the next section.

THEORETICAL EXPLANATION

It is clear that the PSO algorithm itself must provide a bias towards bearings parallel to the coordinate axes. This has to occur where the velocity is updated. We ignore the first term, $\omega \, \vec{V}_i(t)$, because this does not change the bearing of the velocity vector. However, $\Delta \vec{V}_i(t) = c_1 \vec{r}_1 \odot (\vec{P}_i - \vec{X}_i(t)) + c_2 \vec{r}_2 \odot (\vec{G} - \vec{X}_i(t))$ can change the bearing. This can be thought of as a Newtonian force $\vec{F} = m\vec{a}$, where the acceleration of the particles is synonymous with calculating the force on the particles. Specifically, we will examine the expected bearing of $\Delta \vec{V}_i(t)$ to see if there is some

Figure 5. Angular bias with the 20D distance function. The x-axis represents the angle bins. The y-axis represents the frequency counts for the bins. On the upper left $c_1 = c_2 = 1.49$, and $\omega = 0.729$. On the upper right $c_1 = c_2 = 1.49$, and $\omega = 1.0$. On the lower left $c_1 = c_2 = 2.0$, and $\omega = 0.729$. On the lower right $c_1 = c_2 = 2.0$, and $\omega = 1.0$.

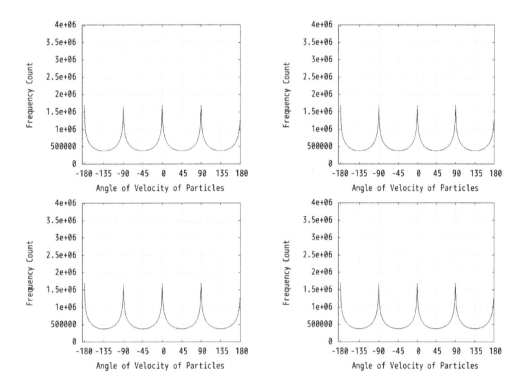

angular bias that would explain the preference for the bearings associated with the coordinate axes.

Since we have shown that the bias holds regardless of the number of dimensions, we will focus on an analysis in two dimensions. Consider again the bearing of the change in velocity of each particle (where the time variable is omitted to simplify notation):

$$\Phi = \arctan\left(\frac{c_1 r_{1,2}(P_{i,2} - X_{i,2}) + c_2 r_{2,2}(G_2 - X_{i,2})}{c_1 r_{1,1}(P_{i,1} - X_{i,1}) + c_2 r_{2,1}(G_1 - X_{i,1})} \right)$$

In the above equation, $r_{i,j}$ represents the jth component of $\vec{r_i}$. Hence, each is implemented via

a separate function call to a $U(0,1)$ random number generator.

Also, in most implementations of PSO, $c_1 = c_2$ so:

$$\Phi = \arctan\left(\frac{r_{1,2}(P_{i,2} - X_{i,2}) + r_{2,2}(G_2 - X_{i,2})}{r_{1,1}(P_{i,1} - X_{i,1}) + r_{2,1}(G_1 - X_{i,1})} \right)$$

A baseline bearing can be obtained by assuming that there are no random numbers generated:

$$\Theta = \arctan\left(\frac{(P_{i,2} - X_{i,2}) + (G_2 - X_{i,2})}{(P_{i,1} - X_{i,1}) + (G_1 - X_{i,1})} \right)$$

Figure 6. The bearing of individual particles on the distance function, over the first 300 steps. The x-axis represents the step number. The y-axis represents the angular bearing of a particle. On the upper left $c_1 = c_2 = 1.49$, and $\omega = 0.729$. On the upper right $c_1 = c_2 = 1.49$, and $\omega = 1.0$. On the lower left $c_1 = c_2 = 2.0$, and $\omega = 0.729$. On the lower right $c_1 = c_2 = 2.0$, and $\omega = 1.0$.

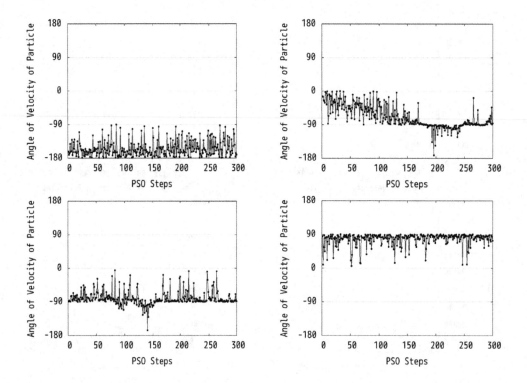

This bearing baseline corresponds to simple vector addition, with the change in velocity of a particle determined by the position of the personal and global best positions. We refer to $\Phi - \Theta$ as the *angular bias* of PSO. We will examine the expectation $E[\Phi - \Theta] = E[\Phi] - \Theta$ to see if it is equal to zero, and if it varies with Θ. We consider various cases.

Case 1

In the first case, $\overrightarrow{X_i} = \vec{G} \neq \overrightarrow{P_i}$. This situation is not possible, since if a particle is at the global best it must also be at its personal best.

Case 2

For the second case, $\overrightarrow{X_i} = \overrightarrow{P_i} = \vec{G}$. This can only occur with the global best particle. In this situation $\Delta \overrightarrow{V_i} = \vec{0}$ and there is no change in bearing.

Case 3

For the third case, $\overrightarrow{X_i} = \overrightarrow{P_i} \neq \vec{G}$. This is often the situation for one of the non-global best particles. In this situation:

$$\Phi = \arctan\left(\frac{r_{1,2}(P_{i,2} - X_{i,2}) + r_{2,2}(G_2 - X_{i,2})}{r_{1,1}(P_{i,1} - X_{i,1}) + r_{2,1}(G_1 - X_{i,1})}\right)$$

Figure 7. The bearing of individual particles on Ackley's function, over the first 300 steps. The x-axis represents the step number. The y-axis represents the angular bearing of a particle. On the upper left $c_1 = c_2 = 1.49$, and $\omega = 0.729$. On the upper right $c_1 = c_2 = 1.49$, and $\omega = 1.0$. On the lower left $c_1 = c_2 = 2.0$, and $\omega = 0.729$. On the lower right $c_1 = c_2 = 2.0$, and $\omega = 1.0$.

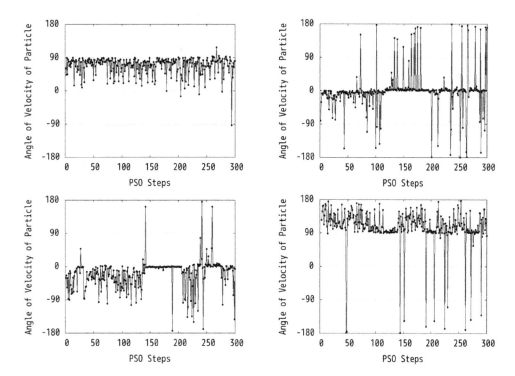

Since $\overrightarrow{X}_i = \overrightarrow{P}_i$ we can simplify:

$$\Phi = \arctan\left(\frac{r_{2,2}(G_2 - X_{i,2})}{r_{2,1}(G_1 - X_{i,1})}\right)$$

The baseline bearing is:

$$\Theta = \arctan\left(\frac{(G_2 - X_{i,2})}{(G_1 - X_{i,1})}\right)$$

We computed the expectation $E[\Phi] - \Theta$ and its standard deviation via simulation. Two points (X and G) were distributed via our $\mathcal{N}(0,1000^2)$ distribution, and Θ was computed. Then, Φ was computed after two calls to U(0,1). This was re-

peated four billion times. Figure 9 shows the results. For both graphs, the horizontal axis is the baseline bearing Θ in degrees. The left graph gives the measured difference $E[\Phi] - \Theta$ in degrees. The right graph gives the standard deviation of that difference in degrees.

For the purposes of verification of our simulation, we were able to calculate the closed form of $E[\Phi] - \Theta$. Note that:

$$\Phi = \arctan\left(\tan(\Theta)\left[\frac{r_{2,2}}{r_{2,1}}\right]\right)$$

Let u denote $r_{2,2}$ and v denote $r_{2,1}$. Then, due to the independence of the two random variables $E[\Phi]$ is expressed as the integral:

Figure 8. The bearing of individual particles on the Griewank function, over the first 300 steps. The x -axis represents the step number. The y -axis represents the angular bearing of a particle. On the upper left $c_1 = c_2 = 1.49$, and $\omega = 0.729$. On the upper right $c_1 = c_2 = 1.49$, and $\omega = 1.0$. On the lower left $c_1 = c_2 = 2.0$, and $\omega = 0.729$. On the lower right $c_1 = c_2 = 2.0$, and $\omega = 1.0$.

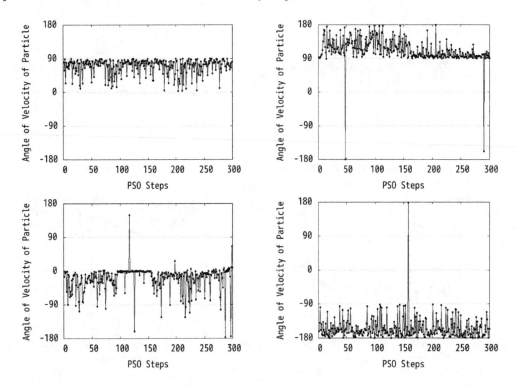

Figure 9. The expected angular bias (left) and the standard deviation (right) of PSO on case 3, determined via simulation

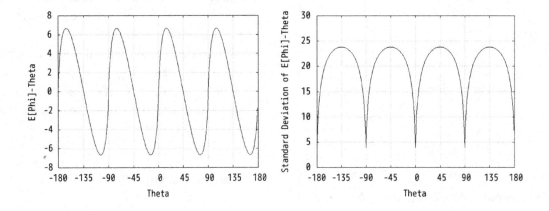

$$E[\Phi] = \int_0^1 \int_0^1 \arctan\left(\tan(\Theta)\frac{u}{v}\right) du\, dv$$

'

With some manipulation it can be shown that $E[\Phi] - \Theta = 0$ when $\Theta = k\pi$, where $k \in \mathbb{Z}$. Otherwise:

$$E[\Phi] - \Theta = \frac{\log((1 + \tan^2\theta)(\tan\theta - \cot\theta)) - 2\tan\theta\log(\tan\theta)}{4}$$

The empirical simulation results have an average absolute error of only 0.006 degrees from theory -- hence this confirms the correctness of the simulation.

Let us examine Figure 9 more carefully. Again, the left graph shows the difference $E[\Phi] - \Theta$. This is zero when $\Theta = k\pi / 4$, where $k \in \mathbb{Z}$. The difference is positive between $0°$ and $45°$, and negative between $45°$ and $90°$. This indicates a bias that tends to push particles *away* from directions parallel to the coordinate axes and *towards* directions parallel with the diagonals, which is opposite that which we expected! However, the right graph indicates that the variation in this difference is very low along directions parallel with the coordinate axes and highest along directions parallel with the diagonals.

Hence, an interesting picture emerges of two contrasting biases, *skew* and *spread* (our use of the term skew differs from that of Poli (2009)). Skew is the expected angular bias $E[\Phi] - \Theta$ (i.e., the first moment of the bias). Spread is the standard deviation of that bias (i.e., the square root of the second moment). If a particle is moving approximately parallel to the coordinate axes, it moves away towards the diagonals (skew). However, if a particle is moving approximately parallel to the diagonals, the high variance (spread) is likely to change that direction quickly. Hence, directions parallel to the coordinate axes act as unstable equilibria (or weak "basins of attraction" (Nix & Vose, 1992) for the particles. These basins are weak because the particles tend to change

direction towards bearings parallel with the diagonals. But the bearings parallel with the diagonals are even more unstable, due to the very high variance. The combination of both biases creates a situation where bearings parallel to the coordinate axes are preferred, but with a lot of noise in the bearings. This is precisely what we saw in the trajectory experiments earlier in the paper.

Note that this discussion is independent of the fitness function. However, from the perspective of function optimization, certain functions will match the biases well, while others will not. We will test our understanding by creating fitness functions that are hard for PSO. However, first we must confirm that these biases are the same for the remaining two cases.

Case 4

For the fourth case, $\overrightarrow{X_i} \neq \overrightarrow{P_i} = \vec{G}$. This is the behavior of the global best particle when it has moved past the best position. In this situation:

$$\Phi = \arctan\left(\frac{r_{1,2}(P_{i,2} - X_{i,2}) + r_{2,2}(G_2 - X_{i,2})}{r_{1,1}(P_{i,1} - X_{i,1}) + r_{2,1}(G_1 - X_{i,1})}\right)$$

Since $\overrightarrow{P_i} = \vec{G}$ we can simplify:

$$\Phi = \arctan\left(\frac{(r_{1,2} + r_{2,2})(P_{i,2} - X_{i,2})}{(r_{1,1} + r_{2,1})(P_{i,1} - X_{i,1})}\right)$$

The baseline bearing is:

$$\Theta = \arctan\left(\frac{(P_{i,2} - X_{i,2})}{(P_{i,1} - X_{i,1})}\right)$$

Again, we computed the expectation $E[\Phi] - \Theta$ and its standard deviation via simulation. Two points (X and P) were distributed via our $\mathcal{N}(0, 1000^2)$ distribution, and Θ was computed. Then Φ was computed after four calls to U(0,1).

Figure 10. The expected angular bias (left) and the standard deviation (right) of PSO on Case 4, determined via simulation

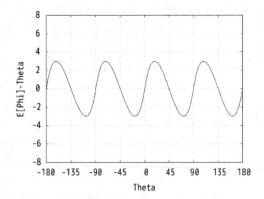
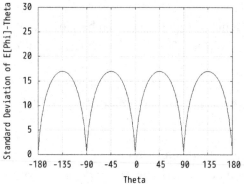

This was repeated four billion times. Figure 10 shows the results. For both graphs, the horizontal axis is the baseline bearing Θ in degrees. The left graph gives the measured difference $E[\Phi] - \Theta$ in degrees. The right graph gives the standard deviation of that difference in degrees.

For the purposes of verification of our simulation, we were able to calculate the closed form of $E[\Phi] - \Theta$. Since it involves a quadruple integral, it is much more difficult to solve than Case 3 and the details are shown in the Appendix A. In this case, the empirical simulation results have an average absolute error of only 0.003 degrees from theory -- once again confirming the correctness of the simulation.

Figure 10 is very similar to Figure 9 and there is no qualitative change in our interpretation of these graphs.

Case 5

For the fifth case, $\vec{X_i} \neq \vec{P_i} \neq \vec{G}$. This is also a situation encountered by non-global best particles.

Φ cannot be simplified:

$$\Phi = \arctan\left(\frac{r_{1,2}(P_{i,2} - X_{i,2}) + r_{2,2}(G_2 - X_{i,2})}{r_{1,1}(P_{i,1} - X_{i,1}) + r_{2,1}(G_1 - X_{i,1})}\right)$$

The baseline bearing is:

$$\Theta = \arctan\left(\frac{(P_{i,2} - X_{i,2}) + (G_2 - X_{i,2})}{(P_{i,1} - X_{i,1}) + (G_1 - X_{i,1})}\right)$$

The simulation results are shown in Figure 11. Again, for both graphs, the horizontal axis is the baseline bearing in degrees. The left graph gives the measured difference $E[\Phi] - \Theta$ in degrees. The right graph gives the standard deviation of that difference in degrees.

Once again, the results are similar to those generated before, other than the standard deviation being higher. This is reasonable since we have the most degrees of freedom in Case 5.

In summary, the theoretical analysis indicates that there is an angular bias in the core PSO algorithm. The bias consists of two parts. The first part, skew, pushes particles towards bearings parallel with the diagonals. However, the second part, spread, indicates that diagonal directions are highly unstable. The combination of the two parts creates a PSO bias that favors particle bearings that are aligned with the coordinate axes.

Figure 11. The expected angular bias (left) and the standard deviation (right) of PSO on case 5, determined via simulation

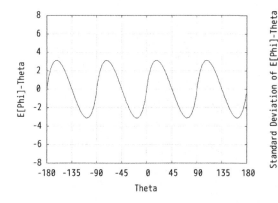 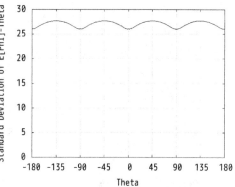

Demonstration of the Skew and Spread Biases

In this subsection, we demonstrate the skew and spread biases that were described earlier. We run PSO on the two-dimensional distance function again. Since we are minimizing, the optimum is at (0,0). A population of size 20 is used, $c_1 = c_2 = 2.0$, $\omega = 1.0$, and $V_{max} = 10.0$. A tight Gaussian cluster of particles is initialized at (300, 0) with $\sigma = 2.0$. The PSO is run for 30 steps, to focus on the behavior before the optimum is found. The PSO is run for 5,000 trials and the trajectories of all the particles are drawn. This is shown in the top left picture of Figure 12. Note that the particles eventually home in on the origin (in the center of the picture), but the spread bias is very clear.

Then the experiment is run again, but with the initial locations of the particles rotated $15°$ counterclockwise around the origin. It is important to note that we use the same random seed as before, so the random number sequence is identical. If the algorithm were rotationally invariant, the picture would look the same as before (other than the rotation). But since it is not rotationally invariant, the image is different (upper right). Note that the spread is increasing, and that more particles are skewed towards the $45°$ bearing.

The experiment was run again, with a rotation of $30°$. Both the spread and skew biases are even more acute (lower left). Finally, in the lower right picture the angle of rotation is $45°$. Now the skew bias is gone, but the spread bias is the greatest.

The only aspect that changed in the above experiments was the rotation of the initial location of the particles. Because PSO is rotationally variant, the behavior and performance of PSO depend on that angle of rotation. We can see this performance difference more clearly in Figure 13. The performance that is monitored is the best fitness seen by 30 steps. For this experiment, 200,000 trials were run for each angle of rotation. It is apparent that the best performance occurs when the initial locations of the particles are rotated by $-180°$, $-90°$, $0°$, $90°$ and $180°$. This is due to the lower spread and lack of skewness. As the initial locations are rotated, and spread and skewness increase, the performance becomes worse. However, at $-135°$, $-45°$, $45°$ and $135°$, performance becomes slightly better again. It is possible that the lack of skewness at $45°$ is causing this improvement. However, there is also another possibility, which we discuss next.

Figure 12. Skew and spread of PSO

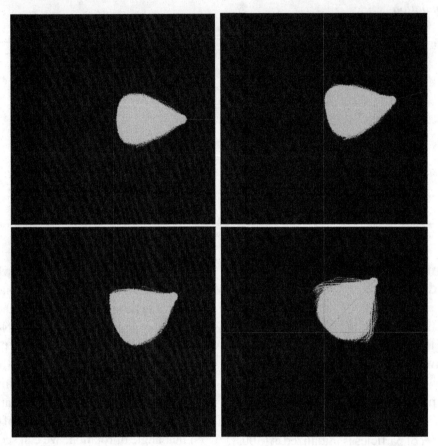

Figure 13. Performance of PSO as the initial locations of the particles are rotated

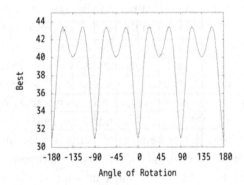

Magnitude Bias

To explain why the performance might improve

at $-135°$, $-45°$, $45°$ and $135°$, we considered the expected magnitude of the change in velocity:

$$E\left[\| c_1 \vec{r_1} \odot (\vec{P_i} - \vec{X_i}(t)) + c_2 \vec{r_2} \odot (\vec{G} - \vec{X_i}(t)) \|\right]$$

Assuming $c_1 = c_2 = c$:

$$cE\left[\| \vec{r_1} \odot (\vec{P_i} - \vec{X_i}(t)) + \vec{r_2} \odot (\vec{G} - \vec{X_i}(t)) \|\right]$$

As before, we computed this expectation via simulation, for two dimensions. However, in this case the radius of the distribution of the initial particles plays an important role. For these experiments, we used a uniform distribution within a circle of radius 10.0. The results are displayed

Figure 14. PSO magnitude bias for Case 3 (left), Case 4 (middle) and Case 5 (right)

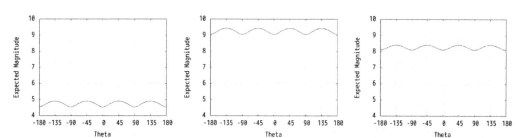

for Cases 3, 4 and 5, in Figure 14. One million samples were generated for each of the three cases.

As can be seen, there is a *magnitude* bias that depends on the baseline angle Θ. The expected magnitude of the change in velocity vector is greater along bearings parallel with the diagonals at $-135°$, $-45°$, $45°$ and $135°$. Hence, on average, the particles move somewhat faster when traveling along those bearings. This appears to at least partially explain the mild improvement in the performance at $-135°$, $-45°$, $45°$ and $135°$ in Figure 13.

It should be noted that if the initialization radius is multiplied by a factor c, the results are also multiplied by that factor. So, what is important is the ratio of the expected maximum magnitude to the expected minimum. This ratio is approximately 1.083 for Case 3, 1.043 for Case 4 and 1.04 for Case 5.

The relative importance of the magnitude bias in comparison to skew and spread is unclear. A further investigation of the magnitude bias will occur in future work. The remainder of this paper will focus on creating fitness functions that will demonstrate how skew and spread can help or hinder PSO performance, depending on the angle of rotation.

RESULTS WITH AN ELLIPSE

Given the skew and spread biases, we decided to test the performance of PSO on a fitness function that is extremely radially asymmetric, namely, a two-dimensional ellipse. We also use the more conventional initialization of particles using a uniform distribution U(-1000, 1000) for both the x and y locations. Again, we used a population size of 20, $c_1 = c_2 = 2.0$ and $V_{max} = 10.0$.

We used a simple hill-climber to adapt the semi-major and semi-minor axes of the ellipse -- to maximize the difference between the best fitness at rotation angles $45°$ and $0°$. In the prior results with the distance function, there was no need to rotate the fitness function (since it is radially symmetric), although the initial locations of the particles were rotated. However, an ellipse is not radially symmetric, hence we need to rotate both the initial location of the particles and the fitness function around the origin of the coordinate system. An example is shown in Figure 15. The left picture shows a portion of the un-rotated ellipse (from $-500 \leq x \leq 500$ and $-400 \leq y \leq 400$). The lighter areas represent higher fitness, and the optimum is at the center of the picture. Note that due to the eccentricity, the structure looks very much like a trough. The right picture illustrates a rotation of $10°$ counter-clockwise around the origin. Note that rotating the "system" refers to rotating the particles and the fitness function simultaneously.

The results are shown in Figure 16, averaged over 20,000 trials. The left graph shows the best performance for all rotation angles, after 500 steps. The right graph shows the performance curves for both $0°$ and $45°$ rotations, over all 500 steps.

Figure 15. A top-down illustration of the elliptical fitness function, rotated 0° *(left) and* 10° *(right)*

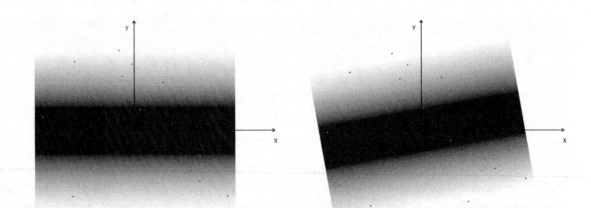

Figure 16. Performance of PSO as the system is rotated, for a very eccentric ellipse

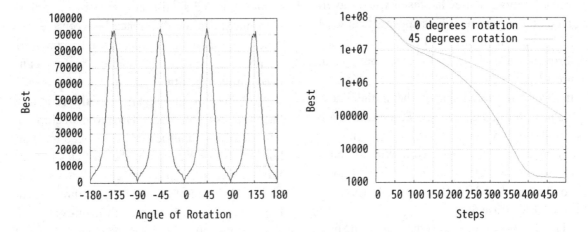

(Note that a logarithmic scale is used for performance.) The performance is approximately 70 times worse when the ellipse is rotated 45°.

RESULTS WITH AN ELLIPSE WITH A MINESHAFT

Finally, we added a deep cylindrical mineshaft to the elliptical fitness function. The hill-climber adapted the semi-major and semi-minor axes, as well as the location and diameter of the mineshaft.

The fitness landscape is shown in Figure 17 ($-500 \leq x \leq 500$ and $-400 \leq y \leq 400$). The mineshaft is located slightly to the right of the center, at $(8, 0)$. The fitness of the mineshaft is $-10,000$. The hill-climber maximized the difference between the probability of finding the mineshaft at rotation angles 45° and 0°. Figure 19 (Appendix B) shows the final fitness function.

The results are shown in Figure 18, averaged over 20,000 trials. The left graph shows the best performance for all rotation angles, after 500 steps. This graph shows that the ellipse must be rotated

Figure 17. A top-down illustration of the elliptical fitness function, with the mineshaft located at (8,0)

Figure 18. Performance of PSO as the system is rotated, for a very eccentric ellipse with a mineshaft

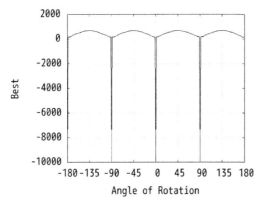
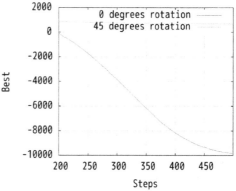

to be aligned exactly with the coordinate axes in order for the optimum to be found (roughly 98% of the time). Even with a $1°$ rotation, the optimum is not found. The right graph shows the performance curves for both $0°$ and $45°$ rotations, over all 500 steps. It is clear that the PSO is making virtually no improvement when the system is rotated $45°$. However, at $0°$ rotation the PSO performance improvement is quite smooth.

CONCLUSION

In this paper, we investigated the claim made by Janson and Middendorf (2007) that when running the traditional PSO algorithm, "most movement steps occurred parallel to one of the coordinate axes." This claim is shown to be true. We then theoretically analyzed the dynamics of PSO by looking at its angular bias. This bias is composed of both skew and spread components -- the two components combined produce the behavior that the bearings of particles tend to be parallel with coordinate axes. A third bias, called the magnitude bias, is also identified.

All of these biases are manifestations of the rotational variance of standard PSO. These biases exist despite changes in standard parameter settings, the number of particles and the number of dimensions.

We use our understanding of these biases to create fitness functions that can be easy or hard for PSO, depending on the angle of rotation. These functions are highly eccentric ellipses that create a trough (or ridge if the fitness function is inverted) in the fitness landscape. Our results indicate that PSO will have difficulty following a trough that is not aligned with the coordinate axes. This occurs because both high spread and skewness tend to push particles out of the trough. This is important if following a trough is necessary for good performance.

The fact that PSO is rotationally variant and hence has associated biases is not surprising. For example, evolutionary algorithms are also rotationally variant (Salomon, 1995). Yet, this does not discourage us from using these algorithms. The point of our paper is not that the standard PSO is "broken" or that it needs to be "fixed." Rather, as with all algorithms, our point is that we need to understand the biases of our algorithms, so that they can be matched to the characteristics of the problems. For example, if PSO is performing poorly, the user may wish to examine the landscape for linear features. If they exist, the landscape may need to be rotated.

Ultimately, what we are seeing is a gradual relaxation of algorithmic properties that used to be deemed necessary. For example, old search algorithms were always sound and complete. The introduction of incomplete algorithms such as PSO and evolutionary algorithms was met with considerable resistance, because, if a solution was not found, we could not say that one does not exist. Similarly, rotational invariance is a property that we used to take for granted. Yet, many of our new algorithms do not possess this property either. This is not necessarily a problem. The key is to analyze the data and see if it has features that do not match the algorithm (Kennedy & Spears, 1998; De Jong et al. 1995). If so, the data needs to be recast, or the algorithm needs to be changed (or another algorithm should be chosen).

ACKNOWLEDGMENT

We thank John Hitchcock for showing us a more elegant solution to Case 3:

$$E[\Phi] - \Theta = \frac{\cot\Theta\log(\cos\Theta) - \tan\Theta\log(\sin\Theta)}{2}$$

REFERENCES

Blackwell, T. M. (2005). Particle swarms and population diversity. *Soft Computing*, *9*(11), 793–802. doi:10.1007/s00500-004-0420-5

Brandstatter, B., & Baumgartner, U. (2002). Particle swarm optimization mass-spring system analogon. *IEEE Transactions on Magnetics*, *38*(2), 997–1000. doi:10.1109/20.996256

Campana, E. F., Fasano, G., Peri, D., & Pinto, A. (2006). Particle swarm optimization: Efficient globally convergent modifications. In *Proceedings of the III European Conference on Computational Mechanics: Solids, Structures and Coupled Problems in Engineering* (pp. 412). New York: Springer.

Campana, E. F., Fasano, G., & Pinto, A. (2006). Dynamic system analysis and initial particles position in particle swarm optimization. In *Proceedings of the IEEE Swarm Intelligence Symposium*, Indianapolis, IN.

Clerc, M. (2001). *PSO: the old bias and its solution*. Retrieved April 28, 2010, from http://clerc.maurice.free.fr/pso/

Clerc, M., & Kennedy, J. (2002). The particle swarm - explosion, stability, and convergence in a multidimensional complex space. *IEEE Transactions on Evolutionary Computation*, *6*(1), 58–73. doi:10.1109/4235.985692

DeJong, K. A., Spears, W. M., & Gordon, D. F. (1995). Using Markov chains to analyze GAFOs. In *Foundations of Genetic Algorithms 3* (pp. 115–137). San Francisco, CA: Morgan Kaufmann.

Eberhart, R., & Shi, Y. (2000). Comparing inertia weights and constriction factors in particle swarm optimization. In *Proceedings of the Congress on Evolutionary Computation* (pp. 84-88).

Eberhart, R., Shi, Y., & Kennedy, J. (2001). *Swarm Intelligence*. San Francisco, CA: Morgan Kaufmann.

Hansen, N., Ros, R., Mauny, N., Schoenauer, M., & Auger, A. (2008). *PSO facing non-separable and ill-conditioned problems* (Tech. Rep. No. 6447). Institut National de Recherche en Informatique et en Automatique (INRIA).

Janson, S., & Middendorf, M. (2007). On trajectories of particles in PSO. In *IEEE Swarm Intelligence Symposium* (pp. 150-155).

Kadirkamanathan, K. S. V., & Fleming, P. J. (2006). Stability analysis of the particle dynamics in particle swarm optimizer. *IEEE Transactions on Evolutionary Computation*, *10*(3), 245–255. doi:10.1109/TEVC.2005.857077

Kennedy, J. (2007). *Personal communication with Dr. W. Spears*.

Kennedy, J., & Eberhart, R. (1995). Particle swarm optimization. In *IEEE International Conference on Neural Networks* (Vol. 4, pp. 1942-1948).

Kennedy, J., & Spears, W. M. (1998). Matching algorithms to problems: An experimental test of the particle swarm and some genetic algorithms on the multimodal problem generator. In *Proceedings of the IEEE Congress on Evolutionary Computation* (pp. 78-83).

Mitchell, T. (1997). *Machine Learning*. New York: McGraw Hill.

Monson, C., & Seppi, K. (2005). Exposing origin-seeking bias in PSO. In *Proceedings of the Conference on Genetic and Evolutionary Computation* (pp. 241-248).

Nix, A., & Vose, M. (1992). Modelling genetic algorithms with Markov chains. *Annals of Mathematics and Artificial Intelligence*, *5*, 79–88. doi:10.1007/BF01530781

Ozcan, E., Cad, S., No, T. S., & Mohan, C. K. (1999). Particle swarm optimization: Surfing the waves. In *Proceedings of the Congress on Evolutionary Computation* (pp. 6-9). Washington, DC: IEEE Press.

Ozcan, E., & Mohan, C. K. (1998). Analysis of a simple particle swarm optimization system. In *Proceedings of the Intelligent Engineering Systems through Artificial. Neural Networks*, *8*, 253–258.

Poli, R. (2009). Mean and variance of the sampling distribution of particle swarm optimizers during stagnation. *IEEE Transactions on Evolutionary Computation*, *13*(4), 712–721. doi:10.1109/TEVC.2008.2011744

Salomon, R. (1995). Reevaluating genetic algorithm performance under coordinate rotation of benchmark functions. *Bio Systems*, *39*(3), 263–278. doi:10.1016/0303-2647(96)01621-8

Shi, Y., & Eberhart, R. (1998). A modified particle swarm optimizer. In *Proceedings of the IEEE World Congress on Computational Intelligence* (pp. 69-73).

Shi, Y., & Eberhart, R. (2008). Population diversity of particle swarms. In *Proceedings of the IEEE Congress on Evolutionary Computation* (pp. 1063-1067).

Shi, Y., & Eberhart, R. (2009). Monitoring of particle swarm optimization. *Frontiers of Computer Science in China*, *3*(1), 31–37. doi:10.1007/s11704-009-0008-4

Trelea, I. (2003). The particle swarm optimization algorithm: Convergence analysis and parameter selection. *Information Processing Letters*, *85*, 317–325. doi:10.1016/S0020-0190(02)00447-7

van den Bergh, F. (2001). *An analysis of particle swarm optimizers*. Unpublished doctoral dissertation, University of Pretoria, Pretoria, South Africa.

van den Bergh, F., & Engelbrecht, A. (2006). A study of particle swarm optimization particle trajectories. *Information Sciences*, *176*(8), 937–971. doi:10.1016/j.ins.2005.02.003

Wilke, D. (2005). *Analysis of the particle swarm optimization algorithm*. Unpublished master's thesis, University of Pretoria, Pretoria, South Africa.

Wolpert, D. H., & Macready, W. G. (1997). No Free Lunch theorems for optimization. *IEEE Transactions on Evolutionary Computation*, *1*(1), 67–82. doi:10.1109/4235.585893

Yasuda, K., Ide, A., & Iwasaki, N. (2003). Adaptive particle swarm optimization. In *Proceedings of the IEEE International Conference on Systems, Man, and Cybernetics* (pp. 1554-1559).

APPENDIX A

Recall that for Case 4:

$$\Phi = \arctan\left(\frac{(r_{1,2} + r_{2,2})(P_{i,2} - X_{i,2})}{(r_{1,1} + r_{2,1})(P_{i,1} - X_{i,1})}\right)$$

Let u denote $r_{1,2}$ and v denote $r_{2,2}$. Furthermore, let w denote $r_{1,1}$ and x denote $r_{2,1}$.

Then, due to the independence of the four random variables $E[\Phi]$ is expressed as the integral:

$$E[\Phi] = \int_0^1 \int_0^1 \int_0^1 \int_0^1 \arctan\left(\tan(\Theta)\frac{u+v}{w+x}\right) du\,dv\,dw\,dx$$

This quadruple integral can be separated into four double integrals by noting that the sum of two U(0,1) random variables is a T(0,1,2) triangular random variable. Let $y = u + v$ and $z = w + x$. Then

$$E[\Phi] = \int_0^1 \int_0^1 \arctan\left(\tan(\Theta)\frac{y}{z}\right) y\,z\,dy\,dz\ +$$
$$\int_1^2 \int_0^1 \arctan\left(\tan(\Theta)\frac{y}{z}\right) y\,(2-z)\,dy\,dz\ +$$
$$\int_0^1 \int_1^2 \arctan\left(\tan(\Theta)\frac{y}{z}\right) (2-y)\,z\,dy\,dz\ +$$
$$\int_1^2 \int_1^2 \arctan\left(\tan(\Theta)\frac{y}{z}\right) (2-y)\,(2-z)\,dy\,dz$$

The solution to the first integral is:

$$\left(\frac{1}{8tan^2(\Theta)}\right)\left(\Theta + tan^3(\Theta) + 2\Theta tan^2(\Theta) - tan(\Theta) - tan^4(\Theta)atan\left(\frac{1}{tan(\Theta)}\right)\right)$$

The solution to the second integral is:

$$-\frac{tan(\Theta)}{8} - \frac{1}{8tan(\Theta)} + \frac{tan(\Theta)}{3}\log(tan^2(\Theta) + 4) - \frac{tan(\Theta)}{3}\log(tan^2(\Theta) + 1)\ +$$

$$\left(-\frac{1}{8}tan^2(\Theta) + \frac{2}{3tan^2(\Theta)} + 1\right)atan\left(\frac{1}{2}tan(\Theta)\right) +$$

$$\left(\frac{1}{8}tan^2(\Theta) - \frac{5}{24tan^2(\Theta)} - \frac{3}{4}\right)\Theta$$

The solution to the third integral is:

$$-\frac{2}{3}tan^2(\Theta)atan\left(\frac{1}{2tan(\Theta)}\right) + \frac{5}{24}tan^2(\Theta)atan\left(\frac{1}{tan(\Theta)}\right) -$$

$$\frac{\log(4tan^2(\Theta)+1)}{3tan(\Theta)} + \frac{\log(tan^2(\Theta)+1)}{3tan(\Theta)} +$$

$$\left(1 - \frac{1}{8tan^2(\Theta)}\right)atan(2tan(\Theta)) + \left(\frac{1}{8tan^2(\Theta)} - \frac{3}{4}\right)\Theta + \frac{1}{8}tan(\Theta) + \frac{1}{8tan(\Theta)}$$

The solution to the fourth integral is:

$$\left(-\frac{2}{3}tan(\Theta) + \frac{4}{3tan(\Theta)}\right)\log(tan^2(\Theta)+4) + \left(\frac{4}{3}tan(\Theta) - \frac{4}{3tan(\Theta)}\right)\log(4tan^2(\Theta)+4) +$$

$$\left(\frac{2}{3}tan(\Theta) - \frac{2}{3tan(\Theta)}\right)\log(tan^2(\Theta)+1) + \left(-\frac{4}{3}tan(\Theta) + \frac{2}{3tan(\Theta)}\right)\log(4tan^2(\Theta)+1) +$$

$$\left(\frac{1}{8tan(\Theta)} - \frac{1}{8}tan(\Theta)\right) + \left(\frac{5}{24}tan^2(\Theta) + \frac{2}{3tan^2(\Theta)} - 3\right)atan\left(\frac{1}{2}tan(\Theta)\right) +$$

$$\left(\frac{2}{3}tan^2(\Theta) + \frac{5}{24tan^2(\Theta)} - 3\right)atan(2tan(\Theta)) + \left(-\frac{7}{8}tan^2(\Theta) - \frac{7}{8tan^2(\Theta)} + \frac{25}{4}\right)\Theta$$

APPENDIX B

Table 1. Fitness functions

```
double FitnessDistance (const double *position, const int dimensions)
{
double sumsqrs = 0.0;
for (int i = 0; i < dimensions; ++i) sumsqrs += position[i] * position[i];
return sqrt(sumsqrs);
}
double FitnessAckley (const double *position)
{
double sum1 = 0.0, sum2 = 0.0;
position[0] = position[0] - 500;
position[1] = position[1] - 500;
sum1 = position[0] * position[0] + position[1] * position[1];
sum2 = cos(2 * PI * position[0]) + cos(2 * PI * position[1]);
return -20.0 * exp(-0.02 * sqrt(sum1/2.0)) - exp(sum2/2.0) + 20 + 2.71828;
}
double FitnessGriewank (const double *position)
{
double sum = 0.0;
position[0] = position[0] - 500;
position[1] = position[1] - 500;
sum = position[0] * position[0] + position[1] * position[1];
return 1.0 + sum * (1.0/4000.0) - cos(position[0]) * cos(position[1] / sqrt(2));
}
double FitnessEllipse (const double *position)
{
double xt = position[0] / 0.000076;
double yt = position[1] / 0.000001;
return sqrt(xt * xt + yt * yt);
}
double FitnessEllipseWithMineshaft (const double *position)
{
double delX = position[0] - 8.0;
double delY = position[1];
if (sqrt(delX * delX + delY * delY) <= 1.0) return -10000.0; // found the shaft! else {
double xt = position[0];
double yt = position[1] / 0.0001;
return sqrt(xt * xt + yt * yt);
} }
```

This work was previously published in International Journal of Swarm Intelligence Research, Volume 1, Issue 2, edited by Yuhui Shi, pp. 34-57, copyright 2010 by IGI Publishing (an imprint of IGI Global)

Chapter 3
Taguchi–Particle Swarm Optimization for Numerical Optimization

T. O. Ting
HKUSpace Global College, China

H. C. Ting
Tunku Abdul Rahman College, Malaysia

T. S. Lee
Multimedia University, Malaysia

ABSTRACT

In this work, a hybrid Taguchi-Particle Swarm Optimization (TPSO) is proposed to solve global numerical optimization problems with continuous and discrete variables. This hybrid algorithm combines the well-known Particle Swarm Optimization Algorithm with the established Taguchi method, which has been an important tool for robust design. This paper presents the improvements obtained despite the simplicity of the hybridization process. The Taguchi method is run only once in every PSO iteration and therefore does not give significant impact in terms of computational cost. The method creates a more diversified population, which also contributes to the success of avoiding premature convergence. The proposed method is effectively applied to solve 13 benchmark problems. This study's results show drastic improvements in comparison with the standard PSO algorithm involving continuous and discrete variables on high dimensional benchmark functions.

INTRODUCTION

The innovative paradigm of behavioral modeling based on the concept of swarm intelligence was proposed by Kennedy and Eberhart (Kennedy & Eberhart, 1995). The particle swarm optimization (PSO) algorithm consists of members sharing information among them, a fact that leads to increased efficiency. A myriad of variants of particle swarm optimizers have been developed with numerous acronyms given by respective researchers. A survey of the variants of PSO discloses some common strategies adopted to achieve better

DOI: 10.4018/978-1-4666-1592-2.ch003

convergence. There are three groups of strategies in these variants. The first strategy is to divide the population into some or many smaller sizes. PSO variants of such a category are:

i.   Co-evolutionary PSO (Co-PSO) (Shi & Krohling, 2002),
ii.   Cooperative PSO (CPSO) (Bergh & Engelbrecht, 2004),
iii.   Concurrent PSO (CONPSO) (Baskar & Suganthan, 2004),
iv.   Dynamic Multi-Swarm PSO (DMS-PSO) (Liang & Suganthan, 2005),
v.   Multi-population Cooperative PSO (MCPSO) (Niu, Zhu, & He, 2005) and
vi.   Species-based PSO (SPSO) (Parrot & Li, 2006)
vii.   NichePSO (Brits, Engelbrecht, & Bergh, 2007),

The second strategy is to design the interaction between particles or sub-swarms. Instead of the normal social learning from local best particle, other leaders from other sub-swarms have the right to influence the optimality search of another sub group. Hierarchical PSO (H-PSO) (Janson & Middendorf, 2005) and MCPSO are typical examples of this approach where hierarchy or master-slave relationship can be observed. In Co-PSO, CONPSO and Comprehensive Learning PSO (CLPSO) (Liang, Qin, Suganthan, & Baskar, n.d.), different social learning are experienced by the particles.

The third strategy is to gradually transform local neighborhood at the beginning of the search into a global one at the end. Unified PSO (UPSO) (Parsopoulos & Vrahatis, 2007) seems to have applied this approach successfully. However, Adaptive Hierarchical PSO (AH-PSO) happens to do exactly the opposite. Other variants such as the Levy PSO (Richer & Blackwell, 2006) and PSO with stretching function (Parsopoulos & Vrahatis, 2004) manipulate the random distribution and

objective functions respectively, instead of the neighborhood topology.

Many of the improved PSO algorithms incorporate some improvement strategies in the algorithms itself (Bergh & Engelbrecht, 2004) (Yao, Liu, & Lin, 1999) (Leung & Wang, 2001) (Vasconcelos, Ramirez, Takahashi, & Saldanha, 2001) (Clerc & Kennedy, 2002) while some improved algorithms are the result of hybridizing two algorithms (Krink & Lovbjerg, 2002) (Tsai, Liu, & Chou, 2004). However, the common drawback of hybridization has been the introduction of complexity in the algorithm thereby increases the computational cost. The unique feature of PSO compared to other algorithms has been signified by its fast convergence capability. However, the drawback is that it does not guarantee global optimum, and in most of the time premature convergence occurs.

To overcome the weakness of PSO above, we incorporate the concept of Taguchi method into PSO to avoid premature convergence while maintaining its fast convergence characteristic. The Taguchi method (Ross, 1989) is an established approach for robust design, applying the idea from statistical experiment design for evaluating and improvements in products, processes and equipment. The key to Taguchi concept is to improve the quality of a product by minimizing the effect of the causes of variation without the elimination of the relevant causes. The two major tools used in the Taguchi method are:

i.   Signal-to-noise ratio (SNR) which measures quality, and
ii.   Orthogonal arrays which are used to study many design parameters simultaneously.

This work adopts the concept of Taguchi method into PSO algorithm to improve its convergence. The hybrid algorithm developed in this work is so called Taguchi-PSO (TPSO) and results on benchmark problems verify the feasibility of Taguchi method in PSO.

Table 1. Orthogonal array of L8(27)

Experiment Number	Factors (Dimension in PSO concept)							SNR (Fitness)
	A	**B**	**C**	**D**	**E**	F	G	**SNR (Fitness)**
1	1	1	1	1	1	1	1	Fit_1
2	1	1	1	2	2	2	2	Fit_2
3	1	2	2	1	1	2	2	Fit_3
4	1	2	2	2	2	1	1	Fit_4
5	2	1	2	1	2	1	2	Fit_5
6	2	1	2	2	1	2	1	Fit_6
7	2	2	1	1	2	2	1	Fit_7
8	2	2	1	2	1	1	2	Fit_8

THE CONCEPT OF TAGUCHI METHOD

Taguchi method has been introduced by Dr. Genichi Taguchi since 1940s. The method is based on several statistical concepts which have proven to be valuable tool in the subject of quality improvement. Many Japanese manufacturers have applied this approach for improving product and process quality with unprecedented success. Taguchi essentially utilizes the conventional statistical tools, which has been simplified by identifying a set of stringent guidelines for experiment layout and the analysis of results. Recently western industries have begun to recognize Taguchi's method as simple but highly effective approach in improving product and process quality. Two major tools used in the Taguchi method are the orthogonal array and the SNR. This paper incorporates the two-level orthogonal arrays (Table 1), whereby the two levels are denoted by number 1 and 2 in the table. The basic concept of the structure and usage of two-level orthogonal arrays are briefly described here. This is adequate in the context of describing the development of the hybrid TPSO algorithm.

The general form of two-level standard orthogonal arrays can be represented by the following mathematical term

$$L_n(2^{n-1}) \qquad\qquad (1)$$

whereby

$n = 2k$ *number of experimental runs;*

k a positive integer greater than 1;

2 *number of levels for each factor;*

n-1 number of columns in the orthogonal array.

The two-level standard orthogonal arrays most often used in practice are L4(23), L8(27), L16(215) and L32(231). Table 1 shows an orthogonal array L8(27), taken from (Ross, 1989), also available in (Tsai, Liu, & Chou, 2004). The number on the left of each row is called the experiment number or run number and it runs from 1 to 8. In fact, each row represents a particle with 7 dimensions (7 factors). The basic idea of Taguchi-PSO is to choose the optimal dimension among two randomly chosen particles from each of the iterations. After choosing two particles randomly, experiments 1 to 8 in Table 1 are performed on these particles to choose the better dimension among the particles to form a new particle with better fitness. The number 1 and 2 represent first and second particle respectively. Therefore, the new particle will have the dimension value from particle 1 and 2. This is a sort of dimension optimization, which is quite a new concept in the area of evolutionary algorithms at this stage.

Besides two-level orthogonal arrays, there exists three-level and four-level orthogonal arrays which can provide better precision to the specified process. However, these higher levels are not used in this work to avoid introducing unnecessary complexity into the proposed algorithm. Instead, two-level orthogonal arrays are adopted in solving benchmark problems as this is simpler and can be easily implemented. The detailed description of how these orthogonal arrays are formed can be found in (Ross, 1989) (Taguchi, Chowdhury, & Taguchi, 2000) (Roy, 1990). Many designed experiments use matrices called orthogonal arrays for each experimental run and for analyzing the dimensional values. The array is called orthogonal because all columns can be evaluated independently of one another, as shown in Table 1. As one row represents a particle, therefore each row has its own fitness value, denoted as $f_1, f_2 \ldots f_8$ in Table 1. These values are important for Taguchi operation which will be elaborated at the end of this paper.

OVERVIEW OF PARTICLE SWARM OPTIMIZATION

Kennedy and Eberhart (Kennedy & Eberhart, 1995) first introduced the particle swarm optimization (PSO) method. Similar to evolutionary computation, a population of candidate solutions is used. The method has been found to be robust in solving real-world problems featuring non-differentiability, high dimension, multiple optima and non-linearity. PSO algorithm is a model that mimics the movement of individuals (fishes, birds, or insects) within a group (school, flock, and swarm). Similar to GA, a PSO consists of a population refining its knowledge of the given search space. PSO is inspired by models of flocking behaviour.

Instead of using evolutionary operators such as selection, mutation and crossover, each particle in the population moves in the search space with velocity which is dynamically adjusted and all particles are assumed to be of no volume. In short, the whole concept of PSO can be concluded in a sentence that is "A population consisting N particles, each particles has d variables (dimensions) which have its own ranges for each value, velocities and positions are updated every iteration until maximum iteration is reached". Each particle keeps track of its own coordinates in the search space, which are associated with the best solution it has achieved in history. This value is known as *pbest*. Another best value that is tracked by the global version of the particle swarm optimizer is the overall best value or the best solution in the population is called *gbest*.

The PSO concept consists of changing the velocity of each particle toward its *pbest* and *gbest* solutions at each time step. The movement is weighted by a random term, with separate random numbers being generated toward *pbest* and *gbest* values. For example the ith particle consisting d dimensions is represented as:

$$X_i = [(X_i 1),(X_i 2), (X_i 3), \ldots, (X_i d)] \quad (2)$$

The same notation applied to the velocity,

$$V_i = [(V_i 1), (V_i 2), (V_i 3), \ldots, (V_i d)] \quad (3)$$

The best previous position of the ith particle is recorded and represented as

$$pbest_i = [(pbest_i 1), (pbest_i 2), (pbest_i 3), \ldots (pbest_i d)] \quad (4)$$

In the case of minimization that we consider in this paper, the value of *pbest_i* with lowest fitness is known as *gbest*. The modification of velocity and position can be calculated using the current velocity and the distance of current position from *pbest$_i$* to *gbest*. This is shown in the following formulas:

$$V_{i,j}^t = wV_i^{t-1} + ñ_1 r_1 (gbest_{i,j} - X_{i,j}^{t-1}) + ñ_2 r_2 \left(pbest_{i,j} - X_{i,j}^{t-1} \right)$$

(5)

$$X_{i,j}^t = X_{i,j}^{t-1} + V_{i,j}^t \qquad (6)$$

where $i \in 1 \ldots N, j \in 1 \ldots d, t \in = 1 \ldots T$ with N is the number of population size, d is the number of dimension and T is the number of maximum generation.

The position, X of each particle is updated for every dimension for all particles in each iteration. This is done by adding the velocity vector to the position vector, as described in equation (6) above. In equation (5), w is known as the inertia weight. This parameter was introduced by Shi and Eberhart (Shi & Eberhart, 1998) to accelerate the convergence of PSO. Suitable selection of w provides a balance between global and local explorations, thus requiring less iteration on average to find sufficiently optimal solution. Low values of w limits the contribution of the previous velocity to the new velocity, limiting step sizes and therefore, limiting exploration. On the other hand, high values of w result in abrupt movement toward targeted search regions.

The parameters ρ_1 and ρ_2 are set to constant values, which are normally given as 2.0 whereas r_1 and r_2 are two random values, uniformly distributed in [0, 1]. The constants, ρ_1 and ρ_2 represent the relative weight of the acceleration that attracts each particle toward *pbest* and *gbest* positions. Since, $\rho_1 = \rho_2 = 2$, therefore the relative attraction towards *pbest* and *gbest* is the same.

TAGUCHI-PARTICLE SWARM OPTIMIZATION

In this section, we illustrate with a simple example the concept of Taguchi-PSO. The flow of TPSO is

as shown in Figure 1. From this figure, it can be observed that the Taguchi method is performed after the entire population is updated via PSO equations.

Following this Taguchi method, further elaborations are given in a list of steps below. The pseudo-codes are implemented in Visual Basic programming language.

1. Choose two particles randomly from the current population, noted as P_1 and P_2.
2. Create 8 new particles; noted as T_1, T_2 … T_8 from P_1 and P_2. (Each particle represents one experiment as shown in Table 1).
3. Assign all the relevant dimensions (columns A-G) to the 8 new particles T_1, T_2 … T_8 from P_1 and P_2 based on these columns in orthogonal array given in Table 1. Number 1 means the relevant dimension of new particle is copied from P_1 whereas number 2 means the relevant dimension is from P_2.
4. Evaluate the fitness of T_1, T_2 … T_8 (refer to last column of Table 1).
5. Calculate the effect of various factors (A, B, …, G) defined as:

$$E(factor, level) = \sum_{\substack{i \in (level=1) \\ or (level=2)}}^{8} f_i$$

$$factor \in [A, B, \ldots G], \quad level \in [1, 2]$$

For instance, for the case of *factor*=B and *level*=1, we have

$$E(B,1) = \sum_{i=1,2,5,6}^{8} f_i = f_1 + f_2 + f_5 + f_6$$

The same calculation is applied to the similar factor with level=2

$$E(B,2) = \sum_{i=3,4,7,8}^{8} f_i = f_3 + f_4 + f_7 + f_8$$

Figure 1. Flow diagram of Taguchi-PSO

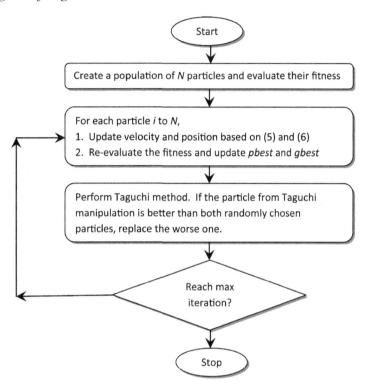

6. Assign the relevant dimension to the optimal particle Po based on the following rule, taking factor=A in this case
   If $E(A,1) < E(A,2)$ **Then** $P^o.x(A)=P_1.x(A)$
   Else
   $P^o.x(A)=P_2.x(A)$
   Endif

7. Replace the worse particle among the two randomly chosen if the optimal particle is better than both. Also, update the gbest as follows.
   If P^o.Fit<P_1.Fit **And** P^o.Fit<P_2.Fit **Then**
   If P_1.Fit>P_2.Fit **Then**
   $P_1 = P^o$
   If P_1.Fit<*gbest*.Fit **Then** *gbest* = P_1
   ElseIf P_2.Fit>P_1.Fit **Then**
   $P_2 = P^o$
   If P_2.Fit<*gbest*.Fit **Then** *gbest* = P_2
   End If
   End If

8. Continue with the next iteration until maximum generation is reached

Step 6 above is important as a better dimension value is assigned to optimal particle P_o from two randomly chosen particles. This technique provides an interesting philosophy of vertical optimization which is very useful for many real world optimization problems. For better performance in regards to convergence, the two particles in step 2 of Taguchi method are randomly chosen from *pbest* vector. As of such, the Taguchi method will therefore improve the dimensions value among *pbest*, an effective way leading to faster convergence and better accuracy. We employ the similar methodology in this work for better performance.

EXPERIMENT SETTINGS

A set of benchmark problems with their mathematical formulas are taken from (Yao, Liu, & Lin, 1999) as test problems to verify the robustness of the proposed strategy. The list in Table 2 shows the mathematical formulation of the test problems with their names and search ranges. The number of dimension is set to 7 for all the benchmark functions. The global minimum and maximum iteration are given in Table 3 and Table 4. In this work, the population size is set to 30 particles as this is sufficient. The inertia weight, w in PSO algorithm is set to 0.5. The maximum velocity is bounded within the search range as specified in Table 2.

RESULTS

A. Results on 7-Dimensional Benchmark Problems

Two sets of results are obtained in this experiment. The first set is the results obtained from standard PSO whereas the second set is the results of TPSO on benchmark problems. Results are averaged over 50 trials recorded as mean best and standard deviation are calculated, as shown in Table 3 below. From these results, the mean best obtained for TPSO shows improvements for all benchmark problems except for f_3 and f_4. The optimal value is obtained by both algorithm in the case of f_6 and f_{12}. This verifies the effectiveness of adopting the Taguchi method in PSO algorithm. From this work, we identify 6 benchmark problems which are very challenging. These are Rosenbrock (f_5), Quartic (f_7), Schwefel (f_8), Rastrigrin (f_9), Ackley (f_{10}) and Griewank (f_{11}). The present of local optima for the case of multimodal problems such as Schwefel, Rastrigrin and Griewank form unavoidable traps in the search landscape, increasing the difficulty in solving these problems. As the Taguchi method is performed only once after all the entire population

is evaluated, these results can be regarded as satisfactory. The convergence graphs for functions with most drastic improvements (Rosenbrock (f_5), Schwefel (f_8), Rastrigrin (f_9) and Griewank (f_{11})) are shown in Figures 2, 3, 4 and 5. The two lines, denoting PSO and TPSO in these graphs are plotted from $\text{Log}_{10}(Error)$ whereby the error (which is actually mean best) here is the average value from 50 trials.

An interesting observation from the results in Table 3 is that the worst result obtained by TPSO is on f_4 (Schwefel 2.21). From the mathematical formula, the function actually chooses the maximum dimension's value as its fitness. For instance, the fitness of a particle with array of dimensions [20, 23, 50, 90, 70, 67, 30, 83] is 90 as this is the largest value from the dimensions. When testing the accuracy of Taguchi method on f_4, it is found that the accuracy of Taguchi method on this function is lowest, 68.6% as recorded in Table 4. The reason of the low accuracy is in fact very simple; there is no relationship between the dimensional values! The dimensional values of f_4 are independent of each other whereas all the other functions have dimensions which are mutually related to one and other. It means that whenever a dimension value varies, so will it affect the fitness of the particle. Only f_4 that does not follow this rule, hence making Taguchi method not workable in this case as the ultimate aim of Taguchi method is to search for optimal dimensional values.

B. Testing the Accuracy of Taguchi Method

To verify the robustness of Taguchi method in solving benchmark functions, we carry out some experiments to determine the accuracy of Taguchi method in selecting the better dimensional value from two particles which are selected randomly for Taguchi operation. For simplicity, the values for the chosen particles (A and B) are given in binary form as depicted in Table 4, Table 5, and Table 6. The complete alternate cases of the di-

Table 2. Benchmark functions

Mathematical term	Search Range & Global Optimum
Sphere $f_1(x) = \sum_{i=1}^{n} x_i^2$	$-100 \le x_i \le 100$ $f_1(0, 0, ..., 0_n) = 0$
Schwefel 2.22 $f_2(x) = \sum_{i=1}^{n} |x_i| + \prod_{i=1}^{n} |x_i|$	$-10 \le x_i \le 10$ $f_2(0, 0, ..., 0_n) = 0$
Schwefel 1.2 $f_3(x) = \sum_{i=1}^{n} \left(\sum_{j=1}^{i} x_j \right)^2$	$-100 \le x_i \le 100$ $f_3(0, 0, ..., 0_n) = 0$
Schwefel 2.21 $f_4(x) = \max |x_i|, 0 \le i \le n$	$-100 \le x_i \le 100$ $f_4(0, 0, ..., 0_n) = 0$
Rosenbrock $f_5(x) = \sum_{i=1}^{n-1} (100(x_{i+1} - x_i^2)^2 + (x_i - 1)^2)$	$-30 \le x_i \le 30$ $f_5(1, 1, ..., 1_n) = 0$
Step $f_6(x) = \sum_{i=1}^{n} \left(\lfloor x_i + 0.5 \rfloor \right)^2$	$-100 \le x_i \le 100$ $f_6(0, 0, ..., 0_n) = 0$
Quartic $f_7(x) = \sum_{i=1}^{n} i x_i^4 + rand[0,1]$	$-1.28 \le x_i \le 1.28$ $f_7(0, 0, ..., 0_n) = 0$
Schwefel $f_8(x) = \sum_{i=1}^{n} -x_i \sin\left(\sqrt{|x_i|} \right)$	$-500 \le x_i \le 500$ $f_8(420.9688, 420.9688, ...,$ $420.9688_n) = -12569.5$
Rastrigin $f_9(x) = \sum_{i=1}^{n} \left(x_i^2 - 10\cos(2\pi x_i) + 10 \right)$	$-5.12 \le x_i \le 5.12$ $f_9(0, 0, ..., 0_n) = 0$
Ackley $f_{10}(x) = -20 \exp\left(-0.2\sqrt{\frac{1}{n} \sum_{i=1}^{n} x_i^2} \right)$ $- \exp\left(\frac{1}{n} \sum_{i=1}^{n} \cos 2\pi x_i \right) + 20 + e$	$-32 \le x_i \le 32$ $f_{10}(0, 0, ..., 0_n) = 0$
Griewank $f_{11}(x) = \frac{1}{4000} \sum_{i=1}^{n} x_i^2 - \prod_{i=1}^{n} \cos\left(\frac{x_i}{\sqrt{i}} \right) + 1$	$-600 \le x_i \le 600$ $f_{11}(0, 0, ..., 0_n) = 0$

Continued on following page

mensional values are tested to verify the 1 and 2 cases given in Table 1. The output from the Taguchi method as described in earlier section is recorded in these tables and the accuracy based on the global optimum is determined.

The accuracy is calculated based on the following formula:

$$\frac{Total\ dimensions - Total\ dimensional\ error}{Total\ dimensions} \times 100\%$$

$$(7)$$

Table 2. Continued

Mathematical term	Search Range & Global Optimum
Penalized P8 $f_{12}(x) = \dfrac{\pi}{n}\{10\sin^2(\pi y_1)$ $\quad + \sum_{i=1}^{n-1}(y_i-1)^2[1+10\sin^2(\pi y_{i+1})]$ $\quad + (y_n-1)^2\} + \sum_{i=1}^{n} u(x_i,10,100,4)$ $y_i = 1 + \dfrac{1}{4}(x_i+1), u(x_i,a,k,m) = \begin{cases} k(x_i-a)^m, & x_i > a, \\ 0, & -a \le x_i \le a, \\ k(-x_i-a)^m, & x_i < -a. \end{cases}$	$-50 \le x_i \le 50$ $f_{12}(-1,-1,...,-1_n) = 0$
Penalized P16 $f_{13}(x) = 0.1\left\{ \sin^2(3\pi x_1) + \sum_{i=1}^{n-1}(x_i-1)^2\left[1+\sin^2(3\pi x_{i+1})\right] \right.$ $\quad \left. +(x_n-1)\left[1+\sin^2(2\pi x_n)\right] \right\} + \sum_{i=1}^{n} u(x_i,5,100,4)$	$-50 \le x_i \le 50$ $f_{13}(0,0,...,0_n) = 0$

Table 3. 7-Dimensional Results of PSO and TPSO (50 trials)

$f(x)$	f_{min}	Max Iteration	PSO Mean best	PSO Std Dev	TPSO Mean best	TPSO Std Dev
f_1	0	375	2.18×10^{-23}	5.21×10^{-23}	3.28×10^{-25}	9.68×10^{-25}
f_2	0	500	3.27×10^{-18}	1.02×10^{-17}	3.63×10^{-20}	1.41×10^{-19}
f_3	0	1250	1.98×10^{-39}	8.14×10^{-39}	1.38×10^{-38}	7.11×10^{-38}
f_4	0	1250	2.77×10^{-30}	8.77×10^{-30}	3.58×10^{-30}	1.04×10^{-29}
f_5	0	5000	8.38×10^{-1}	1.62	3.53×10^{-1}	1.10
f_6	0	375	0	0	0	0
f_7	0	750	1.47×10^{-3}	9.40×10^{-4}	1.10×10^{-3}	6.08×10^{-4}
f_8	-2932.88	2250	-2740.63	113.479	-2905.92	47.66
f_9	0	1250	1.77	1.43	0.30	0.46
f_{10}	0	375	1.07×10^{-6}	9.62×10^{-7}	1.04×10^{-6}	9.54×10^{-7}
f_{11}	0	500	6.17×10^{-2}	3.78×10^{-2}	2.68×10^{-2}	1.35×10^{-2}
f_{12}	0	375	7.55×10^{-19}	0	7.55×10^{-19}	0
f_{13}	0	375	1.51×10^{-19}	4.86×10^{-35}	1.51×10^{-19}	4.86×10^{-35}

Table 4. Taguchi Method on Functions $f_1 - f_5$

No	Particle		Benchmark Functions				
	A	*B*	*f₁*	*f₂*	*f₃*	*f₄*	*f₅*
1	0000000	1111111	0000000	0000000	0000001	0000000	**0101110**
	1111111	0000000	0000000	0000000	0000000	0000000	1111111
2	0010100	1101011	0000000	0000000	0000000	**1101011**	1111111
	1101011	0010100	0000000	0000000	0000000	0010100	**0111110**
3	1001001	0110110	0000000	0000000	0000000	0110110	**0111110**
	0110110	1001001	0000000	0000000	0000000	1001001	1111111
4	1110000	0001111	0000000	0000000	0000000	000**1111**	1111111
	0001111	1110000	0000000	0000000	0000001	0000000	**0101110**
5	0101010	1010101	0000000	0000000	0000000	**1010101**	1111111
	1010101	0101010	0000000	0000000	0000001	0000000	**0101110**
Accuracy (%)			100	100	95.7	68.6	81.4

Remark: The reason for low accuracy on f4 is explained in the last paragraph of Section A above.

Figure 2. Convergence of PSO and TPSO on Rosenbrock (f_3), average out of 50 trials

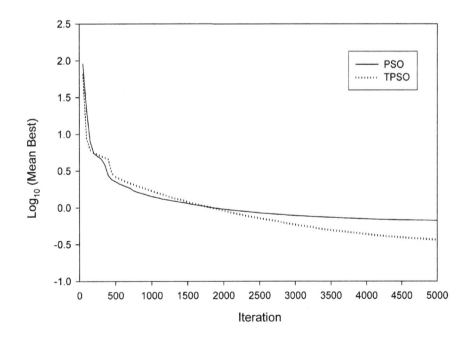

Figure 3. Convergence of PSO and TPSO on Schwefel (f_8), average out of 50 trials

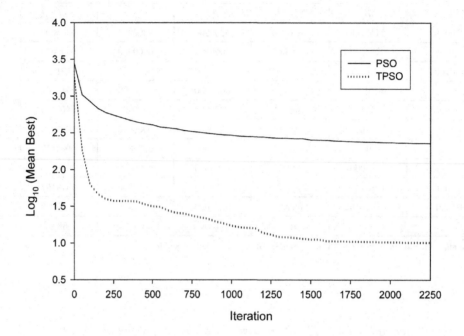

Figure 4. Convergence of PSO and TPSO on Rastrigrin (f_9), average out of 50 trials

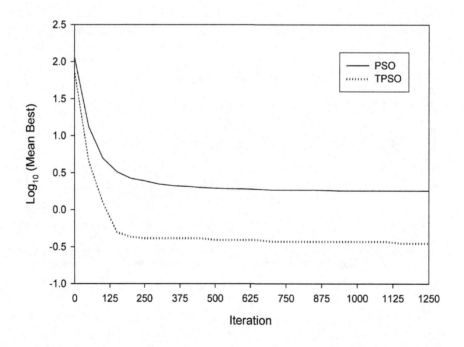

Figure 5. Convergence of PSO and TPSO on Griewank (f₁₁), average out of 50 trials

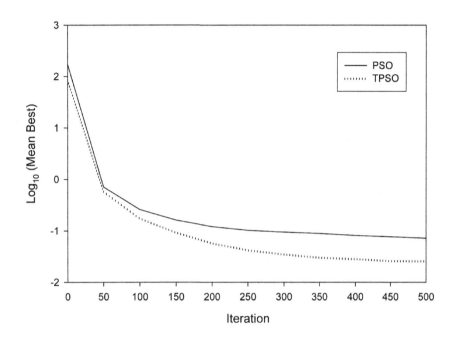

Table 5. Taguchi Method on Functions $f_6 - f_{10}$

No	Particle		Benchmark Functions				
	A	B	f6	f7	f8	f9	f10
1	0000000	1111111	0000000	0000000	1111111	0000000	0000000
	1111111	0000000	0000000	0000000	1111111	0000000	0000000
2	0010100	1101011	0000000	0000000	1111111	0000000	0000000
	1101011	0010100	0000000	0000000	1111111	0000000	0000000
3	1001001	0110110	0000000	0000000	1111111	0000000	0000000
	0110110	1001001	0000000	0000000	1111111	0000000	0000000
4	1110000	0001111	0000000	0000000	1111111	0000000	0000000
	0001111	1110000	0000000	0000000	1111111	0000000	0000000
5	0101010	1010101	0000000	0000000	1111111	0000000	0000000
	1010101	0101010	0000000	0000000	1111111	0000000	0000000
Accuracy (%)			100	100	100	100	100

For instance, when calculating the accuracy of f_3 in Table 4, we have

$$Accuracy\,(\%) = \frac{70-3}{70} \times 100\% = 95.7\%$$

For better clarification, the dimensional errors are bolded in Tables 4-6. From the results in Tables 4-6, we can make the following conclusions in regards to the accuracy of Taguchi method on benchmark problems:

Table 6. Taguchi Method on Functions $f_{11} - f_{15}$

No	Particle		Benchmark Functions		
	A	B	f11	f12	f13
1	0000000	1111111	0000000	0000000	1111111
	1111111	0000000	0000000	0000000	1111111
2	0010100	1101011	0000000	0000000	1111111
	1101011	0010100	0000000	0000000	1111111
3	1001001	0110110	0000000	0000000	1111111
	0110110	1001001	0000000	0000000	1111111
4	1110000	0001111	0000000	0000000	1111111
	0001111	1110000	0000000	0000000	1111111
5	0101010	1010101	0000000	0000000	1111111
	1010101	0101010	0000000	0000000	1111111
Accuracy (%)			100	100	100

1. The method is somehow robust in choosing optimal dimensional values among the two particles A and B in operation for a wide range of benchmark problems. The accuracy recorded by $f_1, f_2, f_6, f_7, f_8, f_9, f_{10}, f_{11}, f_{12}$ and f_{13} are all 100%.

2. The accuracy recorded by f_3, f_4 and f_5 are not 100%. This means that Taguchi method is not 100% reliable in some problems.

3. The result from Taguchi method is different when A and B are swapped. For e.g. when A=0000000 and B=1111111, result on f_5 is 0101110. However, when A=1111111 and B=0101110, the result is 1111111, which is an optimal result.

4. Results on f_4 indicate that dimensional values have to be mutually independent in order for Taguchi method to be effective as this method optimize dimensionally.

Hereby, we suggest some strategies to increase the performance of Taguchi methods. It can be observed that one of the solutions in any pair produces optimal result in f_3 and f_5. Therefore, in any case the Taguchi method can be performed once again after swapping A and B, and only the better solution is accepted for further procedure.

In addition to this strategy, the optimal particle from the Taguchi method is compared to the particles generated from orthogonal array and only the particle with best fitness is updated as optimal particle. Both these strategies are implemented in the simulation on 30-dimensional benchmark problems in the following section which produce encouraging results.

C. Results on 30-Dimensional Benchmark Problems

For 30-dimensional problems, the maximum iteration given in Table 7 is similar to the one available in (Yao, Liu, & Lin, 1999). Results are recorded as average (mean best) out of 50 trials and the standard deviation is calculated, given in Table 7. To cover a dimensional size of 30, the L32(231) orthogonal array which is adopted from (Ross, 1989) is employed here. The extra one column of the orthogonal array is ignored as the size of dimension is 30.

From the results in Table 7, the TPSO shows drastic improvements over the PSO algorithm, obtaining better results for all the 13 benchmark problems tested. In all cases, the mean best recorded by TPSO are closer to the global optimum,

Table 7. 30-Dimensional Results of PSO and TPSO (50 trials)

$f(x)$	f_{min}	Max Iteration	PSO		TPSO	
			Mean best	Std Dev	Mean best	Std Dev
f_1	0	1500	4.36×10^{-14}	7.31×10^{-14}	4.52×10^{-20}	1.12×10^{-19}
f_2	0	2000	1.48×10^{-13}	2.00×10^{-13}	1.92×10^{-20}	3.36×10^{-20}
f_3	0	5000	9.37×10^{-2}	1.08×10^{-1}	2.73×10^{-2}	4.43×10^{-2}
f_4	0	5000	1.19	7.90×10^{-1}	3.85×10^{-2}	3.98×10^{-2}
f_5	0	20000	8.26	14.03	1.57	2.04
f_6	0	1500	4.60×10^{-1}	1.45	0	0
f_7	0	3000	3.71×10^{-1}	2.61×10^{-1}	3.57×10^{-2}	1.56×10^{-2}
f_8	-12569.5	9000	-8769.58	465.03	-11773.4	260.65
f_9	0	5000	41.45	10.12	12.09	4.28
f_{10}	0	1500	5.22×10^{-3}	8.14×10^{-1}	5.35×10^{-6}	1.05×10^{-6}
f_{11}	0	2000	1.38×10^{-2}	1.72×10^{-2}	5.47×10^{-3}	8.40×10^{-3}
f_{12}	0	1500	2.45×10^{-1}	3.71×10^{-1}	6.22×10^{-3}	2.46×10^{-2}
f_{13}	0	1500	2.63×10^{-2}	1.26×10^{-1}	1.76×10^{-3}	4.03×10^{-3}

f_{min} in comparison with the results recorded by PSO. The better convergence of TPSO on these high dimensional problems proves the effectiveness of Taguchi method in improving the quality of a particle by choosing better dimensional values from two particles in operation. Due to the better strategy adopted in TPSO when executing the algorithm for high dimensional problems, it performs quite well on f_4 problem when compared with the low dimensional case. By incorporating Taguchi method, the computational cost by TPSO is slightly higher compared to PSO. Due to the simple methodology of Taguchi, the additional computational cost is not significant and therefore is not included in the results.

CONCLUSION

In this paper, the Taguchi method being incorporated into the PSO has illustrated considerable improvements in comparison with the standard version. The Taguchi method is incorporated after the update via PSO equation, creating a more diversified population, which contributes to the success of avoiding premature convergence, or jumping out from local optima. From our analysis, the Taguchi method improves the respective dimension's value by selecting better value out of two particles in operation which are chosen randomly from *pbest* vector. Results show a better convergence for the majority of the 13 benchmark problems employed in the simulation on low dimensional problems. To tackle more challenging high dimensional problems, two efficient strategies are proposed in this work and results produced are very encouraging on high dimensional problems. Finally, this work proves the feasibility of Taguchi method applied in PSO algorithm to produce a robust approach for numerical optimization.

REFERENCES

Baskar, S., & Suganthan, P. (2004). A novel concurrent particle swarm optimization. In Proceedings of the Congress on Evolutionary Computation, Portland, OR (pp. 792-796).

Bergh, F. v., & Engelbrecht, A. P. (2004). A cooperative approach to particle swarm optimization. *IEEE Transactions on Evolutionary Computation*, 225–239. doi:10.1109/TEVC.2004.826069

Brits, R., Engelbrecht, A. P., & Bergh, F. v. (2007). Locating multiple optima using particle swarm optimization. *Applied Mathematics and Computation*, *189*(2), 1859–1883. doi:10.1016/j.amc.2006.12.066

Clerc, M., & Kennedy, J. (2002). The particle swarm - explosion, stability, and convergence in a multidimensional complex space. *IEEE Transactions on Evolutionary Computation*, *6*(1), 58–73. doi:10.1109/4235.985692

Janson, S., & Middendorf, M. (2005). A hierarchical particle swarm optimizer and its adaptive variant. IEEE Trans on Systems, Man, and Cybernetics-Part B. *Cybernetics*, *35*(6), 1272–1282.

Kennedy, J., & Eberhart, R. C. (1995). Particle Swarm Optimization. In Proceedings of the IEEE Intl. Conf. Neural Network IV (pp. 1942-1948).

Krink, T., & Lovbjerg, M. (2002). The LifeCycle model: Combining Particle Swarm Optimisation, Genetic Algorithms and Hill Climbers. In Proceeding of the Parallel Problem Solving from Nature VII (PPSN-2002) (pp. 621-630).

Leung, Y.-W., & Wang, Y. (2001). An orthogonal Genetic Algorithm with quantization for global numerical optimization. *IEEE Transactions on Evolutionary Computation*, *5*(1), 41–53. doi:10.1109/4235.910464

Liang, J., & Suganthan, P. (2005). Dynamic multi-swarm particle swarm optimizer. In Proceedings of IEEE Swarm Intelligence Symposium, Pasadena, CA (pp. 124-129).

Liang, J. J., Qin, A., Suganthan, P., & Baskar, S. (n.d.). Comprehensive learning particle swarm optimizer for global optimization of multimodal functions. IEEE Trans on Evolutionary Computation, 10(3), 281-295.

Niu, B., Zhu, Y., & He, X. (2005). Multi-population cooperative particle swarm optimization. *Lecture Notes in Computer Science*, *3630*, 874–883. doi:10.1007/11553090_88

Parrot, D., & Li, D. (2006). Locating and tracking multiple dynamic optima by a particle swarm model using speciation. *IEEE Transactions on Evolutionary Computation*, *10*(4), 211–224. doi:10.1109/TEVC.2005.859468

Parsopoulos, K. E., & Vrahatis, M. N. (2004). On the computation of all global minimizers through particle swarm optimization. *IEEE Transactions on Evolutionary Computation*, *8*(3), 211–224. doi:10.1109/TEVC.2004.826076

Parsopoulos, K. E., & Vrahatis, M. N. (2007). Parameter selection and adaptation in unified particle swarm optimization. *Mathematical and Computer Modelling*, *46*(1-2), 193–213. doi:10.1016/j.mcm.2006.12.019

Richer, T. J., & Blackwell, T. (2006). The Levy particle swarm. In Proceedings of the Congress on Evolutionary Computation, Vancouver, Canada (pp. 808-815).

Ross, P. J. (1989). *Taguchi Technique for Quality Engineering*. New York: McGraw-Hill.

Roy, R. (1990). *A Primer on the Taguchi Method*. New York: Van Nostrand Reinhold.

Shi, Y., & Eberhart, R. C. (1998). A modified particle swarm optimizer. In Proceedings of the IEEE International Conference on Evolutionary Computation, Anchorage, AK (pp. 4-9).

Shi, Y., & Krohling, R. (2002). Co-evolutionary particle swarm optimization to solve min-max problems. In Proceedings of the Congress on Evolutionary Computation, Honolulu, HI (pp. 1682-1687).

Taguchi, G., Chowdhury, S., & Taguchi, S. (2000). *Robust Engineering*. New York: McGraw-Hill.

Tsai, J.-T., Liu, T.-K., & Chou, J.-H. (2004). Hybrid Taguchi-Genetic Algorithms for global numerical optimization. *IEEE Transactions on Evolutionary Computation*, 8(4), 365–377. doi:10.1109/TEVC.2004.826895

Vasconcelos, J. A., Ramirez, J. A., Takahashi, R. H., & Saldanha, R. (2001). Improvements in Genetic Algorithms. *IEEE Transactions on Magnetics*, 37(5), 3414–3417. doi:10.1109/20.952626

Yao, X., Liu, Y., & Lin, G. (1999). Evolutionary programming made faster. *IEEE Trans Evolutionay Computation*, 3(2), 82–102. doi:10.1109/4235.771163

This work was previously published in International Journal of Swarm Intelligence Research, Volume 1, Issue 2, edited by Yuhui Shi, pp. 18-33, copyright 2010 by IGI Publishing (an imprint of IGI Global)

Chapter 4
Constraint Handling in Particle Swarm Optimization

Wen Fung Leong
Oklahoma State University, USA

Gary G. Yen
Oklahoma State University, USA

ABSTRACT

In this article, the authors propose a particle swarm optimization (PSO) for constrained optimization. The proposed PSO adopts a multiobjective approach to constraint handling. Procedures to update the feasible and infeasible personal best are designed to encourage finding feasible regions and convergence toward the Pareto front. In addition, the infeasible nondominated solutions are stored in the global best archive to exploit the hidden information for guiding the particles toward feasible regions. Furthermore, the number of feasible personal best in the personal best memory and the scalar constraint violations of personal best and global best are used to adapt the acceleration constants in the PSO flight equations. The purpose is to find more feasible particles and search for better solutions during the process. The mutation procedure is applied to encourage global and fine-tune local searches. The simulation results indicate that the proposed constrained PSO is highly competitive, achieving promising performance.

INTRODUCTION

Recently, there are active studies on using particle swarm optimization (PSO) to solve constrained optimization problems (COPs). Similar to evolutionary algorithms (EAs), the original PSO design lacks a mechanism to handle constraints in an

DOI: 10.4018/978-1-4666-1592-2.ch004

effective manner. Most of the constrained PSO designs adopted the popular constraint handling techniques that are built for EAs (Runarsson & Yao, 2005; Takahama & Sakai, 2006; Cai & Wang, 2006; Wang, Cai, Guo, & Zhou, 2007; Wang, Cai, Zhou, & Zeng, 2008). Evidence shows in recent publications on constraint handling with PSO including penalty methods (Parsopoulus & Vrahatis, 2002), comparison criteria or feasibility tournament (Zielinski & Laur, 2006; He & Wang, 2007; Pulido & Coello Coello, 2004), lagrange-based method (Krohling & Coelho, 2006) lexicographic order (Liu, Wang, & Li, 2008), and multiobjective approach (Lu & Chen, 2006; Li, Li, & Yu, 2008; Liang & Suganthan, 2006; Cushman, 2007), to name a few. The reason of such popularity is credited to its simplicity, easy implementation and rapid convergence capability inherited in PSO design. Most constraint handling techniques such as penalty methods or comparison criteria are treated as an add-on module to be incorporated into any EAs for solving COPs. The PSO's algorithm is built with mechanisms that can be exploited to handle constraints, without imposing any penalty methods or comparison criteria. Motivated by the advantages and its inherited ability, we propose a constrained PSO with design elements that exploit the key mechanisms to handle constraints as well as optimization of the objective function.

Consider a minimization problem; the general form of the COP is given as follows:

Minimize $f\left(\mathbf{x}\right)$, $\mathbf{x} = \left[x_1, x_2, ..., x_n\right] \in \Re^n$ (1)

subject to

$g_j\left(\mathbf{x}\right) < 0, \qquad j = 1, 2, ..., m;$ (2a)

$h_j\left(\mathbf{x}\right) = 0, \qquad j = m+1, ..., p;$ (2b)

$x_i^{\min} \le x_i \le x_i^{\max}, \quad i = 1, 2, ..., n;$ (2c)

where $\mathbf{x}$ is the decision vector of n decision variables. Its upper ($x_i^{\max}$) and lower ($x_i^{\min}$) bounds in Equation (2c) define the search space, $S \subseteq \Re^n$. $g_j\left(\mathbf{x}\right)$ represents the jth inequality constraint while $h_j\left(\mathbf{x}\right)$ represents the jth equality constraint. The inequality constraints that are equal to zero, i.e., $g_j\left(\mathbf{x}^*\right) = 0$, at the global

optimum ($\mathbf{x}^*$) of a given problem are called *active constraints*. The feasible region ($F \subseteq S$) is defined by satisfying all constraints (Equations (2a)-(2b)). A solution in the feasible region ($\mathbf{x} \in F$) is called a feasible solution, otherwise it is considered an infeasible solution.

In this article, we adopt a multiobjective constraint handling techniques in PSO for constraint handling since these techniques require neither penalty factors that need heuristic tuning nor balance the right proportion of selecting feasible and infeasible solutions in the population via selection criteria (Cai & Wang, 2006; Wang et al., 2007; Wang et al., 2008; Mezura-Montes & Coello Coello, 2006). Several design elements are incorporated into the proposed PSO (RCVPSO): 1) two updating procedures are designed to keep track of infeasible and feasible personal best separately; 2) infeasible nondominated solutions along with a best feasible nondominated solution are recorded in the global best archive; 3) the acceleration constants in the PSO flight equation is adjusted based on the feasibility ratio in the personal best memory and the constraint violations corresponding to the members in personal best memory and global best archive; and 4) a mutation operator applied in such the range of the upper and lower bounds of each decision variable is adaptively narrowed over time. This is to promote exploration in early search in order to find any feasible solutions, while encourage exploitation at the later search by local fine tuning in order to find the global optima.

The remaining sections complete the presentation of this article. In Section II, a review of relevant works in this area is presented. Section III elaborates on the proposed constrained PSO (RCVPSO). Comparative study and pertinent discussions are presented in Section IV. Finally, conclusion remarks are drawn in Section V.

RELATED WORKS

In this section, prominent works of PSO adopting multiobjective constraint handling techniques to solve COPs are reviewed.

Multiobjective constraint handling techniques (also called multiobjective approach to handling constraints) are based on multiobjective optimization concepts. The idea is to convert the constraints into one or more unconstrained objective functions and handle them via Pareto dominance relation. From the comprehensive survey conducted by Mezura-Montes and Coello Coello [16], the techniques available in literature are grouped into two main categories.

For the first category, a COP is converted into an unconstrained bi-objective optimization problem where one of the objectives is the original objective function and the other is the sum of the constraint violations. The following works fall into this category: Lu and Chen (2006) proposed a novel constraint handling technique, called dynamic objective method (DOM), which can be easily incorporated into a variety of PSO designs. DOM does not apply Pareto dominance relation, but incorporate a threshold to control when to start the process of optimizing the objective function from the process of minimizing the sum of constraint violations. The threshold is used to update personal and global bests. In addition, the same authors also proposed a restricted velocity particle swarm optimization (RVPSO), in which the PSO equation is modified to incorporate the impact of feasible region on the velocity equation. Experiment results show DOM is efficient in handling constraints and the combined algorithm (DOM+RVPSO) demonstrates promising potential in solving COPs. However, how sensitive for the choice of thresholds to impact the performance over different test problems is not discussed. Li et al. (2008) incorporated goal oriented programming concept to guide the search towards the global optimum (feasible) solution. A feasible tolerance parameter is defined to determine how minimum

does the constraint violations should allow. Selection rules based on Pareto dominance relationship and comparison of constraint violations are proposed to update personal and neighborhood bests. Perturbation with minor probability is applied for diversity maintenance. Simulation results show competitive performance but require prior knowledge of global optimum and user settings of feasible tolerance parameter.

For the second category, a COP is converted into an unconstrained multiobjective optimization problem (MOP), i.e., original objective function and each constraint is treated as a separate objective function. Hence, we will have $p+1$ unconstrained objective functions and the parameter p refers to total number of constraints (see Equations (2a) and (2b)). Liang and Suganthan (2006) proposed a dynamic particle multi-swarm optimization (DMS-PSO). In their design, a sub-swarm or several subswarms are assigned to optimize one objective selected from the objective functions and constrained functions. The assignment of these subswarms changes adaptively and the assignment depends on the complexity of the constraints, e.g. more number of subswarms will be assigned to work on difficult constraints. In addition, the authors applied a local search with sequential quadratic programming (SQP) on a set of five randomly chosen particles' personal best (pbest). Twenty-four benchmark functions are tested and the algorithm is able to obtain the global (feasible) solution efficiently. The drawback is that the user-defined parameters need to be tuned heuristically. In Cushman (2007), the COP is converted into $p+1$ unconstrained objective functions and optimizes these functions as a MOP. The author exploited the information of the "worst" solutions by adding a global worst term to the original velocity equation. The idea is to inform the particles to slightly move away from the center of the least feasible solutions found so far and head towards the direction of global best. The initial experimental results show this approach can obtain global optima for certain benchmark functions. The drawback is the need of extra computation since the 'global worst' is the centroid or the arithmetic mean of the particles' coordinates that computed at every iteration. In future, the author plans to refine the 'global worst' concept by incorporate the information of worst objective function values in the PSO equation.

The reviews briefly outline several methods to exploit PSO inherited mechanism to deal with constraints, i.e., dynamic objective method (Lu & Chen, 2006) for updating personal best and global best, multiple swarms in Liang and Suganthan (2006) to work on different constraints, and adding 'global worst' terms (Cushman, 2007) to nudge particles away from the least infeasible solutions. Hence, considering the experiences gained from the reviews, the proposed PSO design adopts a multiobjective constraint handling technique and modifies the mechanisms to effectively handle constraints as well as optimization of the objective functions.

PROPOSED ALGORITHM

Transform a COP into an Unconstrained Bi-objective Optimization Problem

In this article, multiobjective constraint handling technique is adopted because it requires neither penalty factors that need heuristic tuning nor balance the right proportion of selecting feasible and infeasible solutions in the population via selection criteria.

To transform a COP into a unconstrained bi-objective optimization problem, both the inequality and equality constraints (i.e., $g_j(\mathbf{x})$ and $h_j(\mathbf{x})$, respectively) are treated as one objective and the other objective is the original objective function $f(\mathbf{x})$ (refer to Equation (1)). Hence, Equations (1), (2a) and (2b) are transformed into the following

general form of an unconstrained bi-objective optimization problem:

$$\text{Minimize } \mathbf{f}(\mathbf{x}) = \left[cv(\mathbf{x}), f(\mathbf{x}) \right], \qquad (3)$$

where $cv(\mathbf{x})$ is the scalar constraint violation of a decision vector $\mathbf{x}$ (or particle) [17] and it is mathematically formulated as below:

$$cv(\mathbf{x}) = \frac{1}{p} \sum_{j=1}^{p} \frac{cv_j(\mathbf{x})}{cv_{\max}^j}, \qquad (4)$$

where

$$cv_j(\mathbf{x}) = \begin{cases} \max\left(0, g_j(\mathbf{x})\right), & j = 1, \ldots, m \\ \max\left(0, \left|h_j(\mathbf{x})\right| - \delta\right), & j = m+1, \ldots, p \end{cases}, \qquad (5a)$$

$$cv_{\max}^j = \max_{\mathbf{x} \in CP} cv_j(\mathbf{x}). \qquad (5b)$$

Parameter δ is the tolerance allowed for equality constraints, usually δ is set to 0.001 or 0.0001. If a particle or solution ($\mathbf{x}$) satisfies the jth constraints, then $cv_j(\mathbf{x})$ is set to zero, otherwise it is greater than zero. Note that each jth constraint violation ($cv_j(\mathbf{x})$) is normalized by dividing it by the largest violation of the jth constraint ($cv_{\max}^j$ in Equation 5(b)) in the *current* swarm population (represented by the parameter CP) at every iteration. In solving MOPs, the objective is to find a set of optimum solutions or the Pareto optimal set. Although the Pareto dominance relation is used to solve the bi-objective optimization problem in Equation (3), in this case, we only need to find one global optimum (feasible) solution. This is because if the solution found is infeasible (i.e., $cv(\mathbf{x}) > 0$), it is unacceptable no matter how optimal is the fitness value ($f(\mathbf{x})$). Only the solutions that are landed on the feasible region (i.e., $cv(\mathbf{x}) = 0$) are considered potential solutions.

*Figure 1. Illustration of bi-objective optimization problem (**f(x)**). The feasible region is mapped to the solid segment. The shaded region represents the search space. The global optimum (black circle) is located beat the intersection of the Pareto front and the solid segment [3-5].*

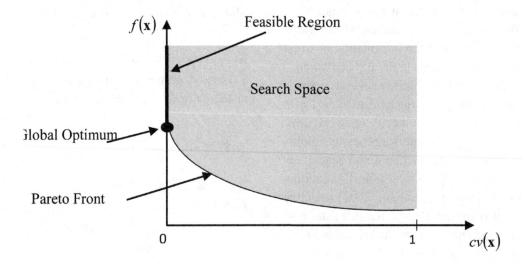

Figure 1 illustrates the feasible region, Pareto front, search space, and the global optimum solution. Note that for the following discussion, we consider minimization for all objective functions unless specified otherwise.

General Framework

All of the existing constraint handling techniques has two goals: 1) to search for feasible solutions and to guide infeasible solutions towards feasibility; and 2) to converge to the global optimal solution. In this design, we have proposed the key design elements to achieve these goals.

The generic procedure of the proposed PSO (RCVPSO) is as follows. First, set user defined parameters (i.e., maximum iterations, and maximum global best archive), and initialize the swarm population and particles' velocities. Then, while the number of iterations has not reached the maximum iterations, the following steps are repeated for all of the particles: 1) calculate the particles' fitness values and scalar constraint violation as explained in Section III.A; 2) find the particles' rank values using the Pareto ranking

scheme; 3) with particles' scalar constraint violation and rank values, particles' personal best memory is updated (see Section III.C and Figure 3); 4) calculate the feasibility ratio of the particles' personal best (parameter r_f) with Equation 7; 5) update the particles' global best archive (See Section III.D and Figure 4); 6) compute the PSO equations (Equations 8-10 in Section III.E); and 7) apply mutation operator by following the procedure presented in Section III.F). These steps are performed until they reach the maximum iteration.

Figure 2 presents the pseudocode of RCVPSO involving the key design elements, which are highlighted in boldface. These design elements are elaborated in the following subsections (Sections III.C –III.F).

Update Personal Best Memory

In Li et al. (2008), the personal best is updated based on the two selection rules: 1) nondominated particles are better than dominated ones; and 2) a particle with lower constraint violation is better than a particle with higher constraint violation.

Figure 3. Pseudocode of updating the particles best memory

Function UpdatePbestMemory(*particle,Pbest_Memory,* $f(\mathbf{x})$, $cv(\mathbf{x})$, $rank(\mathbf{x})$)

/* *particle* = a particles (with decision vector $\mathbf{x}$) in the swarm population
/* *Pbest_Memory* = Recoded personal best
/* $f(\mathbf{x})$ = a Particle's fitness value
/* $cv(\mathbf{x})$ = particle's scalar constraint violation
/* $rank(\mathbf{x})$ = particle's rank value in the current swarm population (obtained from Pareto ranking scheme)

Begin
  Compute $_{RC}$ value for the particle (Equation 6)
  If *Pbest_Memory*= { }   /*an empty set
    /*All are recorded in *Pbest_Memory*
    Record $_{RC}$ value ($pbest\_RC(\mathbf{x})$)
    Record particle's position ($pbest(\mathbf{x})$)
    Record particle's fitness value ($pbest\_fitness(\mathbf{x})$)
    Record particle's constraint violation (*Pbest_cv or* $cv(pbest(\mathbf{x}))$)
  Else
    If $cv(pbest(\mathbf{x}))$ >0 /*infeasible
      If $RC(\mathbf{x}) \le pbest\_RC(\mathbf{x})$
        Update $pbest\_RC(\mathbf{x})$
        Update $pbest(\mathbf{x})$
        Update $pbest\_fitness(\mathbf{x})$
        Update *Pbest_cv or* $cv(pbest(\mathbf{x}))$
      EndIf
    Else /*If $Pbest_i$ is feasible
      If $cv(\mathbf{x}) = 0$ *and* $\{(RC(\mathbf{x}) \le pbest\_RC(\mathbf{x}))\ or\ (f(\mathbf{x}) \le Pbest\_fitness(\mathbf{x}))\}$
        Update $pbest\_RC(\mathbf{x})$
        Update $pbest(\mathbf{x})$
        Update $pbest\_fitness(\mathbf{x})$
        Update *Pbest_cv or* $cv(pbest(\mathbf{x}))$
      EndIf
    EndIf
  EndIf
End

The drawback of these rules is to determine which rule should be prioritized first. If rule one is given higher priority, the progress of searching for feasible region may slow down since personal best indirectly influence the particles' search behavior in the swarm population. On the contrary, if rule two is given higher priority, all infeasible solutions will quickly land on the feasible region but this will indirectly degrade the diversity in the swarm population and may results in premature convergence. Hence it is important to update personal best using both rules at the same time to maintain

Figure 4. Pseudocode of updating the global best archive

Function UpdateGlobalBestArchive(*global_best_archive*, best_*feasible_particle*, *infeasible_nondomparticles*,
nondom_cv, maxglobal)

/* *global_best_archive* = Particle's global best archive
/* best_*feasible_particle* = Current best feasible particle or solution (minimum fitness value for minimizarion
problem)
/* *infeasible_nondomparticles* = infeasible nondominated solutions or particles
/% *nondom_cv* = current scalar constraint violation for infeasible nondominated solutions or particles
/% *Gbest_cv* = Recorded scalar constraint violation for infeasible nondominated solutions or particles
/% *maxglobal* = maximum size of global best archive
/*Assume minimization problems

Begin
    If *global_best_archive* has no recorded feasible solution
        Record best_*feasible_particle*
    Else
    If best_*feasible_particle* < recorded feasible solution
        Record best_*feasible_particle*
    EndIf
    EndIf
    If *global_best_archive* has no recorded infeasible solution
        Record *infeasible_nondomparticles*
        Record *nondom_cv*
    Else
        Remove those *infeasible_nondomparticles* with *nondom_cv* > max(*Gbest_cv*)
        Remove any recorded infeasible solutions in *global_best_archive* that dominated by any
        remaining *infeasible_nondomparticles*
        Add any remaining *infeasible_nondomparticles* that aren't dominated by any infeasible solutions
        in *global_best_archive*
    EndIf
    Compute Harmonic distance [20] for all members in *global_best_archive*
    If the size of *global_best_archive* > *maxglobal*
        Prune the *global_best_archive* by removing the crowded members [21]
    EndIf
End

a balance between convergence to fitter particles and search for feasible region.

In this study, we propose the following equation to incorporate the rank value and the scalar constraint violation of a particle (with decision vector $\mathbf{x}$) to update the personal best if the latest recorded personal best of a particle is in infeasible region.

$$RC(\mathbf{x}) = \left(1 - \frac{1}{rank(\mathbf{x})}\right) + cv(\mathbf{x}), \qquad (6)$$

where $RC(\mathbf{x})$ is the rank-constraint violation indicator of particle with decision vector $\mathbf{x}$, $rank(\mathbf{x})$ represents the current rank value while $cv(\mathbf{x})$ refers to the scalar constraint violation of the particle with decision vector $\mathbf{x}$. The rank values are obtained from applying the Pareto ranking [18] to the swarm population. Refer to Equation (6), the first term indicates the dominant relationship of the particles comparing the others and it is mapped between zero and one, where zero indicates non-dominated particles and any values greater than zero indicates particle is

Figure 2. Pseudocode of the proposed constrained PSO algorithm (RCVPSO)

```
Begin
/*Initialization
Initialize swarm population and velocity
Set maximum global best archive size
Set maximum iterations ( tmax )
Set iteration  t = 0

Record particles' personal best (Section III.C)

While  t < tmax
    Calculate fitness and scalar constrain violation (Equations 4 and 5)
    Find particles' rank values via Pareto ranking [30]
    Update Personal Best Memory (Section III.C)
    Calculate  rf  (See Equation 7)

  Update Global Best Archive (Section III.D)
  Particle Update Mechanism (Section III.E)
  Mutation Operator (Section III.F)
   t = t + 1
EndWhile
Report feasible solution in Global Best Archive
End
```

dominated in various degrees. The purpose is to search for the non-dominated solutions, regardless if the solutions are infeasible, and these solutions will possibly indirectly influence the improvement of the particles in the next iterations in terms of convergence. However, this does not guarantee that the particles will move towards the feasible regions easily since most of the time the searching is spent in the infeasible regions (Runarsson & Yao, 2005). Thus, the second term is added to Equation (6) to emphasize the current state of the particles in terms of their feasibility or the degree of infeasibility in the current population. Note that the range of RC is between 0 and 2, and a particle with smaller RC value indicates better solution in terms of its convergence and feasibility status.

Figure 3 summarizes the procedures of updating the personal best memory at every iteration. Refer to Figure 3, when a recorded personal best

is infeasible, then the updating step depends on Equation (6). On the other hand, if it is feasible, then the updating is done by comparing the rank values (because $cv(\mathbf{x}) = 0$) or fitness values of the particles in the swarm population with those recorded in the personal best memory. Hence, this supports the convergence towards the global optimum in the feasible region.

Once the updating procedure is completed, the feasibility ratio of the particles' personal best (r_f) is updated via the following equation:

$$r_f = \frac{number\ of\ particles'\ personal\ best\ that\ are\ feasible}{swarm\ population\ size}$$

(7)

This parameter will serve as an indicator to guide the particles towards feasibility regions by manipulating the acceleration constants in the PSO equation (Equations (8)-(10) in Section III.E).

Update Global Best Archive

Recent studies have shown the advantage of exploiting infeasible solutions to search for global optimum solution (Mezura-Montes & Coello Coello, 2005). The purpose is to deal with the case where the proportion feasible region is relatively smaller compared to the entire search space and make use of the infeasible solutions to discover such feasible region (Cai & Wang, 2006). Hence, the movement of particles should not only base on feasible global bests but it is also vital to have infeasible global bests to guide particles to search for potential feasible region(s). For such reason, we propose a fixed size global best archive that stores only the best feasible solution found so far and the infeasible nondominated solutions that have minimum constraint violation found so far.

There are two separate procedures to update the global best archive and they are summarized here:

Procedure to update the best feasible solution: If there is no feasible solution in the archive, the best feasible solution (feasible solution with minimum fitness) is immediately accepted in the archive. If the achieve has recorded the best feasible solution in the pervious iteration, then the new best feasible solution in the current iteration is compared. If the recorded one has larger fitness value, then the current best feasible solution will replace the recorded one, otherwise the current one is eliminated.

Procedure to update the infeasible nondominated solutions: If the archive is empty or has no infeasible members, the infeasible nondominated solutions are accepted to fill up the archive. If there are infeasible members in the archive, the scalar constraint violation of the new infeasible nondominated solutions is compared with the largest scalar constraint violation stored in the archive ($\max(Gbest\_cv)$). These new infeasible nondominated solutions with constraint violation exceed the largest scalar constraint violation stored in the archive are removed. Then,

the remaining new infeasible nondominated solutions are compared with respect to any infeasible members in the archive via Pareto dominance concept. If any infeasible new solutions are not dominated by any archive infeasible members, they are accepted into the archive. Similarly, any archive infeasible members dominated by any new infeasible solutions are removed from the archive.

Once the two procedures are completed and if the archive size exceeds the allocated size, then Harmonic distance (Haung, Suganathan, Qin, & Baskar, 2005) is applied to remove the crowded members and to maintain diversity among the archive members. The idea of harmonic average distance is very similar to Deb's crowding distance in NSGA-II (Deb, Pratap, Agarwal, & Meyarivan, 2002), except that the 'harmonic average distance' applied here (in NSGA-II, the term 'crowding distance' is used) is computed using the harmonic mean equation. The harmonic average distance is chosen because the crowding distance may not accurately reflect the crowding degrees of the solutions (Huang, Suganathan, Qin, & Baskar, 2005). Figure 4 presents the pseudocode for updating the global best archive.

In this article, the tournament selection is applied on the harmonic distance value of the archive members to select the global best leaders (*Gbest*) to update the particle velocity and position equations (see Equations (8) and (9)).

Particle Update Mechanism

The movement of particles is influenced by their past experiences, i.e., their personal past experience and successful experience attained by their peers. Cushman (2007) added a global worst term (Gworst) with a very low acceleration constant value (suggested 0.0001) to nudge the particles away from the center (or centroid) of the infeasible solutions. Lu and Chen (2006) replaced the inertial term with personal and global bests in order to restrict the velocity term so that those feasible particles (solutions) will not be moved away from the feasible region(s). Both approaches modified the PSO's velocity equation to either steer the particles away from infeasible region(s) or limit the particles to search within the feasible region(s).

In our approach, the acceleration constants (i.e., c_1 and c_2 in Equation (8)) in the PSO's velocity equation are adjusted based on the feasibility information gather from the personal best memory and the global best archive to guide the particles' movement. The idea is to make use of the feasibility information, which are the feasibility ratio (r_f) and the scalar constraint violation, to guide the particles towards feasibility first and then influence them to search for global optimal solution. The scalar constraint violation belongs to the members in personal best and global best archives.

The PSO equation and the proposed acceleration constants are formulated as follow:

$$v_{i,j}(t+1) = w \times v_{i,j}(t) + c_1 \times r_1 \times \left(pbest_{i,j}(t) - x_{i,j}(t) \right) \\ + c_2 \times r_2 \times \left(Gbest_j(t) - x_{i,j}(t) \right)$$

$$(8)$$

$$x_{i,j}(t+1) = x_{i,j}(t) + v_{i,j}(t+1) \qquad (9)$$

where

$$c_1 = 0.5 \times \left((1 - r_f) + \left(1 - pbest\_cv_i(t) \right) \right) \qquad (10a)$$

$$c_2 = 0.5 \times \left(r_f + \left(1 - Gbest\_cv(t) \right) \right) \qquad (10b)$$

$v_{i,j}(t)$ is the jth dimensional velocity of particle i in iteration t; $x_{i,j}(t)$ is the jth dimensional position of particle i in iteration t; $pbest_{i,j}(t)$ denotes the jth dimensional personal best position of the particle i in iteration t; $pbest\_cv_i(t)$ is the scalar constraint violation of the personal best of par-

ticle i in iteration t, $Gbest_j(t)$ is the jth dimensional $Gbest$ selected from global best archive in iteration t; $Gbest\_cv(t)$ represents the scalar constraint violation of the selected $Gbest(t)$ in iteration t; r_1 and r_2 are random numbers within $[0,1]$ that are regenerated every time they occur; w is the inertial weight, set to varied between 0.1 to 0.5, eliminating the need of fine tuning it [22]; and c_1 and c_2 are the acceleration constants. Please note the PSO flight equations stress the update mechanism of a particle i (so the variable t and subscript i are used). On the other hand, Equations (3)-(5) emphasizes the constraint violation of a particle with decision vector $\mathbf{x}$. Specifically, $pbest\_cv_i(t)$ refers to $cv(pbest(\mathbf{x}))$ in iteration t. Figure 5 presents the pseudocode for updating the particles' velocities and positions.

In general, if c_1 is larger than c_2, the second term in Equation (8), i.e., $c_1 \times r_1 \times \left(Pbest_{i,j}(t) - x_{i,j}(t) \right)$, is emphasized, in which, the movement of a particle depends more on their personal past experience than the global experiences attained by the whole swarm population. With that fact, we exploit the feasibility ratio of the particles' personal best (r_f), i.e., Equation (10), and the amount of constraint violations of the $pbest_{i,j}$ and $Gbest_j$ to influence the value of c_1 and c_2, as shown in Equation (10). Observe Table 1, we can generally conclude with small r_f, the particles are inclined on searching for feasible regions instead of optimum solution, while with small $Gbest\_cv$ and large r_f, the particles are inclined to search for optimum solution. In addition, both $pbest\_cv_i$, and $Gbest\_cv$ will also guide the particles towards feasibility but in an indirect manner.

Mutation Procedure

In Coello Coello, Toscano Pulido, & Lechuga (2004), a time dependent nonlinear equation is

Figure 5. Pseudocode for particle update mechanism

Function ParticleUpdateMechanism(*swarm, velocity, global_best_archive, har_dist Pbest_Memory, r_f*)

/* *swarm* = All the current particles in the swarm population

/* *velocity* = All current particles' velocities in the swarm population

/* *global_best_archive* = Particle's global best archive

/* *har_dist* = harmonic distance of the members in global best archive

/* *Pbest_Memory* = Recoded personal best

/* r_f = the feasibility ratio of the particles' personal best

Begin

    For each particle

        $r_1 = rand[0,1]$

        $r_2 = rand[0,1]$

        Select a *Gbest* via tournament selection and the harmonic distance

        Obtain the scalar constraint violation of selected *Gbest*

        Compute Equations (10a) and (10b)

        Compute Equations (8) and (9)

    EndFor

End

---

*Table 1. Brief summary of the effects of r_f pbest_cv, and **Gbest_cv** on the second and third terms in Equation (8)*

r_f	*pbest_cv*	*Gbest_cv*	**Comments**
small	small	small	$c_1 > c_2$; slightly emphasize on the second term (Both terms will guide the particle towards feasibility)
small	small	large	$c_1 \gg c_2$; emphasize on the second term (Second term guides the particle towards feasibility)
small	large	small	$c_1 \approx c_2$; both terms may have equal emphasis (Both terms will guide the particle towards feasibility and find better solutions)
small	large	large	$c_1 > c_2$; emphasize on the second term (Second term guides the particle towards feasibility)
large	small	small	$c_1 < c_2$; emphasize on the third term (Third term guides the particle to find better solutions)
large	small	large	$c_1 \approx c_2$; both terms may have equal emphasis (Both terms will guide the particle towards feasibility and find better solutions)
large	large	small	$c_1 \ll c_2$; emphasize on the third term (Third term guides the particle to find better solutions)
large	large	large	$c_1 < c_2$; slightly emphasize on the third term (Third term guides the particle to find better solutions)

Figure 6. Graph for percentage range to be reduced against iteration count. (a) Graph for $\beta = 5$ and (b) Graph for $\beta = 20$

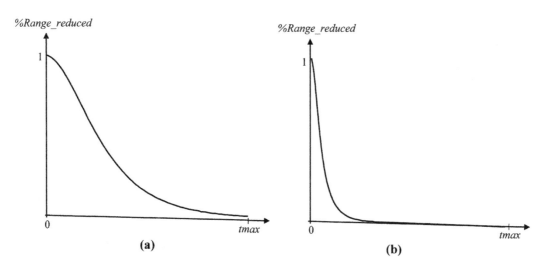

(a)   (b)

introduced to gradually decreases the number of particles in the swarm population that to be affected by the mutation operator. Using the same equation, the mutation operator is applied to the range of each decision variable in order to cover the full range of the full range of the decision variable in the beginning to allow the particles to explore the whole search space and slowly narrow the range over time with a nonlinear equation. The idea is to promote global search in early iterations and encourage fine tuning of the local search during the latter search process. In this article, similar idea of the mutation procedure is employed. In our method, instead of applying mutation directly on the particles in the swarm population, first the *pbest* and/or *Gbest* are randomly selected to be mutated based on certain condition and then apply the mutation operator to all the decision variables of the selected *pbest* and/or *Gbest*. Once the operation is done, the mutated decision variables replace the particle's decision variable. The mutation operator only affects the full range of the decision variables and the reduction rate of their ranges depends on a time dependent nonlinear function (See Equation (11)).

Two reasons why the mutation operator is applied to *pbest* and *Gbest*: 1) *pbest* is mutated to encourage the high probability for the particles to escape the local optima and to promote convergence; and 2) *pbest* and *Gbest* can served as an indicator if the particles aren't exploring the 'right' areas that yield no improvement in the search process to find the global optima. This usually happens during the latter search. If the mutation operator is applied to the selected particles from the swarm population, high chances that the mutated particles will be landed around the search space and not progressing towards the global optima. Hence, applying mutation operator to either *pbest* or *Gbest* is more practical to promote local search around the recorded best feasible solution(s).

The nonlinear equation used to adaptively reduce the range of the decision variable is based on a hyperbolic cooling schedule implemented in the simulated annealing [24]:

$$\%Range\_reduced = \frac{1}{\cosh\left(\dfrac{\beta \times t}{tmax}\right)}, \qquad (11)$$

Figure 7. Pseudocode of mutation operator applies to the swarm population

---

Function MutationOperation(*swarm, current and previous best solutions, global_best_archive, Pbest_Memory*)

/* *swarm* = All the current particles in the swarm population
/* *Pbest_Memory* = Recoded personal best
/*Note: Mutation operator procedure see Coello Coello et al. (2004).

Begin
    Calculate *%Range_reduced* from Equations (11)
    For each particle
      $r_4 = rand[0,1]$
      If $r_4 \leq P_m$
        If *Previous best solution equals to current best solution*
          If rand<0.5
            Apply mutation operator procedure with *%Range_reduced* on   a randomly selected
            Gbest from the *global_best_archive*
          Else
            Apply mutation operator procedure with *%Range_reduced* on the particle's *pbest*
            (from the *Pbest_Memory*)
          EndIf
        Else
          Apply mutation operator procedure with *%Range_reduced* on the particle's *pbest* (from
          the *Pbest_Memory*)
        EndIf
        Replace the current particle with the mutated one
      EndIf
    EndFor
End

---

where *tmax* is the maximum number of iterations; *t* represents the current iteration; and β is a user defined parameter that control how fast to finely narrow the range covered. Figure 6 depicts the Equation (11) and the range reduced or narrowed rate along the iteration count for $\beta = 5$ and $\beta = 20$.

The frequency of mutation procedure is determined by a user-defined mutation probability, P_m. Observe from the pseudocode in Figure 7, during the later stage of the search process, the particles may trap in a local optimum. Hence, the best solution from previous iteration and the best solution from current iteration are compared. If they are the same, then with equal probability, the mutation operator is applied to a randomly selected *Gbest* and replaces the mutated one with a particle in the swarm population; otherwise

the mutation operator is applied to the particle's *pbest*. The idea is to push the particles to create a local search within a vicinity of the *Gbest* or particle's *pbest* and to improve the chances for the particles to advance towards the global optimum solution.

SIMULATION STUDY

Experimental Framework

Twenty-four well-known benchmark functions (Liang et al., 2006) are used to test the performance of the proposed constrained PSO (RCVPSO). Table 2 presents the summary of the main characteristics of all teat functions. It provides the type of objective functions (i.e., linear, nonlinear,

Table 2. Summary of main characteristics of the 24 benchmark functions

Problems	n	Type of function	ρ	LI	NI	LE	NE	a
g01	13	Quadratic	0.0111%	9	0	0	0	6
g02	20	Nonlinear	99.9971%	1	1	0	0	1
g03	10	Nonlinear	0.0000%	0	0	0	1	1
g04	5	Quadratic	52.1230%	0	6	0	0	2
g05	4	Cubic	0.0000%	2	0	0	3	3
g06	2	Cubic	0.0066%	0	2	0	0	2
g07	10	Quadratic	0.0003%	3	5	0	0	6
g08	2	Nonlinear	0.8560%	0	2	0	0	0
g09	7	Nonlinear	0.5121%	0	4	0	0	2
g10	8	Linear	0.0010%	3	3	0	0	3
g11	2	Quadratic	0.0000%	0	0	0	1	1
g12	3	Quadratic	4.7713%	0	9^3	0	0	0
g13	5	Nonlinear	0.0000%	0	0	0	3	3
g14	10	Nonlinear	0.0000%	0	0	3	0	3
g15	3	Quadratic	0.0000%	0	0	1	1	2
g16	5	Nonlinear	0.0204%	4	34	0	0	4
g17	6	Nonlinear	0.0000%	0	0	0	4	4
g18	9	Quadratic	0.0000%	0	13	0	0	6
g19	15	Cubic	33.1761%	0	5	0	0	0
g20	24	Linear	0.0000%	0	6	2	12	16
g21	7	Linear	0.0000%	0	1	0	5	6
g22	22	Linear	0.0000%	0	1	8	11	19
g23	9	Linear	0.0000%	0	2	3	1	6
g24	2	Linear	79.6556%	0	2	0	0	2

cubit, quadratic) subject to specific types of constraint functions (i.e., linear inequality (LI), nonlinear inequality (NI), linear equality (LE), and nonlinear equality (NE)). The parameter **n** represents the number of decision variables, and parameter **a** represents the number of inequality constraints that are active. The parameter ρ is called feasibility ratio. This ratio is determined by calculating the percentage of feasible solutions out of 1,000,000 randomly generated solutions in the entire search space (Cai & Wang, 2006). If the feasibility ratio is very small, this challenges the algorithms to search for feasible solutions.

Parameter configurations of the RCVPSO for each test function are presented in Table 3. For each test function, we perform 350,000 fitness

Table 3. Parameter configurations for the proposed constrained PSO (RCVPSO). Note that all test functions use P_m=0.2 except for g17 and g07, the P_m=0.25

Test Problems	β
g05	9
g03, g09, g10, g22	10
g01, g02, g08, g11, g12, g15, g16, g20	15
g04, g07, g17, g13, g14	20
g06, g23, g24	25
g18	30

function evaluations and conduct 30 independent runs (Zavala, Aguirre, & Diharce, 2007). The experiment is implemented in Matlab software.

Performance Analysis

Table 4 presents the best, median, worst, and mean results obtained by the RCVPSO for each test function. In Table 4, FR represents the number of feasible run; while SR represents successful run in which the best feasible solution **x** * is within 0.0001 of the global optimal [25]. Among the twenty-four test problems, RCVPSO is able to obtain the optimal for g01, g04, g06, g08, g11, g12, g15, g16, g18, and g24. The following test problems: g02, g03, g05, g09, g13, g14, g17, and g19 have the best results that are very close to the optimum. Table 4 also shows that the RCVPSO obtain the poorest results for test functions g20, g21, g22, and g23. For test problem g20, the best reported global optimum is an infeasible solution. Comparing the best solutions of g20 found by PESO (Kirkpatrick, Gelatt, & Vecchi, 1983), RCVPSO obtained best solution closer to the global optima compared to the result reported in PESO. However, both RCVPSO and PESO are unable to obtain any feasible solutions for g22. In fact, to our best knowledge, existing constraint

optimization algorithms published so far are yet to find the global feasible solution for g22. The results presented in Table 4 shows RVPSO is competitive in solving problems with the following types of constraint functions: only linear inequality (LI), only nonlinear inequality (NI), only nonlinear equality (NE), combination of linear inequality (LI) with nonlinear inequality (NI), and combination of linear equality (LE) with nonlinear equality (NE). On the other hand, RVPSO faces difficulty in solving benchmark problem with low very ρ and also has these characteristics: Linear objective function with the combination of nonlinear inequality (NI) and nonlinear equality (NE) constraint functions that most of them are active constraints.

Tables 5 and 6 present the experiment results experiment results for RCVPSO against selected PSO algorithms and selected constrained optimization evolutionary algorithms (COEAs) respectively. The results of thirteen benchmark functions that presented by these selected algorithms are extracted from their publications to avoid biases in comparison. Hence, only thirteen benchmark functions are considered.

RCVPSO is compared against the four selected approaches that are implemented in the PSO algorithm. They are: global worst term in velocity equation (PSO+GlobalWorst) (Cushman, 2007), dynamic-objective method and restricted velocity particle swarm optimization (DOM+RVPSO) (Lu & Chen, 2006), master-slave particle swarm optimization (MSPSO) (Yang, Chen, Zhao, & Han, 2006), and feasibility tournament and perturbing the particle's memory (PESO) (Zavala et al., 2007). Observed Table 5, our algorithm can the achieve same or better performance for some of the selected approaches for the following test problems, g01, g03, g04, g06, g08, g11, and g12. RCVPSO is unable to obtain the best performance compared to some of the selected approaches for these test problems: g02, g05, g07, g09, g10, and g13. However, it is able

*Table 4. Experimental results on the 24 benchmark functions with 30 independent runs. Note that the first column presents the test problem and its global optimal and * indicates infeasible solution*

Problems/optimal	Best	Median	Worst	Mean	Std	FR	SR
g01/ -15.000000	**-15.000000**	-14.999971	-13.000000	-14.933255	3.65E-01	30	25
g02/ -0.803619	-0.803617	-0.769068	-0.718059	-0.765935	2.41E-02	30	1
g03/ -1.000500	-1.000496	-1.000478	-0.997560	-1.000344	5.45E-04	30	26
g04/ -30665.539	**-30665.539**	-30665.539	-33862.302	-31254.539	1.16E+03	30	7
g05/ 5126.4981	5126.4976	5134.6128	5307.0226	5146.3665	3.25E+01	30	0
g06/ -6961.8139	**-6961.8139**	-6961.8139	-6961.8139	-6961.8139	2.93E-06	30	30
g07/ 24.306209	24.348088	24.833433	25.830396	24.893023	3.43E-01	30	0
g08/ -0.095825	**-0.095825**	-0.095825	-0.095825	-0.095825	8.75E-15	30	30
g09/ 680.63006	680.63220	680.64260	680.66231	680.64474	9.04E-03	30	0
g10/ 7049.248	7122.404	7457.766	7954.769	7465.286	1.52E+02	30	0
g11/ 0.749900	**0.749900**	0.749900	0.749900	0.749900	1.36E-08	30	30
g12/ -1.000000	**-1.000000**	-1.000000	-1.000000	-1.000000	0	30	30
g13/ 0.0539498	0.0553445	0.0761482	0.1386873	0.0845082	2.61E-02	30	0
g14/ -47.764888	-47.529873	-45.538150	-42.522880	-45.091196	1.01E+01	30	0
g15/ 961.71502	**961.71502**	961.72424	961.82946	961.73732	3.44E-02	30	6
g16/ -1.905155	**-1.905155**	-1.905154	-1.903892	-1.905066	2.96E-04	30	28
g17/ 8853.5397	8858.9894	8948.3555	8965.5506	8933.8453	3.59E+01	30	0
g18/ -0.866025	**-0.866025**	-0.865215	-0.500484	-0.846145	7.43E-02	30	4
g19/ 32.655592	33.422389	43.043938	49.286338	53.852990	4.86E+00	30	0
g20/ *0.204979	*0.195770	*0.151261	*0.093300	*0.149351	2.86E-02	0	0
g21/ 193.72451	214.44572	277.56500	480.06205	293.25171	5.25E+01	30	0
g22/ 236.43098	*0	*1253.4461	*5081.5722	*1608.5380	1.52E+03	0	0
g23/ -400.0551	-0.13378	-0.00488	-0.00404	-0.01618	2.83E-02	30	0
g24/ -5.508013	**-5.508013**	-5.508013	-5.508013	-5.508013	3.36E-12	30	30

to performance better than MSPSO for test problems g05, g07, and g09, and obtains better performance than DOM+RVPSO for test problems g02. In addition, RCVPSO did better than PSO+GlobalWorst for most of the test functions, except for g08 and g12 that both obtained the same best results. Finally, RCVPSO has the worst results for g10.

Similar to Table 5, Table 6 presents the experiment results for RCVPSO and four selected constrained optimization evolutionary algorithms (COEAs). These selected approaches include stochastic Ranking method (RY) (Runarsson & Yao, 2005), replacement and comparison rules with simplex crossover, and infeasible solution archiving and replacement mechanism (CW) (Cai & Wang, 2006), self-adaptation mechanism and three simple comparison criteria (SMES), and adaptive penalty formulation (Tessema & Yen, 2006). Compare the results with TY, RCVPSO does better for test functions g02, g04, g05, g06, g07, g09, and g11; share the same performance for g08 and g12; while did worst for g10 and g13. The results show that RCVPSO achieves better performance than SMES for test functions g02, g03, and g05 but achieves lesser performance for

Table 5. Comparison of the proposed algorithm with respect to PSO+GlobalWorst (Cushman, 2007), DOM+RVPSO (Lu & Chen, 2006), MSPSO (Yang et al., 2006), and PESO (Zavala et al., 2007)) on 13 benchmark functions. Note that the first column presents the test problem and its global optimal.

Problems/ optimal		DOM+RVPSO [9]	PSO+GlobalWorst [15]	MSPSO [23]	PESO [22]	RCVPSO
g01/ -15.000	Best	**-15.000**	-14.880	**-15.000**	-15.000	-15.000
	Mean	-14.419	-14.057	**-15.000**	-15.000	-14.933
	Worst	-12.453	12.162	**-15.000**	-15.000	-13.000
	St. dev	8.5E-01	NA	4.12E-04	0	3.65E-01
g02/ -0.803619	Best	-0.664028	-0.761717	-0.803020	**-0.803619**	-0.803617
	Mean	-0.413257	-0.530459	-0.800418	**-0.801320**	-0.765935
	Worst	-0.259980	-0.313739	**-0.799342**	-0.786566	-0.718059
	St. dev	1.2E-01	NA	**1.51E-03**	4.59E-03	2.41E-02
g03/ -1.001	Best	-1.005	0.997	1.000	**-1.001**	**-1.001**
	Mean	-1.003	0.981	0.998	**-1.001**	-1.000
	Worst	-0.933	0.939	0.996	-1.000	-0.998
	St. dev	1.3E-02	NA	1.58E-03	3.15E-07	5.45E-04
g04/ -30665.539	Best	**-30665.539**	-30665.395	-30665.537	**-30665.539**	**-30665.539**
	Mean	**-30665.539**	-30634.758	-30663.010	**-30665.539**	-31254.539
	Worst	**-30665.539**	-30435.531	-30658.300	**-30665.539**	-6961.8139
	St. dev	1.2E-11	NA	2.79E+00	0	1.16E+03
g05/ 5126.4981	Best	5126.4842	5144.2083	5126.6051	**5126.4981**	5126.4976
	Mean	5241.0549	5175.3764	5129.8001	**5126.4981**	5146.3665
	Worst	5708.2250	5206.5445	5157.2247	**5126.4981**	5307.0226
	St. dev	1.8E+02	NA	1.25E+01	0	3.25E+01
g06/ -6961.814	Best	**-6961.814**	-6884.630	-6961.830	**-6961.814**	**-6961.814**
	Mean	**-6961.814**	-5866.541259	-6957.760	**-6961.814**	**-6961.814**
	Worst	**-6961.814**	3513.085239	-6954.650	**-6961.814**	**-6961.814**
	St. dev	4.6E-12	NA	2.69E+00	0	2.93E-06
g07/ 24.306	Best	24.306	25.429	24.373	**24.306**	24.348
	Mean	24.317	28.944	24.180	**24.306**	24.893
	Worst	24.385	38.178	23.750	**24.306**	25.830
	St. dev	2.4E-02	NA	2.53E-01	**3.34E-06**	3.43E-01
g08/ -0.095825	Best	**-0.095825**	**-0.095825**	**0.095825**	0.095825	**-0.095825**
	Mean	**-0.095825**	0.095820	**0.095825**	0.095825	**-0.095825**
	Worst	**-0.095825**	0.095775	**0.095825**	0.095825	**-0.095825**
	St. dev	1.4E-17	NA	0	0	8.75E-15
g09/ 680.630	Best	**680.630**	680.647	680.660	**680.630**	680.632
	Mean	**680.630**	681.114	681.002	**680.630**	680.645
	Worst	**680.630**	687.155	684.113	**680.630**	680.662
	St. dev	**5.4E-13**	NA	1.48E+00	0	9.04E-03
g10/ 7049.248	Best	**7049.2480**	7102.69	7051.690	**7049.248**	7122.404
	Mean	7049.2701	8932.347	7054.710	**7049.249**	7465.286
	Worst	7049.5969	19257.649	7059.280	**7049.264**	7954.769
	St. dev	7.9E-02	NA	2.84E+00	3.61E-03	1.52E+02
g11/ 0.750	Best	0.749	0.749	**0.750**	**0.750**	**0.750**
	Mean	0.749	0.749	**0.750**	**0.750**	**0.750**
	Worst	0.749	0.749	**0.750**	**0.750**	**0.750**
	St. dev	2.4E-12	NA	0	0	1.36E-08
g12/ -1.000	Best	**-1.000**	**-1.000**	NA	**-1.000**	**-1.000**
	Mean	**-1.000**	**-1.000**	NA	**-1.000**	**-1.000**
	Worst	**-1.000**	**-1.000**	NA	**-1.000**	**-1.000**
	St. dev	0	NA	NA	0	0
g13/ 0.0539498	Best	0.0538666	0.116590	NA	**0.053950**	0.055345
	Mean	0.0681124	0.300965	NA	**0.053950**	0.084508
	Worst	2.0428924	0.596544	NA	**0.053965**	0.138687
	St. dev	4.0E-01	NA	NA	**2.76E-06**	2.61E-02

Table 6. Comparison of the proposed algorithm with respect to RY (Runarsson & Yao, 2005), CW (Cai & Wang, 2006), SMES (Mezura-Montes & Coello Coello, 2005), and TY (Tessema & Yen, 2006) on 13 benchmark functions. Note that the first column presents the test problem and its global optimal.

Problems/ optimal		RY[1]	CW [3]	SMES [19]	TY [28]	RCVPSO
g01/ -15.000	Best	**-15.000**	**-15.000**	**-15.000**	**-15.000**	**-15.000**
	Mean	**-15.000**	**-15.000**	**-15.000**	-14.552	-14.933
	Worst	**-15.000**	**-15.000**	**-15.000**	-13.097	-13.000
	St. dev	1.3E-13	1.3E-14	0	7.00E-01	3.65E-01
g02/ -0.803619	Best	**-0.803619**	**-0.803619**	-0.803601	-0.803202	-0.803617
	Mean	-0.772078	-0.803220	-0.785238	-0.755798	-0.765935
	Worst	-0.683055	-0.792608	-0.751322	-0.745712	-0.718059
	St. dev	2.6E-02	2.0E-03	1.67E-02	1.33E-01	2.41E-02
g03/ -1.001	Best	**-1.001**	-1.000	-1.000	**-1.001**	**-1.001**
	Mean	**-1.001**	-1.000	-1.000	-0.964	-1.000
	Worst	**-1.001**	-1.000	-1.000	-0.887	-0.998
	St. dev	**6.0E-09**	2.8E-16	2.09E04	3.01E-01	5.45E-04
g04/ -30665.539	Best	**-30665.539**	**-30665.539**	**-30665.539**	-30665.401	**-30665.539**
	Mean	**-30665.539**	**-30665.539**	**-30665.539**	-306659.221	-31254.539
	Worst	**-30665.539**	**-30665.539**	**-30665.539**	-30656.471	-6961.8139
	St. dev	2.2E-11	8.0E-12	0	2.04E+00	1.16E+03
g05/ 5126.4981	Best	5126.497	**5126.4981**	5126.5990	5126.907	5126.4976
	Mean	5126.497	**5126.4981**	5174.4920	5214.232	5146.3665
	Worst	5126.497	**5126.4981**	5304.1670	5564.642	5307.0226
	St. dev	6.2E-12	1.51E-12	50E+00	2.47E+02	3.25E+01
g06/ -6961.814	Best	**-6961.814**	**-6961.814**	**-6961.814**	-6961.046	**-6961.814**
	Mean	**-6961.814**	**-6961.814**	-6961.284	-6953.061	**-6961.814**
	Worst	**-6961.814**	**-6961.814**	-6952.482	-6943.304	**-6961.814**
	St. dev	6.4E-12	1.8E-12	1.85E+00	5.88E+00	2.93E-06
g07/ 24.306	Best	**24.306**	**24.306**	24.327	24.838	24.348
	Mean	**24.306**	**24.306**	24.475	27.328	24.893
	Worst	24.308	**24.306**	24.843	33.095	25.830
	St. dev	2.7E-04	5.7E-12	1.32E-01	2.17E+00	3.43E-01
g08/ -0.095825	Best	**-0.095825**	**-0.095825**	**0.095825**	**0.095825**	**-0.095825**
	Mean	**-0.095825**	**-0.095825**	**0.095825**	0.095635	**-0.095825**
	Worst	**-0.095825**	**-0.095825**	**0.095825**	0.092697	**-0.095825**
	St. dev	4.2E-17	4.2E-17	0	1.06E-03	8.75E-15
g09/ 680.630	Best	**680.630**	**680.630**	680.632	680.773	680.632
	Mean	**680.630**	**680.630**	680.643	681.246	680.645
	Worst	**680.630**	**680.630**	680.719	682.081	680.662
	St. dev	4.6E-13	4.7E-13	1.55E-02	3.22E-01	9.04E-03
g10/ 7049.248	Best	**7049.248**	**7049.248**	7051.903	7069.981	7122.404
	Mean	7049.249	**7049.248**	7253.047	7238.964	7465.286
	Worst	7049.296	**7049.248**	7638.366	7489.406	7954.769
	St. dev	**4.9E-03**	4.0E-09	1.4E+02	1.38E+02	1.52E+02
g11/ 0.750	Best	**0.750**	**0.750**	**0.750**	0.749	**0.750**
	Mean	**0.750**	**0.750**	**0.750**	0.751	**0.750**
	Worst	**0.750**	**0.750**	**0.750**	0.757	**0.750**
	St. dev	1.8E-15	0	1.52E-04	2.00E-03	1.36E-08
g12/ -1.000	Best	**-1.000**	**-1.000**	**-1.000**	**-1.000**	**-1.000**
	Mean	**-1.000**	**-1.000**	**-1.000**	**-1.000**	**-1.000**
	Worst	**-1.000**	**-1.000**	**-1.000**	**-1.000**	**-1.000**
	St. dev	9.6E-10	0	0	1.41E-04	0
g13/ 0.0539498	Best	0.053942	**0.0539498**	0.053986	0.053941	0.055345
	Mean	0.096276	**0.0539498**	0.166385	0.286270	0.084508
	Worst	0.438803	**0.0539498**	0.468294	0.885276	0.138687
	St. dev	1.2E-01	6.5E-17	1.77E-01	2.75E-01	2.61E-02

g07, g10, and g13. For the rest of the test functions, SMES and RCVPSO share the same best results. Regarding the results shown in Figure 6, RCVPSO obtains same best results as RY and CW for functions g01, g03, g04, g06, g11, and g12; while attains inferior performance for the rest of the test functions.

Overall, the RCVPSO is competitive in terms of performance for most of the test functions for the following selected algorithms: PSO+GlobalWorst, DOM+RVPSO, MSPSO, TY, and SMES. However, PESO, RY and CW are better than RCVOPSO in solving the selected test functions.

CONCLUSION AND DISCUSSION

This article proposes a constrained PSO, called RCVPSO, to solve for constrained optimization problems. RCVPSO converts the COP into an unconstrained bi-objective optimization problem. The main contribution RCVPSO is the designed constraint handling techniques are embedded in the key mechanisms of PSO. These techniques include separate procedures to update the infeasible and feasible personal best in the personal best memory in order to guide the infeasible particles towards the feasible regions while promote search for better solutions; store infeasible nondominated solutions along with the best feasible solution in the global archive to assist the search for feasible region and better solutions; the adjustment of the accelerated constants in the PSO equation is based on the number of feasible personal best in the personal best memory and the constraint violations of personal best and global best. The adjustment will influence the search process either to find more feasible solutions (particles) or to search for better solutions; and the range covered for mutation is adaptively reduced over time to encourage global search in early stage of the search process and slowly enter the fine tuning local search in the later stage.

Simulation study shows that RCVPSO is able to obtain quality feasible solutions for most of the test problems while faces difficulty in solving COPs with combination of linear inequality, nonlinear inequality, linear equality and nonlinear equality constraints functions, and the large portion of these constraint functions are also active constraints. This deficiency is contributed by the quick convergence characteristic of PSO and the lacking to support possible search along boundary where the constraints are active constraints. Despite of this deficiency, RCVPSO's performance is observed to be competitive with most of the selected state-of-the-art approaches, particularly the constrained PSOs. Otherwise, it still falls short in performance when compared to two of the constrained optimization evolutionary algorithms (COEA) and a constrained hybrid PSO (PESO).

Future works include improving convergence and diversity issues of PSO by developing criteria to regulate the particles' selection from infeasible to feasible global best, such criteria can based on the feasibility ratio, and to revise the design features to efficiently tackle active constraints. In addition, experiments to examine the effectiveness of the design elements are also considered

REFERENCES

Cai, Z., & Wang, Y. (2006). A multiobjective optimization-based evolutionary algorithm for constrained optimization. *IEEE Transactions on Evolutionary Computation*, *10*(6), 658–674. doi:10.1109/TEVC.2006.872344

Coello Coello, C. A., Toscano Pulido, G., & Lechuga, M. S. (2004). Handling multiple objectives with particle swarm optimization. *IEEE Transactions on Evolutionary Computation*, *8*(3), 256–279. doi:10.1109/TEVC.2004.826067

Cushman, D. L. (2007). *A particle swarm approach to constrained optimization informed by 'Global Worst'*. Unpublished doctoral dissertation, Pennsylvania State University.

Deb, K., Pratap, A., Agarwal, S., & Meyarivan, T. (2002). A fast and elitist multiobjective genetic algorithm: NSGA-II. *IEEE Transactions on Evolutionary Computation*, *6*(2), 182–197. doi:10.1109/4235.996017

Goldberg, D. E. (1989). *Genetic Algorithms in Search, Optimization and Machine Learning*. Reading, MA: Addison-Wesley.

He, Q., & Wang, L. (2007). A hybrid particle swarm optimization with a feasibility-based rule for constrained optimization. *Applied Mathematics and Computation*, *186*, 1407–1422. doi:10.1016/j.amc.2006.07.134

Huang, V. L., Suganathan, P. N., Qin, A. K., & Baskar, S. (2005). *Multiobjective differential evolution with external archive and harmonic distance-based diversity measure* (Tech. Rep. MODE-2005). Singapore: Nanyang Technological University.

Kirkpatrick, S., Gelatt, C. D., & Vecchi, M. P. (1983). Optimization by simulated annealing. *Science*, *220*(4598), 671–680. doi:10.1126/science.220.4598.671

Krohling, R. A., & Coelho, L. D. (2006). Coevolutionary particle swarm optimization using Gaussian distribution for solving constrained optimization problems. *IEEE Transactions on Systems, Man, and Cybernetics. Part B, Cybernetics*, *36*(6), 1407–1416. doi:10.1109/TSMCB.2006.873185

Li, L. D., Li, X., & Yu, X. (2008). A multi-objective constraint-handling method with PSO algorithm for constrained engineering optimization problems. In *Proceedings of IEEE Congress on Evolutionary Computation* (pp. 1528-1535).

Liang, J. J., Runarsson, T. P., Mezura-Montes, E., Clere, M., Suganthan, P. N., Coello Coello, C. A., et al. (2006). *Problem definitions and evaluation criteria*. Paper presented at the CEC2006 special session on constrained real-parameter optimization.

Liang, J. J., & Suganthan, P. N. (2006). Dynamic multi-swarm particle swarm optimizer with a novel constraint-handling mechanism. In *Proceedings of IEEE Congress on Evolutionary Computation* (pp. 9-16).

Liu, Z., Wang, C., & Li, J. (2008). Solving constrained optimization via a modified genetic particle swarm optimization. In *Proceedings of International Workshop on Knowledge Discovery and Data Mining*, Adelaide, Australia (pp. 217-220).

Lu, H., & Chen, W. (2006). Dynamic-objective particle swarm optimization for constrained optimization problems. *Journal of Combinatorial Optimization*, *2*(4), 409–419. doi:10.1007/s10878-006-9004-x

Mezura-Montes, E., & Coello Coello, C. A. (2005). A simple multimembered evolution strategy to solve constrained optimization problems. *IEEE Transactions on Evolutionary Computation*, *9*(1), 1–17. doi:10.1109/TEVC.2004.836819

Mezura-Montes, E., & Coello Coello, C. A. (2006). *A survey of constraint-handling techniques based on evolutionary multiobjective optimization* (Tech. Rep. EVOCINV-04-2006). CINVESTAV-IPN.

Parsopoulus, K. E., & Vrahatis, M. N. (2002) Particle swarm optimization method for constrained optimization problems. In *Technologies- Theory and Applications: New Trends in Intelligent Technologies* (pp. 214-220).

Pulido, G. T., & Coello Coello, C. A. (2004). A constraint-handling mechanism for particle swarm optimization. In *Proceedings of IEEE Congress on Evolutionary Computation* (pp. 1396-1403).

Runarsson, T. P., & Yao, X. (2005). Search biases in constrained evolutionary optimization. *IEEE Transactions on Evolutionary Computation*, *35*(2), 233–243.

Sierra, M. R., & Coello Coello, C. A. (2005). Improving PSO-based multi-objective optimization using crowding, mutation and ε–dominance. In *Proceedings of Evolutionary Multi-Criterion Optimization Conference* (pp. 505-519).

Takahama, T., & Sakai, S. (2006). Constrained optimization by the ε constrained differential evolution with gradient-based mutation and feasible elites. In *Proceedings of IEEE Congress on Evolutionary Computation* (pp. 1-8).

Tessema, B., & Yen, G. G. (2006). A Self Adaptive Penalty Function Based Algorithm for Constrained Optimization. In *Proceedings of IEEE Congress on Evolutionary Computation* (pp. 246-253).

Venkatraman, S., & Yen, G. G. (2005). A generic framework for constrained optimization using genetic algorithms. *IEEE Transactions on Evolutionary Computation*, *9*(4), 424–435. doi:10.1109/TEVC.2005.846817

Wang, Y., Cai, Z., Guo, G., & Zhou, Y. (2007). Multiobjective optimization and hybrid evolutionary algorithm to solve constrained optimization problems. *IEEE Transactions on Systems, Man, and Cybernetics. Part B, Cybernetics*, *37*(3), 560–575. doi:10.1109/TSMCB.2006.886164

Wang, Y., Cai, Z., Zhou, Y., & Zeng, W. (2008). An adaptive trade-off model for constrained evolutionary optimization. *IEEE Transactions on Evolutionary Computation*, *12*(1), 80–92. doi:10.1109/TEVC.2007.902851

Yang, B., Chen, Y., Zhao, Z., & Han, Q. (2006). A master-slave particle swarm optimization algorithm for solving constrained optimization problems. In *Proceedings of the World Congress on Intelligent Control and Automation* (pp. 3208-3212).

Zavala, A. M., Aguirre, A. H., & Diharce, E. V. (2007). Robust PSO-based constrained optimization by perturbing the particle's memory. In T. S. Chan & M. K. Tiwari (Eds.), *Swarm intelligence, focus on ant and particle swarm optimization* (pp. 57-76). Vienna, Austria: I-Tech Education and Publishing.

Zielinski, K., & Laur, R. (2006). Constrained single-objective optimization using particle swarm optimization. In *Proceedings of IEEE Congress on Evolutionary Computation* (pp. 443-450).

This work was previously published in International Journal of Swarm Intelligence Research, Volume 1, Issue 1, edited by Yuhui Shi, pp. 42-63, copyright 2010 by IGI Publishing (an imprint of IGI Global)

Chapter 5
Adaptive Neuro–Fuzzy Control Approach Based on Particle Swarm Optimization

Gomaa Zaki El-Far
Menoufia University, Egypt

ABSTRACT

This paper proposes a modified particle swarm optimization algorithm (MPSO) to design adaptive neuro-fuzzy controller parameters for controlling the behavior of non-linear dynamical systems. The modification of the proposed algorithm includes adding adaptive weights to the swarm optimization algorithm, which introduces a new update. The proposed MPSO algorithm uses a minimum velocity threshold to control the velocity of the particles, avoids clustering of the particles, and maintains the diversity of the population in the search space. The mechanism of MPSO has better potential to explore good solutions in new search spaces. The proposed MPSO algorithm is also used to tune and optimize the controller parameters like the scaling factors, the membership functions, and the rule base. To illustrate the adaptation process, the proposed neuro-fuzzy controller based on MPSO algorithm is applied successfully to control the behavior of both non-linear single machine power systems and non-linear inverted pendulum systems. Simulation results demonstrate that the adaptive neuro-fuzzy logic controller application based on MPSO can effectively and robustly enhance the damping of oscillations.

DOI: 10.4018/978-1-4666-1592-2.ch005

INTRODUCTION

Particle Swarm Optimization (PSO) has been an increasingly hot topic in the area of computational intelligence. PSO is an optimization algorithm that falls under the soft computing umbrella that covers genetic and evolutionary computing algorithms as well. As such, it lends itself as being applicable to a wide variety of optimization problems (Esmin & Torres, 2004;, Parsopoulos & Skokos, 2005; Helwig & Haubelt, 2005; Conradie & Miikkulainen, 2002).

PSO is a population-based algorithm that exploits a population of individuals, to search promising regions of the function space. In this context, the population is called swarm and the individuals are called particles. Each particle moves with an adaptable velocity within the search space, and retains in its memory the best position it ever encountered. In the global variant of the PSO the best position ever attained by all individuals of the swarm is communicated to all the particles. In the local variant, each particle is assigned to a neighborhood consisting of a pre-specified number of particles. In this case, the best position ever attained by the particles that comprise the neighborhood is communicated among them. The PSO like other evolutionary algorithms (e.g., genetic algorithm (GA)) performs searches using a population (called swarm) of individuals (called particles) that are updated from iteration to iteration. Compared to GA, PSO is fast to implement since it has no evolution operators such as crossover and mutation i.e., few parameters to be adjusted.

In Particle Swarm Optimization, each particle moves in the search space and updates its velocity according to best previous positions already found by its neighbors (and itself), trying to find an even better position. This approach has been proved to be powerful but needs tuning parameters predefined by the user (Magoulas & Eldabi, 2002; Mahmoud, 2010; Kiranyaz & Ince, 2010).

Power systems are modeled as large scale non-linear highly structured systems. The high complexity and nonlinearity of power systems have been created a great deal of challenge to power system control engineers for decades. One of the most important problems in the electric power systems is the damping of low-frequency oscillation (dynamic stability). Such oscillations may occur between the electrical and mechanical systems or between large inertia's in the mechanical system. These oscillations are usually initiated by small disturbances such as small changes in the load levels or generator loading. If the disturbance is large (transient stability), the oscillations may be sustained for minutes and grow to cause system separation if no adequate damping at the system oscillating frequency is available (Ahmed, 2000). Therefore, a major effort has to be made to improve power system stabilizers (PSSs) performance and characteristics. PSSs are usually designed once a time, by conventional control methods, which restrict the system model to low order single-input-single-output linear models, where as the power system oscillatory instability is actually a large-scale multivariable problem.

In recent years, renewed interest has been shown in power system control using non-linear control theory, particularly to improve system transient stability (Nassef, 2005). Instead of using an approximate linear model, as in the design of the conventional power system stabilizer, non-linear models are used and non-linear feedback linearization techniques are employed on the power system models, thereby alleviating the operating point dependent nature of the linear designs. Non-linear controllers significantly improve the power system's transient stability. However, non-linear controllers have a more complicated structure and are difficult to implement relative to linear controllers.

Fuzzy logic control systems have the capability of transforming linguistic information and expert knowledge into control signals and are preferred over traditional approaches such as optimal and adaptive control techniques. Despite of the advantages of the conventional fuzzy logic controller (FLC) over traditional approaches, there remain a number of difficulties in the design stages. Hybrid controllers built by combining fuzzy logic with allied technologies like neural networks and genetic algorithms help in overcoming some of these difficulties (Liu & Abraham, 2006, 2007). FLCs are characterized by a number of parameters that are needed to be configured in prior, such as input/output scaling factors, the centre and width of membership functions, and selection of appropriate fuzzy control rules. The complexity in selection of these parameters increases with the complexity of process (Surmann, 2000).

Artificial neural networks, due to their learning capability, are being sought in the development of neuro-fuzzy controllers or adaptive FLCs. This type of knowledge representation does not allow the output variables to be described in linguistic terms. This is one of the major drawbacks of this approach (Fiszelew & Britos, 2007; Goe & Saxena, 2005).

In this paper, a modified approach that uses neural network and MPSO technique to learn and optimize fuzzy logic controllers is proposed. The proposed algorithm is used effectively to learn and optimize on line the fuzzy logic membership function parameters, the rule base and the scaling factors.

A multilayer perceptron model is configured as a neuro-fuzzy network. The consequent terms are represented by linguistic terms, which make this model more intuitive and give more insight into the model structure. To show the performance of the proposed modified technique, it is used effectively to control the behavior of both non-linear single machine power system and non-linear inverted pendulum system. Simulation results on the comparison between MPSO and traditional control approaches demonstrate that the adaptive neuro-fuzzy logic controller application based on MPSO can effectively and robustly enhance the damping of oscillations.

The paper is organized as follows: The following section describes the system. The modified particle swarm optimization is then introduced. Adaptive neuro-fuzzy implementation is described while simulation results are given. Finally, conclusions are given.

SYSTEM DESCRIPTION

Modeling of the Non-Linear Single Machine Infinite Bus System

The non-linear single machine infinite bus system is shown in Figure 1. It consists of one equivalent synchronous machine, transmission system, transformers, excitation system and speed governor.

The generating unit components consist of a synchronous generator, excitation system and a three stages turbine-governor representation. The Park's non-linear current Equations for the synchronous generator are described in Ahmed (2000).

The overall system representation yields 14 differential Equations (Ahmed, 2000). The speed signal error $\Delta\omega$ and its derivative $\Delta\dot{\omega}$ will be used as two inputs to the adaptive neuro-fuzzy logic power system stabilizer.

Modeling of the Non-Linear Inverted Pendulum System

Another example for non-linear system is the cart-pole typed inverted pendulum system. It is described by following state Equations (Nassef, 2005):

$$\dot{x}(t) = [\dot{x}_1(t) \quad \dot{x}_2(t)]^T = [\dot{\theta}(t) \quad \ddot{\theta}(t)]^T \qquad (1)$$

$$x(t) = [x_1(t) \quad x_2(t)]^T = [\theta(t) \quad \dot{\theta}(t)]^T \qquad (2)$$

and

Figure 1. Single machine infinite bus system

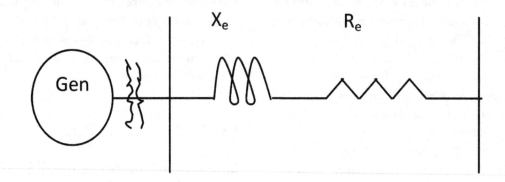

$$\ddot{\theta}(t) = \frac{g \sin(\theta(t)) - aml\dot{\theta}(t)^2 \sin(2\theta(t)) / 2 - a \cos(\theta(t)) u(t)}{4l / 3 - aml \cos^2(\theta(t))}$$

(3)

θ is the angular displacement of the pendulum; $g = 9.8$ m/s^2 is the acceleration due to gravity; $m = 2$ kg is the mass of the pendulum; $M = 8$ kg is the mass of the cart; $2l = 1$m is the length of the pendulum; u is the force applied to the cart and $a = 1/(m+M)$ is a constant.

Problem Formulation

The control objective considered in this paper is to design an adaptive neuro-fuzzy logic controller based on the proposed MPSO approach for both single machine power system and inverted pendulum system such that in the case of the single machine power system, the actual outputs (rotor angle deviation ($\Delta\delta$) and angular speed deviation ($\Delta\omega$)) track the desired performance closely in some sense. Also, in the case of the inverted pendulum, the proposed neuro-fuzzy controller approach can effectively and robustly control the motion of the cart so that the pole can be balanced in the vertical position i.e. $\theta = 0°$ at steady state.

MODIFIED PARTICLE SWARM

Optimization Algorithm

Particle swarm optimization (PSO) is a stochastic, population-based optimization algorithm. It belongs to the class of *swarm intelligence* algorithms, which are inspired from the social dynamics and emergent behavior that arise in socially organized colonies (Skokos & Parsopoulos, 2005). Swarm intelligence is related to the field of evolutionary computation, which consists of algorithms inspired by natural evolution and genetic dynamics, such as genetic algorithms (Garg & Kumar, 2002; Settles & Nathan, 2005). PSO exploits a population, called a *swarm*, and individuals, called *particles*, to probe the search space. Each particle moves with an adaptable velocity within the search space, and retains a memory of the best position it ever encountered. In the *global* variant of PSO, the best position ever attained by all individuals of the swarm is communicated to all the particles. In the *local* variant, each particle is assigned to a neighborhood consisting of prespecified particles. In this case, the best position ever attained by the particles that comprise the neighborhood is communicated among them (Papageorgiou & Parsopoulos, 2005).

Assume a D-dimensional search space, $S \subset \mathbb{R}^D$, and a swarm consisting of M particles. The i-th particle is in effect a D-dimensional vector,

$$X_i = (x_{i1}, x_{i2}, \ldots, x_{iD})^{\mathrm{T}} \in S \qquad (4)$$

The velocity of this particle is also a D-dimensional vector,

$$V_i = (v_{i1}, v_{i2}, \ldots, v_{iD})^{\mathrm{T}} \qquad (5)$$

The best previous position encountered by the i-th particle is a point in S, denoted by

$$P_i = (p_{i1}, p_{i2}, \ldots, p_{iD})^{\mathrm{T}} \in S \qquad (6)$$

Usually, the particles are considered to lie on a ring topology, i.e., X_M and X_2 are considered the immediate neighbors of X1. In this case, the neighborhoods of X_i consist of the particles X_{i-r}. $\ldots, X_i, \ldots, X_{i+r}$, where r is the neighborhood's radius. Assume g_i to be the index of the particle that attained the best previous position among all the particles in the neighborhood of X_i, i.e.

$$f(p_{gi}) \leq f(p_i), \; i = i-r, \ldots, i + r \qquad (7)$$

The swarm approach is manipulated by the following Equations (Papageorgiou & Parsopoulos, 2005),

$$v_i(t+1) = \chi[v_i(t) + c_1 r_1 (p_i(t) - x_i(t)) + \\ c_2 r_2 (p_{gi}(t) - x_i(t))] \qquad (8)$$

$$x_i(t+1) = x_i(t) + v_i(t+1) \qquad (9)$$

Where $i = 1, 2, \ldots, M$, t to be the iteration counter, χ is a parameter called *constriction factor* (Shi & Eberhart, 1998; Clerc, 1999); c_1 and c_2 are two parameters called *cognitive* and *social* parameters, respectively; r_1, r_2, are random vectors with elements uniformly distributed within [0, 1]; and gi is the index of the particle that attained

either the best position of the whole swarm (global version) or the best position in the neighborhood of the i-th particle (local version). All vector operations in Equations (8) and (9) are performed component wise.

The best positions, p_i *(pbest)*, $i = 1, 2, \ldots, M$, are updated as follows:

$$p_i(t+1) = \\ \begin{cases} x_i(t+1), \; if \; f(x_i(t+1)) < f(p_i(t)), \\ p_i(t), \; otherwise. \end{cases} \qquad (10)$$

Alternatively, a different version of the algorithm, which incorporates a parameter called *inertia weight*, is given as (Papageorgiou & Parsopoulos, 2005):

$$v_i(t+1) = \\ w\eta_i(t) + c_1 r_1 (p_i(t) - x_i(t)) + \\ c_2 r_2 (p_{gi}(t) - x_i(t)) \qquad (11)$$

$$x_i(t+1) = x_i(t) + v_i(t+1) \qquad (12)$$

Where w is the inertia weight.

Let us now discuss the role of various parameters that appearing in the above versions. In early versions of PSO (Skokos & Parsopoulos, 2005), there was no actual mechanism to control the magnitude of the velocities of the particles. Thus, they could take arbitrarily high values (swarm explosion), resulting in divergence of the swarm. Another reason for premature convergence of PSO is due to the stagnation of the particles exploration of a new search space. In this situation, a strategy is proposed to drive those lazy particles and let them explore better solutions. So positive parameters $v_{\max}$ and v_c are employed as threshold values on the absolute value of the vector components of the velocity. If a particle's velocity decreases to a threshold value v_c, a modified velocity is assigned using (13),

$$\eta_i(t) = \begin{cases} v_i(t) & if \; |v_i(t) \geq v_c| \\ h(-1,1)v_{max} \, / \, \lambda & if \; |v_i(t) < v_c| \end{cases} \quad (13)$$

where $v_c = e^{-[6(1+h(-1,1))]}$, $h(-1,1)$ is a random number, uniformly distributed with the interval [-1,1], and λ is a tuning factor to control the domain of the particle's oscillation according to v_{max}. v_c is the minimum velocity threshold, a tunable threshold parameter to limit the minimum of the particles' velocity. The minimum velocity threshold can make the particle continue moving until the algorithm converges. The performance of the algorithm is directly correlated to two parameter values, v_c and λ. A large v_c shortens the oscillation period, and it provides a great probability for the particles to leap over local minima using the same number of iterations. But a large v_c compels particles in the quick "flying" state, which leads them not to search the solution and forcing them not to refine the search. In other words, a large v_c facilitates a global search while a smaller value facilitates a local search. By changing it dynamically, the search ability is dynamically adjusted. The value of λ changes directly the particle oscillation domain in which the clustering of the particles can avoid. It is possible for particles not to jump over the local minima if there would be a large local minimum available in the objective search space. But the particle trajectory would more prone to oscillate because of a smaller value of λ. For the desired exploration-exploitation trade-off, the particle search space is divided into three stages. In the first stage the values for v_c and λ are set at large and small values respectively. In the second stage, v_c and λ are set at medium values and in the last stage, v_c is set at a small value and λ is set at a large value. These enable the particles to take very large steps to explore solutions in the early stages, by scanning the whole solution space for good local

minima and then in the final stages particles perform a fine grain search.

Referring to Equations (8) and (11), both the constriction factor χ and the inertia weight w are mechanisms for controlling the magnitude of velocities (Shi & Eberhart, 1998; Clerc, 1999). However, there are some major differences regarding the way of these two factors are computed and applied. The constriction factor χ is derived analytically through the following formula:

$$\chi = \frac{2k}{|\, 2 - \phi - \sqrt{\phi^2 - 4\phi} \, |} \quad (14)$$

for $\phi > 4$, where $\phi = c_1 + c_2$, and $k = 1$. The parameter c_1 determines the effect of the distance between the current position of the particle and its best previous position, P_i *(pbest)*, on its velocity. On the other hand, the parameter c_2 plays a similar role but it concerns the best previous position, P_{gi} *(gbest)*, attained by any particle in the neighborhood. The inertia weight, w, in Equation (11), is employed to manipulate the impact of the previous history of velocities on the current velocity. Therefore, w resolves the trade-off between the exploration (wide-ranging search) and exploitation (more refined local search) abilities of the swarm. A large inertia weight encourages exploration, while a small one promotes exploitation. A suitable value for w which provides the desired balance in the algorithm and improves its effectiveness can be obtained from the following Equation:

$$w = w_{max} - [(w_{max} - w_{min})/iter_{max}] \times iter \quad (15)$$

where w_{max} is the initial value of weighting coefficient; w_{min} is the final value of weighting coefficient; $iter_{max}$ is the maximum number of iterations or generation; $iter$ is the current iteration or generation number.

There are three problems dependent parameters, the inertia weight of the particle w and two trust parameters c_1 and c_2. The inertia parameter controls the exploration properties of the algorithm with larger values facilitating a more global behavior and smaller values facilitation a more local behavior. The trust parameters indicate how much trust a particle has in it self (c_1) and how much it trusts the swarm (c_2). Throughout the present work, slightly more trust is placed in the swarm with $c_1 = 1.5$ and $c_2 = 2.5$. The idea is to start with a more global search and end with a more local search. The initial swarm is created such that the particles are randomly, distributed throughout the design space, using uniform distribution, each with a random initial velocity vector. The random initial position and velocity vectors are obtained from (Liu & Abraham, 2006):

$$x_i(0) = x_{\min} + r_3 (x_{\max} - x_{\min}) \tag{16}$$

$$v_i(0) = \frac{x_{\min} + r_4 (x_{\max} - x_{\min})}{\Delta t} \tag{17}$$

Where r_3 and r_4 are random numbers between 0 and 1, $x_{\min}$ is the vector of lower bound values, $x_{\max}$ is the vector of upper values for the design variables and Δt is the time step value.

The basic particle swarm optimization algorithm is unconstrained algorithm, similar to a genetic algorithm. Typically, constraints are included using a penalty function formulation. However, the particle swarm optimization algorithm used here includes an additional enhancement for dealing with violated design points. The velocity vector of all points that violate constraints is modified as follows:

$$v_i(t+1) = c_1 r_1 \frac{(p_i(t) - x_i(t))}{\Delta t} + c_2 r_2 \frac{(p_{gi}(t) - x_i(t))}{\Delta t} \tag{18}$$

This new velocity vector will point back to the feasible design space in most cases and help the violated design points to overcome their constraint violation more rapidly. A unit time step ($\Delta t = 1$) is used throughout the present work.

The objective function (F) that must be minimized is selected as follows:

$$F(t) = \sum_{i=1}^{N} [w_{ref}(i) - y(i)]^2 \tag{19}$$

Where $w_{ref}(i)$ is the desired reference signal, $y(i)$ is the actual system output and N is the total number of observations. The fitness function is then given by:

$$J(t) = 1/(1+F(t)) \tag{20}$$

ADAPTIVE NEURO-FUZZY LOGIC IMPLEMENTATION

Adaptive Neuro-Fuzzy Logic Controller (ANFLC)

The adaptive fuzzy logic controller can be implemented by neural network as shown in Figure 2.

Controller

- Nodes at layer one are input nodes with crisp inputs e and $\dot{e}$. Where e is the error between the reference input and the actual output of the control system (non-linear inverted pendulum system output and non-linear single machine power system output) and $\dot{e}$ is the derivative of the error. The weights S_e and $S_{\dot{e}}$ are the scaling factors for inputs. The output of the layer is v_e and $v_{\dot{e}} \in [-1, +1]$ which are the normalized values of the inputs.

- Nodes at layer two compute the values of the membership functions, corresponding to v_e and $v_{\dot{e}}$. The layer has the weights L_{ei} and $L_{\dot{e}i}$ which correspond to the central

Figure 2. Adaptive neuro-fuzzy logic

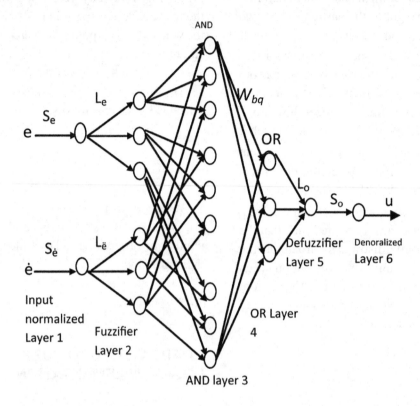

parts of the normalized [- 1, +1] universe of discourse. They are constrained as 0 < L_e < +2 and 0 < $L_{\dot{e}}$ < +2 as shown in Figure 3. Fuzzification will thus vary with the varying weights. Moreover, variation of one parameter, namely L will imply the variation of both the summits and the basis of the fuzzy sets, except of course, the summit of the central one. It reduces considerably the dimension of the problem to be solved.

The output of the nodes j_e, is given by:

$$\mu_{Aje} =$$
$$\begin{cases} (v_e - a_{j_e})/(a_{je} - a_{je-1}) & if\, a_{je-1} \le v_e \le a_{je} \\ (a_{je+1} - v_e)/(a_{je+1} - a_{je}) & if\, a_{je} \le v_e \le a_{je+1} \\ 1 & if\, v_e < a_1\, or\, v_e > a_n \\ 0 & otherwise \end{cases}$$
(21)

Where j_e =1,2, ..., n_e, n_e is the number of fuzzy sets A_{je} associated with input e(t). The output of the nodes $j_{\dot{e}}$ is given by:

$$\mu_{Aj\dot{e}} =$$
$$\begin{cases} (v_{\dot{e}} - a_{j_{\dot{e}}})/(a_{j\dot{e}} - a_{j\dot{e}-1}) & if\, a_{j\dot{e}-1} \le v_{\dot{e}} \le a_{j\dot{e}} \\ (a_{j\dot{e}+1} - v_e)/(a_{j\dot{e}+1} - a_{j\dot{e}}) & if\, a_{j\dot{e}} \le v_{\dot{e}} \le a_{j\dot{e}+1} \\ 1 & if\, v_{\dot{e}} < a_1\, or\, v_{\dot{e}} > a_n \\ 0 & otherwise \end{cases}$$
(22)

Where $j_{\dot{e}}$ =1,2,..., n_e, n_e is the number of fuzzy sets $A_{j\dot{e}}$ associated with input $\dot{e}$. The summits of the fuzzy sets for e, and $\dot{e}$ are given by (Nassef, 2005):

$$a_{je} = ((-1/2) + (j_e-1)/(n_e-1))L_e$$
(23)

and

$$a_{j\dot{e}} = ((-1/2) + (j_{\dot{e}}-1)/(n_{\dot{e}i}-1))L_e$$
(24)

Figure 3. Effect of weighted length L on the universe of discourse

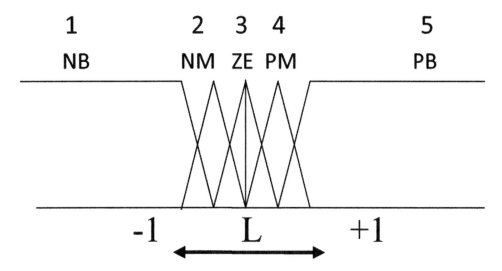

- Nodes at layer three (the AND layer) perform precondition matching of rules of inferences using the algebraic product. The output of an AND node is thus given by:

$$YAND_k = \mu_{A_{je}}(v_e) . \mu_{A_{A_{j\dot{e}}}}(v_{\dot{e}}) \qquad (25)$$

$k = 1, ..., n_t, n_t$ is the total number of the rules. There are no weights to be adjusted at this layer.

- Nodes at layer four, rules with the same consequence are integrated through the fuzzy OR operation for which it is implemented by using the following algebraic sum as:

$$YOR_q = \sum_{b=1}^{nt}(YAND_b)W_{bq} \qquad (26)$$

Where: $q=1, ..., n_o$ and $b=1, ..., n_t$ and W_{bq} are the weights associated with node b of the AND layer and node q of the OR layer, n_o is the number of fuzzy sets associated with the output variable and n_t is the total number of the rule base. Since one rule has only one consequence so:

for b=1, ...,n_t

$$W_{bq} \in \{0,1\} \qquad \forall \; b,q \qquad (27)$$

$$\sum_{q=1}^{n_o} W_{bq} = 1 \qquad (28)$$

- Nodes in layer five realizes defuzzification of fuzzy subsets into normalized data using the centre of gravity formula. Where m_q are the numerical weights corresponding to the midpoints triangular fuzzy sets of the output variable. These weights can be written as:

$$u_{ni} = \frac{\sum_{q=1}^{n_o} m_q . YOR_q}{\sum_{q=1}^{n_o} YOR_q} \qquad (29)$$

$$m_q = (-.\;5 +(q-1)/(no-1))L_o \qquad (30)$$

With the weighted length L_o of the central part of the universe of discourse of the controller output $0< L_o <+2$.

- Finally, node in layer six realizes the denormalization of normalized data. Where $S_o(t)$ is the scaling factor of the controller output and $u_n(t)$ is the normalized network controller output. $u(t)$ is the actual network controller output which is given as:

$$u(t) = u_n(t) \, S_o(t) \tag{31}$$

Adaptive Neuro-Fuzzy Logic Controller Learning Method

The previous section of neural network can be learned on line based on the proposed MPSO algorithm. The block diagram of the closed-loop control system is shown in Figure 4 for either single machine power system or inverted pendulum system. Where ω_{ref}, δ and ω are the reference angular speed, actual rotor angle and actual angular speed of the single machine power system respectively. Also, θ_r, θ and U are the desired angular displacement, actual output angular displacement and the control input signal respectively.

The neuro-fuzzy logic controller parameters, which are needed to be adapted, are:

1. The scaling factors of error (s_e), change of error $\dot{e}$ ($s_{\dot{e}}$), and controller output (s_o).
2. The membership functions of the universe of discourse for e, $\dot{e}$, and u. To save the number of parameters, only the weighting lengths L_e, $L_{\dot{e}}$ and L_o are used. Where L_e, $L_{\dot{e}}$ and L_o are the weighted lengths of error, change of error and controller output respectively. The triangular membership functions are symmetrically distributed in the central part of the continuous normalized [-1,1] universe of discourse with weighting length L as in Figure 3. The membership functions associated with the output fuzziest sets are equal to one. The variation of the parameter L (0 < L < 2) will imply variation of both the summits and the basis of the fuzzy sets, except the summit of central one. Using the last membership function reduces considerably the dimension of the problem to be solved.

3. The used universe of discourse with five fuzzy sets which are Negative Big (NB), Negative Medium (NM), zero (ZE), Positive Medium (PM), and Positive Big (PB) is shown in Figure 3.

SIMULATION RESULTS

Real Code MPSO Learning Method

In the case of two input one output controller with five fuzzy sets, the parameters to be adapted for the case of the non-linear inverted pendulum and the case of non-linear single machine power system are the scaling factors of S_e, $S_{\dot{e}}$, and S_o. Also, the weighted lengths L_e, $L_{\dot{e}}$, and L_o of the fuzzy domains of the error, the derivative of error, and the output of error. Only 4 rules at most are to be adapted at a time. Fuzzy sets of the consequent parts of the firing rules are indicated by R_1, R_2, R_3, and R_4. So, the chromosome consists of [S_e $S_{\dot{e}}$ S_o L_e $L_{\dot{e}}$ L_o R_1 R_2 R_3 R_4] parameters. The population size is taken equal to 50. The real-code is used for coding the population chromosomes. In the swarm technique no genetic operators are used (Goel & Saxena, 2005), but there exist position, and velocity vectors which are updated every iteration.

The proposed MPSO algorithm is used to tune and adjust the neuro-fuzzy logic controller parameters. A suitable initial choice for maximum velocity (V_{max}), v_c, λ, and constriction coefficient (χ) (Shi & Eberhart, 1998; Clerc, 1999), are 0.5, 1e-6, 2, 0.729 respectively.

Figure 4. ANFLC Closed loop block diagram

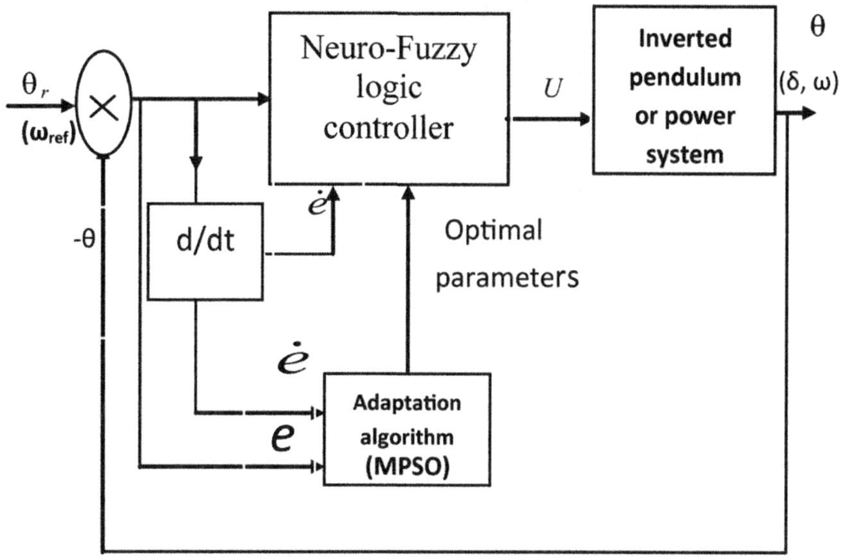

ADAPTIVE NEURO-FUZZY LOGIC CONTROL IMPLEMENTATION

Case 1: Non-Linear Inverted Pendulum System

The parameters of the MPSO are: size of population which is equal to 50 strings, every string represents six parameters (three parameters of scaling factors and another three parameters of weighted lengths). Also, the MPSO algorithm is used to design the adaptive neuro-fuzzy logic controller parameters for the non-linear inverted pendulum system. The controller parameters include the input, and the output scaling factors, membership functions, and rule base. The function of the MPSO is used to choose suitable values for these parameters at every sampling time.

The initial angle of the inverted non-linear pendulum system is 80° with an open loop behavior which is shown in Figure 5 for the states $x_1(t)$ and $x_2(t)$. The output angular deflection θ under control action is shown in Figure 6. Comparison between the proposed MPSO algorithm and GA approach in controlling the behavior of the inverted

pendulum is shown in Figure 7 for the tracking errors. From Figure 7, the proposed modified control approach based on MPSO converges to zero with minimum error for vertical angle θ and the results of MPSO algorithm converges faster than the results of GA approach (Garg & Kumar, 2002). The control signal is shown in Figure 8. Figure 9 and Figure 10 show the scaling factors and the weighted lengths controller parameters respectively. From the obtained results, a superior performance is achieved.

Case 2: Non-Linear Single Machine Power System

The electrical machine is connected to an infinite bus power system through a transmission network. The excitation system is equipped based on the proposed neuro-fuzzy stabilizer based on MPSO algorithm to provide significant damping behavior of the system output.

Figure 5. Open-loop system behaviors

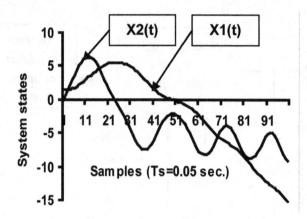

Figure 6. Closed loop output angular deflection 0

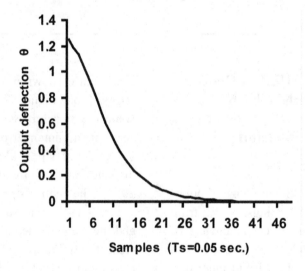

Figure 7. Tracking errors

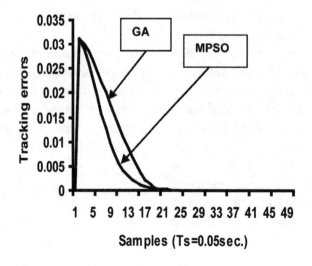

Figure 8. Control signal

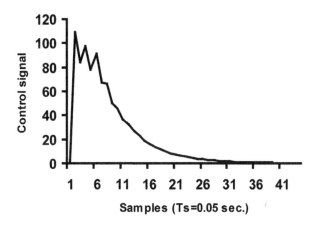

Figure 9. Scaling factors of S$_e$, S$_e$, and So

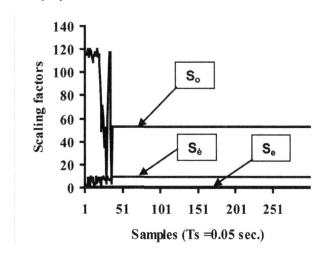

Figure 10. Weighted lengths of Le, L$_e$, and L$_o$

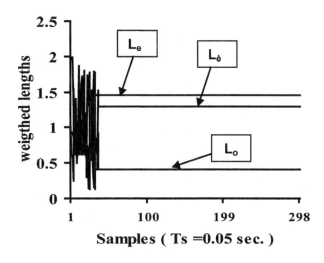

Figure 11. Open loop rotor angle deviation

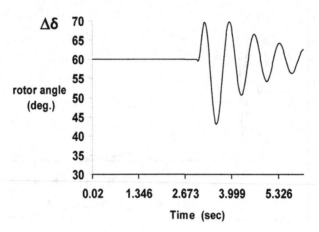

Figure 12. Open loop angular speed deviation

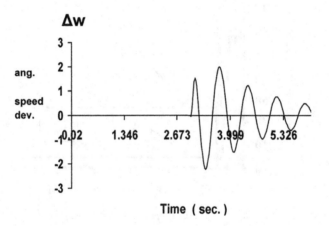

Three Phase Fault at the Generator Bus

The parameters of the non-linear single machine power system with infinite bus are given in Ahmed (2000) and the chosen sampling time Ts=0.01sec. A 3-phase short circuit is applied at the generator bus at the beginning of the second number 3 and cleared after 100 ms. Figure 11 and Figure 12 show the open loop behavior for rotor angle deviation ($\Delta\delta$) (degree) and the open loop behavior for angular speed deviation ($\Delta\omega$) respectively. From the last two figures, the oscillations in the open loop system response may be sustained for

long time and grow to cause system separation. Comparisons between The proposed control approach based on MPSO algorithm and classical fuzzy logic are shown in Figure 13 for closed loop rotor angle deviation and Figure 14 for closed loop angular speed deviation. From Figure 13 and Figure 14, it is clear that the proposed adaptive neuro-fuzzy logic controller based on the proposed MPSO algorithm is efficient approach to control the behavior of the single machine power system effectively and robustly enhances the damping of the oscillations.

Figure 15 shows the scaling factors of the controller inputs error (S_e), the derivative of error

Figure 13. Closed loop rotor angle deviation

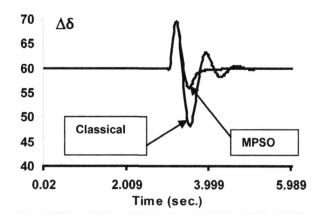

Figure 14. Closed loop angular speed deviation

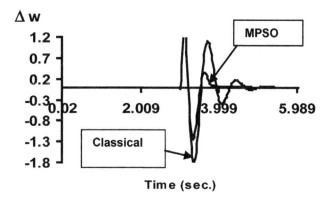

Figure 15. Scaling factors of MPSO

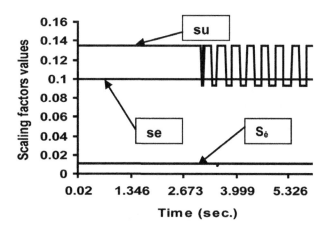

Figure 16. Control signals

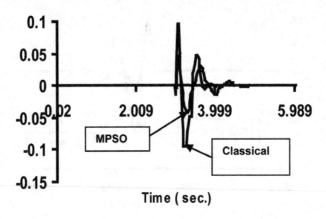

Figure 17. Tracking error $\Delta\delta$

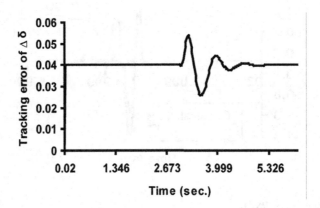

Figure 18. Tracking error $\Delta\omega$

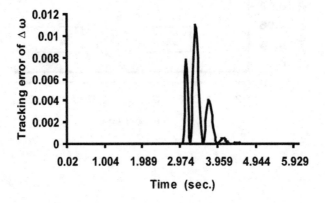

(S_e), and the output of the controller (S_o). The scaling factors of Figure 15 vary during the short circuit to satisfy the demand values for the fuzzy logic controller. Figure 16 shows the control signals based on MPSO algorithm and classical fuzzy logic controller approach. Figure 17 and Figure 18 show the tracking errors for $\Delta\delta$ and $\Delta\omega$ respectively.

From the obtained above results, it is clear that the proposed adaptive neuro-fuzzy logic controller based on MPSO algorithm highly reduces the oscillations of the rotor angle and angular speed deviation of the generator as compared with the classical fuzzy logic approach.

CONCLUSION

A modified particle swarm optimization algorithm to design adaptive neuro-fuzzy logic controller parameters is presented in this paper. The proposed algorithm is used to control the behavior of the non-linear dynamic systems. The modification of the MPSO algorithm includes adding of adaptive weights to the swarm optimization approach which introduced a new update of the algorithm to overcome the premature convergence problems. The proposed algorithm used a minimum velocity threshold to control the velocity of particles, avoided clustering of particles and maintained the diversity of the population in the search space. The basic idea of the proposed algorithm is to control the velocity of the particles to get out of possible local optima and continue exploring optimal search spaces. The minimum velocity threshold can make the particles continue moving until the algorithm converges. To illustrate the adaptation process, the proposed neuro-fuzzy controller based on MPSO algorithm is applied successfully to control the behavior of both non-linear single machine power system and non-linear inverted pendulum system. Simulation results on the comparison between MPSO and traditional control approaches demonstrate that the adaptive

neuro-fuzzy logic controller application based on MPSO can effectively and robustly enhance the damping of oscillations.

ACKNOWLEDGMENT

The author would like to appreciate Prof. Dr. Yuhui Shi and anonymous reviewers for their constructive comments and suggestions which help to improve the quality of this article highly.

REFERENCES

Ahmed, G. S. (2000). *Adaptive fuzzy logic controllers for multimachine power systems.* Unpublished doctoral dissertation, Faculty of Electrical Engineering, Minufiya University.

Clerc, M. (1999). The swarm and the queen: Toward a deterministic and adaptive particle swarm optimization. In *Proceedings of the IEEE International Conference on Evolutionary Computation* (pp. 1951-1957).

Conradie, A. V. E., Miikkulainen, R., & Aldrich, C. (2002). Adaptive control utilizing neural swarming. In *Proceedings of the Genetic and Evolutionary Computation Conference,* New York.

Esmin, A., Aoki, A., & Torres, G. (2004). *Particle swarm optimization versus genetic algorithms for fitting fuzzy membership functions.*

Fiszelew, A., Britos, P., Ochoa, A., Merlino, H., Fernández, E., & García-Martínez, R. (2007). Finding optimal neural network architecture using genetic algorithms. *Research in Computing Science, 27,* 15–24.

Garg, P., & Kumar, M. (2002). Genetic algorithm based PD control and fuzzy logic control of a two link robot. In *Proceedings of IMECCE '02, ASME International Mechanical Engineering Congress & Exposition,* New Orleans, LA (pp. 1-8).

Goel, A., Saxena, S., & Bhanot, S. (2005). A genetic based neuro-fuzzy controller for thermal processes. *Journal of Computer Science & Technology, 5*(1).

Helwig, S., Haubelt, C., & Teich, J. (2005). Modeling and analysis of indirect communication in particle swarm optimization. In *Proceedings of the 2005 IEEE Congress on Evolutionary Computation,* Edinburgh, UK (pp. 1246-1253).

Kiranyaz, S., Ince, T., Yildirim, A., & Gabbouj, M. (2010). Fractional particle swarm optimization in multidimensional search space. *IEEE Transactions on Systems, Man, and Cybernetics. Part B, Cybernetics, 40*(2), 298–319. doi:10.1109/TSMCB.2009.2015054

Liu, H., & Abraham, A. (2007). A hybrid fuzzy variable neighborhood particle swarm optimization algorithm for solving quadratic assignment problems. *Journal of Universal Computer Science, 13*(9), 1309–1331.

Magoulas, G., Eldabi, T., & Paul, R. (2002). Global search strategies for simulation optimization. In *Proceedings of the Winter Simulation Conference* (pp. 1978-1985).

Mahmoud, K. (2010). Design optimization of a bow-tie antenna for 2.45 GHz rfid readers using a hybrid bacterial swarm optimization and nelder-mead algorithm. *Progress in Electromagnetics Research, 100,* 105–117. doi:10.2528/PIER09102903

Nassef, M. (2005). *Genetic algorithm and its Application in control systems.* Unpublished doctoral dissertation, Faculty of Electrical Engineering, Minufiya University. Liu, H., & Abraham, A. (2006). *Fuzzy adaptive turbulent particle swarm optimization.* Dalian, China: Department of Computer Science, Dalian University of Technology.

Papageorgiou, E., Parsopoulos, K., Stylios, C., Groumpos, P., & Vrahatis, M. (2005). Fuzzy cognitive maps learning using particle swarm optimization. *Journal of Intelligent Information Systems, 25*(1), 95–121. doi:10.1007/s10844-005-0864-9

Settles, M., Nathan, P., & Soule, T. (2005, June). Breeding swarms: A new approach to recurrent neural network training. In *Proceedings of GECCO'05,* Washington, DC.

Shi, Y., & Eberhart, R. C. (March 1998). *Parameter selection in particle swarm optimization.* Paper presented at the 7th Annual Conference on Evolutionary Programming, San Diego, CA.

Shi, Y., & Eberhart, R. C. (1998). A modified particle swarm optimizer. In *Proceedings of the IEEE World Congress on Computational Intelligence* (pp. 69-73).

Skokos, C., Parsopoulos, K., Patsis, P., & Vrahatis, M. (2005). Particle swarm optimization: an efficient method for tracking periodic orbits in three-dimensional galactic potentials. *Monthly Notices of the Royal Astronomical Society, 359*(1), 251–260. doi:10.1111/j.1365-2966.2005.08892.x

Surmann, H. (2000, May). Learning a fuzzy rule based knowledge representation. In *Proceedings of the ICSC Symposium on Neural Computation, NC'2000,* Berlin (pp. 349-355).

This work was previously published in International Journal of Swarm Intelligence Research, Volume 1, Issue 4, edited by Yuhui Shi, pp. 1-16, copyright 2010 by IGI Publishing (an imprint of IGI Global)

Chapter 6
Design of Multi-Criteria PI Controller Using Particle Swarm Optimization for Multiple UAVs Close Formation

Xiangyin Zhang
Beijing University of Aeronautics and Astronautics, China

Haibin Duan
Beijing University of Aeronautics and Astronautics, China

Shan Shao
Shenyang Aircraft Design and Research Institute, China

Yunhui Wang
Shenyang Aircraft Design and Research Institute, China

ABSTRACT

Close formation flight is one of the most complicated problems on multiple Uninhabited Aerial Vehicles (UAVs) coordinated control. This paper proposes a new method to achieve close formation tracking control of multiple UAVs by applying Particle Swarm Optimization (PSO) based Proportional plus Integral (PI) controller. Due to its simple structure and effectiveness, multi-criteria PI control strategy is employed to design the controller for multiple UAVs formation, while PSO is used to optimize the controller parameters on-line. With the inclusion of overshoot, rise time, and system accumulated absolute error in the multi-criteria performance index, the overall performance of multi-criteria PI controller is optimized to be satisfactory. Simulation results show the feasibility and effectiveness of the proposed approach.

DOI: 10.4018/978-1-4666-1592-2.ch006

1. INTRODUCTION

Uninhabited Aerial Vehicle (UAV) is an aircraft that flies without a human crew on board the aircraft. Their largest uses are in military applications, especially to replace the human presence in repetitive or dangerous missions (Ambrosino et al., 2009). Multiple UAVs system is being used in a very diverse range of roles, from urban reconnaissance through to high altitude long endurance (HALE) operations (Constantinides et al., 2008). One of the problems particularly interesting to researchers is the automatic cooperative control of a group of UAVs flying in close formation (Duan et al., 2008). When multiple UAVs fly in formation, the formation's initial geometry, including the longitudinal, lateral and vertical separation, should be preserved during maneuvers with heading change, speed change and altitude change. A close formation, also called "tight formation", is the one in which "the lateral separation between UAV is less than a wingspan" (Proud et al., 1999; Pachter et al., 2001). In this case, aerodynamic coupling is introduced into the formation's dynamics. Multiple UAVs flying in a close formation can achieve a significant reduction in power demand, thereby improving cruise performances, such as range and speed, or to increase the payload (Zhang et al., 2010; Binetti et al., 2003). Various control strategies for multiple UAVs formation have been reported in the literatures. Among them, the Leader-Wingman approach has been well recognized and become the most popular approach (Liu et al., 2007): one or more UAVs of the flight formation are selected as leaders and are responsible for guiding the formation, with the rest of UAVs required to follow the leader.

The "Leader-Wingman" formation pattern can be shown with Figure 1.

If the wingman flies close to the leading UAV, the leader's vortices will produce aerodynamic coupling effects, and a reduction in the formation's drag can be achieved. According to the effects of aerodynamic interference, multiple UAVs close

formation flight control is a complex problem with strongly nonlinear and coupling character. The development of a UAV is expensive, and a small error in automatic control can result in a crash (Chen & Chang, 2008). The design and implementation of control methods for multiple UAVs close formation is a hot issue recently. The problem of modeling and control of leader-follower close formation has been studied by many researchers. Many classic and modern control approaches have been applied to solving this problem, including PI controller (Proud et al., 1999; Pachter et al., 2001; Dargan et al., 1992; Buzogany et al., 1993), nonlinear adaptive control (Singh & Pachter, 2000), fuzzy logic (Li et al., 2005), robust control (Li et al., 2006), and receding horizon control (Zhang et al., 2010; Hu et al., 2007).

The conventional Proportional-Integral-Derivative (PID) controller is a widely used industrial controller that uses a combination of proportional, integral and derivative action to control error to form the output of the controller. Due to its simple structure and effectiveness, this control strategy has been being the mainstay for decades among practicing engineers (Duan et al., 2009). After the three parameters have been tuned or set in some way, control parameters of the standard PID controller remain unchanged during the whole control process. Various parameters tuning methods have been presented, which can be classified as: (1) the Ziegler-Nichols (ZN) method and the Internal Model Control (IMC), these methods are treated as empirical methods; (2) analytical methods typified by root locus based techniques; (3) methods basing on optimization such as the iteration feedback tuning (IFT) (Hjalmarsson et al., 1998), genetic algorithm, colonial competitive algorithm (Gargari et al., 2008), and so on. These methods generally adopt some single performance index, and can achieve better frequency-domain characteristics, but the ideal time-domain characteristics can not be achieved simultaneously. Therefore, the single performance index based

Figure 1. Leader-Wingman formation

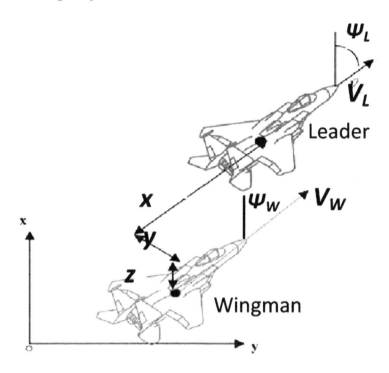

PID parameters tuning method generally cannot meet the system requirements for both frequency- and time-domain characteristics. In this paper, a Particle Swarm Optimization (PSO)-based PI control strategy was presented. The performance index takes into account the overshoot, rise time and the system accumulated absolute error.

PSO algorithm is a population based stochastic optimization technique, which was developed by Dr. Eberhart and Dr. Kennedy in 1995, inspired by social behavior of bird flocking or fish schooling (Kenneedy & Eberhart, 1995; Eberhart & Kennedy, 1995). PSO shares many similarities with evolutionary computation techniques such as Genetic Algorithms (GA). However, unlike GA, PSO has no evolution operators, such as crossover and mutation. It is demonstrated that PSO can get better results in a faster and cheaper way compared with other bio-inspired computational methods.

In this paper, we present a PSO-based PI controller design for multiple UAVs close formation. The rest of this paper is organized as follows:

Section 2 is the model of multiple UAVs close formation, followed by the PI controller scheme design for the close formation in Section 3. Section 4 gives the multi-criteria PSO based PI controller design in detail. The simulation results are given in Section 5, followed by concluding remarks in Section 6.

2. MODEL OF MULTIPLE UAVS CLOSE FORMATION

In this paper, a typical multiple UAVs close formation model established by Proud (Proud et al., 1999) and Pachter (Pachter et al., 2001) is adopted. (see Exhibit 1)

The optimal separation between the Wingman and Leader UAV can be described with $\bar{x} = 2b, \bar{y} = \dfrac{\pi}{4}b, \bar{z} = 0$ (Blake & Multhopp, 1998), where b is the wingspan of the Leader. The close formation model is established basing on the

Exhibit 1.

$$\dot{x} = -\frac{\overline{y}}{\tau_{\psi_W}} \cdot \psi_W - V_W + V_L \cos\psi_E + \frac{\overline{y}}{\tau_{\psi_W}} \cdot \psi_{W_C} + \overline{y}\frac{\overline{q}S}{mV}[\Delta C_{Y_{W_y}} \cdot y + \Delta C_{Y_{W_z}} \cdot z]$$

$$\dot{V}_W = -\frac{1}{\tau_{V_W}} \cdot V_W + \frac{1}{\tau_{V_W}} \cdot V_{W_C} + \frac{\overline{q}S}{m} \cdot \Delta C_{D_{W_z}} \cdot z$$

$$\dot{y} = \frac{\overline{x}}{\tau_{\psi_W}} \cdot \psi_W + V_L \cdot \sin\psi_E - \frac{\overline{x}}{\tau_{\psi_W}} \cdot \psi_{W_C} - \overline{x}\frac{\overline{q}S}{mV}[\Delta C_{Y_{W_y}} \cdot y + \Delta C_{Y_{W_z}} \cdot z]$$

$$\dot{\psi}_W = -\frac{1}{\tau_{\psi_W}} \cdot \psi_W + \frac{1}{\tau_{\psi_W}} \cdot \psi_{W_C} + \frac{\overline{q}S}{mV}[\Delta C_{Y_{W_y}} \cdot y + \Delta C_{Y_{W_z}} \cdot z]$$

$$\dot{z} = \zeta$$

$$\dot{\zeta} = -(\frac{1}{\tau_a} + \frac{1}{\tau_b}) \cdot \zeta - \frac{1}{\tau_a \tau_b} z + \frac{1}{\tau_a \tau_b} h_{W_C} - \frac{1}{\tau_a \tau_b} h_{L_C} + \frac{\overline{q}S}{m} \cdot \Delta C_{L_{W_y}} \cdot y \tag{1}$$

Exhibit 2.

$$\dot{x} = -\frac{\overline{y}}{\tau_{\psi_W}} \cdot \psi_W - V_W + V_L + \frac{\overline{y}}{\tau_{\psi_W}} \cdot \psi_{W_C} + \overline{y}\frac{\overline{q}S}{mV}[\Delta C_{Y_{W_y}} \cdot y + \Delta C_{Y_{W_z}} \cdot z]$$

$$\dot{V}_W = -\frac{1}{\tau_{V_W}} \cdot V_W + \frac{1}{\tau_{V_W}} \cdot V_{W_C} + \frac{\overline{q}S}{m} \cdot \Delta C_{D_{W_z}} \cdot z$$

$$\dot{y} = (\frac{\overline{x}}{\tau_{\psi_W}} - \overline{V}) \cdot \psi_W + \overline{V} \cdot \psi_L - \frac{\overline{x}}{\tau_{\psi_W}} \cdot \psi_{W_C} - \overline{x}\frac{\overline{q}S}{mV}[\Delta C_{Y_{W_y}} \cdot y + \Delta C_{Y_{W_z}} \cdot z]$$

$$\dot{\psi}_W = -\frac{1}{\tau_{\psi_W}} \cdot \psi_W + \frac{1}{\tau_{\psi_W}} \cdot \psi_{W_C} + \frac{\overline{q}S}{mV}[\Delta C_{Y_{W_y}} \cdot y + \Delta C_{Y_{W_z}} \cdot z]$$

$$\dot{z} = \zeta$$

$$\dot{\zeta} = -(\frac{1}{\tau_a} + \frac{1}{\tau_b}) \cdot \zeta - \frac{1}{\tau_a \tau_b} z + \frac{1}{\tau_a \tau_b} h_{W_C} - \frac{1}{\tau_a \tau_b} h_{L_C} + \frac{\overline{q}S}{m} \cdot \Delta C_{L_{W_y}} \cdot y \tag{2}$$

aerodynamic forces on the Wing UAV near the optimal relative position, with a rotating reference frame affixed to the Wingman's instantaneous position and aligned with the Wingman's velocity vector used.

In the close formation model shown in Eq.(1), $\mathbf{X} = (x, V_W, y, \psi_W, z, \zeta)^T$ are the state vectors, where x, y, z denote the longitudinal, lateral and vertical separation between the Leader and Wingman respectively. ψ_W, V_W denote the heading angle and velocity of the Wingman respectively.

$\mathbf{U} = (V_{W_C}, \psi_{W_C}, h_{W_C})$ are the control inputs to Wingman's Heading hold, Mach hold, and Altitude hold autopilot channels, respectively. The Leader's maneuvers are treated as a disturbance, which can be expressed with $\mathbf{U}_L = (V_L, \psi_L, h_{L_C})$.

For the purpose of controller design, linearization of the nonlinear system Eq.(1) yields the linear perturbation equations (see Exhibit 2)

Using the above defined states, control inputs and disturbances, the linear state space representation can be represented by

Figure 2. Multiple UAVs close formation flight control system

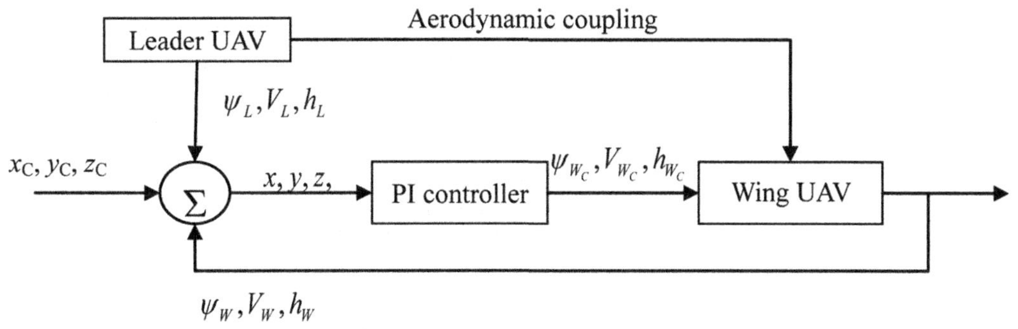

$$\dot{\mathbf{X}} = \mathbf{A} \cdot \mathbf{X} + \mathbf{B} \cdot \mathbf{U} + \mathbf{D} \cdot \mathbf{U}_L$$

Where the dynamics matrix is

$$\mathbf{A} = \begin{bmatrix} 0 & -1 & \bar{y}\dfrac{\bar{q}S}{mV}\Delta C_{Y_{W_s}} & -\dfrac{\bar{y}}{\tau_{\psi_W}} & \bar{y}\dfrac{\bar{q}S}{mV}\Delta C_{Y_{W_s}} & 0 \\[2mm] 0 & -\dfrac{1}{\tau_{V_W}} & \dfrac{\bar{q}S}{m}\Delta C_{D_{W_s}} & 0 & 0 & 0 \\[2mm] 0 & 0 & -\bar{x}\dfrac{\bar{q}S}{mV}\Delta C'_{Y_{W_s}} & \dfrac{\bar{x}}{\tau_{\psi_W}}-\bar{V} & \bar{x}\dfrac{\bar{q}S}{mV}\Delta C_{Y_{W_s}} & 0 \\[2mm] 0 & 0 & \dfrac{\bar{q}S}{mV}\Delta C_{Y_{W_s}} & -\dfrac{1}{\tau_{\psi_W}} & \dfrac{\bar{q}S}{m}\cdot\Delta C_{Y_{W_s}} & 0 \\[2mm] 0 & 0 & 0 & 0 & 0 & 1 \\[2mm] 0 & 0 & \dfrac{\bar{q}S}{m}\cdot\Delta C_{L_{W_s}} & 0 & -\dfrac{1}{\tau_a\cdot\tau_b} & -(\dfrac{1}{\tau_a}+\dfrac{1}{\tau_b})\cdot \end{bmatrix}$$

$$\mathbf{B} = \begin{bmatrix} 0 & \dfrac{\bar{y}}{\tau_{\psi_W}} & 0 \\[2mm] \dfrac{1}{\tau_{\psi_W}} & 0 & 0 \\[2mm] 0 & -\dfrac{\bar{x}}{\tau_{\psi_W}} & 0 \\[2mm] 0 & \dfrac{1}{\tau_{V_W}} & 0 \\[2mm] 0 & 0 & 0 \\[2mm] 0 & 0 & \dfrac{1}{\tau_a\cdot\tau_b} \end{bmatrix}$$

$$\mathbf{D} = \begin{bmatrix} 1 & 0 & 0 \\ 0 & 0 & 0 \\ 0 & \bar{V} & 0 \\ 0 & 0 & 0 \\ 0 & 0 & 0 \\ 0 & 0 & -\dfrac{1}{\tau_a\cdot\tau_b} \end{bmatrix}$$

3. CONTROLLER DESIGN

The block diagram of a multiple UAVs close formation control system is shown in Figure 2.

The formation flight controller is equipped on the Wing UAV. It is an outer-loop controller that receives measurements of separation between the Leader and Wingman, and drives the control signals of the Wingman's three channels: Mach hold, Heading hold and Altitude hold autopilot, that is, x, y and z channels.

The controller for the x channel contains a linear mixer on the x and y error signals and PI action, where the control signal is V_{W_C}. Controller design for the x channel should consider the longitudinal error signal $x_e = x_C - x$, and the velocity error $V_e = V_L - V_W$. Furthermore, considering the close formation pattern, lateral and altitude signals are coupled into the x channel, and thus, the x-channel controller should take into account lateral and altitude errors $y_e = y_C - y$ and $z_e = z_C - z$. The synthesized error for the x-channel is

$$e_x = k_{xx}x_e + k_{xV}V_e + k_{xy}y_e + k_{xz}z_e \tag{3}$$

The generalized error signal of the y-channel controller considers the lateral error signal $y_e = y_C - y$ and the heading error $\psi_e = \psi_L - \psi_W$; moreover, the altitude errors of the z-channel

Figure 3. Architecture of PSO-based control parameters tuning

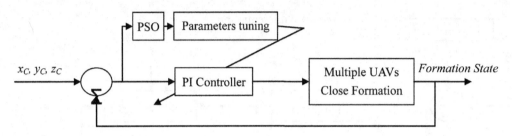

$z_e = z_C - z$ is introduced because of the aerodynamic coupling effect. Therefore, the synthesized error for the *x*-channel is

$$e_y = k_{yy} y_e + k_{y\psi} \psi_e + k_{yz} z_e \qquad (4)$$

The *z*-channel should only consider the altitude error $z_e = z_C - z$, and the generalized error signal is

$$e_z = k_{zz} z_e \qquad (5)$$

Basing on the above error signals, linear PI control laws for the *x*, *y*, and *z* channel are implemented:

$$\begin{cases} V_{W_C} = K_{xP} \cdot e_x + K_{xI} \cdot \int e_x dt \\ \psi_{W_C} = K_{yP} \cdot e_y + K_{yI} \cdot \int e_y dt \\ h_{W_C} = K_{zP} \cdot e_z + K_{zI} \cdot \int e_z dt \end{cases} \qquad (6)$$

There are totally 14 parameters required to be determined for the PI control system, where set $k_{xx} = k_{yy} = k_{zz} = 1$ out of consideration for simplified calculation. Thus, 11 control parameters need to be tuned, namely k_{xV}, k_{xy}, k_{xz}, $k_{y\psi}$, k_{yz}, K_{xP}, K_{xI}, K_{yP}, K_{yI}, K_{zP}, K_{zI}. In this paper, PSO algorithm is adopted to optimize the control parameters by considering a multi-criteria performance index.

4. MULTI-CRITERIA PSO-BASED PI CONTROL DESIGN

Closed-loop PI control scheme is adopted in the multiple UAVs close formation. PSO algorithm is employed to determine these control parameters. The integral action can increase the control signal if there is a small error. The PSO-based control parameters tuning for multiple UAVs close formation system is shown in Figure 3.

4.1 Principle of PSO

The PSO algorithm consists of individuals, named particles, which form a swarm (or population as called in other evolutionary algorithms), and each particle, initialized randomly, represents a candidate solution to the optimization problem. Particles change their positions by flying in a search space with the purpose of looking for the optimal position. During this process, each particle adjusts its position according to its own experience and the information of other particles' to follow the two best value, one of which is the best solution found by the particle itself, called personal best value, and the other is the best solution found by the whole swarm, called global best value (Kennedy et al., 1995). The performance of each particle is measured by an objective function which depends on the problem.

Let *m* particles in a *m*-dimensional search space form a solution swarm, the *i*-th particle of which is represented by $X_i = (x_{i1}, x_{i2}, \cdots, x_{im})$, and its velocity is $V_i = (v_{i1}, v_{i2}, \cdots, v_{im})$. The best position encountered by the i-th particle is $P_i = (p_{i1}, p_{i2}, \cdots, p_{im})$, and the global best solution is $P_g = (p_{g1}, p_{g2}, \cdots, p_{gm})$. In the n-th iteration, each particle updates its position and velocity as follows:

$$V_i^{n+1} = \omega \cdot V_i^n + c_1 \cdot r_1 \cdot (P_i^n - X_i^n) + c_2 \cdot r_2 \cdot (P_g^n - X_i^n) \tag{7}$$

$$X_i^{n+1} = X_i^n + V_i^{n+1} \tag{8}$$

Where ω is the inertia weight; r_1 and r_2 are two random numbers within the range (0, 1); c_1 are c_2 the cognitive and social scaling parameters. In order to improve global searching ability and convergence speed, the velocity of particles should be limited, and the maximum velocity V_{max} is used.

4.2 Multi-Criteria Performance Index

The performance index of the smallest Integrated Time Absolute Error (ITAE) only considers the big initial error, but emphasizes the overshoot and the rise time (Duan et al., 2009). Single performance index can not meet the requirement to the rapidity, accuracy and robustness of the control system (Zhou et al., 2007). Therefore, the multi-criteria performance index, in which all the overshoot, rise time and the accumulated absolute error are considered, was utilized in this paper.

The overshoot of the control system is $\sigma = \dfrac{|y_p - y_{ref}|}{y_{ref}} \times 100\%$, where y_p and y_{ref} are the peak value and the desired value of the output respectively. Especially, as for the z-channel of the formation control system, since $z_{ref} = 0$, set $\sigma_z = |z_p|$.

The rise time of the control system t_s is defined as the minimum time when the output reaches

and won't exceed the error band near y_{ref}. Here, the error band is set as $y_{ref} \pm 5 ft$.

The accumulated absolute error is $e = \int |y(t) - y_{ref}| dt$. Thus, the multi-criteria performance index of the close formation flight control system is as follows:

$$J = w_1 \cdot \sigma + w_2 \cdot t_s + w_3 \cdot e \tag{9}$$

Where w_1, w_2 and w_3 are weight coefficients.

4.3 Searching Space

In order to improve the searching speed and accuracy of PSO algorithm, the searching space shall be limited within a certain range, and every parameter of those particles cannot go beyond this range. In this paper, firstly, a rough parameters value range is set as the initial searching space to constraint the movement of particles, and thus, a set of preliminary optimization parameters can be achieved. Here, the value range of all parameters are the same and can be set wide. For example, the value range is initially set as [-10,10] for all parameters in this work. Secondly, by treating these parameters as the center of the searching space, PSO is employed to find the optimal value for the second time. That is to say, in the second searching process, particles just move within the space around the optimal solution achieved through the last optimization process. By this method, it can make full use of the solution found by PSO itself as the core to narrow the parameter searching space, and thus, in the second searching process, the performance of PSO is improved greatly. Furthermore, the solution achieved in the second searching process can continue to be used as the core in the third searching process, and so on. The utilized PSOs are same. The repetition optimization method can take advantage of the previous results, and is more efficient than simply increasing the number of iterations.

Set K^* as the parameter value achieved after the previous optimization process, α and β are the continuation coefficients. In this paper, we can set $\alpha=0.3$, $\beta=1.6$ according to Zhou et al. (2007) and experiment experience, and thus, the parameter range is determined by:

$$\alpha \cdot K^* \leq K \leq \beta \cdot K^* \qquad (10)$$

4.4 Procedure of PSO-Based PI Controller Parameter Tuning

The procedure of the proposed PSO-based PI controller parameter tuning is as follows:

Step 1: Initilization of the PSO parameters. Set the number of particles $n=100$; the dimensionality of each particle vector is $m=11$; the max iteration $Nc=30$; $c_1 = c_2 = 1.4$; ω decreases form $\omega_{max}=1$ to $\omega_{min}=0.4$ by iterations. In the first optimization process of PSO, set the parameter value range as [-10, 10], and determine the position and velocity of each particle randomly.

Step 2: Compute the objective function value for each particle according to Eq. (9), and then update P_i and P_g.

Step 3: Update the position and velocity vectors for each particle according to Eqs. (7) and (8).

Step 4: Go to Step 2 if the stopping criterion is not satisfied, or else go to next step.

Step 5: Set the optimization solution as the core of the searching space according to Eq. (10), and go to Step 1 to implement the optimization process again.

5. EXPERIMENTAL RESULTS

In order to investigate the feasibility and effectiveness of the proposed PSO-based multi-criteria PI controller parameter tuning approach for multiple UAVs close formation flight system, experiments were conducted using Matlab/Simulink on PC-compatible with 2 GB of RAM under the Microsoft Windows Vista.

In all experiments, the desired separations between Leader and Wingman are $x_C=60$ ft, $y_C=25$ ft, $z_C=0$ ft. The model parameters in Eq.(1) are from Pachter et al. (2001) as follows:

$$A = \begin{bmatrix} 0 & -1 & 0.0057 & -70.6858 & -0.0020 & 0 \\ 0 & -0.2000 & -0.0471 & 0 & 0 & 0 \\ 0 & 0 & -0.0144 & -645.0015 & 0.0050 & 0 \\ 0 & 0 & 0.0002 & -3.0000 & 0.0002 & 0 \\ 0 & 0 & 0 & 0 & 0 & 1 \\ 0 & 0 & 0.4663 & 0 & -0.8447 & -3.5118 \end{bmatrix}$$

$$B = \begin{bmatrix} 0 & 80 & 0 \\ 0.2 & 0 & 0 \\ 0 & -31.4667 & 0 \\ 0 & 1.3333 & 0 \\ 0 & 0 & 0 \\ 0 & 0 & 0.8447 \end{bmatrix},$$

$$D = \begin{bmatrix} 1 & 0 & 0 \\ 0 & 0 & 0 \\ 0 & 825 & 0 \\ 0 & 0 & 0 \\ 0 & 0 & 0 \\ 0 & 0 & -0.8447 \end{bmatrix}$$

Simulation module of multiple UAVs close formation flight control system and the PI controller module under the Matlab Simulink environment are shown in Figure 4 and Figure 5.

5.1 Determine PI Controller Parameters

The PI controller parameters optimized by the first PSO searching is shown in Table 1, and Figure 6 is the evolution curve, with its drawing of partial enlargement shown in Figure 7.

Using the parameters in Table 1 as the core, PSO implement the optimization process for the second time, and yield control parameters in Table 2. Figure 8 is the evolution curve, with its drawing of partial enlargement shown in Figure

Figure 4. Simulation module of multiple UAVs close formation control system

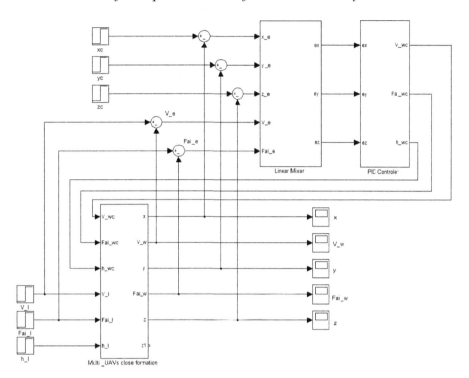

Figure 5. Simulation sub-module of PI controller

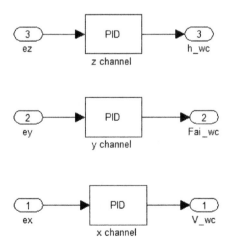

9. These control parameters will be used in the following experiments.

5.2 System Response

1. Given leader UAV's heading angle and velocity are $\psi_L=20°$, $V_L=750$ft/s, which don't change while flying. Experiments were performed with 40s and the following results in Figure 10 show the response curves of the longitudinal, lateral and altitude separation, wing UAV's heading and velocity within the experiment. The time response curves show that the formation can reach the desired state in a short time.

2. Given leader UAV's heading angle and velocity are $\psi_L=20°$, $V_L=750$ft/s at the beginning and the formation fly at the steady state, while at time $t=20$s, the Leader's state steps to $\psi_L=40°$, $V_L=800$ft/s. The response curves are shown in Figure 11.

3. After the formation reaches the steady state, while at time $t=20$s, the Leader's heading angle and velocity begin to change continu-

Table 1. Control parameters optimized by the first time searching

k_{xV}	k_{xy}	k_{xz}	$k_{y\psi}$	k_{yz}	K_{xP}	K_{xI}	K_{yP}	K_{yI}	K_{zP}	K_{zI}
-9.52	10	-2.5	-6.27	-0.19	-3.4	-10	-8.88	-7.1	10	10

Figure 6. Evolution curve of PSO in the first searching process

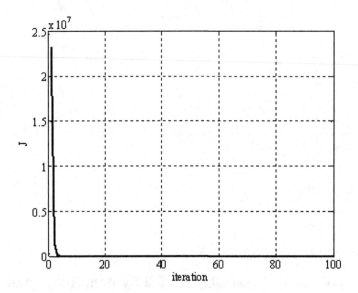

Figure 7. Drawing of partial enlargement shown of Figure 6

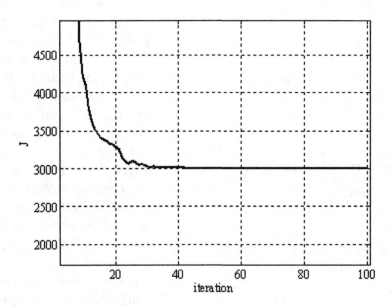

Table 2. Control parameters optimized by the second time searching

k_{xV}	k_{xy}	k_{xz}	$k_{y\psi}$	k_{yz}	K_{xP}	K_{xI}	K_{yP}	K_{yI}	K_{zP}	K_{zI}
-4.01	3	-0.75	-1.88	-0.08	-2.99	-3	-2.66	-3.87	4.46	3

Figure 8. Evolution curve of PSO in the first searching process

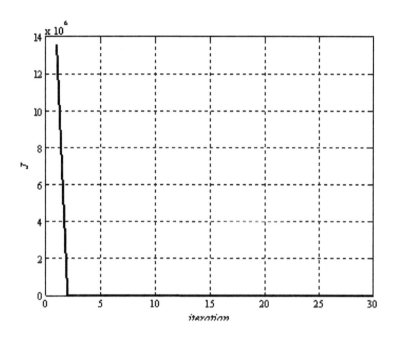

Figure 9. Drawing of partial enlargement shown of Figure 8

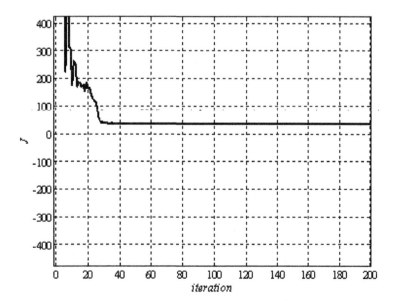

Figure 10. Time response curves of multiple UAVs close formation system with the leader's state unchanging

Figure 11. Time response curves of multiple UAVs close formation system with the leader's state stepping

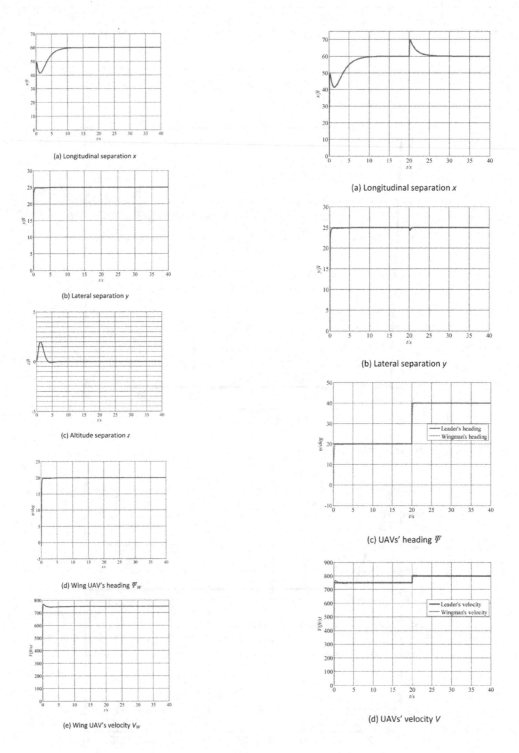

Figure 12. Time response curves of multiple UAVs close formation system with the leader's state changing

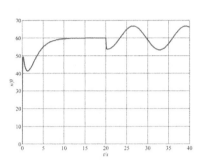

(a) Longitudinal separation *x*

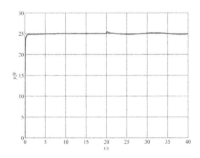

(b) Lateral separation *y*

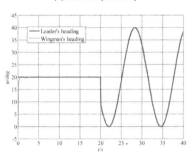

(c) UAVs' heading *Ψ*

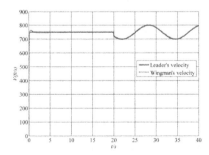

(d) UAVs' velocity *V*

ously, and the response curves are shown in Figure 12.

6. CONCLUDING REMARKS

The close formation aerodynamic coupling effects on the Wingman caused by Leader's wing vortex makes it more difficult for a controller to maintain the formation geometry. In this paper, a multi-criteria performance index is designed for the PI controller parameters tuning and a PI controller is designed for multiple UAVs close formation flight system. PSO algorithm is used to optimize the controller parameter. Experimental results show that the PSO-based parameters for the PI controller of multiple UAVs close formation are effectively. Our future work will focus on developing a more practical close formation model, with the real complicated environments taken into account.

ACKNOWLEDGMENT

This work was partially supported by the Natural Science Foundation of China(NSFC) under grant #60975072 and #60604009, Aeronautical Science Foundation of China under grant #2008ZC01006, Program for New Century Excellent Talents in University of China under grant #NCET-10-0021, Beijing NOVA Program Foundation of China under grant #2007A017, and "New Scientific Star in Blue Sky" Talent Program of Beihang University(BUAA) of China.

REFERENCES

Ambrosino, G., Ariola, M., Ciniglio, U., Corraro, F., Lellis, E. D., & Pironti, A. (2009). Path Generation and Tracking in 3-D for UAVs. *IEEE Transactions on Control Systems Technology, 17*(4), 980–988. doi:10.1109/TCST.2009.2014359

Binetti, P., Ariyur, K. B., Krstic, M., & Bernelli, F. (2003). Formation flight optimization using extremum seeking feedback. *Journal of Guidance, Control, and Dynamics, 26*(1), 132–142. doi:10.2514/2.5024

Blake, W., & Multhopp, D. (1998). Design, performance and modeling considerations for close formation flight. In *Proceedings of AIAA Guidance, Navigation, and Control Conference,* Reston, VA (pp. 476-486).

Buzogany, L. E., Pachter, M., & D'Azzo, J. J. (1993). Automated control of aircraft in formation flight. In *Proceedings of AIAA Guidance, Navigation and Control Conference,* Monterey, CA (pp. 1349-1370).

Chen, Y. M., & Chang, S. H. (2008). An agent-based simulation for multi-UAVs coordinative sensing. *International Journal of Intelligent Computing and Cybernetics, 1*(2), 269–284. doi:10.1108/17563780810874744

Constantinides, C., Parkinson, P., & River, W. (2008). Security challenges in UAV development. In *Proceedings of the IEEE/AAA 27th Digital Avionics Systems Conference (DASC 2008),* Saint Paul, MN (pp. 1-8).

Dargan, J. L., Pachter, M., & D'Azzo, J. J. (1992). Automatic formation flight control. In *Proceedings of AIAA Guidance, Navigation and Control Conference,* Hilton Head Island, SC (pp. 838-857).

Duan, H. B., Liu, S. Q., Wang, D. B., & Yu, X. F. (2009). Design and realization of hybrid ACO-based PID and LuGre friction compensation controller for three degree-of-freedom high precision flight simulator. *Simulation Modelling Practice and Theory, 17*(6), 1160–1169. doi:10.1016/j.simpat.2009.04.006

Duan, H. B., Ma, G. J., & Luo, D. L. (2008). Optimal formation reconfiguration control of multiple UCAVs using improved particle swarm optimization. *Journal of Bionics Engineering, 5*(4), 340–347. doi:10.1016/S1672-6529(08)60179-1

Eberhart, R., & Kennedy, J. (1995). A new optimizer using particle swarm theory. In *Proceedings of the 6th International Symposium on Micro-Machine and Human Science,* Nagoya, Japan (pp. 39-43).

Gargari, E. A., Hashemzadeh, F., Rajabioun, R., & Lucas, C. (2008). Colonial competitive algorithm: a novel approach for PID controller design in MIMO distillation column process. *International Journal of Intelligent Computing and Cybernetics, 1*(3), 337–355. doi:10.1108/17563780810893446

Hjalmarsson, H., Gevers, M., Gunnarsson, S., & Lequin, O. (1998). Iterative feedback tuning: theory and applications. *IEEE Control Systems Magazine, 18*(4), 26–41. doi:10.1109/37.710876

Hu, X. B., Chen, W. H., & Paolo, E. D. (2007). Multiairport capacity management: genetic algorithm with receding horizon. *IEEE Transactions on Intelligent Systems, 8*(2), 254–263. doi:10.1109/TITS.2006.890067

Kennedy, J., & Eberhart, R. (1995). Particle swarm optimization. In *Proceedings of the 1995 IEEE International Conference on Neural Networks,* Perth, Australia (pp. 1942-1948).

Li, B., Liao, X. H., Sun, Z., Li, Y. H., & Song, Y. D. (2006). Robust autopilot for close Formation flight of multi-UAVs. In *Proceedings of the 38th Southeastern Symposium on System Theory,* Cookeville, TN (pp. 294-298).

Li, Y., Li, B., Sun, Z., & Song, Y. D. (2005). Fuzzy technique based close formation flight control. In *Proceedings of the 31st Annual Conference of IEEE Industrial Electronics Society,* New York (pp. 40-44).

Liu, S. C., Tan, D. L., & Liu, G. J. (2007). Formation control of mobile robots with active obstacle avoidance. *Acta Automatica Sinica, 33*(5), 529–535.

Pachter, M., D'Azzo, J. J., & Proud, A. W. (2001). Tight formation flight control. *Journal of Guidance, Control, and Dynamics, 24*(2), 246–254. doi:10.2514/2.4735

Proud, A. W., Pachter, M., & D'Azzo, J. J. (1999). Close formation flight control. In: AIAA Guidance Navigation and Control. In *Proceedings of the AIAA Guidance Navigation and Control and Exhibit,* Portland, OR (pp. 1231-1246).

Singh, S. N., & Pachter, M. (2000). Adaptive feedback linearization nonlinear close formation control of UAVs. In *Proceedings of the American Control Conference,* Chicago (pp. 854-858).

Zhang, X. Y., Duan, H. B., & Yu, Y. X. (2010). Receding horizon control for multi-UAVs close formation control based on differential evolution. *Science China Information Sciences, 53*(2), 223–235. doi:10.1007/s11432-010-0036-6

Zhou, L. X., Zhang, X. H., & Li, W. (2007). Optimal design for PID controller based on differential evolution algorithm. *Machinery & Electronics, 12*, 54–56.

This work was previously published in International Journal of Swarm Intelligence Research, Volume 1, Issue 2, edited by Yuhui Shi, pp. 1-17, copyright 2010 by IGI Publishing (an imprint of IGI Global)

Chapter 7

Oscillation Damping Enhancement via Coordinated Design of PSS and FACTS-Based Stabilizers in a Multi-Machine Power System Using PSO

M. A. Abido
King Fahd University of Petroleum & Minerals, Saudi Arabia

Saleh M. Bamasak
Saudi Electricity Company, Saudi Arabia

ABSTRACT

This paper investigates the enhancement of power system stability via coordinated design of Power System Stabilizers (PSSs), Thyristor Controlled Series Capacitor (TCSC)-based stabilizer, and Static Var Compensator (SVC)-based stabilizer in a multi-machine power system. The design problem of the proposed stabilizers is formulated as an optimization problem. Using the developed linearized power system model, the particle swarm optimization (PSO) algorithm is employed to search for optimal stabilizer settings that maximize the minimum damping ratio of all system oscillating modes. The proposed stabilizers are evaluated on a two-area weakly-connected multi-machine power system with unstable interarea oscillation mode. The nonlinear simulation results and eigenvalue analysis show the effectiveness of the proposed coordinated stabilizers in damping low frequency power system oscillations and enhancing the system stability.

DOI: 10.4018/978-1-4666-1592-2.ch007

INTRODUCTION

Power systems are experiencing low frequency oscillations due to disturbances. These oscillations may sustain and grow to cause system separation if no adequate damping is available (Yu, 1983). In order to damp power system oscillation and increase system oscillation stability, the installation of power system stabilizer (PSS) is both economical and effective (Abido & Magid, 2007; Tse & Tso, 1993).

To date, most major power system plants in many countries are equipped with PSSs. However, PSSs suffer a drawback of being liable to cause great variations in the voltage profile and they may even result in leading power factor operation and losing system stability under severe disturbances. Although a control scheme using PSS has been successfully developed for damping inter-area oscillations in some real power systems like Argentina and Australia electric systems (Cigre Report, 1999), PSSs are not usually effective in damping interarea mode of oscillations and use of other means of solution may be necessary (Feliachi & Yang, 1994).

Recently, FACTS-based stabilizers such as Static Var Compensator (SVC), Thyristor controlled Series Compensation (TCSC), and Thyristor Controlled Phase Shifter (TCPS) offer an alternative way in damping power system oscillations. Although, the damping duty of a FACTS controller often is not its primary function, the capability of FACTS-based stabilizers to increase power system damping characteristics has been extensively investigated. Analysis and identification of the most effective parameter of FACTS controller has been investigated (Abido, 2005). A comparative analysis with minimum singular value, direct component of torque and residue has been presented for finding the most appropriate control input parameters of unified power flow controller for POD (Pandey & Singh, 2009). On the other hand, a dynamic phasor modeling of SVC

has been introduced for system transient stability enhancement (Zhijun et al., 2009).

Several approaches based on modern control theory have been applied to TCSC and SVC controller design. The effectiveness of the series compensation devices on stability enhancement has been presented (Bamasak & Abido, 2004; Chen at al.,1995) presented a state feedback controller for TCSC by using a pole placement technique. (Chang & Chow, 1997) developed a time optimal control strategy for the TCSC where a performance index of time was minimized. A fuzzy logic controller for a TCSC was proposed (Lie et al., 1995). Heuristic optimization techniques have been implemented to search for the optimal TCSC based stabilizer parameters for the purpose of enhancing SMIB system stability (Wang et al., 2002). The power damping enhancement by application of SVC has been analyzed. (Wang & Swift, 1996) used damping torque coefficients approach to investigate the SVC damping control of a SMIB system on the basis of Phillips-Heffron model. It was shown that the SVC damping control provides the power system with negative damping when it operates at a lower load condition than the dead point, the point at which SVC control produces zero damping effect. Robust SVC controllers based on H_∞ also has been presented to enhance system damping (Wang & Tsai, 1998). (Noroozian, 1995, 1994) examined the enhancement of multimachine power system stability by use FACTS. It was concluded that the SVC is more effective for controlling power swings at higher levels of power transfer. However, unlike SVC, TCSC is not sensitive to the load characteristic and when it is designed to damp the inter-area modes; it does not excite the local modes. In some real power systems like the North-South interconnection in the Brazilian system a solution based on FACTS was successfully implemented to solve inter-area oscillations (Gama, et al., 1998).

Some work has been devoted in the literature to study the coordination control of excitation and FACTS stabilizers. (Hiyama et al., 1995) presented a coordinated fuzzy logic-based scheme for PSS and switched series capacitor modules to enhance overall power system stability. Robust coordinated design of excitation and TCSC-based stabilizers using genetic algorithm in a SMIB system was presented (Magid & Abido, 2004). Pourbeik and Gibbard (1998) presented a two-stage method for the simultaneous coordination of PSSs and FACTS-based lead-lag controllers in multi-machine power systems by using the concept of induced damping and synchronizing torque coefficients.

In this paper, a comprehensive assessment of the effectiveness of the individual and co-ordinated design approach of PSSs, TCSC and SVC-based stabilizers on power system stability enhancement has been carried out in a two-area weakly-connected multi-machine power system. The stabilizer design problem is transformed into an optimization problem where PSO is employed to search for the optimal settings of the proposed stabilizer parameters. The locations of PSSs have been investigated using participation factors (PF) method. The eigenvalue analysis and nonlinear simulation results have been carried out to demonstrate the effectiveness of the proposed stabilizers for power system stability enhancement.

SYSTEM MODELING

Generators

In this study, each generator model is comprising of the electromechanical swing equation and the generator internal voltage equation where the ith generator can be modeled as follows.

$$\dot{\delta}_i = \omega_b(\omega_i - 1) \tag{1}$$

$$\dot{\omega}_i = (T_{mi} - T_{ei} - D_i(\omega_i - 1)) / M_i \tag{2}$$

$$\dot{E}'_{qi} = (E_{fdi} - (x_{di} - x'_{di})i_{di} - E'_{qi}) / T'_{doi} \tag{3}$$

$$T_{ei} = v_{qi}i_{qi} + v_{di}i_{di} \tag{4}$$

where: δ and ω are rotor angle and speed respectively; ω_b is the synchronous speed; T_m and T_e are input and output power of the generator respectively; M and D are the inertia constant and damping coefficient respectively; E'_q is the internal voltage; E_{fd} is the field voltage; T'_{do} is the open circuit field time constant, x_d and x'_d are the d-axis reactance and d-axis transient reactance of the generator respectively; v_d, v_q, i_d and i_q are the terminal voltage and armature current d- and q- axis components respectively.

Exciter and PSS

The IEEE Type-ST1 exciter is used in this study. It can be described as:

$$\dot{E}_{fd} = \left(K_A \left(V_{ref} - v + u_{PSS} \right) - E_{fd} \right) / T_A \tag{5}$$

Where: K_A and T_A are the gain and time constant of the excitation system respectively; V_{ref} and v are the reference and terminal voltages respectively.

The widely used lead-lag PSS structure is considered in this study. This structure involves a reset block and lead-lag blocks. The lead-lag blocks provide the appropriate phase-lead characteristic to compensate the phase lag between the exciter input and the generator electrical torque. The structure of the excitation system with a PSS is illustrated in Figure 1 where the stabilizing signal of the PSS is u_{PSS} and the input signal is selected as the generator speed deviation $\Delta\omega$.

FACTS-Based Stabilizer

Figure 2 illustrates the block diagram of TCSC or SVC with a lead-lag compensator. In case of

Figure 1. IEEE type-ST1 excitation system with a lead-lag PSS

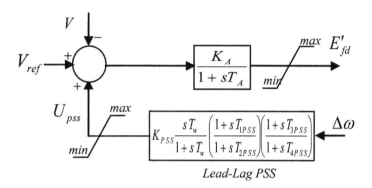

Lead-Lag PSS

TCSC, the FACTS designation in the figure will be replaced by the TCSC reactance X_{TCSC} and in case of SVC, it will be replaced by the SVC susceptance B_{SVC}. Generally, the FACTS device dynamics can be modeled by the first order equation shown in Eq. (6) which found sufficient for dynamic analysis:

$$\overset{\bullet}{FACTS} = \frac{1}{T_s}\left[K_s\left(FACTS_{ref} - U_{FACTS}\right) - FACTS\right]$$

$$(6)$$

where: $FACTS_{ref}$ is the reference reactance of TCSC or the reference susceptance of SVC ; K_s and T_s are the gain and time constant of the FACTS device respectively. As shown in Figure 2, a conventional lead-lag controller is installed in the feedback loop to generate the compensation stabilizer signal U_{FACTS}, i.e., U_{TCSC} or U_{SVC}.

Linearized System Model

In general, a power system can be modeled by a set of nonlinear differential equations as:

$$\overset{\bullet}{X} = f\left(X, U\right)$$

$$(7)$$

where X is the state vector, $X = \left[\delta, \omega, E_q{}', E_{fd}\right]^T$, and U is the input vector, $U = \left[U_{PSS}, U_{FACTS}\right]^T$,

where U_{PSS} and U_{FACTS} are the PSS and FACTS-based stabilizer control signals respectively.

In the design of electromechanical mode damping controllers, the linearized incremental model around a nominal operating point is used (Yu, 1983). Linearizing the system model yields the following state equation.

$$\overset{\bullet}{\Delta X} = A\Delta X + B\Delta U$$

$$(8)$$

where A is $4n \times 4n$ state matrix and equals $\partial f/\partial X$, while B is $4n \times m$ control matrix and equals $\partial f/\partial U$. Here, n is the number of machines and m is the number of stabilizers. Both A and B are evaluated at the nominal operating point.

The driven system can be written as follows:

$$\overset{\bullet}{Z} = A_c Z$$

$$(9)$$

Where A_c is the system augmented matrix and Z is the augmented state vector.

PARTICLE SWARM OPTIMIZATION ALGORITHM

The PSO technique combines social psychology principles in socio-cognition human agents and evolutionary computations. PSO has been motivated by the behavior of organisms such as fish schooling and bird flocking. Generally, PSO is characterized as simple in concept, easy to implement, and computationally efficient. Unlike the other heuristic techniques, PSO has a flexible and well-balanced mechanism to enhance and adapt the global and local exploration abilities (Kennedy, 1997). Therefore, PSO combines the advantages of GA as a global search and the advantages of Tabu search as a local search. In addition, PSO shows superiority performance compared to other heuristic methods (Abido, 2002).

Like evolutionary algorithms, PSO technique conducts search using a population of particles. Each particle represents a candidate solution to the problem. In PSO technique, particles change their positions by flying around in a multi dimensional search space until a relatively unchanging position has been encountered, or until computational limitations are exceeded. In social science context, a PSO system combines a social-only model and a cognition-only model. The social-only component suggests that individuals ignore their own experience and adjust their behavior according to the successful beliefs of individuals in the neighborhood. On the other hand, the cognition-only component treats individuals as isolated beings. The advantages of PSO over other traditional optimization techniques can be summarized as follows:

- PSO is a population-based search algorithm i.e., PSO has implicit parallelism. This property ensures PSO to be less susceptible to getting trapped on local minima.
- PSO uses objective function information to guide the search in the problem space. Therefore, PSO can easily deal with non-differentiable objective functions.
- PSO uses probabilistic transition rules, not deterministic rules. Hence, PSO is a kind of stochastic optimization algorithm that can search a complicated and uncertain

area. This makes PSO more flexible and robust than conventional methods.
- Unlike GA and other heuristic algorithms, PSO has the flexibility to control the balance between the global and local exploration of the search space.

The basic elements of PSO technique are briefly stated and defined as follows:

A. **Particle:** X(t), It is a candidate solution represented by an m-dimensional real-valued vector, where m is the number of optimized parameters. At time t, the jth particle $X_j(t)$ can be described as $X_j(t) = [x_{j,1}(t), ..., x_{j,m}(t)]$, where x's are the optimized parameters and $x_{j,k}(t)$ is the position of the jth particle with respect to the kth dimension, i.e., the value of the kth optimized parameter in the jth candidate solution.

B. **Population:** *pop(t)*,: It is a set of n particles at time t, i.e., $pop(t) = [X_1(t), ..., X_n(t)]^T$.

C. **Swarm:** it is an apparently disorganized population of moving particles that tend to cluster together while each particle seems to be moving in a random direction.

D. **Particle Velocity:** V(t),: It is the velocity of the moving particles represented by an m-dimensional real-valued vector. At time t, the jth particle velocity $V_j(t)$ can be described as $V_j(t) = v_{j,1}(t), ..., v_{j,m}(t)$, where $v_{j,k}(t)$ is the velocity component of the jth particle w.r.t. k^{th} dimension.

E. **Inertia Weight:** w(t),: It is a control parameter that is used to control the impact of the previous velocities on the current velocity. Hence, it influences the trade-off between the global and local exploration abilities of the particles. For initial stages of the search process, large inertia weight to enhance the global exploration is recommended while, for last stages, the inertia weight is reduced for better local exploration.

F. **Individual Best:** X*(t),: As a particle moves through the search space, it compares its fitness value at the current position to the best fitness value it has ever attained at any time up to the current time. The best position that is associated with the best fitness encountered so far is called the individual best, X*(t). For each particle in the swarm, X'(t) can be determined and updated during the search. In a minimization problem with objective function J, the individual best of the Jth particle X*$_j$(t) is determined.

G. **Global Best:** $X^{**}(t)$: It is the best position among all individual best positions achieved so far. Hence, the global best can be determined as $J(X^{**}(t)) < J(X_j^*(t)), j = 1, ..., n$. For simplicity, assume that $J^{**} = J(X^{**}(t))$.

H. **Stopping Criteria:** These are the conditions under which the search will terminate. In this study, the search will stop if one of tile following criteria is satisfied: (a) the number of iterations since the last change of the best solution is greater than a pre specified number; or (b) the number of iterations reaches the maximum allowable number.

In a PSO algorithm, the population has n particles that represent candidate solutions. Each particle is an m-dimensional real-valued vector, where m is the number of optimized parameters. Therefore, each optimized parameter represents a dimension of the problem space. The PSO technique can be described in the following steps:

Step 1: (Initialization): Set the time counter $t = 0$ and generate random n particles, {$X_j(0)$, $j=1,2,...,n$}, where $X_j(0)=[x_{j,1}(0), x_{j,2}(0), ..., x_{j,m}(0)]$, $x_{j,k}(0)$ is generated by randomly selecting a value with uniform probability over the k-th optimized parameter search space [x_k^{min}, x_k^{max}]. Similarly, generate randomly initial velocities of all particles, {$V_j(0)$, $j=1,2,...,n$}, where $V_j(0)=[v_{j,1}(0), v_{j,2}(0), ..., v_{j,m}(0)]$, $v_{j,k}(0)$ is generated by randomly selecting a value with uniform probability over the k-th dimension [$-v_k^{min}, v_k^{max}$]. Each particle in the initial population is evaluated using the objective function, J. For each particle, set $X_j^*(0) = X_j(0)$ and $J_j^* = J_j, J = 1,2,...,n$. Search for the best value of the objective function. Set the particle associated with J_{best} as the global best, X**(0), with an objective function of J^{**}. Set the initial value of the inertia weight $w(0)$.

Step 2: (Time updating): Update the time counter $t = t + 1$.

Step 3: (Weight updating): Update the inertia weight $w(t) = \alpha w(t-1)$.

Step 4: (Velocity updating): Using the global best and individual best, the jth particle velocity in the kth dimension is updated according to the following equation: $v_{j,k}(t) = w(t) v_{j,k}(t-1) + c_1 r_1(x_{j,k}^*(t-1) - x_{j,k}(t-1)) + c_2 r_2(x_{j,k}^{**}(t-1) - x_{j,k}(t-1))$, where c_1 and c_2 are positive constants and r_1 and r_2 are uniformly distributed random numbers in [0,1]. Check the velocity limits. If the velocity violated its limit, set it at its proper limit. It is worth mentioning that the second term represents the cognitive part of PSO where the particle changes its velocity based on its own thinking and memory. The third term represents the social part of PSO where the particle changes its velocity based on the social-psychological adaptation of knowledge.

Step 5: (Position updating): Based on the updated velocities, each particle changes its position according to the following equation: $x_{j,k}(t) = v_{j,k}(t) + x_{j,k}(t-1)$

Step 6: (Individual best updating): Each particle is evaluated according to the updated position. If $J_j < J_j^*, j = 1,2,...,n$, then update individual best as $X_j^*(t) = X_j(t)$ and $J_j^* = J_j$ and go to step 7.

Step 7: (Global best updating): Search for the minimum value J_{min} among J^*_j, where is the index of the particle with minimum objective function value, i.e., min $\in \{j; j=1, 2, ..., n\}$. If $J_{min} < J^{**}$ then update global best as $X^{**} = X_{min}(t)$, and $J^{**} = J_{min}$ and go to step 8.

Step 8: (Stopping criteria): If one of the stopping criteria is satisfied, then stop, or else go to step 2.

PROPOSED DESIGN APPROACH

In this section the proposed approach is illustrated and discussed. Firstly, the locations of the PSSs are identified in a multi-machine system by using the participation factors method. Secondly, the stabilizer parameter tuning problem is formulated as an optimization problem with an eigenvalue based objective function. Then, the PSO is proposed in this work to search for optimal settings of the stabilizer parameters.

PSS Locations

The state equation of the linearized model of undriven system can be rewritten as:

$$\Delta \dot{X} = A \,\Delta X \qquad (10)$$

Then the eigenvalues of the system matrix A can be determined. Out of these eigenvalues, there are $n-1$ modes of oscillations related to machine inertias [1-2]. For the stabilizers to be effective, it is extremely important to identify the eigenvalues associated with electromechanical modes and the machines to which these eigenvalues belong. Identification of electromechanical modes starts with calculating the right and left eigenvectors where the right eigenvector gives the mode shape by describing the activity of the variables when that particular mode is excited while the left eigenvector gives the mode composition by describing

what weighted combination of state variables is needed to construct the mode. Participation factors method that utilizes these eigenvectors has been employed in this work to identify the most effective locations of PSSs.

Problem Formulation

To increase the system damping to the electromechanical modes, an eigenvalue based objective function J is proposed as follows.

$$J = \left\{ \zeta : \zeta \text{ is the minimum electromechanical mode damping ratio} \right\} \qquad (11)$$

It is aimed to maximize the minimum value of the damping ratio among electromechanical modes of all loading conditions considered in the design process. The design problem can be formulated as the following optimization problem.

Maximize J,, Subject to

$$K_{FACTS}{}^{min} \leq K_{FACTS} \leq K_{FACTS}{}^{max}$$

$$K_{PSS}{}^{min} \leq K_{PSS} \leq K_{PSS}{}^{max}$$

$$T_{FACTS1,2,3,4}{}^{min} \leq T_{FACTS1-4} \leq T_{FACTS1-4}{}^{max}$$

$$T_{PSS1,2,3,4}{}^{min} \leq T_{PSS1,2,3,4} \leq T_{PSS1,2,3,4}{}^{max}$$

The minimum and maximum value of the stabilizer gains are set as 0.1 and 100 respectively while the minimum and maximum values of the stabilizer time constants are set as 0.01 and 5.0s respectively. The above formulated optimization problem will be solved by particle swarm optimization technique where all the tuning parameters of all stabilizers are optimized simultaneously. This coordinated design approach avoids the adverse effect among different stabilizers.

PSO Implementation

The proposed PSO based approach was implemented using the MATLAB. Practically, several preliminary experiments have been carried out to select carefully PSO parameters for efficient performance. In our implementation, the initial inertia weight $w(0)$ is selected as 1.0. Other parameters were set as: number of particles n=50, decrement constant α=0.98, c_1=c_2=2, and the search will be terminated if **(a)** the number of iterations since the last change of the best solution is greater than 30; or **(b)** the number of iterations reaches 200.

SIMULATION RESULTS

Test System

The system considered in this paper is the two-area weakly-connected multi-machine power system. The system one-line diagram is shown in Figure 3. The details of the system data used along with load flow results are given in the Appendix. This system consists of two identical areas. Each area includes two 900 MVA generating units equipped with fast static exciters. All four generating units are represented by the same dynamic model. The power transfer from Area 2 to Area 1 over a single tie line is considered.

Modal Analysis and PSS Locations

The open-loop eigenvalues of the electromechanical modes along with their frequencies, damping ratios, and machine participation factors (PF) are given in the Table 1. It can be concluded that the system exhibits three electromechanical modes that can be described as follows.

- A local mode, in area 1, with a frequency of 1.112 Hz. In this mode the machines in Area 1 oscillate against each other.

- A local mode, in area 2, with a frequency of 1.094 Hz. In this mode the machines in Area 2 oscillate against each other.
- An inter-area mode, with a frequency of 0.5098 Hz, in which the generating units in one area oscillate against those in the other area. It can also be seen that the inter-area mode is unstable under the specified loading conditions.

The two generating units in each area have close participation factors with the two local modes as given in Table 1. This is to be expected, since all units are identical, and units in each area are electrically close. Table 1 also shows that the units in Area 1 (the receiving end) have higher participation factors than the units in Area 2 (sending end) to the inter-area mode. For the lightly damped local mode of area 1, generators # 2 is the candidate location as it has the significant participation factors of this mode. Similarly, generator # 4 is the candidate location of PSS for the local mode of area 2. To enhance system damping characteristics to the unstable interarea mode, the candidate location based on participation factors given in the table is generator#1. Therefore, the candidate locations for PSSs are at machines # 1,2, and 4.

The location of SVC controller is selected at the receiving end bus of the tie line, bus 7 and TCSC on the middle of the tie line. Generator #2 speed deviation $\Delta\omega_2$ was chosen as FACTS controller input signal as the nearest machine having high PF to the inter-area mode as given in Table 1.

Stabilizer Design

Having been formulated, the PSO algorithm has been employed to solve the stabilizer design problem. The individual as well as the coordinated design have been investigated. In individual design each stabilizer is designed independently while in coordinated design all stabilizers are designed simultaneously. The coordinated design approach

Table 1. System eigenvalue and participation factor analysis

Eigenvalues	Freq.	Mode	Damping Ratio	Machines Participation Factor			
				G1	G2	G3	G4
-0.660 ±6.9904i	1.1125	Local	0.094	0.7544	1	0.0015	0.0088
-0.7375 ±6.8742i	1.0941	Local	0.1067	0.0133	0.0016	0.8438	1
0.0279 ± 3.2030i	0.5098	Inter-Area	-0.0087	1	0.7869	0.3891	0.2432

Table 2. Optimal parameter settings of coordinated PSSs and TCSC-based stabilizer

Parameters	Coordinated Design			
	PSS1	PSS2	PSS4	TCSC
K	100	100	49.2614	1.064
T_1 (s)	0.0783	0.0702	0.1354	5.0
T_2 (s)	0.01	0.01	0.01	0.021
T_3 (s)	—	—	—	0.01
T_4 (s)	—	—	—	5.0

Figure 3. Two-area 4-machine power system

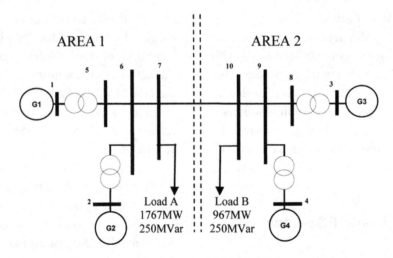

avoids the adverse effect among different stabilizers. The convergence rate of the objective function when PSSs and TCSC-based stabilizer are designed individually and in a coordinated manner is shown in Figure 4, while Figure 5 shows the convergence for PSSs and SVC-based stabilizer. It is clear that the coordinated design approach improves greatly the system damping compared to the individual design scheme. The optimal settings

of the coordinated stabilizer parameters are given in Table 2 and Table 3. It is worth mentioning that in case of PSS, one block is found satisfactory.

Eigenvalue Analysis

The system eigenvalues with the proposed PSSs, TCSC and SVC-based stabilizers when applied individually and in a coordinated manner are given

Figure 4. Objective function convergence with PSSs and TCSC-based stabilizer

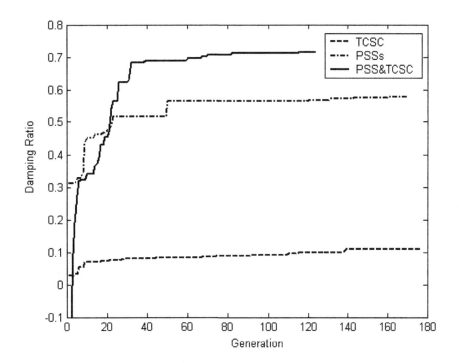

Figure 5. Objective function convergence with PSSs and SVC-based stabilizer

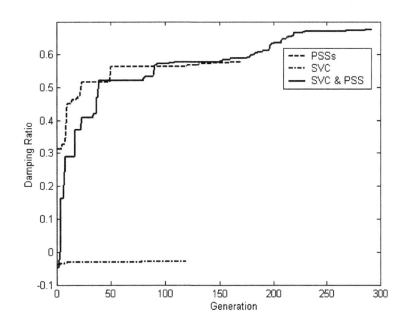

Table 3. Optimal parameter settings of coordinated PSSs and SVC-based stabilizer

Parameters	Coordinated Design			
	PSS1	PSS2	PSS4	SVC
K	26.173	100	51.9935	20.25
T_1 (s)	0.025	0.0548	0.1085	0.9441
T_2 (s)	0.01	0.01	0.01	0.7922
T_3 (s)	—	—	—	5
T_4 (s)	—	—	—	0.01

Table 4. System eigenvalues with individual and coordinated design

PSSs only	TCSC only	SVC only	TCSC & PSSs	SVC & PSSs
-1.7682±1.6360i	-0.509±4.3648i	0.08641±2.9049i*	-1.9658±2.7841i	-2.0859±2.222i
-2.6113±3.0188i	-0.597±5.0238i	0.2752±9.29463i*	-2.390±3.2546i	-2.836±2.7489i
-3.4337±5.4358i	-0.749±6.8431i	-0.4912±6.9342i	-4.423±6.07504i	-3.854±3.568i
-3.9219±5.7975i -7.7989±11.9581i -12.372±17.9649i -17.3096±0.1076i -21.5036±1.8633i -92.0013,-89.364, -81.0185,-76.811, -11.898, -7.4442, -6.2647, -4.9271,-0.2024, -0.2122	-1.614±4.9672i -89.067,-89.41 -79.4,-76.692, -23.969,-21.04, -16.712,-13.89, -13.65,-7.5208, -6.4332,-5.408, -4.908,-0.2000	-16.75 ± 0.69i -89.05,-89.41, -79.5,-76.7, -100,-23.42, -188.2,-13.86, -7.18, -6.67, -6.12, -6.17, -1.65,-0.2	-6.16589±5.0236i -6.4785±9.132i -13.00±15.812i -22.269±4.7965i -100,-100,-0.2, -100, -128.36, -82.48,-100, -20.0,-17.7, -15.8, -12.84,-9.4599,-6.023, -5.328,-2.61	-6.8548±6.432i -16.09±0.836i -34.102±22.03i -125.8±0.9685i -100,-100,-82.5, -84.4, -100, -100, -21.4,-17.7, -2.61, -15.8, -12.8, -1.2, -9.45,-6.0,-5.328

* Unstable modes

in Table 4. In case of individual design, it is clear that PSSs enhance the system damping while the system damping is slightly improved in case of TCSC-based stabilizer. On the other hand, the system with SVC-based stabilizer has a negative damping with unstable electromechanical modes as shown in Table 4.

Moreover, it is evident that the damping of the electromechanical mode eigenvalue is greatly enhanced using the proposed coordinated design approach as the eigenvalues have been shifted more towards the left-hand side of *s*-plane.

Nonlinear Time Domain Simulation

In order to evaluate the effectiveness of the proposed stabilizers, a 6-cycle 3-phase fault dis-

turbance at bus 7 is applied to the system. Figure 6 shows the generators' speed response with the SVC-based stabilizer. It can be seen that the negative damping effect of SVC at this operating condition which agrees with the eigenvalues analysis shown in Table 4 and also confirms the conclusion given in (M. Noroozain & G. Andersson, 1994). Figure 7 shows the system response using TCSC-based stabilizer after being subjected to the same disturbance, it is clear that the system becomes stable. The rotor angle response of generator # 4 is shown in Figure 8 when the proposed stabilizers are applied individually under the same fault disturbance. It is clear that the proposed TCSC-based stabilizer improves the first swing stability while the proposed PSSs reduce greatly the settling time of the system response.

Figure 6. Speed response in (pu) to a 6-cycle fault disturbance with SVC-based stabilizer, individual design

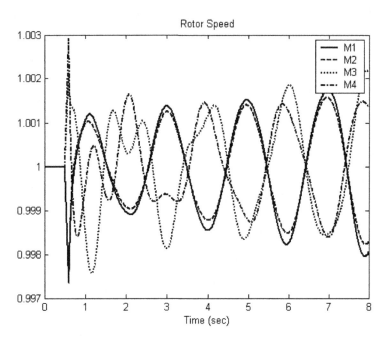

Figure 7. Speed response in (pu) to a 6-cycle fault disturbance with TCSC-based stabilizer, individual design

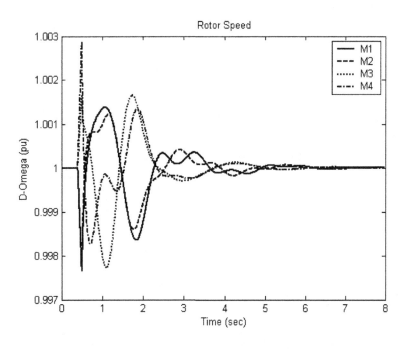

Figure 8. Rotor angle response to a 6-cycle fault disturbance, individual design

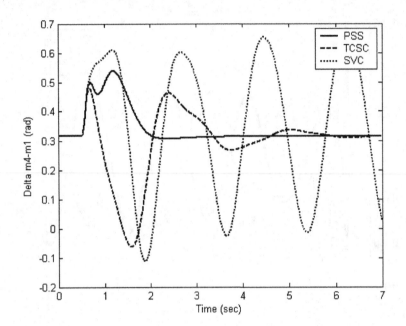

This demonstrates the potential of the proposed coordinated design approach as it hybridizes the advantages of both responses.

On the other hand, Figure 9, Figure 10, Figure 11, and Figure 12 show the system response to a 6-cycle 3-phase fault disturbance at bus 7 with the proposed coordinated stabilizers. The simulation results obtained clearly indicate that the proposed coordinated design approach enhances the system stability in terms of overshoots and settling time. With coordinated design of PSSs and TCSC-based stabilizer, the system response shows improvement in the first swing stability and the settling time is greatly improved. These results confirm the observations drawn from eigenvalue analysis results and demonstrate the effectiveness of the proposed coordinated design approach.

In order to assess the effectiveness of the proposed coordinated design approach to enhance the first swing system stability under a three-phase fault disturbance, the system critical clearing time (CCT) analysis has been carried out. The results

of the simulations are given in Table 5. It is clear that the CCT with the proposed coordinated design approach is quite longer that that with PSS. This confirms also the effectiveness of the coordinated design approach to enhance the system transient stability under such severe disturbances.

CONCLUSION

In this study, individual and coordination design of PSSs and FACTS-based stabilizers have been investigated. The locations of power system stabilizers have been investigated using participation factors method. The stabilizer design problem has been formulated as an optimization problem with an eigenvalue-based objective function. The tuning parameters of the proposed stabilizer have been optimized using particle swarm optimization technique. The proposed stabilizers have been implemented and tested on a two-area weakly-connected multi-machine power system under severe disturbances. The eigenvalue analysis and

Figure 9. Speed response to a 6-cycle fault disturbance with PSSs and TCSC-based stabilizer, coordinated design

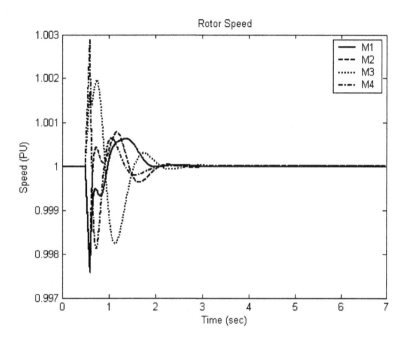

Figure 10. Speed response to a 6-cycle fault disturbance with PSSs and SVC-based stabilizer, coordinated design

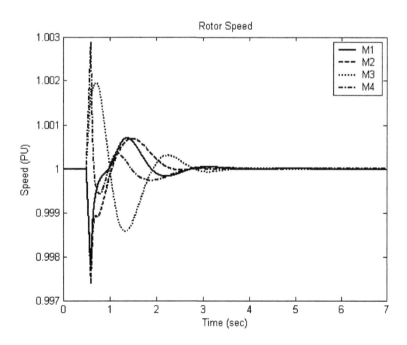

Figure 11. Rotor angle response to a 6-cycle fault disturbance with PSSs and TCSC-based stabilizer, individual and coordinated design

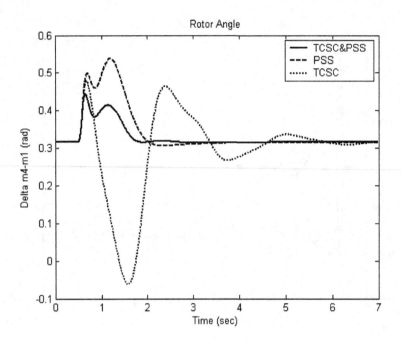

Figure 12. Terminal voltage response for 6-cycle fault with PSS's & TCSC, coordinated design

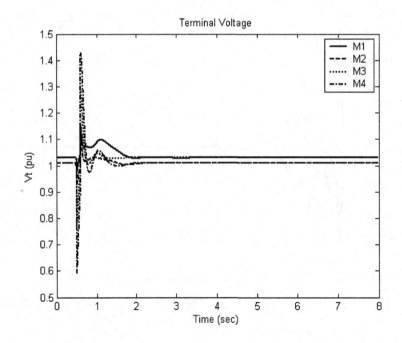

Table 5. CCT analysis

Controller	CCT
PSS	0.294 sec
TCSC	0.386 sec
TCSC & PSS	0.401 sec

the nonlinear time domain simulation results show the effectiveness of the proposed coordinated design approach where the proposed stabilizers improve the damping characteristics of low frequency oscillation and enhance greatly the system stability. In addition, the CCT analysis shows that the proposed coordinated design enhances greatly the system stability margin.

ACKNOWLEDGMENT

The first author would like to acknowledge the support of King Fahd University of Petroleum & Minerals via funded project # IN090019. The second author would like to acknowledge the support of Saudi Electricity Company-SEC.

REFERENCES

Abdel-Magid, Y. L., & Abido, M. A. (2004). Robust coordinated design of excitation and TCSC-based stabilizers using genetic algorithm. *Electric Power Systems Research*, *69*, 129–141. doi:10.1016/j.epsr.2003.06.009

Abido, M. A. (2002, October). Optimal Power Flow Using Particle Swarm Optimization. *International Journal of Electrical Power & Energy Systems*, *24*(7), 563–571. doi:10.1016/S0142-0615(01)00067-9

Abido, M. A. (2005, February). Analysis and assessment of STATCOM-Based damping stabilizers for power system stability enhancement. *Electric Power Systems Research*, *73*(2), 177–185. doi:10.1016/j.epsr.2004.08.002

Abido, M. A., & Abdel-Magid, Y. L. (2007). Dynamic Stability Enhancement of East-Central System in Saudi Arabia via PSS Tuning. *Arabian Journal of Science and Engineering*, *32*, 85–99.

Bamasak, S., & Abido, M. (2004, November). Effectiveness of Series Compensation On Power System Stability Enhancement. *GCC-Cigre Conference, 1*, 65-71.

Chang, J., & Chow, J. (1997). Time Optimal Series Capacitor Control for Damping Inter-Area Modes in Interconnected Power Systems. *IEEE Trans. PWRS*, *12*(1), 215–221.

Chen, X., Annakkage, U., & Kumble, C. (1995). Controlled Series Compensation for Improving the Stability of Multi-machine Power Systems. In. *Proceedings of the IEEE Part C*, *142*, 361–366.

Feliachi, A., & Yang, X. (1994, December). Identification and Control of Inter-Area Modes. In *Proceedings of the 33rd Conference on Decision and Control*, FL (pp. 4061-4066).

Gama, C., et al. (1998). *Brazilian North-South Interconnection – Application of Thyristor Controlled Series Compensation (TCSC) to Damp Inter-Area Oscillation Mode*. Paris: Cigré 37 Session.

Hiyama, T., et al. (1995). Coordinated Fuzzy Logic Contrl for Series Capacitor Modules and PSS to Enhance Stability of Power System. *IEEE Transactions on Power Delivery*, *10*(2), 1098–1104. doi:10.1109/61.400877

Hsu, Y. Y., & Chen, C. L. (1987, May). Identification of optimum location for stabilizer applications using participation factors. In. *Proceedings of the IEEE Part C*, *134*(3), 238–244.

Kennedy, J. (1997). The Particles Swarm: Social Adaptation of Knowledge. In *Proceedings of the 1997 IEEE International Conference on Evolutionary Computation ICEC'97*, Indianapolis, IN (pp. 303-308).

Li, W., & Ming, T. (1998, August). Design of a H∞ static VAr controller for the damping of generator oscillations. In *Proceedings of the 1998 International Conference on Power System Technology (POWERCON '98)* (Vol. 2, pp. 18-21, 785 -789).

Lie, T., Shrestha, G., & Ghosh, A. (1995). Design and Application of Fuzzy Logic Control Scheme for Transient Stability Enhancement In Power System. *Electric Power System Research*, 17-23.

Martins, N., et al. (1999). *Impact of the Interaction among Power System Controls*. CIGRÈ Task Force.

Noroozian, M., & Andersson, G. (1994, October). Damping of Power System Oscillations by use of Controllable Components. *IEEE Transactions on Power Delivery*, *9*(4), 2046–2054. doi:10.1109/61.329537

Noroozian, M., & Andersson, G. (1995, October). Damping of Inter-Area and Local Modes by use Controllable Components. *IEEE Transactions on Power Delivery*, *10*(4), 2007–2012. doi:10.1109/61.473350

Pandey, R., & Singh, N. (2009, July). UPFC control parameter identification for effective power oscillation damping. *International Journal of Electrical Power & Energy Systems*, *31*(6), 269–276. doi:10.1016/j.ijepes.2009.03.002

Pourbeik, P., & Gibbard, M. J. (1998, May). Simultaneous coordination of power system stabilizers and FACTS device stabilizers in a multi-machine power system for enhancing dynamic performance. *IEEE Transactions on PWRS*, *13*(2), 473–479.

Tse, G. T., & Tso, S. K. (1993). Refinement of Conventional PSS Design in Multi-machine System by Modal Analysis. *IEEE Trans. PWRS*, *8*(2), 598–605.

Wang, H. F., & Swift, F. J. (1996). Capability of the static VAR compensator in damping power system oscillations. In *Proceedings of the Gener. Trans. Distrib.*, *143*, 353-358.

Wang, Y., Tan, Y., & Guo, G. (2002, May). Robust nonlinear coordinated excitation and TCSC control for power system. In *Proceedings of Gener. Trans. Distrib.*, *149*(3), 367-372.

Yu, Y. N. (1983). *Electric Power System Dynamics*. New York: Academic Press.

Zhijun, E., et al. (2009). Hybrid simulation of power systems with SVC dynamic phasor model. *International Journal of Electrical Power & Energy Systems*, *31*, 175–180. doi:10.1016/j.ijepes.2009.01.002

APPENDIX

The details of the 4-machine power system data are as follows on MVA base of 100 MVA.

Table 6. System bus data in per unit

Bus no.	Type	Voltage	Angle	Load		Generation	
				P	Q	P	Q
1	1	1.03	0	0	0	0	0
2	2	1.01	0	0	0	7	0
3	2	1.03	0	0	0	7	0
4	2	1.01	0	0	0	7	0
5	3	1	0	0	0	0	0
6	3	1	0	0	0	0	0
7	3	1	0	17.67	2.5	0	0
8	3	1	0	0	0	0	0
9	3	1	0	0	0	0	0
10	3	1	0	9.67	1	0	0

Table 7. System line data in per unit

Line no.	From	To	R	X	B
1	1	5	0	0.0167	0
2	2	6	0	0.0167	0
3	3	8	0	0.0167	0
4	4	9	0	0.0167	0
5	5	6	0.0025	0.025	0.021875
6	8	9	0.0025	0.025	0.021875
7	6	7	0.001	0.01	0.00875
8	9	10	0.001	0.01	0.00875
9	7	10	0.011	0.11	0.384

Table 8. FACTS Data

FACTS	Location	% Compensation
TCSC	Line No. 9	±50% of $X_{7\text{-}10}$
SVC	Bus No. 7	± 1 pu

Table 9. Machine Data

G	H	D	X_d	X_d'	X_q	X_q'	T_d'
1	55.575	0.0	0.2	0.033	0.19	0.016	8
2	55.575	0.0	0.2	0.033	0.19	0.016	8
3	58.5	0.0	0.2	0.033	0.19	0.016	8
4	58.5	0.0	0.2	0.033	0.19	0.016	8
T_q'	K_A	T_A					
0.4	200	0.01					
0.4	200	0.01					
0.4	200	0.01					
0.4	200	0.01					

Table 10. Load flow results in per unit

Bus no.	Voltage	Angle (degree)	Load		Generation	
			P	Q	P	Q
1	1.03	0	0	0	7.2532	2.8008
2	1.01	-10.65	0	0	7	4.4762
3	1.03	27.292	0	0	7	1.7721
4	1.01	17.548	0	0	7	2.155
5	0.99159	-6.8112	0	0	0	0
6	0.94312	-17.7	0	0	0	0
7	0.89954	-27.012	17.67	2.5	0	0
8	1.0077	20.825	0	0	0	0
9	0.98122	10.774	0	0	0	0
10	0.96662	2.4251	9.67	1	0	0

This work was previously published in International Journal of Swarm Intelligence Research, Volume 1, Issue 3, edited by Yuhui Shi, pp. 1-18, copyright 2010 by IGI Publishing (an imprint of IGI Global)

Chapter 8
Compensation of Voltage Sags with Phase–Jumps through DVR with Minimum VA Rating Using PSO based ANFIS Controller

Anil Kumar Ramakuru
IIT MADRAS, India

Siva G. Kumar
IIT MADRAS, India

Kalyan B. Kumar
IIT MADRAS, India

Mahesh K. Mishra
IIT MADRAS, India

ABSTRACT

Dynamic Voltage Restorer (DVR) restores the distribution system load voltage to a nominal balanced sinusoidal voltage, when the source voltage has distortions, sag/swell and unbalances. DVR has to inject a required amount of Volt-Amperes (VA) into the system to maintain a nominal balanced sinusoidal voltage at the load. Keeping the cost effectiveness of DVR, it is desirable to have a minimum VA rating of the DVR, for a given system without compromising compensation capability. In this regard, a methodology has been proposed in this work to minimize VA rating of DVR. The optimal angle at which DVR voltage has to be injected in series to the line impedance so as to have minimum VA loading on DVR as well as the removal of phase jumps in the three-phases is computed by the Particle Swarm Optimization (PSO) technique. The proposed method is able to compensate voltage sags with phase jumps by keeping the DVR voltage and power ratings minimum, effectively. The proposed PSO methodology together with adaptive neuro–fuzzy inference system used to make the DVR work online with minimum VA loading. The proposed method has been validated through detailed simulation studies.

DOI: 10.4018/978-1-4666-1592-2.ch008

INTRODUCTION

Now-a-days, the need of the electrical power is increasing and simultaneously the problems while transmitting the power through the distribution system are also increasing. The consumers are ready to pay for a reliable and quality power. Majority of the problems occurring in the power system are due to the vagaries of the nature and switching on and off of the loads like induction motors connected (Bollen, 2001). The voltage related problems in a distribution network are harmonics, unbalances and sag/swell (Hingorani, 1995). The interest in voltage sags is mainly due to the problems they cause on several types of equipment i.e., adjustable-speed drives, process-control equipment and computers which are very sensitive for voltage. Any short circuit in a transmission system will cause a voltage dip (Nielsen & Blaabjerg, 2001). A short circuit in a power system not only causes a drop in voltage magnitude but also a change in the phase angle relation among the three-phases. This is referred to as phase-angle jump associated with the voltage sag. Phase-angle jumps during three-phase faults are due to the difference in X/R ratio between the source and the feeder. A second cause of phase-angle jumps is the transformation of sags to lower voltage levels (Ghosh & Ledwich, 2001). These problems will affect other sensitive loads of the distribution system. The problems in the distribution system are cleared using custom power devices. Dynamic Voltage Restorer (DVR) is a series connected; custom power device to mitigate the voltage sags with phase jumps. Some methodologies to compensate the voltage sags/swells with phase jumps using DVR are proposed by Nielsen and Blaabjerg (2001) and Ghosh and Ledwich (2001). VA rating minimization for economical operation was not addressed by these methods. In this work, a method is proposed to compensate, the voltage sag/swells with phase jumps by DVR with minimum VA rating. In order to compensate the voltage sag/swell with phase

jumps, the DVR has to inject required amount of Volt-Amperes (VA) into the system. The DVR VA rating is minimized in this work with out compromising its sag/swell compensating capability using particle swarm optimization technique. Since, particle swarm optimization (PSO) is an offline optimization technique; it cannot be used for online applications like DVR. Hence, a PSO based ANFIS is used to find the optimal voltage and angle of injection of DVR in real time for compensating sag/swell with phase-jumps, with minimum VA loading. The proposed methodology is applied on a distribution system and the detailed simulation results are presented.

DYNAMIC VOLTAGE RESTORER

A DVR is a power electronic device, connected in series to the feeder, to protect the loads from typical voltage problems in distribution system. The schematic diagram of a series compensated distribution system is shown in Figure 1. In Figure 1, the source voltage is represented by v_S. The terms L_S and R_S represent feeder inductance and resistance. The terminal voltage and load voltage are represented by v_t and v_p respectively. The DVR is realized by a voltage source inverter with DC capacitor voltage V_{dc} and power electronic switches S_1, S_2, S_3, S_4. The term L_{ts} represents the leakage inductance of the injection transformer and C_f represents the capacitance of the capacitor filter. The operating principle of the DVR is to inject a voltage (v_{DVR}) of required magnitude and phase to compensate sag/swell and distortion in the terminal voltage (v_t) and provide a balanced sinusoidal voltage (v_p) at the load. The reference DVR voltage to be injected (v_{DVR}) is realized by switching S_1, S_2, S_3, S_4 through hysteresis control (Woodley, Morgan, & Sundaram, 1999).

In literature, three methods are proposed to compensate voltage sags (Quirl & Johnson, 2006). These methods are,

Figure 1. Per phase representation of series compensated distribution system

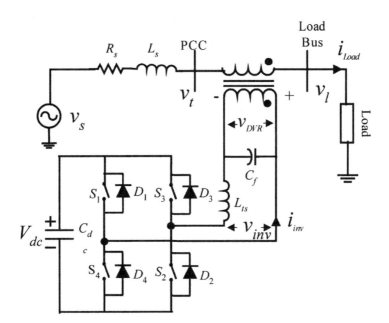

(i)   Pre-Sag compensation
(ii)   In-phase compensation
(iii) Phase advance compensation.

The three methods of compensation of voltage sags can be explained by using the phasor diagram given in Figure 2. Here $V_{S-presag}$ and V_{S-sag} represent the pre-sag and sag voltages of the source respectively. θ represents the phase angle jump, V_l is the load voltage obtained after compensation. ϕ represents the angle between load voltage and source sag voltage. V_{pre}, V_{in} and V_{opt} are the voltages that are injected by the DVR in the pre-sag, in-phase and proposed compensation methods.

Pre-Sag Compensation

In pre-sag compensation method, the DVR voltage (V_{pre}) is injected at an angle θ_{pre} with respect to sag voltage (V_{sag}) such that the vector sum of DVR injected voltage and sag voltage lead to a load voltage in phase with the pre-sag voltage ($V_{S-presag}$). In pre-sag injection method, maximum voltage

injection constraint on DVR limits the compensation even for less severe sags, accompanied with phase jumps (Choi, Li, & Vilathgamuwa, 2005).

In-Phase Compensation

In this method, the DVR injected voltage (V_{in}) is in-phase with that of the sag voltage (V_{S-sag}). In unbalanced sags, in-phase injection tries to restore the nominal load voltage magnitude along the same phase as that of source voltage. But, the active power consumption of DVR should not exceed certain value, since it increases the power rating of DVR. In spite of having maximum voltage boosting capability, this method does not remove the unbalance in three phase network, if the sag is accompanied by phase jumps.

Phase Advance Compensation

In pre-sag compensation and in phase compensation methods, the DVR is supposed to inject active power. This will increase the rating of the capaci-

Figure 2. Phasor diagram representing different compensation methods

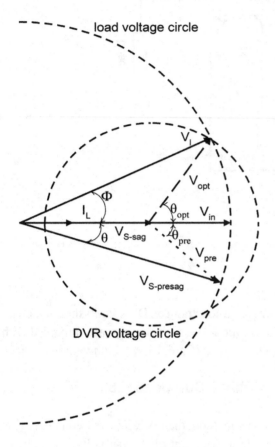

and at the same time the three-phase jumps along with sags/swells should be compensated. In the following section, an optimal function is formulated to minimize VA rating of DVR along with compensating the sag/swell with phase jumps.

DVR VA RATING MINIMIZATION

The rating of the DVR in a three phase system can be expressed as,

$$S_{DVR} = V_{DVR}^a I_{DVR}^a + V_{DVR}^b I_{DVR}^b + V_{DVR}^c I_{DVR}^c \qquad (1)$$

where, $V_{DVR}^{a,b,c}$, are the DVR injected a, b, c phase voltages and I_{DVR}^a, I_{DVR}^b and I_{DVR}^c are the currents through the DVR in each phase. An optimization technique has to be used to minimize the three phase DVR rating given in equation (1). While minimizing DVR rating, compensation of phase jumps should also be considered.

Consider a three phase distribution system as shown in Figure 1, where a three phase balanced voltage sag with phase jumps has occurred. The three-phase source voltages before sag, after sag and the load voltages after compensation through DVR are represented in the phasor diagram as shown in Figure 3.

In Figure 3, V_{sa}, V_{sb} and V_{sc} represent the three-phase pre-sag voltages, V_{sa}^s, V_{sb}^s and V_{sc}^s represent the three phase source sag voltages with phase jumps and V_{la}, V_{lb} and V_{lc} represent the three phase load voltages. The angles θ_a, θ_b and θ_c represent the phase jumps in three phase voltages and ϕ_a, ϕ_b and ϕ_c represent the phase angles of the three phase load voltages with respect to the three phase source sag voltages.

In order to compensate the phase jumps, following equality should hold,

$$\phi_a + \theta_a = \phi_b + \theta_b = \phi_c + \theta_c. \qquad (2)$$

tor which is more expensive. In phase advance compensation, the injected voltage is 90 degrees out of phase with that of the load current, due to which DVR active power supplied will become zero (Choi, Li, & Vilathgamuwa, 2000). In case of three-phase unbalanced voltage sags with phase jumps, the in-phase and phase advance compensation methods will fail (Kumar, Kumar, Kumar, & Mishra 2009). The phase jumps continue to exist in the load voltage and leads to a system with unbalanced load voltages.

A voltage is to be injected by the DVR in such a way that, its magnitude should be as less as possible since it increases the voltage rating

But, as the value of ϕ_a, ϕ_b and ϕ_c increases, the injected voltage magnitudes also increase, as shown in the Figure 3. If the injected voltage exceeds a certain value, the active power consumption of the DVR violates the power limit as explained in Ghosh and Ledwich (2001). Hence, the DVR voltages should not go beyond certain value, which is taken as 0.5 p.u. in this work. This imposes an inequality constraint,

$$abs(V_{DVR}^{a,b,c}) < 0.5 . \qquad (3)$$

Let the fundamental pre-sag source voltage be V_s, and then the fundamental sag source voltage V_s^{sag}, when x is per-unit sag, the following expression can be written.

$$V_s^{sag} = (1-x)V_s . \qquad (4)$$

The injected voltage can be calculated from the phasor diagram shown in Figure 3, using the law of cosines,

$$V_{DVR} = V_s\sqrt{1 + (1-x)^2 - 2(1-x)\cos\phi} . \qquad (5)$$

The angle at which it has to be injected is given by,

$$\alpha = a\tan\left\{\frac{\sin\theta}{\cos\theta - (1-x)}\right\} . \qquad (6)$$

The series active filter VA rating is given as follows.

$$S_{Se} = \sum_{i=a,b,c} V_{inj-i} I_{S2-i}$$
$$= \sum_{i=a,b,c} V_{Li} I_{Li}\left(\sqrt{1 + (1-x_i)^2 - 2(1-x_i)\cos\phi_i}\right) \qquad (7)$$

Thus, the total VA rating of DVR is function of x_i, ϕ_i, I_{Li} and rated fundamental voltage V_{Li}

. The load current is dependent on the load and cannot be controlled. In this function except ϕ_i, remaining all the variables are system dependants. Therefore, the function value i.e., total VA rating of DVR is controlled by varying ϕ_a, ϕ_b and ϕ_c. This can be expressed as a standard optimization problem as given below.

$$\left.\begin{array}{ll} \text{minimize} & f(\phi_i) = S_{DVR} \\ \text{subject to} & -90 < \phi_i < 90, \\ & abs(V_{DVR}^i) < 0.5 \\ \phi_a + \theta_a = \phi_b + \theta_b = \phi_c + \theta_c \\ & i = a,b,c \end{array}\right\} \qquad (8)$$

where, i represents the three phases, abs(V_{DVR}) represents the magnitude of the DVR injected voltage and ϕ_i is the control variable with respect to which the $f(\phi_i)$ has to be minimized. Particle swarm optimization (PSO) method is used in this work to minimize the function $f(\phi_i)$ with constraints given in equation (8). The PSO technique is explained in the following section.

PARTICLE SWARM OPTIMIZATION (PSO)

Particle swarm optimization (PSO) is a population based optimization technique that is originally inspired by the sociological behavior associated with bird flocking and fish schooling. Compared with traditional optimization algorithms, PSO does not need the information of the derivative of functions to be optimized (Kennedy & Eberhart, 1995) or (Shi & Eberhart, 1999) or (Eberhart & Shi, 1998). Unlike classical optimization techniques like gradient search methods, the PSO based optimization does not get stuck up at a local minimum but will always converge to a global minimum, if at all it exists. This algorithm can work as long as fitness values for optimization model can be calculated. Compared with the genetic algorithm,

Figure 3. Phasor diagram representing the three phase voltage sag with phase jumps and load voltages

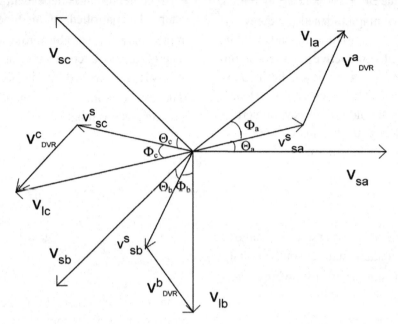

the advantage of PSO is that it is so simple in terms of mathematical expression and understanding. This PSO base technique is fast in converging to a solution when compared to genetic algorithm because of its mathematical simplicity.

In this method, particles are chosen to represent the possible solution of the function to be optimized. These particles are assigned random initial positions and velocities in search space. At each time step (iteration), the velocity of each particle is modified using its current velocity and its distance from pbest (each particle own best fitness value or local best) and gbest (best fitness value among the particles or global best) according to (Robinson & Rahmat-samii, 2004; Shi & Eberhart, 1998),

$$v_i^{k+1} = w v_i^k + c_1 * rand() * (pbest_i - s_i^k)$$
$$+ c_2 * rand() * (gbest_i - s_i^k) \qquad (9)$$

where,

v_i^k where i^{th} velocity component at iteration k
$rand()$ random number between 0 and 1

s_i^k current position in the ith dimension
c_1, c_2 acceleration coefficients.

After the velocity update is done, each particle is allowed to explore the search space of the problem for a better solution as follows:

$$s_i^{k+1} = s_i^k + v_i^{k+1} \qquad (10)$$

The personal best position is updated after the kth iteration according to

$$pbest^{k+1} = \begin{cases} pbest^k & \text{iff} \quad f(s^{k+1}) \geq f(pbest^k) \\ s^{k+1} & \text{iff} \quad f(s^{k+1}) < f(pbest^k) \end{cases} \qquad (11)$$

The global best position among the particles personal best position is updated after the kth iteration as given follows.

$$gbest^{k+1} = \begin{cases} pbest^{k+1} & \text{iff} \quad f(pbest^{k+1}) \leq f(gbest^k) \\ gbest^k & \text{iff} \quad f(pbest^{k+1}) > f(gbest^k) \end{cases} \qquad (12)$$

Inertia weight and acceleration coefficients are the only parameters to be adjusted. For the value of inertia weight (w), it is assumed to decrease linearly during the course of the simulation from 0.95 to 0.4 according to

$$w = w_{max} - \left(\frac{w_{max} - w_{min}}{iter_{max} - 1}\right) * \left(iter - 1\right) \qquad (13)$$

where,

w inertia weight for current iteration
w_{min} is the minimum inertia weight
w_{max} is the maximum inertia weight
$iter$ current iteration
$iter_{max}$ total number of iterations.

Using PSO, the rating of the DVR can be minimized but it cannot work for online conditions because the voltage sag appears only for few cycles and the distribution system will retain its original value after the sag disappears. Hence the DVR should dynamically solve the problem of voltage sags with phase jumps. This can be accomplished using adaptive neural network techniques (ANFIS). The ANFIS is one of the adaptive neural techniques which is used to make the above mentioned PSO system applicable to real time implementation of the DVR.

ADAPTIVE NEURO-FUZZY INFERENCE SYSTEM (ANFIS)

Fuzzy inference is the process of formulating the mapping from a given input to an output using fuzzy logic. The basic method involves converting inputs into fuzzy sets through membership functions. This process is called as fuzzification. On the basis of weighed fuzzified inputs, rules are framed. The outcome of the rules is defuzzified to get the actual output. Mamdani and Sugeno are two types of such fuzzy inference systems. ANFIS utilizes the Sugeno type fuzzy inference system.

ANFIS requires a set of input data and output data. It provides a set of membership functions for mapping the input data to output. The membership function chosen should be able to minimize the error between the actual output data and ANFIS input mapped output data. The parameters associated with the membership functions will change through the learning process.

ANFIS Architecture

An adaptive network is a feedforward network structure consisting of nodes and links connecting the nodes. Each node performs a particular function on incoming signals as well as a set of parameters of that node. Some of the nodes are adaptive which means, the node parameters are dependent on the other nodes where as some of the nodes are fixed nodes, where the node parameters are independent. The node function and node output are represented by O_i^k and is given by the following expression,

$$O_i^k = O_i^k(O_1^{k-1}, ...O_{\#k-1}^{k-1}, ..., a, b, c...) \qquad (14)$$

where, O_i^k is the output node at the ith node of the kth layer. O_i^{k-1}, O_i^{k-2} are the incoming signals, and a, b, c are the parameters (Jang, 1993).

For simplicity, the fuzzy inference system is considered to have two inputs x, y and one output z as proposed by Takagi and Sugeno (1983). The ANFIS structure for Sugeno type (Type 3) fuzzy inference system is given in Figure 4. The rules are given as follows.

Rule 1: If x is A1 and y is B1 then f1 = p1x + q1y + r1

Rule 2: If x is A2 and y is B2 then f2 = p2x + q2y + r2

Figure 4. Sugeno type ANFIS structure

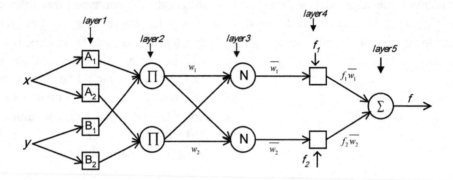

For the above fuzzy inference system, the node functions at each layer can be explained as follows.

Layer 1: In this layer, the node is represented by square node. The node function is nothing but the membership function which specifies the degree to which the given x satisfies the linguistic label associated with this node function (A_i).

$$O_i^1 = \mu_{A_i}(x) \tag{15}$$

The membership function can be any continuous and piecewise differential functions such as, trapezoidal, pi, sigma and Gaussian membership functions (Wang, 1992; Wang & Mendel, 1992). Parameters in this layer are referred as premise parameters.

Layer 2: The function of this node is to multiply the incoming signals and send to third layer. This can be expressed as follows,

$$w_i = \mu_{A_i}(x) \times \mu_{B_i}(y), \ i = 1, 2 \tag{16}$$

Layer 3: The node in this layer is a circular node and the ith node calculates the ratio of the ith rule firing strength to the sum of all rules firing strengths.

$$\overline{w_i} = \frac{w_i}{w_1 + w_2}, \ i = 1, 2 \tag{17}$$

Layer 4: This node is a square node with function given as,

$$O_i^4 = \overline{w_i} f_i \tag{18}$$

Parameters in the above function are called consequent parameters.

Layer 5: The node in this layer is a circular node which gives final output. The function is given as,

Final output, $O_i^5 = \sum_i \overline{w_i} f_i$ (19)

For a given training data with P entries the error measure for the pth entry ($1 <= p <= P$) of the data can be expressed using an error function given by,

$$E_p = \sum_{m=1}^{l} (O_{mp}^l - T_{mp})^2 \tag{20}$$

Where O_{mp}^l is the mth component of the actual output vector obtained after presenting p^{th} input, T_{mp} is the mth component of the target output vector and l represents the total number of layers.

The overall error measure for all the p entries is given by,

$$E = \sum_{p=1}^{P} E_p. \tag{21}$$

Now if α is a parameter of the given adaptive network, then the update formula for the generic parameter can be given by,

$$\Delta\alpha = -\eta \frac{\partial E_p}{\partial \alpha} \qquad (22)$$

in which η is the learning rate and

$$\frac{\partial E_p}{\partial \alpha} = \sum_{o^* \in S} \frac{\partial E_p}{\partial O^*} \frac{\partial O^*}{\partial S} \qquad (23)$$

where S is the set of the nodes whose output is dependent on parameter α. The above type of updating is referred to as pattern learning (online learning). In the case of offline learning, the update action takes place only after the whole training data set is presented. For the offline learning the update formula is given by,

$$\frac{\partial E}{\partial \alpha} = \sum_{p=1}^{P} \frac{\partial E_p}{\partial \alpha} \qquad (24)$$

STATE SPACE MODEL OF DVR

Consider the DVR structure as shown in the Figure 1. In order to express the dynamics of the above series compensated system in state space form, a state vector is defined below.

$$x^T = \begin{bmatrix} v_f & i_o \end{bmatrix}$$

for this state vector the state space model of the system given in Figure 1 can be written as

$$\dot{x} = \begin{bmatrix} 0 & 1/C_f \\ -1/L_T & -R_{in}/L_T \end{bmatrix} x + \begin{bmatrix} 0 & -1/C_f \\ V_{dc}/L_T & 0 \end{bmatrix} \begin{bmatrix} u \\ i_s \end{bmatrix} \qquad (25)$$

where, L_T denotes the leakage inductance of the transformer, C_f is the capacitance of the filter capacitor and R_{in} denotes the switching losses of each inverter. The term u is the switching logic with a value of +1 or -1.

Deadbeat Control

The state space model given in (25) can be discretized as,

$$x(k+1) = Fx(k) + Gu(k) \qquad (26)$$

F and G are in matrix form. The output variable is taken as v_r. Defining the elements of the matrix F as f_{ij} and G as g_{ij}, then,

$$F = \begin{bmatrix} f_{11} & f_{12} \\ f_{21} & f_{22} \end{bmatrix} \text{ and } G = \begin{bmatrix} g_{11} & g_{12} \\ g_{21} & g_{22} \end{bmatrix}. \qquad (27)$$

The above equation is converted into the discrete form,

$$v_r(k+1) = f_{11}v_r(k) + f_{12}i_o(k) + g_{11}u(k) + g_{12}i_s(k). \qquad (28)$$

The value of $u(k)$ is obtained by minimizing the cost function given below.

$$J = \left\{ v_r(k) - v_{ref}(k) \right\}^2$$

The minimization results in the following equation,

$$u(k) = \frac{-v_{ref}(k+1) + f_{11}v_r(k) + f_{12}i_o(k) + g_{12}i_s(k)}{2g_{11}} \qquad (29)$$

The control variable $u(k)$ is used as a switching controller for the voltage source inverter. The reference voltage and switching control scheme are discussed below.

Reference Voltage Generation

The DVR reference voltage as considered in the equations (5), (6) is calculated from the Figure 3. The reference voltage during the sag interval is calculated separately and is given by,

$$v_{ref} = v_{sag} + v_{DVR}. \tag{30}$$

where, v_{sag} is the source sag voltage and v_{DVR} is the DVR injected voltage which is calculated in the previous section (DVR VA rating minimization). The switching control scheme is explained in the next section.

Switching Control Scheme

The inverter output voltages $+V_{dc}$ and $-V_{dc}$ are referred to be the switching states +1 and −1 respectively. The switching control is done using the concept of hysteresis band control by using the following relationships,

$$if\ u(k) > h, \quad sw = +1 \\ and\ if\ u(k) < -h, \quad sw = -1 \tag{31}$$

where, h is the hysteresis band magnitude prespecified and sw is the switching state (Jowder, 2007).

SIMULATION STUDIES

Simulation study is carried out for the power distribution system shown in Figure 1. The system parameters for simulation studies are given in Table 1.

A three-phase balanced voltage sag with phase jumps is created. Voltage sag of 20% with phase jumps of 10, 12, and 14 degrees in the three

phases is considered during the time interval 0.06 s to 0.12 s. The load is considered to be linear. The PCC voltage without compensation is shown in the Figure 5. An optimization function as given in equation (8) is formulated for the system parameters given in Table 1. The PSO method is used to optimize the function with constraints. The PSO parameters used in simulation are summarized in Table 2.

The optimal DVR injected voltages and angles along with the DVR VA rating obtained from PSO and pre-sag compensation are given in Table 3.

It can be observed from Table 3 that the VA rating of DVR with pre-sag compensation is 0.232 p.u. higher than PSO based compensation. Also, the voltage injected by the DVR is shown in the Figure 6. The reference values are calculated by the deadbeat control method (Ghosh & Ledwich, 2001). It can be observed from Figure 7 that the load voltage during sag after compensation is at its nominal voltage and perfectly balanced.

Using PSO method, the sag cannot be compensated online. Using an ANFIS controller the problem can be solved. Data collected in different operating conditions with different voltage sags and phase jumps as inputs and DVR injected voltages calculated using PSO as outputs are given as training data to the ANFIS. For three outputs, three ANFISs are used. Few samples of the training data given to ANFIS is tabulated in Table 4.

A set of 200 samples of data having different magnitudes of voltage sags and phase jumps and corresponding DVR injected voltage phase angles obtained from PSO are given to train the ANFIS Controller. The ANFIS is checked with different membership functions like triangular, trapezoidal, pi, sigma, and gauss membership functions. The error is minimum with gauss membership function. With the above mentioned membership function, the ANFIS is trained for given number of epochs. As the number of epochs increases the error reduces. After the first epoch, the training error is around 0.08 and it has reached 0.04 by

Table 1. System parameters

System Parameters	Values
System voltage	282 V (peak)
Loads	Z_a =80+j59.66 Ω, Z_b =100 + j 79.75 Ω, Z_c = 40 + j 100 Ω
Feeder impedance	Z_{sa} = 2 + j 120 Ω, Z_{sb} = 2 + j 12 Ω, Z_{sc} = 2 + j 12.089 Ω
Control signal hysteresis band (lim)	.01
Filter capacitor	C_d=80 μF
Filter Inductance	L_d= 0.0127 H, R_d= 6 ohms

Table 2. PSO parameters

Parameter	Value
no of particles	30
maximum inertia weight	0.95
minimum inertia weight	0.4
number of iterations	100
c_1 and c_2	1.43

Figure 5. Source voltage with sag

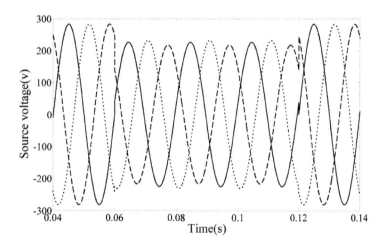

Table 3. Comparison between PSO and pre-sag compensation methods

	Voltage Sag in p.u. in phases			Phase Jumps in phases			DVR injected voltages in p.u. using proposed pso and pre-sag methods						DVR Rating In p.u.
	a	*B*	*c*	*a*	*b*	*c*	V_{inj}^a	α_a α_a (deg)	V_{inj}^b	α_b (deg)	V_{inj}^c	α_c (deg)	
PSO	0.8	0.8	0.8	10	12	14	0.2032	2.83	0.2000	0.336	0.2018	-2.165	0.6055
presag	0.8	0.8	0.8	10	12	14	0.2535	-33.21	0.2738	-37.41	0.2958	-40.85	0.823

Figure 6. DVR injected voltage

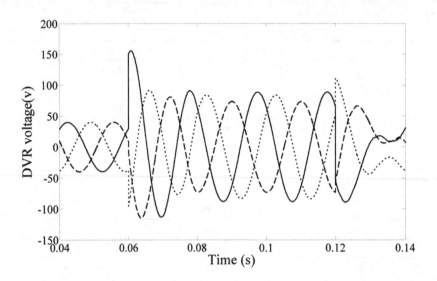

Figure 7. Load voltages after compensation

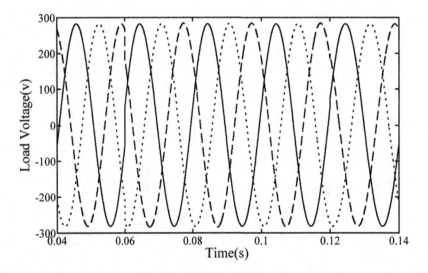

the end of tenth epoch. A graph displaying the training error for each epoch can be seen in Figure 8.

After training the ANFIS, the ANFIS is tested with given data. The DVR injected voltages obtained from ANFIS controller and presag compensation for different testing data are compared. The simulation results obtained using ANFIS controller and presag compensation are tabulated in Table 5 and Table 6 respectively.

A threshold of 45% sag is considered with phase jumps of 10, 12 and 14 degrees and the DVR rating obtained is 1.3524 p.u. using proposed method whereas the VA rating of DVR obtained through pre-sag compensation with the same system parameters is 1.429 p.u.. This is 5.1%

Table 4. Training data given to ANFIS

Voltage Sag in p.u. in phases			Phase Jump in phases			DVR series injected voltage phase angles from PSO		
a	b	c	a	b	c	α_a (deg)	α_b (deg)	α_c (deg)
0.6	0.6	0.6	25	10	5	-21.1587	4.5007	12.9837
0.7	0.7	0.7	2	10	10	7.5544	-3.914	-3.914
0.8	0.8	0.8	25	10	5	-15.3687	3.6981	10.0324
0.9	0.9	0.9	10	2	10	-2.5581	6.3568	-2.5581
0.6	0.6	0.6	15	5	10	-8.5344	8.2174	-0.1561

Table 5. DVR injected voltages with ANFIS controller

Voltage Sag in p.u. in phases			Phase Jump in phases			DVR injected voltages in p.u. using proposed pso based ANFIS controller						DVR Rating in p.u.
a	b	c	a	b	c	V_{inj}^a	α_a (deg)	V_{inj}^b	α_b (deg)	V_{inj}^c	α_c (deg)	
0.8	0.8	0.8	10	12	14	0.2032	2.83	0.2000	0.336	0.2018	-2.165	0.6055
0.7	0.7	0.7	10	12	14	0.3046	5.195	0.3009	2.327	0.3000	-0.531	0.9057
0.6	0.6	0.6	10	12	14	0.4011	3.594	0.4000	0.258	0.4008	-3.077	1.2019
0.55	0.55	0.55	10	12	14	0.4501	1.3242	0.4503	-2.313	0.4520	-5.9644	1.3524

Table 6. DVR injected voltages using presag method

Voltage Sag in p.u. in phases			Phase Jump in phases			DVR injected voltages in p.u. using pre-sag compensation						DVR Rating in p.u.
a	b	c	a	b	c	V_{inj}^a	α_a (deg)	V_{inj}^b	α_b (deg)	V_{inj}^c	α_c (deg)	
0.8	0.8	0.8	10	12	14	0.2535	-33.21	0.2738	-37.41	0.2958	-40.85	0.823
0.7	0.7	0.7	10	12	14	0.3336	-21.37	0.347	-24.77	0.3627	-27.82	1.0433
0.6	0.6	0.6	10	12	14	0.422	-14.28	0.4315	-16.80	0.442	-19.16	1.2955
0.55	0.55	0.55	10	12	14	0.4682	-11.77	0.4759	-13.90	0.4849	-15.92	1.429

higher than the DVR rating obtained through the proposed method. The VA rating obtained using proposed method for 20% sag with phase-jumps of 10, 12 and 14 degrees is 0.6055 whereas the VA rating obtained that of pre-sag compensation with the same system parameters is 0.823. This is 14.5% higher than the rating obtained using proposed method. This clearly shows that the proposed method will lead to an optimal VA rat-

ing of DVR simultaneously compensating sags with phase jump.

CONCLUSION

A new methodology is proposed to minimize the DVR rating during voltage sags with phase jumps in a three phase distribution system using Particle

Figure 8. Plot representing training error with respect to epochs

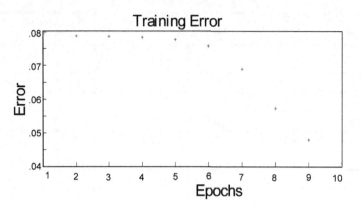

swarm optimization. Simulations were done on a three-phase distribution system and the results were presented. PSO based methodology is made applicable online by implementation of adaptive-neuro fuzzy controller (ANFIS). The DVR rating for different sag depths using the proposed method is studied thoroughly.

The VA rating of DVR with the proposed method is also compared with that of pre-sag compensation. It was observed that for a sag depth of 20% the VA rating of DVR computed by pre-sag compensation method was 14.1% higher as compared to proposed method. The load voltages after compensation with the proposed method were perfectly balanced and have nominal reference rms values.

ACKNOWLEDGMENT

We sincerely acknowledge the financial support given by Department of Science and Technology, India (Project No. DST:SR/S3/EECE/048/2008).

REFERENCES

Bollen, M. H. J. (2001). *Understanding Power Quality Problems: Voltage Sags and Interruptions*. Washington, DC: IEEE Press.

Choi, S. S., Li, B. H., & Vilathgamuwa, D. M. (2000). Dynamic voltage restoration with minimum energy injection. *IEEE Transactions on Power Systems*, *15*(1), 51–57. doi:10.1109/59.852100

Choi, S. S., Li, J. D., & Vilathgamuwa, D. M. (2005). A generalized voltage compensation strategy for mitigating the impacts of voltage sags/swells. *IEEE Transactions on Power Delivery*, *20*(3), 2289–2297. doi:10.1109/TP-WRD.2005.848442

Eberhart, R. C., & Shi, Y. (1998). Comparison between Genetic Algorithm and Particle swarm optimization. In *Proceedings of 7th annual conference on evolutionary programming VII*, San Diego, CA (pp. 611-616).

Ghosh, A., & Ledwich, G. (2001). Structures and control of dynamic voltage restorer. *Power Engineering Society Winter Meeting, 3*, 1027-1032.

Ghosh, A., & Ledwich, G. (2002). *Power Quality Enhancement Using Custom Power Devices*. Dordrecht, The Netherlands: Kluwer.

Hingorani, N. G. (1995). Introducing custom power. *IEEE Spectrum*, 41–48. doi:10.1109/6.387140

Jang, J. S. R. (1993). ANFIS: adaptive-network-based fuzzy inference system. *IEEE Transactions on Systems, Man, and Cybernetics*, *23*(3), 665–685. doi:10.1109/21.256541

Jowder, F. A. L. (2007). Modeling and simulation of Dynamic Voltage Restorer (DVR) based on Hysteresis Voltage Control. In *Proceedings of the Industrial Electronics Society, IECON 2007, 33rd Annual conference of IEEE* (pp. 1726-1731).

Kennedy, J., & Eberhart, R. (1995). Particle swarm optimization. In *Proceedings of IEEE international conference on neural networks, IEEE service centre,* Piscataway, NJ (Vol. 4, pp. 1942-1948).

Kumar, R. A., Kumar, G. S., Kumar, B. K., & Mishra, M. K. (2009). Compensation of voltage sags with phase-jumps through DVR with minimum VA rating using PSO. In *Proceedings of TENCON 2009-2009 IEEE Region 10 conference* (pp. 1-6).

Nielsen, J. G., & Blaabjerg, F. (2001). Control Strategies for dynamic voltage restorer compensating voltage sags with phase jump. In *Proceedings of the Sixteenth Annual IEEE, Applied Power Electronics Conference and Exposition* (Vol. 2, pp. 1267-1273).

Quirl, B. J., Johnson, B. K., & Hess, H. L. (2006). Mitigation of voltage sags with phase jump using a dynamic voltage restorer. In *Proceedings of the Power Symposium 2006, NAPS 2006, 38th North American* (pp. 647-654).

Robinson, J., & Rahmat-Samii, Y. (2004). Particle swarm optimization in electromagnetics. *IEEE Transactions on Antennas and Propagation, 52*(2), 397–407. doi:10.1109/TAP.2004.823969

Shi, Y., & Eberhart, R. (1998). A modified particle swarm optimizer. *Evolutionary Computer Proceedings, IEEE International conference* (pp. 69-73).

Shi, Y., & Eberhart, R. C. (1999). Empirical study of Particle Swarm Optimization. In *Proceedings of the 1999 Congress on Evolutionary Computation* (CEC 99).

Takagi, T., & Sugeno, M. (1983). Derivation of fuzzy control rules from human operator's control actions. In *Proceedings of the IFAC Symp. Fuzzy Inform., Knowledge Representation and Decision Analysis* (pp. 55-60).

Wang, L.-X. (1992). Fuzzy systems are universal approximators. In *Proceedings of the Fuzzy Systems, IEEE international conference* (pp. 1163-1170).

Wang, L.-X., & Mendel, J. M. (1992). Fuzzy basis function, universal approximation, and orthogonal least squares learning. *IEEE Transactions on Neural Networks, 3*(5), 807–814. doi:10.1109/72.159070

Woodley, N. H., Morgan, L., & Sundaram, A. (1999). Experience with an inverter-based dynamic voltage restorer. *IEEE Transactions on Power Delivery, 14*(3), 1181–1186. doi:10.1109/61.772390

This work was previously published in International Journal of Swarm Intelligence Research, Volume 1, Issue 3, edited by Yuhui Shi, pp. 19-33, copyright 2010 by IGI Publishing (an imprint of IGI Global)

Chapter 9

Optimal Power Flow with TCSC and TCPS Modeling using Craziness and Turbulent Crazy Particle Swarm Optimization

P. K. Roy
National Institute of Technology

S. P. Ghoshal
National Institute of Technology

S. S. Thakur
National Institute of Technology

ABSTRACT

This paper presents two new Particle swarm optimization methods to solve optimal power flow (OPF) in power system incorporating flexible AC transmission systems (FACTS). Two types of FACTS devices, thyristor-controlled series capacitor (TCSC) and thyristor controlled phase shifting (TCPS), are considered. In this paper, the problems of OPF with FACTS are solved by using particle swarm optimization with the inertia weight approach (PSOIWA), real coded genetic algorithm (RGA), craziness based particle swarm optimization (CRPSO), and turbulent crazy particle swarm optimization (TRPSO). The proposed methods are implemented on modified IEEE 30-bus system for four different cases. The simulation results show better solution quality and computation efficiency of TRPSO and CRPSO algorithms over PSOIWA and RGA. The study also shows that FACTS devices are capable of providing an economically attractive solution to OPF problems.

DOI: 10.4018/978-1-4666-1592-2.ch009

INTRODUCTION

Flexible AC transmission systems (FACTS) devices are integrated in power systems to control power flow, increase transmission line capability to its thermal limit, and improve the security of transmission systems. In addition to controlling the power flow in specific lines, FACTS devices could be used to minimize the total generator fuel cost in optimal power flow (OPF) problem. In OPF the main objective is to minimize the costs of meeting the load demand for the power system while satisfying all the security constraints. Traditional optimization techniques such as linear Programming (Taranto, Pinto, & Pereira, 1992; Ge & Chung, 1998; Ge & Chung, 1999), Newton Rapshon method (Fuerte-Esquivel, Acha, Tan, & Rico, 1998; Fuerte-Esquivel, Acha, & Ambriz-Perez, 2000a; Fuerte-Esquivel, Acha, & Ambriz-Perez, 2000b) and Newton's method (Ambriz-Perez, Acha, Fuerte-Esquivel, & De la Torre, 1998; Ambriz-Perez, Acha, & Fuerte-Esquivel, 2000) are used to solve the problem of OPF with FACTS assuming continuous, differentiable and monotonically increasing cost function. However, these methods have failed in handling non-convex and nonlinear engineering optimization problems and tend to get stuck at local optimum solutions. Since OPF incorporating FACTS devices with valve point discontinuities is a highly non-linear problem with non-differentiable feature, stochastic search algorithms such as GA (Ippolito, Cortiglia, & Petrocelli, 2006; Chung & Li, 2001; Cai & Erlich, 2003; Leung & Chung, 2000; Narmatha Banu & Devaraj, 2008), particle swarm optimization (PSO) (Benabid, Boudour, & Abido, 2009; Hu & Eberhart, 2002; Mollazei, Farsangi, Nezamabadi-pour, & Lee, 2007; Saravanan, Slochanal, Venkatesh, Stephen, & Abraham, 2007), differential evolution (DE) (Basu, 2008), tabu search (TS) & simulated annealing (SA) (Bhasaputra & Ongsakul, 2002), evolutionary programming (EP) (Ma, 2003), ant colony optimization (ACO) (Song, Chou, & Stonham, 1999) and bacteria foraging optimization (BFO) (Ghoshal, Chatterjee, & Mukherjee, 2009) are used as techniques to solve problems of OPF incorporating FACTS.

Amongst the above population based algorithms, the annealing schedule of SA should be tuned carefully; otherwise it may produce suboptimal solutions. The GA method is usually faster than SA method because GA has parallel search technique. Traditional GA also differs from EP in two aspects; EP primarily relies on mutation and selection, but no crossover like traditional GA and EP uses the real values of control parameters but not their coding as in traditional GA. Hence, considerable computation time may be saved in EP. Real coded GA (RGA) (Gaing & Huang, 2004) has been introduced to solve the OPF problems more efficiently with significant reduction in the computation time. ACO is based on foraging behavior of ant species. Solution candidates, called ants in ACO, communicate with other members of the ant colony by depositing pheromone to mark a path. High concentrations of pheromones indicate more favorable paths that other members should follow in order to reach the optimal solution. BFO is a bio-inspired technique, applied to solve power system optimization problems by Ghoshal et al. (Ghoshal, Chatterjee, & Mukherjee, 2009), but its optimization time is very high. PSO is one of the modern heuristic algorithms and has a great potential to solve complex optimization problems. PSO algorithm is highly robust yet remarkably simple to implement Thus, it has become usual to apply the PSO, with more new modifications (Roy, Ghoshal, & Thakur, 2009a; Roy, Ghoshal, & Thakur, 2009b) in velocity, to achieve better optimization and handle the power system problems more efficiently. But conventional PSO also suffers from achieving the global best solution in possible shortest time.

In this paper two new PSO algorithms have been employed which are more effective and capable of solving nonlinear optimization problems faster and with better accuracy in detecting the

Figure 1. Circuit model of TCSC connected between i^{th} bus and j^{th} bus

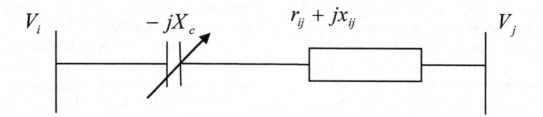

global best solution. The new PSO algorithms (TRPSO and CRPSO) are implemented to minimize the generator fuel cost in optimal power flow with multiple type FACTS devices. Modified IEEE 30-bus system with single and multiple TCSC and TCPS devices in different locations are presented to show the algorithms' flexibility and reliability towards the convergence. The results obtained by the proposed PSO algorithms are compared to the results of PSOIWA and RGA to establish the optimization superiority of the proposed algorithms.

STATIC MODEL OF FACTS DEVICES

Static models of the FACTS devices that are used in this work are described below.

Thyristor Controlled Series Compensator (TCSC)

The effect of TCSC on a network may be represented by a controllable reactance inserted in the related transmission line. Active power flow through the compensated transmission line can be maintained at a specified level under a wide range of operating conditions. The static model of the network with TCSC placed in transmission line that connected between the ith bus and j^{th} bus is shown in Figure 1.

The power flow equations of the branch having TCSC can be derived as follows:

$$P_{ij} = V_i^2 g_{ij} - V_i V_j \left(g_{ij} \cos \partial_{ij} + b_{ij} \sin \partial_{ij} \right) \quad (1)$$

$$Q_{ij} = -V_i^2 b_{ij} - V_i V_j \left(g_{ij} \sin \partial_{ij} - b_{ij} \cos \partial_{ij} \right) \quad (2)$$

Where $g_{ij} = \dfrac{r_{ij}}{r_{ij}^2 + \left(x_{ij} - x_c \right)^2}$ and

$b_{ij} = \dfrac{\left(x_{ij} - x_c \right)}{r_{mn}^2 + \left(x_{ij} - x_c \right)^2}$

P_{ij}, Q_{ij}: active and reactive power flows respectively from i^{th} bus to j^{th} bus,

V_i, V_j: voltage magnitudes at i^{th} bus and j^{th} bus respectively,

∂_{ij}: the angle deference between i^{th} bus and j^{th} bus voltages,

r_{ij}, x_{ij}: resistance and reactance respectively of line that connected between i^{th} bus and j^{th} bus,

x_c: reactance of TCSC placed in transmission line that connected between m^{th} bus and n^{th} bus.

Thyristor Controlled Phase Shifter (TCPS)

The static model of a TCPS connected between i^{th} bus and j^{th} bus, having a complex tapping ratio, $1:1\angle\alpha$ and series admittance of $y_{ij} = \left(g_{ij} - jb_{ij} \right)$ of the transformer is shown in Figure 2.

The real and reactive power flows from i^{th} bus to j^{th} bus may be expressed as:

Figure 2. Circuit model of TCPS connected between i^{th} bus and j^{th} bus

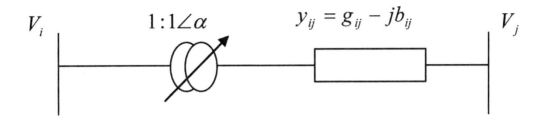

Figure 3. Injected power model of TCPS connected between bus and bus

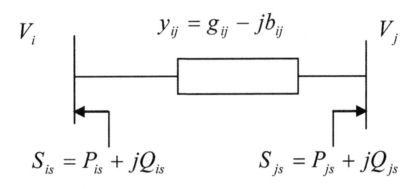

$$P_{ij} = \frac{V_i^2 g_{ij}}{a^2} - \frac{V_i V_j}{a}\left[g_{ij}\cos\left(\partial_{ij} + \alpha\right) + b_{ij}\sin\left(\partial_{ij} + \alpha\right)\right]$$

(3)

$$Q_{ij} = -\frac{V_i^2 B_{ij}}{a^2} - \frac{V_i V_j}{a}\left[g_{ij}\sin\left(\partial_{ij} + \alpha\right) - b_{ij}\cos\left(\partial_{ij} + \alpha\right)\right]$$

(4)

Similarly, the real and reactive power flows from j^{th} bus to i^{th} bus may be expressed as follows:

$$P_{ji} = V_j^2 g_{ij} - \frac{V_i V_j}{a}\left[g_{ij}\cos\left(\partial_{ij} + \alpha\right) - b_{ij}\sin\left(\partial_{ij} + \alpha\right)\right]$$

(5)

$$Q_{ji} = -V_j^2 b_{ij} + \frac{V_i V_j}{a}\left[g_{ij}\sin\left(\partial_{ij} + \alpha\right) + b_{ij}\cos\left(\partial_{ij} + \alpha\right)\right]$$

(6)

where $a = \cos\alpha$

The injected power model of TCPS is shown in Figure 3.

The injected real and reactive powers of TCPS at i^{th} bus and j^{th} bus are as follow:

$$P_{is} = -k^2 V_i^2 g_{ij} - k V_i V_j\left[g_{ij}\sin\left(\partial_{ij}\right) - b_{ij}\cos\left(\partial_{ij}\right)\right]$$

(7)

$$Q_{is} = k^2 V_i^2 b_{ij} + k V_i V_j\left[g_{ij}\cos\left(\partial_{ij}\right) + b_{ij}\sin\left(\partial_{ij}\right)\right]$$

(8)

$$P_{js} = -kV_iV_j\left[g_{ij}\sin(\partial_{ij}) + b_{ij}\cos(\partial_{ij})\right] \quad (9)$$

$$Q_{js} = -kV_iV_j\left[g_{ij}\cos(\partial_{ij}) - b_{ij}\sin(\partial_{ij})\right] \quad (10)$$

where $k = \tan\alpha$,

g_{ij}, b_{ij} : conductance and susceptance of transmission line connected between i^{th} bus and j^{th} bus.

MATHEMATICAL PROBLEM FORMULATION

Objective Function

The conventional formulation of OPF problem with TCSC and TCPS determines the optimal settings of control variables such as real power generations, generators' terminal voltages, transformers' tap settings, reactive power injections of shunt regulators, reactance value of TCSC and phase shifting angle of TCPS while minimizing the total fuel cost while satisfying all equality and inequality constraints. Total fuel cost of generating units having quadratic cost function is given by:

$$FC = \sum_{i=1}^{NG}\left(a_iP_{gi}^2 + b_iP_{gi} + c_i\right) \quad (11)$$

For more practical and accurate model of the cost function, multiple valve steam turbines are incorporated for flexible operational facilities. Total generation cost of generating units with valve point discontinuities is given by:

$$FC = \sum_{i=1}^{NG}a_iP_{gi}^2 + b_iP_{gi} + c_i + \left|d_i \times \sin\left(e_i \times \left(P_{gi_{min}} - P_{gi}\right)\right)\right| \quad (12)$$

where a_i, b_i, c_i, d_i, e_i : cost coefficients of ith generator,

P_{gi} : active power generation of ith generator,

$P_{gi_{min}}$: minimum active power generation limit of ith generator.

Constraints

The OPF with TCSC and TCPS is subjected to the following constraints.

Equality Constraints

These constraints represent the load flow equations as given below:

$$\begin{cases} \sum_{i=1}^{nb}(P_{gi} - P_{li}) + \sum_{i=1}^{ntcps}P_{is} = \sum_{i=1}^{nb}\sum_{j=1}^{nb}|V_i||V_j||Y_{ij}|Cos(\theta_{ij} - \delta_{ij}) \\ \sum_{i=1}^{nb}Q_{gi} - Q_{li} + \sum_{i=1}^{ntcpsS}Q_{is} = -\sum_{i=1}^{nb}\sum_{j=1}^{nb}|V_i||V_j||Y_{ij}|Sin(\theta_{ij} - \delta_{ij}) \end{cases} \quad (13)$$

P_{li} : active power demand of ith bus,

Q_{gi}, Q_{li} : reactive power generation and demand respectively of ith bus,

P_{is}, Q_{is} : injected active and reactive powers respectively of TCPS at i^{th} bus,

Y_{ij} : admittance of transmission line connected between i^{th} bus and j^{th} bus,

θ_{ij} : admittance angle of transmission line connected between i^{th} bus and j^{th} bus,

nb : number of buses, $ntcps$: number of TCPS.

INEQUALITY CONSTRAINTS

Generator Constraints:

$$\begin{cases} V_{gi_{\min}} \le V_{gi} \le V_{gi_{\max}} \\[2mm] P_{gi_{\min}} \le P_{gi} \le P_{gi_{\max}} \qquad i \in ng \\[2mm] Q_{gi_{\min}} \le Q_{gi} \le Q_{gi_{\max}} \end{cases} \qquad (14)$$

Load Bus Constraint:

$$V_{li_{\min}} \le V_{li} \le V_{li_{\max}} \qquad i \in nl \qquad (15)$$

Transmission Line Constraint:

$$S_{Li} \le S_{Li_{\max}} \qquad i \in ntl \qquad (16)$$

Transformer tap Constraint:

$$T_{i_{\min}} \le T_i \le T_{i_{\max}} \qquad i \in nt \qquad (17)$$

Shunt Compensator Constraint:

$$Q_{ci_{\min}} \le Q_{ci} \le Q_{ci_{\max}} \qquad i \in nc \qquad (18)$$

TCSC reactance constraint:

$$X_{ci_{\min}} \le X_{ci} \le X_{ci_{\max}} \qquad i \in nt\,\mathrm{csc} \qquad (19)$$

TCPS phase shift constraint:

$$\alpha_{i_{\min}} \le \alpha_i \le \alpha_{i_{\max}} \qquad i \in ntcps \qquad (20)$$

where $V_{gi_{\min}}, V_{gi_{\max}}$: minimum and maximum voltage limits respectively of ith generator bus,

$P_{gi_{\min}}, P_{gi_{\max}}$: minimum and maximum active power generation limits respectively of ith bus,

$Q_{gi_{\min}}, Q_{gi_{\max}}$: minimum and maximum reactive power generation limits respectively of ith bus,

$V_{li_{\min}}, V_{li_{\max}}$: minimum and maximum voltage limits respectively of ith load bus,

$S_{Li}, S_{Li_{\max}}$: apparent power flow and maximum apparent power flow respectively of ith branch,

$T_{i_{\min}}, T_{i_{\max}}$: minimum and maximum tap setting limits respectively of ith regulating transformer,

$Q_{ci_{\min}}, Q_{ci_{\max}}$: minimum and maximum reactive power injection limits of ith shunt compensator,

$X_{ci_{\min}}, X_{ci_{\max}}$: minimum and maximum reactance limits respectively of ith TCSC,

$\alpha_{i_{\min}}, \alpha_{i_{\max}}$: minimum and maximum phase shift angle limits respectively of ith TCPS,

ng : number of generator buses,

nl : number of load buses,

ntl : number of transmission line,

nt : number of regulating transformers,

nc : number of shunt compensators,

$nt\,\mathrm{csc}$: number of TCSC, $ntcps$: number of TCPS.

ALGORITHMS

Real Coded Genetic Algorithm (RGA)

Traditional binary coded GA suffers from few drawbacks when applied to multi-dimensional and high-precision numerical problems. The situation can be improved if GA is used with real number data (called as RGA). Each chromosome is coded as a vector of floating point numbers that has the same length as the solution vector. Different steps of RGA are

- Real coded initialization of each chromosome.

- Selection operation based on computation of fitnesses and merit ordering
- Crossover and Mutation operation
- Sorting of the fitness values in increasing order among parents and off-springs
- Selection of the better chromosomes as parents of the next generation
- Updating of genetic cycle and stopping criterion.

Overview of PSO Algorithm

In PSO each candidate solution is associated with a velocity. In PSO algorithms, each particle moves with an adaptable velocity within the regions of decision space and retains a memory of the best position it ever encountered. The best position ever attained by each particle of the swarm is communicated to all other particles. The particles find the optimal solution by cooperation and competition among them. Each particle of the population modifies its position and velocity according to the following mathematical equations:

$$v_i^{k+1} = w \times v_i^k + c1 \times r1 \times (pBest_i - x_i^k) + c2 \times r2 \times (gBest - x_i^k) \tag{21}$$

$$x_i^{k+1} = x_i^k + v_i^{k+1} \tag{22}$$

where, x_i^k: current position of the ith particle at k^{th} iteration,

x_i^{k+1}: modified position of the ith particle,

v_i^k: current velocity of the ith particle at k^{th} iteration,

v_i^{k+1}: modified velocity of the ith particle,

$c1, c2$: the cognitive and the social parameters, respectively,

$r1, r2$: random numbers uniformly distributed within [0, 1],

$pBest_i$: position best of the ith particle,

$gBest$: group best, w: inertia weight factor.

Particle Swarm Optimization with Inertia Weight Approach (PSOIWA)

With some modifications in the basic PSO algorithm, better quality solution may be attributed. In PSOIWA, the inertia weight parameter w which controls the global and local exploration capabilities of the particle is modified. A large inertia weight factor is used at initial stages to enhance the global exploration and this value is gradually reduced as the search progresses to enhance local exploration. The inertia weighting factor for the velocity of particles is defined by the inertia weight approach and is given by

$$w = w_{max} - \frac{w_{max} - w_{min}}{iter_{max}} \times iter \tag{23}$$

where w_{max}, w_{min}: limits of inertia weight factor,

$iter_{max}$: maximum iteration cycles,

$iter$: current iteration number.

Craziness Based Particle Swarm Optimization (CRPSO)

In basic PSO, particle updates its velocity and position according to its own best position and the group's best position. During the searching process, most particles contract quickly to a certain specific position and if it is a local optimal, it is not easy for the particle to escape from it. Research shows that as the iteration goes on, particles become very similar and almost have no ability to explore new area. In CRPSO, this situation is overcome by introducing a predefined craziness probability to maintain the diversity of the directions of search.

The global search ability of PSO algorithm may be enhanced by the following modifications.

Position and Velocity Updating: In velocity equation of basic PSO, the second term represents the cognitive part of PSO where the particle changes its velocity based on its own memory and the third term represents the social part of PSO where the particle changes its velocity based on the social psychological adaptation of knowledge. As $r1$ and $r2$ are random numbers within [0, 1], these might be too large or too small. If these two random numbers are too large, personal and social experiences will be over used and that may drive the particles too far away from the global optimum. While on the other hand, if these two random numbers are too small, the two experiences will not be fully utilized and may reduce the convergence speed. So instead of taking two independent random numbers, one random number $r1$ is chosen which acts balancing between over use and under use of social and personal experiences. If $r1$ is small, $(1 - r1)$ will be large and vice versa. Local and global searches are balanced by random number $r2$ as stated in (24).

$$v_i^{k+1} = r2 \times v_i^k + (1 - r2) \times c1 \times r1 \times (pBest_i - x_i^k)$$
$$+ (1 - r2) \times c2 \times (1 - r1) \times (gBest - x_i^k)$$
$$(24)$$

Change in the direction in velocity may be modeled as in (25).

$$v_i^{k+1} = r2 \times sign(r3) \times v_i^k + (1 - r2) \times c1 \times r1 \times (pBest_i - x_i^k) +$$
$$(1 - r2) \times c2 \times (1 - r1) \times (gBest - x_i^k)$$
$$(25)$$

where $r3$ may be defined as follows

$$sign(r3) = \begin{cases} -1, & (r3 \leq 0.05) \\ 1, & (r3 > 0.05) \end{cases} \qquad (26)$$

Inclusion of Craziness: Diversity in the direction of swarm may be handled in traditional PSO with inclusion of a predefined craziness probability. The particles may be crazed in accordance with (27) before updating its position.

$$v_i^{k+1} = v_i^{k+1} + \Pr ob(r4) \times sign(r4) \times v_i^{craziness}$$
$$(27)$$

where, $\Pr ob(r4)$, $sign(r4)$ and $v_i^{craziness}$ may be defined as follow

$$\Pr ob(r4) = \begin{cases} 1, & (r4 \leq P_{craz}) \\ 0, & (r4 > P_{craz}) \end{cases} \qquad (28)$$

$$sign(r4) = \begin{cases} 1, & (r4 \geq 0.5) \\ -1, & (r4 < 0.5) \end{cases} \qquad (29)$$

$$v_i^{crazziness} = v_{min}^{crazziness} + (v_{max}^{crazziness} - v_{min}^{crazziness}) \times r(0, 1)$$
$$(30)$$

The judicious selection of $v_{min}^{craziness}$ and $v_{max}^{craziness}$ is very necessary to control oscillations at the final convergence stage.

Turbulent Crazy Particle swarm Optimization (TRPSO)

This algorithm utilizes a minimum velocity threshold to control the velocity of particles. To explore new search spaces (better solution), turbulence mechanism being similar to a turbulent pump, supplies some power to the swarm system to explore new search spaces for better solutions.

It is claimed by some research groups that some premature convergence degrades the performances of PSO algorithm. One of the main reasons for this premature convergence of PSO is due to the stagnation of lazy particles during later stage of exploration of a new search space. To drive those lazy particles and let them explore better solutions, turbulence i.e. giving extra power to lazy particles is reported. A new velocity is assigned as in (31), if a particle's velocity reaches to minimum threshold velocity v_c. Thus, the turbulent crazy particle swarm optimization is presented using a new velocity update equation of (31).

$$v_i^k = \begin{cases} v_i^k & if \left| v_i^k \right| \geq v_c \\ \dfrac{r5 \times v^{\max}}{\rho} & if \left| v_i^k \right| < v_c \end{cases}$$

(31)

and

$$
\begin{array}{llll}
v_c = v_{c1}, & \rho = \rho_1 & if & cycles(k) \leq \dfrac{\max cylces}{3} \\[2mm]
v_c = v_{c2} < v_{c1}, & \rho = \rho_2 > \rho_1 & if & \dfrac{\max cycles}{3} < cycles(k) \leq \dfrac{2 \times \max cycles}{3} \\[2mm]
v_c = v_{c3} < v_{c2}, & \rho = \rho_3 > \rho_2 & if & \dfrac{2 \times \max cycles}{3} < cycles(k) \leq \max cycles
\end{array}
$$

(32)

where $r5$: a random number uniformly distributed within the interval [-1, 1],

ρ : the scaling factor to control the domain of the particles' oscillations according to $v^{\max}$.

The minimum velocity threshold v_c is a tunable threshold parameter to limit the particles' minimum velocities. Experiment shows that the performance of the algorithm is greatly dependent on v_c and ρ. A large v_c provides a great probability for the particles to jump over local minima during iteration cycles. But, on the other hand, a large value of v_c compels particles in the quick "flying" state, that leads them not to search the solution and forcing them not to refine the search. In other words, a large v_c facilitates a global search while a smaller value facilitates a local search. By changing it dynamically, the search ability is dynamically adjusted. A small value of ρ makes the search trajectory more prone to oscillate. So, ρ is increased in steps after a fixed number of iteration cycles. The value of v_c is also decreased in steps after a fixed number of iteration cycles as defined by (32).

PSO Algorithm Applied to OPF with TCSC and TCPS Devices

The algorithm of the PSO is as enumerated below.

Step 1: The independent variables such as active powers of all generators except slack bus, generators' voltages, tap settings of regulating transformers, reactive power injections, power flow through the transmission lines where TCSC & TCPS devices are placed and power injections of TCPS devices of each particle should be randomly selected while satisfying different equality and inequality constraints of OPF. Several numbers of particles depending upon the population size are being generated. Each particle represents a potential solution.

Step 2: Perform load flow with TCSC and TCPS using any classical technique and determine all dependent variables such as load voltages, active power of slack bus, generators' reactive powers, reactance of TCSC and phase shifting angle of TCPS etc. In this paper load flow is performed by Newton-Raphson method.

Step 3: Evaluate the value of objective function for each particle of the population set and record the individual best particles $pBest_i$ and global best particle $gBest$.

Step 4: Compute new velocity and update position of each particles.

Step 5: Sort the population from best to worst.

Step 6: Feasibility of a problem solution is verified i.e., each controlled variables should satisfy equality and inequality constraints. The infeasible solutions are replaced by copying the best feasible solutions.

Step 7: Go to step 2 for the next iteration.

Step 8: Stop iterations after a predefined number of iterations.

Table 1. Input parameters of different algorithms

RGA	PSOIWA	CRPSO	TRPSO
Mutation probability:0.001 cross-over: 0.8	$c1, c2 \;\; : 2.05\,;$ $w_{max} : 0.9;\;\; w_{min} : 0.4$	$v_{min}^{craziness} : 0.1\,;$ $v_{max}^{craziness} : 0.4\,;$ $P_{craz} \;\; : 0.25\,.$	$v^{max} : 250\,;vc1 : 50\,;vc2 : 10\,;$ $vc3 : 1\,;\rho1 : 1\,;\;\rho2 : 10\,;\rho3 : 50$

INPUT PARAMETERS

A population size of 50 and iteration cycles of 100 are taken for all the algorithms. After several runs, the input control parameters as shown in Table 1 are found to be best for optimal performance of the different algorithms.

SIMULATION RESULTS AND DISCUSSIONS

The applicability and validity of all the algorithms have been tested on IEEE 30-bus system for OPF problems having multiple numbers of TCSC and TCPS devices. All the programs are developed using MATLAB language, using MATLAB 7.1 and the system configuration is on core 2 duo processor, 2.0 GHz with 1GB RAM.

IEEE 30-bus system contains 6 generating units connected at bus no. 1, 2, 5, 8, 11 & 13; 30 buses, 4 regulating transformers connected between the line numbers 6-9, 6-10, 4-12 & 27-28; 2 shunt compensators connected at bus no. 10 & 14; 41 transmission lines. The full system data are taken form (Basu, 2008) and the generators' capacities and cost coefficient data including valve point discontinuities are also shown in Table 2. The generators' active powers (except slack bus-1) & generators' voltages, tap settings of the regulating transformers, Var injections of the shunt capacitors, power flow through the transmission lines where TCSC & TCPS devices are placed and power injections of TCPS devices are con-

sidered as controlled variables. The voltage magnitudes of all buses are considered within the range of [$0.95p.u, 1.05p.u.$]. Tap settings of regulating transformers are within the range of [$0.9p.u., 1.1p.u.$]. The Var injection of the shunt capacitors are taken within the interval of [0 MVar, 30 MVar]. The reactance limits of TCSC devices in p.u. are $0 \leq x_t \leq 0.10$. The limits of phase shift angle (radian) of TCPS devices are taken as $-0.05 \leq \alpha \leq 0.05$. The feasibility of the proposed method is tested on IEEE 30- bus system in four different cases as given below. The simulation results shown in the different tables are the best solutions obtained in fifty runs.

Case 1: OPF without FACTS Devices

The objective function of minimization of fuel cost without any FACTS devices is considered in this case. The simulation results of controlled variables like active powers & voltages of generator buses, tap settings of the regulating transformers, Var injections of the shunt capacitors and total fuel cost are given in Table 3. The results show that the total fuel cost found by the proposed TRPSO & CRPSO methods are less (821.3521 $/hr & 821.5686 $/hr respectively) than PSOIWA (823.0141$/hr.) and RGA (822.8868 $/hr.). Thus TRPSO gives the best results amongst all the algorithms. However, CRPSO results are very much comparable with TRPSO.

Table 2. Generating unit capacity, cost coefficient

Bus No	P_{gi}^{min} (MW)	P_{gi}^{max} (MW)	Q_{gi}^{min} (MW)	Q_{gi}^{max} (MW)	a_i ($/hr.)	b_i ($/MWh)	c_i ($/MW2h)	d_i ($/hr.)	e_i (rad/MW)
1	50	250	-20	10	0	2.000	0.0037	18	0.0370
2	20	80	-20	50	0	1.750	0.0175	16	0.0380
5	15	50	-15	40	0	1.000	0.0625	14	0.0400
8	10	35	-15	40	0	3.250	0.0083	12	0.0450
11	10	30	-10	24	0	3.000	0.0250	13	0.0420
13	12	40	-15	24	0	3.000	0.0250	13.5	0.0410

Table 3. Comparison of control variable settings and objective function, obtained by PSOIWA, RGA, CRPSO and TRPSO (Case 1)

Algorithms	PSOIWA	RGA	CRPSO	TRPSO
PG_1 (MW)	220.0189	219.6631	218.6078	219.8879
PG_2 (MW)	23.0680	25.4220	27.4810	25.5210
PG_5 (MW)	19.2620	15.5430	16.6980	16.9770
PG_8 (MW)	10.0000	11.6600	10.0000	10.0000
PG_{11} (MW)	10.4760	10.0000	10.0000	10.4220
PG_{13} (MW)	12.0000	12.6930	12.1030	12.0000
V_1 (p.u.)	1.0946	1.0923	1.0965	1.0983
V_2 (p.u.)	1.0624	1.0757	1.0704	1.0738
V_5 (p.u.)	1.0334	1.0511	1.0432	1.0361
V_8 (p.u.)	1.0436	1.0574	1.0420	1.0505
V_{11} (p.u.)	1.0918	1.0706	1.0522	1.0859
V_{13} (p.u.)	1.0988	1.0336	1.0823	1.0965
QC_{10} (MVAR)	27.7513	14.1171	25.3134	28.0398
QC_{24} (MVAR)	11.1286	12.2254	11.6544	10.7844
TC_{6-9}	0.9966	1.0849	1.0557	0.9851
TC_{6-10}	0.9360	0.9922	0.9697	1.0493
TC_{4-12}	0.9499	1.0401	1.0300	1.0073
TC_{27-28}	0.9294	1.0194	0.9938	0.9637
Total Fuel Cost ($/hr)	823.0141	822.8868	821.5686	821.3521

Case 2: OPF with Three TCSC

In this case, three TCSC are placed in the transmission lines those connected between buses 4-12, 16-17 & 27-28. The optimal settings of control variables (i.e. active power & voltage of generator buses, tap settings of the regulating transformers, Var injection of the shunt capacitors, reactance of

Table 4. Comparison of control variable settings and objective function, obtained by PSOIWA, RGA, CRPSO and TRPSO (Case 2)

Algorithms	PSOIWA	RGA	CRPSO	TRPSO
PG_1 (MW)	219.5664	219.6040	219.8283	219.7963
PG_2 (MW)	27.4040	27.3780	25.4830	26.7060
PG_5 (MW)	15.1980	15.6270	16.5720	15.9160
PG_8 (MW)	10.0570	10.0000	10.2370	10.0390
PG_{11} (MW)	10.6020	10.3120	10.1660	10.0340
PG_{13} (MW)	12.1200	12.0720	12.4030	12.2770
V_1 (p.u.)	1.0947	1.0925	1.1000	1.1000
V_2 (p.u.)	1.0738	1.0708	1.0841	1.0798
V_5 (p.u.)	1.0425	1.0462	1.0557	1.0531
V_8 (p.u.)	1.0518	1.0537	1.0625	1.0611
V_{11} (p.u.)	1.0983	1.0939	1.0922	1.0737
V_{13} (p.u.)	1.0972	1.0874	1.0997	1.1000
QC_{10} (MVAR)	13.3178	14.8367	29.9234	29.9834
QC_{24} (MVAR)	15.7368	13.0423	10.5086	9.9678
TC_{6-9}	0.9586	1.0170	1.0630	1.0134
TC_{6-10}	1.0713	1.0239	0.9361	1.0221
TC_{4-12}	0.9993	0.9804	0.9638	0.9958
TC_{27-28}	0.9767	0.9702	0.9508	0.9696
$TCSC_{4-12}$ reactance (p.u.)	0.025756	0.014236	0.023638	0.010637
$TCSC_{16-17}$ reactance (p.u.)	0.094081	0.016569	0.068536	0.064136
$TCSC_{27-28}$ reactance (p.u.)	0.035761	0.043879	0.049738	0.023667
Total Fuel Cost ($/hr)	821.5594	821.4758	821.0688	820.7397

TCSC) and the total fuel cost that are obtained by the different methods are shown in Table 4. The results clearly show that the cost obtained by all methods significantly improved in this case compare to case 1. The simulation results also show that CRPSO and TRPSO methods gives lower fuel cost (821.0688 $/hr & 820.7397 $/hr respectively) than PSOIWA (821.5594 $/hr.) and RGA (821.4758 $/hr.). Figure 4 gives the convergence characteristics of all the algorithms.

Case 3: OPF with Three TCSC and One TCPS

In this case, three TCSC are placed in the transmission line that connected between the buses 4-12, 16-17 & 27-28 and one TCPS is placed in the transmission line connected between the buses 2-5. The simulation results that are obtained by the different methods are shown in Table 5. It can be inferred from the results that the fuel cost obtained by the proposed TRPSO (820.2560 $/hr.) and CRPSO (820.3649 $/hr) methods are better than PSOIWA (821.4178 $/hr) and RGA (821.2751 $/

Figure 4. Convergence characteristics with PSOIWA, RGA, CRPSO and TRPSO algorithms of Case 2

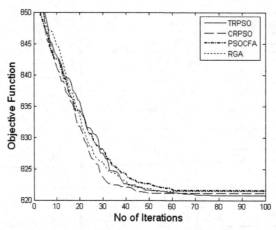

Figure 5. Convergence characteristics with PSOIWA, RGA, TRPSO and CRPSO algorithms of Case-3

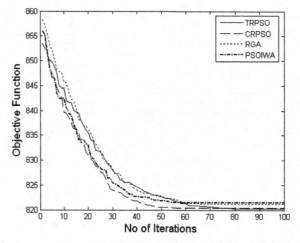

Figure 6. Convergence characteristics with PSOIWA, RGA, TRPSO and CRPSO algorithms of Case-4

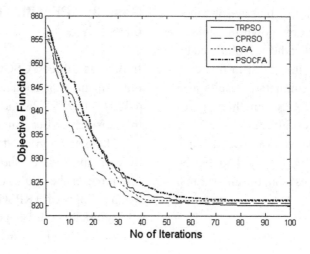

Table 5. Comparison of control variable settings and objective function, obtained by PSOIWA, RGA, CRPSO and TRPSO (Case 3)

Algorithms	PSOIWA	RGA	CRPSO	TRPSO
PG_1 (MW)	219.0952	219.7908	219.8114	219.8108
PG_2 (MW)	26.2730	26.3920	26.8980	27.2810
PG_5 (MW)	17.3180	16.5010	15.8560	15.5390
PG_8 (MW)	10.0540	10.0310	10.1040	10.0010
PG_{11} (MW)	10.0740	10.1560	10.0210	10.0881
PG_{13} (MW)	12.0000	12.0410	12.0270	12.0000
V_1 (p.u.)	1.0887	1.0975	1.0988	1.0993
V_2 (p.u.)	1.0704	1.0691	1.0832	1.0847
V_5 (p.u.)	1.0453	1.0415	1.0562	1.0591
V_8 (p.u.)	1.0527	1.0397	1.0641	1.0643
V_{11} (p.u.)	1.0594	1.0511	1.0799	1.0881
V_{13} (p.u.)	1.0965	1.0983	1.1000	1.0997
QC_{10} (MVAR)	28.2787	27.5951	28.5806	29.6575
QC_{24} (MVAR)	9.3618	12.8132	10.0994	10.1730
TC_{6-9}	1.0687	0.9802	1.0079	1.0626
TC_{6-10}	0.9303	1.0328	1.0395	0.9392
TC_{4-12}	1.0106	0.9964	0.9951	0.9684
TC_{27-28}	0.9698	0.9979	0.9732	0.9598
$TCSC_{4-12}$ reactance (p.u.)	0.012883	0.026237	0.010134	0.002357
$TCSC_{16-17}$ reactance (p.u.)	0.046096	0.058782	0.087007	0.033593
$TCSC_{27-28}$ reactance (p.u.)	0.021768	0.078609	0.015691	0.013622
$TCPS_{2-5}$ angle (radian)	0.039432	0.038944	0.034220	0.033437
Total Fuel Cost ($/hr)	821.4178	821.2751	820.3649	820.2560

hr.). The convergence characteristics of the best solution obtained by the different methods are shown in Figure 5.

Case 4: OPF with three TCSC & three TCPS

To investigate the effectiveness of the proposed algorithms for more complicated system, three TCSC and three TCPS are incorporated in IEEE 30 bus system in this case. The three TCSC are placed in the transmission lines connected between buses 4-12, 16-17 and 27-28. The three TCPS are placed in the transmission lines connected between buses 2-5, 6-10 and 14-15. The optimal values of the control variable settings and fuel cost obtained are given in Table 6. The convergence characteristics of fuel cost with different algorithms are shown in

Table 6. Comparison of control variable settings and objective function, obtained by PSOIWA, RGA, CRPSO and TRPSO (Case 4)

Algorithms	PSOIWA	RGA	CRPSO	TRPSO
PG_1 (MW)	219.6451	219.1632	219.8152	219.8159
PG_2 (MW)	24.9140	27.5830	27.5240	26.8770
PG_5 (MW)	17.8390	16.0430	15.3910	15.9850
PG_8 (MW)	10.1040	10.0000	10.0120	10.0000
PG_{11} (MW)	10.0580	10.0610	10.0060	10.0000
PG_{13} (MW)	12.1230	12.0290	12.0000	12.0000
V_1 (p.u.)	1.0991	1.0926	1.1000	1.1000
V_2 (p.u.)	1.0723	1.0738	1.0841	1.0842
V_5 (p.u.)	1.0503	1.0426	1.0557	1.0575
V_8 (p.u.)	1.0532	1.0538	1.0638	1.0639
V_{11} (p.u.)	1.0792	1.0581	1.0694	1.0945
V_{13} (p.u.)	1.0965	1.0934	1.1000	1.0998
QC_{10} (MVAR)	26.3642	28.7840	28.5436	27.2618
QC_{24} (MVAR)	9.3729	9.8549	9.9435	10.3945
TC_{6-9}	1.0654	0.9658	1.0483	1.0509
TC_{6-10}	0.9612	1.0182	0.9572	0.9493
TC_{4-12}	1.0057	0.9865	1.0036	0.9769
TC_{27-28}	0.9705	0.9978	0.9989	0.9628
$TCSC_{4-12}$ reactance (p.u.)	0.031443	0.035754	0.031813	0.021196
$TCSC_{16-17}$ reactance (p.u.)	0.017852	0.069244	0.084754	0.026409
$TCSC_{27-28}$ reactance (p.u.)	0.057472	0.084744	0.101339	0.032744
$TCPS_{2-5}$ angle (radian)	0.018290	0.035754	0.034178	0.032160
$TCPS_{6-10}$ angle (radian)	0.008995	0.016431	0.021687	0.010152
$TCPS_{14-15}$ angle (radian)	-0.007088	-0.005838	-0.003627	-0.005482
Total Fuel Cost ($/hr)	821.2413	821.1233	820.2639	820.1587

Figure 6. It is found from results that the fuel costs are reduced further for all the algorithms in this case compared to the other cases. It is also noticed that proposed algorithms give the better results for fuel cost which demonstrate the effectiveness of the proposed TRPSO and CRPSO algorithms.

CONCLUSION

In this paper two new PSO algorithms are proposed to solve problems of Optimal Power Flow (OPF) incorporating TCSC and TCPS devices and valve point discontinuities. The feasibility of the proposed TRPSO and CRPSO methods are demonstrated using modified IEEE 30-bus system for five different cases. Their results are compared to those of other well established algorithms like, PSOIWA and RGA. It is revealed that among all the algorithms, TRPSO gives optimal cost in all cases. However, the performance of CRPSO is very comparable to TRPSO. Considering all the results, it may finally be concluded that the proposed algorithms are very promising evolutionary optimization algorithms for solving OPF incorporating FACTS problems in power system.

REFERENCES

Ambriz-Perez, H., Acha, E., & Fuerte-Esquivel, C. R. (2000). Advanced SVC models for Newton–Raphson load flow and Newton optimal power flow studies. *IEEE Transactions on Power Systems, 15*(1), 129–136. doi:10.1109/59.852111

Ambriz-Perez, H., Acha, E., Fuerte-Esquivel, C. R., & De la Torre, A. (1998). Incorporation of a UPFC model in an optimal power flow using Newton's method. *IEE Proceedings. Generation, Transmission and Distribution, 145*(3), 336–344. doi:10.1049/ip-gtd:19981944

Basu, M. (2008). Optimal power flow with FACTS devices using differential evolution. *International Journal of Electrical Power & Energy Systems, 30*, 150–156. doi:10.1016/j.ijepes.2007.06.011

Benabid, R., Boudour, M., & Abido, M. A. (2009). Optimal location and setting of SVC and TCSC devices using non-dominated sorting particle swarm optimization. *Electric Power Systems Research, 79*(12), 1668–1677. doi:10.1016/j.epsr.2009.07.004

Bhasaputra, P., & Ongsakul, W. (2002). Optimal Power Flow with Multi-type of FACTS Devices by Hybrid TS/SA Approach. In *Proceedings of IEEE ICIT'02*, Bangkok, Thailand (pp. 285-290).

Cai, L. J., & Erlich, I. (2003). Optimal choice and allocation of FACTS devices using genetic algorithms. In *Proceedings on Twelfth Intelligent Systems Application to Power Systems Conference* (pp. 1-6).

Chung, T. S., & Li, Y. Z. (2001). A hybrid GA approach for OPF with consideration of FACTS devices. *IEEE Power Engineering Review, 21*(2), 47–50. doi:10.1109/39.896822

Fuerte-Esquivel, C. R., Acha, E., & Ambriz-Perez, H. (2000). Integrated SVC and step-down transformer model for Newton–Raphson load flow studies. *IEEE Power Engineering Review, 20*(2), 45–46. doi:10.1109/39.819916

Fuerte-Esquivel, C. R., Acha, E., & Ambriz-Perez, H. A. (2000). Comprehensive Newton–Raphson UPFC model for the quadratic power flow solution of practical power networks. *IEEE Transactions on Power Systems, 15*(1), 102–109. doi:10.1109/59.852107

Fuerte-Esquivel, C. R., Acha, E., Tan, S. G., & Rico, J. J. (1998). Efficient object oriented power system software for the analysis of large-scale networks containing FACTS-controlled branches. *IEEE Transactions on Power Systems, 13*(2), 464–472. doi:10.1109/59.667370

Gaing, Z., & Huang, H. S. (2004). Real-coded mixed integer genetic algorithm for constrained optimal power flow. *In IEEE TENCON Region 10 conference* (pp. 323-326).

Ge, S. Y., & Chung, T. S. (1998). Optimal active flow incorporating FACTS devices with power flow control constraints. *International Journal of Electrical Power & Energy Systems, 20*(5), 321–326. doi:10.1016/S0142-0615(97)00081-1

Ge, S. Y., & Chung, T. S. (1999). Optimal active power flow incorporating power flow control needs in flexible AC transmission systems. *IEEE Transactions on Power Systems, 14*(2), 738–744. doi:10.1109/59.761906

Ghoshal, S. P., Chatterjee, A., & Mukherjee, V. (2009). Bio-inspired fuzzy logic based tuning of Power system stabilizer. *Expert Systems with Applications*, *36*(5), 9281–9292. doi:10.1016/j.eswa.2008.12.004

Hu, X., & Eberhart, R. (2002). Multiobjective optimization using dynamic neighborhood particle swarm optimization. In *Proceedings of the Congress on Evolutionary Computation IEEE Service Center*, Piscataway, NJ (pp. 1677-1681).

Ippolito, L., Cortiglia, A. L., & Petrocelli, M. (2006). Optimal allocation of FACTS devices by using multi-objective optimal power flow and genetic algorithms. *International Journal of Emerging Electric Power Systems*, *7*(2). doi:10.2202/1553-779X.1099

Leung, H. C., & Chung, T. S. (2000). Optimal power flow with a versatile FACTS controller by genetic algorithm approach. In *Proceedings of IEEE Power Engineering Society Winter Meeting* (pp. 2806-2811.

Ma, T. T. (2003). Enhancement of power transmission systems by using multiple UPFC on evolutionary programming. *In IEEE Bologna Power Tech Conference* (Vol. 4).

Mollazei, S., Farsangi, M. M., Nezamabadi-pour, H., & Lee, K. Y. (2007). Multi-objective optimization of power system performance with TCSC using the MOPSO algorithm. In *Proceedings of the IEEE Power Engineering Society General Meeting*, Tampa, FL (pp. 24-28).

Narmatha Banu, R., & Devaraj, D. (2008). Genetic Algorithm Approach for Optimal Power Flow with FACTS devices. In *Proceedings of the 4th International IEEE Conference Intelligent Systems* (pp. 11-15).

Roy, P. K., Ghoshal, S. P., & Thakur, S. S. (2009). Turbulent Crazy Particle swarm Optimization Technique for Optimal Reactive Power Dispatch. In *Proceedings of the 2009 World Congress on Nature & Biologically Inspired Computing (NaBIC 2009)* (pp. 1219-1224).

Roy, P. K., Ghoshal, S. P., & Thakur, S. S. (2009). Constrained Optimal Power Flow using Craziness Based Particle Swarm Optimization Considering Valve Point Loading and Prohibited Operating Zone. *In Proceedings of the 3rd International Conference on Power Systems*, Kharagpur, India.

Saravanan, M. S., Slochanal, M. R., Venkatesh, P., Stephen, J., & Abraham, P. (2007). Application of particle swarm optimization technique for optimal location of FACTS devices considering cost of installation and system loadability. *Electric Power Systems Research*, *77*(3), 276–283. doi:10.1016/j.epsr.2006.03.006

Song, Y. H., Chou, C. S., & Stonham, T. J. (1999). Combined heat and power economic dispatch by improved ant colony search algorithm. *Electric Power Systems Research*, *52*(2), 115–121. doi:10.1016/S0378-7796(99)00011-5

Taranto, G. N., Pinto, L. M. V. G., & Pereira, M. V. F. (1992). Representation of FACTS devices in power system economic dispatch. *IEEE Transactions on Power Systems*, *7*(2), 572–576. doi:10.1109/59.141761

This work was previously published in International Journal of Swarm Intelligence Research, Volume 1, Issue 3, edited by Yuhui Shi, pp. 34-50, copyright 2010 by IGI Publishing (an imprint of IGI Global)

Chapter 10
Congestion Management Using Hybrid Particle Swarm Optimization Technique

Sujatha Balaraman
Government College of Engineering, India

N. Kamaraj
Thiagarajar College of Engineering, India

ABSTRACT

This paper proposes the Hybrid Particle Swarm Optimization (HPSO) method for solving congestion management problems in a pool based electricity market. Congestion may occur due to lack of coordination between generation and transmission utilities or as a result of unexpected contingencies. In the proposed method, the control strategies to limit line loading to the security limits are by means of minimum adjustments in generations from the initial market clearing values. Embedding Evolutionary Programming (EP) technique in Particle Swarm Optimization (PSO) algorithm improves the global searching capability of PSO and also prevents the premature convergence in local minima. A number of functional operating constraints, such as branch flow limits and load bus voltage magnitude limits are included as penalties in the fitness function. Numerical results on three test systems namely modified IEEE 14 Bus, IEEE 30 Bus and IEEE 118 Bus systems are presented and the results are compared with PSO and EP approaches in order to demonstrate its performance.

DOI: 10.4018/978-1-4666-1592-2.ch010

INTRODUCTION

Deregulation is a new paradigm in the electric power industry. The goal of deregulation is to enhance competition and bring consumer's new choices and economic benefits. Power system security, congestion management, power quality and power regulations are major concepts that draw the attention of power researchers in deregulated surroundings. In deregulated electricity market, most of the time power system operates near its rated capacity as each player in the market is trying to gain as much as possible by full utilization of existing resources. Congestion in the transmission lines is one of the technical problems that appear particularly in the deregulated environment. Congestion management methods reported in literature are as follows.

OPF based Congestion management is proposed in (Alfredo, Cuello-reyna, & Jose, 2005) using differential evolution as an optimization tool. (Conejo, Milano, & Garcia-Bertrand, 2006) addressed congestion management using classical approach considering voltage stability. Congestion management based on multi objective particle swarm optimization method is reported by (Hazra & Sinha, 2007; Dutta & Singh, 2008) discussed congestion management by optimal rescheduling of generators using PSO. However security loading margin is not considered. Multi objective market clearing procedure is discussed by (Milano, canizares, & Invernizzi, 2003). Moreover this work does not give marginal prices directly since the objective function is neither a cost nor a social welfare, whereas the technique used in our paper computes marginal prices directly, if applied to the market-clearing problem. Congestion management based on sensitivity methods are reported in (Christie, Wollenberg, & Wangensteen, 2000; Singh, Hao, & Papalexopoulos, 1998; Sinha & Hazarika, 2001). Congestion management based on optimum generation rescheduling and load shedding schemes are reported in (Sinha & Hazarika, 2001; Talukdar, Sinha, Mukhopadhyay,

& Bose, 2005. Reference (Kumar, Srivastava, & Singh, 2004) proposed zonal based congestion management approach, where zones are determined based on transmission congestion distribution factors.

Since the proposed problem is a complex, combinatorial optimization problem use of heuristic algorithm is inevitable. Population based co-operative and competitive stochastic search algorithms are very popular in the recent years in the research area of computational intelligence. Careful survey on literature reveals that the application of Genetic Algorithm and Evolutionary Programming, PSO are successfully implemented to solve complex problems such as congestion management in efficient and effective manner. These techniques do not depend on the first and second derivatives of the objective function of the problem to be optimized Most of the population based search approaches are motivated by evaluation as seen in nature. Evolutionary Programming is a technique based on the mechanics of natural selections. It is a powerful and general global optimization method (Xin, Yong, & Guangming, 1999). EP can provide a good solution even the problem has many local optimum solutions at the beginning. Application of EP in the field of Power Systems is reported in (Wong & Yuryevich, 1998; Pathom, Hiroyuki, Eiichi, & Jun Hasegawa, 2002; Somasundaram & Kuppusamy, 2005).

The PSO algorithm was first introduced by Eberhart and Kennedy (1995). PSO is yet another optimization algorithm that falls under the soft computing umbrella that covers genetic and evolutionary algorithm as well. Unlike in genetic algorithms, evolutionary programming, and evolution strategies, in PSO, the selection operation is not performed. Also PSO technique can generate a high-quality solution within shorter calculation time and stable convergence characteristic than other stochastic methods (Eberhart & Kennedy, 1995; Shi & Eberhart, 1998). References (Saravanan, Slochanal, Venkatesh, & Abraham, 2007; Lee, 2007; Yoshida, Kawata, & Fukuyama, 2000) provide application of PSO to various Power System problems. (Ahmed, Germano, & Antonio, 2005) propose hybrid PSO method for loss minimization problem.

This paper proposes a new approach for solving transmission congestion management problem using hybrid particle swarm optimization technique for a pool based day-ahead electric energy market. In the proposed approach the global searching capability is improved by embedding EP in PSO algorithm and also the premature convergence in local minima is prevented.

The proposed algorithm effectively alleviate line overloads with minimum adjustments in generations. However if generation adjustment alone is not sufficient, then load shedding has been done at the appropriate load buses. The feasibility and robustness of the proposed method is demonstrated on modified IEEE 14, IEEE 30 and IEEE 118 bus systems

PROBLEM FORMULATION

This paper consider a day-ahead electric energy market based on a pool. Within this pool, producers and consumers submit production and consumption bids to the market operator, which clears the market using an appropriate market-clearing procedure which results in 24 hourly energy prices to be paid by consumers and to be charged by producers. Equation (1) represents total cost for congestion management which is a sum of increment in revenues for producers for adjusting power production (up and down) and revenues for consumers for adjusting power consumptions (up and down). This cost might be either allocated among all market participants, generators, and demands or it might be allocated to those generators and demands that do not contribute to the actual congestion relieving by changing their productions or consumptions.

Objective Function

The objective function is the cost incurred in up/down power adjustments by the ISO to ensure a secure operation which is defined as

Minimize

$$F = \sum_{j \in g} (C_{Gj}^{up} \Delta P_{Gj}^{up} + C_{Gj}^{down} \cdot \Delta P_{Gj}^{down}) + \sum_{i \in d} (C_{Di}^{down} \cdot \Delta P_{Di}^{down}) \$ / hr \tag{1}$$

where

ΔP_{Di}^{down} Active power decrement in demand i due to congestion management.

ΔP_{Gj}^{up} Active power increment in generation j due to congestion management.

ΔP_{Gj}^{down} Active power decrement in generation j due to congestion management.

C_{Di}^{down} Price offered by demand i to decrease its pool power schedule for congestion management

C_{Gj}^{up} Price offered by generator j to increase its pool power schedule for congestion management

C_{Gj}^{down} Price offered by generator j to decrease its pool power schedule for congestion management

Constraints

The set of equality and in equality constraints considered in this study are given below.

$$P_{Gi} - P_{Di} = p_i(V, \theta); \forall i \in NB \tag{2}$$

$$P_{SGi} - P_{SDi} = p_{Si}(V_S, \theta_S); \forall i \in NB \tag{3}$$

$$Q_{Gi} - Q_{Di} = q_i(V, \theta); \forall i \in NB \tag{4}$$

$$Q_{SGi} - Q_{SDi} = q_{Si}(V_S, \theta_S) \forall i \in NB \tag{5}$$

$$Q_{Di} = P_{Di} \cdot \tan(\varphi_{Di}); \forall i \in d \tag{6}$$

$$P_{SGj} = (1 + \lambda) P_{Gj}, \forall j \in g \tag{7}$$

$$P_{sDi} = (1 + \lambda) P_{Di}, \forall i \in d \tag{8}$$

$$Q_{SDi} = (1 + \lambda) Q_{Di}, \forall i \in d \tag{9}$$

$$P_{Gj}{}^{min} \leq P_{Gj} \leq P_{Gj}{}^{max}, \forall j \in g \tag{10}$$

$$P_{Gj}{}^{min} \leq P_{SGj} \leq P_{Gj}{}^{max}, \forall j \in g \tag{11}$$

$$Q_{Gj}{}^{min} \leq Q_{Gj} \leq Q_{Gj}{}^{max}, \forall j \in g \tag{12}$$

$$Q_{Gj}{}^{min} \leq Q_{SGj} \leq Q_{Gj}{}^{max}, \forall j \in g \tag{13}$$

$$V_n{}^{min} \leq V_n \leq V_n{}^{max}, \forall n \in NL \tag{14}$$

$$V_n{}^{min} \leq V_{sn} \leq V_n{}^{max}, \forall n \in NL \tag{15}$$

$$\lambda \geq \lambda_{min} \tag{16}$$

$$P_{ij} \leq P_{ij}^{max} \quad \& \quad P_{Sij} \leq P_{ij}^{max} \tag{17}$$

Also

$$P_{Gj} = P_{Gj}{}^C + \Delta P_{Gj}{}^{up} - \Delta P_{Gj}{}^{down}; j \in g \tag{18}$$

$$P_{Di} = P_{Di}{}^C + \Delta P_{Di}{}^{down}; i \in d \tag{19}$$

$$\Delta P_{Gj}{}^{up} \geq 0; \Delta P_{Gj}{}^{down} \geq 0 \ \& \ \Delta P_{Di}{}^{down} \geq 0 \tag{20}$$

Where

P_{Di} Final active power consumed by demand i as determined by the market clearing procedure.

P_{Gj} Final active power produced by generator j as determined by the market clearing procedure

P_{SGj} Active power produced by generator j under security loading condition.

P_{SDi} Active power consumed by demand i under security loading condition.

Q_{Gj} Reactive power produced by generator j under normal loading condition.

Q_{SGj} Reactive power produced by generator j under security loading condition.

Q_{Di} Reactive power consumption of demand i.

V_i Vector of node voltage magnitudes.

$V_n{}^{min}$ & $V_n{}^{max}$ maximum and minimum limit for voltages at n^{th} bus.

λ Loading Margin

λ_{min} minumum loading Margin

"S" denotes Security loading Condition

$P_{Gj}{}^{min}$ & $P_{Gj}{}^{max}$ Minimum and maximum real power output of generator j.

$P_{Gj}{}^C$ Active power produced by generator j as determined by the market clearing procedure.

$P_{Di}{}^C$ Active power consumed by demand i as determined by the market clearing procedure.

d & g no. of participating loads and generators.

NB Total number of buses.

Nl Total lines in the system.

P_{ij} Real power flow in line i-j under current loading conditions.

P_{Sij} Real power flow in line i-j under security loading condition.

$P_{ij}{}^{max}$ Maximum loading limit of line i-j

Constraints (2) and (3) represents active power balances at all buses for the current loading and security loading conditions, respectively. Constraints (4) and (5) corresponds to reactive power balances at all buses for the current loading and security loading conditions. Constraint

(6) ensures constant power factor of the loads. Current loading and security loading are related through constraints (7) to (9). Constraints (10) to (13) provide operational limits for real and reactive power of generators for current loading and security loading conditions. Constraints (14) and (15) establish threshold limits for load bus voltages. Constraint (16) ensures minimum distance between current operating point and maximum loading. Constraint (17) establish line loading limit for current loading and security loading conditions. Constraints (18) to (19) express final powers in terms of market clearing values. Finally constraint(20) ensures that the increment and decrement in powers are positive.

The main scope of this work is to alleviate overloads in transmission lines and also to regulate load bus voltages by means of generation rescheduling. If congestion cannot be overcome by generation adjustment alone, then load shedding has been made finally. Hence in this study up, down adjustments required for the generators are taken as control variables.

Fitness Function

Fitness function adopted for evaluating the fitness of each individual in the population is expressed in (21). When dealing with constrained optimization problems, penalty functions are often used. A common technique is the method of static penalties, which requires fixed user – supplied penalty parameters because of its simplicity and easy for implementation.

Minimize

$$Z = F + P \tag{21}$$

Where F is the objective function and P is the penalty function.

Usually, the penalty function is based on the distance of a solution from the feasible region or on the effort to repair the solution.

$$P = (K_P \cdot \sum_{i=1}^{Nl} max(0, P_l) + K_V \cdot \sum_{j=1}^{NB} max(0, P_V)) \tag{22}$$

Where K_p and K_V are the user defined weights, prescribing how severely constraint violations are weighted. P_l and P_V are expressed as

$$P_l = \begin{cases} 0; & if\ P_{sij} \le P_{ij}^{max} \\ (P_{sij} - P_{ij}^{max})^2; & if\ P_{sij} > P_{ij}^{max} \end{cases} \tag{23}$$

$$P_V = \begin{cases} 0\ ; & if\ V_n^{min} \le V_{sn} \le V_n^{max} \\ (V_n^{min} - V_{sn})^2; & if\ V_{sn} \le V_n^{min} \\ (V_{sn} - V_n^{max})^2; & if\ V_{sn} \ge V_n^{max} \end{cases} \tag{24}$$

PROPOSED HYBRID PARTICLE SWARM OPTIMIZATION TECHNIQUE

Particle Swarm Optimization

Swarm Intelligence (SI) originated from the study of colonies or swarms of social organisms. It is an intelligence technique based around the study of collective behavior in decentralized, self-organized systems. Studies of the social behavior of organisms (individuals) in swarms prompted the design of very efficient optimization and clustering algorithms.PSO is one of the modern heuristic algorithms. It was developed through simulation of a simplified social system and has been found to be robust in solving continuous nonlinear optimization problems. PSO as an optimization tool provides a population-based search procedure in which individuals, called particles, change their position (states) with time. In a PSO system, particles fly around in a multidimensional search space during flight, each particle adjusts its position according to its own experience and the experience of neighboring particles, making use of the best position encountered by itself and its neighbors. The PSO technique can generate high-quality solution within shorter calculation time and more stable convergence characteristics than other stochastic methods. Many researchers are still in progress for providing its potential in solving complex power system problems (Lee, 2007; Saravanan, Slochanal, Venkatesh, & Prince, 2007; Dutta & Sinha, 2006).

The global optimizing model proposed by Kennedy and Eberhart (1999) is as follows:

$$v_j^{(t+1)} = \omega.v_j^{(t)} + C1.R1(pbest_j^{(t)}$$
$$-x_j^{(t)}) + C2.R2.(gbest^{(t)} - x_j^{(t)}) \qquad (25)$$

$$x_j^{(t+1)} = x_j^{(t)} + v_j^{t+1} \qquad (26)$$

Where $v_j^{(t+1)}$ is the velocity of the particle j, $x_j^{(t)}$ is the jth particle position in iteration t, ω is the inertial weight. $C1$ and $C2$ are the positive constant parameters namely cognitive parameter and social parameter and its value usually lies between [0-4], $R1$ and $R2$ are the random values in the range [0,1], $pbest_j$ is the best position of jth particle and $gbest$ is the best position among all particles in the swarm. The velocity of each agent is modified according to (25) and the position of each agent is modified according to (26).In general, the inertia weight ω is set according to the following equation:

$$\omega = \omega_{max} - \frac{\omega_{max} - \omega_{min}}{iter_{max}} * iter \qquad (27)$$

Evolutionary Programming

EP is different from conventional optimization methods. It does not need to differentiate objective function and constraints. It uses probabilistic transition rules to select generations. Evolutionary Programming seeks the optimal solution of an optimization problem by evolving a population of candidate solutions over a number of generations or iterations. A new population is formed from an existing population through the use of a mutation operator. This perturbs each component of every solution in the population by a random operator amount to produce new solutions. The degree of optimality of each of the new candidate solutions or individuals is measured by its fitness. Through the use of a competition scheme, the individuals in each population compete with each other. The winning individuals will form a resultant population which is regarded as the next generation. An offspring population is generated from each parent using (28).

$$X_j^{(t+1)} = X_j^{(t)} + N(0, \sigma_j^2) \qquad (28)$$

Where $N(0, \sigma_j^2)$ represents a gaussian random variable with mean zero and variance σ^2.

$$\tilde{A}_j = {}^2 * (Z_j / Z_{min}) * (X_{jmax} - X_{jmin}) \qquad (29)$$

where β is a scaling factor, Z_j is the value of the fitness function corresponding to X_j.

Z_{min} is the minimum fitness function value among the parent population. In each iteration the scaling factor β is decreased from maximum value in a suitable step size of g given in (30) which will improve the search and offspring fitness.

$$g = \frac{\beta max - \beta min}{iter_{max}} * iter \qquad (30)$$

Proposed Hybrid PSO Method

In this study hybrid particle swarm optimization model is proposed for relieving line overloads in an economical manner. Few modifications are incorporated in PSO, so that it becomes more robust.

Such modifications arise, not because a bird may follow a different direction by itself but because the local information (position) this bird carries may be faced as a prematuration. Combining EP with PSO will make PSO to jump out of the local optima and also to enhance the computational efficiency. Also the global searching capability of PSO is improved in search space. In the proposed method the velocity of particle is modified as

$$
\begin{aligned}
v_j^{(t+1)} = \ &\omega.v_j^{(t)} + C1.R1(pbest_{jnew}^{(t)} \\
&-x_{jnew}^{(t)}) + C2.R2.(gbest^{(t)} - x_{jnew}^{(t)})
\end{aligned}
\tag{31}
$$

where X_{jnew} is the particles computed from competition and selection pool as follows. The N_p individuals obtained from EP are combined with N_p individuals obtained from PSO and the best N_p particles are selected based on their fitness values and they are stored as X_{jnew}.

PSUEDO CODE

Step 1: Set iteration $k=1$. Initialize the parameters of PSO and EP such as $C1, C2, R1, R2, \omega_{max}$, ω_{min}, initial velocity, particle size N_p, maximum iterations $k_{max}, \beta_{max}, \beta_{min}$.
Step 2: Randomly generate the control variables $X_i^{(k)}$ (i.e., parent population) within the limit.
Step 3: Creation of new particles.

// PSO

Find $pbest$, $gbest$. Update velocity $V_i^{(k+1)}$ using (25). Compute N_p particles of $X_i^{(k+1)}$ Using (26) and evaluate fitness function for $X_i^{(k+1)}$ using (21).
// EP

N_p offsprings $X_i^{(k+1)}$ are generated from the parent population $X_i^{(k)}$ created in step 2 using (28) and evaluate the corresponding fitness values.
// HPSO

Step 4: Competition and Selection:

Combine the N_p individuals obtained from EP and N_p individuals from PSO.

Arrange the particles ($2.N_p$) in ascending order based on their fitness values. First N_p particles will survive and are transcribed along with their elements to form the basis of the next generation. It is stored as $X_{jnew}^{(k)}$. Update velocity using (31). Compute new particle Xjnewk+1.

$$
X_{jnew}^{(k+1)} = X_{jnew}^{(k)} + v_j^{k+1}
\tag{33}
$$

Evaluate fitness value and update $gbest_{new}$ and $pbest_{jnew}$.

Step 5: Increment iteration count k.
Step 6: Check for $k=k_{max}$. If yes store the $gbest_{new}$ as optimal solution and terminate the program. Otherwise repeat from step 3.

CONGESTION MANAGEMENT USING HPSO

The implementation of HPSO method for congestion management is discussed in this section.

Parameters:

Population size =20
$C1=2$ and $C2=2$
Inertia constants $\omega_{max} = 0.9$, $\omega_{min} = 0.4$
Mutation scaling factor $\beta_{min} = 0.005$, $\beta_{max} = 1.0$
Maximum iterations= 250 (IEEE 14 and IEEE 30 bus system)
Maximum iterations= 400 (IEEE 118 bus system)
Penalty factors K_p and $K_V = 10,000$

Notations and Terminologies

N Number of control variables
N_p Population size
k iteration number

ΔP_{ij} up/down adjustment of jth variable in i^{th} particle.

V_{ij} velocity of jth variable in i^{th} particle.

g_{best} best value obtained so far by any particle in the population.

Implementation of Proposed Algorithm

Step 1: Input system data, lower and upper boundaries of each variables, active power produced at generator buses and active power consumed at load buses as determined by market clearing procedure.

Step 2: Initialize the HPSO parameters. These parameters are chosen for the proposed method based on the pre simulation conducted for the base case without any contingency for various trials.

Step 3: When applying evolutionary computation algorithm, the first step is to decide the control variables embedded in the individuals. These control variables should be the same as those of the problem to be optimized. In our studies, the set of control variables includes generator active power outputs except slack bus with all control variables $\Delta P_{ij}^{k} = (\Delta P_{ij}^{up}, \Delta P_{ij}^{down})$,

where $j=1,..N$ and $i=1,2,..N_p$ satisfied their practical operation constraints.

Step 4: Update velocity and position using PSO. The velocity of each particle is modified using (25) and the position of each particle is modified according to (26). If any particle violates its limits then the particle can be fixed at its limits by the following equation.

$$\Delta P_{ij}^{K+1} = \begin{cases} \Delta P_{ij}^{min}; if(\Delta P_{ij}^{K} + V_{ij}^{(K+1)}) \leq \Delta P_{ij}^{min} \\ \Delta P_{ij}^{max}; if(\Delta P_{ij}^{K} + V_{ij}^{(K+1)}) \geq \Delta P_{ij}^{max} \\ (\Delta P_{ij}^{K} + V_{ij}^{(K+1)}) \quad; Otherwise \end{cases}$$

(34)

Step 5: Offspring creation using EP. An offspring population is created for the parent population generated in step3 using mutation operator given in (28).

Step 6: Competition and selection. Combine the N_p individuals from EP and N_p individuals from PSO. Compute fitness value for 2. N_p individuals by running NR power flow. Arrange the particles in ascending order based on their fitness values. First N_p population size of the particles will survive and are transcribed along with their elements to form the basis of the next generation.

Step 7: Stopping criteria: If any one of the end conditions given below is satisfied, then terminate the process. Otherwise, the N_p individuals generated in Step 6 can be treated as parent for the next iteration and repeat Steps 4 to 6.

a) The final best individual obtained satisfies the condition that $P = 0$ (term defined in the fitness function) which means that the line flows and load bus voltages are within their maximum and minimum limits.

b) When maximum number of iteration is reached.

Step 8: Print the particle that generates the latest $gbest_{new}$ value at the end of maximum iteration as optimal solution.

Step 9: Finally if the line overloads are not completely relieved by means of generation adjustments alone then load shedding has been made at the appropriate buses.

Table 1. Overloaded line status for various simulated cases

System	Case name	Simulated case	Over loaded lines	Actual power flow (MW)	Amount of power violation (MW)	Maximum power flow limit (MW)
IEEE 14 Bus	A	Overload simulation for outage of line 3-4	1 – 2 2 – 3	89.92 45.11	39.92 5.11	50 40
	B	Overload simulation for outage of line 1-2.	1-5 4-5	141.88 91.29	81.88 11.29	60 80
IEEE 30 Bus	C	Overload simulation for outages of line 1-3 & transformer unit 6-9.	1-2	141.49	11.49	130
	D	Overload simulation for outage of line 10-22, and by reducing capacity of line 1-2 to 75MW	1-2	88.66	13.66	75
IEEE 118 Bus	E	Overload simulation by reducing capacity of line 4-5 to 80 MW	4-5	91.12	11.12	80

Table 2. Post congestion operation schedule details for Case A with λmin = 0.1

Participating Gen. Bus No	Initial generation (MW)	Final Up/down adjustments in Generators (MW)		
		EP	PSO	HPSO
1(slack)	134.53	-56.447	-56.306	-56.268
2	40	+26.466	+27.823	+34.368
3	50	+17.058	+16.064	+9.845
6	40	+11.017	+10.543	+10.345
Total cost ($/hr)		2743.04	2707.9	**2581.3**

RESULTS AND DISCUSSION

For examining the proposed approach modified IEEE 14, IEEE 30 and IEEE 118 bus systems are taken. System data and demands are taken from (Zimmerman & Gan, 1997). Base case demands are considered as initial solutions provided by the market clearing, $P_{Di}{}^C$. Price bids by generators *($/MWhr)* to alter their scheduled productions and consumptions (as determined in the day-ahead market) are given in Appendix. These values have been selected arbitrarily close to the corresponding marginal cost values. For generators up cost is taken slightly more than down cost and opposite for demands. The upper and lower limit for the load bus voltages are taken as 1.1 p.u and 0.9 p.u.

The program has been implemented using Mat lab 7.0. Details of simulation cases considered in this study for various test systems are given in Table 1. Overloads are simulated either by simulating line/transformer outage or by reducing the maximum power flow limit of the line.

Table 1 summarizes number of overloaded lines and the actual power flows, line loading limit and power violations for various test cases.

IEEE 14 Bus System

This system consists of 4 generators, 11 loads and 20 branches with total load of 259 MW. For this system, base case generation values $P_{Gj}{}^C$ are given in Table 2, which are considered as initial market clearing values. Table 2 shows the power

Table 3. Payment particulars- IEEE 14 bus system

Case	λ_{min}	Method	Total Power Loss (MW)		Power flow in the congested lines after congestion management		Total cost ($/hr)
			Before congestion management	After congestion management	Line	MW	
A	0.1	EP	5.461	3.624	1-2 2-3	45.25 27.54	2743.04
		PSO		3.654	1-2 2-3	45.25 28.55	2707.9
		HPSO		3.820	1-2 2-3	45.23 34.93	**2581.3**
	0.2	EP	5.461	3.536	1-2 2-3	41.24 31.46	3158.8
		PSO		3.556	1-2 2-3	41.25 32.27	3144.5
		HPSO		3.584	1-2 2-3	41.25 33.25	**3119.5**
B	0.1	EP	12.879	3.866	1-5 4-5	54.13 53.97	3734.0
		PSO		4.099	1-5 4-5	54.13 50.65	3363.4
		HPSO		4.27	1-5 4-5	54.11 51.98	**3166.3**

adjustments required in the generators for relieving line overloads for the contingency case A.

In Case A, outage of line between 3 and 4 results in overloading of two branches namely 1-2 and 2-3. The actual power flow in these lines are 89.92 MW and 45.11 MW. The total power violation is 45.03 MW. To alleviate these overloads the total cost required is 2581.3 $/hr as reported by HPSO method. The proposed method yield more economical solution than PSO (2707.9 $/hr) and EP (2743.04 $/hr). This solution also ensures security with loading margin of 0.1 i.e. the system can withstand further increase of 10% of load without any congestion. Also there is a significant reduction in real power loss from 5.461 MW to 3.82 MW. The power flows in the congested lines after congestion relieving is reported in Table 3 which summarizes cost particulars for this system for various security margin.

It is revealed from Table 3, for Case A payments to producers increases with security margin, since higher the system security, the higher the power adjustments. For Case B also the proposed method yield high quality solution of 3166.3 $/hr than PSO and EP.

It is shown from Figure 1 that PSO has good searching capability than EP in Case A. However the proposed method finds global solution in the earlier iteration when compared with other approaches. It is clear from figure that the searching capability of PSO is improved by hybridization.

IEEE 30 Bus System

This system consists of 6 generators, 21 loads and 41 branches with total load of 283.4 MW. Base case generation values (i.e., initial market clearing values) are reported in Table 4.

In Case C, line 1-2 get congested by 11.49 MW due to outage of line 1-3 and transformer unit 6-9. The detailed post congestion schedule are summarized in Table 4 for this case.

Figure 1. Fitness convergence characteristics-Case A with λmin = 0.1

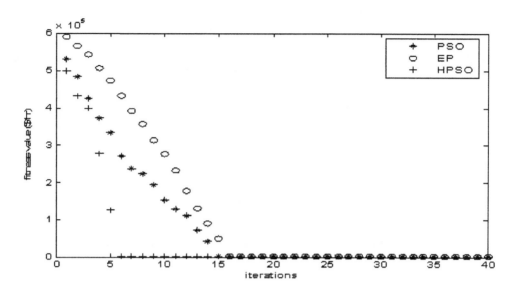

Table 4. Post congestion operation schedule details for Case C with λmin = 0.2

Participating Gen.Bus No	Initial generation (MW)	Final Up/down adjustments in Generators (MW)		
		EP	PSO	HPSO
1(slack)	138.54	-32.05	-39.265	-32.043
2	57.56	+10.41	+30.009	+16.042
5	24.56	+4.69	+10.997	+1.156
8	35.00	+3.67	+0.569	+2.598
11	17.93	+7.73	-1.807	+4.534
13	16.91	+5.74	NP	+8.223
Total cost ($/hr)		1718.03	1886.6	**1606.0**

From Table 4 it is clear that PSO method relieves overload completely with the total cost of 1886.6 $/hr, Whereas EP method results economical solution than PSO with total cost of 1718.03 $/hr. The solution also ensures minimum security of λ_{min}=0.2 (i.e., system can withstand further 20% of load increase without any line violation). However the proposed HPSO method yield high quality solution with minimum cost of 1606 $/hr for the same level of security.

From Figure 2 it is reveal that performance of EP is better than PSO for Case C. But the proposed method finds global solution in the earlier itera-tion when compared with other approaches. It is clear that hybridization of EP with PSO prevent the premature convergence of PSO in local optima and thereby enhance the search ability.

Table 5 depicts the payment particulars for two simulated cases of IEEE 30 bus system considering security margin in order to ensure mini-mum distance from current operating point to maximum loading point.

Figure 2. Fitness convergence characteristics-Case C with λmin = 0.2

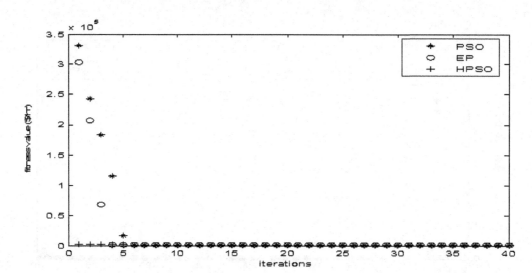

Table 5. Payment particulars- IEEE 30 bus system

Case	λ_{min}	Method	Total Power Loss (MW)		Power flow in the congested lines after congestion management (MW)		Total cost ($/hr)
			Before congestion management	**After congestion management**	**Line**	**MW**	
C	0.2	EP	10.046	7.293	1-2	106.49	1718.03
		PSO		7.654	1-2	99.32	1886.6
		HPSO		7.659	1-2	106.55	**1606.0**
D	0.1	EP	7.238	6.059	1-2	67.67	1436.6
		PSO		6.075	1-2	67.7	1208.2
		HPSO		6.5	1-2	67.71	**1027.7**
	0.2	EP	7.238	5.419	1-2	61.69	1926.6
		PSO		6.075	1-2	61.57	1745.7
		HPSO		6.269	1-2	61.54	**1401.9**

IEEE 118 Bus System

IEEE 118 bus system consists of 54 generators and 186 branches with total load of 4242 MW. Base case generation values are taken from (Dutta & Sinha, 2006).

For case E out of 54 only 8 generators are participated (except slack bus) for congestion management. These generators are selected based on their sensitivities to real power flow in the congested lines (Dutta & Singh, 2008). The participating generators with their bus numbers and the initial market clearing values are given in Table 6.

Line 4-5 get congested by 11.12 MW. In this case also the proposed method gives more economical solution and result with minimum cost of 2473.3 $/hr when compared with PSO and EP.

Table 6. Post congestion operation schedule details for Case E with λmin = 0.1

Participating Gen. Bus No.	Initial generation (MW)	Final Up/down adjustments in Generators (MW)		
		EP	PSO	HPSO
4	10.0	+20.866	+20.796	+20.732
12	79.6707	+7.916	+11.153	+11.970
15	10.0	+7.919	-8.697	+0.668
25	198.4896	+7.634	+10.439	+6.401
26	296.6821	+9.521	+10.452	+3.972
31	10.7	+1.981	+4.516	+0.463
32	10.2288	+11.824	-0.862	+3.912
49	201.1425	+7.439	+5.6414	+3.589
69(slack)	487.8	-78.065	-54.835	-53.852
Total cost ($/hr)		3590.7	3159.7	**2473.3**

Table 7. Payment Particulars-118 bus system

λ_{min}	Method	Real Power Loss (MW)		Power flow in the congested lines after congestion management		Total cost ($/hr)
		Before congestion management	After congestion management	Line	MW	
0.1	EP	109.31	106.351	4-5	72.46	3590.7
	PSO		107.919	4-5	72.82	3159.7
	HPSO		107.179	4-5	72.37	**2473.3**
0.2	EP	109.31	106.558	4-5	66.53	4846.0
	PSO		105.034	4-5	66.75	5070.8
	HPSO		105.778	4-5	66.47	**4372.4**

Figure 3. Fitness convergence characteristics-Case E with λmin = 0.2

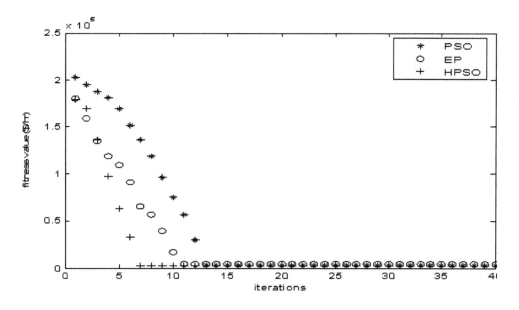

The solution also ensures reasonable security margin of 0.1 i.e., the system can withstand at least 10% of load increase without violating any operational limits.

Table 7 illustrates real power loss before and after congestion management, line flows in the congested lines after congestion relieving and payment details for 118 bus system with different security margin. Figure 3 shows the convergence characteristics of Case E with λ_{min}=0.2.

In this case EP method shows better performance than PSO. But the rate of convergence is faster in proposed method than EP. Hence HPSO approach finds more economical solution in an efficient manner.

CONCLUSION

In this paper an attempt is made to alleviate line overload in the pool based electricity market using Hybrid PSO. For each case of outages considered in this study, the proposed approach relieves congestion economically by means of minimum power adjustments in generations without any load sheds. The inclusion of loading margin in the power flow equations ensures minimum distance of current operating point to the maximum loading point and thereby enhances system security. Feasibility and robustness of the proposed method is demonstrated on three test systems namely IEEE 14, IEEE 30, and IEEE118 Bus system considering line outages. Numerical results obtained from HPSO method confirm the effectiveness of the proposed approach.

REFERENCES

Ahmed, A. A., Lambert-Torres, E. G., & Zambroni de Souza, A. C. (2005). A hybrid Particle Swarm Optimization applied to Loss Power minimization. *IEEE Transactions on Power Systems, 20*(2), 859–866. doi:10.1109/TPWRS.2005.846049

Attaviriyanupap, P., Kita, H., Tanaka, E., & Hasegawa, J. (2002). A Hybrid EP and SQP for dynamic economic dispatch with non smooth fuel cost function. *IEEE Transactions on Power Systems, 17*(2). doi:10.1109/TPWRS.2002.1007911

Christie, R. D., Wollenberg, B., & Wangensteen, I. (2000). Transmission congestion management in the deregulated environment. *Proceedings of the IEEE, 88*(2), 170–195. doi:10.1109/5.823997

Conejo, A. J., Milano, F., & Garcia-Bertrand, R. (2006). Congestion management ensuring voltage stability. *IEEE Transactions on Power Systems, 21*(1), 357–364. doi:10.1109/TP-WRS.2005.860910

Cuello-Reyna, & Jose, R. (2005). OPF framework for congestion management in deregulated environments using differential evolution. *International Journal of Power and Energy Systems,* 127-133.

Dutta, P., & Sinha, A. K. (2006). Voltage Stability constrained Multi-objective Optimal Power Flow using Particle Swarm Optimization. In *Proceedings of the First International Conference on Industrial and Information Systems* (pp. 161-166).

Dutta, S., & Singh, S. P. (2008). Optimal Rescheduling of Generators for Congestion Management based on Particle Swarm Optimization. *IEEE Transactions on Power Systems, 23*(4), 1560–1569. doi:10.1109/TPWRS.2008.922647

Hazra, J., & Avinash Sinha, K. (2007). Congestion Management using multi objective Particle Swarm Optimization. *IEEE Transactions on Power Systems, 22*(4), 1726–1734. doi:10.1109/TPWRS.2007.907532

Kennedy, J., & Eberhart, R. (1995). Particle Swarm Optimization. In *Proceedings of the IEEE Int. Conf. Neural Networks* (Vol. 4, pp. 1942-1948).

Kumar, A., Srivastava, S. C., & Singh, S. N. (2004). A zonal Congestion Management Approach using ac transmission congestion distribution factors. *Electric Power Systems Research, 72,* 85–93. doi:10.1016/j.epsr.2004.03.011

Milano, F., Canizares, C. A., & Invernizzi, M. (2003). Multiobjective optimization for Pricing system security in electricity markets. *IEEE Transactions on Power Systems, 18*(2), 596–604. doi:10.1109/TPWRS.2003.810897

Miranda, V., Srinivasan, D., & Proenca, L. M. (1998). Evolutionary computation in Power Systems. *Electr. Power and Energy syst., 20*(2), 89-98.

Saravanan, M., Slochanal, M. R., Venkatesh, P., & Abraham, P. S. J. (2007). Application of Particle Swarm Optimization technique for optimal location of FACTS devices considering cost of installation and system load ability. *Electric Power Systems Research, 77,* 276–283. doi:10.1016/j.epsr.2006.03.006

Shi, Y., & Eberhart, R. (1998). A modified particle swarms optimizer. In *Proceedings of the IEEE Int. Conf. on Evolutionary Computation* (pp. 69-73).

Singh, H., Hao, S., & Papalexopoulos, A. (1998). Transmission congestion Management in Competitive electricity markets. *IEEE Transactions on Power Systems, 13*(2), 672–680. doi:10.1109/59.667399

Sinha, A. K., & Hazarika, D. (2001). A fast algorithm for line overload alleviation in Power System. *IE (I) JEL, 8,* 67-71.

Somasundaram, P., & Kuppusamy, K. (2005). Application of Evolutionary Programming to Security constrained economic dispatch. *Electrical Power and Energy systems, 27,* 343-351.

Sood, Y. R., Pandhy, N. P., Gupta, H. O., Abdel Moamen, M. A., & Kumar, M. (2002). *A hybrid model for congestion management with real and reactive power transaction* (pp. 1366–1372). IEEE Proc.

Srinivasa, R. V., Singh, S. P., & Raju, G. S. (2008, December). Active and Reactive Power Rescheduling for Congestion Management Using Descent Gradient Method. In *Proceedings of the Fifteenth National Power systems Conference (NPSC), IIT Bomba.*

Taher, S. A., & Besharat, H. (2008). Transmission congestion Management by determining optimal location of FACTS devices in deregulated power systems. *American Journal of Applied Sciences, 5*(3), 242–247. doi:10.3844/ajassp.2008.242.247

Talukdar, B. K., Sinha, A. K., Mukhopadhyay, S., & Bose, A. (2005). A computationally simple method for cost-efficient generation rescheduling and load shedding for Congestion Management. *Electrical Power and Energy Systems, 27,* 379–388. doi:10.1016/j.ijepes.2005.02.003

Tsung-Ying, L. (2007). Optimal Spinning Reserve for a Wind-Thermal Power System using EIPSO. *IEEE Transactions on Power Systems, 22*(4).

Wei, S., & Vittal, V. (2005). Corrective switching algorithm for relieving overloads and voltage violations. *IEEE Transactions on Power Systems, 20*(4), 1877–1885. doi:10.1109/TPWRS.2005.857931

Wong, K. P., & Yuryevich, J. (1998). Evolutionary Programming based algorithm for Environmentally constrained economic dispatch. *IEEE Transactions on Power Systems, 13*(2).

Yao, X., Liu, Y., & Lin, G. (1999). Evolutionary Programming made faster. *IEEE Transactions on Evolutionary Computation, 3*(2).

Yoshida, H., Kawata, K., & Fukuyama, Y. (2000). A particle swarm optimization for reactive Power and voltage control considering voltage security assessment. *IEEE Transactions on Power Systems*, *15*, 1232–1239. doi:10.1109/59.898095

Zimmerman, R. D., & Gan, D. (1997). *MATPOW-ER: A Mat lab Power System Package*. Retrieved from http://www.pserc.cornell.edu/Matpower

APPENDIX

Price bids submitted by generators (*$/MWhr*)

Bus no.	IEEE 14 Bus		IEEE 30 Bus	
	C_{Gj}^{up}	C_{Gj}^{down}	C_{Gj}^{up}	C_{Gj}^{down}
1	22	17	22	18
2	22	18	21	19
3	42	37	-	-
5	-	-	42	38
6	44	39	-	-
8			43	37
11			43	35
13			41	39

IEEE 118 BUS SYSTEM											
Bus no.	C_{Gj}^{up}	C_{Gj}^{down}	Bus no.	C_{Gj}^{up}	C_{Gj}^{down}	Bus no.	C_{Gj}^{up}	C_{Gj}^{down}	Bus no	C_{Gj}^{up}	C_{Gj}^{down}
1	40	38	32	24	18	66	26	18	92	44	36
4	43	35	34	43	37	69	28	15	99	43	37
6	41	38	36	44	36	70	43	39	100	42	16
8	44	39	40	43	35	72	47	38	103	24	17
10	22	17	42	47	38	73	44	36	104	44	38
12	23	18	46	45	35	74	43	39	105	43	39
15	45	35	49	25	18	76	44	36	107	42	38
18	41	38	54	32	30	77	47	38	110	43	37
19	44	36	55	42	36	80	23	15	111	22	18
24	45	35	56	43	37	85	43	39	112	42	38
25	27	18	59	23	17	87	25	17	113	47	33
26	23	18	61	26	16	89	44	36	116	45	35
27	41	39	62	44	36	90	42	38			
31	45	35	65	25	17	91	41	38			

This work was previously published in International Journal of Swarm Intelligence Research, Volume 1, Issue 3, edited by Yuhui Shi, pp. 51-66, copyright 2010 by IGI Publishing (an imprint of IGI Global)

Chapter 11

Particle Swarm Optimization Algorithms Inspired by Immunity–Clonal Mechanism and Their Applications to Spam Detection

Ying Tan
Peking University, China

ABSTRACT

Compared to conventional PSO algorithm, particle swarm optimization algorithms inspired by immunity-clonal strategies are presented for their rapid convergence, easy implementation and ability of optimization. A novel PSO algorithm, clonal particle swarm optimization (CPSO) algorithm, is proposed based on clonal principle in natural immune system. By cloning the best individual of successive generations, the CPSO enlarges the area near the promising candidate solution and accelerates the evolution of the swarm, leading to better optimization capability and faster convergence performance than conventional PSO. As a variant, an advance-and-retreat strategy is incorporated to find the nearby minima in an enlarged solution space for greatly accelerating the CPSO before the next clonal operation. A black hole model is also established for easy implementation and good performance. Detailed descriptions of the CPSO algorithm and its variants are elaborated. Extensive experiments on 15 benchmark test functions demonstrate that the proposed CPSO algorithms speedup the evolution procedure and improve the global optimization performance. Finally, an application of the proposed PSO algorithms to spam detection is provided in comparison with the other three methods.

DOI: 10.4018/978-1-4666-1592-2.ch011

INTRODUCTION

Particle swarm optimization (PSO) is a stochastic global optimization technique inspired by social behavior of bird flocking or fish schooling. In the conventional PSO suggested in Kennedy and Eberhart (1995) and Eberhart and Kennedy (1995), each particle in a population adjusts its position in the search space according to the best position it has found so far, and the position of the known best-fit particle in the entire population. Compared to other population-based algorithms, i.e., genetic algorithms, the PSO does not need genetic operators such as crossover and mutation. Thus it has advantages of easy implementation, fewer parameters to be adjusted, strong capability to escape from local optima as well as rapid convergence. As a result, the PSO outperforms other population-based algorithms in many real-world application domains.

In recent years, the PSO has been increasingly used as an efficient technique for solving complicated and hard optimization problems, such as function optimization, evolving artificial neural networks, fuzzy system control, optimization in dynamic and noisy environments, blind source separation, machine learning, games, to name a few. Furthermore, the PSO has also been found to be robust and fast in solving non-linear, non-differentiable and multi-modal problems (Ge & Zhou, 2005). Therefore, it is very important and necessary to exploit some new mechanisms and principles to improve and promote the performance of the conventional PSO for a variety of problems in practice. In this article, the clonal mechanism found in natural immune system of creatures is introduced into the PSO, resulting in a novel clonal PSO (CPSO, for short). In addition, in order to improve the CPSO further, an advance-and-retreat(AR) strategy and the concept of random black hole(RBH) are then introduced into the CPSO, resulting in two variants of the CPSO, called CPSO with AR strategy (AR-CPSO, for short) and RBH model (RBH-PSO, for short).

This article is an extended version of our earlier short paper (Tan & Xiao, 2007), in which a basic idea of the CPSO is briefly presented. Here, we have extended it substantially and included two variants with some deep discussions, comprehensive experimental studies as well as our application to spam detection.

The remainder of this article is organized as follows. Section II describes the conventional PSO algorithm and its related modification versions. Section III presents the proposed CPSO by introducing the clonal mechanism in NIS into the conventional PSO and its implementation. Section IV improves the CPSO by introducing the AR strategy and the RBH model. Section V gives several experimental results to illustrate the effectiveness and efficiency of the proposed algorithms in comparison with the conventional PSO. An application of spam detection is also given in details in section VI. Finally, concluding remarks are drawn in Section VII.

RELATED WORKS

Conventional PSO

In the conventional PSO algorithm, each potential solution to an optimization problem is considered as a particle in the search space, and a population of particles called a swarm is used to explore the search space. All of particles in the swarm have their fitness values which are evaluated by a fitness function related to the optimization problem to be solved. Therefore, the PSO algorithm is originally initialized with a swarm of particles randomly placed on the search space. Then the randomly initialized swarm is getting to start to search for the optimal solution to the optimization problem by evolving iteratively. In each iteration, the position and the velocity of each particle are updated according to its own previous best position ($P_{iBd}(t)$) and the current best position of all particles($P_{gBd}(t)$) in the swarm. The update formula for the velocity and position of each particle in the conventional PSO is written as

$$V_{id}(t+1) = wV_{id}(t) + c_1 r_1(P_{iBd}(t) - X_{id}(t))$$

$$+c_2 r_2(P_{gBd}(t) - X_{id}(t)), \qquad (1)$$

$$X_{id}(t+1) = X_{id}(t) + V_{id}(t+1), \qquad (2)$$

where $i = 1, 2, \cdots, n$, n is the number of particles in the swarm, $d = 1, 2, \cdots, D$, and D is the dimension of solution space.

In Eqs. (1) and (2), the learning factors $c1$ and $c2$ are nonnegative constants, $r1$ and $r2$ are random numbers uniformly distributed in the interval $[0,1]$, $V_{id} \in [-v_{max}, V_{max}$, where V_{max} is a $_{des}$ignated maximum velocity which is a constant preset by users according to the objective function of optimization. The velocity on one dimension which exceeds the maximum will be set to Vmax. This $_{par}$ameter controls the convergence rate of the PSO and can prevent it from growing too fast. The parameter $w \in [0, 1]$ in Eq. (1) is the inertia weight used to balance the global and local search abilities. A large inertia weight is more appropriate for global search while a small inertia weight facilitates local search.

The termination criterion for iterations in the PSO is determined by whether reaching the fixed maximum number of fitness evaluations or a designated value of the fitness.

For convenience, we call the PSO in Eqs. (1) and (2) as standard PSO (abbreviated as SPSO) in the remainder of this article.

Improvements of the PSO

Since its invention, the PSO has attracted an extensive attentions and interests of researchers from different scientific and engineering domains. Many researchers have worked on improving its performance in various ways, thereby deriving many interesting improvements of the PSO.

One of the improvements introduced a linearly decreasing inertia weight over the course of search by Shi and Eberhart (1998) and gave a good convergence performance. A smart technique for creating a binary PSO suggested by Kennedy and Eberhart in 1997 used the concept of velocity as a probability that a bit takes on one or zero. Furthermore, by analyzing the convergence behavior of the PSO, a variant of the PSO with a constriction factor was introduced by Clerc and Kennedy (2002), which guarantees the convergence and improves the convergence speed sharply simultaneously. Parsopoulos and Vrahatis proposed a unified particle swarm optimizer (UPSO) which combined both the global version and local version together (Parsopoulos, & Vrahatis, 2004). A cooperative particle swarm optimizer was also proposed in (Bergh & Engelbrecht, 2004). Furthermore, El-Abd and Kamel proposed a hierarchal cooperative particle swarm optimizer (El-Abd & Kamel, 2006). In Peram, Veeramachaneni and Mohan (2003), proposed the fitness-distance-ratio based particle swarm optimization (FDR-PSO), by defining the "neighborhood" of a particle as the n closest particles of all particles in the population. In Pereira and Fernandes (2005) and Ismael and Fernandes (2005), a SAPSO algorithm combined the particle swarm optimization with the simulated annealing. The SAPSO can narrow the field of search and speedup the rate of convergence continuously during the optimizing process. Recently, a comprehensive learning particle swarm optimizer (CLPSO) was proposed to improve the performance of the conventional PSO on multi-modal problems by a novel learning strategy (Liang, Qin, Suganthan & Baskar, 2006). A stretching technique was introduced into the PSO by Parsopoulos, Plagianakos, Magoulas and Vrahatis (2001), which applied a two-stage transformation to the shape of the fitness function that eliminates undesired local minima but preserves the global minimum.

Although there are numerous improved versions of the PSO, they almost need much time to accomplish the evaluations of fitness function, and give similar results in the early phase of convergence. Hence, we here choose the improvement of the PSO with the inertia weight as a foundation of our standard PSO for further comparisons in the rest of this article.

CLONAL PARTICLE SWARM OPTIMIZATION

Clonal Expansion Process in Nature Immune System

Artificial immune system (AIS) is a novel computational intelligence paradigm inspired by the natural immune system (NIS). Like artificial neural networks and genetic algorithm, AIS are highly abstract models of their biological counterparts applied to solve a number of complex problems in different domains. Some work processes in NIS are used as metaphors to develop novel computing models in computational intelligence, such as negative selection, clonal selection, to name a few, to solve many complex problems in science and engineering domain (Dasgupta & Attoh-Okine, 1997; Castro & Timmis, 2003; Castro, 2002).

Originally, according to clonal selection theory, when the B-and T-lymphocytes in NIS recognize an antigen as non-self, the NIS will start to proliferate by cloning upon recognition of such antigen. When a B cell is activated by binding an antigen, many clones are produced in response, via a process called clonal expansion. The resulting cells can undergo somatic hyper mutation, creating offspring B cells with mutated receptors. The higher the affinity of a B cell to the available antigens, the more likely it will clone. This is called as a Darwinian process of variation and selection, i.e., affinity maturation (Dasgupta & Attoh-Okine, 1997; Castro & Timmis, 2003).

The essence of the SPSO is to use these particles with best known positions to guide the swarm or the population to converge to a single optimum in the search space. However, how to choose the best-fit particle to guide each particle in the swarm is a critical issue. This becomes even more acute when the problem to be solved has multiple optima since the entire swarm could potentially be misled to local optima. In order to deal with this case, a clonal expansion in NIS is probably a good way to guide or direct the SPSO escaping from local optima whilst searching for the global optima efficiently. Therefore, here we want to introduce the clonal expansion process in NIS into the SPSO to strength the interaction between particles in a swarm for improving its convergent performances and global optimization capability greatly.

Clonal Particle Swarm Optimization Algorithm

According to the clonal expansion process in NIS discussed above, we propose a clonal operator for the SPSO. The clonal operator is at first to clone one particle as N same particles in the solution space according to its fitness function, then generate N new particles via clonal mutation and selection processes which are related to the concentration mechanisms used for antigens and antibodies in NIS. Here we call the SPSO with such clonal operator as clonal particle swarm optimization (for short, CPSO) algorithm. For simplification in presentation, we will use the abbreviated CPSO algorithm directly later on.

As indicated in Liang, Qin, Suganthan and Baskar (2006), CLPSO's learning strategy abandons the global best information, the past best information of other particles is used to update the particles' velocity instead. In such a way, the CLPSO can significantly improve the performance of the SPSO on multi-modal problems.

Here in order to present our CPSO clearly and efficiently, we adopt the similar definitions used in

AIS paradigms. Antigen, antibody, and the affinity between antigen and antibody are corresponding to objective optimization function, solution candidate, and the fitness value of the solution on the objective optimization function, respectively. The clonal operator is used to duplicate one point as N same points according to its fitness function, and then generate N new particles by undergoing mutation and selection operations. In general, the state transition process of a swarm of particles in the CPSO can be schematically expressed as follows.

$$P(t)\xrightarrow{\ clone\ }C(t)\xrightarrow{\ mutation\ }M(t)\xrightarrow{\ sel\ }P(t+1)$$
(3)

where the arrow represents the transition process between two states while symbols over the arrows show the operations needed for the transition processes.

Notice that the population of particles $P(t)$ at time t can be transited as $C(t)$ via a clonal process, then next generation population $P(t+1)$ can be generated by using mutation and selection processes for the cloned population $C(t)$.

Briefly, the CPSO algorithm can be summarized in Algorithm 1.

Algorithm 1 CPSO Algorithm

Step 1: Initialization. Assume $a=1$, $c1=2$, $c2=2$, and w be from 0.9 to 0.4 linearly.

Step 2: The state evolution of particles is iteratively updated according to Eqs. (1) and (2).

Step 3: Memory the global best-fit particle of each generation, P_{gb}, as a mother particle of the clonal operator in Step 4.

Step 4: After M generations, clone the memorized M global best particles, P_{gB} ($i=1, \cdots, M$.

Step 5: Mutation Process. All of the cloned particles are mutated to some extents to differentiate with original or mother particle by using some random disturbances such as Gaussian noise. Assume P_{gBk} be the k-*th* entry of the vector P_{gB} and μ is an Gaussian random variable with zero mean and unity variance, then one can have the following random mutation process

$$P_{gB_k} = P_{gB_k} + s * (1 - \mu) * V_{\max}$$
(4)

where s is the scale of mutation and Vm_{ax} is the max velocity.

Step 6: Selection Process. We store the current P_{gB} in memory, but the other particles are selected according to a strategy of the diversity keeping of the concentration mechanism so that in next generation of particles, a certain concentration of particles will be maintained for each fitness layer. Here the concentration of i-th particle are defined as follows.

$$D(x_i) = (\sum_{j=1}^{N+M} | f(x_i) - f(x_j) |)^{-1},$$

$$i = 1, 2, ..., N + M$$
(5)

where xi and $f(xi)$ in Eq. (5) denote the i-*th* particle and its fitness value, respectively. According to above Eq. (5), one can derive a selection probability in terms of the concentration of particles as

$$p(x_i) = \frac{\dfrac{1}{D(x_i)}}{\sum_{j=1}^{N+M} \dfrac{1}{D(x_j)}}, i = 1, 2, ..., N + M$$
(6)

Step 7: Termination. The algorithm can be terminated by some common stop criteria such as a given maximum number of fitness evaluations or a presetting accuracy of the solution. In our experiments in the article, we adopt the former stop criterion, i.e. a maximum number of fitness evaluations, which is 1,200,000.

It can be seen from Eqs. (5) and (6) that the more the particles are similar to the antibody *i*, the less the probability the particle *i* can be chosen, and vice versa. In such a way, the particle with low fitness value also has an opportunity to evolve. Therefore, this kind of probability selection mechanism in terms of the concentration of particles in the swarm is able to guarantee the diversity of antibodies theoretically and endows the method with the ability of escaping from local minima.

Through keeping current global optima, the proposed CPSO algorithm can guarantee to maintain the good convergent performance of original SPSO. In the meantime, the essence of the clonal operator is to generate a new particle swarm near the promising candidate solution according to the value of the fitness function such that the search space are enlarged greatly and the diversity of clones is increased to avoid trapping in local minima. So, the speed of convergence and the global optimization capability can be raised rapidly.

Analysis of the CPSO

The essence of the CPSO is making full use of the area around the current best particle, denoted as x_{gB}, in depth, which works well for two reasons. First of all, we assume the probability that the actual global solution lies in the range around the current best particle would be probably greater than that in the other space. Secondly, when the SPSO converges to one solution, it is supposed to be the current best-fit position x_{gB}. If x_{gB} is the global best particle, the CPSO will speed up the convergence of the evolving swarm, because we have cloned more particles which are very close to x_{gB}, and search the area around x_{gB} more thoroughly and completely. If x_{gB} falls into a local optimum, which means a premature for the SPSO, the CPSO can give x_{gB} another chance to escape from trapping in the local minima by using the

mutation and selection operations that keep the diversity of the swarm.

However, the clones may be not efficient enough to find nearby minima in an enlarged unknown space after the clonal operation. Moreover, as can be seen, the above CPSO algorithm has complex operations which lead to much more computational time and preserve more memory. In addition, the clonal selection cannot be tuned easily for a specific task. So, by introducing the advance-and-retreat (AR) strategy, and random black hole (RBH) model into the CPSO, we propose two variants, i.e., AR-CPSO and RBH-PSO (Zhang, Xiao, Tan & He, 2008; Zhang, Liu, Tan, & He, 2008), to overcome these two limitations.

In the AR-CPSO, the AR strategy endows the clones with faster speed to find nearby local basins by using the history information of each particle's last performance of "flying" after each clonal operation. In the next clonal operation, clonal mutation and selection of the best individual of a number of succeeding generations enlarge the search space greatly and increase the diversity of clones to avoid being trapped in local minima. Thus, the clones have more chances to find and flee the nearby local basins with fast speed.

Black hole model in physics is inspired by the concept of black holes in the outer space. A black hole is a highly dense star that exerts a strong force on other stars and matter around it. It is impossible to see a black hole directly because no light can escape from it, so it is always black. But when it passes through a cloud of interstellar matter, or is close to another "normal" star, the black hole can accrete matter into itself. So we can estimate the position of the black hole according to the X-ray emission curves of matter which is being magnetized by it (NASA, n.d.). Here we still use the clonal operation, but in each generation, we clone one particle of x_{gB}, which is set to be more powerful but more stochastic, like a black hole in outer space in physics. In such a way, we can accelerate the convergence rate considerably. On the other hand, instead of the mutation and selection operations in the CPSO, our black hole model employs the randomness to keep the diversity of the swarm and enlarge the search space in the meantime, which is very simple and effective.

TWO VARIANTS OF CPSO

CPSO with AR Strategy

Many researches focus on improving the convergent capability of the PSO by a variety of methods. In Liu, Qin and Shi (2004), golden division algorithm is introduced into the particle swarm optimization algorithm. In PSO-LS (Chen, Qin, Liu & Lu, 2005), each particle has a chance of self-improvement by applying local search algorithm before it communicates with other particles in the swarm. Hybrid Gradient descent PSO (HGPSO) (Noel & Jannett, 2004) algorithm makes use of gradient information to achieve a fast convergence. In this combination, the third part of the original evolving equation, i.e., local best solution is replaced by a gradient term. Multi-Local PSO (MLPSO) algorithm (Vaz & Fernandes, 2005) uses gradient descent directions to drive each particle to a nearby local minimum for locating multiple solutions. The second part of the original PSO equation, called global best solution, is replaced by the steepest descent direction evaluated at the best ever particle position. In these two methods, the gradient or the approximate gradient is used to increase the convergent ability in the PSO.

1. AR Strategy: The AR strategy is a simple and effective method for the problem of one-dimensional search. One-dimensional search is also called linear search for optimization of a single-variable objective function. The iterative formula in one-dimension search is as follows.

$$x_{k+1} = x_k + v_k d_k \tag{7}$$

where x_k denotes the position of a solution, v_k the velocity of a solution and d_k the direction of the velocity. The bottleneck problem in Eq. (7) is how to determine the search direction d_k and the step-size v_k. Let

$$\varphi(v_k) = f(x_k + v_k d_k) \tag{8}$$

where $\varphi(.)$ denotes the function value of the velocity v_k, f is the objective function.

The problem of how to determine the step-size v_k and the search direction d_k in Eq.(8) is just an one-dimensional search problem such that makes

$$\varphi(v_k) < \varphi(0) \tag{9}$$

The step-size v_k could be optimal if the step-size v_k minimizes the objective function along the search direction d_k as in Eq. (10).

$$\varphi(v_k) = \min_v \varphi(v), v > 0 \tag{10}$$

In practice, the optimal step-size is hard to determine analytically, and often requires expensive computational cost. Therefore, an approximate one-dimensional search with less cost becomes increasingly popular.

It is well known that the AR strategy is a simple and effective method in one-dimensional search, whose main principle is to start a particle from one point with a certain step-size to determine three points of 'high-low-high', then calculate the distance from the point of 'low', i.e., the approximate optimal step-size. If a particle succeeds in one direction, its search direction remains unchanged. Otherwise, it will return and search along its opposite direction. Finally, algorithm 2 outputs an interval which contains the minimum of an unimodal function. In summary, Algorithm 2 shows steps of the AR strategy in detail.

Algorithm 2 Advance-and-Retreat Algorithm

Step 1: Initialization: $v_0 \in [0, \infty)$, $h_0 > 0$, acceleration factor $\alpha > 1$, compute $\varphi(v0)$, k=0.

Step 2: Compare Fitness Values:

$v_{k+1} = v_k + h_k$

$\varphi k_{+1} = \varphi(v_{k+1})$

if $\varphi k+1 <_\varphi k$ the$_n$

   go Step3

else

   go Step4

end if

Step 3: Advance:

$h_{k+1} = a \, h_k$

$v = v_k$

$v_k = v_{k+1}$

$\varphi k = \varphi_{k+1}$

$k = k + 1$

go Step2

Step 4: Retreat:

if $k = 0$ **then**

h$k = - hk$ //reverse the search direction vk

$= vk+1$

   go Step2

else

   stop

end if

Step 5:

$a = min\{v, v_{k+1}\}$

$b = max\{v, v_{k+1}\}$

output [a,b]

2. AR-CPSO: In each iteration, we use the AR strategy to replace the first part (i.e., the previous velocity of a particle) of Eq. (1) in SPSO just for the cloned particles. When the fitness value turns better after the last "flying", the cloned particle advances according to Eq. (1). On contrary, when the fitness value turns worse after the last "flying", the cloned particle then retreats the searches in the reverse direction of the last "flying" with a smaller step-size of the previous velocity, which can be formulated as

$$V_{id}(t+1) = w(-\alpha V_{id}(t)) + c_1 r_1 (P_{iBd}(t) - X_{id}(t))$$

$$+ c_2 r_2 (P_{gBd}(t) - X_{id}(t)) \tag{11}$$

where $a < 1$.

The AR-CPSO algorithm is the same as the CPSO algorithm in Algorithm 1 except for replacing its Step2 with the following step.

Step2: The state evolution of particles is iteratively updated according to Eqs. (1), (2) and (11).

With the inertia weight$w$ decreasing with the evolution of the swarm, clones may be restricted in a decreasing local area for searching nearby local minima. Due to the influence of the global best position and the local best positions, clones change their tracks randomly. Noticeably, the AR strategy is just applied to the cloned particles.

The AR strategy in the AR-CPSO on Ackley benchmark test function is schematically shown in Figure 1. As can be seen, a particle starts from $p1$, after the 1st step, the particle advances in the 2nd step and retreats in the 3rd step. Thus, the clones do not scatter over the search space, but fly toward the nearby local basin quickly. Therefore, the AR strategy enables each clone to predict the next direction to the local optima according to its own history information rather than just memorizing the last velocity without any judgement of the last "flying". In such a way, the clones are restricted to the search space around nearby local optima, so the individual convergent capability of each clone is able to be enhanced greatly.

Particle Swarm Optimization with Random Black Hole

For each dimension in every generation, we randomly generate a particle close to the current best particle. We regard it as a black hole by giving a threshold p drawn in the interval [0, 1], to decide its capability of magnetism. In each dimension of a particle in the swarm, we randomly generate

Figure 1. Convergent performance of one particle on Ackley benchmark function within 4 generations using the AR-CPSO

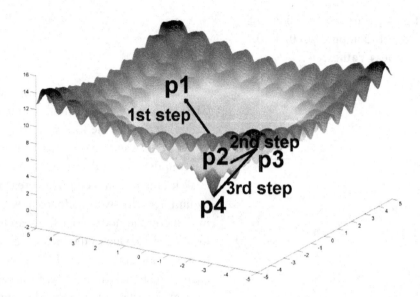

a value l, which is drawn from an uniform distribution over interval [0, 1]. If l is smaller than p, we let the particle be arrested by the black hole, i.e. the coordinate of the particle in this dimension is directly set to the coordinate of the black hole. At the same time, the velocities of other particles in the swarm in calculation of the SPSO are kept unchanged, which will be used in the next generation. The transition of a particle x from the t-*th* to the (t+1)-*t*h generation in the RBH-PSO is schematically shown in Figure 2, where x_{gB} the position of current best-fit particle in the entire population. x(t) is the position of x in current t- th generation, x(t + 1) is the position that x is supposed to be in the next generation in the SPSO, and $\tilde{x}$ (t + 1) is its actual position in the next generation after using our random black hole operation. s is randomly drawn from an uniform distribution over the interval [-r, r], *and* r is the radius of the area around xgB, in $_{wh}$ich the black hole is generated randomly. r is de*t*ermined according to the attributes of test functions, which will be discussed in section IV in detail.

As shown in Figure 2, if the particle x(t) is randomly chosen to be magnetized to the black hole, i.e., $l < p$, th*e* actual position $\tilde{x}$ (t + *1*) in our RBH-PSO would be calculated by Eq. (12). Otherwise, x(t + *1*) will be as same as that in the SPSO according to Eq. (13). This operation is carried out in each dimension for all particles in the swarm. So, from the point of view of high-dimensionality, the black hole gives another direction for some particles in some dimensions to converge in a probability threshold p.

$$\tilde{x}(t+1) = x_{gB} + s, if \ l < p \qquad (12)$$

$$\tilde{x}(t+1) = x(t+1), if \ l \geq p \qquad (13)$$

Briefly, the RBH-PSO algorithm can be summarized in Algorithm 3.

Figure 2. Schematic Graph of the Position Transformation of $x(t)$ in the RBH-PSO

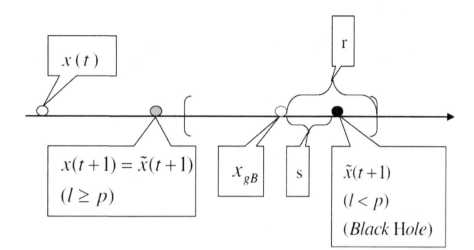

Algorithm 3 RBH-PSO Algorithm

Step 1: Initialization. Assume $c_1 = 2$, $c_2 = 2$, and w be from 0.9 to 0.4 linearly.

Step 2: The state of particles evolves iteratively according to Eqs. (1) and (2).

Step 3: Find the current best-fit particle x_{gB}, and generate a new particle close to x_{gB} as a random black hole in the range of r. Determine r as the radius of the range, and then choose s randomly from an uniform distribution in interval [-r,r].

Step 4: For each particle x in the swarm, randomly give it an evaluation l, and determine the threshold of the black hole p. Then update the position of x according to Eqs. (12) and (13). Accordingly, the velocity is updated by Eq. (1).

Step 5: Termination. The algorithm can be terminated by a given maximum number of fitness evaluations, i.e., 1,200,000 in this study. If the termination condition is not met, go to step 2.

The essence of the RBH-PSO is to randomly clone and mutate another new best particle to guide all particles in the swarm. This new guide is consid-

ered to represent the actual best-fit position which exists but not found so far, just like a black hole in physics which has a huge quality (Black hole). We do not know where the real solution should be, but according to our analysis and knowledge so far, the small range around the current best-fit particle is considered to be the best candidate of the real solution, and randomness is employed to enhance the feasibility. As the SPSO evolves, we expect x_{gB} in certain generations would converge to the solution of the problem at hand. If this is achieved, our black hole model will enhance the convergent speed because it is right next to x_{gB} in each generation, and help x_{gB} to magnetize other particles strongly. If the SPSO would converge to local optima, the black hole will give all particles another chance to fly out of the trapped local optima and keep evolving continuously.

Comparisons among CPSO and Its Variants

For the AR-CPSO, a clonal operator is used to generate a new particle swarm near the promising candidate solution according to the value of the fitness function so that the search space is enlarged greatly and the diversity of clones is increased to avoid being trapped in local minima. Meanwhile, the essence of the AR strategy is to speed up clone for greatly finding nearby minima in an enlarged unknown space. Convergent rate and global optimization performance could be raised significantly. The RBH-PSO is also inspired by the clone and selection mechanism, which not only keep the diversity of the swarm but also accelerate the local search at the same time. Because the two clonal operations are complicated highly and need more computational time and preserve much more memory, therefore, a simple model, RBH-PSO, is proposed to find a more reasonable tradeoff between the convergent speed and global optimization capability.

In summary, during the iteration procedure of the three proposed algorithms, the local search space is enlarged significantly by the corresponding clonal operations around x_{gB}, which accelerate the local search greatly. Meanwhile, we not only keep the velocity of the original particles but also keep the diversity of the swarm for global search.

EXPERIMENTS AND ANALYSIS

Experimental Setup

1. Fifteen Benchmark Test Functions: To test and verify the performance of the proposed CPSO and its variants, fifteen benchmark functions and their corresponding parameters listed in Figure 3 are used for our following simulations. Besides the global optimum of Shaffer f6 function is 1, the global optimum of the other fourteen benchmark test functions are 0. Since the optimization cost in real-world applications is usually dominated by the evaluations of the objective function, so the presetting expected number of fitness evaluations ($F Es$) is retained as the main algorithmic performance measure. The stop criterion in algorithms, i.e. the maximum number of fitness evaluations, is set to 1,200,000 in our simulations. In addition,

we fix the number of particles in a swarm to be 40 for the convenience of comparisons later on. In Figure 3, $F Es$ denotes the number of the fitness evaluations and D the dimension of test functions.

The column 'Ini. Space' in the figure shows the spaces where the initializations lie in. For concrete expressions of the fifteen benchmark test functions used in our experiments, and more complex and compound benchmark test functions (see Liang, Qin, Suganthan & Baskar, 2006; Kennedy & Mendes, 2002).

2. Experimental Platforms: All experiments in this article are conducted on two PCs with AMD Athlon 3200+ CPU and 1G RAM under Windows XP OS. Accuracy, precision, recall and miss rates are used as performance indices for spam detection.

LIBSVM software package is used for implementing our SVM under an environment of MATLAB version R2007a.

Determination of Parameters in Algorithms

A best trade-off between exploration and exploitation strongly depends on properties of objective functions to be optimized, such as the number of local optima, the distance to the global optimum, the position of the global optimum in the search space (for example, at center, near borders, etc.), the size of the search area, the accuracy required in location of the optimum, etc. It is probably impossible to find a unique set of algorithmic parameters that work well in all cases (Trelea, 2003). Therefore, usually, a tentative method is adopted to determine the parameters in terms of three representative test functions, i.e., the Sphere function with only one optimum, the Rosenbrock function with slow slope, and the Schwefel function being rotated. Actually, all fifteen benchmark test functions are used to verify and test the validation of the parameters determined above in our experiments.

Figure 3. List of fifteen benchmark test functions and their parameters for our following simulations

Functions	Exp.	D	Search Space	V_{max}	Ini. Space
Shaffer f6	F_1	30	$[-100, 100]^D$	100	$[15, 30]^D$
Sphere	F_2	30	$[-100, 100]^D$	100	$[15, 30]^D$
Rosenbrock	F_3	30	$[-100, 100]^D$	100	$[15, 30]^D$
Griewangk	F_4	30	$[-100, 100]^D$	100	$[15, 30]^D$
Ellipse	F_5	30	$[-100, 100]^D$	100	$[15, 30]^D$
Cigar	F_6	30	$[-100, 100]^D$	100	$[15, 30]^D$
Tablet	F_7	30	$[-100, 100]^D$	100	$[15, 30]^D$
Sumcan	F_8	30	$[-0.16, 0.16]^D$	0.16	$[0.03, 0.1]^D$
Schwefel	F_9	30	$[-100, 100]^D$	100	$[15, 30]^D$
Ackley	F_{10}	30	$[-32, 32]^D$	32	$[10, 20]^D$
Non. Rastrigin	F_{11}	30	$[-100100]^D$	100	$[15, 30]^D$
Rastrigrin RT	F_{12}	30	$[-100100]^D$	100	$[15, 30]^D$
Griewangk RT	F_{13}	30	$[-100, 100]^D$	100	$[15, 30]^D$
Schwefel RT	F_{14}	30	$[-100, 100]^D$	100	$[15, 30]^D$
Ncrastrigrin RT	F_{15}	30	$[-100100]^D$	100	$[15, 30]^D$

1. Number of Generations of Clones Versus Performance: For the number of generations of clones, denoted by symbol n, being 2, 5, 10, 20 and 30, respectively, the performances of the CPSO on Sphere and Rotated Schwefel functions are illustrated in Figure 4.

   It can be seen from Figure 4 that the best performances of the proposed CPSO on both Sphere and Rotated Schwefel functions are obtained when 'n=10'.

2. Mutation Scale of Clones Versus Performance: For the mutation scale of clones s from 0.001 to 0.0000001, when the retreat step a is equal to 0.4 and the generation of clones is set to 10, the performances of the CPSO on Rosenbrock and Rotated Schwefel functions are illustrated in Figure 5. It can be seen from Figure 5 that s =0.000001 has better performance. As a result, in the following

experiments, let s be 0.000001 for the CPSO and the AR-CPSO.

3. Retreat Step-size Versus Performance of AR-CPSO: For the retreat step-size a, in Eq. (11), being from 0.1 to 0.5, when the mutation scale of clones is equal to 0.000001 and the number of generations of clones is 10, the performances of the AR-CPSO on Rosenbrock and Rotated Schwefel functions are illustrated in Figure 6. It can be seen that the best performance is achieved as a =0.4. So, in the following experiments, a is assumed to be 0.4 for the AR-CPSO.

4. Generations of Clones Versus Performance for AR-CPSO: For the number of generations of clones, denoted by n, from 10 to 50, when the mutation scale of clones is equal to 0.000001 and the retreat step is equal to 0.4, the performances of the AR-CPSO on

Figure 4. Convergent Performances of the CPSO on Rosenbrock and Rotated Schwefel Functions with Different Generations of Clones (Denoted by n)

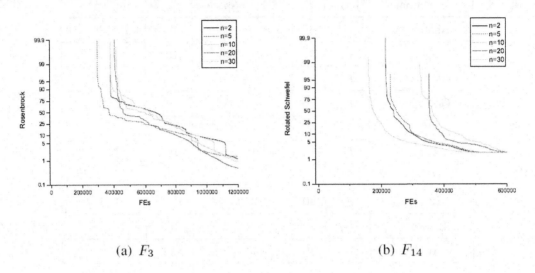

(a) F_3 (b) F_{14}

Figure 5. Convergent Performances of the CPSO on Rosenbrock and Rotated Schwefel Functions with Different Mutation Scales (Denoted by s)

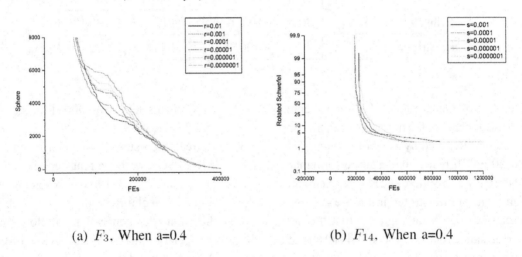

(a) F_3. When a=0.4   (b) F_{14}. When a=0.4

Rosenbrock and Rotated Schwefel functions are illustrated in Figure 7. It can be seen that $n = 10$ has better performance. So in the following experiments, let n be 10 for the AR-CPSO and CPSO.

5. Determination of Parameters in the RBH-PSO: Two parameters in the RBH-PSO need to be determined, i.e., p and r, which represent the probability of a black hole and the radius of the interval, respectively. For simplification and convenience, three benchmark functions are chosen to test their effects. Sphere function and Rosenbrock function both have one single optimum, but the former has a "large scale" curvature while the latter has a flat bottom. Rotated Rastringrin function has multiple optima scattering over the entire search space.

Figure 6. Convergent Performances of the CPSO on Rosenbrock and Rotated Schwefel Functions with Different Retreat Step-size (Denoted by a)

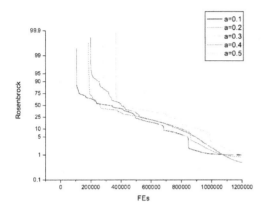

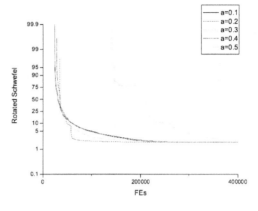

(a) F_3, When s=0.000001   (b) F_{14}, When s=0.000001

With a fixed p =0.05, the performance of the RBH-PSO on the three functions with different initial values of r are illustrated in Figures 8 (a)-8 (c). It can be seen from Figures 8 (a)-8 (c) that the best performance for all the three benchmark functions is achieved at r =0.000001. In Figures 8(d)-8(f), with a fixed r=0.000001, it is obvious that p =0.1 would be a good choice. Therefore, the parameters in the RBH-PSO are finally chosen as p =0.1 and r =0.000001 which will be used in our following experiments.

Performance Comparisons among CPSO, AR-CPSO, RBH-PSO and SPSO

The comparisons of performance among the CPSO, the AR-CPSO, the RBH-PSO and the SPSO on fifteen typical benchmark test functions are shown in Figure 9. These convergent curves are drawn from the averaged values of 50 independent runs. In such a way, these curves can give the stable performances of the CPSO, the AR-CPSO, the RBH-PSO and the SPSO completely and reliably. As can be seen from Figure 9, the proposed CPSO, AR-CPSO and RBH-PSO have

much faster convergence speed and much more accurate solution than that of the SPSO on all fifteen benchmark test functions.

Furthermore, in order to verify the validation and efficiency of our proposed three algorithms, by 50 independent runs, we give the statistical means and standard deviations, in Figure 10, of our obtained solutions of the fifteen benchmark test functions listed in Figure 3, by using the proposed CPSO, AR-CPSO, RBH-PSO and the original SPSO, respectively. It turns out that the proposed CPSO, AR-CPSO and RBH-PSO has much more accurate solution than that of the SPSO on all fifteen benchmark test functions.

Specifically, the relationship of the convergent speed among the CPSO, the AR-CPSO, the RBH-PSO and the SPSO can be obviously observed from Figure 9, which could be expressed as follows.

$$AR - CPSO \succ CPSO \succ RBH - PSO \succ SPSO \tag{14}$$

where symbol $\succ$ denotes a relation of partial order such as 'faster than' in convergence speed.

Figure 7. Convergent Performances of the CPSO on Rosenbrock and Rotated Schwefel Functions with Different Generations of Clones (Denoted as n)

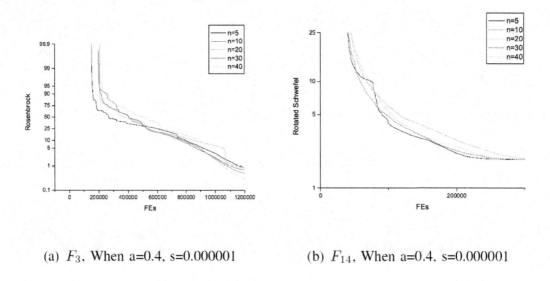

(a) F_3, When a=0.4, s=0.000001   (b) F_{14}, When a=0.4, s=0.000001

Figure 8. Convergent Performances of the RBH-PSO on Sphere, Rosenbrock and Rotated Rastringrin Functions with Different Parameters

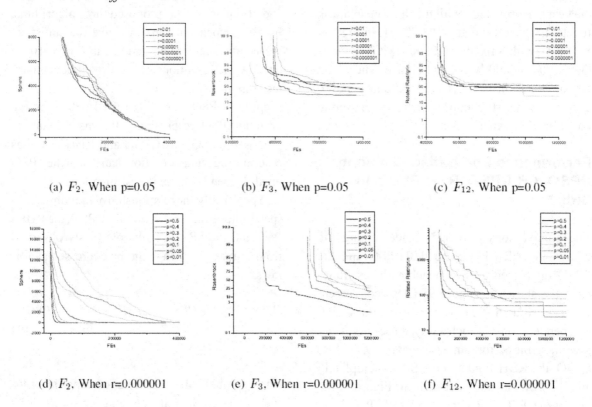

(a) F_2, When p=0.05   (b) F_3, When p=0.05   (c) F_{12}, When p=0.05

(d) F_2, When r=0.000001   (e) F_3, When r=0.000001   (f) F_{12}, When r=0.000001

Figure 9. The Average Performance of the RBH-PSO and SPSO on F1 − F15 ͺn Figure 3 with 40 Particles in a Swarm over 50

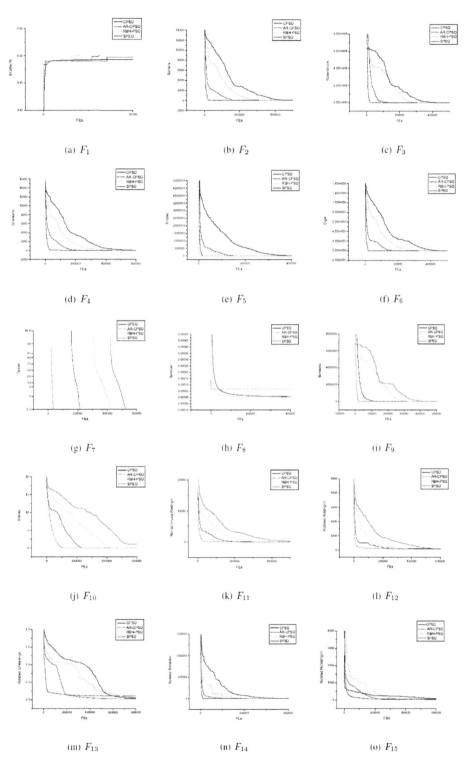

(a) F_1 (b) F_2 (c) F_3

(d) F_4 (e) F_5 (f) F_6

(g) F_7 (h) F_8 (i) F_9

(j) F_{10} (k) F_{11} (l) F_{12}

(m) F_{13} (n) F_{14} (o) F_{15}

According to Eq.(14), one can easily capture a clear picture of relations among the CPSO, AR-CPSO, RBH-PSO as well as the SPSO.

In a same way, the relationship among the proposed CPSO, AR-CPSO, RBH-PSO and the SPSO in global exploration capability is also easily observed from Figure 10, as follows.

$$RBH - PSO \succ CPSO \succ AR - CPSO \succ SPSO \tag{15}$$

where symbol $\succ$ denotes a relation of partial order such as 'stronger than' in global exploration capability.

As can be seen from Figure 10 and Eq. (15), the proposed CPSO, the AR-CPSO and the RBH-PSO has stronger global optimization capability than that of the SPSO on almost all fifteen benchmark test functions. Specifically, the CPSO achieves better global solution than the SPSO on twelve test functions. The AR-CPSO achieves better global

solution than the SPSO on eleven test functions. The RBH-PSO achieves better global solution than the SPSO on all fifteen test functions.

Therefore, we can conclude that the proposed CPSO and its two variants are able to accelerate the convergence tremendously whilst keeping a good global search capability with much more accuracy. All of the simulation results in experiments have shown that the introduction of the clonal mechanism in NIS into the PSO leads to a promising performance.

Analysis and Discussion

By inspired by immunity-clonal mechanism, the CPSO and its two variants, i.e., AR-CPSO and RBH-PSO, use a clonal operation to generate new particles near the promising candidate solution according to the fitness value so that the search space is able to be enlarged greatly and further the diversity of clones is increased to avoid being trapped in local minima. In such a way, conver-

Figure 10. Statistical means (M) and standard deviations (STD) of the solutions of fifteen benchmark test functions, listed in Figure 3, given by the AR-CPSO, the CPSO, the RBH-PSO and the SPSO over 50 independent runs, where FEs denote the fitness evaluations.

Functions	FEs.	CPSO's M ± Std	AR-CPSO's M ± Std	RBH-PSO's M ± Std	SPSO's M ± Std
Shaffer f6	20, 120	0.9949 ± 0.004	0.9922 ± 0.003	1 ± 0	0.9924 ± 0.003
Sphere	315, 331	0.000002 ± 0.000001	0 ± 0	81.361 ± 51.58	1025.55 ± 372.70
Rosenbrock	1, 200, 000	1.01 ± 1.72	0.49 ± 1.23	32.01 ± 35.87	45.64 ± 54.51
Griewangk	1, 200, 000	7.31 ± 3.52	4.576811 ± 2.69	4.57 ± 2.69	18.80 ± 4.95
Ellipse	492, 820	0.000001 ± 0	0± 0	0.000069 ± 0.00008	53 ± 38
Cigar	549, 000	0.000002 ± 0.000002	0.000001 ± 0.000001	0 ± 0	15.7 ± 17.63
Tablet	353, 010	0.000001 ± 0	0 ± 0	55.98 ± 24.79	857.36 ± 362.3
SumCan	1, 200, 000	0.000004 ± 0	0.000022 ± 0	0.000002 ± 0	0.0000030 ± 0
Schwefel	427, 999	0 ± 0	0.000001 ± 0	51.2 ± 40.1	11989.14 ± 8907
Ackley	594, 336	0 ± 0	0.000001 ± 0	0.000001 ± 0	1.02 ± 4.48
Nonc. Rastrigin	1, 200, 000	0.95 ± 0.97	0.35 ± 0.65	1.95 ± 3.29	5.9 ± 3.89
Rastrigrin RT	1, 200, 000	82.12 ± 79.07	103.95 ± 74.58	34.18 ± 1.33	52.76± 24.56
Griewangk RT	1, 200, 000	0.025 ± 0.03	0.11 ± 0.13	0.013 ± 0.000046	0.034 ± 0.027
Schwefel RT	1, 200, 000	1.898378 ± 0.000001	1.898377 ± 0.000001	1.898374 ± 0	1.89839 ± 0.00002
Ncrastrigrin RT	1, 200, 000	31.06± 19.29	58.41 ± 51.52	8.9 ± 3.92	25.32 ± 7.16

gent rate and global exploration capability can be greatly raised simultaneously.

As we know, those fifteen functions listed in Figure 3 are of very much different characteristics and properties. Some of them have a single minimum, and others have multiple local minima. Several functions are of a large-scale curvature which guides the search toward the global minimum, while others are essentially flat except the area near the global minimum. So, these functions are usually used as powerful and useful benchmark test functions to test the newly developed algorithms thoroughly and objectively. In spite of the complexities of these functions, it turns out from the comparisons of performances among the CPSO, the AR-CPSO, the RBH-PSO and the SPSO, that the CPSO and its two variants not only has a faster convergence speed but also has more accurate optimal solution than that of the SPSO on almost all of the benchmark test functions, which strongly support our contributions introducing the clonal mechanism into the PSO.

In particular, the proposed CPSO, the AR-CPSO and the RBH-PSO do not need to stop the evolving of the swarm (Liu, Qin & Shi, 2004; Chen, Qin, Liu & Lu, 2005) for a local search. Furthermore, the CPSO and its two variants do not need to calculate the gradient of the objective function, which is computationally expensive cost, and change the structure of the conventional PSO (Noel & Jannett, 2004; Vaz & Fernandes, 2005). Most recently, we have developed parallelism implementations of the PSO algorithms based on graphics processing unit (GPU) in a personal computer and obtained a more than 20 times of speedup for the PSO algorithm for a specific task (Zhou & Tan, 2009).

What follows is an application of the proposed CPSO-like algorithms on spam detection.

SPAM DETECTION APPLICATION

Spam, usually defined as unsolicited commercial e-mail, or unsolicited bulk e-mail, or uninterested e-mail from the perspective of individual e-mail user, has been regarded as an increasingly serious problem to the infrastructure of Internet. According to the statistics from International Telecommunication Union (ITU), about 70% to 80% of the present emails in Internet are spam. Numerous spams not only occupy valuable communications bandwidth and storage space, but also threaten the network security as it is often used as a carrier of viruses and malicious codes. Meanwhile, spam wastes much user's time to tackle with them so that the productivity is reduced considerably. Therefore, spam detection has attracted many attentions in Internet research community from academia as well as industry. Theoretical analysis and many practical algorithms, tools, and system level solutions have been successfully developed. In summary, they can be classified into three categories: simple approaches, intelligent approaches and hybrid approaches.

Simple approaches include munging, listing, aliasing and challenging. These techniques are easy to implement while are also prone to be deceived by tricks of spammers. Intelligent approaches play an increasingly important role in anti-spam in recent years for their ability of self learning and good performance, which include Naïve Bayes (Androutsopoulos, Koutsias, Chandrinos & Spyropoulos, 2000; Sahami, Dumais, Heckerman & Horvitz, 1998), Support Vector Machine (SVM) (Ruan & Tan, 2007; Drucker, Wu & Vapnik, 1999; Tan & Wang, 2004), Artificial Neural Network (ANN) (Clark, Koprinska & Poon, 2003; Stuart, Cha & Tappert, 2004), Artificial Immune System (AIS) (Ruan & Tan, 2008; Oda & White, 2003; Secker, Freitas & Timmis, 2003; Bezerra & Barra, 2006; Tan, 2006; Sirisanyalak & Sornil, 2007) and DNA Computing (Rigoutsos & Huynh, 2004). As an anti-spam shield with one technique alone can be easily intruded in practice, consequently, several hybrid approaches by combining two or more techniques together are proposed (Leiba & Borenstein, 2004; Wu, Huang, Lu, Chen & Kuo, 2005) for better overall performance.

Support Vector Machine (SVM) has already proved its superiority in pattern recognition for its generalization performance, which is based on the Structural Risk Minimization principle from statistical learning theory (Vapnik, 1995; Drucker, Burges, Kauffman, Smola & Vapnik, 1997). The goal of SVM is to find an optimal hyper plane for which the lowest true error can be guaranteed. In what follows, the SVM is used as the classifier for spam detection.

Natural immune system has some desirable properties for spam detection, including pattern recognition, dynamically changing coverage and noise tolerance, etc, some of which are drawn for our algorithm. So, inspired by human immune system, a concentration based feature construction (CFC) approach is constructed to characterize each e-mail through a two-element feature vector (Tan, Deng & Ruan, 2009). In the CFC approach, 'self' concentration and 'non-self' concentration are constructed by using 'self' gene library and 'non-self' gene library, respectively. Subsequently, they are used to form a two-element concentration vector which characterizes the e-mail efficiently and concisely.

Two corpus used to test the CFC approaches are the PU1 corpus (Androutsopoulos, Koutsias, Chandrinos & Spyropoulos, 2000) and Ling corpus[1] (Androutsopoulos, Koutsias, Chandrinos, Paliouras & Spyropoulos, 2000). PU1 corpus consists of 1,099 messages, with spam rate 43.77%, Ling corpus consists of 2,893 messages, with spam rate 16.63%. All the messages in both corpora have header fields, attachment and HTML tags removed, leaving only subject line and mail body text. In PU1, each token is mapped to a unique integer to ensure the privacy of the content while keeping its original form in Ling. Each corpus is divided into ten partitions with approximately equal amount of messages and spam rate. The

version with stop-word removal is used in our experiments.

LIBSVM software package is used as an implementation of the SVM (Chang & Lin, 2001). Polynomial kernel with three parameters, i.e., gamma, coef0 and degree, is adopted. Together with the cost parameter C, there are four parameters to be optimized.

The proposed CPSO, AR-CPSO, and RBH-PSO as well as three typical algorithms are used to tune the above four parameters. A corresponding test function model with four parameters as input and classification accuracy as output is established. The classification accuracy, measured by 10-fold cross validation, serves as the objective function. The CPSO-like algorithms terminate when the fitness value of the global best particle does not change in consecutive 50 generations.

Comparisons of performances among the CPSO, the AR-CPSO, the RBH-PSO are made and shown in Figure 11, where the accuracy of the CPSO, the AR-CPSO, the RBH-PSO, Nave Bayesian, Linger-V and SVM-IG on corpus PU1 and Ling are listed in digits (Androutsopoulos, Koutsias, Chandrinos & Spyropoulos, 2000; Clark, Koprinska & Poon, 2003; Androutsopoulos, Koutsias, Chandrinos, Paliouras & Spyropoulos, 2000; Koprinska, Poon, Clark & Chan, 2007). Where, Linger-V is a NN-based system for automatic e-mail classification. All these results are obtained by using 10-fold validation. For Naïve Bayesian, 50 words with the highest mutual information scores are selected. LINGER-V and SVM-IG uses variance (V) and information gain (IG) as the criteria of feature selection, respectively, and the best-scoring 256 features are chosen. It can be seen from Figure 11 that the proposed CPSO-like algorithms is indeed used to tune the parameters of SVM classifier and raise the accuracy of classification greatly.

Furthermore, the corresponding solutions of the four parameters, i.e., gamma, coef0, degree and C, optimized by the CPSO, the AR-CPSO and the RBH-PSO, respectively, are given in

Figure 11. Performances of CPSO, AR-CPSO, RBH-PSO, Naïve Bayesian (NB), Linger-V and SVM-IG on corpus PU1 and Ling, by using 10-fold cross-validation

Dat Sets	CPSO (%)	AR-CPSO (%)	RBH-PSO (%)	NB (%)	Linger-V(%)	SVM-IG(%)
PU1	**99.09**	**99.09**	98.99	91.07	93.45	93.18
Ling	**99.82**	**99.82**	**99.82**	96.40	98.2	96.85

Figure 12. The corresponding solutions of the four parameters, i.e., gamma, coef0, degree and c, found by the CPSO, AR-CPSO and RBH-PSO in Figure 11 on corpus PU1,using 10-fold cross-validation

Parameters	CPSO	AR-CPSO	RBH-PSO
C	1	3	169.38
gamma	6.21	0.19	0.87
coef0	178.94	21.19	142.76
degree	8	4	10

Figure 13. The corresponding solutions of the four parameters, i.e., gamma, coef0,degree and c, found by the CPSO, AR-CPSO and RBH-PSO in Figure 11 on corpus Ling, using 10-fold cross-validation

Parameters	CPSO	AR-CPSO	RBH-PSO
C	201	11.52	201
gamma	17.13	19.97	20
coef0	88.25	27.79	67.1
degree	7	8	3

Figure 12 for corpus PU1 and in Figure 13 for corpus Ling. In one word, we succeed in applying the proposed PSO algorithms to optimize the parameters of the SVM, which gives much higher classification accuracy than that of current methods.

CONCLUSION

Inspired by immunity-clonal strategies, a clonal particle swarm optimization (CPSO) and its two variants are proposed and implemented in details in this article. By cloning the best individuals of every several successive generations, the proposed CPSO algorithms have better optimization solving capability and convergence performance than the conventional SPSO in terms of a number of experiments on fifteen benchmark test functions. Two variants to the CPSO, i.e., AR-CPSO and RBH-CPSO, are developed to enhance the convergent ability. For the three proposed algorithms, the local search space is enlarged significantly by the corresponding clonal operations, which accelerate the local search greatly whilst we not only keep the velocity of the original particles but also keep the diversity of the swarm for global search. Furthermore, an application to spam detection by a SVM classifier, optimized by the proposed PSO algorithms, is completely conducted to achieve a promising result, which implies that the proposed PSO algorithms will find themselves helpful in many real-world applications in future.

ACKNOWLEDGMENT

This work was supported by the National High Technology Research and Development Program of China (863 Program), with grants No.2007AA01Z453, and also supported by the National Natural Science Foundation of China under grant No.60875080 and No.60673020. The author would like to appreciate Prof. Yuhui Shi andanonymous reviewers for their constructive comments and suggestions which help to improve the quality of this article highly. The author also thanks my students in my CIL at Peking University, Dr. Junqi Zhang, Mr. Kun Liu, Mr. Guangchen Ruan and Mr. Zhongmin Xiao for their efforts in conducting all experiments.

REFERENCES

Androutsopoulos, I., Koutsias, J., Chandrinos, K. V., Paliouras, G., & Spyropoulos, C. D. (2000). *An evaluation of naive bayesian anti-spam filtering*. Paper presented at the European Conference on Machine Learning (ECML'00).

Androutsopoulos, I., Koutsias, J., Chandrinos, K. V., & Spyropoulos, C. D. (2000). An experimental comparison of naive bayesian and keyword-based anti-spam filtering with personal e-mail messages. In *Proceedings of the 23rd Annual International ACM SIGIR Conference on Research and Development in Information Retrieval* (pp. 160-167).

Bergh, F. V. D., & Engelbrecht, A. P. (2004). A cooperative approach to particle swarm optimization. *IEEE Transactions on Evolutionary Computation, 8*, 225–239. doi:10.1109/TEVC.2004.826069

Bezerra, G. B., Barra, T. V., et al. (2006). *An immunological filter for spam*. Paper presented at the International Conference on Artificial Immune Systems (ICARIS'06).

Castro, L. N. D. (2002). Learning and optimization using the clonal selection principle. *IEEE Transactions on Evolutionary Computation, 6*, 239–251. doi:10.1109/TEVC.2002.1011539

Castro, L. N. D., & Timmis, J. I. (2003). Artificial immune system as a novel soft computing paradigm. *Soft Computing Journal, 7*(8), 526–544.

Chang, C.-C., & Lin, C.-J. (2001). *LIBSVM: a Library for Support Vector Machines*. Retrieved from http://www.csie.ntu.edu.tw/~cjlin/libsvm

Chen, J., Qin, Z., Liu, Y., & Lu, J. (2005). Particle swarm optimization with local search. In *Proceedings of the IEEE International Conference on Neural Networks and Brains* (pp. 481-484).

Clark, J., Koprinska, I., & Poon, J. (2003). A neural network based approach to automated e-mail classification. In *Proceedings of the IEEE International Conference on Web Intelligence (WI'03)* (pp. 702-705).

Clerc, M., & Kennedy, J. (2002). The particle swarm-explosion, stability, and convergence in a multidimensional complex space. *IEEE Transactions on Evolutionary Computation, 6*(1), 58–73. doi:10.1109/4235.985692

Dasgupta, D., & Attoh-Okine, N. (1997). Immunity-based systems: A survey. In *Proceedings of the IEEE International Conference on Systems, Man, and Cybernetics.*

Drucker, H., Burges, C. J. C., Kauffman, L., Smola, A., & Vapnik, V. N. (1997). Support vector regression machines. *Advances in Neural Information Processing Systems, 9,* 155–161.

Drucker, H., Wu, D., & Vapnik, V. N. (1999). Support vector machines for spam categorization. *IEEE Transactions on Neural Networks, 10,* 1048–1054. doi:10.1109/72.788645

Eberhart, R. C., & Kennedy, J. (1995). A new optimizer using particle swarm theory. In *Proceedings of the 6th International Symposium on Mcro Machine Human Science* (pp. 39-43).

El-Abd, M., & Kamel, M. S. (2006). A hierarchal cooperative particle swarm optimizer. In *Proceedings of the Swarm Intelligence Symposium* (pp. 43-47).

Ge, H. W., Lu, Y. H., Zhou, Y., Guo, X. C., & Liang, Y. C. (2005). A particle swarm optimization-based algorithm for job-shop scheduling problem. *International Journal of Computational Methods, 2*(3), 419–430. doi:10.1142/S0219876205000569

Ismael, A. I. F., Pereira, A. I. P. N., & Fernandes, E. M. G. P. (2005). Particle swarm and simulated annealing for multi-global optimization. *WSEAS Transactions on Information Science and Applications, 2,* 534–539.

Kennedy, J. (1997). The particle swarm: Social adaption of knowledge. In *Proceedings of the IEEE International Conference on Evolutionary Computation.*

Kennedy, J., & Eberhart, R. (1995). Particle swarm optimization. In *Proceedings of the IEEE International Conference on Neural Networks* (pp. 1942-1948).

Kennedy, J., & Mendes, R. (2002). Population structure and particle swarm performance. In *Proceedings of the IEEE Congress on Evolutionary Computation* (pp. 1671-1676).

Koprinska, I., Poon, J., Clark, J., & Chan, J. (2007). Learning to classify e-mail. *Information Science.* (n.d.)., 2167–2187. doi:10.1016/j.ins.2006.12.005

Leiba, B., & Borenstein, N. (2004). *A multifaceted approach to spam reduction.* In Proceedings of the First Conference on Email and AntiSpam (CEAS'04).

Liang, J. J., Qin, A. K., Suganthan, P. N., & Baskar, S. (2006). Comprehensive learning particle swarm optimizer for global optimization of multimodal functions. *IEEE Transactions on Evolutionary Computation, 10,* 281–296. doi:10.1109/TEVC.2005.857610

Liu, Y., Qin, Z., & Shi, Z. (2004). Hybrid particle swarm optimizer with line search. In *Proceedings of the IEEE International Conference on Systems, Man and Cybernetics* (pp. 3751-3755).

NASA. (n.d.). *Black hole.* From http://imagine.gsfc.nasa.gov/docs/science/knowl2/blackholes.html

Noel, M. M., & Jannett, T. C. (2004). Simulation of a new hybrid particle swarm optimization algorithm. In *Proceedings of the thirty-sixth Southeastern Symposium,* Mumbai, India (pp. 150-153).

Oda, T., & White, T. (2003). Increasing the accuracy of a spam-detecting artificial immune system. In *Proceedings of the IEEE Congress on Evolutionary Computation (CEC'03)* (Vol. 1, pp. 390-396).

Parsopoulos, K. E., Plagianakos, V. P., Magoulas, G. D., & Vrahatis, M. N. (2001). Stretching technique for obtaining global minimizers through particle swarm optimization. In *Proceedings of the Workshop on Particle Swarm Optimization* (pp. 22-29).

Parsopoulos, K. E., & Vrahatis, M. N. (2004). Upso-a united particle swarm optimization scheme. In *Lecture Series on Computational Sciences* (pp. 868-873).

Peram, T., Veeramachaneni, K., & Mohan, C. K. (2003). Fitness-distance-ratio based particle swarm optimization. In *Proceedings of the Swarm Intelligence Symposium* (pp. 174-181).

Pereira, A. I. P. N., & Fernandes, E. M. G. P. (2005). A new algorithm to identify all global maximizers based on simulated annealing. In *Proceedings of the 6th World Congresses of Structural and Multidisciplinary Optimization*.

Rigoutsos, I., & Huynh, T. (2004). Chung-kwei: A pattern-discovery-based system for the automatic identification of unsolicited e-mail messages(spam). In *Proceedings of the first Conference on Email and AntiSpam (CEAS'04)*.

Ruan, G. C., & Tan, Y. (2007). Intelligent detection approaches for spam. In *Proceedings of Third International Conference on Natural Computation (ICNC'07)*.

Sahami, M., Dumais, S., Heckerman, D., & Horvitz, E. (1998). A bayesian approach to filtering junk e-mail. In *Proceedings of the AAAI Workshop on Learning for Text Categorization* (pp. 55-62).

Secker, A., Freitas, A. A., & Timmis, J. (2003). AISEC: An artificial immune system for email classification. In *Proceedings of the IEEE Congress on Evolutionary Computation (CEC'031)* (Vol. 1, pp. 131-139).

Shi, Y. H., & Eberhart, R. (1998). A modified particle swarm optimizer. In *Proceedings of the IEEE World Congress on Computational Intelligence* (pp. 69-73).

Sirisanyalak, B., & Sornil, O. (2007). An artificial immune-based spam detection system. In *Proceedings of the IEEE Congress on Evolutionary Computation (CEC'07)*.

Stuart, I., Cha, S.-H., & Tappert, C. (2004). A neural network classifier for junk e-mail. In *Document Analysis Systems VI* (LNCS 3163, pp. 442-450).

Tan, Y. (2006). Multiple-point bit mutation method of detector generation for snsd model. In *Advances in Neural Networks - ISNN 2006* (LNCS 3973, pp. 340-345).

Tan, Y., Deng, C., & Ruan, G. C. (2009). Concentration based feature construction approach for spam detection. In *Proceedings of the International Joint Conference of Neural Networks (IJCNN'09)* (pp. 3088-3093).

Tan, Y., & Wang, J. (2004). A support vector network with hybrid kernel and minimal vapnik-chervonenkis dimension. *IEEE Transactions on Knowledge and Data Engineering, 26*, 385–395.

Tan, Y., & Xiao, Z. M. (2007). Clonal particle swarm optimization and its applications. In *Proceedings of the IEEE Congress on Evolutionary Computation* (pp. 2303-2309).

Trelea, I. C. (2003). The particle swarm optimization algorithm: Convergence analysis and parameter selection. *Information Processing Letters*, (n.d.), 317–325. doi:10.1016/S0020-0190(02)00447-7

Vapnik, V. (1995). *The Nature of Statistical Learning Theory.* New York: Springer-Verlag.

Vaz, A. F., & Fernandes, E. M. G. P. (2005). *Particle swarm algorithms for multi-local optimization.* Paper presented at the Congresso de Estatistica e Investigacao Operacional da Galiza e Norte de Portugal.

Wu, M.-W., Huang, Y., Lu, S.-K., Chen, I.-Y., & Kuo, S.-Y. (2005). A multi-faceted approach towards spam-resistible mail. In *Proceedings of the IEEE Pacific Rim International Symposium on Dependable Computing* (pp. 208-218).

Zhang, J. Q., Liu, K., Tan, Y., & He, X. G. (2008). Random black hole particle swarm optimization and its application. In *Proceedings of the IEEE International Conference on Neural Networks for Signal Processing (ICNNSP2008)* (pp. 359-365).

Zhang, J. Q., Xiao, Z. M., Tan, Y., & He, X. G. (2008). Hybrid particle swarm optimizer with advance and retreat strategy and clonal mechanism for global numerical optimization. In *Proceedings of the IEEE World Congress on Computational Intelligence (WCCI'2008—IEEE CEC'2008)* (pp. 2059-2066).

Zhou, Y., & Tan, Y. (2009). GPU-based parallel particle swarm optimization. In *Proceedings of the 2009 IEEE Congress on Evolutionary Computation* (pp. 1493-1500).

ENDNOTE

[1]   The PU1 corpus and Ling corpus may be downloaded from http://www.iit.demokritos.gr/skel/iconfig/

This work was previously published in International Journal of Swarm Intelligence Research, Volume 1, Issue 1, edited by Yuhui Shi, pp. 64-86, copyright 2010 by IGI Publishing (an imprint of IGI Global)

Section 2
Other Algorithms

Chapter 12
Unit Commitment by Evolving Ant Colony Optimization

K. Vaisakh
Andhra University, India

L. R. Srinivas
S.R.K.R. Engineering College, India

ABSTRACT

Ant Colony Optimization is more suitable for combinatorial optimization problems. ACO is successfully applied to the traveling salesman problem, and multistage decision making of ACO has an edge over other conventional methods. In this paper, the authors propose the Evolving Ant Colony Optimization (EACO) method for solving unit commitment (UC) problem. The EACO employs Genetic Algorithm (GA) for finding optimal set of ACO parameters, while ACO solves the UC problem. Problem formulation takes into consideration the minimum up and down time constraints, start up cost, spinning reserve, and generation limit constraints. The feasibility of the proposed approach is demonstrated on the systems with number of generating units in the range of 10 to 60. The test results are encouraging and compared with those obtained by other methods.

INTRODUCTION

The task of unit commitment (UC) involves scheduling of the generating units for minimizing the overall cost of the power generation over the scheduled time horizon while satisfying a set of system constraints. UC problem is a nonlinear, combinatorial optimization problem. The global

optimal solution can be obtained by complete enumeration, which is not applicable to large power systems due to its excessive computational time requirements (Wood & Wollenberg, 1996). So far many methods have been developed for solving the UC problem such as priority list methods (Burns & Gibson, 1975; Sheble, 1990), integer programming (Dillon, Edwin, Kochs, & Taud, 1978; Garver, 1963), dynamic programming (DP) (Lowery, 1983; Ouyang & Shahidepour, 1991;

DOI: 10.4018/978-1-4666-1592-2.ch012

Snyder, Powel, & Rayburn, 1987), branch-and-bound methods (Cohen & Yoshimura, 1983), mixed-integer programming (Muckstadt & Wilson, 1986). These methods have only been applied to small UC problems and have required major assumptions which limit the solution space (Sen & Kothari, 1998; Sheble & Fahd, 1994). Lagrangian Relaxation (LR) (Fisher, 1981; Merlin & Sandrin, 1983; Zhuang & Galiana, 1988) can be applied to large UC problems due to its faster computational time. However, it suffers from numerical convergence and solution quality problems in the presence of identical units. Furthermore, solution quality of LR depends on the method to initialize and update Lagrange multipliers (Dekrajangpetch, Sheble, & Conejo, 1999).

In addition to the above methods, there is another class of numerical techniques applied to the UC problem. These are (GA) (Kazarlis, Bakirtzis, & Petridis, 1996), evolutionary programming (EP) (Juste, Kita, Tanaka, & Hasegawa, 1999) and simulated annealing (SA) (Zhuang & Galiana, 1990). These are general-purpose searching techniques based on principles inspired from natural systems. These methods have the advantage of accommodating more complicated constraints and are claimed to have better solution quality.

Ant colony optimization (ACO) was proposed by M. Dorigo et al to solve the difficult combinatorial optimization problems. ACO is a random stochastic population based algorithm that simulates the behavior of ants for cooperation and learning in finding shortest paths between food sources and their nest (Bonabeau, Dorigo, & Theraulaz, 1999; Dorigo, Mahiezzo, & Colorni, 1996; Dorigo & Gambardella, 1997; Dorigo, Di Caro, & Gambardella, 1999). In ACO, the ants' behavior is simulated to solve the combinatorial problems such as traveling salesman problem and quadratic assignment problem (Dorigo, Mahiezzo, & Colorni, 1996; Dorigo & Gambardella, 1997). The ACO is applied to solve the UC problem by Simon, Padhy, and Anand (2006) and Yu, Chou, and Song, 1998).

This paper proposes a new method, Evolving Ant Colony optimization (EACO) for solving UC problem for a period of 24 hours. In this approach, the ACO is used to obtain the unit commitment schedule and genetic algorithm technique is used to find optimal set of parameters required for ACO. The Lagrangian multiplier method is applied to obtain the economic dispatch for the 24-hour schedule. The proposed method is tested on systems having 10 to 60 generating units to illustrate its effectiveness and simulation results are presented and compared with other methods.

PROBLEM FORMULATION

The objective of unit commitment problem is to minimize the production cost over the scheduled time horizon (24hours) under the generator operational and spinning reserve constraints. The objective function to be minimized is

$$F(P_i^t, U_{i,t}) = \sum_{t=1}^{T} \sum_{i=1}^{N} [F_i(P_i^t) + ST_{i,t}(1 - U_{i,t-1})]U_{i,t}$$

(1)

subject to the following constraints:

Power balance constraint

$$\sum_{i=1}^{N} P_i^t U_{i,t} = P_D^t$$

(2)

Spinning reserve constraint

$$\sum_{i=1}^{N} P_{i,max} U_{i,t} \geq P_D^t + R^t$$

(3)

Generator limit constraints

$$P_{i,min} U_{i,t} \leq P_i^t \leq P_{i,max} U_{i,t}, \quad i = 1, ..., N$$

(4)

Minimum up and down time constraints

$$U_{i,t} = \begin{cases} 1, & if \ T_{i,on} < T_{i,up}, \\ 0, & if \ T_{i,off} < T_{i,down}, \\ 0 \ or \ 1, & otherwise \end{cases} \quad (5)$$

Startup cost

$$ST_{i,t} = \begin{cases} HSC_i & if \ T_{i,down} \leq T_{i,off} \leq T_{i,cold} + T_{i,down}, \\ CSC_i & if \ T_{i,off} > T_{i,cold} + T_{i,down} \end{cases}$$

$$(6)$$

IMPLEMENTATION OF THE PROPOSED METHOD

The implementation of EACO algorithm for solving UC problem involves two phases. In the first phase, all possible states of the tth hour (using exhaustive enumeration) that satisfy the load demand with spinning reserve constraints are found. For 10-unit system, a maximum of 256 eligible states are found in any hour by taking first two generators as base units. i.e., first two generators are in 'on' condition for 24 hours and only 256 feasible states (size of pheromone matrix) are available for remaining eight generators. From 20-unit case onwards exhaustive enumeration is not possible. The base load units are always in switched on condition. In the remaining units for 20-unit case, the peak units are not considered for light load conditions to try the combinations. In that way, a maximum of 1024 feasible states are found in any hour for 20-unit case. For 40-unit case onwards the ant search space becomes large. To reduce the search space, some of the intermediate load units are also not considered to try the combinations. Which intermediate load units are not to be considered is decided based on the results of 10 and 20-unit systems. In this way, for 40-unit & 60-unit cases a maximum of 4096 feasible states are found in any hour. Because search grows space further, this

method is applied up to 60 units only. Economic dispatch using Lagrangian multiplier method is carried out for all feasible states to calculate the optimal generator output and production cost for each hour and startup cost is added for production to get transition cost for each hour. This process is continued for the complete scheduling period of 24 hours to get total cost for each state of all feasible states which constitutes the Ant Search Space (ASS).

The ASS which involves multi decision states is given in Figure 1. S_t is the eligible state satisfying load demand and spinning reserve at t^{th} hour. Once the search space is identified, the second phase involves the artificial ants allowed to pass continuously through the ASS. Each ant starts its journey from the starting node (initial condition, i.e., 1st hour), reaches the final node (24th hour) to complete its tour. Whenever an ant reaches the final node, overall generation cost for 24 hours including start-up cost is calculated.

For each transit stage (t to t+1 hour), the ant selects a state satisfying minimum uptime, minimum down time constraints etc. The generation cost together with start-up cost is calculated for all units which becomes transition cost.

This process is continued till the time period becomes T (24 hours) and a tour is completed for that particular ant. Whenever a tour is completed by an individual ant and if the total generation cost is found is lesser than the minimum cost paths taken by the previous ants, the present cost path is captured. The procedure is continued for all the remaining ants available at the starting nodes, which enables to trace the optimal path.

WORKING OF EACO

The evolving ant colony search mechanism can be mainly divided into initialization, pseudo random probabilistic transition rule, fitness function and genetic algorithm, pheromone update rule. These steps are given below:

Figure 1. Multi decision space

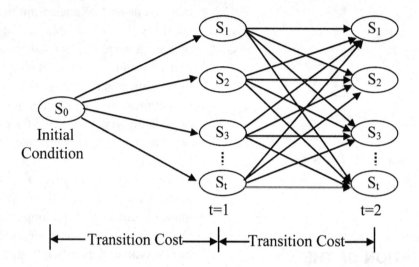

Initialization

During initialization, the parameters such as number of ants m, the relative importance of the pheromone trail α, relative importance of the visibility β, amplifying or decaying factor for updating of pheromone γ, evaporation factor ρ, the exploitation probability q_0 and scaling factor for the modification of the trail Q are randomly generated as binary strings to be subjected to GA search and are converted into the values within the limits shown in Table 1 as mentioned in Botee and Bonabeau (1998) and pheromone trail τ_0 is initialized heuristically to a small value.

Transition Strategy

The transition strategy used as given in Bonabeau, Dorigo, and Theraulaz (1999).The transition probability for the kth ant from one state i to next state j is given by

$$j = \begin{cases} \arg\max_{u \in J_i^k} \left\{ [\tau_{iu}(t)]^\alpha [\eta_{iu}]^\beta \right\} & if \ q \leq q_0 \\ J & if \ q > q_0 \end{cases}$$

(7)

where τ_{ij} trail intensity on edge (i,j); $\eta_{ij} = (1/C_{ij})$ is called heuristic function; C_{ij} is the production cost occurred for that particular stage; q is a random variable in the interval [0, 1]; q_0 is a tunable parameter. $J \in J_i^k$ is a state that is randomly selected according to the probability,

$$P_{iJ}^k(t) = \frac{[\tau_{iu}(t)]^\alpha [\eta_{iJ}]^\beta}{\sum_{u \in J_i^k} [\tau_{iu}(t)]^\alpha [\eta_{iJ}]^\beta}$$

(8)

when $q \leq q_0$ which corresponds to an exploitation of the knowledge available about the problem, that is the heuristic knowledge about cost between states and the learned knowledge memorized in the form of pheromone trails, whereas $q > q_0$ favors more exploitation. Cutting exploration by tuning q_0 allows the activity of the system to concentrate on the best solutions instead of letting it explore constantly. Here 'u' is the allowable states (Bonabeau, Dorigo, & Theraulaz, 1999; Dorigo, Di Caro, & Gambardella, 1999).

Table 1. Parameters evolved and their ranges

Sl.No	Range
1	$1 \leq m \leq 2n$
2	$0.0 \leq \alpha \leq 5.0$
3	$0.0 \leq \beta \leq 10.0$
4	$0.1 \leq \gamma \leq 3.0$
5	$0.0 \leq \rho \leq 1.0$
6	
7	$0.0 \leq q_0 \leq 1.0$
8	$0.0 \leq Q \leq 100.0$

Fitness Function and Genetic Algorithm

The fitness function of genetic algorithm used in this method is given in reference (Botee & Bonabeau, 1998). In the GA, each colony, characterized by a set of parameters, is an individual. Colonies are in competition to make it to the next generation. The fitness function F used in this study is the weighted sum of the components given below.

$$F = \sum_{i=1}^{3} c_i F_i \qquad (9)$$

where c_i is the weight of component i.

(1) $F_1 = 1 / (L + 1 - L_+)$, where L is the best cost found by the colony and L_+ is the best cost found by all of the colonies thus far. This component is relative to the performance of other colonies. $c_1 = 2.0 - 3.0$

(2) $F_2 = e^{-\frac{v}{5n}}$, where v is the iteration in which best tour was found. F_2 reflects fact that it is important for the best tour to be found quickly. $c_2 = 0.5 - 0.8$.

(3) $F_3 = e^{-\frac{m}{10n}}$ encourages m to be as small as possible. It is important to try to minimize m as the CPU time per iteration scales linearly with m. $c_3 = 0.5$. F_3 does not di-

rectly depend on how well the algorithm performs but rather on parameters that influence its speed of convergence toward a good solution. Here standard GA implementation is used which includes reproduction by Roulette-wheel selection, crossover and mutation procedures to find the optimal set of parameters for ACO. The parameters taken for GA search are: the length of the strings 16, the crossover probability 0.95 and the mutation probability 0.01.

Pheromone Update Rule

The ant that performed the best tour since the beginning of the trail is allowed to globally update the concentrations of pheromone on corresponding edges. In ACO the global trail updating rule is

$$\tau_{ij}(t+1) \leftarrow (1-\rho)\,\tau_{ij}(t) + \rho\,\Delta\tau_{ij}(t) \qquad (10)$$

where ρ is a parameter governing trail decay and

$$\Delta\tau_{ij}(t) = \begin{cases} \dfrac{Q}{(L_+)^\gamma} & if\ (i,j) \in T_+ \,, \\ 0 & otherwise \end{cases} \qquad (11)$$

where Q is the scaling factor for the modification of the trail and T_+ is the best tour since the beginning of the trail and L_+ is best cost. Only the best tour is reinforced through the global update.

Local updates are also performed, so that other solutions also emerge. It is performed as follows: when, while performing a tour, ant k is in state i and selects a state $j \in J_i^k$, the pheromone concentration of (i, j) is updated by the following equation:

$$\tau_{ij}(t) \leftarrow (1-\rho)\,\tau_{ij}(t) + \rho\,\tau_0\,. \qquad (12)$$

Figure 2. Flowchart of the proposed method

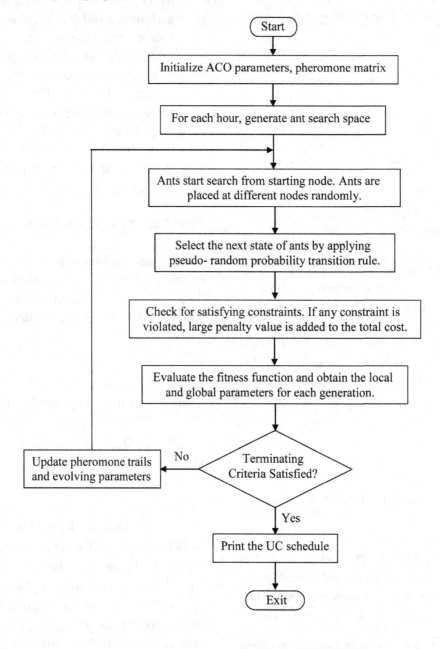

where τ_0 initial value of the pheromone trail. The flowchart for the EACO approach is shown in Figure 2.

SIMULATION RESULTS

All simulations have been run on MATLAB environment with Pentium-IV, 2.66 GHz computer with 512 MB RAM. Base ten-unit characteristics are taken from Ongsakul and Petcharaks (2004) and are given in Table 2. Load data is given in Table 3. The spinning reserve requirement is considered to be 10% of the load demand; cold startup cost is double that of hot startup cost and total scheduling period is 24 hours. The simulations include test runs for 10, 20, 40 & 60-unit systems. The 20, 40 & 60-unit data are formed

Table 2. Unit data for the ten-unit system

	Unit 1	Unit 2	Unit 3	Unit 4	Unit 5
$P_{max}(MW)$	455	455	130	130	162
$P_{min}(MW)$	150	150	20	20	25
$a\ (\$/h)$	1000	970	700	680	450
$b\ (\$/MWh)$	16.19	17.26	16.60	16.50	19.70
$c\ (\$/MW^2-h)$	0.00048	0.00031	0.002	0.00211	0.00398
min up (h)	8	8	5	5	6
min down (h)	8	8	5	5	6
hot start cost ($)	4500	5000	550	560	900
cold start cost ($)	9000	10000	1100	1120	1800
cold start hours (h)	5	5	4	4	4
initial status (h)	8	8	-5	-5	-6
	Unit 6	Unit 7	Unit 8	Unit 9	Unit 10
$P_{max}(MW)$	80	85	55	55	55
$P_{min}(MW)$	20	25	10	10	10
$a\ (\$/h)$	370	480	660	665	670
$b\ (\$/MWh)$	22.26	27.74	25.92	27.27	27.79
$c\ (\$/MW^2-h)$	0.00712	0.00079	0.00413	0.00222	0.00173
min up (h)	3	3	1	1	1
min down(h)	3	3	1	1	1
hot start cost ($)	170	260	30	30	30
cold start cost ($)	340	520	60	60	60
cold start hours (h)	2	0	0	0	0
initial status (h)	-3	-3	-1	-1	-1

by duplicating the base ten unit case and load demands are adjusted proportionately to the system size. Maximum generations are 100 for 10-unit system and 50 for remaining cases. The solution is tested for different weights of the fitness function within the ranges mentioned previously. Based

Table 3. Load data for the ten-unit system

Hour	1	2	3	4	5	6	7	8	9	10	11	12
Load (MW)	700	750	850	950	1000	1100	1150	1200	1300	1400	1450	1500
Hour	13	14	15	16	17	18	19	20	21	22	23	24
Load (MW)	1400	1300	1200	1050	1000	1100	1200	1400	1300	1100	900	800

Table 4. Optimal set of ACO parameters

ACO Parameter	10 unit system	20 unit system	40 unit system	60 unit system
m	428	1305	5212	7094
α	2.6127	1.9054	2.8713	0.0459
β	7.1177	3.8413	5.7723	8.3796
γ	0.5408	0.3016	1.7289	0.5314
ρ	0.1663	0.5747	0.7434	0.4255
q_0	0.9342	0.6721	0.5885	0.6125
Q	54.8196	97.6349	66.1814	81.8311

Table 5. Comparison of total cost

No. of Units	Total Cost ($)								
	LR[15]	GA[15]	EP[14]	LRGA [4]	GAUC[22]	ELR[19]	ICGA[6]	HPSO[27]	EACO
10	565825	565825	564551	564800	563977	563977	566404	563942	563938
20	1130660	1126243	1125494	1122622	1125516	1123297	1127244	----	1123297
40	2258503	2251911	2249093	2242178	2249715	2244237	2254123	----	2242882
60	3394066	3376625	3371611	3371079	3375065	3363491	3378108	----	3362854

on the results, $c_1 = 2.1$, $c_2 = 0.8$ and $c_3 = 0.5$ are chosen, as EACO performed best with these settings. Population size of 20 is taken 10 and 20-unit cases and 10 for remaining systems for evolving ACO parameters.

In normal ACO procedure the ant colony parameters $m, \alpha, \beta, \gamma, \rho, q_0, Q$ are fixed. Generally, it is not easy to find optimal set of parameters for ACO. This is to be done heuristically through trial and error procedure. In this paper, these parameters are not fixed, but are evolved using genetic algorithm (Botee & Bonabeau, 1998) so that optimal parameters for better solution can be found. The optimal set of ACO parameters obtained by GA is given in Table 4. The number of ants m is included for evolving because it is unclear how many ants are necessary to find a very good solution in an efficient way for a problem of given size. The exploitation probability q_0 is included

Table 6. Units on/off schedule for the 60-unit case

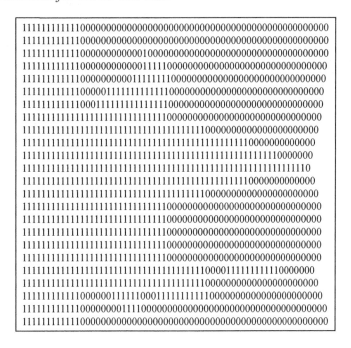

```
11111111111110000000000000000000000000000000000000000000000000
11111111111110000000000000000000000000000000000000000000000000
11111111111110000000000010000000000000000000000000000000000000
11111111111100000000000011110000000000000000000000000000000000
11111111111100000000001111111000000000000000000000000000000000
11111111111100000111111111111000000000000000000000000000000000
11111111111100011111111111111100000000000000000000000000000000
11111111111111111111111111111100000000000000000000000000000000
11111111111111111111111111111111111000000000000000000000000000
11111111111111111111111111111111111111111111110000000000000000
11111111111111111111111111111111111111111111111111111110000000
11111111111111111111111111111111111111111111111111111111111110
11111111111111111111111111111111111111111111111110000000000000
11111111111111111111111111111111111111000000000000000000000000
11111111111111111111111111111111110000000000000000000000000000
11111111111111111111111111111111110000000000000000000000000000
11111111111111111111111111111111110000000000000000000000000000
11111111111111111111111111111111110000000000000000000000000000
11111111111111111111111111111111110000000000000000000000000000
11111111111111111111111111111111111111111110000111111111110000000
11111111111111111111111111111111111111110000000000000000000000
11111111111110000001111100011111111111100000000000000000000000
11111111111110000000001110000000000000000000000000000000000000
11111111111110000000000000000000000000000000000000000000000000
```

Figure 3. Convergence of total cost for 60-unit system

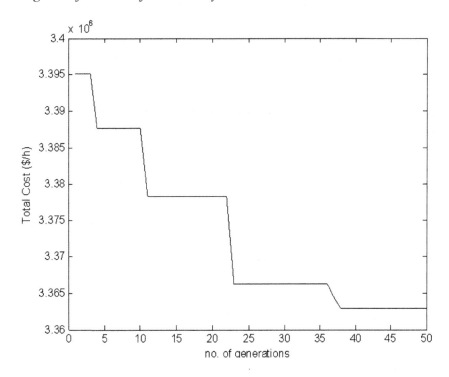

for evolving because its optimal value is also unclear.

Table 5 shows comparison of the proposed method with other methods. Units' on/off status for 60-unit system is given in Table 6. Results EACO performs well in obtaining better solution. It is to be observed that ramp rate limit constraints (Wang & Shahidehpour, 1993) are not taken into account in this paper since we would like to compare the solutions with previous works (Kazarlis, Bakirtzis, & Petridis, 1996; Juste, Kita, Tanaka, & Hasegawa, 1999; Cheng, Liu, & Liu, 2000; Serjyu, Yamashiro, Uezato, & Funabashi, 2002; Ongsakul & Petcharaks, 2004; Damousis, Bakirtzis, & Dokopoulos, 2004; Ting, Rao, & Lou, 2006; Cheng, Liu, & Liu, 2000). The total cost characteristics for 60-unit system is shown in Figure 3.

CONCLUSION

ACO is more suitable for combinatorial optimization problems. In this paper, evolving ACO is proposed and effectively implemented to solve the UC problem. The effectiveness of this proposed method is tested on 10 to 60-unit systems. Results demonstrate that EACO is a very competent method to solve the UC problem. EACO generates better solutions because the ACO parameters are evolved instead of fixing them. The results obtained from simulation are most encouraging in comparison with other methods and EACO production costs are found to be less expensive. Accordingly, EACO is very suitable for UC problem due to the production cost savings.

NOMENCLATURE

CSC_i Cold startup cost of unit i.

F_i^t Generator fuel cost in quadratic form.

$F_i^t = a_i + b_i P_i^t + c_i (P_i^t)^2$ Fuel cost in \$/h.

HSC_i Hot startup cost of unit i.

N Total number of generator units.

$P_{i,min}$ Minimum real power generation of unit i (in megawatts).

$P_{i,max}$ Maximum real power generation of unit i (in megawatts).

P_i^t Real power generation of unit i at hour t (in megawatts).

P_D^t Load demand at hour t (in megawatts).

R^t Spinning reserve at hour t (in megawatts).

ST_i^t Startup cost of unit i at hour t.

T Total number of hours.

$T_{i,cold}$ Cold start hours of unit i (in hours).

$T_{i,down}$ Minimum down time of unit i (in hours).

$T_{i,off}$ Continuously off time of unit i (in hours).

$T_{i,on}$ Continuously on time of unit i (in hours).

$T_{i,up}$ Minimum up time of unit i (in hours).

$U_{i,t}$ Status of unit i at hour t (on = 1, off = 0).

m Number of ants

τ Pheromone intensity

C_{ij} Production Cost occurred during a stage

η_{ij} Heuristic function for visibility

n Number of eligible states (size of pheromone matrix)

REFERENCES

Bonabeau, E., Dorigo, M., & Theraulaz, G. (1999). *Swarm Intelligence: From Natural to Artificial Systems*. New York: Oxford University Press.

Botee, H. M., & Bonabeau, E. (1998). Evolving ant colony optimization. *Advances in Complex Systems*, *1*, 149–159. doi:10.1142/S0219525998000119

Burns, R. M., & Gibson, C. A. (1975). Optimization of priority lists for a unit commitment program. In *Proceedings of the IEEE Power Engineering Society summer meeting* (Vol. 75, pp. 453-1).

Cheng, C. P., Liu, C. W., & Liu, C. C. (2000). Unit Commitment by Lagrangian Relaxation and Genetic algorithms. *IEEE Transactions on Power Systems*, *15*(2), 707–713. doi:10.1109/59.867163

Cohen, A. I., & Yoshimura, M. (1983). A branch-and-bound algorithm for unit commitment. *IEEE Transactions on Power Apparatus and Systems*, *2*, 444–451. doi:10.1109/TPAS.1983.317714

Damousis, I. G., Bakirtzis, A. G., & Dokopoulos, P. S. (2004). A solution to the Unit Commitment Problem using Integer-Coded Genetic Algorithm. *IEEE Transactions on Power Systems*, *19*(2), 1165–1172. doi:10.1109/TPWRS.2003.821625

Dekrajangpetch, S., Sheble, G. B., & Conejo, A. J. (1999). Auction implementation problems using Lagrangian relaxation. *IEEE Transactions on Power Systems*, *14*, 82–88. doi:10.1109/59.744488

Dillon, T. S., Edwin, K. W., Kochs, H. D., & Taud, R. J. (1978). Integer programming approach to the problem of optimal unit commitment with probabilistic reserve determination. *IEEE Transactions on Power Apparatus and Systems*, *6*, 2154–2166. doi:10.1109/TPAS.1978.354719

Dorigo, M., Di Caro, G., & Gambardella, L. M. (1999). Ant Algorithms for Distributed Discrete Optimization. *Artificial Life*, *5*(3), 137–172. doi:10.1162/106454699568728

Dorigo, M., & Gambardella, L. M. (1997). Ant colony system: a cooperative learning approach to the traveling salesman. *IEEE Transactions on Evolutionary Computation*, *1*(1), 53–65. doi:10.1109/4235.585892

Dorigo, M., Maniezzo, V., & Colorni, A. (1996). The ant system: optimization by a colony of cooperating agents. *IEEE Trans Systems Man Cybernetics. Part B*, *26*(2), 29–41.

Fisher, M. L. (1981). The Lagrangian relaxation method for solving integer programming problems. *Management Science*, *27*, 1–18. doi:10.1287/mnsc.27.1.1

Garver, L. L. (1963). Power generation scheduling by integer programming development of theory. *IEEE Transactions on Power Apparatus and Systems*, *6*, 730–735.

Juste, K. A., Kita, H., Tanaka, E., & Hasegawa, J. (1999). An Evolutionary Programming Solution to the Unit Commitment Problem. *IEEE Transactions on Power Systems*, *14*, 1452–1459. doi:10.1109/59.801925

Kazarlis, A., Bakirtzis, A. G., & Petridis, V. (1996). A Genetic Algorithm Solution to the Unit Commitment Problem. *IEEE Transactions on Power Systems*, *11*(1), 83–92. doi:10.1109/59.485989

Lowery, P. G. (1983). Generation unit commitment by dynamic programming. *IEEE Transactions on Power Apparatus and Systems*, *102*, 1218–1225.

Merlin, A., & Sandrin, P. (1983). A new method for unit commitment at Electricite De France. *IEEE Transactions on Power Systems*, *102*, 1218–1225. doi:10.1109/TPAS.1983.318063

Muckstadt, J. A., & Wilson, R. C. (1968). An application of mixed-integer programming duality to scheduling thermal generating systems. *IEEE Transactions on Power Apparatus and Systems*, 1968–1978. doi:10.1109/TPAS.1968.292156

Ongsakul, W., & Petcharaks, N. (2004). Unit Commitment by Enhanced Adaptive Lagrangian Relaxation. *IEEE Transactions on Power Systems*, *19*(1), 620–628. doi:10.1109/TPWRS.2003.820707

Ouyang, Z., & Shahidepour, S. M. (1991). An intelligent dynamic programming for unit commitment application. *IEEE Transactions on Power Systems*, *6*(3), 1203–1209. doi:10.1109/59.119267

Sen, S., & Kothari, D. P. (1998). Optimal thermal generating unit commitment: a review. *Electrical Power & Energy Systems, 20*(7), 443–451. doi:10.1016/S0142-0615(98)00013-1

Senjyu, T., Yamashiro, H., Uezato, K., & Funabashi, T. (2002). A Unit Commitment Problem by Genetic Algorithm based on Unit Characteristic Classification. In. *Proceedings of the Power Engineering Society Winter Meet, 1*, 58–63.

Sheble, G. B. (1990). Solution of the unit commitment problem by the method of unit periods. *IEEE Transactions on Power Systems, 5*(1), 257–260. doi:10.1109/59.49114

Sheble, G. B., & Fahd, G. N. (1994). Unit commitment literature synopsis. *IEEE Transactions on Power Systems, 9*, 128–135. doi:10.1109/59.317549

Simon, S. P., Padhy, N. P., & Anand, R. S. (2006). An Ant Colony System Approach for Unit Commitment Problem. *Electrical Power and Energy Systems, 28*, 315–323. doi:10.1016/j.ijepes.2005.12.004

Snyder, W. L. Jr, Powel, H. D. Jr, & Rayburn, J. C. (1987). Dynamic programming approach to unit commitment. *IEEE Transactions on Power Apparatus and Systems, 2*, 339–350.

Ting, T. O., Rao, M. V. C., & Loo, C. K. (2006). A Novel Approach for Unit Commitment Problem via an Effective Hybrid Particle Swarm Optimization. *IEEE Transactions on Power Systems, 21*(1), 411–418. doi:10.1109/TPWRS.2005.860907

Wang, C., & Shahidehpour, S. M. (1993). Effects of ramp rate limits on unit commitment and economic dispatch. *IEEE Transactions on Power Systems, 8*(3), 1341–1350. doi:10.1109/59.260859

Wood, A. J., & Wollenberg, B. F. (1996). *Power Generation, Operation & Control* (2nd ed.). New York: Wiley.

Yu, I.-K., Chou, C. S., & Song, Y. H. (1998). Applications of the ant colony search algorithm to short-term generation scheduling problem of thermal units. In *IEEE Proceedings.* doi0-7803-4754-4/98

Zhuang, F., & Galiana, F. D. (1988). Toward a more rigorous and practical unit commitment by Lagrangian relaxation. *IEEE Transactions on Power Systems, 3*(2), 763–770. doi:10.1109/59.192933

Zhuang, F., & Galiana, F. D. (1990). Unit commitment by simulated annealing. *IEEE Transactions on Power Systems, 5*(1), 311–317. doi:10.1109/59.49122

This work was previously published in International Journal of Swarm Intelligence Research, Volume 1, Issue 3, edited by Yuhui Shi, pp. 67-77, copyright 2010 by IGI Publishing (an imprint of IGI Global)

Chapter 13
Bacterial Foraging Optimization

Kevin M. Passino
The Ohio State University, USA

ABSTRACT

The bacterial foraging optimization (BFO) algorithm mimics how bacteria forage over a landscape of nutrients to perform parallel nongradient optimization. In this article, the author provides a tutorial on BFO, including an overview of the biology of bacterial foraging and the pseudo-code that models this process. The algorithms features are briefly compared to those in genetic algorithms, other bio-inspired methods, and nongradient optimization. The applications and future directions of BFO are also presented.

1. INTRODUCTION: BACTERIAL FORAGING: E. COLI

The *E. coli* bacterium has a plasma membrane, cell wall, and capsule that contain, for instance, the cytoplasm and nucleoid. The pili (singular, pilus) are used for a type of gene transfer to other *E. coli* bacteria, and flagella (singular, flagellum) are used for locomotion. The cell is about $1\mu m$ in diameter, and $2\mu m$ in length. The *E. coli* cell only weighs about 1 picogram, and is composed of about 70% water. *Salmonella typhimurium* is a similar type of bacterium.

The *E. coli* bacterium is probably the best understood microorganism. Its entire genome has been sequenced; it contains 4,639,221 of the A, C, G, and T "letters"—adenosine, cytosine, guanine, and thymine—arranged into a total of 4,288 genes. When *E. coli* grows, it gets longer, then divides in the middle into two "daughters." Given sufficient food and held at the temperature of the human gut (one place where they live) of 37 deg. C, *E. coli* can synthesize and replicate everything it needs to make a copy of itself in about 20 min.; hence, growth of a population of bacteria is exponential with a relatively short "time to double" the population size. For instance,

DOI: 10.4018/978-1-4666-1592-2.ch013

following (Berg, 2000), if at noon today you start with one cell and sufficient food, by noon tomorrow there will be $2^{72} = 4.7 \times 10^{21}$ cells, which is enough to pack a cube 17 meters on one side. (It should be clear that with enough food, at this reproduction rate, they could quickly cover the entire earth with a knee-deep layer!)

The *E. coli* bacterium has a control system that enables it to search for food and try to avoid noxious substances (the resulting motions are called "taxes"). For instance, it swims away from alkaline and acidic environments, and towards more neutral ones. To explain the motile behavior of *E. coli* bacteria, we will explain its actuator (the flagella), "decision-making," sensors, and closed-loop behavior (i.e., how it moves in various environments—its "motile behavior"). You will see that *E. coli* perform a type of "saltatory search."

1.1 Swimming and Tumbling via Flagella

Locomotion is achieved via a set of relatively rigid flagella that enable it to "swim" via each of them rotating in the same direction at about $100 - 200$ revolutions per second (in control systems terms, we think of the flagella as providing for actuation). Each flagellum is a left-handed helix configured so that as the base of the flagellum (i.e., where it is connected to the cell) rotates counterclockwise, as viewed from the free end of the flagellum looking towards the cell, it produces a force against the bacterium so it pushes the cell. You may think of each flagellum as a type of propeller. If a flagellum rotates clockwise, then it will pull at the cell. From an engineering perspective, the rotating shaft at the base of the flagellum is quite an interesting contraption that seems to use what biologists call a "universal joint" (so the rigid flagellum can "point" in different directions, relative to the cell). In addition, the mechanism that creates the rotational forces to spin the flagellum in either direction is described

by biologists as being a biological "motor" (a relatively rare contraption in biology even though several types of bacteria use it). The motor is quite efficient in that it rotates a complete revolution using only about 1000 protons and thereby *E. coli* spends less than 1% of its energy budget for motility.

An *E. coli* bacterium can move in two different ways: it can "run" (swim for a period of time) or it can "tumble," and it alternates between these two modes of operation its entire lifetime (i.e., it is rare that the flagella will stop rotating). First, we explain each of these two modes of operation. Following that, we will explain how it decides how long to swim before it tumbles.

If the flagella rotate clockwise, each flagellum pulls on the cell and the net effect is that each flagellum operates relatively independent of the others and so the bacterium "tumbles" about (i.e., the bacterium does not have a set direction of movement and there is little displacement). To tumble after a run, the cell slows down or stops first; since bacteria are so small they experience almost no inertia, only viscosity, so that when a bacterium stops swimming, it stops within the diameter of a proton. Call the time interval during which a tumble occurs a "tumble interval." Under certain experimental conditions (an isotropic, homogeneous medium—one with no nutrient or noxious substance gradients) for a "wild type" cell (one found in nature), the mean tumble interval is about 0.14 ± 0.19 sec.(mean $\pm$ standard deviation, and it is exponentially distributed) (Berg, 1972, 2000). After a tumble, the cell will generally be pointed in a random direction, but there is a slight bias toward being placed in a direction it was traveling before the tumble.

If the flagella move counterclockwise, their effects accumulate by forming a "bundle" (it is thought that the bundle is formed due to the viscous drag of the medium) and hence, they essentially make a "composite propeller" and push the bacterium so that it runs (swims) in one direction. On a run, bacteria swim at a rate of about

$10 - 20$ μ meters/sec., or about 10 body lengths per second (assuming the faster speed and an *E. coli* that is 2 μ meters long, a typical length), but in a rich medium they can swim even faster (Lowe, Meister, & Berg, 1987). This is a relatively fast rate for a living organism to travel; consider how fast you could move through water if you could swim at 10 of your body lengths per second. Call the time interval during which a run occurs the "run interval." Under certain experimental conditions (an isotropic, homogeneous medium---the same as the one mentioned above) for a wild type cell, the mean run interval is about 0.86 ± 1.18 sec.(and it is exponentially distributed) (Berg, 1972, 2000). Also, under these conditions, the mean speed is 14.2 ± 3.4 $\mu m / sec$. Runs are not perfectly straight since the cell is subject to Brownian movement that causes it to wander off course by about 30 deg. in 1 sec. in one type of medium, so this is how much it typically can deviate on a run. In a certain medium, after about 10 sec. it drifts off course more than 90 deg. and hence, essentially forgets the direction it was moving (Berg, 1972). Finally, note that in many bacteria, the motion of the flagella can induce other motions, e.g., rotating the bacteria about an axis.

1.2 Bacterial Motile Behavior: Climbing Nutrient Gradients

The motion patterns (called "taxes") that the bacteria will generate in the presence of chemical attractants and repellents are called "chemotaxes." For *E. coli*, encounters with serine or aspartate result in attractant responses, while repellent responses result from the metal ions Ni and Co, changes in pH, amino acids like leucine, and organic acids like acetate. What is the resulting emergent pattern of behavior for a whole group of *E. coli* bacteria? Generally, as a group they will try to find food and avoid harmful phenomena, and when viewed under a microscope, you will get a sense that a type of intelligent behavior has

emerged, since they will seem to intentionally move as a group.

To explain how chemotaxis motions are generated, we simply must explain how the *E. coli* decides how long to run since, from the above discussion, we know what happens during a tumble or run. First, note that if an *E. coli* is in some substance that is neutral, in the sense that it does not have food or noxious substances, and if it is in this medium for a long period of time (e.g., more than one minute), then the flagella will simultaneously alternate between moving clockwise and counterclockwise so that the bacterium will alternately tumble and run. This alternation between the two modes will move the bacterium, but in random directions, and this enables it to "search" for nutrients. For instance, in the isotropic homogeneous environment described above, the bacteria alternately tumble and run with the mean tumble and run lengths given above, and at the speed that was given. If the bacteria are placed in a homogeneous concentration of serine (i.e., one with a nutrient but no gradients), then a variety of changes occur in the characteristics of their motile behavior. For instance, mean run length and mean speed increase and mean tumble time decreases. They do, however, still produce a basic type of searching behavior; even though it has some food, it persistently searches for more. As an example of tumbles and runs in the isotropic homogeneous medium described above, in one trial motility experiment lasting 29.5 sec., there were 26 runs, the maximum run length was 3.6 sec., and the mean speed was about 21 $\mu m / sec$. (Berg, 1972, 2000).

Next, suppose that the bacterium happens to encounter a nutrient gradient (e.g., serine). The *change* in the concentration of the nutrient triggers a reaction such that the bacterium will spend more time swimming and less time tumbling. As long as it travels on a positive concentration gradient (i.e., so that it moves towards increasing nutrient concentrations) it will tend to lengthen the time it spends swimming (i.e., it runs farther). The directions of movement are "biased" towards increasing nutrient gradients. The cell does not change its *direction* on a run due to changes in the gradient—the tumbles basically determine the direction of the run, aside from the Brownian influences mentioned above.

On the other hand, typically if the bacterium happens to swim down a concentration gradient (or into a positive gradient of noxious substances), it will return to its baseline behavior so that essentially it tries to search for a way to climb back up the gradient (or down the noxious substance gradient). For instance, under certain conditions, for a wild-type cell swimming up serine gradients, the mean run length is 2.19 ± 3.43 sec., but if it swims down a serine gradient, mean run length is 1.40 ± 1.88 sec. (Berg, 2000). Hence, when it moves up the gradient, it lengthens its runs. The mean run length for swimming down the gradient is the one that is expected, considering that the bacteria are in this particular type of medium; they act basically the same as in a homogeneous medium so that they are engaging their search/ avoidance behavior to try to climb back up the gradient.

Finally, suppose that the concentration of the nutrient is constant for the region it is in, after it has been on a positive gradient for some time. In this case, after a period of time (not immediately), the bacterium will return to the same proportion of swimming and tumbling as when it was in the neutral substance so that it returns to its standard searching behavior. It is never satisfied with the amount of surrounding food; it always seeks higher concentrations. Actually, under certain experimental conditions, the cell will compare the concentration observed over the past 1 sec. with the concentration observed over the 3 sec. before that and it responds to the difference (Berg, 1972). Hence, it uses the past 4 sec. of nutrient concentration data to decide how long to run (Segall, Block, & Berg, 1986). Considering the deviations in direction due to Brownian movement

discussed above, the bacterium basically uses as much time as it can in making decisions about climbing gradients (Berg, 1993). In effect, the run length results from how much climbing it has done recently. If it has made lots of progress and hence, has just had a long run, then even if for a little while it is observing a homogeneous medium (without gradients), it will take a longer run. After a certain time period, it will recover and return to its standard behavior in a homogeneous medium.

Basically, the bacterium is trying to swim from places with low concentrations of nutrients to places with high concentrations. An opposite type of behavior is used when it encounters noxious substances. If the various concentrations move with time, then the bacteria will try to "chase" after the more favorable environments and run from harmful ones. Clearly, nutrient and noxious substance diffusion and motion will affect the motion patterns of a group of bacteria in complex ways.

1.3 Underlying Sensing and Decision-Making Mechanisms

The sensors are the receptor proteins, which are signaled directly by external substances (e.g., in the case for the pictured amino acids) or via the "periplasmic substrate-binding proteins." The "sensor" is very sensitive, in some cases requiring less than 10 molecules of attractant to trigger a reaction, and attractants can trigger a swimming reaction in less than 200 ms. You can then think of the bacterium as having a "high gain" with a small attractant detection threshold (detection of only a small number of molecules can trigger a doubling or tripling of the run length). On the other hand, the corresponding threshold for encountering a homogeneous medium after being in a nutrient rich one is larger. Also, there is a type of time-averaging that is occurring in the sensing process. The receptor proteins then affect signaling molecules inside the bacterium. Also, there is in effect an "adding machine" and an ability to compare values and to arrive at an overall decision about which mode the flagella should operate in; essentially, the different sensors add and subtract their effects, and the more active or numerous have a greater influence on the final decision. Even though the sensory and decision-making system in *E. coli* is probably the best understood one in biology, we are ignoring the underlying chemistry that is needed for a full explanation.

It is interesting to note that the "decision-making system" in the *E. coli* bacterium must have some ability to sense a *derivative*, and hence, it has a type of memory! At first glance it may seem possible that the bacterium senses concentrations at both ends of the cell and finds a simple difference to recognize a concentration gradient (a spatial derivative); however, this is not the case. Experiments have shown that it performs a type of sampling, and roughly speaking, it remembers the concentration a moment ago, compares it with a current one, and makes decisions based on the difference (i.e., it computes something like an Euler approximation to a time derivative). Actually, in Yi, Huang, Simon, and Doyle (2000) the authors show how internal bacterial decision-making processes involve some type of integral feedback control mechanism.

In summary, we see that with memory, a type of addition mechanism, an ability to make comparisons, a few simple internal "control rules," and its chemical sensing and locomotion capabilities, the bacterium is able to achieve a complex type of searching and avoidance behavior. Evolution has designed this control system. It is robust and clearly very successful at meeting its goals of survival when viewed from a population perspective.

1.4 Elimination and Dispersal Events

It is possible that the local environment where a population of bacteria lives changes either gradually (e.g., via consumption of nutrients) or suddenly due to some other influence. There can

be events such that all the bacteria in a region are killed or a group is dispersed into a new part of the environment. For example, local significant increases in heat can kill a population of bacteria that are currently in a region with a high concentration of nutrients (you can think of heat as a type of noxious influence). Or, it may be that water or some animal will move populations of bacteria from one place to another in the environment. Over long periods of time, such events have spread various types of bacteria into virtually every part of our environment, from our intestines, to hot springs and underground environments, and so on.

What is the effect of elimination and dispersal events on chemotaxis? It has the effect of possibly destroying chemotactic progress, but it also has the effect of assisting in chemotaxis since dispersal may place bacteria near good food sources. From a broad perspective, elimination and dispersal is part of the population-level motile behavior.

1.5 Evolution of Bacteria

Mutations in *E. coli* occur at a rate of about 10^{-7} per gene, per generation. In addition to mutations that affect its physiological aspects (e.g., reproductive efficiency at different temperatures), *E. coli* bacteria occasionally engage in a type of "sex" called "conjugation," where small gene sequences are unidirectionally transferred from one bacterium to another. It seems that these gene sequences apparently carry good fitness characteristics in terms of reproductive capability, so conjugation is sometimes thought of as a transmittal of "fertility." To achieve conjugation, a pilus extends to make contact with another bacterium, and the gene sequence transfers through the pilus.

It is important to note that there are some very basic differences in evolution for higher organisms and bacteria. While conjugation apparently spreads "good" gene sequences, the "homogenizing effect" on gene frequency from conjugation is relatively small compared to how sex works in other organisms. This is partly since conjugation is relatively rare, and partly since the rate of reproduction is relatively high, on the order of hours depending on environmental conditions. Due to these characteristics, population genetics for *E. coli* may be dominated by selection sweeps triggered by the acquisition, via sex, of an adaptive allele.

1.6 Taxes in Other Swimming Bacteria

While most bacteria are motile and many types have analogous taxes capabilities to *E. coli* bacteria, the specific sensing, actuation, and decision-making mechanisms are different (Armitage, 1999; Neidhardt, Ingraham, & Schaechter, 1990). For instance, while the proton-driven motor on *E. coli* rotates at a few hundred revolutions per second, Na^+-driven motors on some bacteria rotate at speeds up to 1000 revolutions per second, and on some species, the motor can turn in either direction or stop. Different types of bacteria can sense different phenomena and have different underlying decision-making, so they may search for and try to avoid different phenomena. Some bacteria can sense their own metabolic state and only respond to compounds currently required for growth and their pattern of responses may change based on their environment. Studies of the mechanisms for decision and control in various bacteria do, however, indicate that they have common features and hence, some have suggested that there was a single early evolutionary event that resulted in the swimming capability of bacteria. Swimming generally moves a bacterium to a more favorable environment for growth, or it maintains it in its current position, and hence, it gives the bacteria a survival advantage. Some scientists have suggested that the shapes of motile bacteria developed to allow efficient swimming. Some bacteria even change their shape to reduce the adverse effects of moving through more viscous media. Even though there can be significant differences between species, all swimming bacteria seem to have similar swimming patterns, where there is an alternation between smooth swimming and a change in direction (i.e., a type of saltatory search). Next, several examples of other types of sensing and taxes in swimming bacteria are provided.

Some bacteria can search for oxygen, and hence their motility behavior is based on "aerotaxis," while others search for desirable temperatures resulting in "thermotaxis." Actually, the *E. coli* is capable of thermotaxis in that it seeks warmer environments with a temperature range of 20 deg. to 37 deg. C. Other bacteria, such as *Thiospirillum jenense*, search for or avoid light of certain wavelengths and this is called "phototaxis" Actually, the *E. coli* tries to avoid intense blue light, so it is also capable of phototaxis. Some bacteria swim along magnetic lines of force that enter the earth, so that when in the northern hemisphere, they swim towards the north magnetic pole, and in the southern hemisphere, they swim towards the south magnetic pole. (This is due to the presence of a small amount of magnetic material *in the cell* that essentially acts as a compass to passively reorient the cell.)

There are square-shaped bacteria that are propelled either forward or backward via flagella, and when multiple such bacteria naturally collide, their flagella can become "clumped," and this seems to be responsible for their tumbling. Hence, their motility behavior is characterized by forward movement, followed by either forward or backward movement, and an intermittent change in direction via tumbling (Alam, Claviez, Oesterhelt, & Kessel, 1984). *Vibrio alginolyticus* move differently when free-living versus living on a surface. Free-living *Vibrio alginolyticus* swims using a Na^+-driven motor on its flagella but when it is on the surface of a liquid, it senses the increased viscosity via the flagellar motor and then synthesizes many proton-driven flagella, which then allow the cell to move over surfaces (Armitage, 1999). The cells move as groups ("rafts"), since this is thought to help overcome viscous drag and surface tension. In other bacteria, flagella can be synthesized and discarded as they are needed.

1.7 Other Group Phenomena in Bacteria

A particularly interesting group behavior has been demonstrated for several motile species of bacteria, including *E. coli* and *S. typhimurium*, where intricate stable spatio-temporal patterns (swarms)[1] are formed in semi-solid nutrient media (Armitage, 1999; Budrene & Berg, 1995a, 1995b; Woodward, Tyson, Myerscough, Murray, Budrene, & Berg, 1995; Blat & Eisenbach, 1995). When a group of *E. coli* cells is placed in the center of a semi-solid agar with a single nutrient chemo-effector (sensor), they move out from the center in a traveling ring of cells by moving up the nutrient gradient created by consumption of the nutrient by the group. Moreover, if high levels of the nutrient called succinate are used as the nutrient, then the cells release the attractant aspartate, so that they congregate into groups and hence, move as concentric patterns of groups with high bacterial density. (Note that many cells in those groups permanently lose motility.) The spatial order results from outward movement of the ring and the local releases of the attractant; the cells provide an attraction signal to each other so they swarm together. Pattern formation can be suppressed by a background of aspartate (since it seems that this will in essence scramble the chemical signal by eliminating its directionality). The pattern seems to form based on the dominance of two stimuli (cell-cell signaling and foraging).

The role of these patterns in natural environments is not understood; however, there is evidence that stress to the bacteria results in them releasing chemical signals that other bacteria are chemotactic towards. If enough stress is present,

then a whole group can secrete the chemical signal strengthening the total signal, and hence, an aggregate of the bacteria forms. It seems that this aggregate forms to protect the group from the stress (e.g., by effectively hiding many cells in the middle of the group). It seems that the aggregates of the bacteria are not necessarily stationary; under certain conditions they can migrate, split, and fuse. This has led researchers to hypothesize that there may be other communication methods being employed that are not yet understood.

As another example, there are "biofilms" that can be composed of multiple types of bacteria (e.g., *E. coli*) that can coat various objects (e.g., roots of plants or medical implants). It seems that both motility and "quorum sensing" are involved in biofilm formation. A biofilm is a mechanism for keeping a bacterial species in a fixed location, avoiding overcrowding, and avoiding nutrient limitation and toxin production by packing them at a low density in a "polysaccharide matrix." Secreted chemicals provide a mechanism for the cells to sense population density, but motility seems to assist in the early stages of biofilm formation. It is also thought that chemotactic responses are used to drive cells to the outer edges of the biofilm, where nutrient concentrations may be higher.

In a variety of bacteria, including *E. coli*, complex patterns result primarily not from motility, but from reproduction (Shapiro, 1997). In some bacteria, it seems that there is a type of signaling that occurs and results in the formation of regular patterns as the culture of bacteria grows. Formation of such patterns is sometimes thought of as a type of multicellular "morphogenesis." For example, the formation of the "fruiting bodies" by *Myxococcus xanthus* can be viewed as a type of morphogenesis, but one that seems to be primarily based on motility and cell deaths rather than reproduction (Shimkets & Dworkin, 1997).

Other types of bacteria exhibit group behaviors (Losick & Kaiser, 1997). For instance, there are luminous bacteria that will emit no light until the population reaches a certain density. For instance, the bacteria *Vibrio fischeri* lives in the ocean at low concentrations and its secreted "autoinducer" chemical signal is quite dilute. However, the squid *Euprymna scolopes* selects these bacteria to grow in its light organ. When a sufficiently large population is cultivated in its light organ, the autoinducer chemical signals given off by each bacterium effectively add to result in a high concentration of this chemical and, when it reaches a certain threshold, each cell will switch on its luminescence property so that as a group they emit a visible light (Losick & Kaiser, 1997). The squid, which is a nocturnal forager, benefits since the light camouflages it from predators below, since its light resembles moonlight and hence, effectively eliminates its shadow. The bacteria benefit by getting nourishment and shelter. The bacteria and squid are in a symbiont relationship (i.e., they live together to benefit each other).

Also, the soil-dwelling *streptomycete* colonies can grow a branching network of long fiber-like cells that can penetrate and degrade vegetation and then feed on the resulting decaying matter. (In terms of combinatorial optimization, you may think of finding optimal trees or graphs.) Under starvation conditions, they can cooperate to produce spores on a structure called an "aerial mycelium" that may be carried away.

As another example, in *Proteus mirabilis* the rod-shaped cells exist as "swimmers" that are driven by fewer than 10 flagella when they are in liquid media and they have chemotactic responses analogous to those of *E. coli*. If, however, these swimmers are placed on a solid surface, the swimmer cell "differentiates" (changes) into a "swarmer cell" that is an elongated rod (of roughly the same diameter) with more than 10,000 flagella. On solid surfaces, the cells aggregate and exhibit swarm behavior in foraging via group chemotaxis. If they are then placed back in a liquid medium, there is a process of "consolidation" where swarmer cells split into swimmer cells. Moreover, when swarming they exhibit the "Dienes phenomenon," where swarms of the same

type of bacteria try to avoid each other. (The mechanisms of this apparent territorial behavior are not well-understood.)

2. E. COLI BACTERIAL SWARM FORAGING FOR OPTIMIZATION

Suppose that we want to find the minimum of $J(\theta)$, $\theta \in \Re^p$, where we do not have measurements, or an analytical description, of the gradient $\nabla J(\theta)$. Here, we use ideas from bacterial foraging to solve this "nongradient" optimization problem. First, suppose that θ is the position of a bacterium and $J(\theta)$ represents the combined effects of attractants and repellents from the environment, with, for example, $J(\theta) < 0$, $J(\theta) = 0$, and $J(\theta) > 0$ representing that the bacterium at location θ is in nutrient-rich, neutral, and noxious environments, respectively. Basically, chemotaxis is a foraging behavior that implements a type of optimization where bacteria try to climb up the nutrient concentration (find lower and lower values of $J(\theta)$) and avoid noxious substances and search for ways out of neutral media (avoid being at positions θ where $J(\theta) \geq 0$).

2.1 An Optimization Model for *E. coli* Bacterial Foraging

To define our optimization model of *E. coli* bacterial foraging, we need to define a population (set) of bacteria, and then model how they execute chemotaxis, swarming, reproduction, and elimination/dispersal. After doing this, we will highlight the limitations (inaccuracies) in our model.

2.1.1 Population and Chemotaxis

Define a chemotactic step to be a tumble followed by a tumble or a tumble followed by a run. Let j be the index for the chemotactic step. Let k be the index for the reproduction step. Let ℓ be the index of the elimination-dispersal event. Let

$$P(j,k,\ell) = \left\{ \theta^i(j,k,\ell) \mid i = 1,2,...,S \right\}$$

represent the positions of each member in the population of the S bacteria at the jth chemotactic step, k^{th} reproduction step, and ℓ^{th} elimination-dispersal event. Here, let $J(i,j,k,\ell)$ denote the cost at the location of the ith bacterium $\theta^i(j,k,\ell) \in \Re^p$ (sometimes we drop the indices and refer to the ith bacterium position as θ^i). Note that we will interchangeably refer to J as being a "cost" (using terminology from optimization theory) and as being a nutrient surface (in reference to the biological connections). For actual bacterial populations, S can be very large (e.g., $S = 10^9$), but $p = 3$. In computer simulations, we will use much smaller population sizes and will keep the population size fixed. We will allow $p > 3$, so we can apply the method to higher dimensional optimization problems.

Let N_c be the length of the lifetime of the bacteria as measured by the number of chemotactic steps they take during their life. Let $C(i) > 0$, $i = 1,2,...,S$, denote a basic chemotactic step size that we will use to define the lengths of steps during runs. To represent a tumble, a unit length random direction, say $\phi(j)$, is generated; this will be used to define the direction of movement after a tumble. In particular, we let

$$\theta^i(j+1,k,\ell) = \theta^i(j,k,\ell) + C(i)\phi(j)$$

so that $C(i)$ is the size of the step taken in the random direction specified by the tumble. If at $\theta^i(j+1,k,\ell)$ the cost $J(i,j+1,k,\ell)$ is better (lower) than at $\theta^i(j,k,\ell)$, then another step of size $C(i)$ in this same direction will be taken, and again, if that step resulted in a position with a better cost value than at the previous step, another step is taken. This swim is continued as long

as it continues to reduce the cost, but only up to a maximum number of steps, N_s . This represents that the cell will tend to keep moving if it is headed in the direction of increasingly favorable environments.

2.1.2 Swarming Mechanisms

The above discussion was for the case where no cell-released attractants are used to signal other cells that they should swarm together. Here, we will also have cell-to-cell signaling via an attractant and will represent that with $J_{cc}^i(\theta, \theta^i(j,k,\ell))$, $i = 1,2,...,S$, for the ith bacterium. Let

$$d_{attract} = 0.1$$

be the depth of the attractant released by the cell (a quantification of how much attractant is released) and

$$w_{attract} = 0.2$$

be a measure of the width of the attractant signal (a quantification of the diffusion rate of the chemical). The cell also repels a nearby cell in the sense that it consumes nearby nutrients and it is not physically possible to have two cells at the same location. To model this, we let

$$h_{repellent} = d_{attract}$$

be the height of the repellent effect (magnitude of its effect) and

$$w_{repellent} = 10$$

be a measure of the width of the repellent. The values for these parameters are simply chosen to illustrate general bacterial behaviors, not to represent a particular bacterial chemical signaling scheme. The particular values of the parameters are chosen with the nutrient profile in mind. For instance, the depth and width of the attractant is small relative to the nutrient concentrations represented in the cost function. Let J_cc(,P(j,k,)) = _i=1^SJ_cc^i(,^i(j,k,))

= _i=1^S [-d_attract (-w_attract _m=1^p(_m-_m^i)^2)]

+ _i=1^S [h_repellent (-w_repellent _m=1^p(_m-_m^i)^2)] denote the combined cell-to-cell attraction and repelling effects, where $\theta = [\theta_1,...,\theta_p]^T$ is a point on the optimization domain and θ_m^i is the mth component of the ith bacterium position θ^i (for convenience, we omit some of the indices). Note that as each cell moves, so does its $J_{cc}^i(\theta,\theta^i(j,k,\ell))$ function, and this represents that it will release chemicals as it moves. Due to the movements of all the cells, the $J_{cc}(\theta,P(j,k,\ell))$ function is *time-varying* in that, if many cells come close together, there will be a high amount of attractant and hence, an increasing likelihood that other cells will move towards the group. This produces the swarming effect. When we want to study swarming, the ith bacterium, $i = 1,2,...,S$, will hill-climb on

$$J(i,j,k,\ell) + J_{cc}(\theta,P)$$

(rather than the $J(i,j,k,\ell)$ defined above) so that the cells will try to find nutrients, avoid noxious substances, and at the same time try to move towards other cells, but not too close to them. The $J_{cc}(\theta,P)$ function dynamically deforms the search landscape as the cells move to represent the desire to swarm (i.e., we model mechanisms of swarming as a minimization process).

2.1.3 Reproduction and Elimination/Dispersal

After N_c chemotactic steps, a reproduction step is taken. Let N_{re} be the number of reproduction steps to be taken. For convenience, we assume that S is a positive even integer. Let S_r=S2 be the number of population members who have had sufficient nutrients so that they will reproduce (split in two) with no mutations. For reproduction, the population is sorted in order of ascending accumulated cost (higher accumulated cost represents that it did not get as many nutrients during its lifetime of foraging and hence, is not as "healthy" and thus unlikely to reproduce); then the S_r least healthy bacteria die and the other S_r healthiest bacteria each split into two bacteria, which are placed at the same location. Other fractions or approaches could be used in place of Equation (2.1.3); this method rewards bacteria that have encountered a lot of nutrients, and allows us to keep a constant population size, which is convenient in coding the algorithm.

Let N_{ed} be the number of elimination-dispersal events, and for each such elimination-dispersal event, each bacterium in the population is subjected to elimination-dispersal with probability p_{ed}. We assume that the frequency of chemotactic steps is greater than the frequency of reproduction steps, which is in turn greater in frequency than elimination-dispersal events (e.g., a bacterium will take many chemotactic steps before reproduction, and several generations may take place before an elimination-dispersal event).

2.1.4 Foraging Model Limitations

Clearly, we are ignoring many characteristics of the actual biological optimization process in favor of simplicity and capturing the gross characteristics of chemotactic hill-climbing and swarming. For instance, we assume that consumption does not affect the nutrient surface (e.g., while a bacterium is in a nutrient-rich environment, we do not increase the value of J near where it has consumed nutrients) where clearly in nature, bacteria modify the nutrient concentrations via consumption. A tumble does not result in a perfectly random new direction for movement; however, here we assume that it does. Brownian effects buffet the cell, so that after moving a small distance, it is within a pie-shaped region of its start point at the tip of the piece of pie. Basically, we assume that swims are straight, whereas in nature they are not. Tumble and run lengths are exponentially distributed random variables, not constant, as we assume. Run-length decisions are actually based on the past 4 sec. of concentrations, whereas here we assume that at each tumble, older information about nutrient concentrations is lost. Although naturally asynchronous, we force synchronicity by requiring, for instance, chemotactic steps of different bacteria to occur at the same time, all bacteria to reproduce at the same time instant, and all bacteria that are subjected to elimination and dispersal to do so at the same time. We assume a constant population size, even if there are many nutrients and generations. We assume that the cells respond to nutrients in the environment in the same way that they respond to ones released by other cells for the purpose of signaling the desire to swarm. (A more biologically accurate model of the swarming behavior of certain bacteria is given in Woodward et al., 1995.) Clearly, other choices for the criterion of which bacteria should split could be used (e.g., based only on the concentration at the end of a cell's lifetime, or on the quantity of noxious substances that were encountered). We are also ignoring conjugation and other evolutionary characteristics. For instance, we assume that $C(i)$, N_s, and N_c remain the same for each generation. In nature it seems likely that these parameters could evolve for different environments to maximize population growth rates.

2.2 Bacterial Foraging Optimization Algorithm

For initialization, you must choose p, S, N_c, N_s, N_{re}, N_{ed}, p_{ed}, and the $C(i)$, $i = 1,2,...,S$. If you use swarming, you will also have to pick the parameters of the cell-to-cell attractant functions. Also, initial values for the θ^i, $i = 1,2,...,S$, must be chosen. Choosing these to be in areas where an optimum value is likely to exist is a good choice. Alternatively, you may want to simply randomly distribute them across the domain of the optimization problem. The algorithm that models bacterial population chemotaxis, swarming, reproduction, elimination, and dispersal is given below (initially, $j = k = \ell = 0$). For the algorithm, note that updates to the θ^i automatically result in updates to P. Clearly, we could have added a more sophisticated termination test than simply specifying a maximum number of iterations.

Elimination-dispersal loop: $\ell = \ell + 1$ Reproduction loop: $k = k+1$ Chemotaxis loop: $j = j+1$ For $i = 1,2,...,S$, take a chemotactic step for bacterium i as follows. Compute $J(i,j,k,\ell)$. Let

$$J(i,j,k,\ell) = J(i,j,k,\ell) + J_{cc}(\theta^i(j,k,\ell), P(j,k,\ell))$$

(i.e., add on the cell-to-cell attractant effect to the nutrient concentration). Let $J_{last} = J(i,j,k,\ell)$ to save this value, since we may find a better cost via a run. Tumble: generate a random vector $\Delta(i) \in \Re^p$ with each element $\Delta_m(i)$, $m = 1,2,...,p$, a random number on $[-1,1]$. Move: let

$$\theta^i(j+1,k,\ell) = \theta^i(j,k,\ell) + C(i)\frac{\Delta(i)}{\sqrt{\Delta^T(i)\Delta(i)}}$$

This results in a step of size $C(i)$ in the direction of the tumble for bacterium i. Compute $J(i,j+1,k,\ell)$, and then let

$$J(i,j+1,k,\ell) = J(i,j+1,k,\ell)$$
$$+J_{cc}(\theta^i(j+1,k,\ell),P(j+1,k,\ell))$$

Swim (note that we use an approximation, since we decide swimming behavior of each cell as if the bacteria numbered $\{1,2,...,i\}$ have moved, and $\{i+1,i+2,...,S\}$ have not; this is much simpler to simulate than simultaneous decisions about swimming and tumbling by all bacteria at the same time): Let $m=0$ (counter for swim length). While $m < N_s$ (if have not climbed down too long)

Let $m=m+1$. If $J(i,j+1,k,\ell) < J_{last}$ (if doing better), let $J_{last} = J(i,j+1,k,\ell)$ and let

$$\theta^i(j+1,k,\ell) = \theta^i(j+1,k,\ell) + C(i)\frac{\Delta(i)}{\sqrt{\Delta^T(i)\Delta(i)}}$$

and use this $\theta^i(j+1,k,\ell)$ to compute the *new* $J(i,j+1,k,\ell)$ as we did in (f) above. Else, let $m=N_s$. This is the end of the while statement.

Go to next bacterium ($i+1$) if $i \neq S$ (i.e., go to (b) above to process the next bacterium).

If $j < N_c$, go to step 3. In this case, continue chemotaxis, since the life of the bacteria is not over.

Reproduction: For the given k and ℓ, and for each $i=1,2,...,S$, let

$$J_{health}^i = \sum_{j=1}^{N_c+1} J(i,j,k,\ell)$$

be the health of bacterium i (a measure of how many nutrients it got over its lifetime and how successful it was at avoiding noxious substances). Sort bacteria and chemotactic parameters $C(i)$ in order of ascending cost J_{health} (higher cost means lower health). The S_r bacteria with the highest J_{health} values die and the other S_r bacteria with the best values split (and the copies that are made are placed at the same location as their mother).

If $k < N_{re}$, go to step 2. In this case, we have not reached the number of specified reproduction steps, so we start the next generation in the chemotactic loop.

Elimination-dispersal: for $i=1,2,...,S$, with probability p_{ed}, eliminate and disperse each bacterium (this keeps the number of bacteria in the population constant). To do this, if you eliminate a bacterium, simply disperse one to a random location on the optimization domain.

If $\ell < N_{ed}$, then go to step 1; otherwise end.

Matlab code for this can be obtained at: http://www.ece.osu.edu/passino/

2.3 Guidelines for Algorithm Parameter Choices

The bacterial foraging optimization algorithm requires specification of a variety of parameters. First, you can pick the size of the population, S. Clearly, increasing the size of S can significantly increase the computational complexity of the algorithm. However, for larger values of S, if you choose to randomly distribute the initial population, it is more likely that you will start at least some bacterium near an optimum point, and over time, it is then more likely that many bacterium will be in that region, due to either chemotaxis or reproduction.

What should the values of the $C(i)$, $i=1,2,...,S$, be? You can choose a biologically motivated value; however, such values may not be the best for an engineering application. If the $C(i)$ values are too large, then if the optimum value lies in a valley with steep edges, it will tend to jump out of the valley, or it may simply miss possible local minima by swimming through them without stopping. On the other hand, if the $C(i)$ values are too small, then convergence can be slow, but if it finds a local minimum, it will typically not deviate too far from it. You should think of the $C(i)$ as a type of "step size" for the optimization algorithm.

The size of the values of the parameters that define the cell-to-cell attractant functions J_{cc}^i will define the characteristics of swarming. If the attractant width is high and very deep, the cells will have a strong tendency to swarm (they may even avoid going after nutrients and favor swarming). On the other hand, if the attractant width is small, and the depth shallow, there will be little tendency to swarm and each cell will search on its own. Social versus independent foraging is then dictated by the balance between the strengths of the cell-to-cell attractant signals and nutrient concentrations.

Next, large values for N_c result in many chemotactic steps, and, hopefully, more optimization progress, but of course, more computational complexity. If the size of N_c is chosen to be too short, the algorithm will generally rely more on luck and reproduction, and in some cases, it could more easily get trapped in a local minimum ("premature convergence"). You should think of N_s as creating a bias in the random walk (which would not occur if $N_s = 0$), with large values tending to bias the walk more in the direction of climbing down the hill.

If N_c is large enough, the value of N_{re} affects how the algorithm ignores bad regions and focuses on good ones, since bacteria in relatively nutrient-poor regions die (this models, with a fixed population size, the characteristic where bacteria will tend to reproduce at higher rates in favorable environments). If N_{re} is too small, the algorithm may converge prematurely; however, larger values of N_{re} clearly increase computational complexity.

A low value for N_{ed} dictates that the algorithm will not rely on random elimination-dispersal events to try to find favorable regions. A high value increases computational complexity but allows the bacteria to look in more regions to find good nutrient concentrations. Clearly, if p_{ed} is large, the algorithm can degrade to random exhaustive search. If, however, it is chosen appropriately, it can help the algorithm jump out of local optima and into a global optimum.

2.4 Relations to Other Nongradient Optimization Methods

There are *algorithmic analogies* between the genetic algorithm and the above optimization model for foraging. There are analogies between the fitness function and the nutrient concentration function (both a type of "landscape"), selection and bacterial reproduction (bacteria in the most favorable environments gain a selective advantage for reproduction), crossover and bacterial splitting (the children are at the same concentration, whereas with crossover they generally end up in a region around their parents on the fitness landscape), and mutation and elimination and dispersal. However, the algorithms are not equivalent, and neither is a special case of the other. Each has its own distinguishing features. The fitness function and nutrient concentration functions are *not* the same (one represents likelihood of survival for given phenotypic characteristics, whereas the other represents nutrient/noxious substance concentrations, or for other foragers predator/prey characteristics). Crossover represents mating and resulting differences in offspring, something we ignore in the bacterial foraging algorithm (we could, however, have made less than perfect copies of the bacteria to represent their splitting). Moreover, mutation represents gene mutation and the resulting phenotypical changes, not physical dispersal in an environment.

From one perspective, note that all the typical features of genetic algorithms could augment the bacterial foraging algorithm by representing evolutionary characteristics of a forager in their environment. From another perspective, foraging algorithms can be integrated into evolutionary algorithms and thereby model some key survival activities that occur during the lifetime of the population that is evolving (i.e., foraging success can help define fitness, mating characteristics, etc.). For the bacteria studied here, foraging happens to entail hill-climbing via a type of biased random walk, and hence, the foraging algorithm can be viewed as a method to integrate a type of approximate stochastic gradient search (where only an approximation to the gradient is used, not analytical gradient information) into evolutionary algorithms. Of course, standard gradient methods, quasi-Newton methods, etc., depend on the use of an explicit analytical representation of the gradient, something that is not needed by a foraging or genetic algorithm. Lack of dependence on analytical gradient information can be viewed as an advantage (fewer assumptions), or a disadvantage (e.g., since, if gradient information is available, then the foraging or genetic algorithm may not exploit it properly).

You probably also recognize some similarities between certain features of the foraging algorithm and simultaneous perturbation stochastic approximation algorithm (SPSA) (Spall, Hill, & Stark, 2000). What are they? What are the relationships to other nongradient methods (pattern search methods)? There are in fact many approaches to "global optimization" when there is no explicit gradient information available; however, it is beyond the scope of this article to evaluate the relative merits of foraging algorithms to the vast array of such methods that have been studied for many years. To start such a study, it makes sense to begin by considering the theoretical convergence guarantees for certain types of evolutionary algorithms, stochastic approximation methods, and pattern search methods (e.g., see Spall et al., 2000, for work along these lines), and then proceed to consider foraging algorithms in this context. It also seems useful to consider how well the foraging algorithms will perform for time-varying nutrient landscapes, which occurs in the underlying biological problem and many engineering problems.

3. CONCLUSION: BFO APPLICATIONS AND DIRECTIONS

Since its initial development and introduction and popularization via the book (Passino, 2002, 2004), BFO has been used in a number of applications: Optimization over continuous surfaces (cost functions) (Passino, 2002); Algorithmic extensions: Hybrid approach (Kim, Abrahamb, & Choa, 2007); Comparative analysis with other methods, in particular particle swarm optimization (PSO) (Biswas, Dasgupta, Das, & Abrahamb, 2008); Adaptive control: Introduction of the idea and application to liquid level control (Passino, 2002); proportional-integral-derivative (PID) controller tuning (Kim & Cho, 2005); Harmonic estimation (Mishra, 2005); Active power filter for load optimization (Mishra & Bhende, 2007); Transmission loss reduction: Application in power systems (Tripathy, Mishra, Lai, & Zhang, 2006); Optimizing power loss and voltage stability limits: Application in power systems (Tripathy & Mishra, 2007). These are the most popular applications as measured by the number of citations to them on Google. Applications to fuzzy controller construction/tuning, neural network training, job-shop scheduling, electromagnetics, stock market predication, optimal power flow, motor control, temperature control, system identification, and others have also been studied but apparently have not received as much attention to-date. The reader is encouraged to search the internet since more such applications seem likely in the coming years.

Finally, additional applications and studies of the method still holds potential: Optimization: There is still a wide variety of domains in which BFO could be useful for. For instance, it would be useful to study its use in energy efficiency optimization for buildings and distributed energy generation. Comparative analysis: There is a need for a comprehensive Monte-Carlo-based evaluation of its performance relative to other nongradient methods (e.g., the genetic algorithm). This should include evaluation for a large data base of cost functions. Adaptive control: The method holds potential to solve more challenging adaptive control problems, yet it needs to be compared to "genetic adaptive control methods" (see Passino, 2004, or the publications at: http://www.ece.osu.edu/passino/).

REFERENCES

Alam, M., Claviez, M., Oesterhelt, D., & Kessel, M. (1984). Flagella and motility behavior of square bacteria. *The EMBO Journal, 13*(12), 2899–2903.

Armitage, J. P. (1999). Bacterial Tactic Responses. *Advances in Microbial Physiology, 41,* 229–290. doi:10.1016/S0065-2911(08)60168-X

Berg, H. C. (1993). *Random Walks in Biology, New Expanded Edition*. Princeton, NJ: Princeton University Press.

Berg, H. C. (2000). Motile Behavior of Bacteria. *Physics Today*, 24–29. doi:10.1063/1.882934

Berg, H. C., & Brown, D. A. (1972). Chemotaxis in *Escherichia coli* Analysed by Three-Dimensional Tracking. *Nature, 239,* 500–504. doi:10.1038/239500a0

Biswas, A., Dasgupta, S., Das, S., & Abraham, A. (2008). Synergy of PSO and Bacterial Foraging Optimization--A Comparative Study on Numerical Benchmarks. *Advances in Soft Computing. Innovations in Hybrid Intelligent Systems, 44,* 255–263. doi:10.1007/978-3-540-74972-1_34

Blat, Y., & Eisenbach, M. (1995). Tar-Dependent and Independent Pattern Formation by *Salmonella typhimurium. Journal of Bacteriology, 177,* 1683–1691.

Budrene, E. O., & Berg, H. C. (1995a). Complex Patterns Formed by Motile Cells of *Escherichia coli. Nature, 349,* 630–633. doi:10.1038/349630a0

Budrene, E. O., & Berg, H. C. (1995b). Dynamics of formation of symmetrical patterns by chemotactic bacteria. *Nature, 376,* 49–53. doi:10.1038/376049a0

Kim, D. H., Abrahamb, A., & Choa, J. H. (2007). A hybrid genetic algorithm and bacterial foraging approach for global optimization. *Information Sciences, 177*(18), 3918–3937. doi:10.1016/j.ins.2007.04.002

Kim, D. H., & Cho, J. H. (2005). Adaptive Tuning of PID Controller for Multivariable System Using Bacterial Foraging Based Optimization. In *Advances in Web Intelligence* (LNCS 3528, pp. 231-235).

Losick, R., & Kaiser, D. (1997). Why and How Bacteria Communicate. *Scientific American, 276*(2), 68–73. doi:10.1038/scientificamerican0297-68

Lowe, G., Meister, M., & Berg, H. (1987). Rapid Rotation of Flagellar Bundles in Swimming Bacteria. *Nature, 325,* 637–640. doi:10.1038/325637a0

Mishra, S. (2005). A hybrid least square-fuzzy bacterial foraging strategy for harmonic estimation. *IEEE Transactions on Evolutionary Computation, 9*(1), 61–73. doi:10.1109/TEVC.2004.840144

Mishra, S., & Bhende, C. N. (2007). Bacterial Foraging Technique-Based Optimized Active Power Filter for Load Compensation. *IEEE Transactions on Power Delivery, 22*(1), 457–465. doi:10.1109/TPWRD.2006.876651

Neidhardt, F. C., Ingraham, J. L., & Schaechter, M. (1990). *Physiology of the Bacterial Cell: A Molecular Approach*. Sunderland, MA: Sinauer Associates.

Passino, K. M. (2002). Biomimicry of Bacterial Foraging for Distributed Optimization and Control. *IEEE Control Systems Magazine, 22*(3), 52–67. doi:10.1109/MCS.2002.1004010

Passino, K. M. (2004). *Biomimicry for Optimization, Control, and Automation*. London: Springer-Verlag.

Segall, J. E., Block, S. M., & Berg, H. C. (1986). Temporal Comparisons in Bacterial Chemotaxis. *Proceedings of the National Academy of Sciences of the United States of America, 83*, 8987–8991. doi:10.1073/pnas.83.23.8987

Shapiro, J. A. (1997). Multicellularity: The Rule, Not the Exception. In J. A. Shapiro & M. Dworkin (Eds.), *Bacteria as Multicellular Organisms* (pp. 14-49). New York: Oxford University Press.

Shimkets, L. J., & Dworkin, M. (1997). Myxobacterial Multicellularity. In J. A. Shapiro & M. Dworkin (Eds.), *Bacteria as Multicellular Organisms* (pp. 220-244). New York: Oxford University Press.

Spall, J. C., Hill, S. D., & Stark, D. R. (2000). Some Theoretical Comparisons of Stochastic Optimization Approaches. In *Proceedings of the American Control Conference*, Chicago.

Tripathy, M., & Mishra, S. (2007). Bacteria Foraging-Based Solution to Optimize Both Real Power Loss and Voltage Stability Limit. *IEEE Transactions on Power Systems, 22*(1), 240–248. doi:10.1109/TPWRS.2006.887968

Tripathy, M., Mishra, S., Lai, L. L., & Zhang, Q. P. (2006). Transmission Loss Reduction Based on FACTS and Bacteria Foraging Algorithm. In *Parallel Problem Solving from Nature - PPSN IX* (LNCS 4193, pp. 222-231).

Woodward, D. E., Tyson, R., Myerscough, M. R., Murray, J. D., Budrene, E. O., & Berg, H. C. (1995). Spatio-temporal patterns generated by Salmonella typhimurium. *Biophysical Journal, 68*, 2181–2189. doi:10.1016/S0006-3495(95)80400-5

Yi, T.-M., Huang, Y., Simon, M. I., & Doyle, J. C. (2000). Robust Perfect Adaptation in Bacterial Chemotaxis Through Integral Feedback Control. *Proceedings of the National Academy of Sciences of the United States of America, 97*(9), 4649–4653. doi:10.1073/pnas.97.9.4649

ENDNOTE

[1] Actually, microbiologists reserve the term "swarming" for other characteristics of groups of bacteria. Here, we abuse the terminology and favor using the terminology that is used for higher forms of animals such as bees.

This work was previously published in International Journal of Swarm Intelligence Research, Volume 1, Issue 1, edited by Yuhui Shi, pp. 1-16, copyright 2010 by IGI Publishing (an imprint of IGI Global)

Chapter 14
Networks Do Matter:
The Socially Motivated Design of a 3D Race Controller Using Cultural Algorithms

Robert G. Reynolds
Wayne State University, USA

Leonard Kinniard-Heether
Wayne State University, USA

ABSTRACT

This article describes a socially motivated evolutionary algorithm, Cultural Algorithms, to design a controller for a 3D racing game for use in a competitive event held at the 2008 IEEE World Congress. The controller was modeled as a state machine and a set of utility functions were associated with actions performed in each state. Cultural Algorithms are used to optimize these functions. Cultural Algorithms consist of a Population Space, a collection of knowledge sources in the Belief Space, and a communication protocol connecting the components together. The knowledge sources in the belief space vie to control individuals in the population through the social fabric influence function. Here the population is a network of chromosomes connected by the LBest topology. This LBest configuration was employed to train the system on an example oval track prior to the contest, but it did not generalize to other tracks. The authors investigated how other topologies performed when learning on each of the contest tracks. The square network (a type of small world network) worked best at distributing the influence of the knowledge sources, and reduced the likelihood of premature convergence for complex tracks.

DOI: 10.4018/978-1-4666-1592-2.ch014

Figure 1. Example of the "pack" rounding a turn in close formation during a simulated race

INTRODUCTION

This article investigates the use of Computational Intelligence techniques to generate socially motivated behavior in a controller for a 3D racing game. The resultant controller was submitted to the Car Racing Competition at the 2008 World Congress held in Hong Kong China (Loiacono et al., 2008). The goal was to design a controller that can take advantage of the social context in which the race is run. That is, the driver/controller is part of a "pack" of racers during the race as can be seen in the Figure 1.

In order to do this certain aspects of the "individual" were minimized in order to allow for more computational support for the social component. For example, while the controller can get in-race information about the location nearby track edges, if they are aware of the position of the adjacent cars then they can "infer" track boundaries as well as other pieces of information without having to process specific sensory information. This will give the controller more time to aggregate its behavioral experience into its

knowledge base in order to make higher-level strategic decisions.

Given this "tabula raza" the intent was to gradually add in higher levels of social knowledge and behavior over time. The key was then to identify a social learning technique that can support learning at a variety of different spatial and temporal scales. Recently, a number of socially motivated algorithms have been used to solve optimization problems. Some of the example algorithms are the Particle Swarm Algorithm (Kennedy & Eberhart, 1995), the Ant Colony Algorithm (Dorigo, Maniezzo, & Colorni, 1996), and the Cultural Algorithm (Reynolds, 1978). These three algorithms all use a population-based model as the backbone of the algorithm, and solve problems by sharing information via social interaction among agents in the population. The difference between them is the diversity of scales over which social learning and interaction can take place.

Since Cultural Algorithms encompass the scale of activities for each of the other social learning systems, we selected that as the learning framework here. In this article we will demon-

Figure 2. Scales of social interaction: The emergent properties depend upon the scale at which the interaction takes place.

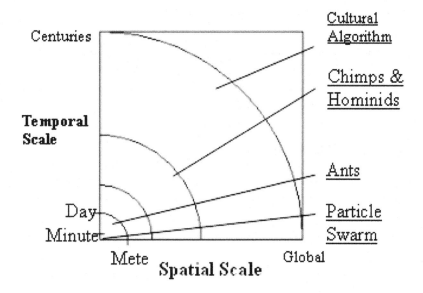

strate how the social learning process will take place by examining how to optimize a low level aspect of the system using Cultural Algorithms. In doing so, aspects of particular swarm optimization technology will be used. In future work, we anticipate using techniques that will support the integration of higher level strategic actions such as co-evolution as suggested by Togelius and Lucas (2006).

Specifically, we start with our minimal state machine framework for a controller. Each of its states employs a set of functions in order to accomplish its goals. There are some utility functions that are shared across all of the states and employ a basic set of variables. Our goal is to use Cultural Algorithms with a network of problem solvers in its population to learn to optimize performance. The network employed initially to train the system for the competition was "Lbest". However, it was of interest to examine the impact that the use of other network topologies will have on the learning process if any.

In section II the basic design of the controller is presented. Then, in section III the instantiation of

the Cultural Algorithm used to "train" the system offline is described. Next, section IV gives the results of the learning activities. The emergence (see Figure 2) of "bridging" performance levels in the system during the initial learning process is highlighted. Next, how the results generalize to the new tracks during the competition is discussed. Finally, the system is used to learn the control parameters for each of the competition tracks using different social topologies. We demonstrate that the square topology, a kind of "small world network" outperforms the Lbest and Gbest topologies in the complex tracks. Section V presents our conclusions.

DESIGNING THE DRIVER CONTROL STATE MACHINE

The TORCS Car Racing Game

The TORCS system is a state-of-the art open source racing game that combines aspects of a high-level 3D racing environment with features

Figure 3. The Architecture of the TORCS interface for the Competition

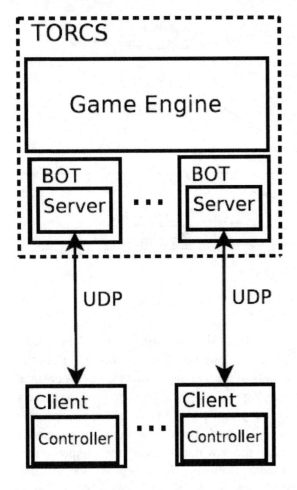

of a simulator (Espi'e & Guionneau, 2008). Our controller was designed to interface with a specialized version of the TORCS system that supports multiple plug and play controllers as shown in Figure 3 (Loiacono, Togelius, & Lanzi, 2009).

The TORCS system is composed of a sophisticated physics engine along with a 3D graphics engine for race visualization. It also possesses extensive game content in terms of many different tracks on which to run the competitions. Therefore, a successful controller will need to be able to generalize its behavior sufficiently in order to perform well on tracks that it has not been trained on before.

In addition to generality, a successful controller needed to traverse a sufficient amount of the track in order to be a candidate for the head to head phase of the competition. Thus, we focused our training and learning on maximizing our distance travelled in the time trials. We assumed that in the actual competition we might even do better since we will rely on information from those around us to make decisions.

During each game "tic", information is exchanged via the interface between the controller and the system. The system provides the controller with raw sensor data as shown in Table 1. Our goal was to employ a small subset of this sensor data in order to reduce the processing time for the controller in each step. Our assumption was that other values can be derived or inferred from these variables within a "pack" like setup.

The controller on the other hand can respond through the use of the effector functions that are shown in Table 2. Only the first four are employed here. The last function requests a race restart and it was assumed that as a contestant we would not be allowed to control that functionality.

The Basic Controller State Machine

Given the TORCS performance environment described above, the initial phase of the project was to design a basic controller and its associated kinematics. The state machine is designed so that there is a centralized controller that selects the appropriate state based upon values of the state variables. This makes state recognition and change more efficient than allowing each state to detect a change. The selector state is labeled as the "idle state in Figure 4. The length of the "idle" state can be instantaneous in some transitions and take additional time to make other transitions.

The idle selector state was used to switch the system between four basic states: On_target, Off track, Stuck, and Off target. Associated with each of these states are four kinematic algorithms: steering, shifting, orientation, and collision avoid-

Table 1. The basic raw sensor data provided to the controller by the TORCS environment

Name	Description
angle	Angle between the car direction and the direction of the track axis.
curLapTime	Time elapsed during current lap.
damage	Current damage of the car (the higher the value, the higher the damage).
distFromStartLine	Distance of the car from the start line along the track line.
distRaced	Distance covered by the car from the beginning of the race
fuel	Current fuel level.
gear	Current gear: -1 is reverse, 0 is neutral and the gear from 1 to 6.
lastLapTime	Time to complete the last lap
opponents	Vector of 18 sensors that detects the opponent distance in meters (range is [0,100]) within a specific 10 degrees sector. Each sensor covers 10 degrees, from -_/2 to +_/2 in front of the car.
racePos	Position in the race with to respect to other cars.
rpm	Number of revolutions per minute of the car engine.
speedX	Speed of the car along the longitudinal axis of the car.
speedY	Speed of the car along the transverse axis of the car.
track	Vector of 19 range finder sensors: each sensor represents the distance between the track edge and the car. Sensors are oriented every 10 degrees from -_/2 and +_/2 in front of the car. Distances are in meters within a range of 100 meters. When the car is outside of the track (i.e., pos is less than -1 or greater than 1), these values are not reliable!
trackPos	Distance between the car and the track axis. The value is normalized with respect to the track width: it is 0 when car is on the axis, -1 when the car is on the left edge of the track and +1 when it is on the right edge of the car. Values greater than 1 or smaller than -1 means that the car is outside of the track.
wheelSpinVel	Vector of 4 sensors representing the rotation speed of the wheels.

Table 2. The basic effector actions for TORCS

Name	Description
accel	Virtual gas pedal (0 means no gas, 1 full gas).
brake	Virtual brake pedal (0 means no brake, 1 full brake).
gear	Gear value.
steering	Steering value: -1 and +1 means respectively full left and right, that corresponds to an angle of 0.785398 rad.
meta	This is meta-control command: 0 do nothing, 1 ask the competition server to restart the race.

ance. The key was to parameterize the kinematic functions in each situation so as to produce a consistent path of movement around the track.

Notice that two of the kinematics, orientation and collision avoidance, provide the behaviors necessary to maintain an objects position within a swarm or flock of agents. These two kinematic functions will be useful in the second phase when we use Cultural Algorithms to develop the system's Social Intelligence. That is, Cultural Algorithms

Figure 4. The hierarchy of basic controller states

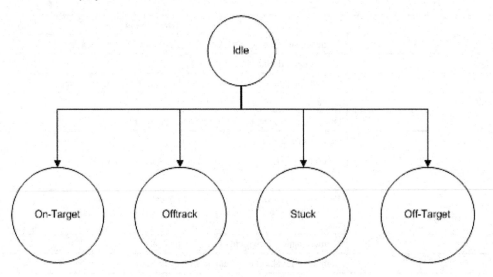

Table 3. Basic Set of Parameters Used in the Controller

Sensors	trackPos, rpm, gear, angle, speedX, angle
Effectors	accel, brake, gear, steering

Table 4. Intermediate Values Generated from the values in Table 3

turnAngle	the angle with the furthest distance to edge of the track (in the trackPos variable)
maxSpeed	determined by turnAngle, or an error correction state

are best at learning socially motivated decision making. Here, we view the collection of cars and drivers as a "pack" or "swarm". Our goal is to navigate through the "swarm" and establish the car near the front of the pack.

One advantage of this social embedding here is that we need not use all of the parameters present since we can rely on other individuals to be performing those calculations. While the raw variables may be available to a solo driver, the driver's cognitive abilities will be reduced when in a "pack." So we will need to infer this missing information based on our position in the pack. Thus, knowing our position relative to others will be an important factor in making these calculations. In fact, during the actual competition, our controller did better on the "Streets1" track in the head to head competition than during the time trials. This was due, in part, to the fact that

the presence of the other individuals filled in gaps in its knowledge about the track which had some difficult 90 degree turns.

The basic set of parameters used in the minimal configuration of the base state machine is given below (see Table 3) using the same parameter abbreviation presented earlier.

The controller also makes use of some intermediate variables that are calculated from the above parameters and other data. These are shown in Table 4.

The following pseudo-code diagrams (see Figures 5, 6, 7 and 8) give the functions used in the On-Target state. Although the other states make use of these functions as well to perform their respective activities, we will illustrate their use in terms of the most frequently occurring state, On_Track.

Figure 5. The steering function pseudocode

```
steering(turnAngle)
    if turnAngle = 0
        steering = 0
    else
        steering = (turnAngle/10) / 9
```

Figure 6. The shifting function

```
shifting(gear, rpm)
    if gear = 0 or (gear = 2 and rpm < 3000)
        gear = 1
    else if gear > 0 and rpm > 7500
        gear = gear + 1
    else if gear > 2 and rpm < 4000
        gear = gear -1
```

Figure 7. The acceleration function

```
acceleration(speedX, maxSpeed)
    if(speedX < maxSpeed)
        accel = 1
    else
        accel = 0
```

Figure 8. The braking function

```
braking(speedX, maxSpeed)
    if(speedX > maxSpeed + 30)
        brake = 1
    else
        brake = 0
```

Figure 9. Pseudocode of the Off Target state

```
offtarget(angle)
    If angle > 0.5 or angle < -0.5
        the car is off-target
    else
        the car is on-target
```

Figure 10. Pseudocode of the Offtrack state

```
offtrack(trackPos)
    if trackPos > 1 or trackPos < -1
        the car is offtrack
        maxSpeed = 30
    else
        the car is on-target
```

Figure 11. Pseudocode of the Stuck state

```
stuck()
    if speedX < 10 for more than 10 turns
        the car is stuck
```

The steering function works by finding the furthest distance to the edge of the track by using the distance readings gained from communication with the server. The angle that corresponds to the furthest distance is then used as the current steering angle (normalized to fit within a range of [-1, 1].) This calculation is made every game turn or tic, thus reducing the chance of over-steering. The controller will modify the turning angle as the car passes through a turn, due to the fact that the angle corresponding to the furthest distance to the edge of the track will tend to move toward 0 degrees (straight) as the turn progresses. In this way, the controller finds an adequate, if not the best, method of navigating a turn.

The shifting function is based on readings retrieved from the server for the current Revolutions per Minute (RPM) reading for the car. When the RPM reading reaches a certain point, the controller will send a signal to either shift up or down. In this phase, it was required that the controller wait a short period of time after shifting to decide whether or not to shift again. This lag was added to prevent cycling between up-shifting and down-shifting due to the drop in the RPM reading that occurs immediately after up-shifting.

With the exception of the steering function, all of the functions rely directly on the maxSpeed variable. The steering function relies indirectly on maxSpeed which is governed by angle. Thus, the maxSpeed variable is the key to coordinating the behaviors of the states, and was the variable that was focused on during the Cultural Algorithm learning phase.

When the controller is not in the on-target state, the following pseudo-code (Figures 9, 10 and 11) is used in the Off-Target, Offtrack, and Stuck states respectively in order to correct errors and return the controller to the On-Target state.

Each of these functions was hardcoded into the controller. The learning process here then focuses on tuning the common parameters used by these functions, maxspeed and turn angle, in order to coordinate state activity and optimize performance.

Error correction in the controller is specific to each of three states; whether or not the car is "stuck", whether or not the car is "off the track", and whether or not the car is going in the wrong direction. If multiple error states are detected simultaneously, the controller handles them hierarchically. The "stuck" state takes the highest precedence, followed by the "off_target" state, and then the "off the track" state.

If the car does not move farther than ten meters over one game tick, the controller increments a counter to indicate that the car may be in the "stuck" state. When this counter reaches a certain level, the car is declared stuck and stuck state actions are performed by the controller. The controller then directs the car to drive in reverse for a number of game turns. By doing this, the car should have backed up far enough to be able to turn out of the situation that led it to get stuck.

If the car is beyond the boundary of the track based on trackPos sensor information, then the system is in the "off the track" state. In this case the controller will direct the car to slow down, and to turn in the opposite direction of the side of the track that contains the boundary that it has just crossed. The impetus behind reducing the speed is that, typically when the car is off the track, the ability of the tires to grip the road surface is reduced, thus increasing the possibility that the car's wheels will spin and the controller will not be able to control the car.

If using the angle sensor the controller detects that the car is traveling at an angle that is greater than +/-90 degrees from the track normal

(0 degrees), the controller indicates that the car is traveling in the wrong direction and is in the "off target" state. The controller then directs the car to reduce its speed and turn in the direction that will provide it with the fastest way of returning to the correct direction. The reduction in speed is necessary to ensure that the car has enough room to successfully turn around. Notice that we are assuming symmetry relative to the maximum speed possible at each turn angle. That is, we are assuming a flat track in the initial design of the learning system. However, in future versions it is possible to change this assumption when it is clear that the track is not flat.

THE CULTURAL ALGORITHM LEARNING PHASE

Overview of the Cultural Algorithm

Once the kinematic algorithms for the basic driver state machine were produced, the next step was to parameterize the algorithms in order to optimize their performance. Though several methods were considered initially, the decision was made to train the controller so as to optimize the distance travelled in a given time frame. This corresponds to the first phase of the contest, where an individual driver's performance was assessed based upon the distance that they travelled over a set of runs on each of the available tracks.

The performance function was conditioned or constrained by certain physical constraints. For example, it was desirable that the driver not exceed a maximum speed around a curve as a function of the curve angle. In order to accomplish this, the concept of a speed limit, or "governor system", was introduced. Essentially, this concept provides that the controller must not direct the car to travel faster than a certain speed that corresponds to the angle of the turn it is currently navigating. How-

Figure 12. The Cultural Algorithm framework

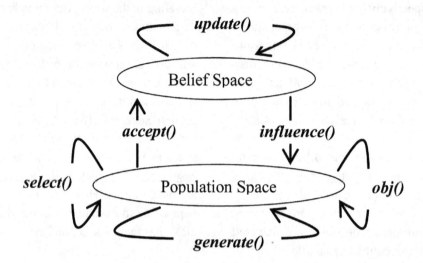

Figure 13. The Cultural Algorithm pseudo-code

```
Begin
    t = 0;
    initialize Bt, Pt
    repeat
        evaluate Pt {obj()}
        update(Bt, accept(Pt))
        generate(Pt, influence(Bt))
        t = t + 1
        select Pt from Pt – 1
    until (termination condition achieved)
End
```

ever, the goal is to drive as close to that optimum speed as possible.

The controller currently uses 10 values for the speed limits, each corresponding to degree angle values from 0 to 90 degrees. In order to simplify the computation, we encoded both positive and negative angles using the same index. Thus, +10 and -10 mapped to the same governor constraint. This reflected our assumption concerning the symmetry for turning on a flat track. Learning the speed values for tracks with a slope can be done by changing the representation to allow right and left turns to produce different speeds.

The goal of the Cultural Algorithm learning activity is then to learn these governor constraints for each of the 10 angle classes. The Cultural Algorithm is a framework in which to perform socially motivated learning activities. A schematic view

Figure 14. The update process for the five knowledge source categories

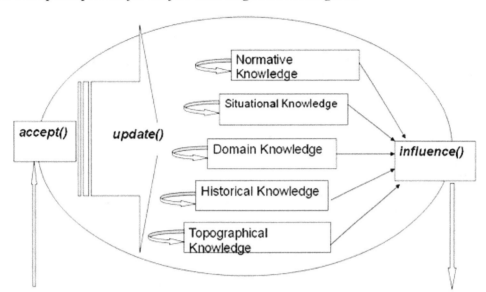

Figure 15. The social fabric influence function: Each of the knowledge sources vie to influence individuals in the network.

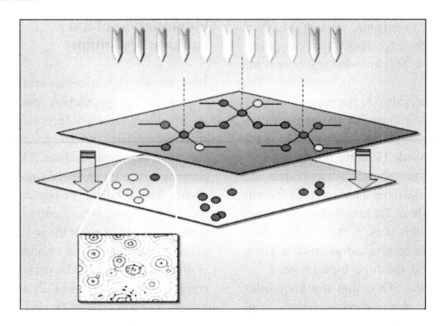

of the Cultural Algorithm and associated pseudo-code is given in Figures 12 and 13 (Reynolds & Ali, 2008):

The key to the Cultural Algorithm is that culture is the aggregation of individual behavior.

Individuals are viewed as behavior configurations. The knowledge concerning the performance of each of the individuals is collected into the Belief Space by the acceptance function. That knowledge is used to update each of the five basic categories of knowledge sources as shown in Figure 14. The

Figure 16. An example chromosome

TurnAngle	0°	±10°	±20°	±30°	±40°	±50°	±60°	±70°	±80°	±90°
MaxSpeed	209.32	160.60	131.83	114.05	115.80	107.87	35.69	86.04	27.50	145.86

update process can vary from a basic statistical aggregation activity to a symbolic learning or inference activity.

Each knowledge source category can be viewed as one way of influencing an individual or generating a new set of behaviors. The current influence function used here is called the social fabric influence function, SFI. This is illustrated in Figure 15. Each knowledge source has a normalized performance value based upon the performance of the individuals that it influenced in the last generation. As such, each knowledge source occupies a portion of a roulette wheel. So for each individual in the population, we spin the wheel and select a knowledge source that can potentially influence it. This knowledge source is the direct bidder.

Once each individual in the population has a direct bidder, that information is communication to those individuals that it is connected to in the social fabric network. Here, we just pass the bid to its immediate neighbors. Each individual add up its direct bid and those it has received from its immediate neighbors. The knowledge source with the majority of bids wins. If there is a tie, then various rules can be invoked to break it. Here, when there is a tie, the direct bidder wins.

The key to the SFI is that if a knowledge source produces above average choices those can disseminate through the population faster and allow the system to focus its search efforts on more desirable places. Currently we support the topologies commonly used in particle swarm optimization, lbest, gbest, and square. Lbest is a ring topology that connects each individual to two others, gbest connects each individual to all others in the population, and square connects each individual with four other neighbors.

Gbest produces faster convergence but may lead to false peaks since one knowledge source may tend to dominate the dissemination process, whereas Lbest produces slower convergence but is less likely the a single knowledge source will be able to dominate the dissemination process. The Square topology was selected as a middle ground that allows faster dissemination than LBest but still makes it difficult for one knowledge source to dominate the influence process.

Instantiation of the Cultural Algorithm

Here the population component was a Genetic Algorithm. The population space consists of a set of chromosomes where each chromosome specified a set of candidate parameter values for the controller state machine. The chromosome consists of maximum speed values for ten angle classes from 0 to 90. The non-zero angles serve a double purpose as they contain the maximum speed for a turn of either the positive or negative values of that angle. An example chromosome is given in Figure 16. The performance of each chromosome is in terms of distance travelled in meters for each generation, and the values sent to the Belief Space by the acceptance function.

The Belief Space component consists of a collection of knowledge sources that are used to influence changes in the population of chromosomes via the Social Fabric influence function. Here, the influence function controls the genetic operators and their application. The contents of the knowledge sources are "updated" by "accepting" a subset of experiences of individuals within the population. Five basic categories of knowledge are supported in the system: Normative, Situational, Domain, Topographic (spatial) and Historic (temporal).

Normative knowledge corresponds to ranges of acceptable values for the parameters. Some are hard coded such as speed for given angles, while other ranges can be learned. Normative knowledge will generate a new individual chromosome that fits within the current ranges of the target parameters. These ranges can be indexed by different track surfaces.

Situational knowledge corresponds to example chromosomes with exemplary behavior, e.g. best and/or worst. Here, configurations that perform best on each of the various tracks are recorded and used to direct modifications of individuals in the population relative to these exemplars.

Domain knowledge corresponds to details about the social or physical context in which the problem is being solved. Here, each of the three tracks has a different set of speed controls relative to angle that were encoded manually. For example, in order to allow the controller to recognize what track it is currently using, readings were taken from the first four starting positions, of the distances to the edge of the track recorded by the server before the race starts. These are used by the state machine to index the appropriate track and governor constraints and are applied to the corresponding speed limit variables for that track.

Although initially we attempted to have a generalized set of governor constraints for all of the tracks, the differences in track structure and composition made it difficult to apply a standard set to all of them without getting some "weaving" of the car as it drove around the track since it designed to stay as close to the middle of the track as possible. This meant that we needed to have more specific information about each track. This was encoded in domain knowledge. Also, as new tracks were encountered, the corresponding

domain constraints and track indexing information can be stored there as well.

For example, in the case that the track was new and could not be determined, the controller has three levels of speed limits from which to start from: fast, medium, and slow. The controller starts out using the fast level speeds. Once a certain level of damage was accrued by the car, the controller assumes that its current speed is too fast and switches to the medium speed level. If the car continues to take damage, the speed is slowed further. This method works rather well because damage usually comes from car-wall collisions, rather than car-car collisions. The resultant constraints along with the first four racing positions are sufficient to add the track to the domain knowledge.

History knowledge can be used to keep track of the races run on various tracks and the results obtained for each. This information can be used to make predictions about racing conditions and strategies at the start of the race. One such decision, as mentioned earlier is to infer what track one is using. If the start points do not match precisely, the system can also predict that it is on the track with the best match.

Topographic information here can encode maps of the tracks which can be used for navigation purposes. For simplicity, topographic information is used here only implicitly as part of the speed/angle constraints found in the domain knowledge in the current version. However, it can be useful with uneven terrain and different road surfaces and will be augmented in future versions of the system.

TRAINING THE CONTROLLER

The Initial Training for WCCI

The controller was trained for each track provided with the TORCS system using the Cultural Algorithm (CAT) toolkit (Reynolds, Ali, & Jayyousi, 2008). Figure 17 gives a snapshot of a car on a

Figure 17. A training segment from an oval track

Figure 18. The Lbest topology

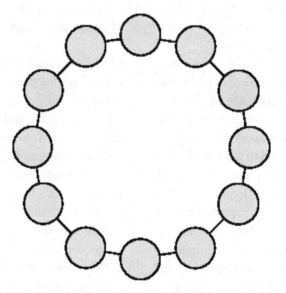

training lap for an oval track. The toolkit was initialized to run for 100 generations, with a population of 100 chromosomes. The CAT toolkit uses a Social Fabric influence function that assumes that an individual is linked to others in the population via a network. Here we use the standard Lbest topology taken from the Particle Swarm Optimization.

In the Lbest topology, each individual is connected to two other individuals as given in Figure 18. In this framework the Knowledge sources vie to influence chromosomes or individuals in the network. If a Knowledge Source were to influence an individual in the network, that information is distributed to its two immediate neighbors in this case. The extent of the distribution is called a

Figure 19. Learning for a run over the oval track

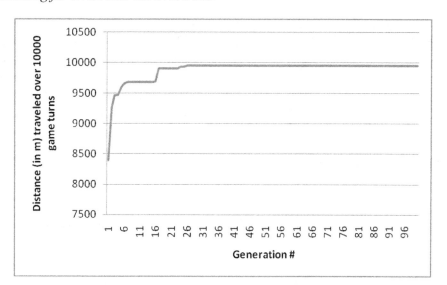

"hop". In our case distribution is only one hop although multiple hops are possible.

An example of a learning curve for a given Cultural Algorithm run is given in Figure 19 for the Oval Track.

Notice the incremental nature of the learning process here. This is a phenomena often observed in physical system. The ability to achieve one performance level provided the system with an opportunity to build on that, and achieve a higher level of performance. The phenomenon is called bridging behavior. Bridging behavior is a stable performance interval within which new adaptations can be tried out. For example, one must be able to balance a bicycle before steering behavior can be learned. Likewise, once you can balance and steer in the right direction, then pushing the pedals can produce acceleration. The next step is to learn to use the brakes. Here, one must learn to stay on track before learning to deal with the transient exceptional conditions.

Here, we observe a series of increments in performance during the learning process. These increments reflect improvements in the repertoire of system behaviors relative to the performance function. First, around generation 3 we get an initial

increment. This corresponds to the establishment of a set of values from the initial random set that keeps the car on the track. Next, from generation 7 through 17 we observe a second increment and resultant plateau. This increment deals with learning to accelerate. This is most easily done on straight-aways. Since the performance function is distance traveled, acceleration on straight-aways will have a strong impact on performance.

Around generation 17, the system begins to add braking activities in to the repertoire. That is, the car can accelerate and then brake. This is what happens when curves or turns are negotiated. Between generations 25 and 31 the system looks at other behavioral sequences, such as braking and then accelerating. This starts to allow the system to deal with different types of track segments. In future work we intend to add components to the performance function that will support more detailed learning of other track segments.

The Competition Results: How did Learning Generalize?

The actual competition for the event was carried out on three selected tracks. The tracks are shown

Figure 20. The Oval D-Speedway track

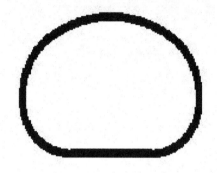

Figure 21. The Streets1 track that contains right angle turns similar to a city street

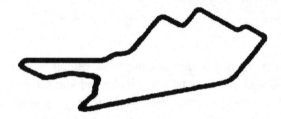

Figure 22. The Ruudskogen track

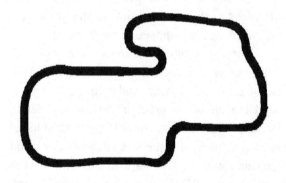

below in Figures 20 through 22. Each of these tracks, designated D-Speedway, Street1, and Ruudskogen, represent a different type of race track. The first, D-Speedway, is a classic oval track design commonly used in NASCAR, or Indy Series type races. It contains steeply banked turns, and is designed for high speed driving. Street1 is an urban track, similar to those set up in many major cities for Formula 1 Grand Prix races. It is a narrow track, designed to represent the feel of a typical metropolitan street, with non-permanent concrete barriers. This track is flat, and does not contain banked turns. It also contains two very sharp turns that include a gravel shoulder.

The Ruudskogen track is designed to represent the track at the Rudskogen Motorsenter located near Rakkestad, Norway. This track is slightly wider than Street1, but not as wide as D-Speedway. It contains many unbanked turns, and also has multiple elevation changes, something that sets it apart from the other two tracks.

Table 5 gives the results of the time trials for the competition. It gives the median score for each of the contestants over 10 runs for each track. Since our controller was trained exclusively on a type of oval track, the results suggest that the learning behavior transfers over well to the other different tracks. The Ruudskogen and Speedway (D-Oval) are similar to the track that we trained on, and the system generalized well to them on its own. It did not generalize as well to the Street-1 track in the time trials.

Table 6 gives the results of the head to head races. The score for each contestant was the median place over 10 runs for each of the tracks. Notice that while the system still performed well on the speedway, the performance on the other two tracks was reversed. Its ranking on the Street-1 track improved, while its ranking on the Ruudskogen declined. The reasons for this reflect the basic assumptions there were made in the design and training of the system.

First, the decline in performance on the Ruudskogen reflected the fact that even though the surface was uneven, if the car was centered on the track the effects of the unevenness were reduced. On the other hand, when bumped by other cars during the head to head, it can end up at many different angles on the surface which will violate the symmetry assumptions and cause performance problems.

Table 5. The median number of meters for each of 10 runs for each of the 5 competitors over the three tracks

Entry	Ruudskogen	Street-1	D-Speedway
Kinnaird-Heether et al.	6716.7	3692.9	14406.9
Lucas	4134.2	5502.8	12664.5
Simmerson	5934.0	6477.8	12523.3
Perez et al.	3786.9	2984.8	-317.3
Tan et al.	3443.5	2998-5	10648.2
C++ Sample Controller	4465.1	4928.8	7464.5
Java Sample Controller	5593.8	2963.2	5689.9

Table 6. The median scores of performance for 10 runs on each track, three laps around. 10 points for first, 8 for second etc

Entry	Ruudskogen	Street-1	D-Speedway	Total
Simmerson	10	10	6	26
Kinnaird-Heether et al.	4	8	10	22
Lucas	6	6	8	20
Tan et al.	5	5	5	15
Perez et al.	5.5	4.5	5	14

Second, the improvement in performance for the Street1 track reflected the additional presence of competitors that gave the controller opportunities to infer more information about the track. This, in fact was consistent with the assumption that the controller needs to be part of the pack.

Learning to Optimize Performance on Each Track

The systems performance in the competition was based on the use of the LBest topology. In this section we use the LBest. GBest, and Square topologies to learn the turn parameters for each of the tracks selected for the race. The goal here is to see whether the topology used in the Social Fabric has an effect on the systems performance and which topology is suitable for learning with the more complex tracks.

The tests performed focused on changing only the network structure, so all of the other variables were held constant. All tests were done using a population size of 100 over the course of 100 years. Each track was tested in turn with each of these three network configurations. During the training process using the CAT toolkit, sets of speed variables were produced that guided the car along is path through the track. Each set of speed variables was then given a fitness value that was equal to how many meters that it traveled from the start of the track as before.

The first track tested was D-Speedway. Figure 23 shows the maximum fitness achieved over time by each of the three methods. Tables 7, 8 and 9 show the years in which the maximum fitness changes for each of the three topologies. The other years are not shown since their values were unchanged from the previous maximum value.

Table 7. Fitness value changes on the D-Speedway track for the L-Best network configuration

Year	1	2	3	7	36	41	74
Fitness	14569.4	15055.0	16358.4	16359.6	16361.8	16363.8	16365.9

Table 8. Fitness value changes on the D-Speedway track for the Square network configuration

Year of Change	1	2	4	13	20	65
Fitness	15134.0	15142.5	16358.4	16359.6	16361.4	16362.1

Table 9. Fitness value changes on the D-Speedway track for the G-Best network configuration

Year of Change	1	14	16	19	20
Fitness	16358.4	16359.1	16361.8	16363.0	16364.7

Figure 23. The results of the training for the D-Speedway track using the different network configurations

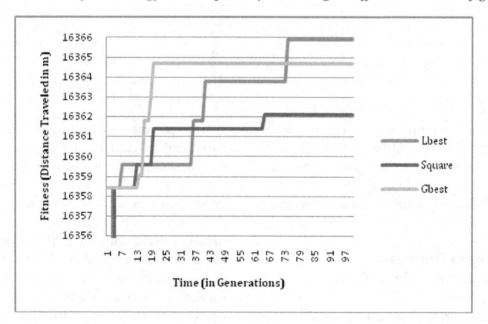

The results show that the D-Speedway track can be learned by any of the network configurations, with very little difference in the final results. Also, the results are comparable with the results produced in the actual competition time trials for our controller. This is not unexpected since the D-Speedway track is by far the easiest track to learn, and the track that produced the highest fitness. However, GBest reached a stable performance plateau before the other two as can be seen by looking at the changes in fitness that corresponds to new bridging levels in Table 9. It means that for simple oval tracks a GBest approach can produce near optimal performanc faster than the other two.

Table 10. Fitness value changes on the Street1 track for the L-Best network configuration

Year of Change	1	2	4
Fitness	6698.71	6923.5	7180.22

Table 11. Fitness value changes on the Street1 track for the Square network configuration

Year	1	4	13	17	20	29	61	72
Fitness	6670.91	6865.96	6895.25	6957.65	7087.51	7432.13	7435.71	7527.01

Table 12. Fitness value changes on the Street1 track for the G-Best network configuration

Year	1	2	3	4	5	11	28	95
Fitness	643296	6926.97	7133.71	7298.12	7393.67	7427.97	7429.12	7429.67

Figure 24. The results of the training for the Street1 track using the different network configurations

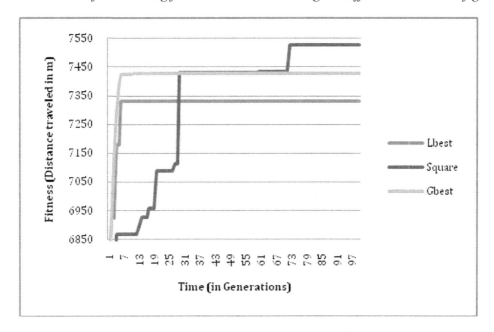

Figure 24 presents the results for the Street1 track. All three topologies produced maximum scores that are better than the median scores for the controller in the contest. Tables 10, 11 and 12 gives the bridges produced in each. For this track notice that LBest, which was the one used for the contest, performed the worst of the three and managed to generate just three performance bridges. GBest stabilized first, but at a false peak since the square topology passed it later on.

As mentioned earlier, the GBest approach has a tendency to prematurely converge. Here, the square topology, which can be viewed as form of small world network, worked best. Its score was twice that of the score produced in the time trials for the controller.

Table 13. Fitness value changes on the Ruudskogen track for the L-Best network configuration

Year of Change	1	2	5	7	9	10	100
Fitness	6906.1	6922.92	7024.85	7154.67	7165.88	7556.6	7562.75

Table 14. Fitness value changes on the Ruudskogen track for the Square network configuration

Year	1	4	9	21	22	42	85	100
Fitness	6917.49	7129.37	7188.83	7237.47	7481.15	7516.42	7694.93	8036.91

Table 15. Fitness value changes on the Ruudskogen track for the G-Best network configuration

Year	1	6	8	14	27	41	48	65
Fitness	7097.76	7193.15	7245.98	7396.95	7534.35	7795.66	7820.92	7829.73

Figure 25. The results of the training for the Ruudskogen track using the different network configurations

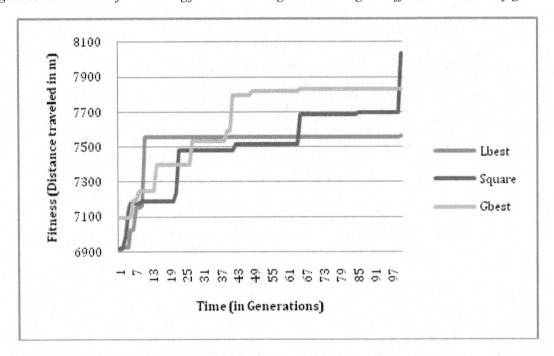

The learning curves for the Ruudskogen are shown in Figure 25. Tables 13, 14 and 15 give the maximum fitness value changes for each of the three topologies. Notice that again the scores for the three topologies are all better than the median score produced by the controller in the time trials. However, again LBest performs the worst of the three, lagging far behind in the generation of bridging levels and producing only small increments in improvements over the runs. GBest again exhibited the most improvements early on, but again reached a false peak. The square topology still outperformed them both, producing

Figure 26. Flocking behavior in TORCS

relatively stable bridges with constant increments in improvement.

Overall, the results show that any of the three configurations can be used to train for the D-Speedway, due to the relative simplicity of the track. Of the three, the LBest is the least complex and was a good fit for the contest relative to this track in terms of efficient processing speed. For the other tracks, the Square configuration appears to be the best and is less likely to converge prematurely. This can be explained by the nature of the networks, coupled with the complex nature of the tracks.

The LBest configuration quickly finds a set of variable values that produced an increment in fitness level. Often LBest has the highest overall fitness in the early generations of a training cycle. However, due to the fact that this network is less connected than the other networks, when better sets of speed variables are found by a knowledge source, it is less able to spread its influence across

the network than the other two. In fact, the lack of connection prevents the network from finding better solutions to more complicated tracks.

The Square topology on the other hand has no problem finding better solutions to the complicated tracks. This network configuration takes longer than LBest, and in contrast to LBest, often has the lowest overall fitness in the early years of a training cycle. However, it continues to find better solutions, and is still coming up with better solutions after the other network configurations have converged prematurely as seen in the results for Street1. This could be explained by the fact that it is more strongly connected than LBest, so a high performing knowledge source will be able to spread its influence through the network more quickly.

The GBest configuration is completely connected which means that there is a tendency for a knowledge source that is dominant early to spread its influence across the network without the other knowledge sources being given sufficient opportunity to provide their own influences. For a simple track like the Oval this produces quick convergence to the best solutions. For complex tracks it can produce early convergence.

In summary, the small world style network, the Square, works the best of the three across the board although for the oval track all three perform similarly. This is interesting since one frequently finds a small world network present in a variety of different societies. An interesting conjecture is that it emerges in a variety of settings because of its ability to circulate influence in an optimal way relative to other network structures.

CONCLUSION

In this article we proposed a socially motivated design for a 3D race controller. In Figure 26 we see an example of the controller (the red car) exhibiting flocking style behavior as it passes another car in a sample race. We proceeded to optimize the performance of its utility functions with a Cultural Algorithm using the simple LBest topology on an oval style track. The learned parameters generalized very well to the oval track variant used in the contest but had difficulty with the more complex tracks.

We then repeated the learning process, using the three tracks from the contest, but employing different topologies for the social fabric influence function. The results suggest that a Square topology is less likely to converge prematurely for each of the three tracks and exhibited performance improvements over the LBest score for the tournament.

The Square topology works well across the three different tracks suggest that it is able to provide the knowledge sources with sufficient opportunities to distribute their influence across the network over time. As a result, it is less likely

that a particular knowledge source can take over early and lead the system to reduced performance.

The fact that we commonly observe networks of 4-6 connections in real-world systems suggests that the ubiquity of the network in the real world reflects its ability to fairly distributed influence and information through a network of problems solvers.

ACKNOWLEDGMENT

This work was supported in part by N.S.F. IGERT Grant # DGE-0654014.

REFERENCES

Dorigo, M., Maniezzo, V., & Colorni, A. (1996). Ant system: optimization by a colony of cooperating agents. *IEEE Transactions on Systems, Man, and Cybernetics*, 26(1), 29–41. doi:10.1109/3477.484436

Espi'e, E., & Guionneau, C. (2008). *TORCS: The open racing car simulator*. Retrieved May 7, 2009, from http://torcs.sourceforge.net/

Kennedy, J., & Eberhart, R. C. (1995). Particle Swarm Optimization. In *Proceedings of the IEEE International Conference on Neural Networks*, Perth, Australia (pp. 12-13). Washington, DC: IEEE Computer Society.

Kohler, T., Gummerman, G., & Reynolds, R. G. (2005). Virtual Archaeology. *Scientific American*, 293(1), 76–84. doi:10.1038/scientificamerican0705-76

Loiacono, D., Togelius, J., & Lanzi, P. (2009). *Software manual of the car racing competition*. Retrieved May 7, 2009, from http://voxel.dl.sourceforge.net/project/cig/Championship2009 Manual/1.0/manual-1.0.pdf

Loiacono, D., Togelius, J., Lanzi, P., Kinnaird-Heether, L., Lucas, S., Simmerson, M., et al. (2008). Survival of the Fastest: The WCCI 2008 Simulated Car Racing Competition. In *Proceedings of the 2008 IEEE Workshop on Computational Intelligence in Games*.Washington, DC: IEEE Computer Society.

Reynolds, R. G. (1978). On modeling the evolution of hunter-gatherer decision-making systems. *Geographical Analysis*, *10*(1), 31–46.

Reynolds, R. G., & Ali, M. Z. (2008). Computing with the Social Fabric: The Evolution of Social Intelligence within a Cultural Framework. *IEEE Computational Intelligence Magazine*, *3*(1), 18–30. doi:10.1109/MCI.2007.913388

Reynolds, R. G., Ali, M. Z., & Jayyousi, T. (2008). Mining the Social Fabric of Archaic Urban Centers with Cultural Algorithms. *Computer*, *41*(1), 64–72. doi:10.1109/MC.2008.25

Togelius, J., & Lucas, S. M. (2006). Arms races and car races. In *Parallel Problem Solving from Nature IX* (pp. 613-622). Heidelberg, Germany: Springer.

This work was previously published in International Journal of Swarm Intelligence Research, Volume 1, Issue 1, edited by Yuhui Shi, pp. 17-41, copyright 2010 by IGI Publishing (an imprint of IGI Global)

Chapter 15
Honey Bee Swarm Cognition:
Decision–Making Performance and Adaptation

Kevin M. Passino
Ohio State University, USA

ABSTRACT

A synthesis of findings from neuroscience, psychology, and behavioral biology has been recently used to show that several key features of cognition in neuron-based brains of vertebrates are also present in bee-based swarms of honey bees. Here, simulation tests are administered to the honey bee swarm cognition system to study its decision-making performance. First, tests are used to evaluate the ability of the swarm to discriminate between choice options and avoid picking inferior "distractor" options. Second, a "Treisman feature search test" from psychology, and tests of irrationality developed for humans, are administered to show that the swarm possesses some features of human decision-making performance. Evolutionary adaptation of swarm decision making is studied by administering swarm choice tests when there are variations on the parameters of the swarm's decision-making mechanisms. The key result is that in addition to trading off decision-making speed and accuracy, natural selection seems to have settled on parameters that result in individual bee-level assessment noise being effectively filtered out to not adversely affect swarm-level decision-making performance.

DOI: 10.4018/978-1-4666-1592-2.ch015

1. INTRODUCTION

The "collective intelligence" or "super-organism" perspectives have been used for both animals and humans to discuss fully integrated group functioning, especially group decision-making (Hölldobler & Wilson, 2008, 1990; Levine et al., 1993; Franks, 1989; Seeley, 1989, 1995; Hinsz et al., 1997; Wilson, 2000; Camazine et al., 2001; Surowiecki, 2004). But, how does a group of organisms implement a "mind" that supports group decision-making? Recently, this question has been partially answered. Viewing the honey bee super-organism as a single decision-maker, a detailed explanation of the honey bee nest-site selection process has been used to identify the key elements and functional organization of swarm cognition (Passino et al., 2008). It was shown that the swarm has identifiable elements that correspond to neurons, action potentials, inter-neuron communications, lateral inhibition, short-term memory, neural images, and layers of processing (Kandel et al., 2000). Functional similarities to the networks of neurons that perform certain attention, perception, and choice functions (Gazzaniga et al., 1998; Kandel et al., 2000) in solitary animals were identified. It was shown that the swarm's short-term memory ("group memory") is on average a representation of the relative quality of the discovered nest sites that leads to good choice performance. Then, two basic properties of the swarm's choice process were tested: discrimination (the ability to distinguish between nest sites of different quality) and distraction (the ability to ignore nest sites of inferior quality). The focus of this paper is to analyze swarm decision-making performance and adaptation to provide additional evidence that bee-based swarms have a cognition process that shares key features with neuron-based brains.

The key experimental work in the area of honey bee nest-site selection is in (Seeley & Buhrman, 1999; Camazine et al., 1999; Seeley & Buhrman, 2001; Seeley, 2003; Seeley & Visscher, 2003, 2004a). A number of models of the nest-site selection process have been published. First, there are the ODE models introduced in (Britton et al., 2002) to study the issue of whether bees make direct comparisons between the qualities of more than one nest in order to make a decision (which they do not). There is a discrete-time population matrix model introduced in (Myerscough, 2003). A simulation model that was validated for a range of experiments (those in (Seeley & Buhrman, 1999; Camazine et al., 1999; Seeley & Buhrman, 2001; Seeley, 2003; Seeley & Visscher, 2003, 2004a)) is introduced in (Passino and Seeley, 2006) and used to study the speed-accuracy trade-off in the choice process. In Perdriau and Myerscough (2007) the authors introduce a density-dependent Markov process model of honey bee nest-site selection and study the effects of site quality, competition between sites, and delays in site discovery. Next, the work in (Janson et al., 2007) introduces an individual-based model and studies the swarm's scouting behavior and the impact of distance on choice. Ant colonies performing nest-site selection have some broad similarities to the bees' nest-site selection process (e.g., a speed-accuracy trade-off), and corresponding models and simulations have been developed (Mallon et al., 2001; Pratt et al., 2002; Franks et al., 2003; Pratt, 2005; Pratt et al., 2005). Finally, note that recently a common framework was introduced to study the optimality of decision-making in the brain along with nest-site selection in both ants and bees (Marshall et al., 2009).

In this paper, the simulator from (Passino & Seeley, 2006) is used to administer tests to the swarm to evaluate its decision-making performance and adaptation. First, basic properties of discrimination and distraction and their interaction are studied by administering swarm choice tests. Then, it is shown that choice performance analogous to what humans possess is found if the Treisman feature search test for humans (Treisman & Gelade, 1980) is given to the swarm. In particular, the Treisman test illustrates how swarm cognition dynamics operate in parallel in early processing and how cognition delays can occur in the presence of many inferior choices. Next, it is determined whether swarms exhibit "irrational" choice behavior commonly found in (individual) human decision making (Luce & Suppes, 1965; Huber et al., 1982; Tversky, 1972; Simonson, 1989; Simonson & Tversky, 1992) in the presence of context-dependent effects (i.e., certain patterns of choice alternatives that can conspire to mislead the decision-maker). Irrationality has already been studied in the field of behavioral ecology. In hoarding gray jays, simultaneous choice errors decrease as the rate of availability of choices decreases, since then choice errors are costly (Waite, 2001; Waite & Field, 2000; Waite, 2002). Honey bees and gray jays have been shown to exhibit context-dependent decision making (Shafir et al., 2002). In these studies errors ("irrationality") seem to arise due to sensory noise, cognitive processing limitations, and physical constraints (which all cause choice errors in nest-site selection also). Context-dependence has also been studied for human group decision making (Steiner, 1966; Laughlin & Ellis, 1986; Kerr & Tindale, 2004; Hastie & Kameda, 2005) as summarized in (Hinsz et al., 1997). Here, analogous to the studies in (Ratcliff et al., 1999; Ratcliff & Smith, 2004; Roe et al., 2001; Busemeyer & Townsend, 1993) for humans, context-dependent decision making is studied for a reaction-time test (quick choice of the best-of-N nest sites). For a very wide variety of nest-site quality patterns, simulations here show that the swarm cannot be tricked into misordering its choice percentages in relation to the nest-site quality pattern. This implies that violations of strong stochastic transitivity (Luce & Suppes, 1965) will not occur. Next, it is shown that for a special nest-site quality pattern (where a discrimination-distraction interaction is induced) the attraction effect (Huber et al., 1982) can occur. However, this leads to *improved* choice performance.

Finally, using a cognitive ecological perspective (Dukas, 1998) swarm-level choice performance is studied when individual-level bee behavioral parameters are perturbed (a "pseudo-mutated" swarm (Passino & Seeley, 2006)). Simulations show how natural selection seems to have settled on cognition mechanisms that balance the speed and accuracy of nest-site choice and filter error-prone individual bee decisions. From a broad perspective, this last part of the paper provides an initial synthesis of ideas from group decision making and cognitive ecology (Dukas, 1998), which has been previously thought to only apply to neuron-based brains.

2. NEST-SITE SELECTION BY HONEY BEES

The simulation model from (Passino & Seeley, 2006) is used here to administer all choice tests and to study adaptation. This model was validated using the experiments in (Seeley & Buhrman, 1999; Camazine et al., 1999; Seeley & Buhrman, 2001; Seeley, 2003; Seeley & Visscher, 2003, 2004a) and is summarized here to explain the nest-site selection process and set the notation for our analysis.

In nest-site selection (reviewed in (Seeley & Visscher, 2004b; Seeley et al., 2006; Passino et al., 2008)), the colony splits itself when the queen and about half the old colony depart and assemble as a cluster nearby, typically on a tree branch. Assume $B = 100$ "scout" bees take on different roles (explorer, observer, committed, rester, and dead) in the nest-site selection process that occurs on the surface of the cluster of bees. Let k be the time step index. A scout bee can conduct one expedition from the swarm cluster per time step. When a scout, functioning as an "explorer," successfully finds a candidate nest site (e.g., a hollow of a tree) it evaluates its attributes to form a quality assessment based on cavity volume, entrance height, entrance area, and other attributes that are correlated with colony success. Denote the quality of site j as $N^j \in [0,1]$ with "1" representing a perfect site. Let the position of scout bee i be θ^i, and let $J(\theta)$ denote the "landscape" of site quality, with $\theta = [0,0]^\top$ the position of the cluster. Then $J(\theta^i) = N^j$ if scout i is at site j. Scout i has assessment noise $w^i(k)$, and a quality threshold $\epsilon_t = 0.2$ below which it will ignore a site. Hence, scout i's assessment of a site at time step k is $S^i(k) = J(\theta^i(k)) + w^i(k)$, if $J(\theta^i(k)) + w^i(k) > \epsilon_t$, and zero otherwise. Here, $w^i(k)$ is uniformly distributed on $(-01,01)$ to represent errors up to $\pm 10\%$ in the scout's assessment of nest-site quality (a normal distribution is inappropriate because large but unlikely deviations from the mean do not seem to exist in nature). Any scout bee that finds an above-threshold nest site dances for it (recruits other bees to it) and hence becomes "committed" to that site. Bees die with a small probability $p_d = 0.0016$ on each expedition so that less than 10% die over the whole nest-site selection process.

An unsuccessful explorer returns to the cluster and seeks to observe a dance. The time step that scout bee i first discovers site j is k_j^i and if the assessed quality of the site is above the quality threshold, this bee returns to the cluster and dances with a "strength" (number of waggle runs, with each run communicating the angle and radial distance to the nest site via the angle the run makes relative to the sun and the duration of the run) of $L^{ij}(k_j^i) = \gamma S^i(k_j^i)$ waggle runs where $\gamma = 150$; hence dance strength is correlated with nest quality. The dances recruit other bees to visit the site. After dancing, this committed bee returns to the site, and then back to the cluster, possibly making several such round trips between the swarm cluster and nest site; however, each time it returns to the cluster it dances on average $\epsilon_s = 15$ fewer waggle runs than the previous time. The sequence of waggle runs produced by scout bee i over the whole process is L^i and the total

number of waggle runs produced on the cluster for all sites at time step k is $L_t(k)$. Let $\sum L_t$ denote the total number of waggle runs over the entire process. A sequence of dances by one scout bee for one site, from the time of the initial dance to when the dance strength decays to zero, is called a "dance decay series." After a committed scout's dance strength has decayed to zero it rests and rejoins the process (by seeking to observe a dance) at each expedition with a probability $p_m = 0.25$. Scout bees that seek to observe a dance will end up exploring instead with probability

$$p_e(k) = \exp\left(-\frac{1}{2}\frac{L_t^2(k)}{\sigma^2}\right)$$ where $\sigma = 4000$, repre-

senting that when there is not much dancing on the cluster (small $L_t(k)$, meaning few good sites have been found), then there will be more exploring, and vice versa. There are $B_r(k)$ resters, $B_e(k)$ explorers, $B_o(k)$ bees that seek to observe, $B_u(k) = B_o(k) + B_r(k)$ uncommitted bees, and $B_c(k)$ committed bees. With probability $1 - p_e(k)$ observer bees will observe dances, and with probability $p_i(k) = \dfrac{L^i(k)}{\sum\limits_{i=1}^{B_c(k)} L^i(k)}$ they will be recruited by

the ith dancing bee; this means that recruits will be proportioned across candidate sites based on the site's relative proportion of recruiters, with better sites thereby getting more recruits. Bees recruited to site j will visit and dance for it back at the cluster according to their own assessment, as described above.

Key parts of the whole process are occurring simultaneously with the scouts performing and observing dances on the cluster and sensing at each candidate nest site the number of other bees at the site. When the quorum threshold $\epsilon_q = 20$ is reached at one of the sites (the time at which quorum achieved is called the "agreement time" and it is denoted with T_a), the bees there return to the cluster and produce piping signals that elicit heating by the quiescent (non-scout) bees in preparation for flight. Eventually, the entire swarm lifts off and flies to the chosen site, guided by the scout bees. There is significant time-pressure to complete the nest-site selection process as fast as possible since weather and energy losses pose significant threats to an exposed colony. However, enough time must be dedicated to ensure that many bees can conduct independent evaluations of the site and enough must agree that it is the best site found. Hence, during nest-site selection the swarm optimizes a balance between time minimization and site quality choice maximization (Passino & Seeley, 2006).

Each expedition by a scout bee is assumed to take 30 min, and the maximum amount of time for the swarm to make its choice is set at 32 hrs, so there are up to 64 time steps. Due to the possibility of simultaneous quorum achievement at two or more sites there can be "split decisions." In this case, the process is restarted by having the swarm lift off, fail to fly away, and then reform the cluster. Also, the process can fail to come to agreement before 64 time steps are completed, which is called a "no-decision failure." These failures can arise if a site of sufficient quality, one that will generate a recruitment rate that will assemble the required ϵ_q bees at a nest site, is not discovered early enough.

3. DISCRIMINATION AND DISTRACTION PROPERTIES

Viewing the swarm as a cognitive unit, its choice performance is evaluated in this and the two following sections. Choice performance of swarms is considered for several landscapes of nest-site quality. For each landscape and each choice test, 100 nest-site selection processes that terminate with a single site chosen are used. Then statistics are computed from the resulting data.

3.1 Discrimination Amplification

Let all sites have zero quality, except sites 5 and 6, which both start out at a quality of $N^6 = N^5 = 0.65$ and differentially move to 0.4 and 0.9. When both sites are at a quality of 0.65, the top-right plot of Figure 1 shows that it is equally likely that each site is chosen. As the two sites have increasingly different quality values, the swarm is increasingly better at discriminating between them. When the site quality difference is above 0.3 the swarm is always correct in its choice of the best site. Next, see the top- and bottom-left plots of Figure 1. There is a slight decrease in the median value of T_a and mean value of $\sum L_t$ since in this case the quality of site 5 is much lower so that it is not nearly as viable of a candidate; hence, it is easier to choose the best site (i.e., without as much deliberation that takes time). The bottom-right plot of Figure 1 shows that the number of bees not visiting sites goes up slightly as differential quality increases. This demonstrates that fewer bees are needed to join the process of selection when there are clear quality differences in the field of possible nest site qualities.

The results in Figure 1 also show that discrimination ability goes up relative to Figure 3 in Passino et al. (2008), indicated by increased slope on the percentage of times the correct site (site 6) is chosen as they move away from each other (in the initial part of the top-right plot, the slope is approximately (1-0.5)/0.3=5/3, compared to 5/4 when the sites start at 0.75). Hence, discrimination is better when site qualities are lower since mistakes are more costly. Notice that compared to Figure 3 in Passino et al. (2008) there is more coupling in the process here due to more bees abandoning the low quality site and switching to the high quality site (here, for some values of differential quality about 11/40=27.5% dance for two sites).

Figure 1. Amplified discrimination effect: Top-left: middle line in each box is the median value of T_a, boxes with notches that do not overlap represent that the medians of the two groups differ at the 5% significance level (i.e., a pairwise statistical hypothesis test), whiskers (dashed lines) represent 1.5 times the interquartile range, and outliers are designated with a " + ". Top-right: percentage of times each nest site is chosen (black lines), with site 1 designated by $\triangleright$ ("tR" represents "triangle right", a right-pointing triangle), site 2 by $\triangle$ ("tU" represents "triangle up"), site 3 by $\square$ ("dia"), site 4 by $\square$ ("sq"), site 5 by $\circ$, and site 6 by $*$. The gray lines with markers show the relative site qualities, $N^j / \sum_j N^j$.

Bottom-left: left-vertical axis and the black lines show the mean $\sum L_t$ (solid line, dots), and its standard deviation (dash-dot line, + marker), while gray lines and right-vertical axis show the number of split decision ($\times$) and no-decision ($\circ$) cases that occur for the 100 nest site selection processes that terminate with a single choice. Bottom-right: left-vertical axis and the black lines show the mean number of bees out of the 100 total that visit 0 sites (designated with $\triangleright$), 1 site ($\triangle$), 2 sites ($\square$), 3 sites ($\square$), 4 sites ($\circ$), 5 sites ($*$), and 6 sites ($\times$), and right-vertical axis shows via the gray lines the mean number B_c of committed scouts ($\times$) and mean number of explorers B_e (+) at the agreement time T_a.

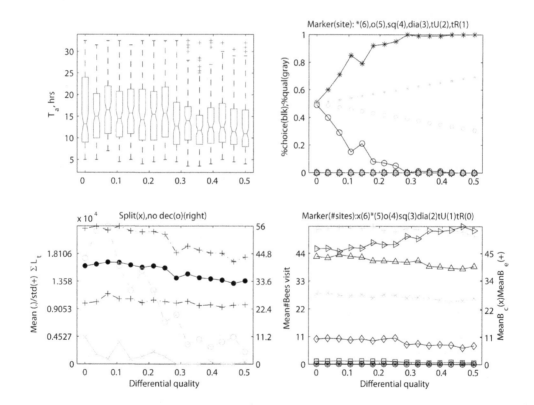

Figure 2. Effect of number of distractors, with perfect site present (see Figure 1 caption for axes explanation)

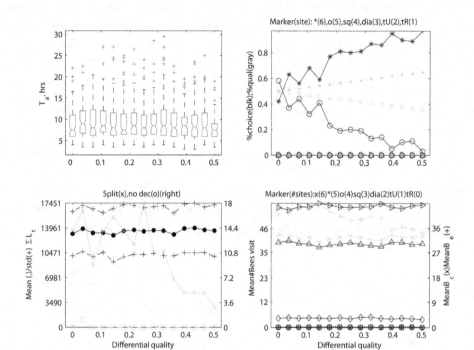

3.2 Effect of Number of Distractors: Treisman Feature Search Test

Let $N^6 = 1$ and $N^5 = 0.55$, then successively add sites 1, 2, 3, and 4 as additional distractors of quality 0.55. So, there are a total of 2, 3, 4, and 5 distractors. This is a Treisman feature search test (Treisman and Gelade, 1980) with one "target" (the best site) that should be chosen, and a variable number of distractors. The results in Figure 2 show that as more distractors of such a low quality are added there is little effect on the percent of correct choices (see top-right plot) relative to when there are only two distractors; however, this comes at the cost of an increased mean $\sum L_t$ for the swarm to try to resolve the differences (see bottom-left plot). Treisman and others took this as evidence of early *parallel* neural processing of alternatives, early enough that it was not at the level of consciousness. Clearly, the swarm is

processing the distractors in parallel also and this test shows that this has a positive effect on swarm choice performance.

The main result, however, comes from comparing with the case where everything is the same as in the previous test, but $N^6 = 0$, that is, when the target is removed. In standard feature search tests human subjects are asked to decide if the target is there or not, something that cannot be requested from the swarm. Instead, the swarm comes to a decision for this case and the results are compared to the last case. The results in the top-right plot of Figure 3 show that as expected, with two distractors each is chosen 50% of the time, 3 are each chosen about 33% of the time, 4 are chosen around 25% of the time, and 5 about 20% of the time. The mean $\sum L_t$ increases with more distractors but the median T_a goes up, then comes down since it becomes easier to make the

Figure 3. Effect of number of distractors, without perfect site present (see Figure 1 caption for axes explanation)

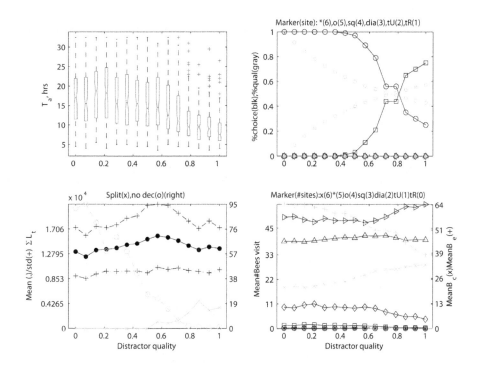

Figure 4. Distraction can attenuate discrimination (see Figure 1 caption for axes explanation)

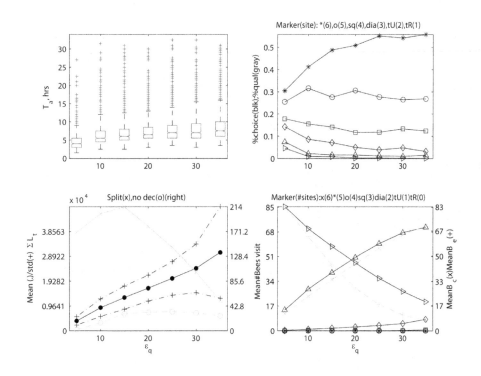

errors that occur with 5 distractors. Also, comparing Figures 2 and 3, the median T_a values are *higher* for the case when there is no target compared to when the target is present. An analogous result is obtained in tests for humans, and Treisman hypothesized that humans switched to a "sequential search mode" where by a process of elimination they decided that the target was not present (Treisman & Gelade, 1980; Gazzaniga et al., 1998). For the swarm such a mode switch is not possible. The swarm simply takes longer to decide due to the internal dynamics of the decision-making process being slowed by a more lengthy evaluation of the evidence gathered.

4. DISCRIMINATION-DISTRACTION INTERACTIONS

The tests in the last section were designed to illustrate *isolated* swarm discrimination abilities and distractor effects. In other nest-site quality landscapes, however, both effects are present and interact with each other as shown next.

4.1 A Distractor Can Attenuate Discrimination

First, it is shown that distraction can attenuate discrimination. Let all sites have zero quality, except let site 4 have a quality of 0.5 and let sites 5 and 6 both start out at a quality of 0.75 and differentially move to 0.5 and 1. Site 4 is considered to be a distractor since it should not be chosen. Notice that in the top-right plot of Figure 4 the region of "generalization" (i.e., quality range where the swarm treats qualities as similar) (Gazzaniga et al., 1998) grows relative to Figure 1 and Figure 3 in (Passino et al., 2008) and the slope of the line representing correct choices is about 1 (lower than in Figure 1 and Figure 3 in (Passino et al., 2008)) so that discrimination is attenuated by the relatively low quality distractor. This at-tenuation occurs while all other key variables (e.g., median T_a and mean $\sum L_t$) stay relatively constant. This illustrates that the generalization effect is solely coming from the effect of site 4 as a distractor.

4.2 Discrimination Tries to Overcome Distraction

Let the quality of site 5 be 0.75, let the quality of site 4 vary as $N^4 = D \subset [0,1]$ and consider site 4 to be a distractor for the range $D \in [0,0.75]$ since it should not be chosen for that range of values, but it is the best site for $D \in (075,1]$ when you can view site 5 as the distractor (this is a case of nonlinearly decreasing differential quality). Of course, you could view the basic task as one of discriminating between the two sites. The results are in Figure 5. First, note that discrimination level is asymmetric in the sense that the swarm is better at discriminating when $D \in [0,0.75]$, but discrimination is not as good for $D \in (075,1]$ (mistakes are not as costly in that region). There is a small region of generalization around 0.75. It is interesting that the median T_a values are relatively high until the quality of the sites approach each other, and then the amount of dancing $\sum L_t$ increases in order to discriminate between the sites, but then decreases as the sites move apart again. Also, the median T_a value decreases in the range $D \in [0.8,1]$ (since it is easier to make a quick but incorrect decision) and note that there are fewer outliers. There are many no-decision cases when site 4 has a low quality; this is due to the difficulties of finding the *single* relatively good site 5. Overall, this shows that distraction tends to have an effect on choice performance degradation that discrimination tries to overcome (i.e., the "tension" between choice performance enhancement via good discrimination and choice performance degradation via distraction is balanced).

Figure 5. Nonlinear differential quality (see Figure 1 caption for axes explanation)

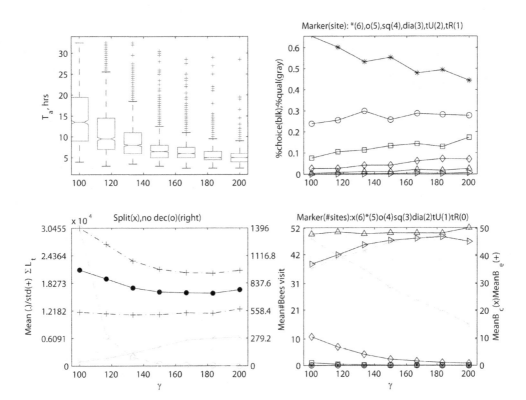

4.3 Context Dependence: Transitivity

A broad range of nest-site quality landscapes were tested to see if the swarm would ever misorder the percentages of choices for sites in comparison to the order of relative nest-site qualities. These tests included all the simulation results shown in the discrimination and distraction tests above, the general class of landscapes described at the beginning of the next section, the cases considered in (Passino & Seeley, 2006), and many landscapes not reported here. The tests were never able to "trick" the swarm: the percentage choice order is always given by the ordering of the relative qualities of the nest sites (to see this, review all plots of choice performance in this paper). Hence, the swarm never violates "strong stochastic tran-

sitivity" (Luce & Suppes, 1965) which can lead to choice errrors.

5. ADAPTIVE TUNING OF SWARM COGNITION PROCESSES

To gain more insights into the mechanisms of swarm decision making, their evolutionary adaptation is studied. First, the adaptive tuning of the parameters of the individual bees' decision-making is studied. This helps to further validate the model and serves to show how speed accuracy trade-offs emerge from the adaptive tuning of the swarm's cognition process. Second, the effect of the amount of individual bee nest-site assessment noise on the swarm's choice performance and speed-accuracy trade-off is studied.

To study the adaptive tuning of individual bee-level behavioral parameters, their values are changed ("pseudo-mutated") from experimentally-determined ones, and the average time/energy costs and choice performance are evaluated. Six sites with qualities uniformly distributed on $[\epsilon_t, 1]$, where $\epsilon_t = 0.2$ is the threshold quality, are used. The randomly generated qualities are ordered so that site 1 is the lowest quality, site 2 is the second worst one, and so on, and this makes site 6 the best site. Each nest-site quality landscape generated this way is highly likely to produce interacting distraction and discrimination effects and hence generally more challenging choice tests than in (Passino & Seeley, 2006). Seven values of each behavioral parameter are considered, and for each of these, 1000 nest-site selection processes are run (each for a randomly generated landscape). Performance is characterized using statistics of the 1000 runs for each parameter.

5.1 Effect of Quorum Threshold Size

Figure 6 shows that small ϵ_q values result in fast decisions (top-left plot) and relatively few dances (bottom-left plot), but relatively frequent errors (top-right plot) since only a few bees evaluate the chosen site. High ϵ_q values result in slower decisions, more dancing, and relatively low error rates since many bees evaluate the chosen site. The experimentally-determined quorum threshold value (in the range of 10-20 (Seeley and Visscher, 2003)) is the adaptive result of balancing the trade-off between keeping the median T_a and mean $\sum L_t$ values low and the percent of correct choices high (Passino & Seeley, 2006). This range of ϵ_q also keeps (bottom-right plot) enough bees involved in the process by visiting sites and evaluating them, enough explorers in the role of searching for sites, yet relatively few bees that visit two sites since that can lead to degraded performance in some cases.

5.2 Effect of Initial Dance Strength and Model Validation

For the effect of variation of γ see Figure 7. This shows that the value of 150 waggle runs for the initial dance strength from an excellent site found in experiments (Seeley, 2003) is the result of a trade off between keeping the median T_a and mean $\sum L_t$ values low (high γ values) and the percent of correct choices high (low γ values), while at the same time avoiding split and no-decision cases. This provides a more complete verification that the values used in (Passino & Seeley, 2006) (and here) are in the range settled on by evolution since the class of quality landscapes considered here is considerably broader. Similar results are found for ϵ_s and σ. The results here also help to verify the model in Passino and Seeley (2006) since ϵ_q, ϵ_s, and γ (a parameter not studied in Passino & Seeley, 2006) are the ones found in experiments (Seeley & Buhrman, 1999, 2001; Seeley, 2003; Seeley & Visscher, 2003, 2004a, 2004b).

Overall, from a swarm cognition perspective, the results here show that individual-level bee behavioral parameters related to "early" (γ and ϵ_s) and "late" (ϵ_q) processing (Gazzaniga et al., 1998) have values that are the result of balancing a swarm-level choice speed and accuracy trade-off.

5.3 Effects of Other Behavioral Parameters

Results for considering the tendency to seek to observe dances, $p_m \in [0,1]$ show that this parameter has little effect on most variables. Increasing it does, however, increase the number of split decisions and decrease the number of no-decision cases since there is an increase in coupling in the process that leads to build-up for similar sites to be closer, and helps to ensure that some site will have enough bees to reach a quorum. If site

Figure 6. Effect of ϵ_q (see Figure 1 caption for axes explanation)

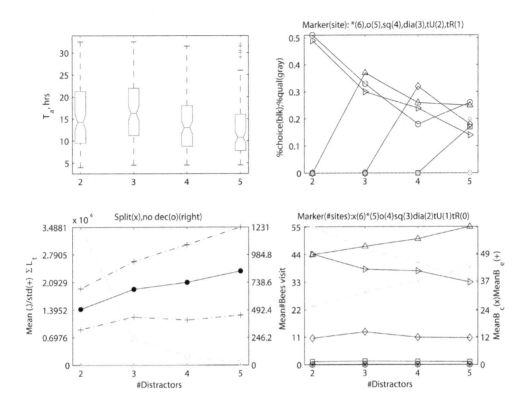

qualities are generated on $[0.2, 1]$ but $\epsilon_t \in [0, 0.4]$, there is little effect on the choice performance since higher values of ϵ_t simply eliminate inferior alternatives that the swarm is already quite capable of eliminating. Simulations show that all low values of p_d have no major impact on choice performance.

5.4 Effect of Individual Bee Assessment Noise Magnitude

The effect of varying the magnitude w of the bee assessment noise $w^i \in [-w, w]$ is shown in Figure 8. If w increases, the choice error rate does not degrade or improve much over the case where $w = 0.1$, the value from (Passino & Seeley, 2006). It is physiologically impossible for the individu-

al bees to have $w = 0$ and there is little choice performance degradation when w increases to $w = 0.1$. For $w > 0.1$ the choice performance stays nearly the same (and most importantly, does not decrease a lot), but the swarm needs a higher median value of T_a and mean $\sum L_t$ to reach agreement. This is due to a slowing of the decision process due to resolving the differences due to noise. For increasing noise magnitudes, the number of split decisions goes down (since it becomes more unlikely there will be simultaneous agreement) and the number of no-decision cases generally goes up (due to too much confusion caused by the noise). Also, an increasing noise magnitude results in more cross-inhibition as seen in the mean number of bees that visit two sites. This occurs since the noise perturbs the system away

Figure 7. Effect of γ (see Figure 1 caption for axes explanation)

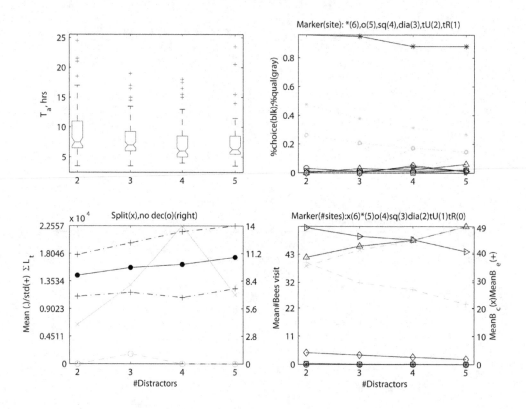

from a quick decision and thereby avoids "locking" onto a low quality site. Noise results in more *deliberation* so that on average better sites will be found (i.e., deliberation allows more time for search and consideration).

From a swarm cognition perspective, since group memory is more accurate when more bees are committed to a site (Passino et al., 2008), and choices are made based on group memory, the swarm effectively filters individual level assessment errors especially for the chosen site (even for unrealistically large quality assessment error magnitudes such as $w = 0.5$). However, natural selection seems to have favored a reduction in individual bee site assessment noise magnitude because that leads to shorter agreement times and less dancing, without much degradation in choice accuracy.

5.5 Effect of Individual Bee Assessment Noise Magnitude on Discrimination

The results in Section 5.4 for the effects of noise magnitude are for a very general class of nest-site quality landscapes. The effect can be amplified for specific and common landscapes. For instance, it seems likely that the swarm will often face discrimination problems for relatively close quality sites. To study the effect of noise magnitude on discrimination, the case of Figure 3 in (Passino et al., 2008) is modified to have all site qualities be zero, except $N^6 = 0.76$ and $N^5 = 0.74$, a differential quality of only 0.02 (which by the results in Figure 3 in (Passino et al., 2008) results in around 50% of the time the swarm choosing each of the two sites). That is, the sites are in the region of generalization and it is difficult for the

Figure 8. Effect of w (see Figure 1 caption for axes explanation)

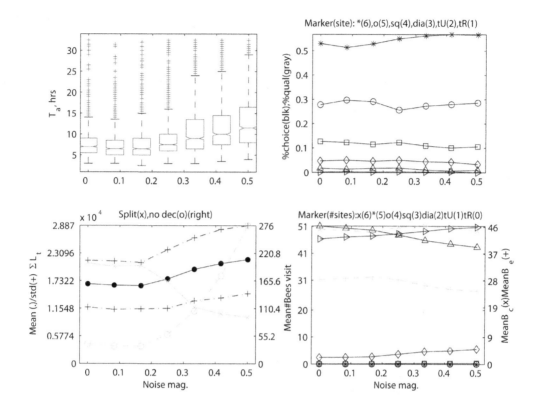

swarm to discriminate between the two since their quality is so close. Figure 9 shows that by increasing the amount of individual assessment noise, choice performance for the best site stays almost the same as the noise magnitude increases. Notice that in this case 1000 simulations are performed for each parameter value so that at $w = 0.1$ there is about a 5% difference in the choice rates for the two sites. In the region above $w > 0.3$ there is about a 10% difference in the rates of choice for the two sites; hence, the noise has increased the ability of the swarm discriminate between these close-quality sites. This increase in performance comes, however, at the expense of a higher median T_a and mean $\sum L_t$, and an increased number of no-decision cases. These results further confirm the conclusions reached for the general class of landscapes in the last subsection.

6. CONCLUSION

The swarm choice performance and adaptation studies in this paper provide additional evidence that bee-based swarms have a cognition process that shares key features with neuron-based brains. It was shown that the ability to discriminate depends not only on the differential quality, but also on the absolute quality. In particular, discrimination performance improves for lower quality sites. Next, it was shown that distractors can attenuate the ability of the swarm to discriminate and that discrimination mechanisms try to overcome the negative impacts of distractors. The Treisman feature search test showed that choice performance only degrades slightly if relatively low quality distractors are added to the task of finding the best quality site. The original idea that this provides evidence of parallel process-

Figure 9. Effect of w, $N^6 = 0.76$ *and* $N^5 = 0.74$ *case (see Figure 1 caption for axes explanation)*

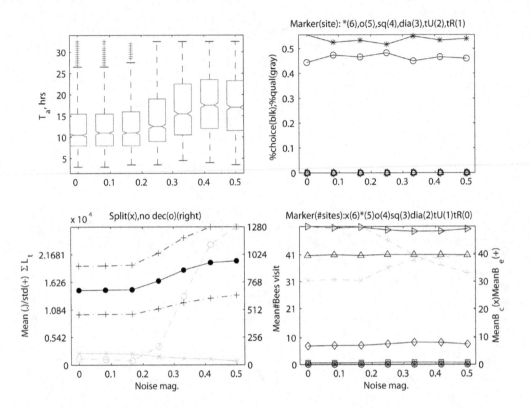

ing in the brain clearly also holds for the swarm. Moreover, it was shown that if the high quality site is removed, the swarm takes much longer to decide which site to choose. It was proposed that this was due to a switch in humans to a sequential search mode. Here, however, the delay is clearly induced by the dynamics of the process that leads to deliberation. This provides an alternative way to interpret the delays that occur in reaction time tests, and this may be useful to infer mental dynamics and structure in other species. The existence of irrational choice behavior commonly found in human decision making in the presence of context-dependent effects was studied. It was shown that for the nest-site selection task, the swarm possesses strong stochastic transitivity and the attraction effect, which both provide evidence that the swarm makes good choices on average.

The analysis of the adaptive "tuning" of the processes underlying swarm cognition was a study of the cognitive ecology of the honey bee swarm. It was shown that several behavioral parameters underlying swarm cognition have values evidently shaped by natural selection to balance speed and accuracy of choice. Moreover, it is shown that swarm-level choice performance is insensitive to bee-level assessment errors.

There are a number of directions for future work. First, consideration of the work in (Shafir et al., 2002) on honey bees begs the question if, for the same task and species, context-dependent effects are amplified or attenuated when comparing cases of social and solitary choice. Second, in this paper it was assumed that the number of scouts is $B = 100$. In nature, however, swarms come in different sizes, so that the resulting number of scouts could be in the range $75 \leq B \leq 1000$. It is not known how the size of B and particularly large values of B affect the decision-making process as there have not been experiments conducted to investigate this issue. In fact, it is very difficult to perform such experiments; hence, the investigation of the size of B is likely best done in simulation. This raises a number of questions. For instance, will a larger swarm be more effective at discrimination between the quality of two sites? Will it more effectively eliminate distractors from consideration? What will be the effect on context-dependent decision-making? How will the speed-accuracy trade-off be affected? Will a larger size swarm use a higher quorum threshold? Third, it would be useful to conduct a full statistical analysis of the results in this paper (using analysis of variance and the Tukey procedure for multiple comparisons). All these questions await further study.

ACKNOWLEDGMENT

The author would like to thank Thomas D. Seeley of Cornell University for many fruitful and enjoyable discussions on the nest-site selection process and swarm cognition in honey bees. The author would also like to thank Roger Ratcliff of Ohio State University for inputs on the psychology and neuroscience of decision-making, and Benjamin E. Keller for giving me edits on the document.

REFERENCES

Britton, N. F., Franks, N. R., Pratt, S. C., & Seeley, T. D. (2002). Deciding on a new home: how do honey bees agree? *Proceedings. Biological Sciences*, *269*, 1383–1388. doi:10.1098/rspb.2002.2001

Busemeyer, J. R., & Townsend, J. T. (1993). Decision field theory: A dynamic-cognitive approach to decision making in an uncertain environment. *Psychological Review*, *100*(3), 432–459. doi:10.1037/0033-295X.100.3.432

Camazine, S., Deneubourg, J.-L., Franks, N. R., Sneyd, J., Theraulaz, G., & Bonabeau, E. (2001). *Self-Organization in Biological Systems*. Princeton, NJ: Princeton University Press.

Camazine, S., Visscher, P. K., Finley, J., & Vetter, R. S. (1999). House-hunting by honey bee swarms: collective decisions and individual behaviors. *Insectes Sociaux*, *46*, 348–360. doi:10.1007/s000400050156

Dukas, R. (Ed.). (1998). *Cognitive Ecology*. Chicago: University of Chicago Press.

Franks, N. R. (1989). Army ants: A collective intelligence. *American Scientist*, *77*, 138–145.

Franks, N. R., Dornhaus, A., Fitzsimmons, J. P., & Stevens, M. (2003). Speed versus accuracy in collective decision making. *Proceedings. Biological Sciences*, *270*, 2457–2463. doi:10.1098/rspb.2003.2527

Gazzaniga, M. S., Ivry, R. B., & Mangun, J. R. (1998). *Cognitive Neuroscience: The Biology of the Mind*. New York: W. W. Norton and Co.

Hastie, R., & Kameda, T. (2005). The robust beauty of majority rules in group decisions. *Psychological Review*, *112*(2), 494–508. doi:10.1037/0033-295X.112.2.494

Hinsz, V. B., Tindale, R. S., & Vollrath, D. A. (1997). The emerging conceptualization of groups as information processors. *Psychological Bulletin*, *121*(1), 43–64. doi:10.1037/0033-2909.121.1.43

Hölldobler, B., & Wilson, E. O. (1990). *The Ants*. Cambridge, MA: Belknap Press of Harvard University Press.

Hölldobler, B., & Wilson, E. O. (2008). *The Superorganism: The Beauty, Elegance, and Strangeness of Insect Societies*. New York: W.W. Norton and Co.

Hub, J., Payne, W., & Puto, C. (1982). Adding asymmetrically dominated alternatives: Violations of regularity and the similarity hypothesis. *The Journal of Consumer Research, 9*, 90–98. doi:10.1086/208899

Janson, S., Middendorf, M., & Beekman, M. (2007). Searching for a new home–scouting behavior of honeybee swarms. *Behav Ecol, 18*, 384–392. doi:10.1093/beheco/arl095

Kandel, E. K., Schwartz, J. H., & Jessell, T. M. (Eds.). (2000). *Principles of neural science*. New York: McGraw-Hill.

Kerr, N. L., & Tindale, R. S. (2004). Group performance and decision making. *Annual Review of Psychology, 55*, 623–655. doi:10.1146/annurev.psych.55.090902.142009

Laughlin, P. R., & Ellis, A. L. (1986). Demonstratability and social combination processes on mathematical intellective tasks. *Journal of Experimental Social Psychology, 22*, 177–189. doi:10.1016/0022-1031(86)90022-3

Levine, J. M., Resnik, L. B., & Higgins, E. T. (1993). Social foundations of cognition. *Annual Review of Psychology, 44*, 585–612. doi:10.1146/annurev.ps.44.020193.003101

Luce, R. D., & Suppes, P. (1965). Preference, utility, and subjective probability. In Luce, R. D., Bush, R. R., & Galanter, E. (Eds.), *Handbook of mathematical psychology* (*Vol. 3*, pp. 249–410). New York: Wiley.

Mallon, E. B., Pratt, S. C., & Franks, N. R. (2001). Individual and collective decision-making during nest site selection by the ant *Leptothorax albipennis. Behavioral Ecology and Sociobiology, 50*, 352–359. doi:10.1007/s002650100377

Marshall, J. A., Bogacz, R., Dornhaus, A., Planque, R., Kovacs, T., & Franks, N. R. (2009, February). On optimal decision-making in brains and insect societies. *J Roy. Soc. Interface*, 1-10. doi:10.1098/rsif.2008.0511

Myerscough, M. R. (2003). Dancing for a decision: a matrix model for nest-site choice by honey bees. *Proceedings. Biological Sciences, 270*, 577–582. doi:10.1098/rspb.2002.2293

Passino, K. M., & Seeley, T. D. (2006). Modeling and analysis of nest-site selection by honey bee swarms: The speed and accuracy trade-off. *Behavioral Ecology and Sociobiology, 59*(3), 427–442. doi:10.1007/s00265-005-0067-y

Passino, K. M., Seeley, T. D., & Visscher, P. K. (2008). Swarm cognition in honey bees. *Behavioral Ecology and Sociobiology, 62*(3), 401–414. doi:10.1007/s00265-007-0468-1

Perdriau, B. S., & Myerscough, M. R. (2007). Making good choices with variable information: a stochastic model for nest-site selection by honeybees. *Biology Letters, 3*, 140–143. doi:10.1098/rsbl.2006.0599

Pratt, S. C. (2005). Quorum sensing by encounter rates in the ant *Temnothorax albipennis. Behav Ecol, 16*, 488–496. doi:10.1093/beheco/ari020

Pratt, S. C., Mallon, E. B., Sumpter, D. J. T., & Franks, N. R. (2002). Quorum sensing, recruitment, and collective decision-making during colony emigration by the ant *Leptothorax albipennis. Behavioral Ecology and Sociobiology, 52*, 117–127. doi:10.1007/s00265-002-0487-x

Pratt, S. C., Sumpter, D. J. T., Mallon, E. B., & Franks, N. R. (2005). An agent-based model of collective nest choice by the ant *Temnothorax albipennis. Animal Behaviour, 70*, 1023–1036. doi:10.1016/j.anbehav.2005.01.022

Ratcliff, R., & Smith, P. L. (2004). A comparison of sequential sampling models for two-choice reaction time. *Psychological Review, 111*(2), 333–367. doi:10.1037/0033-295X.111.2.333

Ratcliff, R., VanZandt, T., & McKoon, G. (1999). Connectionist and diffusion models of reaction time. *Psychological Review, 106*(2), 231–300. doi:10.1037/0033-295X.106.2.261

Roe, R. M., Busemeyer, J. R., & Townsend, J. T. (2001). Multialternative decision field theory: A dynamic connectionist model of decision making. *Psychological Review, 108*(2), 370–392. doi:10.1037/0033-295X.108.2.370

Seeley, T. D. (1989). The honeybee as a superorganism. *American Scientist, 77*, 546–553.

Seeley, T. D. (1995). *The Wisdom of the Hive.* Cambridge, MA: Harvard University Press.

Seeley, T. D. (2003). Consensus building during nest-site selection in honey bee swarms: the expiration of dissent. *Behavioral Ecology and Sociobiology, 53*, 417–424.

Seeley, T. D., & Buhrman, S. C. (1999). Group decision making in swarms of honey bees. *Behavioral Ecology and Sociobiology, 45*, 19–31. doi:10.1007/s002650050536

Seeley, T. D., & Buhrman, S. C. (2001). Nest-site selection in honey bees: how well do swarms implement the "best-of-n" decision rule? *Behavioral Ecology and Sociobiology, 49*, 416–427. doi:10.1007/s002650000299

Seeley, T. D., & Visscher, P. K. (2003). Choosing a home: how the scouts in a honey bee swarm perceive the completion of their group decision making. *Behavioral Ecology and Sociobiology, 54*, 511–520. doi:10.1007/s00265-003-0664-6

Seeley, T. D., & Visscher, P. K. (2004a). Quorum sensing during nest-site selection by honey bee swarms. *Behavioral Ecology and Sociobiology, 56*, 594–601. doi:10.1007/s00265-004-0814-5

Seeley, T. D., & Visscher, P. K. (2004b). Group decision making in nest-site selection by honey bees. *Apidologie, 35*, 1–16. doi:10.1051/apido:2004004

Seeley, T. D., Visscher, P. K., & Passino, K. M. (2006, May/June). Group decision making in honey bee swarms. *American Scientist, 94*(3), 220–229.

Shafir, S., Waite, T. A., & Smith, B. (2002). Context-dependent violations of rational choice in honeybees (apis mellifera) and gray jays (perisoreus canadensis). *Behavioral Ecology and Sociobiology, 51*, 180–187. doi:10.1007/s00265-001-0420-8

Simonson, I. (1989). Choice based on reasons: The case of attraction and compromise effects. *The Journal of Consumer Research, 16*, 158–174. doi:10.1086/209205

Simonson, I., & Tversky, A. (1992). Choice in context: Tradeoff contrast and extremeness aversion. *JMR, Journal of Marketing Research, 24*, 281–295. doi:10.2307/3172740

Steiner, I. D. (1966). Models for inferring relationships between group size and potential group productivity. *Behavioral Science, 11*, 273–283. doi:10.1002/bs.3830110404

Surowiecki, J. (2004). *The wisdom of crowds.* New York: Doubleday.

Treisman, A., & Gelade, G. (1980). A feature-integration theory of attention. *Cognitive Psychology, 12*, 97–136. doi:10.1016/0010-0285(80)90005-5

Tversky, A. (1972). Elimination by aspects: A theory of choice. *Psychological Review, 79*, 281–289. doi:10.1037/h0032955

Waite, T. A. (2001). Background context and decision making in hoarding gray jays. *Behav Ecol, 12*, 318–324. doi:10.1093/beheco/12.3.318

Waite, T. A. (2002). Interruptions improve choice performance in gray jays: prolonged information processing versus minimization of costly errors. *Animal Cognition, 5*, 209–214.

Waite, T. A., & Field, K. L. (2000). Erroneous choice and foregone gains in hoarding gray jays. *Animal Cognition, 3*, 127–134. doi:10.1007/s100710000073

Wilson, D. S. (2000). Animal movement as group-level adaptation. In Boinski, S., & Garber, P. A. (Eds.), *On the Move: How and Why Animals Travel in Groups* (pp. 238–258). Chicago: University of Chicago Press.

This work was previously published in International Journal of Swarm Intelligence Research, Volume 1, Issue 2, edited by Yuhui Shi, pp. 80-97, copyright 2010 by IGI Publishing (an imprint of IGI Global)

Chapter 16
A Theoretical Framework for Estimating Swarm Success Probability Using Scouts

Antons Rebguns
The University of Wyoming, USA

Diana Spears
Swarmotics LLC, USA

Richard Anderson-Sprecher
University of Wyoming, USA

Aleksey Kletsov
East Carolina University, USA

ABSTRACT

This paper presents a novel theoretical framework for swarms of agents. Before deploying a swarm for a task, it is advantageous to predict whether a desired percentage of the swarm will succeed. The authors present a framework that uses a small group of expendable "scout" agents to predict the success probability of the entire swarm, thereby preventing many agent losses. The scouts apply one of two formulas to predict – the standard Bernoulli trials formula or the new Bayesian formula. For experimental evaluation, the framework is applied to simulated agents navigating around obstacles to reach a goal location. Extensive experimental results compare the mean-squared error of the predictions of both formulas with ground truth, under varying circumstances. Results indicate the accuracy and robustness of the Bayesian approach. The framework also yields an intriguing result, namely, that both formulas usually predict better in the presence of (Lennard-Jones) inter-agent forces than when their independence assumptions hold.

DOI: 10.4018/978-1-4666-1592-2.ch016

INTRODUCTION

This paper presents a novel theoretical framework for swarm risk assessment. The framework is applied to a scenario consisting of a swarm of agents that needs to travel from an initial location to a goal location, while avoiding obstacles. Before deploying the entire swarm, we would like to have a certain level of confidence that a desired portion of the swarm will successfully reach the goal. If not, then perhaps the swarm should not be deployed. For example, for a swarm of moving robots, the environment itself can pose a significant risk (rough terrain, sudden changes in elevation that agents are not equipped to handle, water, etc.) and, as with any hardware, circuit and mechanical failures can prevent agents from successfully reaching their destination. It is alternatively plausible that the swarm consists of software agents trying to achieve a more abstract goal, such as a successful transaction, while avoiding obstacles, such as provisions or constraints. For simplicity, in our simulation agents are modeled as robots and obstacles are modeled as physical objects.

The environment in which the agents are deployed is assumed to be static, though it may be completely or partially unknown. This environment can be highly unstructured as well, as in Mondada et al. (2005). Additionally, deployment of the entire swarm is potentially hazardous, e.g., due to the possible loss or corruption of agents – for example, some of the obstacles might contain explosives, agents could fall into inescapable holes as in Dorigo et al. (2006), or there could be environmental hazards as in Tatomir and Rothkrantz (2006). In these and many similar situations it is advantageous to do a preliminary phase of *risk assessment* before deploying the full swarm. The information gained from this phase will help the practitioner decide what deployment strategy to use, e.g. what starting location works best, how many agents to deploy in order to ensure a desired success rate, and whether the task at hand is worth the risk of losing a possibly large portion of the swarm.

The solution proposed here is the use of a group of expendable agent "scouts" to predict the success probability for the swarm, during the risk assessment phase. For practical reasons, only a few (less than 20) scouts are sent from the swarm, which may consist of hundreds of agents. A human or artificial agent, called the "sender," deploys the scouts. Then, an agent (e.g., a person, an artificial scout, or a sensing device), called the "receiver," counts the fraction of scouts that arrive at the goal successfully. The sender and receiver must be able to communicate with each other – to report the scout success rate, but no other agents require the capability of communicating messages. Using the fraction of *scouts* that successfully reach the goal, we apply a formula that predicts the probability that a desired percentage of the *entire swarm* will reach the goal. Based on this probability, the sender can decide whether or not to deploy the full swarm. Alternatively, based on this probability the sender can decide how many agents to deploy in order to yield a high probability that a desired number of agents will reach the goal.

Our theoretical framework is based on two formulas that use agent scouts as "samples" for making predictions regarding the success probability of a swarm. The first approach is the standard Bernoulli trials formula, and the second is a novel Bayesian formula. We report conclusions regarding the predictive accuracy of these formulas, based on an extensive set of experiments during which parameters were varied methodically. Our measure of predictive accuracy is the *mean squared error (MSE)* of each formula's predictions versus "ground truth." Experimental conclusions include the value of a uniform prior for the Bayesian formula in knowledge-lean situations, and the accuracy and robustness to changes in the environment of the Bayesian approach. This paper also reports an intriguing result, namely, that both formulas usually predict better in the presence of inter-agent forces (when a Lennard-Jones inter-agent force law is used) than when their independence assumptions hold. Inter-agent forces are useful for initiating and sustaining multi-agent formations while traveling to a target location. We conclude that these formulas, and especially our Bayesian formula, provide extremely practical solutions for solving "the swarm success rate prediction problem" in a variety of real-world situations. Additionally, this paper provides conclusions which lead to advice on selecting the values of controllable parameters in order to help the practitioner apply our framework.

The most notable contributions of this research are:

- A novel theoretical framework for swarm *risk assessment,* using very few scouts to predict the swarm success probability, is presented. For the first time, scouts are used to predict the probability that a given portion of a swarm will achieve its objective. Although our framework has been applied to a particular navigation task in this paper, there is nothing about our approach that depends on this specific task.
- A novel Bayesian formula for success probability calculation is introduced, along with its mathematical derivation.
- A full factorial experimental design has been employed to evaluate and compare the Bernoulli and Bayesian formulas.

RELATED WORK

Our framework is applicable to a wide range of tasks, including search-and-rescue, navigation, surveillance, optimization, and so on. It assumes that each agent within the swarm will succeed or fail at the task, and that this binary outcome can be determined. This research instantiates our framework by applying it to a simulation in which the agents' task is to navigate through a field of obstacles to get to a goal location.

For our control strategy, we chose *physicomimetics*, also called *artificial physics (AP)*, invented by Spears and Gordon (1999). This was a serendipitous choice. Alternative control strategies that could have been employed include *behavior-based*, *rule-based* or *biomimetic*. As will be seen in the experimental results below, there appears to be a favorable relationship between our scouts approach and physicomimetics control (using a Lennard-Jones control law).

Our scouts framework is related to statistical sampling. The process of sampling from a population to infer conclusions about the general population has a long and very important history in the field of statistics, starting in the early 1800s with census taking (Wright & Farmer, 2000). The Bernoulli formula applied in this work is a fundamental formula from the literature on statistical sampling (Zwillinger, 2002). Statistical sampling has permeated a wide array of social and scientific fields, including artificial intelligence (AI). For example, search and evolutionary algorithms depend fundamentally on stochastic sampling (Russell & Norvig, 2003). Also, inductive inference within machine learning uses sampling theory (Hastie et al., 2001; Kearns & Vazirani, 1994). Furthermore, our Bayesian formula is related to Bayesian statistical approaches in AI, including Bayesian inference/updating (Russell & Norvig, 2003).

There has been little prior research on agent scouts. Most studies are found in natural science – because scouts are a popular mechanism for assisting biological swarms. One noteworthy example is that of Greene and Gordon (2007), who published a study of red harvest ants that use a group of "patrollers" as scouts before sending out the full swarm of ants. These patrollers establish a path for foraging. Our scouts also act as "patrollers," but they quantify the probability of success for the swarm rather than setting the path. Future work will include merging the use of scouts for predicting the success rate and for subsequently guiding the swarm.

Scouts are particularly relevant for search-and-rescue applications (Rybski et al., 2001), for remote reconnaissance, and within the context of swarms they are relevant for distributed sensor networks (Tikanmäki et al., 2006) and swarm "nest assessment" (Şahin & Franks, 2002). Like this previous work, our approach also uses scouts for assessing the safety of the environment for the swarm. We have not, however, been able to find any prior research on the topic of sending out a small set of scout agents specifically for the purpose of predicting the *probability* of swarm success. The ability to predict the swarm success rate is fundamental for tasks in which the loss of a substantial fraction of the swarm would be costly or might prevent completion of the task.

Predicting Swarm Success Rate With Scouts

Our objective is to predict the probability that y or more out of a total of n agents will successfully navigate through an obstacle field and get to a goal location within a time limit (Rebguns et al., 2008). We predict this probability by sending out a sample of k scout agents (which, we assume, are not part of the n swarm agents, although modifying our formulas if they are a subset of the swarm is straightforward). For practical reasons, we assume that $k \ll n$.

The Formalized Prediction Problem

Formally, the problem being addressed in this paper is the following. Assume that k scouts are used to find an estimate $\hat{p} = \dfrac{Successes}{k}$ of p, where *Successes* is the number of scouts successfully reaching the goal, and p is the true probability of one agent succeeding in the time limit. We use p as a measure of environmental difficulty, which, in the simplest case is related to the number of obstacles to be avoided by the agents. Given $\hat{p}$ as input, we want our approach (using one of the

formulas below) to output the following probability:

$$P(Y \geq y \mid \hat{p})$$

where Y is a random variable and y is a problem-dependent lower bound parameter whose value is given by the system user.

Bernoulli Trials Formula

The process of predicting the swarm success rate can be considered to be a Bernoulli trials process. Assume that k scouts are sent out to estimate $\hat{p} = \dfrac{Successes}{k}$. Then the standard formula (Zwillinger, 2002), which we call P_{Bern}, for predicting the probability of y or more successes in n independent trials is directly applicable:

$$P_{Bern} = P(Y \geq y \mid \hat{p}) = \sum_{j=y}^{n} \binom{n}{j} \hat{p}^{j}(1 - \hat{p})^{n-j}$$

Novel Bayesian Formula

This paper assumes that the number k of scouts is between 3 and 15. Our rationale is that we specifically want to investigate the case of scouts being a valuable and expensive commodity, and sending more is problematic. By modeling few scouts, we are able to address the real-world situation faced by practitioners of whether it is worthwhile sending any scouts at all if only a few can afford to be sent. A well-known problem with using P_{Bern} is that k should be large, perhaps more than 20 scouts, to get a reasonable estimate $\hat{p}$ of p. Our reason for mentioning the number 20 in particular is that when k is less than 20, the variance of P_{Bern} tends to be high and there is a substantial chance that either all or no scouts will reach the goal, typically leading to poor predictions of swarm behavior. As an example, consider the case of three scouts. There is always a risk that all three will fail, even if the environment is very easy, i.e., tiny samples can be skewed. To overcome this limitation of P_{Bern}, we provide a Bayesian formula called P_{Bayes}.

P_{Bayes} assumes a prior distribution over the probability p of a single agent reaching the goal. A prior distribution initializes with prior information (if such information is available), reduces the variance of the predictions (and this lower variance has been demonstrated experimentally), and "evens out" the random perturbations of small samples thereby enabling greater accuracy with small k. We use a Beta distribution $\mathcal{B}(\alpha, \beta)$ over $(0, 1)$ for the prior (Zwillinger, 2002), which is a good choice because it can represent a variety of prior shapes when the possible values are on the finite interval $(0, 1)$. No other standard family of distributions has these properties. If the Beta distribution parameters α and β are both 1, then the distribution is uniform. The probability density function (pdf) $\mathcal{P}(p)$ corresponding to the Beta distribution is given by:

$$\mathcal{P}(p) = \frac{p^{\alpha-1}(1-p)^{\beta-1}}{B(\alpha, \beta)}$$

where $B(\alpha, \beta)$ is the (complete) Beta function defined by $\int_0^1 z^{\alpha-1}(1-z)^{\beta-1}dz$, which in the case where α and β are positive integers reduces to $\frac{(\alpha-1)!(\beta-1)!}{(\alpha+\beta-1)!}$. The next section and Appendix A describe our approach to methodically varying the parameters of the $\mathcal{B}(\alpha, \beta)$ distribution and hence the shape of its pdf $\mathcal{P}(p)$.

Recall that our objective is to find the probability of y or more successes out of n agents. We are allowed to observe k scouts, and their performance yields a fraction $\hat{p}$ of successes that is used to predict the true probability p of one agent reaching the goal. Our Bayesian formula is (for the derivation, see Appendix B):

$$P_{Bayes} = P(Y \geq y \mid \hat{p}) =$$

$$\int_0^1 \int_0^p M \cdot z^{y-1}(1-z)^{n-y} p^{r-1}(1-p)^{s-1} dz dp$$

where $M = \{B(r,s) \cdot B(y, n-y+1)\}^{-1}$

$$r = k\hat{p} + \alpha$$

$$s = k(1 - \hat{p}) + \beta$$

where p takes on all possible values in the outer integral, and z is a variable that ranges from 0 to p, given the particular p chosen by the outer integral. Note that this formula is not the same formula as one would obtain by plugging the posterior mean of p into the formula for P_{Bern}. It is the posterior mean of the probability that y or more scouts will reach the goal, assuming a Beta prior for p with parameters α and β. The inner integral gives the probability of y or more successes out of n trials for a given p, weighted by the prior for p. The form of the integrand may not be intuitive because it replaces the usual sum of Binomial probabilities with an equivalent incomplete Beta form. The outer integral averages over all possible values p of environmental difficulty, which ranges from 0 to 1. Note that with a uniform prior and a large sample size, P_{Bayes} will reduce to P_{Bern} (Ferguson, 1996). The advantage of P_{Bayes} (even with a uniform prior) over P_{Bern} is in applications with few scouts.

P_{Bayes} is implemented in our simulation using numerical methods; specifically, we use the *n-point Gaussian quadrature rule* (Cheney & Kincaid, 2003; Press et al., 1994; Zwillinger, 2002). The implementation of this rule was rigorously tested against hand-calculated values, and found to be accurate and correct within expected bounds of precision (Rebguns, 2008).

The Prior Distribution for the Bayesian Formula

The experiments described later in the paper are designed to determine how the predictive accuracy of the formulas changes as a function of parametric variations. One of the parameters that can be varied in P_{Bayes} is the prior distribution. This distribution can be either more or less confident, and more or less accurate. Confidence is measured in terms of prior *strength*, and accuracy in terms of prior *correctness*. See Appendix A for our methodology for varying the prior strength and correctness. The final seven priors and their strength and correctness are (see Appendix A for the derivation):

1. Uniform ($\alpha = \beta = 1$). Weakest prior.
2. $\alpha = 2.1$ and $\beta = 18.9$. Weak, and almost correct for $p = 0.1$.
3. $\alpha = 10.9$ and $\beta = 98.1$. Strong, and almost correct for $p = 0.1$.
4. $\alpha = 2.5$ and $\beta = 2.5$. Weak, and almost correct for $p = 0.5$.
5. $\alpha = 14.5$ and $\beta = 14.5$. Strong, and almost correct for $p = 0.5$.
6. $\alpha = 18.9$ and $\beta = 2.1$. Weak, and almost correct for $p = 0.9$.
7. $\alpha = 98.1$ and $\beta = 10.9$. Strong, and almost correct for $p = 0.9$.

The uniform prior is neither correct nor incorrect; it is "non-informative."

Figures 1, 2, and 3 show graphs of the $\mathcal{P}(p)$ probability density functions (pdf) for three different values of environmental difficulty p: 0.1, 0.5 and 0.9 respectively. The level of environmental difficulty was hand-crafted -- by choosing the goal location, and the number, sizes, shapes and locations of the obstacles, and the location of the starting square for the agents.

Finally, note that a prior that is correct for a particular value of p will be incorrect for any *other* value of p. For example, a prior that is correct for $p = 0.1$ will be incorrect if the true p is 0.3, and will be even more incorrect if the true p is 0.5 or especially 0.9. This incorrectness is exacerbated if the prior is strong. Also, the reason for "almost" correct is that it is usually too hard to design environments that have a precise level of difficulty.

Swarm Navigation Simulator

Our 2D simulation (see Figures 4 and 5) consists of a distributed, decentralized swarm of agents (the dots), a goal location (square), and a set of obstacles (circles/disks), whose locations can be varied. Agents sense the goal at any distance. They sense obstacles and other agents in any direction, but only within their *sensing range*, which is $1.5R$, where R is 50 pixels. The choice of this particular sensing range optimizes the formation of triangular (i.e., hexagonal if one assumes no agent in the middle of the hexagon) agent lattices. The value of 50 pixels for R was determined empirically; it led to good performance.

The following is a formalization of *Navigation Through Obstacles to Goal* problem that is addressed here. An agent i succeeds at the problem if and only if it satisfies the following objective after the *time limit* has been reached (where the arrows denote backwards implication read as "if," and only the first matching clause executes, as in the computer language Prolog):

1. **goal_reached(i) = true**, where *goal_reached* is defined recursively as:
   goal_reached(agent) ←*d(agent, goal)* < *1.5R;*
   goal_reached(agent) ←

there exists agent2 such that ([d(agent, agent2) ≤ 1.5R] & goal_reached(agent2))

Furthermore, the agent i must try to achieve the following objectives (using its force law -- see

Figure 1. Graph of Beta pdf for p = 0.1, with mean μ = 0.1 and C is defined in Appendix A

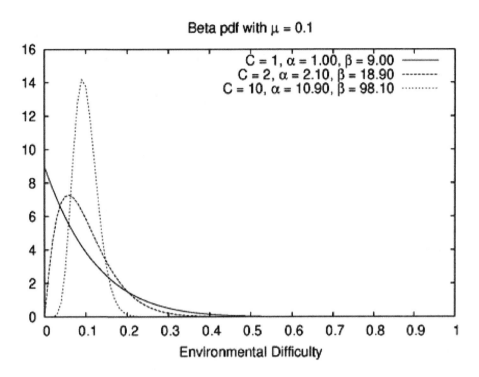

Figure 2. Graph of Beta pdf for p = 0.5, with mean μ = 0.5 and C is defined in Appendix A

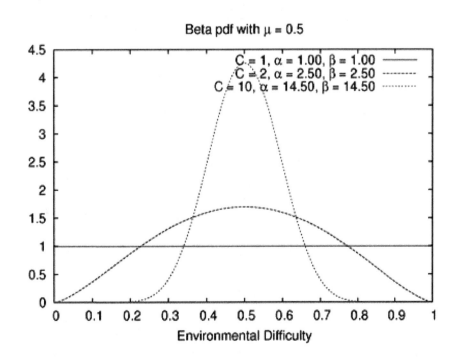

Figure 3. Graph of Beta pdf for p = 0.9, with mean μ = 0.9 and C is defined in Appendix A

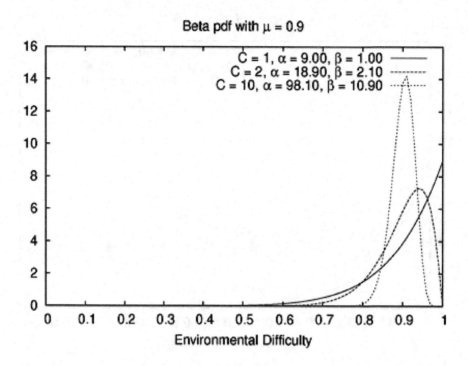

Figure 4. Swarm simulation screen-shot, with no inter-agent forces. Large circles represent obstacles, the square represents the goal and the small dots represent agents.

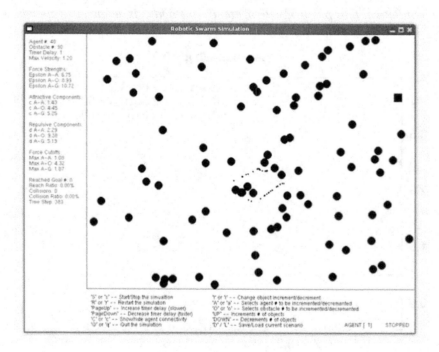

Figure 5. Swarm simulation screen-shot, with inter-agent forces. Large circles represent obstacles, the square represents the goal and the small dots represent agents.

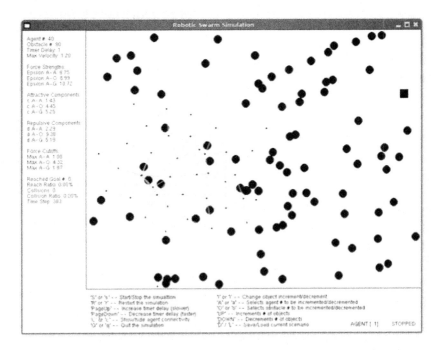

below) during as many time steps of the simulation as possible:

2. **Stay in formation**, i.e., *d(i, j)* = *R* for all agents *j* within sensing range, where *j* ≠ *i*
3. **Avoid obstacles**, i.e., *d(i, o)* ≥ *R* for all objects *o* within sensing range

The control algorithm that we use for achieving these problem objectives is physicomimetics, also called "artificial physics" (AP). We provide a brief overview here. *Potential fields (PF)* described in Khatib (1986) is the earliest approach to applying physics to agent control. AP and PF evolved along similar lines, in parallel, although PF tends to be more control theoretic than AP (Leonard & Fiorelli, 2001).

With physicomimetics, virtual physics forces drive a swarm to a desired configuration or state. The desired configuration is one that minimizes overall system potential energy, and the system

acts as a dynamics $\vec{F} = m\vec{a}$ simulation. Each agent has a position $\vec{p}$ and a velocity $\vec{v}$. We use a discrete-time approximation to the continuous behavior of the agents, with time-step Δt. At each time step, the position of each agent undergoes a perturbation $\Delta\vec{p}$. The perturbation depends on the agent's velocity, i.e., $\Delta\vec{p} = \vec{v}\Delta t$. The velocity of each agent at each time step also changes by $\Delta\vec{v}$. The change in velocity is controlled by the force on the agent, i.e., $\Delta\vec{v} = \vec{F}\Delta t / m$, where m is the mass of that agent and $\vec{F}$ is the force on that agent. A frictional force is included for self-stabilization.

Researchers have experimented with a wide variety of virtual forces for physicomimetics (Spears & Gordon, 1999; Spears et al., 2004, 2005). Here we use a generalization of the Lennard-Jones (LJ) force law (Lennard-Jones, 1931) to represent the force between *i* and *j*:

$$F_{i,j} = 24\epsilon \left[\frac{2dR^{12}}{d(i,j)^{13}} - \frac{cR^6}{d(i,j)^7} \right]$$

where the parameter ϵ affects the strength of the force between the entities, $d(i,j)$ is the actual distance between i and j, R is the desired distance between i and j, and c and d control the relative balance between attractive and repulsive forces, respectively. We have chosen the LJ force because it is extremely effective for agents staying in geometric formations while navigating around obstacles to get to a goal location. We use optimal parameter settings for LJ, evolved for this task by Hettiarachchi (2007). The values of all parameters used in our simulation can be seen on the left-hand side of Figures 4 and 5. Agents sense the range and bearing to nearby obstacles, neighboring agents, and to the goal location.

Initially, all agents begin at uniformly randomly chosen locations within a starting square of side length 100 pixels, approximately 1,000 pixels from the goal.[1] The simulation area is 800 pixels wide and 600 pixels tall, with the starting square located in the lower left corner and the goal in the upper right corner. The simulation ends after $t = 1,500$ time steps, which is the time limit. The simulation has two modes: one where the agents are completely independent of each other (see Independent Agents section for details) and another where there are virtual LJ inter-agent forces (see Interacting Agents section for details). Figure 4 shows the simulation with independent agents (inter-agent forces disabled), and Figure 5 shows the simulation with dependent agents (inter-agent forces enabled). Lines are shown in the graphics to visualize the virtual inter-agent forces. With inter-agent forces, the agents stay in a geometric (triangular) lattice formation while avoiding obstacles and navigating to the goal location.

EXPERIMENTAL DESIGN

The Performance Metric

Our primary experimental objective is to evaluate and compare the quality (predictive accuracy) of the standard Bernoulli trials formula, which we call P_{Bern} and our Bayesian formula, which we call P_{Bayes}. Evaluating the quality of a formula implies comparing its value against a form of "ground truth." For fairness, P_{Bern} or P_{Bayes} and ground truth all use the same parameter values during comparisons.

The mean squared error (*MSE*) is our performance metric because it includes *both* the error and the variance of the error. The *MSE* is a function of the "absolute error," which is the difference between the estimate and the truth. Assuming X is the true value and $\hat{X}$ is an estimate of X, the *MSE* is defined as:

$$MSE(\hat{X}, X) = E[(\hat{X} - X)^2]$$

where E denotes the expected value.

To measure the *MSE*, we need a form of "ground truth." Our ground truth, which is called P_{Truth}, is the fraction out of 1,000 runs of the simulation in which y or more of the n agents reach the goal. To compare with ground truth, we use the performance metrics $MSE(P_{Bern}, P_{Truth})$ and $MSE(P_{Bayes}, P_{Truth})$.

Experimental Parameters

Our secondary experimental objective is to vary the parametric conditions and measure how the *MSE* varies. A full factorial experimental design has been performed, i.e. we vary one parameter at a time and evaluate how varying that parameter affects performance over *all* combinations of *all* other parameter values. The following list enumerates the parameters (the *independent variables*) whose values are varied:

- **Total number of agents:** One variable is n, the total number of agents in the swarm. We expect n to have a negligible effect on the errors. The values of n are 100, 200, 300, 400, and 500. These particular swarm size values were chosen because they are variations of the precedents that we found in the swarm agents literature (Berman et al., 2007).

- **Number of scouts:** Perhaps the most important independent variable is k, the number of scouts. The values of k are 3, 5, 10, and 15. These values for the number of scouts were selected because they are sufficiently small that we believe they would be practical for many real-world applications. Normally, for methodical variation, we would select 5, 10, and 15. But the value 3 was added also in order to include the smallest reasonable number of scouts that one might wish to employ.

- **Desired number of successes:** Here, y is the desired number out of the n swarm agents that are required to succeed. This varies exhaustively from 1 to n.

- **Environmental difficulty:** We also vary p, the "true" probability of one agent succeeding, which is found using 1,000 runs of the simulation of n agents each. Three environments were hand-crafted (by choosing the goal location, and the number, sizes, shapes and locations of the obstacles, and the location of the starting square for the agents) in order to get the following values of p: 0.1, 0.5, and 0.9. These particular numbers reflect the need to include reasonable values for the easiest (0.9) environment, the hardest (0.1) environment, and a mid-level of difficulty (0.5) environment. Note that throughout the paper, the particular value of p can vary, although it is close to 0.1, 0.5, or 0.9. For example, sometimes we use 0.51 and other times 0.55. The reason for p varying slightly is that with hand-

crafted environments we were not always able to get perfectly precise values of environmental difficulty.

- **Strength of the prior distribution:** Recall that we use a Beta prior probability distribution for P_{Bayes}. The "strength" of this prior is quantified as $1/\sigma^2$, where σ^2 denotes the variance. In other words, a lower variance yields a "stronger" prior.

- **Correctness of the prior distribution:** Another variable is the prior "correctness." Correctness is the degree to which the prior is well-matched to the truth (p). Here, correctness is measured as the absolute value of the difference between the mean of the prior distribution and the true value of p. The smaller the difference, the more correct the chosen prior distribution is considered to be.

- **Independence of the agent:.** This parameter is Boolean. If its value is true, the agents are assumed to be completely independent of each other.

The Experimental Algorithms

Next, we describe our algorithms used in the experiments. Each experiment measures the $MSE(P_{Bern}, P_{Truth})$ and $MSE(P_{Bayes}, P_{Truth})$ with a single choice of values for all parameters, for multiple runs.

The algorithm for P_{Truth} was described above. The following is the algorithm for P_{Bayes} and P_{Bern}:

Step 1: Using the k scout agents obtain $\hat{p}$, which is an estimate of p.

Step 2: Apply the implemented formula for $P(Y \geq y \,|\, \hat{p})$, using the $\hat{p}$ obtained from Step 1.

When P_{Bern} and P_{Bayes} are calculated in the real world, the value of $\hat{p}$, which is the estimate of p found using k scouts, is unknown until the scouts are sent out. However for the experimental evaluation of our framework, this needs to be modified for fair comparisons. One way to obtain $\hat{p}$ in our experiments would be to deploy the k scouts in the simulation to get $\hat{p}$ as the fraction out of the k scouts that succeeded, and then plug $\hat{p}$ into the formulas for P_{Bern} and P_{Bayes}. The problem with doing this is that it does not predict performance *in expectation*. The correct solution is to treat $\hat{p}$ as a random variable for the experiments (though this would obviously not be done in the real-world situation). The expectation E is calculated as an average over 1,000 runs. For each run, we randomly vary the agent locations within the starting square. The *dependent variable MSE* is calculated as follows. Let P_B be P_{Bern} or P_{Bayes}. Then

$$Bias = E(P_B) - P_{Truth}$$

$$Variance = E[(P_B - E(P_B))^2]$$

$$MSE = E[(P_B - P_{Truth})^2] = Bias^2 + Variance$$

In the next two sections we formulate and test hypotheses for independent, and then dependent, agent scouts and swarms. There is only room here to show a few of the most interesting and representative results. In the graphs, the horizontal axis is one of the independent variables and, unless otherwise stated, the vertical axis is the *MSE*. Each curve shows the *MSE* estimated by averaging over 1,000 runs.

Independent Agents: Experimental Results

The case of independent agents is practical for some search and rescue problems, as well as chemical plume tracing tasks where the agents use *anemotaxis* (Zarzhitsky et al., 2004, 2005).

Before we formulate our hypotheses, consider the graphs of *MSE* and how it changes across all values of y. We focus first on variations of y because the graphs have an interesting characteristic shape that generally remains invariant as the values of all other parameters vary. Figure 6 shows the $MSE(P_{Bayes}, P_{Truth})$ as y varies. Note the bimodal curves in Figure 6, which tend to be a common characteristic of our error curves when y is varied along the horizontal axis. To understand this bimodal pattern, it is useful to look at the graph of P_{Bayes} versus P_{Truth} that was used to create one of the curves in Figure 6. Figure 7 provides the intuition for the bimodal pattern. Compare the curve for P_{Bayes} with the curve for P_{Truth} in Figure 7. Notice that there is an abrupt shift in ground truth (P_{Truth}) probability from 1 to 0, analogous to a sigmoid function (but reversed), around $y = 55$. We call this a "phase transition." In particular, if $y < np$, then y or more agents are guaranteed to reach the goal – because the environment (captured by p) supports such success. If $y > np$, then it is nearly impossible (probability close to 0) for y or more agents to reach the goal. P_{Truth} accurately reflects this phase transition. On the other hand, the curve for P_{Bayes} very roughly approximates the transition, i.e., rather than an abrupt drop in the curve it shows a smaller slope in going from a 1 to 0 probability of success. This explains the curves for *MSE*. Near the transition point where $y = np$, the curves for P_{Truth} have an abrupt phase shift but the curves for P_{Bayes} have a more gradual shift, which causes the bimodal errors around the point $y = np$. The same phenomenon occurs in all the graphs comparing P_{Bern} with P_{Truth} as well. For example, see Figure 8 for the *MSE* graph and Figure 9 for the probability graph. Although these graphs show results for only one particular set of parameters, our factorial experiments have confirmed that this characteristic bimodal pattern holds regardless of *all* the other parameter settings, when y is the independent variable. (The odd wavy forms seen in Figures 8 and 9 for

Bernoulli estimators with small k are an artifact of the property that only $k+1$ possible estimates exist for k scouts.)

The variable y is not the focus of any of our hypotheses below (and therefore we usually average over it) because we understand its behavior

Figure 6. Graph of MSE(P_{Bayes}, P_{Truth}) with p = 0.55 and n = 100 (Rebguns et al., 2008) (© 2008, IEEE. Used with permission.)

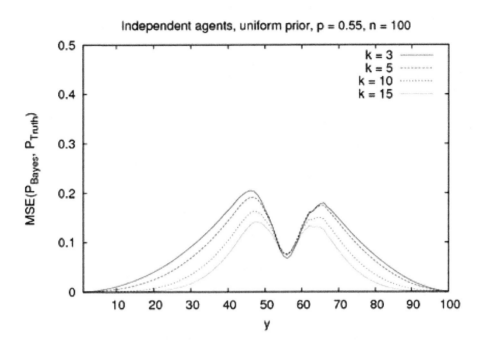

Figure 7. Graph of P_{Bayes} and P_{Truth} with p = 0.55, n = 100, and k = 5 (Rebguns et al., 2008) (© 2008, IEEE. Used with permission.)

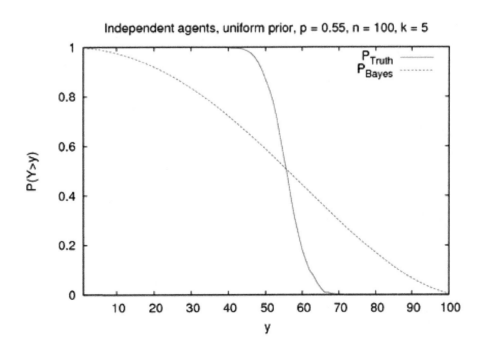

Figure 8. Graph of MSE(P_{Bern}, P_{Truth}) with p = 0.55 and n = 100

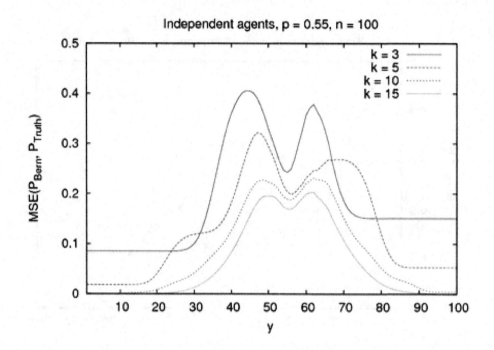

Figure 9. Graph of P_{Bern} and P_{Truth} with p = 0.55, n = 100, and k = 5

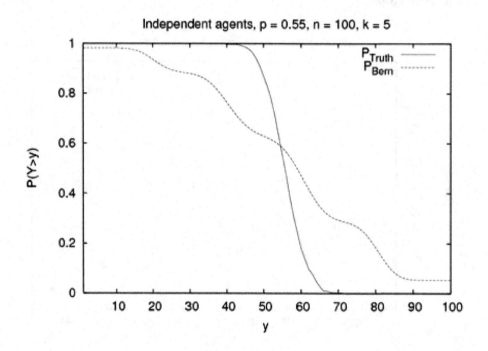

based on the above discussion, and because the proximity (which predicts the MSE) of y to np is not controllable by the practitioner (because p is unknown). The remaining graphs show variations in other parameters besides y.

We next formulate and test four hypotheses regarding performance, measured with the *MSE*, as parameters values are varied. Throughout this paper, we will consider a hypothesis to be "confirmed" if it is true for the overall trends in the graphs, even if it does not necessarily hold for every data point on every curve of every graph. In other words, our hypotheses capture performance trends/patterns, rather than absolute performance guarantees.

To test each hypothesis, we vary the parameter of interest and hold the others (except y) constant. When y is not on the horizontal axis, each curve is an average over all values of y (called "Average MSE" on the vertical axis). Conclusions about both the $MSE(P_{Bern}, P_{Truth})$ and $MSE(P_{Bayes}, P_{Truth})$ are presented.

The first hypothesis is about how the predictive accuracy varies when the number of scout agents is varied. Scout and swarm agents are both independent.

Hypothesis 1 (about the number of scouts)
Increasing the number of scouts, k, will improve the predictive accuracy.

For independent agents, this hypothesis is intuitive. A bigger sample size produces a better estimator/predictor of truth. The experimental results confirm that this hypothesis is indeed correct for both P_{Bern} and P_{Bayes}. Let us consider Figure 6 more carefully. It shows the graph of how the *MSE* of P_{Bayes} varies as we change the number of scouts k, namely, as we increase k from 3 to 15 the maximum *MSE* decreases from about 0.20 to about 0.12. Next, look at Figure 8, which shows the graph of how the *MSE* of P_{Bern} varies as we change the number of scouts k, namely, as we increase k from 3 to 15 the maximum *MSE*

decreases from about 0.40 to about 0.19. Note that P_{Bern} is much more dependent on the number of scouts for its predictions, whereas this effect is much less pronounced for the P_{Bayes} formula. For P_{Bayes}, the prior distribution compensates for a small sample size.

The reduction in error with more scouts can be explained with the Law of Large Numbers. In particular, the Law of Large Numbers states that as the sample size increases, the sample means converge to the true mean of the population. The fraction of successes found by the scouts can be considered a sample mean, which is estimating the true mean found by ground truth. Two phenomena occur as k increases. First, the sample mean approaches the true mean. Second, our Bayesian formula for P_{Bayes} puts more emphasis on the samples than on the prior when k is large.

The following three hypotheses have also been tested and confirmed with independent scouts/ agents:

Hypothesis 2 (about the prior distribution for P_{Bayes})
1. *It is better to have a correct rather than incorrect prior.*
2. *If the prior is incorrect it is better to be weak rather than strong. Also, the non-informative uniform (weakest) prior is better than any incorrect prior.*

3. *If the prior is correct it is better to be strong than weak.*

As is well known in Bayesian statistics, a strong correct prior is optimal, and a uniform prior is the best solution when prior knowledge is weak or lacking. Our results confirm this.

Based on our confirmation of Hypotheses 1 and 2, we find that there are two main ways to reduce *MSE* in the predictions made by P_{Bayes}. One is to increase the number k of scouts, which increases the sample size, and the other is to choose a better prior distribution.

Hypothesis 3 (about swarm size/scalability) *If the ratio k/n is held constant, then increasing the swarm size will not significantly increase the prediction error.*

Hypothesis 4 (about environmental difficulty/ robustness) *The predictions will be robust (i.e., will not change significantly in value) across a wide range of environmental difficulties.*

Both Hypotheses 3 and 4 have been confirmed in all of our experiments, which demonstrated that both formulas are good predictors, and P_{Bayes} is usually better than P_{Bern} – even with a uniform prior. In particular, the $MSE(P_{Bayes}, P_{Truth})$ is usually lower than the $MSE(P_{Bern}, P_{Truth})$, and in many cases *much* lower. Interestingly, based on further experimental results we have found that with few exceptions, the variance for P_{Bayes} is *much* lower than for P_{Bern}.

Interacting Agents: Experimental Results

This section assumes dependent swarm agents and dependent scout agents (so that the scout behavior is representative of the swarm behavior).

Here, we test the same four hypotheses that were tested for the independent agents case. The conclusions are more interesting in the case of dependent agents. To test each hypothesis, the parameter of interest is varied and the other parameter values (except y) are held constant. When y is not on the horizontal axis, each curve is an average over all values of y. Conclusions about both the $MSE(P_{Bern}, P_{Truth})$ and $MSE(P_{Bayes}, P_{Truth})$ are presented.

Recall Hypothesis 1, which predicts that increasing the number of scouts will increase the predictive accuracy of the formulas. Although this hypothesis is intuitive and holds for the independent agents case, the results are surprisingly mixed for dependent agents for both formulas, P_{Bern} and P_{Bayes}. Figure 10 shows a typical result where

Hypothesis 1 is violated. In this figure the swarm size n is held constant and the number of scouts k is varied. By watching the simulation one can see *why* Hypothesis 1 is violated for dependent scouts. It is because the scouts stay in formation and act as a quasi-unit (just like the swarm does). The scouts are predictive, but because they act as a quasi-unit, adding more usually does not increase their predictive ability. However the harder the environment, the more it helps to use additional scouts. This is because the quasi-unit gets fractured in hard environments (e.g., with many obstacles) and it becomes more like the case of independent agents.

In general, we have found that very few scouts are needed for a very good assessment of the swarm success rate, and adding more scouts does little to improve the predictions in the case of dependent agents. This is fortunate because it implies that just a few scouts are enough to obtain a good estimate of the swarm success rate.

Next, recall Hypothesis 2 about the prior distribution for P_{Bayes}. It states that a correct prior is preferable if one is available and, if correct, then it should be strong. On the other hand, if a correct prior is unavailable then it is better to choose a weak incorrect prior than a strong one. Hypothesis 2 has been confirmed by our experimental results. For example, Figure 11 confirms that if a prior is correct (or almost correct), then it should be strong; the confirmation is over most values of y, where y is varied along the horizontal axis. Overall, we have found that a strong, correct prior is optimal, and a uniform prior is the best choice when prior knowledge is lacking and an incorrect prior must be used.

In Figure 11 we show P_{Bayes} with different priors. We show one curve per prior, which means that we were able to vary y along the horizontal axis in the graph. For the sake of conciseness of comparisons of P_{Bayes} versus P_{Bern} we hereafter resume the convention of showing curves that average over all values of y and vary the parameter of interest along the horizontal axis.

Figure 10. Graph of MSEs with p = 0.51, n = 300, k ranging from 3 to 15, with inter-agent forces (Rebguns et al., 2008) (© 2008, IEEE. Used with permission.)

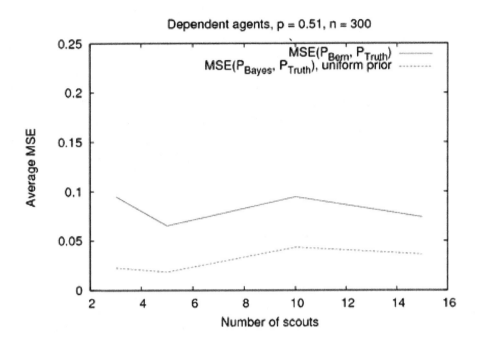

Figure 11. Graph for Hypothesis 2, part 3, with p = 0.55, n = 100, k = 5, and inter-agent forces (Rebguns et al., 2008) (© 2008, IEEE. Used with permission.)

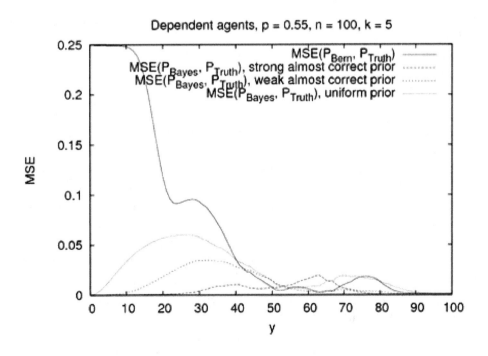

Next, consider Hypothesis 3, which states that increasing the swarm size will not significantly increase the prediction error, if the ratio k/n is maintained as a constant. The results from our tests of this hypothesis display characteristic trends, and these trends depend upon the environmental difficulty. We report three trends corresponding to easy, moderate, and hard environments, respectively. The uniform prior is used with P_{Bayes} because we wish to show worst case results, and in the worst case when there is no knowledge to help select a prior the uniform can always be used to get the best results overall.

Figure 12 shows typical results for an easy environment, where $p = 0.9$. As we can see in the figure, for easy environments the *MSE* actually *decreases* when going from 100 to 300 agents, and then it increases somewhat when going from 300 to 500 agents, but with 500 agents the *MSE* is still less than with 100 agents. This assumes a constant k/n ratio of 0.03.

Figure 13 shows a typical result in a moderate environment, where $p = 0.5$. There is a slight increase in *MSE* for P_{Bayes} as the swarm size scales up while the ratio of scouts to swarm agents is held constant. The maximum increase in *MSE* in either curve is less than 0.0025, which is tiny.

Finally, consider the typical Figure 14, where the environment is most difficult ($p = 0.1$). In this case as the number of agents increases while the ratio is maintained, the *MSE* is reduced for P_{Bern} and reduced or maintained for P_{Bayes}, except for a second peak when there are 400 agents. With $P_{Bayes,}$ the MSE is highest with the fewest (100) agents. This demonstrates nice scalability.

Hypothesis 3 is true in almost all of our experiments, for both $MSE(P_{Bayes}, P_{Truth})$ (with any prior, though the results with a strong almost correct prior are, as usual, much better than with a uniform prior) and for $MSE(P_{Bern}, P_{Truth})$. Note that P_{Bayes} has a lower *MSE* than P_{Bern}, except when the environment is maximally difficult with $p = 0.1$ (see Figures 12, 13, and 14). This latter issue will be addressed in the next hypothesis regarding environmental difficulty.

Finally, consider Hypothesis 4, which states that the predictions will be robust, i.e., not change significantly in value, despite wide variations in the level of environmental difficulty. There are two trends in the graphs when varying the environmental difficulty along the horizontal axis. Figure 15 exemplifies the first pattern. Note the contrast between the predictions of P_{Bayes} with a uniform prior and P_{Bern}, as the environmental difficulty varies in Figure 15. P_{Bayes} is considerably more robust than P_{Bern} over the range of environments. This figure and all those similar to it confirm Hypothesis 4 for P_{Bayes}, e.g., in this figure $MSE(P_{Bayes}, P_{Truth})$ never goes significantly above 0.05. On the other hand, the predictive ability of P_{Bern} degrades a lot in easy environments, e.g., $MSE(P_{Bern}, P_{Truth}) \rightarrow$ 0.09 as $p \rightarrow 0.9$ in Figure 15. P_{Bayes} with a uniform (but not strong correct) prior performs worse than P_{Bern} in the most difficult environment ($p = 0.1$), *but* both perform well at that extreme.

Figure 16 is typical of the second trend. In the set of graphs typifying this trend, both the P_{Bern} and P_{Bayes} with uniform prior curves have a similar shape, but the $MSE(P_{Bern}, P_{Truth})$ is much higher for moderate environments than the $MSE(P_{Bayes}, P_{Truth})$ with a uniform prior. Again, P_{Bayes} with a uniform prior performs worse than P_{Bern} when the environment is most difficult, but otherwise it performs better than P_{Bern}.

We conclude that when averaged over all environments (which is an uncontrollable parameter), P_{Bayes} appears to be preferable. P_{Bern} shows a lack of robustness that can make it barely acceptable in moderate to easy environments.

Finally, note that both Figure 15 and Figure 16 reinforce the value of a strong, almost correct prior – if feasible to obtain. The *MSE* is always lower, and often much lower, when the prior is well-matched to the environment.

Figure 12. Graph of MSE with varying n and k, k/n = 0.03, p = 0.9, uniform prior for P_{Bayes}, and inter-agent forces

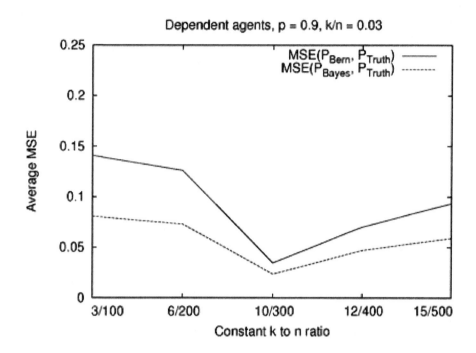

Figure 13. Graph of MSE with varying n and k, k/n = 0.03, p = 0.5, uniform prior for P_{Bayes}, and inter-agent forces

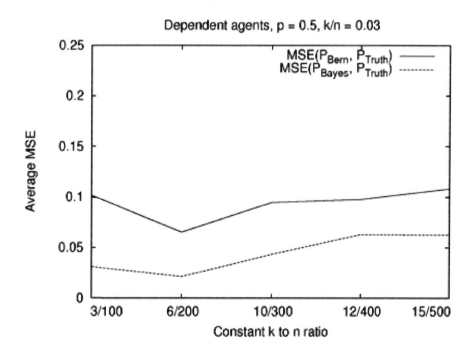

Figure 14. Graph of MSE with varying n and k, k/n = 0.03, p = 0.1, uniform prior for P_{Bayes}, and inter-agent forces

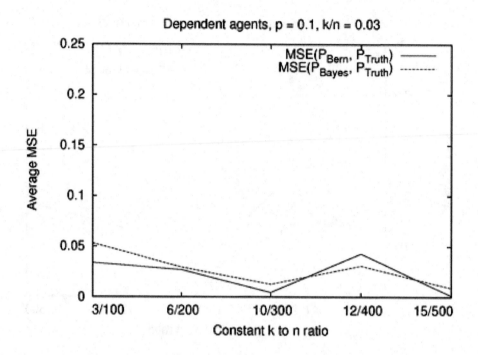

Figure 15. Graph of MSE(P_{Bern}, P_{Truth}) and MSE(P_{Bayes}, P_{Truth}), with inter-agent forces, as environmental difficulty varies. The first trend (Rebguns et al., 2008) (© 2008, IEEE. Used with permission.)

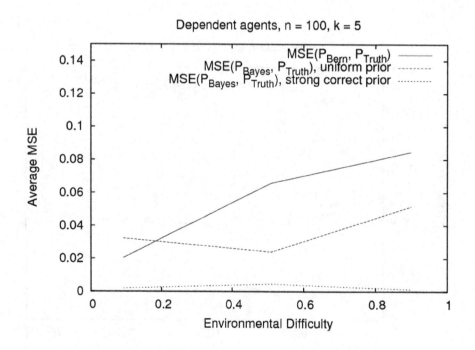

Figure 16. Graph of MSE(P$_{Bern}$, P$_{Truth}$) and MSE(P$_{Bayes}$, P$_{Truth}$), with inter-agent forces, as environmental difficulty varies. The second trend (Rebguns et al., 2008) (© 2008, IEEE. Used with permission.)

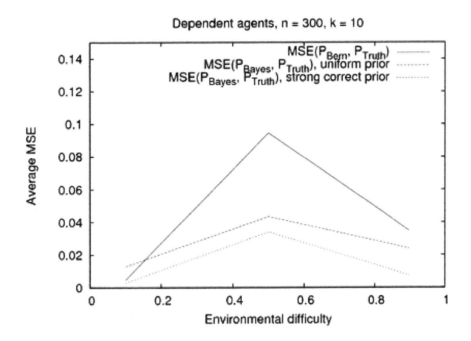

Independent Versus Dependent Agents: Experimental Results

The most interesting result obtained from our experiments is that although our two formulas make independence assumptions, when these assumptions are violated (and the LJ force law is used) the predictions of both formulas usually improve! Figures 17 and 18 illustrate this result. All parameter values are identical (and the value of p is nearly identical) in these two figures, other than inter-agent (in)dependence (which is the same for both the scouts and the swarm).

This result is both surprising and exciting. It is surprising because any mathematical formula will typically be more accurate when its assumptions hold, and are not violated. Note that we are not stating that the swarm performance is better when the agents are dependent – that would be intuitively obvious. Rather, we are stating that the formulas' predictions are closer to "ground truth," which is not at all obvious. In hindsight, we have

a better intuitive understanding for why dependent scouts are so adept at predicting the performance of dependent swarm agents.

In the case of independent agents, the only forces affecting agents are the attractive goal force, which is felt from any distance, and the repulsive forces of obstacles, which are felt when an agent gets close enough to an obstacle. In this situation the initial (starting) position of every agent in the swarm is very important. Figure 19 illustrates the independent agents case. (Here, as in simulation screen-shots in Figures 4 and 5, a square denotes the goal, big circles denote obstacles, and small circles denote agents; arrows show the direction of movement that an agent is likely to take.) It is very likely that agents 1, 2 and 3 will get stuck behind the cul-de-sac that lies between them and the goal, and the rest of swarm will successfully reach the goal. If we send out three scouts that start out from the same positions as agents 1, 2 and 3, and they also get stuck, then this is certainly not representative of the swarm. The variance is high

Figure 17. Graph of MSEs with p = 0.55, n = 300, k ranging from 3 to 15, with no inter-agent forces (Rebguns et al., 2008) (© 2008, IEEE. Used with permission.)

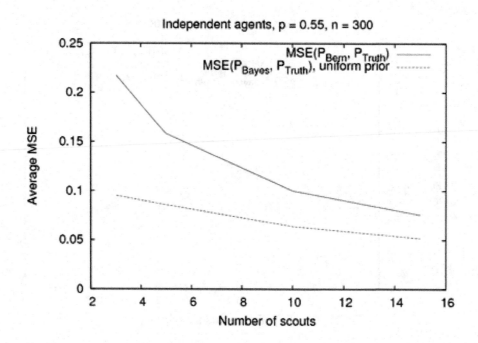

Figure 18. Graph of MSEs with p = 0.51, n = 300, k ranging from 3 to 15, with inter-agent forces. Identical to Figure 10 but shown here again for ease of comparison with Figure 17.

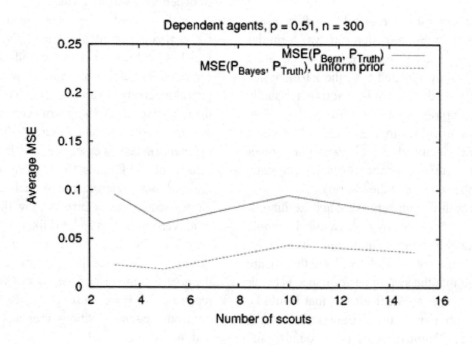

Figure 19. Independent agents; initial position is very important

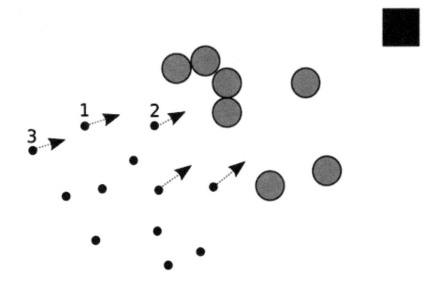

– as you change the scout starting positions, the results differ drastically. With inter-agent forces enabled, on the other hand, the starting position does not matter as much; variations in the starting positions do not affect how the swarm as a whole moves (see Figure 20; small lighter dots are other possible starting positions). Another way to think about it is as if we were reducing the size of the starting square, and hence reducing the variance. Reduced variance improves the results.

Another explanation of this phenomenon is related to the Lennard-Jones force law used for dependent agents. LJ produces swarm behavior similar to the flow of a liquid. Liquid agent movement is advantageous because:

1. A small drop of liquid behaves similarly to a large body of liquid. Analogously, scouts behave very similarly to the swarm when using LJ.
2. Liquid particles interact, whereas gas particles do not. Interacting particles (or agents) are more predictable than independent ones.

Interacting particles can behave like a liquid or a solid. To test whether LJ liquid-like forces improve the predictions with dependent agents, we applied the Newtonian virtual force law of Spears and Gordon (1999), which generates solid-like swarm behavior. Our results (which agree with the earlier results of Hettiarachchi, 2007) demonstrate that small groups of agents can squeeze through tight paths between obstacles, whereas larger solid-like groups get stuck. This implies that scouts and swarms will often behave differently when using a Newtonian force. In fact, when using the Newtonian law our formulas do not produce better predictions with dependent than with independent agents. Therefore, our choice of the Lennard-Jones force law, in particular, is responsible for the outstanding predictive accuracy of our swarms with dependent agents.

EXPERIMENTAL CONCLUSIONS

The following results/conclusions hold for both independent and dependent agents:

Figure 20. Dependent agents; initial position not as important

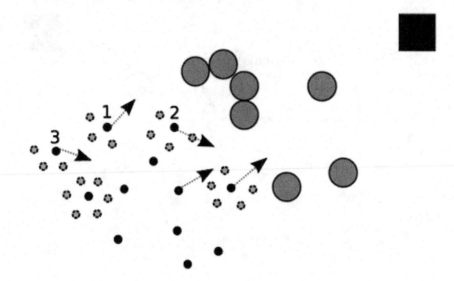

1. Both formulas are usually good predictors. Their accuracy can be seen in all of our graphs.

2. Observations about prior distribution selection for our Bayes formula are:
   ◦ It is better to have a correct rather than an incorrect prior.
   ◦ If the prior is incorrect it is better to be weak rather than strong. Uniform is the best incorrect prior.
   ◦ If the prior is correct it is better to be strong than weak.

3. P_{Bayes} with a uniform prior is usually better (i.e., has a lower *MSE*) than P_{Bern}, and is often much better. This conclusion has significant practical implications. It means that even in the case when prior knowledge is absent, P_{Bayes} typically outperforms P_{Bern}. All graphs in this paper that compare P_{Bayes} with P_{Bern} provide evidence to support this conclusion. Of course, theoretically we know that as the number of scouts gets large, the difference between P_{Bayes} and P_{Bern} will vanish to 0. Therefore, the advantage of P_{Bayes} is for situations of few scouts.

4. Increasing the swarm size *n* with a proportional increase in the number of scouts (i.e., holding the ratio *k/n* constant) has a negligible effect on predictability.

5. P_{Bayes} is "robust" across wide variations in environmental difficulty. By "robust" we mean that the *MSE* does not substantially increase as the environmental difficulty is varied. P_{Bern} is less robust than P_{Bayes}. In particular, when averaged over all environments (which is an uncontrollable parameter), P_{Bayes} appears to be preferable. P_{Bern} shows a lack of robustness that can make it barely acceptable in moderate to easy environments.

6. With the Lennard-Jones force law, P_{Bern} and P_{Bayes} predict better when the agents are dependent, i.e., when their independence assumptions are violated.

Porting to Real Robots

Our theoretical framework is a general approach to risk assessment for swarm applications. It models agents at an abstract level. Agents are "abstract" because the types and levels of sensor and actuator noise, vehicle limitations and dynamics, and the environmental details are not modeled. However, note that in terms of the probability of success, which is the meta-parameter of variation here, noise that causes performance degradation is equivalent (at an abstract level) to a "hard" environment, which is in fact modeled in our simulator. Furthermore, if AP is used then we have confidence (based on applying AP with real robots) that the success rate will not be significantly adversely affected by sensor noise, even if the noise level is quite high (e.g., see Maxim et al. (2009) for robust simulated multi-robot chain formations despite 50% sensor noise and 50% motor noise, and robust real multi-robot chain formations despite unknown but very high noise levels; furthermore, W. Spears and D. Green - personal communication - found AP to be exceptionally robust in simulated swarm optimization problems where throughout the environment the sensor noise exceeds the signal).

Therefore, it is our hypothesis that our scouts approach will carry over to realistically simulated robots, as well as to real robots, provided a sampling assumption holds. This sampling assumption states that the scouts are "typical" of the swarm, i.e., the scout vehicle imperfections closely match those of the swarm vehicles. If the scouts are randomly selected from the pool of swarm vehicles, then this assumption will be likely to hold. Our hypothesis of portability to real robots (or even realistically-simulated robots) has not yet been tested, but will be done as future work.

CONCLUSION

Our theoretical framework is very useful for predicting the success rate of a swarm of agents before it is deployed, especially in difficult or dangerous situations -- when sending the entire swarm at once is inadvisable and may result in a loss of a substantial part of the swarm. In other words, our scouts framework has significant practical implications for agent swarm *risk assessment*.

As part of our framework, we introduced a novel Bayesian formula for success probability calculation, along with its mathematical derivation (in Appendix B). The derivation shows how this formula is a Bayesian variant of the standard Bernoulli trials formula for predicting success rate, and how it employs a prior distribution to reduce the variance and increase the robustness of the formula's predictions. We have designed and implemented a swarm agent simulator that uses both Bernoulli and Bayesian formulas to predict the swarm success rate. The simulator has parameterization capabilities for running rigorous experiments. We have implemented and executed a full factorial experimental design for evaluating both the Bernoulli and Bayesian formulas, in the context of the navigation task. Both formulas were compared against "ground truth," using the mean-squared error as an evaluation metric. The results were analyzed and presented along with several important conclusions, including the accuracy and robustness of our Bayesian formula as compared to the standard Bernoulli trials formula, and the effectiveness of both formulas for swarms of interacting agents using a Lennard-Jones force law. The latter conclusion is surprising because both formulas assume independence; we have provided an explanation for this surprising result.

Future work includes transitioning our framework to a swarm of real robots. We also plan to design strategies for increasing the success rate when a low rate is predicted. We could, for example, record successful scout paths for the swarm members to follow. In this case, scouts would not only predict the success rate for the swarm, but they would also provide advice to the swarm regarding which paths are preferable and which should be avoided. We could also add further complexity to the interactions between agents, e.g., by merging the DAEDALUS multi-agent online evolution approach described in Hettiarachchi (2007) with scouts and path planning. Another important direction for future research would be to apply our predictions to behavior-based, rule-based and biomimetic swarms, and compare on other (e.g., benchmark optimization) problems. So far we have seen that predictions improve when coupled with a physicomimetic control strategy for inter-agent cooperation, but it would be useful to see if the same holds for other control strategies.

In conclusion, our theoretical framework that uses scouts for predicting swarm success rate is an important contribution that could, in the future, be complemented with a variety of control strategies, as well as with the use of scouts for transmitting additional learning and planning information to the swarm. Future work will focus on these directions, as well as application to other tasks.

ACKNOWLEDGMENT

This research was funded in part by the Office of the Secretary of Defense Joint Ground Robotics Enterprise (JGRE) program.

REFERENCES

Berman, S., Halasz, A., Kumar, V., & Pratt, S. (2007). Bio-inspired group behaviors for the deployment of a swarm of robots to multiple destinations. In *Proceedings of the IEEE International Conference on Robotics and Automation* (pp. 2318-2323). Piscataway, NJ: IEEE Press.

Cheney, E. W., & Kincaid, D. R. (2003). *Numerical mathematics and computing* (5th ed.). Salt Lake City, UT: Brooks Cole.

Dorigo, M., Tuci, E., Trianni, V., Groß, R., Nouyan, S., & Ampatzis, C. (2006). SWARM-BOT: Design and implementation of colonies of self-assembling robots. In Yen, G. Y., & Fogel, D. B. (Eds.), *Computational intelligence: Principles and practice* (pp. 103–135). New York: IEEE Computational Intelligence Society.

Ferguson, T. S. (1996). *A course in large sample theory*. Boca Raton, FL: Chapman and Hall/CRC.

Greene, M., & Gordon, D. (2007). How patrollers set foraging direction in harvester ants. *American Naturalist, 170*, 943–948. doi:10.1086/522843

Hastie, T., Tibshirani, R., & Friedman, J. (2001). *The elements of statistical learning*. New York, NY: Springer-Verlag.

Hettiarachchi, S. (2007). *Distributed evolution for swarm robotics*. Unpublished doctoral dissertation, University of Wyoming, Laramie, WY.

Kearns, M., & Vazirani, U. (1994). *An introduction to computational learning theory*. Cambridge, MA: The MIT Press.

Khatib, O. (1986). Real-time obstacle avoidance for manipulators and mobile robots. *The International Journal of Robotics Research, 5*(1), 90–98. doi:10.1177/027836498600500106

Lennard-Jones, J. (1931). Cohesion. *Proceedings of the Physical Society, 43*(5), 461–482. doi:10.1088/0959-5309/43/5/301

Leonard, N., & Fiorelli, E. (2001). Virtual leaders, artificial potentials and coordinated control of groups. In *Proceedings of the 40th IEEE Conference on Decision and Control* (Vol. 3, pp. 2968-2973).

Maxim, P., Spears, W., & Spears, D. (2009). Robotic chain formations. In *Proceedings of the IFAC Workshop on Networked Robotics (NetRob'09)* (pp. 19-24).

Mondada, F., Gambardella, L., Floreano, D., & Dorigo, M. (2005). The cooperation of swarm-bots: Physical interactions in collective robotics. *Robotics and Automation Magazine, 12*(2), 21–28. doi:10.1109/MRA.2005.1458313

Press, W. H., Flannery, B. P., Teukolsky, S. A., & Vetterling, W. T. (1994). *Numerical recipes in C.* Cambridge, MA: Cambridge University Press.

Rebguns, A. (2008). *Using scouts to predict swarm success rate.* Unpublished master's thesis, University of Wyoming, Laramie, WY.

Rebguns, A., Anderson-Sprecher, R., Spears, D., Spears, W., & Kletsov, A. (2008). Using scouts to predict swarm success rate. In *Proceedings of the IEEE Swarm Intelligence Symposium* (pp. 1-8). Piscataway, NJ: IEEE Press.

Russell, S., & Norvig, P. (2003). *Artificial intelligence: A modern approach* (2nd ed.). Upper Saddle River, NJ: Prentice Hall.

Rybski, P. E., & Burt, I. Drenner. A., Kratochvil, B., Mcmillen, C., Stoeter, S., et al. (2001). *Evaluation of the scout robot for urban search and rescue.* Paper presented at the AAAI 2001 Mobile Robot Competition and Exhibition Workshop, Seattle, WA.

Şahin, E., & Franks, N. R. (2002). Simulation of nest assessment behavior by ant scouts. In *Proceedings of the 3rd International Workshop on Ant Algorithms (ANTS'2)* (pp. 274-281). New York: Springer-Verlag.

Spears, W., & Gordon, D. (1999). Using artificial physics to control agents. In *Proceedings of the International Conference on Information Intelligence and Systems (ICIIS'99)* (pp. 281-288). Washington, DC: IEEE Computer Society.

Spears, W. M., Spears, D. F., Hamann, J. C., & Heil, R. (2004). Distributed, physics-based control of swarms of vehicles. *Autonomous Robots, 17*(2-3), 137–162. doi:10.1023/B:AURO.0000033970.96785.f2

Spears, W. M., Spears, D. F., Heil, R., Kerr, W., & Hettiarachchi, S. (2005). An overview of physicomimetics. In E. Şahin & W. Spears (Eds.), *Swarm Robotics* (LNCS 3342, pp. 84-97).

Tatomir, B., & Rothkrantz, L. (2006). Ant based mechanism for crisis response coordination. In *Proceedings of the 5th International Conference on Ant Colony Optimization and Swarm Intelligence (ANTS'06)* (pp. 380-387). New York: Springer-Verlag.

Tikanmäki, A., Haverinen, J., Kemppainen, A., & Röning, J. (2006). Remote-operated robot swarm for measuring an environment. In *Proceedings of the International Conference on Machine Automation (ICMA'06)*, Seinäjoki, Finland.

Wright, T., & Farmer, J. (2000). *A bibliography of selected statistical methods and development related to census 2000 (Statistical Research Rep. Series No. RR 2000/2).* Washington, DC: U.S. Census Bureau.

Zarzhitsky, D., Spears, D., & Spears, W. (2005). Distributed robotics approach to chemical plume tracing. In *Proceedings of the IEEE/RSJ International Conference on Intelligent Robots and Systems (IROS'05)* (pp. 4034-4039). Piscataway, NJ: IEEE Press.

Zarzhitsky, D., Spears, D. F., Spears, W. M., & Thayer, D. R. (2004). A fluid dynamics approach to multi-robot chemical plume tracing. In *Proceedings of the 3rd International Joint Conference on Autonomous Agents and Multiagent Systems (AAMAS'04)* (pp. 1476-1477). Washington, DC: IEEE Computer Society.

Zwillinger, D. (2002). *CRC standard mathematical tables and formulae* (31st ed.). Boca Raton, FL: Chapman & Hall/CRC. doi:10.1201/9781420035346

ENDNOTE

[1] These numbers of pixels were chosen because they led to a reasonable running time and helped the agents and their path show up nicely on the graphical interface.

APPENDIX A: DERIVATION OF PRIORS

This appendix is from Rebguns (2008). The following methodology is used to vary prior strength and correctness. We quantify the "strength" of a prior as $1/\sigma^2$, where σ^2 denotes the variance, and the correctness of a prior as the degree to which the prior is well-matched to "ground truth" (p). Recall from above that we use a Beta distribution for our priors, which has parameters α and β. When we vary these two parameters the shape of the probability density function $\mathcal{P}(p)$ changes. The mean of this Beta distribution is $\mu = \dfrac{\alpha}{\alpha + \beta}$ and the variance is $\sigma^2 = \dfrac{\alpha\beta}{(\alpha + \beta)^2(\alpha + \beta + 1)} = \dfrac{(1-\mu)\mu^2}{(\alpha + \mu)} = \dfrac{\mu(1-\mu)^2}{(\beta + 1 - \mu)}$. It is expected that in actual usage, the prior belief will be unimodal. The weakest unimodal prior with mean μ has one parameter equal to 1 and the other ≥ 1:

$$\mu < 0.5\text{:}\ \alpha = 1, \beta = \frac{1-\mu}{\mu}, \text{ and } \sigma^2 = \frac{\beta}{(\beta+1)^2(\beta+2)} = \frac{(1-\mu)\mu^2}{(1+\mu)}$$

$$\mu \geq 0.5\text{:}\ \alpha = \frac{\mu}{1-\mu}, \beta = 1, \text{ and } \sigma^2 = \frac{\alpha}{(\alpha+1)^2(\alpha+2)} = \frac{(1-\mu)^2\mu}{(2-\mu)}$$

To strengthening the prior, we shrink the variance by a factor C:

$\mu < 0.5$: To reduce the variance from $\dfrac{(1-\mu)\mu^2}{(1+\mu)}$ to $\dfrac{(1-\mu)\mu^2}{C(1+\mu)}$ we solve the equation $\dfrac{(1-\mu)\mu^2}{(\alpha^* + \mu)} = \dfrac{(1-\mu)\mu^2}{C(1+\mu)}$ for α^* and then solve for $\beta^* = \dfrac{1-\mu}{\mu}\alpha^*$. The results are $\alpha^* = (C(1+\mu)-\mu)$ and $\beta^* = \dfrac{1-\mu}{\mu}(C(1+\mu)-\mu)$.

. $\mu \geq 0.5$: To reduce the variance from $\dfrac{(1-\mu)^2\mu}{(2-\mu)}$ to $\dfrac{(1-\mu)^2\mu}{C(2-\mu)}$ we solve the equation $\dfrac{\mu(1-\mu)^2}{(\beta^* + 1 - \mu)} = \dfrac{(1-\mu)^2\mu}{C(2-\mu)}$ for β^* and then solve for $\alpha^* = \dfrac{\mu}{1-\mu}\beta^*$. The results are $\alpha^* = \dfrac{\mu}{1-\mu}(C(2-\mu)-(1-\mu))$ and $\beta^* = (C(2-\mu)-(1-\mu))$.

Using the solutions to these equations, we have selected α^*, β^*, and C to find six priors (plus uniform makes seven) that represent a good variability along the strength and correctness dimensions.

APPENDIX B: BAYESIAN FORMULA AND DERIVATION

This appendix, which is from Rebguns et al. (2008), provides our derivation of the P_{Bayes} formula. Here, we use f to denote probability functions, and we employ the common statistics convention of letting the argument determine which probability function is meant by f, i.e. f varies depending on the context. Also, we use π rather than f for the *prior* distribution in particular, as is traditional in the statistics literature.

The intuition behind the derivation of the Bayesian formula is as follows. We start by deriving the probability of *exactly* x out of n successes, given our estimate $\hat{p}$ from the fraction of k scouts that successfully reached the goal, using the standard Bernoulli trials formula. We apply the Beta distribution prior assumption, and perform mathematical simplification operations on it to get a simplified version of the formula for exactly x out of n successes. To find the probability $P(Y \geq y)$ of y or more successes (where y is a lower bound on the desired number of successes), we next take the sum of this expression, from x equals y to x equals n. Applying the relation between the cumulative Binomial probability and the incomplete Beta function, along with other mathematical operations, we simplify the expression to get our final formula. The full detailed formula derivation follows.

Let Y be a binomial random variable, where $Y \mid p \sim \mathcal{B}(n,p)$ and p is the probability of one agent reaching the goal and n is the total number of agents. Let $\hat{p}$ be an estimate of p based on k trials. Then $k\hat{p} \mid p \sim \mathcal{B}(k,p)$, and these variables are independent. From the Bernoulli trials formula, we have:

$$f(x \mid p) = \binom{n}{x} p^x (1-p)^{n-x}$$

$$f(\hat{p} \mid p) = \binom{k}{k\hat{p}} p^{k\hat{p}} (1-p)^{k(1-\hat{p})}$$

$$f(x \mid \hat{p}) = \frac{f(x,\hat{p})}{f(\hat{p})} = \frac{\int_0^1 f(x,\hat{p},p)dp}{\int_0^1 f(\hat{p},p)dp} = \frac{\int_0^1 f(x,\hat{p} \mid p)\pi(p)dp}{\int_0^1 f(\hat{p} \mid p)\pi(p)dp}$$

$$\int_0^1 f(x,\hat{p} \mid p)\pi(p)dp = \int_0^1 f(x \mid p)f(\hat{p} \mid p)\pi(p)dp$$

$$= \int_0^1 \binom{n}{x} p^x (1-p)^{n-x} \binom{k}{k\hat{p}} p^{k\hat{p}} (1-p)^{k(1-\hat{p})} \frac{1}{B(\alpha,\beta)} p^{\alpha-1}(1-p)^{\beta-1} dp$$

Then, expand the denominator:

$$\int_0^1 f(\hat{p} \mid p)\pi(p)dp =$$

$$\int_0^1 \binom{k}{k\hat{p}} p^{k\hat{p}} (1-p)^{k(1-\hat{p})} \frac{1}{B(\alpha,\beta)} p^{\alpha-1}(1-p)^{\beta-1} dp =$$

$$\binom{k}{k\hat{p}} \frac{1}{B(\alpha,\beta)} \int_0^1 p^{k\hat{p}+\alpha-1}(1-p)^{k(1-\hat{p})+\beta-1} dp =$$

$$\binom{k}{k\hat{p}} \frac{B(k\hat{p}+\alpha, k(1-\hat{p})+\beta)}{B(\alpha,\beta)}$$

Because the denominator is free of *x*, we will temporarily refer to it as *D*. Now, for exactly *x* success we have:

$$f(x \mid \hat{p}) = \frac{\int_0^1 f(x,\hat{p} \mid p)\pi(p)dp}{D}$$

Thus, $P(y) = \dfrac{1}{D} \displaystyle\sum_{x=y}^{n} \int_0^1 f(x,\hat{p} \mid p)\pi(p)dp =$

$$\frac{1}{D} \int_0^1 \sum_{x=y}^{n} \binom{n}{x} p^x (1-p)^{n-x} \binom{k}{k\hat{p}} p^{k\hat{p}}(1-p)^{k(1-\hat{p})} \frac{1}{B(\alpha,\beta)} p^{\alpha-1}(1-p)^{\beta-1} dp =$$

$$\frac{1}{D} \binom{k}{k\hat{p}} \frac{1}{B(\alpha,\beta)} \int_0^1 \sum_{x=y}^{n} \binom{n}{x} p^x (1-p)^{n-x} p^{k\hat{p}}(1-p)^{k(1-\hat{p})} p^{\alpha-1}(1-p)^{\beta-1} dp$$

$$\sum_{x=y}^{n} \binom{n}{x} p^x (1-p)^{n-x} = I_p(y, n-y+1) =$$

$$\frac{1}{B(y, n-y+1)} \int_0^p z^{y-1}(1-z)^{n-y} dz$$

$$P(y) = \frac{1}{D} \binom{k}{k\hat{p}} \frac{1}{B(\alpha,\beta)B(y, n-y+1)} \times$$

$$\int_0^1 \int_0^p z^{y-1}(1-z)^{n-y}\, p^{k\hat{p}+\alpha-1}(1-p)^{k(1-\hat{p})+\beta-1}\, dz\, dp$$

Returning to D,

$$\frac{1}{D}\binom{k}{k\hat{p}}\frac{1}{B(\alpha,\beta)B(y,n-y+1)} =$$

$$\frac{\binom{k}{k\hat{p}}\dfrac{1}{B(\alpha,\beta)B(y,n-y+1)}}{\binom{k}{k\hat{p}}\dfrac{B(k\hat{p}+\alpha,k(1-\hat{p})+\beta)}{B(\alpha,\beta)}} =$$

$$\frac{\dfrac{1}{B(y,n-y+1)}}{B(k\hat{p}+\alpha,k(1-\hat{p})+\beta)} =$$

$$\frac{1}{B(y,n-y+1)B(k\hat{p}+\alpha,k(1-\hat{p})+\beta)}$$

Therefore,

$$P(y) = \frac{\int_0^1 \int_0^p z^{y-1}(1-z)^{n-y}\, p^{k\hat{p}+\alpha-1}(1-p)^{k(1-\hat{p})+\beta-1}\, dz\, dp}{B(y,n-y+1)B(k\hat{p}+\alpha,k(1-\hat{p})+\beta)}$$

When simplified, this becomes our Bayesian formula from the previous section:

$$P(y) = \int_0^1 \int_0^p M \cdot z^{y-1}(1-z)^{n-y}\, p^{r-1}(1-p)^{s-1}\, dz\, dp$$

where $M = \{B(r,s)\cdot B(y,n-y+1)\}^{-1}$

$r = k\hat{p} + \alpha$

$s = k(1-\hat{p}) + \beta$

This work was previously published in International Journal of Swarm Intelligence Research, Volume 1, Issue 4, edited by Yuhui Shi, pp. 17-45, copyright 2010 by IGI Publishing (an imprint of IGI Global)

Chapter 17
Distributed Multi-Agent Systems for a Collective Construction Task based on Virtual Swarm Intelligence

Yan Meng
Stevens Institute of Technology, USA

Yaochu Jin
University of Surrey, UK

ABSTRACT

In this paper, a virtual swarm intelligence (VSI)-based algorithm is proposed to coordinate a distributed multi-robot system for a collective construction task. Three phases are involved in a construction task: search, detect, and carry. Initially, robots are randomly located within a bounded area and start random search for building blocks. Once the building blocks are detected, agents need to share the information with their local neighbors. A distributed virtual pheromone-trail (DVP) based model is proposed for local communication among agents. If multiple building blocks are detected in a local area, agents need to make decisions on which agent(s) should carry which block(s). To this end, a virtual particle swarm optimization (V-PSO)-based model is developed for multi-agent behavior coordination. Furthermore, a quorum sensing (QS)-based model is employed to balance the tradeoff between exploitation and exploration, so that an optimal overall performance can be achieved. Extensive simulation results on a collective construction task have demonstrated the efficiency and robustness of the proposed VSI-based framework.

DOI: 10.4018/978-1-4666-1592-2.ch017

INTRODUCTION

One main challenge for multi-agent systems is to create intelligent agents that are able to adapt their behaviors to changing environments and to improve their skills in performing tasks over time. Such abilities are crucial for agents under dynamic environments, where unpredictable task scenarios may happen, or for those required to perform the same action repeatedly over a large area, where agents need to work together to achieve a global task.

Centralized control methods for multi-agent systems usually require to maintain a complete overview of the situation and a plan of action for every agent (Koenig et al., 2001), which is unpractical. In contrast, distributed control methods are more attractive and feasible for these systems due to their robustness, flexibility, and adaptability. Distributed control methods have been proposed for solving a wide range real-world applications, such as foraging (Krieger et al., 2000), box-pushing (Mataric et al., 1995), aggregation and segregation (Martinoli et al., 1999), shape formation (Balch & Arkin, 1998; Guo et al., 2009), cooperative mapping (Yamauchi, 1999), soccer tournaments (Weiger et al., 2002), collective cleaning (Meng & Gan, 2007; Wagner et al., 1999; Wagner et al., 2008), site preparation (Parker & Zhang, 2006), sorting (Holland & Melhuish, 1999), collective construction and assembly (Stewart & Russell, 2006; Werfel & Nagpal, 2006; Matthey et al., 2009), cooperative searching and exploration and coverage (Correll & Martinoli, 2007; Franchi et al., 2007; Hsiang et al., 2007; Mclurkin & Smith, 2004; Rutishauser et al., 2009). All these systems consist of multiple robots or embodied simulated agents acting autonomously based on their own individual decisions.

In this paper, we focus on developing a distributed control algorithm to coordinate a multi-agent system for a collective construction task. In this task, a few building blocks are randomly distributed in a closed area. Agents are required to search, detect, and carry these building blocks to a predefined base.

A number of challenges much be addressed to develop a distributed, self-adaptive multi-agent system for collective construction tasks. First, since blocks are randomly distributed within a large-scale environment, it is nontrivial to efficiently search and detect the blocks. Second, since small, inexpensive agents have limited communication capability, each agent can only share information with its local neighbors and makes its decisions individually. It is thus tricky to control the communication costs among the agents in a large-scale system, while maximizing the information sharing among agents. Finally, it is not straightforward to achieve an optimal global performance, i.e., to accomplish the construction task as soon as possible by means of local control of the individual agents.

To address the above-mentioned challenges, researchers have turned to biological systems (Pfeifer et al., 2007; Bonabeau et al., 1997; Camazine et al., 2001; Chialvo & Millonas, 1995). For example, swarm intelligence was inspired from behaviors of social insects. Among other applications, swarm intelligence has shown to be successful in controlling multi-agent systems (Doctor et al., 2004; Koening et al., 2001; Payton et al., 2001; Wagner et al., 1999; Keriger et al., 2000; Kumar & Sahin, 2003; Meng & Gan, 2007; Meng & Gan, 2008; Pugh & Martinoli, 2007). However, these work mainly focused on mimicking the behaviors of biological systems by treating each agent in multi-agent systems as an artificial ant or an artificial particle, which usually involve extensive random movements of agents. Furthermore, in some of these work, agents either need to deposit artificial pheromone trails physically in the environment for information sharing (which is usually not feasible in the real-world applications or special sensors have to be developed), or using some global information such as virtual pheromone gradients for information sharing (which is not feasible for distributed systems). In the collective construction tasks, efficient distributed local communication and dynamic task allocation mechanisms are critical for the success of the tasks.

This paper proposes a framework for distributed control of multi-agent systems based on virtual swarm intelligence (VSI), which has the following main features. First, a distributed virtual pheromone-trail (DVP)-based model is developed for local communication among agents, which allows agents to share their local information about the environment to improve the efficiency of exploration. In addition, an optimal overall system performance can be achieved through a virtual particle swarm optimization (V-PSO)-based model, which dynamically allocates agents to different blocks to improve the exploitation capability. Finally, a quorum sensing (QS)-based model allows the agents to achieve an optimal balance between exploration and exploitation.

Although we mainly focus on collective construction tasks in this work, the proposed control framework can be easily extended to other multi-agent systems where robustness and scalability is essential yet only limited communication is allowed, such as exploration of an environment for hazardous waste cleanup, surveillance of multiple buildings, large scale environmental monitoring, urban search and rescue, reconnaissance and exploration missions.

The rest of the paper is organized as follows. Section 2 summarizes the related work. The problem statement is formulated in Section 3. Section 4 discusses the DVP-based communication mechanism. In Section 5, the virtual swarm intelligence (VSI) based coordination framework is presented, which consists of a V-PSO-based method for dynamic task allocation and a QS-based strategy for exploration-exploitation balance. Theoretical analysis of the convergence of the V-PSO is also provided in this section. Simulation results and analysis are presented in Section 6 to evaluate the efficiency, scalability and robustness of the proposed framework. The conclusion and future work are discussed in Section 7.

RELATED WORK

Recently, increasing researchers have been interested in developing self-organizing systems inspired from biological systems. Flocks of migrating birds and schools of fish are good examples of spatially self-organized patterns formed by living organisms through social foraging. Such aggregation patterns are observed in various colonies, such as single-cell bacteria, social insects like ants and termites, birds and fish (Chowdhury et al., 2004).

Considerable bio-inspired methods are based on the behaviors of ant colony. A well-known computational paradigm, i.e., Ant Colony Optimization (ACO), was proposed by Dorigo et al. (1996). This ant system model provides a new and powerful approach to stochastic combinational optimization. The ACO algorithm is essentially an algorithm that simulates the natural behavior of ants, including mechanisms of cooperation and adaptation. The involved agents are steered toward local and global optimization through a feedback mechanism via simulated pheromones and pheromone intensity processing.

Accordingly, many researchers have applied ant behavior-inspired methods to multi-agent systems. In (Koenig et al., 2001), real-time heuristics search methods were proposed for ant-like robots in vacuum cleaning based on ant behaviors through pheromone trails, where physical pheromone trails were deposited within the environment. Instead of spreading chemical landmarks in the environment, Payton et al. (Payton et al., 2001; Payton et al., 2005) proposed a virtual pheromone mechanism, which was simulated by a population of robots, for spreading information and creating gradients in the information space. By using these virtual pheromones, the agents can send and receive directional communications to each other.

Wagner and his colleagues (Altshuler et al., 2005; Wagner et al., 1999) proposed swarm-based algorithms with theoretical bounds using ant heuristics for solving the area-coverage problem using robots for a floor cleaning application. Foraging-based task allocation for a group of robots was proposed in (Keieger et al., 2000), where an ant-derived algorithm was investigated to check if it allows several robots to accomplish tasks in a cooperative manner. The essential components of social organization governing ant colonies were used to program swarms of robots foraging from a central nest. A foraging strategy of ant systems was proposed by Kumar and Sahin (2003) to build the cognitive maps in swarm robots for mine detection applications.

Meanwhile, cooperative multi-agent methods have been proposed inspired by a social analogy, such as bird flocking or fish schooling. Reynolds (1987) built up a computer simulation algorithm to model the motion of a flock of birds, called *boids*. He believed that the motion of boids, as a whole, was the result of the actions of each individual member that follows some simple rules. Ward et al. (2001) evolved *e-boids*, groups of artificial fish capable of displaying schooling behavior. Spector et al. (2003) used a genetic programming algorithm to evolve group behaviors for flying agents in a simulated environment.

One well-known optimization method, particle swarm optimization (PSO), inspired by flocking, herding, and schooling behavior in animal populations, was proposed by Kennedy and Eberhart (1995). PSO has been applied to solving problems in various areas, such as clustering, data mining, dynamic task allocation, and optimization (Lhotska et al., 2006). Pugh and Martinoli (2007) developed a PSO-based multi-robot system, where they treated each robot as a physical particle and used a conventional PSO method to coordinate multi-robot behaviors. PSO-based methods have also been applied to multi-robot systems in various applications, such as collective search (Doctor et al., 2004), odor source localization (Jatmiko et al., 2006), and olfactory guided search (Marques et al., 2006).

A closely related work was proposed by (Halasz et al. 2007), where they proposed a top-down approach to dynamic assignment and reassignment of a swarm of robots to multiple sites, which was inspired by ant behaviors in ant house hunting scenarios. A stochastic control policy was developed to distribute the robots between multiple candidate sites in a pre-specified robot/site ratio.

In our previous work, instead of applying ACO-based methods or PSO-based methods to a multi-agent system individually, control approaches were suggested to integrate these two mechanisms for a multi-robot hazardous waste cleanup task (Meng & Gan, 2007) and a collective construction task (Meng & Gan, 2008). However, there are two major limitations in our previous work. First, communication cost is not scalable to the number of robots in the system. Second, each robot was treated as one physical particle in the system, and PSO was directly applied for task allocation among the robots. This mechanism usually causes extensive random movement of robots that may lead to expensive power consumption of robots.

To address these issues, we extend our previous work in this paper in the following manner. First, we propose a distributed virtual pheromone-trail (DVP) model to reduce the communication cost and make the system scalable to large-scale systems. Second, instead of applying the PSO method directly to the coordination of the velocities of agents at the steering layer, we introduce a virtual PSO (V-PSO) mechanism to coordinate the behaviors of agents at the behavior layer so that the V-PSO model can dynamically allocate multiple agents to multiple tasks. Third, to prevent the agents to overly exploit one particular subarea, which might lead to getting stuck in a local minimum, a quorum sensing (QS)-based model is applied to balance the tradeoff between the exploitation and exploration.

Figure 1. Multi agents (red circles) search for building blocks/targets (black squares) and move the targets to the Base in a bounded environment in a collective construction task

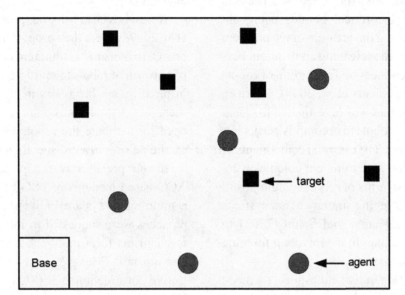

PROBLEM STATEMENT

The problem we are looking at in this paper is to develop a distributed multi-agent system for a collective construction task in a bounded area. As shown in Figure 1, in a collective construction task, a group of agents is deployed in a bounded area where the building blocks (i.e., targets) are randomly placed. The agents will coordinate in a distributed manner to search, detect, and move the targets to a predefined base as soon as possible. Here, tasks are defined as searching for new targets and moving the detected targets to a predefined base. Normally, there are three layers of coordination involved in a multi-agent system: behavior layer (multiple agents behave differently and coordinately to finish a common task), steering layer (such as a formation control task where multiple agents follow the same velocity), and locomotion layer (such as a modular robot where multiple modules work together to move the robot). In this paper, we will focus on the coordination in the behavior layer and ignore the locomotion constraints of the agents in the real-world applications.

In this system, each agent makes its own decisions based on its interaction with neighboring agents and its local environment. The challenging problem is how to define local heuristic control rules for each individual agent to achieve a desired global behavior emerged from local interactions, i.e. searching for and detecting the building blocks and moving them to a predefined base as soon as possible.

We need to make the following assumptions before we present the proposed method. (1) Robots are homogeneous in terms of the agent's capability and asynchronous in terms of their decision making for behaviors; (2) Each agent has its own identification; (3) A bounded environmental map is given to agents in advance, while the locations of building blocks are randomly distributed within the environment and unknown to agents; (4) All agents are randomly distributed within the environment initially, and each agent knows its own initial position within the map; (5) Each agent can self-localize itself using its onboard sensors using an odometry method, and can detect building blocks (the target) and the expected rectangle shape, and estimate the relative distance of the target from itself within its sensor range.

The next step is to define the tasks and the agents. The behavior of agents is self-organized and self-adaptive. Each agent has its onboard sensors, actuators, and controllers, and is able to perform meaningful tasks alone. Each agent has its own goal or interest, which is expressed in terms of a utility function. The state of each agent can be expressed using variable $x(t)$, which is assumed to be an element of a compact subset X of R^n. The utility function of each agent depends on its current position, its strategies, its neighbor' current positions and strategies, and available tasks, which can be defined as $g_i\{x_.(t),...,x_n(t),u_i(t)\} = g_i\{\mathbf{x}(t),u_i(t)\}$, $i = 1,2,...,$ n, where n is the number of neighbors of an agent. At each time step, each agent needs to choose its strategy $u_i(t)$ in order to maximize its own utility function. The state of each agent evolves over time, and its dynamics can be described by heuristic local rules developed in this paper. Here the neighboring agents of a particular agent are defined as all the agents located within the communication range of the said agent.

The tasks can be defined as searching and moving the targets to the base. The detected tasks known to an agent i are defined as $r^i(t)$, which is a subset of R^n, and consists of a set of elements: $r^i(t) = \{r_1^i(t),...,r_m^i(t)\}, i = 1,2,...,m$, where m is the number of tasks known by agent i.

For a collective construction task, basically, each agent has two states: exploration and exploitation. In the exploration state, the agent searches and detects new targets. In the exploitation state, the agent communicates with its neighbors to dynamically allocate the detected targets, and moves the target to the predefined base. For each agent, these two states are interleaved with each other. No agent needs to synchronize its states with others. Each agent stores a grid-based map represented by a matrix $\mathbf{M}$ within its local memory as the global reference coordinate for the agent localization system.

DECENTRALIZED VIRTUAL PHEROMONE-TRAIL (DVP)-BASED COMMUNICATION MECHANISM

The local communication among agents is important for the coordination of a distributed multi-agent system. How to develop a scalable distributed mechanism for local communication among agents is a challenging problem. In natural systems, pheromone trails are chemical markers, which can mediate inter-insect interactions through artifacts or indirect communication. The pheromone trails, which are a kind of environmental synergy where information can be gathered from work in progress, provide a decentralized incremental learning and memory mechanism among the society. A pheromone trail dissipates through an evaporative process. As a result, the strength of the pheromone trials decays with an increasing distance from the source in both spatial and temporal dimensions. Spatial decay maintains locality of communication, and temporal decay reduces the system complexity by ensuring that obsolete information can be removed from the system over time.

This spatiotemporal decaying feature of the pheromone trails is attractive since it allows agents to share information locally in a distributed manner without flooding the pheromone trail information to all agents in the system. Only those agents close to the pheromone source will be informed. Due to the dynamic changing environment, only those newly updated pheromone trails will be propagated and those old pheromone trails will be removed from the system over time. This feature provides the system higher robustness and adaptability to adapt to dynamic environments. Inspired by these features, a *distributed virtual pheromone-trail (DVP)* based communication mechanism is

Table 1. DVP structure stored in an agent

Target location	Source agent ID	Initial deposit time	Value	Agent intensity
l_1	a_{id_1}	t_1	s_1	n_1
l_2	a_{id_2}	t_2	s_2	n_2
...				
l_b	a_{id_b}	t_b	s_b	n_b

Note: b is the total number of targets detected so far by an agent.

proposed here for the message passing scheme among agents.

Distributed Virtual Pheromone (DVP)

Each agent has its local memory storing its own DVPs matrix, where each DVP is associated with one detected target. Each DVP is deposited when the associated target is initially detected, and will be reinforced if the associated target is detected by more agents later or evaporated over time if the associated target is not detected by any agent. Whenever an agent detects a new target, it would update its own DVPs matrix and propagate the corresponding DVP to its neighboring agents. The DVP mechanism consists of the following four components.

- **Deposition and aggregation:** If an agent detects a target, the agent deposits new pheromone value on the associated DVP. By aggregating multiple pheromone values into a single DVP, the superposition of the same pheromone trails can be achieved in a distributed manner.
- **Evaporation:** Pheromone trails gradually fade over time unless new deposits reinforce them.
- **Propagation:** In principle, agents could propagate the pheromone trail information to neighboring agents spatially, with the maximum concentration of a deposit

remaining at the original deposit point. Meanwhile, due to the dynamic environments, we also allow agents to propagate the pheromone trail information temporally.

- **Sensing:** Each agent makes decisions based on the values of the pheromone trails it senses in its local environment. If multiple pheromone sources (i.e., targets) are detected, it has to decide which one to approach.

A simple data structure of DVPs stored in each agent can be defined in Table 1. Initially, the DVP strength is set to be 0. To emulate the reinforcement and evaporation process of the pheromone trails in nature, the strength of DVPs can be updated by the following equation (Dorigo et al. 1996):

$$s_i(t+e) = \rho s_i(t) + \Delta s_i \qquad (1)$$

where s_i represents the pheromone value of ith DVP. $0 < \rho < 1$ is the DVP decay parameter, where $(1 - \rho)$ represents the evaporation of DVP between time t and $t+e$. Δs_i is the aggregated pheromone value of ith DVP deposited by multiple agents, which can be estimated by:

$$\Delta s_i = \sum_{k=1}^{N} \Delta s_i^k \qquad (2)$$

where Δs_i^k is the unit quantity of ith DVP that agent k deposits between time t and $t+e$. N is the total number of agents that have deposited on ith DVP. Basically, the first term on the right-hand side of Equation (1) is used for DVP evaporation and the second term is used for the DVP reinforcement.

Deposition Update

When a DVP is deposited with value s, Table 1 will be checked for a hit on the target location and agent source. There are three possible cases: (1) If there is no hit, the data is stored and scheduled for transmission as a DVP update with value s. (2) If the hit has the value which is less than s, the "no-hit" action (1) is taken. (3) If the hit has the value which is greater than s, the deposition is ignored.

Propagation Models

When an agent receives a new DVP update, it decides whether it will propagate this information to its neighbors according to the two propagation models: spatial propagation model (SPM) and temporal propagation model (TPM). In SPM, it is desirable that the value of the DVP decays with increasing distance from the DVP source (i.e. target location). This encodes the physical distance from the detected target and limits the range over which the data will be propagated. When the distance of an agent from the DVP source is greater than a predefined threshold, this DVP will not be propagated by this agent. In TPM, it is desirable that the value of the DVP decays over time. This model encodes the time since the pheromone trail deposition, which favors newer information while allowing old information to persist at a low level. When the value of a DVP is below a predefined threshold, this DVP will not be propagated.

Broadcast Suppression

To limit redundant transmissions among agents, a broadcast suppression mechanism is needed. Since it is assumed that each agent has a unique ID, an ID-traced method is proposed to tackle this issue. Basically, if a new DVP package is generated, the IDs of all the agents along the routing path of this DVP will be added into the DVP package. The agent will only broadcast this DVP package to those neighbors that have not received this DVP before.

Intermediate Summary

In summary, scalability of a multi-agent system requires localized communication and efficient coordination among local neighboring agents. The DVP-based communication mechanism would coordinate the agents in both exploration and exploitation phases. Once a target is detected by an agent, the agent would deposit a certain DVP value associated with this target, and propagate this DVP information to its neighbors using both SPM and TPM. If the detected targets need multiple agents to move, some agents stop exploration and move the detected targets if multiple agents are needed for the detected targets. In this way, the fuel cost of agents can be saved. During the exploitation phase, either the utility-based method or the virtual PSO-based method will be applied to the coordination of the agent behaviors using the DVP mechanism, which will be discussed in the next subsection. Furthermore, the encoding of spatial and temporal information in the DVP value, combined with superposition of the same DVP, allows neighboring agents to coordinate in a distributed manner without requiring expensive point-to-point protocols, which are vulnerable to faults.

DISTRIBUTED COORDINATION

During the exploration phase, since agents have not detected any target yet and the targets may be dynamically added in or removed from the environment, a simple strategy for agents to take is "random walk". Since it is assumed that the search environment is modeled as a strongly connected (and degree bounded) planar graph, in this environment, the computational complexity of the random walks to cover a graph (i.e., finding new targets for the agents) is $O(n^2)$.

The Utility-Based Method

During the exploitation phase, agents have detected one or more targets within one time step. The utility function of a detected target for an agent can be defined as:

$$\mu_{ij}^k(t) = \frac{\omega_{ij}^k(t)}{d_{ij}^k(t)} e^{-s_{ij}^k(t)}, \tag{3}$$

where $\mu_{ij}^k(t)$ is the utility value of the target located at (i, j) for agent k. $\omega_{ij}^k(t)$ is the weight of the target, which means the number of agents required to process the target at (i, j). $d_{ij}^k(t)$ is the distance between agent k and the target at (i, j). $s_{ij}^k(t)$ is the DVP value of the target at (i, j), which is defined in Equation (1). Basically, the greater the DVP value associated with the target, the more agents may potentially approach to the target, which may reduce the utility value of the target for each agent so that agent congestion around this target can be prevented. The greater the travel cost to the target, the less attractive the target is for the agent.

If a target is detected by an agent, this agent would share the target information with its neighbors. If this is the only target that has been detected within its local neighborhood, a simple task allocation strategy is adopted. It is assumed that each agent has an assignment flag, which is set to be on-duty if the agent has been assigned to a target; otherwise, it is available. Then, based on the weight of the detected target, if multiple agents are needed to move this target, the initiated agent, which first detected this target, would pick the required number of agents with the highest utility value(s) for this target from available neighbors. If multiple targets have been detected within a local neighborhood, agents in this neighborhood have to decide which agent moves which target, which is an NP-hard dynamic task allocation problem. Therefore, we need to develop an advanced task allocation method for this case.

V-PSO-Based Task Allocation Method

To tackle this above-mentioned problem, we turned our attention to Particle Swarm Optimization (PSO) (Keneedy & Eberhart, 1995) methods. In a PSO, particles explore the n-dimensional search space S of an optimization problem with the objective function $f : S \subseteq \mathbf{R}^n \to \mathbf{R}$. Without loss of generality, we assume it is a maximization problem. Each particle has a position $x_i(t)$, a velocity $v_i(t)$, and a fitness function $f(x_i(t))$, where t is the iteration counter. A position $x_1(t) \in S$ is called better than $x_2(t) \in S$ if and only if $f(x_1(t)) > f(x_2(t))$. The best search position particle i has visited until t is its private guide $p_{best}(t)$. For each particle, a subset of all particles is assigned as its neighbors. The best private guide of all neighbors of particle i is called its local guide $l_{best}(t)$. At each iteration, position and velocity of each particle i are updated according to the following equations:

$$\begin{aligned} v_{i,t} = w \cdot v_{i,t-1} &+ c_1 \cdot r_1 \cdot ((p_{best})_{i,t-1} - x_{i,t-1}) \\ &+ c_2 \cdot r_2 \cdot ((l_{best})_{i,t-1} - x_{i,t-1}) \end{aligned} \tag{4}$$

$$x_{i,t} = x_{i,t-1} + v_{i,t} \tag{5}$$

Figure 2. Assigning three targets to four agents

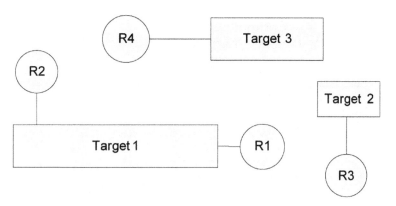

where w, c_1, and c_2 are predefined constant factors. r_1 and r_2 are vectors of random real numbers uniformly chosen between 0 and 1, and independently drawn every time they occur.

In PSO, each particle, which is a candidate solution, moves in the search space and updates its velocity according to its best private guide (self-experience) and the local guide achieved by its neighbors (and itself), trying to find a better position. This approach combines private search methods (through own private experience) and local search methods (through neighboring experiences), and has been proved to be powerful in finding global optima provided the parameters are well predefined.

One of the key issues in designing a successful PSO algorithm for a specific problem is to find a suitable mapping between the problem solutions and the PSO particles. A simple mapping is to treat each agent as one particle, as in our previous work (Meng & Gan, 2007; Meng & Gan, 2008). However, this kind of mapping has its weaknesses. For example, the performance of the PSO can be flatten out with a loss of diversity in the search space as the overall result since only two dimensions are used. And it is difficult to hill-climb the solution space due to the lack of dynamic velocity adjustment mechanism. Furthermore, many random movements of particles will consume too much onboard power, which is

especially undesirable for mobile robot systems where onboard power is very limited.

To cope with this problem, we develop a virtual PSO approach to dynamic task allocation. First, we set up a search space with R dimensions. Then the search problem reduces to finding an optimal solution to the assignment of N detected targets to R agents. Each dimension has a discrete set of possible values P_k, which represents the target assigned to each dimension (i.e. agent). And the value of P_k is limited to $O = \{P_k \mid 1 \leq k \leq N\}$, where N is the number of targets. One example of assigning 3 targets to 4 agents is shown in Figure 2, and the corresponding assignment mapping using the particle representation is depicted in Figure 3.

Basically, if there are L particles used in the PSO algorithm, the particle population can be represented by an array consisting of L numbers of 2-dimensional assignment instance. As shown in Figure 3, in each assignment instance, the first number indicates the agent and the second number indicates the target assigned to this agent. For example, the variable (2, 1) means assigning target 1 to agent 2. Here, to make it simple, we use one number to represent the targets instead of 2D values of target locations. But, in the agent programs, the targets are identified using their locations within a global coordinate.

Now the problem is converted to finding an optimal solution to the assignment of N detected

Figure 3. The mapping of target assignment to a PSO particle

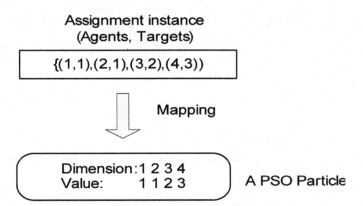

targets to R agents that are available. We adopt a virtual PSO (V-PSO) based method for this purpose, where each particle represents one possible array of assignment instances, for example, $\{(1,1),(2,1),(3,2),(4,3)\}$, and there are L particles in total, which means that there are L possible assignment solutions.

Initially, the PSO algorithm generates L particles with randomly generated potential solutions for the problem. The fitness function of each particle is the sum of the utility values of all the assignment instances within the array, which can be defined as:

$$f_p(t) = \sum_{j=1}^{N} \sum_{i=1}^{R} \eta_j^i(t). \tag{6}$$

where $\eta_j^i(t)$ is the utility value of assigning agent i to target j. Then each particle follows the dynamics defined in Equations (4) and (5) to converge to some optimal solutions.

Since this is a distributed system, each agent can only detect its local environment and share information with its local neighbors. How do we apply the V-PSO method to this distributed system? We propose an initiator-based method described below. Whenever an agent detects a target (we call this agent as initiator), it will initiate a local-team call to see if there is any neighbors available to join its team for this local task allocation. Once an agent decides to join a team, its assignment flag should be on-duty; otherwise, it is available. Only those available agents can join a new team for a local task allocation. This regulation can avoid assignment overlapping and simplify the overall system design.

If an available agent receives multiple local-team calls simultaneously from different initiators, this agent will pick a target with the highest utility value. From the system point of view, there may be multiple initiators running the V-PSO method at the same time, where each one is trying to achieve its local global optimal solution.

After checking with its neighbors, the initiator will start to run a V-PSO-based method for this local task allocation. In this way, a distributed task allocation approach is built up, where only the initiators can run the V-PSO algorithm for a local team. The size of the team only depends on the current available agents within the initiator's neighborhood. For each initiator, the pseudo code of the V-PSO based dynamic task allocation algorithm is summarized as follows:

For each particle
Initialize particles with random solutions;
Initialize $p_{best}(t)$ with the current solution;
End

Do

For each particle

Calculate the fitness value;

If the fitness value is better than the best fitness value $p_{best}(t)$ in history

Set current value as the new $p_{best}(t)$;

End

Choose the particle with the best fitness value of all the particles as the $g_{best}(t)$;

For each particle

Calculate particle velocity according Equation (7);

Update particle position according Equation (8);

End

While maximum iterations or minimum error criteria is not attained.

Theoretical Convergence Analysis of the V-PSO-based Method

Now we need to prove the convergence of the V-PSO-based method theoretically to ensure that an optimal solution for task allocation can be achieved. The PSO behaviors under different conditions have been discussed extensively in [37]. Here only a brief analysis is given. Since each particle is updated independently in Equations (4) and (5), without loss of generality, one-dimensional particle movements can be used for our analysis. So Equations (4) and (5) can be rewritten as:

$$v_t = w \cdot v_{t-1} + c_1 \cdot ((p_{best})_{t-1} - x_{t-1}) + c_2 \cdot ((l_{best})_{t-1} - x_{t-1}) \tag{7}$$

$$x_t = x_{t-1} + v_t \tag{8}$$

Here the random factors r_1 and r_2 are omitted so that Equations (7) and (8) actually represent a deterministic version of the PSO algorithm, which can be qualitatively discussed. If we defined

$$c = \frac{c_1 + c_2}{2} \tag{9}$$

$$g = \frac{(c_1 \cdot p_{best} + c_2 \cdot l_{best})}{(c_1 + c_2)}, \tag{10}$$

Equation (10) can be simplified to be:

$$v_t = w \cdot v_{t-1} + c \cdot (g - x_{t-1}) \tag{11}$$

Combining Equations (8), (9), (10), and (11), the PSO can be expressed in a matrix form as follows:

$$\begin{bmatrix} x_t \\ v_t \end{bmatrix} = \begin{bmatrix} 1-c & w \\ -c & w \end{bmatrix} \begin{bmatrix} x_{t-1} \\ v_{t-1} \end{bmatrix} + g \begin{bmatrix} c \\ c \end{bmatrix} \tag{12}$$

Applying the dynamic system theory and the eigenvalue analysis to Equation (12), the equilibrium state of Equation (13) can be achieved as:

$$\begin{bmatrix} x_{eq} \\ v_{eq} \end{bmatrix} = \begin{bmatrix} g \\ 0 \end{bmatrix} \tag{13}$$

If $w < 1 \quad c > 0 \quad$ and $2w - c + 2 > 0 \tag{14}$

The conclusion in Equation (14) is intuitively correct. At the beginning, particles are distributed all over the search space; then move around and finally converge to the equilibriums. The equilibriums not only rely on particles' own private experience but also on the local best from their neighbors. When the convergence is achieved, velocities of particles become zeros.

Quorum Sensing (QS)-based Strategy to Balance Exploration and Exploitation

We have proposed rules for exploration and exploitation phases separately, now the question is how each agent decides when to switch from one phase to another. This poses a tradeoff between exploration and exploitation.

For example, the utility-based methods may result in greedy behaviors of an agent since the agent would rather move to a distant target with a higher utility value rather than explore new areas, which may lead to the situation in which some targets are left undiscovered. To tackle this problem, a quorum sensing (QS)-based technique is proposed to provide an optimal balance between the exploration and exploitation.

Seeley and Visscher (2004) proposed a quorum-sensing hypothesis for the nest-site selection process of honeybee swarms: the scouts do this by noting when one of the potential nest sites under consideration is being visited by a sufficiently large number of scouts. It was suggested that the quorum size was a parameter of the bees' decision-making process that has been tuned by natural selection to provide an optimal balance between speed (favored by a small quorum) and accuracy (favored by a large quorum). With respect to speed, the requirement of a quorum means that preparations for takeoff can begin as soon as enough bees have approved of one of the potential nest sites, even if some others are still scouting other sites. With respect to accuracy, the quorum requirement evidently promotes a high level accuracy, for it appears that scouts will not begin producing piping signals for takeoff preparations until the number of bees present simultaneously outside a nest cavity reaches 10-15.

This mechanism of quorum sensing can be used by agents in the decision-making procedure to coordinate group behaviors. The basic idea is that if there is more than one detected target, the agents have a higher tendency to approach targets. Otherwise, the agents should explore new areas for new targets. Here, we define the quorum sensing variable θ_{qs} as the ratio of the detected target weights and the number of available agents in a local neighborhood, which can be defined as:

$$\theta_{qs} = \frac{\sum_{i=1}^{n_t} \varpi_{t,i}}{n_l}, \tag{15}$$

where $\omega_{ij}^k(t)$ is the weight of target i, which indicates the number of agents needed for target i. n_t is the total number of detected targets in the local neighborhood. n_l is the number of the available agents in the local neighborhood. The threshold of θ_{qs} is defined as θ_{qs_t}. If $\theta_{qs} \geq \theta_{qs\_t}$, it means that if there is more than one target in the local neighborhood need to be processed, the agent needs to switch to the exploitation phase to process those targets. Otherwise, it means that sufficient agents have been assigned to the detected targets, and the agent should switch to exploration of new targets.

Algorithm Summary

To summarize, each agent makes its own decision for its behaviors based on the following rules. When no target is detected, the agents are in exploration phase and move around randomly to search for new targets. Once one or several targets are detected by an agent or its neighbors, the agents have to decide whether to switch to exploitation phase to process the target or continue its exploration for new targets using QS-based strategy. If the agents decide to switch to the exploitation phase, the utility-based method defined in Equation (3) is applied in the one-target cases, and the V-PSO method is applied for multi-targets cases. After the agents accomplish the task regarding the targets assigned them, they use the QS-based strategy to decide weather to process another target if there is any or switch to the exploration phase searching for new targets. This procedure continues until all the targets have been processed if we know the total number of the building blocks need to

Figure 4. One snapshot of the SwarmSim. 84 homogeneous agents (black dots) search, detect and move randomly distributed 24 target blocks (red rectangles) with various weights to a predefined base (yellow rectangle). Each agent is equipped with a camera system for target detection and a wireless communication card for local information sharing.

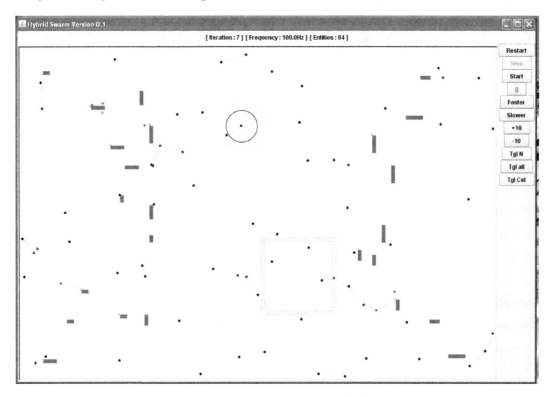

be moved to the base or a predefined maximum iteration is reached.

Simulation Results and Analysis

To evaluate the performance of the proposed algorithm in a distributed multi-agent system, we developed a JAVA-based simulator, SwarmSim, as shown in Figure 4.

SwarmSim works with a bounded area of a size of 994m x 672m, where agents are supposed to search and detect building blocks (red rectangles), and move the blocks (targets) to a base location (yellow rectangle) as soon as possible. Two criteria can be used to evaluate the system performance: finish time and power consumption. The finish time is defined as the time to finish the task, in other words, how long the system needs to move all the blocks to the base. The power consumption is defined as the total power is needed for the robots to finish the task, which consists of communication cost and movement cost. In the following simulation, we use both criteria to evaluate the system performance. The communication range is set up as 30m and the vision range is set up as 10m.

Several parameters need to be tuned in the V-PSO method. To speed up the decision making process for real-time performance, based on the experimental trials, the population size of particles is set as 15 and $w = 0.732$ and $c_1 = c_2 = 1.496$. The stopping condition for the V-PSO is the predefined maximum number of iterations (i.e., 1600).

Figure 5. The number of inter-agent communication package passing using different methods with different agent populations. The * represent the mean values, and the corresponding error-bars represent the associated standard deviations.

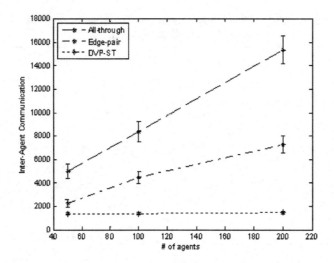

DVP Mechanism with Spatial and Temporal Constraints

To evaluate the proposed DVP mechanism with SPM and TPM (we call it DVP-ST for short) and the ID-traced broadcast suppression method, a comparison with two alternative methods is conducted. First one is called all-through method where all messages are transferred without any elimination. Second one is the edge-pair method used in our previous work (Meng & Gan, 2007), where the messages are ignored if these messages have been received from the same neighbors before. Three different populations of agents have been used, 50, 100, and 200, for 10 targets in the simulation, and each population runs for 35 times. The numbers of the inter-agent package passing for three different methods are shown in Figure 5.

It can be seen from Figure 5 that the proposed DVP-ST method can reduce the communication cost significantly compared to other two methods. Furthermore, while the communication costs of all-through and edge-pair methods increase considerably as the number of agent increases, the

communication costs of the DVP-ST method largely remains constant with different population sizes. In other words, the DVP-ST method is scalable to system scale.

V-PSO Task Allocation Combined with QS-based Switching Strategy

To evaluate the performance of the proposed V-PSO method with QS-based switching strategy, the following methods are implemented for comparison.

- Random approach. All agents search for targets in a random fashion with no explicit communication among the agents. Once the target is detected by an agent, the agent moves the target directly. If multiple agents are needed for a target, the target can only be moved when enough agents are around.
- DPSO approach. We use the method proposed in our previous work (Meng and Gan, 2008), where each particle represents

*Figure 6. Comparisons of the mean-values and the standard deviations of the finish time using different algorithms with different agent populations. The * represents the mean value and error-bar associated with the * represents the standard deviation.*

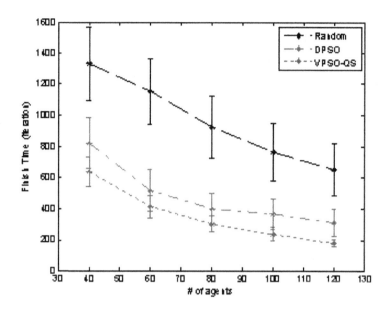

one agent and the agents' movements are controlled by PSO directly.

- VPSO-QS approach. This is the proposed approach in this paper, where a random search method is applied in the exploration phase, a V-PSO method is applied in exploitation phase, and a quorum sensing (QS) method is applied to balance the exploration and exploitation.

It is assumed that both DPSO and VPSO-QS methods use the same DVP-based mechanism for sharing local information among agents. We run the simulations 35 times with different swarm populations for the three compared methods. The simulation results of the finish time are shown in Figure 6. The running iterations in the simulation are considered as the finish time.

From Figure 6, it is observed that the proposed VPSO-QS method outperforms the other two methods, where the random method is the worst. This is because, in the DPSO method, the agents

have to search for the local best and global best positions physically through the agents' movements, where more time is needed for the system to converge to the global best. Meanwhile, the agents using the VPSO-QS method can skip this convergence procedure since the VPSO is implemented virtually on the local initiators. The initiators virtually estimate the global best within its local team using VPSO, and send the assignment results to their available neighbors. In this manner, the agents would approach to and move the assigned targets directly, which can save time for search considerably and lead to a much smaller finish time.

To further evaluate the performance of the proposed method, the comparison of the power consumption is needed. For simplicity, the power consumption is measured in SimWatt, where one SimWatt is the power required for one agent to move one meter. Since the communication costs have been compared in Figure 5, here, we only consider the travel cost contributed to the agent

Figure 7. The mean and standard deviation of the power consumption of all agents using different methods. The * represents the mean value and error-bar associated with the * represents the standard deviation.

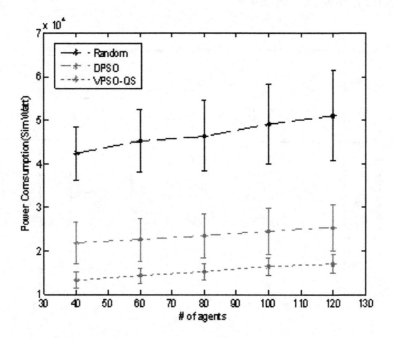

power consumption. The simulation results are shown in Figure 7.

It can be seen from Figure 7 that the VPSO-QS method consumes much less power than the other two methods. Obviously, the random search would consume more power due to the random movements of the agents. In the DPSO method, the exploration and exploitation phases are integrated in the PSO method without explicitly distinguishing from each other. In the VPSO-QS method, QS method is applied to dynamically switch between the exploration and exploitation, which would improve the overall search performance. It is also observed that, for all three methods, the total travel costs only increase slightly with the increase of the agent population. This is because as more agents join the search, more movements are involved. Meanwhile, the overall finish time decreases as the number of the agents increases, thus the total travel time is reduced, which leads to a lower power consumption.

The final power consumption is the balance of these two factors.

Robustness Test

To show that the proposed VPSO-QS method can be applied to various dynamic environments, the following four environments are tested:

1. **Dense targets, dense agents (DTDS):** 24 targets and 100 agents
2. **Dense targets, sparse agents (DTSA):** 24 targets and 50 agents
3. **Sparse targets, dense agents (STDA):** 12 targets and 100 agents
4. **Sparse targets, sparse agents (STSA):** 12 targets and 50 agents

We conducted 35 independent runs for each environmental configuration. The results in terms of the mean and standard deviation of the finish time are listed in Table 2 for different configura-

Table 2. The finish time (iterations) using the VPSO-QS method under different environmental configurations

Method	Finish time (Mean)	Finish time (STD)
DTDS	352	32
DTSA	556	57
STDA	312	27
STSA	373	34

Table 3. Simulation results of dynamic environments

Method	Finish time (Mean)	Finish time (STD)
Targets: 12 → 24 Agents: 100	375	38
Targets: 24 → 12 Agents: 100	232	21
Agents: 100 → 110 Target: 12	303	29
Agents: 100 → 90 Targets: 12	324	35

Note: The targets/agents are added or removed randomly after the simulation running. The finish time is represented by iterations.

Table 4. Mean and standard deviation of the finish time when the self-localization is subject to noise

	Without noise	5% noise	10% noise
Mean	315	319	326
STD	25	29	31

tions. It can be seen that more finish time is needed for dense-target cases.

To demonstrate the capability of the self-organization and robustness of the VPSO-QS method, the following two cases are studied. First, the targets are added or removed dynamically on the fly while keeping the same agent population. Second, the agents are added or removed dynamically on the fly while keeping the same number of targets. The simulation results are listed in Table 3. Both cases demonstrate that the agents can adapt to changing environments effectively.

In the problem statement, we assume that agents can self-localize themselves within a global coordinate and can detect targets and the relative distance to targets. When we apply the VPSO-QS method to the real-world applications, more constraints have to be taken into account, which include noise in distance measurement and self-localization. To consider the influence of sensory noise, noise is deliberately added to the sensory measurements and localization. 35 independent runs are conducted using 84 agents and 24 targets. We then calculate the mean and standard deviation of the finish time with 5% and 10% noise level added in the agent localization and distance measurement, as listed in Table 4 and Table 5, respectively. From these results, we can

Table 5. Mean and standard deviation of the finish time when the distance measurements are subject to noise

	Without noise	5% noise	10% noise
Mean	315	321	334
STD	25	24	29

Figure 8. The comparison of the mean and standard deviation of the finish time with different particle populations using the VPSO-QS method

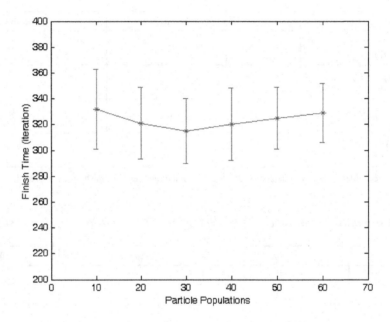

conclude that the system is robust to the noise in the localization measurements.

Parameter Influence Test

In the parameter setup, we use 15 particles for the VPSO-QS method. To evaluate the influence of the number of particles in VPSO-QS on the system performance, we conduct another set of simulations. For each simulation, we have 24 targets and 100 agents. Again, we conducted 35 independent simulation runs with a particle population of 10, 20, 30, 40, 50, and 60. The results describing the mean and standard deviation of the finish time are presented in Figure 8. It can be seen that

particle population size in the VPSO-QS method does not have significant influence on the system performance. However, if the population size is too small or too big, the processing speed of the system may slow down.

CONCLUSION

In this paper, we propose a virtual swarm intelligence based framework for distributed multi-agent systems to coordinately work in a collective construction task. Basically, the proposed framework consists of two processes: the interaction of short-range positive-feedback activation processes (autocatalysis) and longer-range inhibitory (antagonistic) processes. The rules for these processes depend on local cues only – there is no global control unit or plan for agents to consult. The global behaviors emerge as the cumulative effect of the individual agents interacting with each other and with their local environment. More specifically, three models are proposed in this framework: a distributed DVP-ST model for agents to communicate with their neighbors, a V-PSO model to dynamically allocate the detected targets to local agents, and a QS-based model to balance exploration and exploitation. The proposed framework is well suited for multi-agent systems where each agent is equipped with only limited communication and computational capabilities. Since other algorithms which are closely related to our work in this paper have different simulation/experimental scenarios, it is hard to provide the comparison results with other approaches. We will build a benchmark for collective construction tasks in the future to provide comparison results with other methods.

While the proposed framework shows advantages in system robustness, scalability, and individual simplicity, some issues remain to be resolved. For example, the search process used by the swarm intelligence methods is usually unbiased. The performance of swarm intelligence methods can be improved considerably if domain knowledge is incorporated to reduce the search space. We will investigate this issue in our future work.

REFERENCES

Altshuler, Y., Bruckstein, A. M., & Wagner, I. A. (2005). Swarm robotics for a dynamic clearning problem. In *Proceedings of the IEEE Swarm Intelligence Symposium* (pp. 209-216).

Balch, T., & Arkin, R. C. (1998). Behavior-based formation control for multi-agent teams. *IEEE Transactions on Robotics and Automation, 14*(6), 926–939. doi:10.1109/70.736776

Bonabeau, E., Theralauz, G., Deneubourg, J. L., & Camazine, S. (1997). Self-organization in social insects. *Trends in Ecology & Evolution, 12*(5), 188–193. doi:10.1016/S0169-5347(97)01048-3

Camazine, S., Deneubourg, J. L., Franks, N. R., Sneyd, J., Gheraulaz, G., & Bonabeau, E. (2001). *Self-organization in biological systems. Princeton Studies in Complexity*. Princeton, NJ: Princeton University Press.

Chialvo, D. R., & Millonas, M. M. (1995). How swarms build cognitive maps. In Steels, L. (Ed.), *The Biology and Technology of Intelligent Autonomous Agents* (*Vol. 144*, pp. 439–450). New York: Springer.

Chowdhury, D., Nishinari, K., & Schadschneider, A. (2004). Self-organized patterns and traffic flow in colonies of organisms from bacteria and social insects to vertebrates. *Phase Transitions, 77*, 601–624. doi:10.1080/01411590410001672567

Correll, N., & Martinoli, A. (2007). Robust decentralized coverage using a swarm of miniature robots. In *Proceedings of the IEEE International Conference on Robotics and Automation* (pp. 379-384).

Doctor, S., Venayagamoorthy, G., & Gudise, V. (2004, June 19-23). Optimal PSO for Collective Robotic Search Applications. In *Proceedings of the IEEE Congress on Evolutionary Computation*, Portland, OR (pp. 1390-1395).

Dorigo, M., Maniezzo, V., & Colorni, A. (1996). Ant system: optimization by a colony of cooperating agents. *IEEE Transactions on Systems, Man, and Cybernetics. Part B, Cybernetics, 26*(1), 29–41. doi:10.1109/3477.484436

Franchi, A., Freda, L., Oriolo, G., & Vendittelli, M. (2007). A randomized strategy for cooperative robot exploration. In *Proceedings of the IEEE International Conference on Robotics and Automation*, Rome, Italy (pp. 768-774).

Guo, H., Meng, Y., & Jin, Y. (2009). A Cellular Mechanism for Multi-Robot Construction via Evolutionary Multi-Objective Optimization of a Gene Regulatory Network. *Bio Systems, 98*(3), 193–203. doi:10.1016/j.biosystems.2009.05.003

Halasz, A., Hsieh, M. A., Berman, S., & Kumar, V. (2007). Dynamic Redistribution of a Swarm of Robots Among Multiple Sites. In *Proceedings of the 2007 IEEE/RSJ International Conference on Intelligent Robots and Systems*.

Holland, O. E., & Melhuish, C. (1999). Stigmergy, self-organization, and sorting in collective robotics. *Artificial Life, 5*, 173–202. doi:10.1162/106454699568737

Hsiang, T., Arkin, E., Bender, M., Fekete, S., & Mitchell, J. (2007). *Algorithms for rapidly dispersing robot swarms in unknown environments*.

Jatmiko, W., Sekiyama, K., & Fukuda, E. (2006). A PSO-based Mobile Sensor Network for Odor Source Localization in Dynamic Environment: Theory, Simulation and Measurement. In *Proceedings of the IEEE Congress on Evolutionary Computation*, Vancouver, Canada (pp. 1036-1043).

Kennedy, J., & Eberhart, R. (1995). Particle swarm optimization. *IEEE Conference on Neural Networks*.

Khoshnevis, B., & Bekey, G. A. (1998). Centralized sensing and control of multiple mobile robots. *Computers & Industrial Engineering, 35*(3-4), 503–506. doi:10.1016/S0360-8352(98)00144-2

Koenig, S., Szymanski, B., & Liu, Y. (2001). Efficient and inefficient ant coverage methods. *Annals of Mathematics and Artificial Intelligence, 31*(1-4), 41–76. doi:10.1023/A:1016665115585

Krieger, M., Billeter, J., & Keller, L. (2000). Ant-like task allocation and recruitment in cooperative agents. *Nature, 406*, 992–995. doi:10.1038/35023164

Kumar, V., & Sahin, E. (2003). Cognitive maps in swarm robots for the mine detection application. In *Proceedings of the IEEE International Conference on Systems, Man and Cybernetics* (pp. 3364-3369).

Lhotská, L., Macaš, M., & Burša, M. (2006). PSO and ACO in Optimization Problems. In E. Corchado et al. (Eds.), *Intelligent Data Engineering and Automated Learning* (LNCS 4224, pp. 1390-1398).

Marques, L., Nunes, U., & de Almeida, A. (2006). Particle swarm-based olfactory guided search. *Autonomous Robots, 20*, 277–287. doi:10.1007/s10514-006-7567-0

Martinoli, A., Ijspeert, A., & Mondada, F. (1999). Understanding collective aggregation mechanisms: from probabilistic modeling to experiments with real agents. *Robotics and Autonomous Systems, 29*, 51–63. doi:10.1016/S0921-8890(99)00038-X

Mataric, M., Nilsson, M., & Simsarian, K. (1995). Cooperative multi-agent box-pushing. In *Proceedings of the IEEE/RSJ International Conference on Intelligent Agents and Systems*.

Mathhey, L., Berman, S., & Kumar, V. (2009). Stochastic strategies for a swarm robotic assembly system. In *Proceedings of the IEEE International Conference on Robotics and Automation*.

Mclurkin, J., & Smith, J. (2004). Decentralized algorithms for dispersion in indoor environments using a swarm of autonomous mobile robots. In *Proceedings of the 7th International Symposium on Decentralized Autonomous Robotic Systems*, Toulouse, France.

Meng, Y., & Gan, J. (2007). LIVS: Local Interaction via Virtual Stigmergy Coordination in Distributed Search and Collective Cleanup. In *Proceedings of the IEEE/RSJ International Conference on Intelligent Robots and Systems,* San Diego, CA.

Meng, Y., & Gan, J. (2008). A Distributed Swarm Intelligence based Algorithm for a Cooperative Multi-Robot Construction Task. In *Proceedings of the IEEE Swarm Intelligence Symposium,* St. Louis, MO.

Parker, C., & Zhang, H. (2006). Collective robotic site preparation. *Adaptive Behavior, 14*(1), 5–19. doi:10.1177/105971230601400101

Payton, D., Daily, M., Estowski, R., Howard, M., & Lee, C. (2001). Pheromone robotics. *Autonomous Robots, 11*(3), 319–324. doi:10.1023/A:1012411712038

Payton, D., Estkowski, R., & Howard, M. (2005). Pheromone robotics and the logic of virtual pheromones. In E. Sahin & E. M. Spears (Eds.), *Swarm Robotics* (LNCS 3342, pp. 45-57).

Pfeifer, R., Lungarella, M., & Iida, F. (2007). Self-organization, embodiment, and biologically inspired robotics. *Science, 318*, 1088–1093. doi:10.1126/science.1145803

Pugh, J., & Martinoli, A. (2007). Inspiring and Modeling Multi-Robot Search with Particle Swarm Optimization. In *Proceedings of the 2007 IEEE Swarm Intelligence Symposium.*

Reynolds, C. (1987). Flocks, herds, and schools: a decentralized behavioral model. *Computer Graphics, 21*(4), 25–34. doi:10.1145/37402.37406

Rutishauser, S., Correll, N., & Martinoli, A. (2009). Collaborative coverage using a swarm of networked miature robots. *Robotics and Autonomous Systems, 57*(5), 517–525. doi:10.1016/j.robot.2008.10.023

Seeley, T. D., & Visscher, P. K. (2004). Quorum sensing during nest-site selection by honeybee swarms. *Behavioral Ecology and Sociobiology, 56*, 594–601. doi:10.1007/s00265-004-0814-5

Spector, L., Klein, J., Perry, C., & Feinstein, M. (2003). Emergence of collective behavior in evolving populations of flying agents. In E. Cantu-Paz et al. (Eds.), *Proceedings of the Genetic and Evolutionary Computation Conference (GECCO),* Berlin (pp. 61-73).

Stewart, R., & Russell, R. (2006). A decentralized feedback mechanism to regulate wall construction by a robotic swarm. *Adaptive Behavior, 14*(1), 21–51. doi:10.1177/105971230601400104

Trelea, I. C. (2003). The Particle Swarm Optimization Algorithm: Convergence Analysis and Parameter Selection. *Information Processing Letters, 85*, 317–325. doi:10.1016/S0020-0190(02)00447-7

Wagner, I., Lindenbaum, M., & Bruckstein, A. (1999). Decentralized covering by ant-robots using evaporating traces. *IEEE Transactions on Robotics and Automation, 15*(5), 918–933. doi:10.1109/70.795795

Wagner, I. A., Altshuler, Y., Yanovski, V., & Bruckstein, A. M. (2008). Cooperative cleaners: a study in ant robotics. *The International Journal of Robotics Research, 27*(1), 127–151. doi:10.1177/0278364907085789

Ward, C., Gobet, F., & Kendall, G. (2001). Evolving collective behavior in an artificial ecology. *Artificial Life, 7*(2), 191–209. doi:10.1162/106454601753139005

Weigel, T., Gutmann, J., Dietl, M., Kleiner, A., & Nebel, B. (2002). CS Freiburg: coordinating agents for successful soccer playing. *IEEE Transactions on Robotics and Automation, 18*(5), 685–699. doi:10.1109/TRA.2002.804041

Werfel, J., & Nagpal, R. (2006). Extended stigmergy in collective construction. *IEEE Intelligent Systems*, *21*(2), 20–28. doi:10.1109/MIS.2006.25

Yamauchi, B. (1999). Decentralized coordination for multi-agent exploration. *Robotics and Autonomous Systems*, *29*(1), 111–118. doi:10.1016/S0921-8890(99)00046-9

This work was previously published in International Journal of Swarm Intelligence Research, Volume 1, Issue 2, edited by Yuhui Shi, pp. 58-79, copyright 2010 by IGI Publishing (an imprint of IGI Global)

Compilation of References

Abdel-Magid, Y. L., & Abido, M. A. (2004). Robust coordinated design of excitation and TCSC-based stabilizers using genetic algorithm. *Electric Power Systems Research, 69*, 129–141. doi:10.1016/j.epsr.2003.06.009

Abido, M. A. (2002, October). Optimal Power Flow Using Particle Swarm Optimization. *International Journal of Electrical Power & Energy Systems, 24*(7), 563–571. doi:10.1016/S0142-0615(01)00067-9

Abido, M. A. (2005, February). Analysis and assessment of STATCOM-Based damping stabilizers for power system stability enhancement. *Electric Power Systems Research, 73*(2), 177–185. doi:10.1016/j.epsr.2004.08.002

Abido, M. A., & Abdel-Magid, Y. L. (2007). Dynamic Stability Enhancement of East-Central System in Saudi Arabia via PSS Tuning. *Arabian Journal of Science and Engineering, 32*, 85–99.

Ahmed, G. S. (2000). *Adaptive fuzzy logic controllers for multimachine power systems.* Unpublished doctoral dissertation, Faculty of Electrical Engineering, Minufiya University.

Ahmed, A. A., Lambert-Torres, E. G., & Zambroni de Souza, A. C. (2005). A hybrid Particle Swarm Optimization applied to Loss Power minimization. *IEEE Transactions on Power Systems, 20*(2), 859–866. doi:10.1109/TPWRS.2005.846049

Alam, M., Claviez, M., Oesterhelt, D., & Kessel, M. (1984). Flagella and motility behavior of square bacteria. *The EMBO Journal, 13*(12), 2899–2903.

Altshuler, Y., Bruckstein, A. M., & Wagner, I. A. (2005). Swarm robotics for a dynamic clearning problem. In *Proceedings of the IEEE Swarm Intelligence Symposium* (pp. 209-216).

Ambriz-Perez, H., Acha, E., & Fuerte-Esquivel, C. R. (2000). Advanced SVC models for Newton–Raphson load flow and Newton optimal power flow studies. *IEEE Transactions on Power Systems, 15*(1), 129–136. doi:10.1109/59.852111

Ambriz-Perez, H., Acha, E., Fuerte-Esquivel, C. R., & De la Torre, A. (1998). Incorporation of a UPFC model in an optimal power flow using Newton's method. *IEE Proceedings. Generation, Transmission and Distribution, 145*(3), 336–344. doi:10.1049/ip-gtd:19981944

Ambrosino, G., Ariola, M., Ciniglio, U., Corraro, F., Lellis, E. D., & Pironti, A. (2009). Path Generation and Tracking in 3-D for UAVs. *IEEE Transactions on Control Systems Technology, 17*(4), 980–988. doi:10.1109/TCST.2009.2014359

Androutsopoulos, I., Koutsias, J., Chandrinos, K. V., & Spyropoulos, C. D. (2000). An experimental comparison of naive bayesian and keyword-based anti-spam filtering with personal e-mail messages. In *Proceedings of the 23rd Annual International ACM SIGIR Conference on Research and Development in Information Retrieval* (pp. 160-167).

Androutsopoulos, I., Koutsias, J., Chandrinos, K. V., Paliouras, G., & Spyropoulos, C. D. (2000). *An evaluation of naive bayesian anti-spam filtering.* Paper presented at the European Conference on Machine Learning (ECML'00).

Armitage, J. P. (1999). Bacterial Tactic Responses. *Advances in Microbial Physiology, 41*, 229–290. doi:10.1016/S0065-2911(08)60168-X

Attaviriyanupap, P., Kita, H., Tanaka, E., & Hasegawa, J. (2002). A Hybrid EP and SQP for dynamic economic dispatch with non smooth fuel cost function. *IEEE Transactions on Power Systems, 17*(2). doi:10.1109/TPWRS.2002.1007911

Balch, T., & Arkin, R. C. (1998). Behavior-based formation control for multi-agent teams. *IEEE Transactions on Robotics and Automation, 14*(6), 926–939. doi:10.1109/70.736776

Bamasak, S., & Abido, M. (2004, November). Effectiveness of Series Compensation On Power System Stability Enhancement. *GCC-Cigre Conference, 1*, 65-71.

Baskar, S., & Suganthan, P. (2004). A novel concurrent particle swarm optimization. In Proceedings of the Congress on Evolutionary Computation, Portland, OR (pp. 792-796).

Basu, M. (2008). Optimal power flow with FACTS devices using differential evolution. *International Journal of Electrical Power & Energy Systems, 30*, 150–156. doi:10.1016/j.ijepes.2007.06.011

Benabid, R., Boudour, M., & Abido, M. A. (2009). Optimal location and setting of SVC and TCSC devices using non-dominated sorting particle swarm optimization. *Electric Power Systems Research, 79*(12), 1668–1677. doi:10.1016/j.epsr.2009.07.004

Berg, H. C. (1993). *Random Walks in Biology, New Expanded Edition*. Princeton, NJ: Princeton University Press.

Berg, H. C. (2000). Motile Behavior of Bacteria. *Physics Today*, 24–29. doi:10.1063/1.882934

Berg, H. C., & Brown, D. A. (1972). Chemotaxis in *Escherichia coli* Analysed by Three-Dimensional Tracking. *Nature, 239*, 500–504. doi:10.1038/239500a0

Bergh, F. V. D., & Engelbrecht, A. P. (2004). A cooperative approach to particle swarm optimization. *IEEE Transactions on Evolutionary Computation, 8*, 225–239. doi:10.1109/TEVC.2004.826069

Bergh, F. v., & Engelbrecht, A. P. (2004). A cooperative approach to particle swarm optimization. *IEEE Transactions on Evolutionary Computation*, 225–239. doi:10.1109/TEVC.2004.826069

Berman, S., Halasz, A., Kumar, V., & Pratt, S. (2007). Bio-inspired group behaviors for the deployment of a swarm of robots to multiple destinations. In *Proceedings of the IEEE International Conference on Robotics and Automation* (pp. 2318-2323). Piscataway, NJ: IEEE Press.

Bezerra, G. B., Barra, T. V., et al. (2006). *An immunological filter for spam*. Paper presented at the International Conference on Artificial Immune Systems (ICARIS'06).

Bhasaputra, P., & Ongsakul, W. (2002). Optimal Power Flow with Multi-type of FACTS Devices by Hybrid TS/SA Approach. In *Proceedings of IEEE ICIT '02*, Bangkok, Thailand (pp. 285-290).

Binetti, P., Ariyur, K. B., Krstic, M., & Bernelli, F. (2003). Formation flight optimization using extremum seeking feedback. *Journal of Guidance, Control, and Dynamics, 26*(1), 132–142. doi:10.2514/2.5024

Biswas, A., Dasgupta, S., Das, S., & Abraham, A. (2008). Synergy of PSO and Bacterial Foraging Optimization--A Comparative Study on Numerical Benchmarks. *Advances in Soft Computing. Innovations in Hybrid Intelligent Systems, 44*, 255–263. doi:10.1007/978-3-540-74972-1_34

Blackwell, T., & Richer, T. J. (2006). The Lévy particle swarm. In *Proceedings of the IEEE Congress on Evolutionary Computation (CEC '06)*, Vancouver, BC, Canada (pp. 808-815). Washington, DC: IEEE Computer Society.

Blackwell, T. M. (2005). Particle swarms and population diversity. *Soft Computing, 9*(11), 793–802. doi:10.1007/s00500-004-0420-5

Blake, W., & Multhopp, D. (1998). Design, performance and modeling considerations for close formation flight. In *Proceedings of AIAA Guidance, Navigation, and Control Conference*, Reston, VA (pp. 476-486).

Blat, Y., & Eisenbach, M. (1995). Tar-Dependent and Independent Pattern Formation by *Salmonella typhimurium*. *Journal of Bacteriology, 177*, 1683–1691.

Bollen, M. H. J. (2001). *Understanding Power Quality Problems: Voltage Sags and Interruptions*. Washington, DC: IEEE Press.

Bonabeau, E., Dorigo, M., & Theraulaz, G. (1999). *Swarm Intelligence: From Natural to Artificial Systems*. New York: Oxford University Press.

Bonabeau, E., Theralauz, G., Deneubourg, J. L., & Camazine, S. (1997). Self-organization in social insects. *Trends in Ecology & Evolution, 12*(5), 188–193. doi:10.1016/S0169-5347(97)01048-3

Botee, H. M., & Bonabeau, E. (1998). Evolving ant colony optimization. *Advances in Complex Systems, 1*, 149–159. doi:10.1142/S0219525998000119

Brandstatter, B., & Baumgartner, U. (2002). Particle swarm optimization mass-spring system analogon. *IEEE Transactions on Magnetics, 38*(2), 997–1000. doi:10.1109/20.996256

Bratton, D., & Kennedy, J. (2007). Defining a standard for particle swarm optimization. In *Proceedings of the IEEE Swarm Intelligence Symposium* (pp. 120-127). Washington, DC: IEEE Computer Society.

Brits, R., Engelbrecht, A. P., & Bergh, F. v. (2007). Locating multiple optima using particle swarm optimization. *Applied Mathematics and Computation, 189*(2), 1859–1883. doi:10.1016/j.amc.2006.12.066

Britton, N. F., Franks, N. R., Pratt, S. C., & Seeley, T. D. (2002). Deciding on a new home: how do honey bees agree? *Proceedings. Biological Sciences, 269*, 1383–1388. doi:10.1098/rspb.2002.2001

Budrene, E. O., & Berg, H. C. (1995a). Complex Patterns Formed by Motile Cells of *Escherichia coli. Nature, 349*, 630–633. doi:10.1038/349630a0

Budrene, E. O., & Berg, H. C. (1995b). Dynamics of formation of symmetrical patterns by chemotactic bacteria. *Nature, 376*, 49–53. doi:10.1038/376049a0

Burns, R. M., & Gibson, C. A. (1975). Optimization of priority lists for a unit commitment program. In *Proceedings of the IEEE Power Engineering Society summer meeting* (Vol. 75, pp. 453-1).

Busemeyer, J. R., & Townsend, J. T. (1993). Decision field theory: A dynamic-cognitive approach to decision making in an uncertain environment. *Psychological Review, 100*(3), 432–459. doi:10.1037/0033-295X.100.3.432

Buzogany, L. E., Pachter, M., & D'Azzo, J. J. (1993). Automated control of aircraft in formation flight. In *Proceedings of AIAA Guidance, Navigation and Control Conference,* Monterey, CA (pp. 1349-1370).

Cai, L. J., & Erlich, I. (2003). Optimal choice and allocation of FACTS devices using genetic algorithms. In *Proceedings on Twelfth Intelligent Systems Application to Power Systems Conference* (pp.1-6).

Cai, Z., & Wang, Y. (2006). A multiobjective optimization-based evolutionary algorithm for constrained optimization. *IEEE Transactions on Evolutionary Computation, 10*(6), 658–674. doi:10.1109/TEVC.2006.872344

Camazine, S., Deneubourg, J. L., Franks, N. R., Sneyd, J., Gheraulaz, G., & Bonabeau, E. (2001). *Self-organization in biological systems. Princeton Studies in Complexity.* Princeton, NJ: Princeton University Press.

Camazine, S., Visscher, P. K., Finley, J., & Vetter, R. S. (1999). House-hunting by honey bee swarms: collective decisions and individual behaviors. *Insectes Sociaux, 46*, 348–360. doi:10.1007/s000400050156

Campana, E. F., Fasano, G., & Pinto, A. (2006). Dynamic system analysis and initial particles position in particle swarm optimization. In *Proceedings of the IEEE Swarm Intelligence Symposium*, Indianapolis, IN.

Campana, E. F., Fasano, G., Peri, D., & Pinto, A. (2006). Particle swarm optimization: Efficient globally convergent modifications. In *Proceedings of the III European Conference on Computational Mechanics: Solids, Structures and Coupled Problems in Engineering* (pp. 412). New York: Springer.

Castro, L. N. D. (2002). Learning and optimization using the clonal selection principle. *IEEE Transactions on Evolutionary Computation, 6*, 239–251. doi:10.1109/TEVC.2002.1011539

Castro, L. N. D., & Timmis, J. I. (2003). Artificial immune system as a novel soft computing paradigm. *Soft Computing Journal, 7*(8), 526–544.

Chang, C.-C., & Lin, C.-J. (2001). *LIBSVM: a Library for Support Vector Machines.* Retrieved from http://www.csie.ntu.edu.tw/~cjlin/libsvm

Chang, J., & Chow, J. (1997). Time Optimal Series Capacitor Control for Damping Inter-Area Modes in Interconnected Power Systems. *IEEE Trans. PWRS, 12*(1), 215–221.

Chen, J., Qin, Z., Liu, Y., & Lu, J. (2005). Particle swarm optimization with local search. In *Proceedings of the IEEE International Conference on Neural Networks and Brains* (pp. 481-484).

Chen, X., Annakkage, U., & Kumble, C. (1995). Controlled Series Compensation for Improving the Stability of Multi-machine Power Systems. In. *Proceedings of the IEEE Part C, 142*, 361–366.

Cheney, E. W., & Kincaid, D. R. (2003). *Numerical mathematics and computing* (5th ed.). Salt Lake City, UT: Brooks Cole.

Cheng, C. P., Liu, C. W., & Liu, C. C. (2000). Unit Commitment by Lagrangian Relaxation and Genetic algorithms. *IEEE Transactions on Power Systems, 15*(2), 707–713. doi:10.1109/59.867163

Chen, Y. M., & Chang, S. H. (2008). An agent-based simulation for multi-UAVs coordinative sensing. *International Journal of Intelligent Computing and Cybernetics, 1*(2), 269–284. doi:10.1108/17563780810874744

Chialvo, D. R., & Millonas, M. M. (1995). How swarms build cognitive maps. In Steels, L. (Ed.), *The Biology and Technology of Intelligent Autonomous Agents* (Vol. 144, pp. 439–450). New York: Springer.

Choi, S. S., Li, B. H., & Vilathgamuwa, D. M. (2000). Dynamic voltage restoration with minimum energy injection. *IEEE Transactions on Power Systems, 15*(1), 51–57. doi:10.1109/59.852100

Choi, S. S., Li, J. D., & Vilathgamuwa, D. M. (2005). A generalized voltage compensation strategy for mitigating the impacts of voltage sags/swells. *IEEE Transactions on Power Delivery, 20*(3), 2289–2297. doi:10.1109/TPWRD.2005.848442

Chowdhury, D., Nishinari, K., & Schadschneider, A. (2004). Self-organized patterns and traffic flow in colonies of organisms from bacteria and social insects to vertebrates. *Phase Transitions, 77*, 601–624. doi:10.1080/01411590410001672567

Christie, R. D., Wollenberg, B., & Wangensteen, I. (2000). Transmission congestion management in the deregulated environment. *Proceedings of the IEEE, 88*(2), 170–195. doi:10.1109/5.823997

Chung, T. S., & Li, Y. Z. (2001). A hybrid GA approach for OPF with consideration of FACTS devices. *IEEE Power Engineering Review, 21*(2), 47–50. doi:10.1109/39.896822

Clark, J., Koprinska, I., & Poon, J. (2003). A neural network based approach to automated e-mail classification. In *Proceedings of the IEEE International Conference on Web Intelligence (WI'03)* (pp. 702-705).

Clerc, M. (1999). The swarm and the queen: Toward a deterministic and adaptive particle swarm optimization. In *Proceedings of the IEEE International Conference on Evolutionary Computation* (pp. 1951-1957).

Clerc, M. (2001). *PSO: the old bias and its solution.* Retrieved April 28, 2010, from http://clerc.maurice.free.fr/pso/

Clerc, M. (2003, October). *TRIBES - Un exemple d'optimisation par essaim particulaire sans paramètres de contrôle.* Paper presented at OEP'03 (Optimisation par Essaim Particulaire), Paris, France.

Clerc, M. (2006a). Particle Swarm Optimization. *ISTE. International Scientific and Technical Encyclopedia.* doi:10.1002/9780470612163

Clerc, M. (2006b). *Stagnation analysis in particle swarm optimization or what happens when nothing happens.* Retrieved July 25, 2010, from http://hal.archives-ouvertes.fr/hal-00122031

Clerc, M. (2010). *Balanced PSO, variable PSO.* Retrieved July 23, 2010, from http://clerc.maurice.free.fr/pso/

Clerc, M., & Kennedy, J. (2002). The Particle Swarm - Explosion, Stability, and Convergence in a Multidimensional Complex Space. *IEEE Transactions on Evolutionary Computation, 6*(1), 58–73. doi:10.1109/4235.985692

Clerc, M., & Kennedy, J. (2002). The particle swarm - explosion, stability, and convergence in a multidimensional complex space. *IEEE Transactions on Evolutionary Computation, 6*(1), 58–73. doi:10.1109/4235.985692

Coello Coello, C. A., Toscano Pulido, G., & Lechuga, M. S. (2004). Handling multiple objectives with particle swarm optimization. *IEEE Transactions on Evolutionary Computation, 8*(3), 256–279. doi:10.1109/TEVC.2004.826067

Cohen, A. I., & Yoshimura, M. (1983). A branch-and-bound algorithm for unit commitment. *IEEE Transactions on Power Apparatus and Systems, 2*, 444–451. doi:10.1109/TPAS.1983.317714

Conejo, A. J., Milano, F., & Garcia-Bertrand, R. (2006). Congestion management ensuring voltage stability. *IEEE Transactions on Power Systems, 21*(1), 357–364. doi:10.1109/TPWRS.2005.860910

Conradie, A. V. E., Miikkulainen, R., & Aldrich, C. (2002). Adaptive control utilizing neural swarming. In *Proceedings of the Genetic and Evolutionary Computation Conference,* New York.

Constantinides, C., Parkinson, P., & River, W. (2008). Security challenges in UAV development. In *Proceedings of the IEEE/AAA 27th Digital Avionics Systems Conference (DASC 2008)*, Saint Paul, MN (pp. 1-8).

Cooren, Y., Clerc, M., & Siarry, P. (2009). Performance evaluation of TRIBES, an adaptive particle swarm optimization algorithm. *Swarm Intelligence, 3*, 149–178. doi:10.1007/s11721-009-0026-8

Correll, N., & Martinoli, A. (2007). Robust decentralized coverage using a swarm of miniature robots. In *Proceedings of the IEEE International Conference on Robotics and Automation* (pp. 379-384).

Cuello-Reyna, & Jose, R. (2005). OPF framework for congestion management in deregulated environments using differential evolution. *International Journal of Power and Energy Systems,* 127-133.

Cushman, D. L. (2007). *A particle swarm approach to constrained optimization informed by 'Global Worst'.* Unpublished doctoral dissertation, Pennsylvania State University.

Damousis, I. G., Bakirtzis, A. G., & Dokopoulos, P. S. (2004). A solution to the Unit Commitment Problem using Integer-Coded Genetic Algorithm. *IEEE Transactions on Power Systems, 19*(2), 1165–1172. doi:10.1109/TPWRS.2003.821625

Dargan, J. L., Pachter, M., & D'Azzo, J. J. (1992). Automatic formation flight control. In *Proceedings of AIAA Guidance, Navigation and Control Conference,* Hilton Head Island, SC (pp. 838-857).

Dasgupta, D., & Attoh-Okine, N. (1997). Immunity-based systems: A survey. In *Proceedings of the IEEE International Conference on Systems, Man, and Cybernetics.*

Deb, K., Pratap, A., Agarwal, S., & Meyarivan, T. (2002). A fast and elitist multiobjective genetic algorithm: NSGA-II. *IEEE Transactions on Evolutionary Computation, 6*(2), 182–197. doi:10.1109/4235.996017

DeJong, K. A., Spears, W. M., & Gordon, D. F. (1995). Using Markov chains to analyze GAFOs. In *Foundations of Genetic Algorithms 3* (pp. 115–137). San Francisco, CA: Morgan Kaufmann.

Dekrajangpetch, S., Sheble, G. B., & Conejo, A. J. (1999). Auction implementation problems using Lagrangian relaxation. *IEEE Transactions on Power Systems, 14*, 82–88. doi:10.1109/59.744488

Dillon, T. S., Edwin, K. W., Kochs, H. D., & Taud, R. J. (1978). Integer programming approach to the problem of optimal unit commitment with probabilistic reserve determination. *IEEE Transactions on Power Apparatus and Systems, 6*, 2154–2166. doi:10.1109/TPAS.1978.354719

Doctor, S., Venayagamoorthy, G., & Gudise, V. (2004, June 19-23). Optimal PSO for Collective Robotic Search Applications. In *Proceedings of the IEEE Congress on Evolutionary Computation*, Portland, OR (pp. 1390-1395).

Dorigo, M., Di Caro, G., & Gambardella, L. M. (1999). Ant Algorithms for Distributed Discrete Optimization. *Artificial Life, 5*(3), 137–172. doi:10.1162/106454699568728

Dorigo, M., & Gambardella, L. M. (1997). Ant colony system: a cooperative learning approach to the traveling salesman. *IEEE Transactions on Evolutionary Computation, 1*(1), 53–65. doi:10.1109/4235.585892

Dorigo, M., Maniezzo, V., & Colorni, A. (1996). Ant system: optimization by a colony of cooperating agents. *IEEE Transactions on Systems, Man, and Cybernetics, 26*(1), 29–41. doi:10.1109/3477.484436

Dorigo, M., Tuci, E., Trianni, V., Groß, R., Nouyan, S., & Ampatzis, C. (2006). SWARM-BOT: Design and implementation of colonies of self-assembling robots. In Yen, G. Y., & Fogel, D. B. (Eds.), *Computational intelligence: Principles and practice* (pp. 103–135). New York: IEEE Computational Intelligence Society.

Drucker, H., Burges, C. J. C., Kauffman, L., Smola, A., & Vapnik, V. N. (1997). Support vector regression machines. *Advances in Neural Information Processing Systems, 9,* 155–161.

Drucker, H., Wu, D., & Vapnik, V. N. (1999). Support vector machines for spam categorization. *IEEE Transactions on Neural Networks, 10,* 1048–1054. doi:10.1109/72.788645

Duan, H. B., Liu, S. Q., Wang, D. B., & Yu, X. F. (2009). Design and realization of hybrid ACO-based PID and LuGre friction compensation controller for three degree-of-freedom high precision flight simulator. *Simulation Modelling Practice and Theory, 17*(6), 1160–1169. doi:10.1016/j.simpat.2009.04.006

Duan, H. B., Ma, G. J., & Luo, D. L. (2008). Optimal formation reconfiguration control of multiple UCAVs using improved particle swarm optimization. *Journal of Bionics Engineering, 5*(4), 340–347. doi:10.1016/S1672-6529(08)60179-1

Dukas, R. (Ed.). (1998). *Cognitive Ecology*. Chicago: University of Chicago Press.

Dutta, P., & Sinha, A. K. (2006). Voltage Stability constrained Multi-objective Optimal Power Flow using Particle Swarm Optimization. In *Proceedings of the First International Conference on Industrial and Information Systems* (pp. 161-166).

Dutta, S., & Singh, S. P. (2008). Optimal Rescheduling of Generators for Congestion Management based on Particle Swarm Optimization. *IEEE Transactions on Power Systems, 23*(4), 1560–1569. doi:10.1109/TPWRS.2008.922647

Eberhart, R. C., & Kennedy, J. (1995). A new optimizer using particle swarm theory. In *Proceedings of the 6th International Symposium on Mcro Machine Human Science* (pp. 39-43).

Eberhart, R. C., & Shi, Y. (1998). Comparison between Genetic Algorithm and Particle swarm optimization. In *Proceedings of 7th annual conference on evolutionary programming VII,* San Diego, CA (pp. 611-616).

Eberhart, R., & Shi, Y. (2000). Comparing inertia weights and constriction factors in particle swarm optimization. In *Proceedings of the Congress on Evolutionary Computation* (pp. 84-88).

Eberhart, R., Shi, Y., & Kennedy, J. (2001). *Swarm Intelligence.* San Francisco, CA: Morgan Kaufmann.

El-Abd, M., & Kamel, M. S. (2006). A hierarchal cooperative particle swarm optimizer. In *Proceedings of the Swarm Intelligence Symposium* (pp. 43-47).

Esmin, A., Aoki, A., & Torres, G. (2004). *Particle swarm optimization versus genetic algorithms for fitting fuzzy membership functions.*

Espi'e, E., & Guionneau, C. (2008). *TORCS: The open racing car simulator.* Retrieved May 7, 2009, from http://torcs.sourceforge.net/

Feliachi, A., & Yang, X. (1994, December). Identification and Control of Inter-Area Modes. In *Proceedings of the 33rd Conference on Decision and Control,* FL (pp. 4061-4066).

Ferguson, T. S. (1996). *A course in large sample theory.* Boca Raton, FL: Chapman and Hall/CRC.

Fisher, M. L. (1981). The Lagrangian relaxation method for solving integer programming problems. *Management Science, 27,* 1–18. doi:10.1287/mnsc.27.1.1

Fiszelew, A., Britos, P., Ochoa, A., Merlino, H., Fernández, E., & García-Martínez, R. (2007). Finding optimal neural network architecture using genetic algorithms. *Research in Computing Science, 27,* 15–24.

Franchi, A., Freda, L., Oriolo, G., & Vendittelli, M. (2007). A randomized strategy for cooperative robot exploration. In *Proceedings of the IEEE International Conference on Robotics and Automation,* Rome, Italy (pp. 768-774).

Franks, N. R. (1989). Army ants: A collective intelligence. *American Scientist, 77,* 138–145.

Franks, N. R., Dornhaus, A., Fitzsimmons, J. P., & Stevens, M. (2003). Speed versus accuracy in collective decision making. *Proceedings. Biological Sciences, 270,* 2457–2463. doi:10.1098/rspb.2003.2527

Fuerte-Esquivel, C. R., Acha, E., & Ambriz-Perez, H. (2000). Integrated SVC and step-down transformer model for Newton–Raphson load flow studies. *IEEE Power Engineering Review, 20*(2), 45–46. doi:10.1109/39.819916

Fuerte-Esquivel, C. R., Acha, E., & Ambriz-Perez, H. A. (2000). Comprehensive Newton–Raphson UPFC model for the quadratic power flow solution of practical power networks. *IEEE Transactions on Power Systems, 15*(1), 102–109. doi:10.1109/59.852107

Fuerte-Esquivel, C. R., Acha, E., Tan, S. G., & Rico, J. J. (1998). Efficient object oriented power system software for the analysis of large-scale networks containing FACTS-controlled branches. *IEEE Transactions on Power Systems, 13*(2), 464–472. doi:10.1109/59.667370

Gacôgne, L. (2002). Steady state evolutionary algorithm with an operator family. In *Proceedings of EISCI* (pp. 373-379), Kosice, Slovakia.

Gaing, Z., & Huang, H. S. (2004). Real-coded mixed integer genetic algorithm for constrained optimal power flow. *In IEEE TENCON Region 10 conference* (pp. 323-326).

Gama, C., et al. (1998). *Brazilian North-South Interconnection – Application of Thyristor Controlled Series Compensation (TCSC) to Damp Inter-Area Oscillation Mode*. Paris: Cigré 37 Session.

Garg, P., & Kumar, M. (2002). Genetic algorithm based PD control and fuzzy logic control of a two link robot. In *Proceedings of IMECCE'02, ASME International Mechanical Engineering Congress & Exposition,* New Orleans, LA (pp. 1-8).

Gargari, E. A., Hashemzadeh, F., Rajabioun, R., & Lucas, C. (2008). Colonial competitive algorithm: a novel approach for PID controller design in MIMO distillation column process. *International Journal of Intelligent Computing and Cybernetics, 1*(3), 337–355. doi:10.1108/17563780810893446

Garver, L. L. (1963). Power generation scheduling by integer programming development of theory. *IEEE Transactions on Power Apparatus and Systems, 6*, 730–735.

Gazzaniga, M. S., Ivry, R. B., & Mangun, J. R. (1998). *Cognitive Neuroscience: The Biology of the Mind*. New York: W. W. Norton and Co.

Ge, H. W., Lu, Y. H., Zhou, Y., Guo, X. C., & Liang, Y. C. (2005). A particle swarm optimization-based algorithm for job-shop scheduling problem. *International Journal of Computational Methods, 2*(3), 419–430. doi:10.1142/S0219876205000569

Ge, S. Y., & Chung, T. S. (1998). Optimal active flow incorporating FACTS devices with power flow control constraints. *International Journal of Electrical Power & Energy Systems, 20*(5), 321–326. doi:10.1016/S0142-0615(97)00081-1

Ghosh, A., & Ledwich, G. (2001). Structures and control of dynamic voltage restorer. *Power Engineering Society Winter Meeting, 3*, 1027-1032.

Ghosh, A., & Ledwich, G. (2002). *Power Quality Enhancement Using Custom Power Devices*. Dordrecht, The Netherlands: Kluwer.

Ghoshal, S. P., Chatterjee, A., & Mukherjee, V. (2009). Bio-inspired fuzzy logic based tuning of Power system stabilizer. *Expert Systems with Applications, 36*(5), 9281–9292. doi:10.1016/j.eswa.2008.12.004

Goel, A., Saxena, S., & Bhanot, S. (2005). A genetic based neuro-fuzzy controller for thermal processes. *Journal of Computer Science & Technology, 5*(1).

Goldberg, D. E. (1989). *Genetic Algorithms in Search, Optimization and Machine Learning*. Reading, MA: Addison-Wesley.

Greene, M., & Gordon, D. (2007). How patrollers set foraging direction in harvester ants. *American Naturalist, 170*, 943–948. doi:10.1086/522843

Guo, H., Meng, Y., & Jin, Y. (2009). A Cellular Mechanism for Multi-Robot Construction via Evolutionary Multi-Objective Optimization of a Gene Regulatory Network. *Bio Systems, 98*(3), 193–203. doi:10.1016/j.biosystems.2009.05.003

Halasz, A., Hsieh, M. A., Berman, S., & Kumar, V. (2007). Dynamic Redistribution of a Swarm of Robots Among Multiple Sites. In *Proceedings of the 2007 IEEE/RSJ International Conference on Intelligent Robots and Systems*.

Hansen, N., Ros, R., Mauny, N., Schoenauer, M., & Auger, A. (2008). *PSO facing non-separable and ill-conditioned problems* (Tech. Rep. No. 6447). Institut National de Recherche en Informatique et en Automatique (INRIA).

Hastie, R., & Kameda, T. (2005). The robust beauty of majority rules in group decisions. *Psychological Review*, *112*(2), 494–508. doi:10.1037/0033-295X.112.2.494

Hastie, T., Tibshirani, R., & Friedman, J. (2001). *The elements of statistical learning*. New York, NY: Springer-Verlag.

Hazra, J., & Avinash Sinha, K. (2007). Congestion Management using multi objective Particle Swarm Optimization. *IEEE Transactions on Power Systems*, *22*(4), 1726–1734. doi:10.1109/TPWRS.2007.907532

Helwig, S., & Wanka, R. (2007). Particle Swarm Optimization in High-Dimensional Bounded Search Spaces. In *Proceedings of the IEEE Swarm Intelligence Symposium* (pp.198-205). Washington, DC: IEEE Computer Society.

Helwig, S., & Wanka, R. (2008). Theoretical analysis of initial particle swarm behavior. In *Proceedings of the 10th International Conference on Parallel Problem Solving from Nature (PPSN 2008)*, Dortmund, Germany (pp. 889-898). Berlin: Springer.

Helwig, S., Haubelt, C., & Teich, J. (2005). Modeling and analysis of indirect communication in particle swarm optimization. In *Proceedings of the 2005 IEEE Congress on Evolutionary Computation*, Edinburgh, UK (pp. 1246-1253).

He, Q., & Wang, L. (2007). A hybrid particle swarm optimization with a feasibility-based rule for constrained optimization. *Applied Mathematics and Computation*, *186*, 1407–1422. doi:10.1016/j.amc.2006.07.134

Hettiarachchi, S. (2007). *Distributed evolution for swarm robotics*. Unpublished doctoral dissertation, University of Wyoming, Laramie, WY.

Hingorani, N. G. (1995). Introducing custom power. *IEEE Spectrum*, 41–48. doi:10.1109/6.387140

Hinsz, V. B., Tindale, R. S., & Vollrath, D. A. (1997). The emerging conceptualization of groups as information processors. *Psychological Bulletin*, *121*(1), 43–64. doi:10.1037/0033-2909.121.1.43

Hiyama, T., et al. (1995). Coordinated Fuzzy Logic Contrl for Series Capacitor Modules and PSS to Enhance Stability of Power System. *IEEE Transactions on Power Delivery*, *10*(2), 1098–1104. doi:10.1109/61.400877

Hjalmarsson, H., Gevers, M., Gunnarsson, S., & Lequin, O. (1998). Iterative feedback tuning: theory and applications. *IEEE Control Systems Magazine*, *18*(4), 26–41. doi:10.1109/37.710876

Holland, O. E., & Melhuish, C. (1999). Stigmergy, self-organization, and sorting in collective robotics. *Artificial Life*, *5*, 173–202. doi:10.1162/106454699568737

Hölldobler, B., & Wilson, E. O. (1990). *The Ants*. Cambridge, MA: Belknap Press of Harvard University Press.

Hölldobler, B., & Wilson, E. O. (2008). *The Superorganism: The Beauty, Elegance, and Strangeness of Insect Societies*. New York: W.W. Norton and Co.

Hsiang, T., Arkin, E., Bender, M., Fekete, S., & Mitchell, J. (2007). *Algorithms for rapidly dispersing robot swarms in unknown environments*.

Hsu, Y. Y., & Chen, C. L. (1987, May). Identification of optimum location for stabilizer applications using participation factors. In. *Proceedings of the IEEE Part C*, *134*(3), 238–244.

Hu, X., & Eberhart, R. (2002). Multiobjective optimization using dynamic neighborhood particle swarm optimization. In *Proceedings of the Congress on Evolutionary Computation IEEE Service Center*, Piscataway, NJ (pp. 1677-1681).

Huang, V. L., Suganathan, P. N., Qin, A. K., & Baskar, S. (2005). *Multiobjective differential evolution with external archive and harmonic distance-based diversity measure* (Tech. Rep. MODE-2005). Singapore: Nanyang Technological University.

Hub, J., Payne, W., & Puto, C. (1982). Adding asymmetrically dominated alternatives: Violations of regularity and the similarity hypothesis. *The Journal of Consumer Research*, *9*, 90–98. doi:10.1086/208899

Hu, X. B., Chen, W. H., & Paolo, E. D. (2007). Multiairport capacity management: genetic algorithm with receding horizon. *IEEE Transactions on Intelligent Systems*, *8*(2), 254–263. doi:10.1109/TITS.2006.890067

Ippolito, L., Cortiglia, A. L., & Petrocelli, M. (2006). Optimal allocation of FACTS devices by using multi-objective optimal power flow and genetic algorithms. *International Journal of Emerging Electric Power Systems*, *7*(2). doi:10.2202/1553-779X.1099

Ismael, A. I. F., Pereira, A. I. P. N., & Fernandes, E. M. G. P. (2005). Particle swarm and simulated annealing for multi-global optimization. *WSEAS Transactions on Information Science and Applications, 2*, 534–539.

Jang, J. S. R. (1993). ANFIS: adaptive-network-based fuzzy inference system. *IEEE Transactions on Systems, Man, and Cybernetics, 23*(3), 665–685. doi:10.1109/21.256541

Janson, S., & Middendorf, M. (2007). On trajectories of particles in PSO. In *IEEE Swarm Intelligence Symposium* (pp. 150-155).

Janson, S., & Middendorf, M. (2005). A hierarchical particle swarm optimizer and its adaptive variant. IEEE Trans on Systems, Man, and Cybernetics-Part B. *Cybernetics, 35*(6), 1272–1282.

Janson, S., Middendorf, M., & Beekman, M. (2007). Searching for a new home–scouting behavior of honeybee swarms. *Behav Ecol, 18*, 384–392. doi:10.1093/beheco/arl095

Jatmiko, W., Sekiyama, K., & Fukuda, E. (2006). A PSO-based Mobile Sensor Network for Odor Source Localization in Dynamic Environment: Theory, Simulation and Measurement. In *Proceedings of the IEEE Congress on Evolutionary Computation*, Vancouver, Canada (pp. 1036-1043).

Jowder, F. A. L. (2007). Modeling and simulation of Dynamic Voltage Restorer (DVR) based on Hysteresis Voltage Control. In *Proceedings of the Industrial Electronics Society, IECON 2007, 33rd Annual conference of IEEE* (pp. 1726-1731).

Juste, K. A., Kita, H., Tanaka, E., & Hasegawa, J. (1999). An Evolutionary Programming Solution to the Unit Commitment Problem. *IEEE Transactions on Power Systems, 14*, 1452–1459. doi:10.1109/59.801925

Kadirkamanathan, K. S. V., & Fleming, P. J. (2006). Stability analysis of the particle dynamics in particle swarm optimizer. *IEEE Transactions on Evolutionary Computation, 10*(3), 245–255. doi:10.1109/TEVC.2005.857077

Kandel, E. K., Schwartz, J. H., & Jessell, T. M. (Eds.). (2000). *Principles of neural science*. New York: McGraw-Hill.

Kazarlis, A., Bakirtzis, A. G., & Petridis, V. (1996). A Genetic Algorithm Solution to the Unit Commitment Problem. *IEEE Transactions on Power Systems, 11*(1), 83–92. doi:10.1109/59.485989

Kearns, M., & Vazirani, U. (1994). *An introduction to computational learning theory*. Cambridge, MA: The MIT Press.

Kennedy, J. (1997). The particle swarm: Social adaption of knowledge. In *Proceedings of the IEEE International Conference on Evolutionary Computation.*

Kennedy, J. (2007). *Personal communication with Dr. W. Spears.*

Kennedy, J., & Eberhart, R. (1995). Particle swarm optimization. In *Proceedings of the IEEE International Conference on Neural Networks* (pp. 1942-1948).

Kennedy, J., & Eberhart, R. C. (1995). Particle Swarm Optimization. In Proceedings of the IEEE Intl. Conf. Neural Network IV (pp. 1942-1948).

Kennedy, J., & Mendes, R. (2002). Population structure and particle swarm performance. In *Proceedings of the IEEE Congress on Evolutionary Computation* (pp. 1671-1676).

Kennedy, J., & Spears, W. M. (1998). Matching algorithms to problems: An experimental test of the particle swarm and some genetic algorithms on the multimodal problem generator. In *Proceedings of the IEEE Congress on Evolutionary Computation* (pp. 78-83).

Kerr, N. L., & Tindale, R. S. (2004). Group performance and decision making. *Annual Review of Psychology, 55*, 623–655. doi:10.1146/annurev.psych.55.090902.142009

Khatib, O. (1986). Real-time obstacle avoidance for manipulators and mobile robots. *The International Journal of Robotics Research, 5*(1), 90–98. doi:10.1177/027836498600500106

Khoshnevis, B., & Bekey, G. A. (1998). Centralized sensing and control of multiple mobile robots. *Computers & Industrial Engineering, 35*(3-4), 503–506. doi:10.1016/S0360-8352(98)00144-2

Kim, D. H., & Cho, J. H. (2005). Adaptive Tuning of PID Controller for Multivariable System Using Bacterial Foraging Based Optimization. In *Advances in Web Intelligence* (LNCS 3528, pp. 231-235).

Kim, D. H., Abrahamb, A., & Choa, J. H. (2007). A hybrid genetic algorithm and bacterial foraging approach for global optimization. *Information Sciences*, *177*(18), 3918–3937. doi:10.1016/j.ins.2007.04.002

Kiranyaz, S., Ince, T., Yildirim, A., & Gabbouj, M. (2010). Fractional particle swarm optimization in multidimensional search space. *IEEE Transactions on Systems, Man, and Cybernetics. Part B, Cybernetics*, *40*(2), 298–319. doi:10.1109/TSMCB.2009.2015054

Kirkpatrick, S., Gelatt, C. D., & Vecchi, M. P. (1983). Optimization by simulated annealing. *Science*, *220*(4598), 671–680. doi:10.1126/science.220.4598.671

Koenig, S., Szymanski, B., & Liu, Y. (2001). Efficient and inefficient ant coverage methods. *Annals of Mathematics and Artificial Intelligence*, *31*(1-4), 41–76. doi:10.1023/A:1016665115585

Kohler, T., Gummerman, G., & Reynolds, R. G. (2005). Virtual Archaeology. *Scientific American*, *293*(1), 76–84. doi:10.1038/scientificamerican0705-76

Koprinska, I., Poon, J., Clark, J., & Chan, J. (2007). Learning to classify e-mail. *Information Science*. (n.d)., 2167–2187. doi:10.1016/j.ins.2006.12.005

Krieger, M., Billeter, J., & Keller, L. (2000). Ant-like task allocation and recruitment in cooperative agents. *Nature*, *406*, 992–995. doi:10.1038/35023164

Krink, T., & Lovbjerg, M. (2002). The LifeCycle model: Combining Particle Swarm Optimisation, Genetic Algorithms and HillClimbers. In Proceeding of the Parallel Problem Solving from Nature VII (PPSN-2002) (pp. 621-630).

Krohling, R. A., & Coelho, L. D. (2006). Coevolutionary particle swarm optimization using Gaussian distribution for solving constrained optimization problems. *IEEE Transactions on Systems, Man, and Cybernetics. Part B, Cybernetics*, *36*(6), 1407–1416. doi:10.1109/TSMCB.2006.873185

Kumar, R. A., Kumar, G. S., Kumar, B. K., & Mishra, M. K. (2009). Compensation of voltage sags with phase-jumps through DVR with minimum VA rating using PSO. In *Proceedings of TENCON 2009-2009 IEEE Region 10 conference* (pp. 1-6).

Kumar, V., & Sahin, E. (2003). Cognitive maps in swarm robots for the mine detection application. In *Proceedings of the IEEE International Conference on Systems, Man and Cybernetics* (pp. 3364-3369).

Kumar, A., Srivastava, S. C., & Singh, S. N. (2004). A zonal Congestion Management Approach using ac transmission congestion distribution factors. *Electric Power Systems Research*, *72*, 85–93. doi:10.1016/j.epsr.2004.03.011

Langdon, W., & Poli, R. (2005). Evolving problems to learn about particle swarm and other optimisers. In *Proceedings of the Congress on Evolutionary Computation* (pp. 81-88).

Laughlin, P. R., & Ellis, A. L. (1986). Demonstratability and social combination processes on mathematical intellective tasks. *Journal of Experimental Social Psychology*, *22*, 177–189. doi:10.1016/0022-1031(86)90022-3

Leiba, B., & Borenstein, N. (2004). *A multifaceted approach to spam reduction*. In Proceedings of the First Conference on Email and AntiSpam (CEAS'04).

Lennard-Jones, J. (1931). Cohesion. *Proceedings of the Physical Society*, *43*(5), 461–482. doi:10.1088/0959-5309/43/5/301

Leonard, N., & Fiorelli, E. (2001). Virtual leaders, artificial potentials and coordinated control of groups. In *Proceedings of the 40th IEEE Conference on Decision and Control* (Vol. 3, pp. 2968-2973).

Leung, H. C., & Chung, T. S. (2000). Optimal power flow with a versatile FACTS controller by genetic algorithm approach. In *Proceedings of IEEE Power Engineering Society Winter Meeting* (pp. 2806-2811.

Leung, Y.-W., & Wang, Y. (2001). An orthogonal Genetic Algorithm with quantization for global numerical optimization. *IEEE Transactions on Evolutionary Computation*, *5*(1), 41–53. doi:10.1109/4235.910464

Levine, J. M., Resnik, L. B., & Higgins, E. T. (1993). Social foundations of cognition. *Annual Review of Psychology*, *44*, 585–612. doi:10.1146/annurev.ps.44.020193.003101

Lhotská, L., Macaš, M., & Burša, M. (2006). PSO and ACO in Optimization Problems. In E. Corchado et al. (Eds.), *Intelligent Data Engineering and Automated Learning* (LNCS 4224, pp. 1390-1398).

Li, B., Liao, X. H., Sun, Z., Li, Y. H., & Song, Y. D. (2006). Robust autopilot for close Formation flight of multi-UAVs. In *Proceedings of the 38th Southeastern Symposium on System Theory,* Cookeville, TN (pp. 294-298).

Li, L. D., Li, X., & Yu, X. (2008). A multi-objective constraint-handling method with PSO algorithm for constrained engineering optimization problems. In *Proceedings of IEEE Congress on Evolutionary Computation* (pp. 1528-1535).

Li, W., & Ming, T. (1998, August). Design of a H∞ static VAr controller for the damping of generator oscillations. In *Proceedings of the 1998 International Conference on Power System Technology (POWERCON '98)* (Vol. 2, pp. 18-21, 785 -789).

Li, Y., Li, B., Sun, Z., & Song, Y. D. (2005). Fuzzy technique based close formation flight control. In *Proceedings of the 31st Annual Conference of IEEE Industrial Electronics Society,* New York (pp. 40-44).

Liang, J. J., & Suganthan, P. N. (2006). Dynamic multi-swarm particle swarm optimizer with a novel constraint-handling mechanism. In *Proceedings of IEEE Congress on Evolutionary Computation* (pp. 9-16).

Liang, J. J., Qin, A., Suganthan, P., & Baskar, S. (n.d.). Comprehensive learning particle swarm optimizer for global optimization of multimodal functions. IEEE Trans on Evolutionary Computation, 10(3), 281-295.

Liang, J. J., Runarsson, T. P., Mezura-Montes, E., Clere, M., Suganthan, P. N., Coello Coello, C. A., et al. (2006). *Problem definitions and evaluation criteria.* Paper presented at the CEC2006 special session on constrained real-parameter optimization.

Liang, J., & Suganthan, P. (2005). Dynamic multi-swarm particle swarm optimizer. In Proceedings of IEEE Swarm Intelligence Symposium, Pasadena, CA (pp. 124-129).

Liang, J. J., Qin, A. K., Suganthan, P. N., & Baskar, S. (2006). Comprehensive learning particle swarm optimizer for global optimization of multimodal functions. *IEEE Transactions on Evolutionary Computation, 10,* 281–296. doi:10.1109/TEVC.2005.857610

Lie, T., Shrestha, G., & Ghosh, A. (1995). Design and Application of Fuzzy Logic Control Scheme for Transient Stability Enhancement In Power System. *Electric Power System Research,* 17-23.

Liu, Y., Qin, Z., & Shi, Z. (2004). Hybrid particle swarm optimizer with line search. In *Proceedings of the IEEE International Conference on Systems, Man and Cybernetics* (pp. 3751-3755).

Liu, Z., Wang, C., & Li, J. (2008). Solving constrained optimization via a modified genetic particle swarm optimization. In *Proceedings of International Workshop on Knowledge Discovery and Data Mining,* Adelaide, Australia (pp. 217-220).

Liu, H., & Abraham, A. (2007). A hybrid fuzzy variable neighborhood particle swarm optimization algorithm for solving quadratic assignment problems. *Journal of Universal Computer Science, 13*(9), 1309–1331.

Liu, S. C., Tan, D. L., & Liu, G. J. (2007). Formation control of mobile robots with active obstacle avoidance. *Acta Automatica Sinica, 33*(5), 529–535.

Loiacono, D., Togelius, J., & Lanzi, P. (2009). *Software manual of the car racing competition.* Retrieved May 7, 2009, from http://voxel.dl.sourceforge.net/project/cig/Championship 2009 Manual/1.0/manual-1.0.pdf

Loiacono, D., Togelius, J., Lanzi, P., Kinnaird-Heether, L., Lucas, S., Simmerson, M., et al. (2008). Survival of the Fastest: The WCCI 2008 Simulated Car Racing Competition. In *Proceedings of the 2008 IEEE Workshop on Computational Intelligence in Games.* Washington, DC: IEEE Computer Society.

Losick, R., & Kaiser, D. (1997). Why and How Bacteria Communicate. *Scientific American, 276*(2), 68–73. doi:10.1038/scientificamerican0297-68

Lowe, G., Meister, M., & Berg, H. (1987). Rapid Rotation of Flagellar Bundles in Swimming Bacteria. *Nature, 325,* 637–640. doi:10.1038/325637a0

Lowery, P. G. (1983). Generation unit commitment by dynamic programming. *IEEE Transactions on Power Apparatus and Systems, 102*, 1218–1225.

Luce, R. D., & Suppes, P. (1965). Preference, utility, and subjective probability. In Luce, R. D., Bush, R. R., & Galanter, E. (Eds.), *Handbook of mathematical psychology* (*Vol. 3*, pp. 249–410). New York: Wiley.

Lu, H., & Chen, W. (2006). Dynamic-objective particle swarm optimization for constrained optimization problems. *Journal of Combinatorial Optimization, 2*(4), 409–419. doi:10.1007/s10878-006-9004-x

Ma, T. T. (2003). Enhancement of power transmission systems by using multiple UPFC on evolutionary programming. *In IEEE Bologna Power Tech Conference* (Vol. 4).

Magoulas, G., Eldabi, T., & Paul, R. (2002). Global search strategies for simulation optimization. In *Proceedings of the Winter Simulation Conference* (pp. 1978-1985).

Mahmoud, K. (2010). Design optimization of a bow-tie antenna for 2.45 GHz rfid readers using a hybrid bacterial swarm optimization and nelder-mead algorithm. *Progress in Electromagnetics Research, 100*, 105–117. doi:10.2528/PIER09102903

Mallon, E. B., Pratt, S. C., & Franks, N. R. (2001). Individual and collective decision-making during nest site selection by the ant *Leptothorax albipennis. Behavioral Ecology and Sociobiology, 50*, 352–359. doi:10.1007/s002650100377

Marques, L., Nunes, U., & de Almeida, A. (2006). Particle swarm-based olfactory guided search. *Autonomous Robots, 20*, 277–287. doi:10.1007/s10514-006-7567-0

Marshall, J. A., Bogacz, R., Dornhaus, A., Planque, R., Kovacs, T., & Franks, N. R. (2009, February). On optimal decision-making in brains and insect societies. *J Roy. Soc. Interface*, 1-10. doi:10.1098/rsif.2008.0511

Martinoli, A., Ijspeert, A., & Mondada, F. (1999). Understanding collective aggregation mechanisms: from probabilistic modeling to experiments with real agents. *Robotics and Autonomous Systems, 29*, 51–63. doi:10.1016/S0921-8890(99)00038-X

Martins, N., et al. (1999). *Impact of the Interaction among Power System Controls*. CIGRÈ Task Force.

Mataric, M., Nilsson, M., & Simsarian, K. (1995). Cooperative multi-agent box-pushing. In *Proceedings of the IEEE/RSJ International Conference on Intelligent Agents and Systems*.

Mathhey, L., Berman, S., & Kumar, V. (2009). Stochastic strategies for a swarm robotic assembly system. In *Proceedings of the IEEE International Conference on Robotics and Automation*.

Maxim, P., Spears, W., & Spears, D. (2009). Robotic chain formations. In *Proceedings of the IFAC Workshop on Networked Robotics (NetRob '09)* (pp. 19-24).

Mclurkin, J., & Smith, J. (2004). Decentralized algorithms for dispersion in indoor environments using a swarm of autonomous mobile robots. In *Proceedings of the 7th International Symposium on Decentralized Autonomous Robotic Systems*, Toulouse, France.

Meng, Y., & Gan, J. (2007). LIVS: Local Interaction via Virtual Stigmergy Coordination in Distributed Search and Collective Cleanup. In *Proceedings of the IEEE/RSJ International Conference on Intelligent Robots and Systems*, San Diego, CA.

Meng, Y., & Gan, J. (2008). A Distributed Swarm Intelligence based Algorithm for a Cooperative Multi-Robot Construction Task. In *Proceedings of the IEEE Swarm Intelligence Symposium*, St. Louis, MO.

Merlin, A., & Sandrin, P. (1983). A new method for unit commitment at Electricite De France. *IEEE Transactions on Power Systems, 102*, 1218–1225. doi:10.1109/TPAS.1983.318063

Mezura-Montes, E., & Coello Coello, C. A. (2006). *A survey of constraint-handling techniques based on evolutionary multiobjective optimization* (Tech. Rep. EVOCINV-04-2006). CINVESTAV-IPN.

Mezura-Montes, E., & Coello Coello, C. A. (2005). A simple multimembered evolution strategy to solve constrained optimization problems. *IEEE Transactions on Evolutionary Computation, 9*(1), 1–17. doi:10.1109/TEVC.2004.836819

Milano, F., Canizares, C. A., & Invernizzi, M. (2003). Multiobjective optimization for Pricing system security in electricity markets. *IEEE Transactions on Power Systems, 18*(2), 596–604. doi:10.1109/TPWRS.2003.810897

Miranda, V., Srinivasan, D., & Proenca, L. M. (1998). Evolutionary computation in Power Systems. *Electr. Power and Energy syst., 20*(2), 89-98.

Mishra, S. (2005). A hybrid least square-fuzzy bacterial foraging strategy for harmonic estimation. *IEEE Transactions on Evolutionary Computation, 9*(1), 61–73. doi:10.1109/TEVC.2004.840144

Mishra, S., & Bhende, C. N. (2007). Bacterial Foraging Technique-Based Optimized Active Power Filter for Load Compensation. *IEEE Transactions on Power Delivery, 22*(1), 457–465. doi:10.1109/TPWRD.2006.876651

Mitchell, T. (1997). *Machine Learning*. New York: McGraw Hill.

Mollazei, S., Farsangi, M. M., Nezamabadi-pour, H., & Lee, K. Y. (2007). Multi-objective optimization of power system performance with TCSC using the MOPSO algorithm. In *Proceedings of the IEEE Power Engineering Society General Meeting*, Tampa, FL (pp. 24-28).

Mondada, F., Gambardella, L., Floreano, D., & Dorigo, M. (2005). The cooperation of swarm-bots: Physical interactions in collective robotics. *Robotics and Automation Magazine, 12*(2), 21–28. doi:10.1109/MRA.2005.1458313

Monson, C., & Seppi, K. (2005). Exposing origin-seeking bias in PSO. In *Proceedings of the Conference on Genetic and Evolutionary Computation* (pp. 241-248).

Muckstadt, J. A., & Wilson, R. C. (1968). An application of mixed-integer programming duality to scheduling thermal generating systems. *IEEE Transactions on Power Apparatus and Systems*, 1968–1978. doi:10.1109/TPAS.1968.292156

Myerscough, M. R. (2003). Dancing for a decision: a matrix model for nest-site choice by honey bees. *Proceedings. Biological Sciences, 270*, 577–582. doi:10.1098/rspb.2002.2293

Narmatha Banu, R., & Devaraj, D. (2008). Genetic Algorithm Approach for Optimal Power Flow with FACTS devices. In *Proceedings of the 4th International IEEE Conference Intelligent Systems* (pp. 11-15).

NASA. (n.d.). *Black hole*. From http://imagine.gsfc.nasa.gov/docs/science/knowl2/blackholes.html

Nassef, M. (2005). *Genetic algorithm and its Application in control systems*. Unpublished doctoral dissertation, Faculty of Electrical Engineering, Minufiya University.

Liu, H., & Abraham, A. (2006). *Fuzzy adaptive turbulent particle swarm optimization*. Dalian, China: Department of Computer Science, Dalian University of Technology.

Neidhardt, F. C., Ingraham, J. L., & Schaechter, M. (1990). *Physiology of the Bacterial Cell: A Molecular Approach*. Sunderland, MA: Sinauer Associates.

Nielsen, J. G., & Blaabjerg, F. (2001). Control Strategies for dynamic voltage restorer compensating voltage sags with phase jump. In *Proceedings of the Sixteenth Annual IEEE, Applied Power Electronics Conference and Exposition* (Vol. 2, pp. 1267-1273).

Niu, B., Zhu, Y., & He, X. (2005). Multi-population cooperative particle swarm optimization. *Lecture Notes in Computer Science, 3630*, 874–883. doi:10.1007/11553090_88

Nix, A., & Vose, M. (1992). Modelling genetic algorithms with Markov chains. *Annals of Mathematics and Artificial Intelligence, 5*, 79–88. doi:10.1007/BF01530781

Noel, M. M., & Jannett, T. C. (2004). Simulation of a new hybrid particle swarm optimization algorithm. In *Proceedings of the thirty-sixth Southeastern Symposium*, Mumbai, India (pp. 150-153).

Noroozian, M., & Andersson, G. (1994, October). Damping of Power System Oscillations by use of Controllable Components. *IEEE Transactions on Power Delivery, 9*(4), 2046–2054. doi:10.1109/61.329537

Noroozian, M., & Andersson, G. (1995, October). Damping of Inter-Area and Local Modes by use Controllable Components. *IEEE Transactions on Power Delivery, 10*(4), 2007–2012. doi:10.1109/61.473350

Oda, T., & White, T. (2003). Increasing the accuracy of a spam-detecting artificial immune system. In *Proceedings of the IEEE Congress on Evolutionary Computation (CEC '03)* (Vol. 1, pp. 390-396).

Ongsakul, W., & Petcharaks, N. (2004). Unit Commitment by Enhanced Adaptive Lagrangian Relaxation. *IEEE Transactions on Power Systems, 19*(1), 620–628. doi:10.1109/TPWRS.2003.820707

Onwubolu, G. C., & Babu, B. V. (2004). *New Optimization Techniques in Engineering*. Berlin: Springer.

Ouyang, Z., & Shahidepour, S. M. (1991). An intelligent dynamic programming for unit commitment application. *IEEE Transactions on Power Systems, 6*(3), 1203–1209. doi:10.1109/59.119267

Ozcan, E., Cad, S., No, T. S., & Mohan, C. K. (1999). Particle swarm optimization: Surfing the waves. In *Proceedings of the Congress on Evolutionary Computation* (pp. 6-9). Washington, DC: IEEE Press.

Ozcan, E., & Mohan, C. K. (1998). Analysis of a simple particle swarm optimization system. In *Proceedings of the Intelligent Engineering Systems through Artificial. Neural Networks, 8*, 253–258.

Pachter, M., D'Azzo, J. J., & Proud, A. W. (2001). Tight formation flight control. *Journal of Guidance, Control, and Dynamics, 24*(2), 246–254. doi:10.2514/2.4735

Pandey, R., & Singh, N. (2009, July). UPFC control parameter identification for effective power oscillation damping. *International Journal of Electrical Power & Energy Systems, 31*(6), 269–276. doi:10.1016/j.ijepes.2009.03.002

Papageorgiou, E., Parsopoulos, K., Stylios, C., Groumpos, P., & Vrahatis, M. (2005). Fuzzy cognitive maps learning using particle swarm optimization. *Journal of Intelligent Information Systems, 25*(1), 95–121. doi:10.1007/s10844-005-0864-9

Parker, C., & Zhang, H. (2006). Collective robotic site preparation. *Adaptive Behavior, 14*(1), 5–19. doi:10.1177/105971230601400101

Parrot, D., & Li, D. (2006). Locating and tracking multiple dynamic optima by a particle swarm model using speciation. *IEEE Transactions on Evolutionary Computation, 10*(4), 211–224. doi:10.1109/TEVC.2005.859468

Parsopoulos, K. E., & Vrahatis, M. N. (2004). Upso-a united particle swarm optimization scheme. In *Lecture Series on Computational Sciences* (pp. 868-873).

Parsopoulos, K. E., Plagianakos, V. P., Magoulas, G. D., & Vrahatis, M. N. (2001). Stretching technique for obtaining global minimizers through particle swarm optimization. In *Proceedings of the Workshop on Particle Swarm Optimization* (pp. 22-29).

Parsopoulos, K. E., & Vrahatis, M. N. (2004). On the computation of all global minimizers through particle swarm optimization. *IEEE Transactions on Evolutionary Computation, 8*(3), 211–224. doi:10.1109/TEVC.2004.826076

Parsopoulos, K. E., & Vrahatis, M. N. (2007). Parameter selection and adaptation in unified particle swarm optimization. *Mathematical and Computer Modelling, 46*(1-2), 193–213. doi:10.1016/j.mcm.2006.12.019

Parsopoulus, K. E., & Vrahatis, M. N. (2002) Particle swarm optimization method for constrained optimization problems. In *Technologies- Theory and Applications: New Trends in Intelligent Technologies* (pp. 214-220).

Passino, K. M. (2004). *Biomimicry for Optimization, Control, and Automation.* London: Springer-Verlag.

Passino, K. M. (2002). Biomimicry of Bacterial Foraging for Distributed Optimization and Control. *IEEE Control Systems Magazine, 22*(3), 52–67. doi:10.1109/MCS.2002.1004010

Passino, K. M., & Seeley, T. D. (2006). Modeling and analysis of nest-site selection by honey bee swarms: The speed and accuracy trade-off. *Behavioral Ecology and Sociobiology, 59*(3), 427–442. doi:10.1007/s00265-005-0067-y

Passino, K. M., Seeley, T. D., & Visscher, P. K. (2008). Swarm cognition in honey bees. *Behavioral Ecology and Sociobiology, 62*(3), 401–414. doi:10.1007/s00265-007-0468-1

Payton, D., Estkowski, R., & Howard, M. (2005). Pheromone robotics and the logic of virtual pheromones. In E. Sahin & E. M. Spears (Eds.), *Swarm Robotics* (LNCS 3342, pp. 45-57).

Payton, D., Daily, M., Estowski, R., Howard, M., & Lee, C. (2001). Pheromone robotics. *Autonomous Robots, 11*(3), 319–324. doi:10.1023/A:1012411712038

Peram, T., Veeramachaneni, K., & Mohan, C. K. (2003). Fitness-distance-ratio based particle swarm optimization. In *Proceedings of the Swarm Intelligence Symposium* (pp. 174-181).

Perdriau, B. S., & Myerscough, M. R. (2007). Making good choices with variable information: a stochastic model for nest-site selection by honeybees. *Biology Letters, 3*, 140–143. doi:10.1098/rsbl.2006.0599

Pereira, A. I. P. N., & Fernandes, E. M. G. P. (2005). A new algorithm to identify all global maximizers based on simulated annealing. In *Proceedings of the 6th World Congresses of Structural and Multidisciplinary Optimization.*

Pfeifer, R., Lungarella, M., & Iida, F. (2007). Self-organization, embodiment, and biologically inspired robotics. *Science, 318,* 1088–1093. doi:10.1126/science.1145803

Poli, R. (2009). Mean and variance of the sampling distribution of particle swarm optimizers during stagnation. *IEEE Transactions on Evolutionary Computation, 13*(4), 712–721. doi:10.1109/TEVC.2008.2011744

Pourbeik, P., & Gibbard, M. J. (1998, May). Simultaneous coordination of power system stabilizers and FACTS device stabilizers in a multi-machine power system for enhancing dynamic performance. *IEEE Transactions on PWRS, 13*(2), 473–479.

Pratt, S. C. (2005). Quorum sensing by encounter rates in the ant *Temnothorax albipennis. Behav Ecol, 16,* 488–496. doi:10.1093/beheco/ari020

Pratt, S. C., Mallon, E. B., Sumpter, D. J. T., & Franks, N. R. (2002). Quorum sensing, recruitment, and collective decision-making during colony emigration by the ant *Leptothorax albipennis. Behavioral Ecology and Sociobiology, 52,* 117–127. doi:10.1007/s00265-002-0487-x

Pratt, S. C., Sumpter, D. J. T., Mallon, E. B., & Franks, N. R. (2005). An agent-based model of collective nest choice by the ant *Temnothorax albipennis. Animal Behaviour, 70,* 1023–1036. doi:10.1016/j.anbehav.2005.01.022

Press, W. H., Flannery, B. P., Teukolsky, S. A., & Vetterling, W. T. (1994). *Numerical recipes in C.* Cambridge, MA: Cambridge University Press.

Proud, A. W., Pachter, M., & D'Azzo, J. J. (1999). Close formation flight control. In: AIAA Guidance Navigation and Control. In *Proceedings of the AIAA Guidance Navigation and Control and Exhibit,* Portland, OR (pp. 1231-1246).

PSC. (2010). *Particle Swarm Central.* Retrieved July 25, 2010, from http://www.particleswarm.info

Pugh, J., & Martinoli, A. (2007). Inspiring and Modeling Multi-Robot Search with Particle Swarm Optimization. In *Proceedings of the 2007 IEEE Swarm Intelligence Symposium.*

Pulido, G. T., & Coello Coello, C. A. (2004). A constraint-handling mechanism for particle swarm optimization. In *Proceedings of IEEE Congress on Evolutionary Computation* (pp. 1396-1403).

Quirl, B. J., Johnson, B. K., & Hess, H. L. (2006). Mitigation of voltage sags with phase jump using a dynamic voltage restorer. In *Proceedings of the Power Symposium 2006, NAPS 2006, 38th North American* (pp. 647-654).

Ratcliff, R., & Smith, P. L. (2004). A comparison of sequential sampling models for two-choice reaction time. *Psychological Review, 111*(2), 333–367. doi:10.1037/0033-295X.111.2.333

Ratcliff, R., VanZandt, T., & McKoon, G. (1999). Connectionist and diffusion models of reaction time. *Psychological Review, 106*(2), 231–300. doi:10.1037/0033-295X.106.2.261

Rebguns, A. (2008). *Using scouts to predict swarm success rate.* Unpublished master's thesis, University of Wyoming, Laramie, WY.

Rebguns, A., Anderson-Sprecher, R., Spears, D., Spears, W., & Kletsov, A. (2008). Using scouts to predict swarm success rate. In *Proceedings of the IEEE Swarm Intelligence Symposium* (pp. 1-8). Piscataway, NJ: IEEE Press.

Reynolds, C. (1987). Flocks, herds, and schools: a decentralized behavioral model. *Computer Graphics, 21*(4), 25–34. doi:10.1145/37402.37406

Reynolds, R. G. (1978). On modeling the evolution of hunter-gatherer decision-making systems. *Geographical Analysis, 10*(1), 31–46.

Reynolds, R. G., & Ali, M. Z. (2008). Computing with the Social Fabric: The Evolution of Social Intelligence within a Cultural Framework. *IEEE Computational Intelligence Magazine, 3*(1), 18–30. doi:10.1109/MCI.2007.913388

Reynolds, R. G., Ali, M. Z., & Jayyousi, T. (2008). Mining the Social Fabric of Archaic Urban Centers with Cultural Algorithms. *Computer, 41*(1), 64–72. doi:10.1109/MC.2008.25

Richer, T. J., & Blackwell, T. (2006). The Levy particle swarm. In Proceedings of the Congress on Evolutionary Computation, Vancouver, Canada (pp. 808-815).

Rigoutsos, I., & Huynh, T. (2004). Chung-kwei: A pattern-discovery-based system for the automatic identification of unsolicited e-mail messages(spam). In *Proceedings of the first Conference on Email and AntiSpam (CEAS'04)*.

Robinson, J., & Rahmat-Samii, Y. (2004). Particle swarm optimization in electromagnetics. *IEEE Transactions on Antennas and Propagation, 52*(2), 397–407. doi:10.1109/TAP.2004.823969

Roe, R. M., Busemeyer, J. R., & Townsend, J. T. (2001). Multialternative decision field theory: A dynamic connectionist model of decision making. *Psychological Review, 108*(2), 370–392. doi:10.1037/0033-295X.108.2.370

Ross, P. J. (1989). *Taguchi Technique for Quality Engineering*. New York: McGraw-Hill.

Roy, P. K., Ghoshal, S. P., & Thakur, S. S. (2009). Constrained Optimal Power Flow using Craziness Based Particle Swarm Optimization Considering Valve Point Loading and Prohibited Operating Zone. *In Proceedings of the 3rd International Conference on Power Systems*, Kharagpur, India.

Roy, P. K., Ghoshal, S. P., & Thakur, S. S. (2009). Turbulent Crazy Particle swarm Optimization Technique for Optimal Reactive Power Dispatch. In *Proceedings of the 2009 World Congress on Nature & Biologically Inspired Computing (NaBIC 2009)* (pp. 1219-1224).

Roy, R. (1990). *A Primer on the Taguchi Method*. New York: Van Nostrand Reinhold.

Ruan, G. C., & Tan, Y. (2007). Intelligent detection approaches for spam. In *Proceedings of Third International Conference on Natural Computation (ICNC'07)*.

Runarsson, T. P., & Yao, X. (2005). Search biases in constrained evolutionary optimization. *IEEE Transactions on Evolutionary Computation, 35*(2), 233–243.

Russell, S., & Norvig, P. (2003). *Artificial intelligence: A modern approach* (2nd ed.). Upper Saddle River, NJ: Prentice Hall.

Rutishauser, S., Correll, N., & Martinoli, A. (2009). Collaborative coverage using a swarm of networked miature robots. *Robotics and Autonomous Systems, 57*(5), 517–525. doi:10.1016/j.robot.2008.10.023

Rybski, P. E., & Burt, I. Drenner. A., Kratochvil, B., Mcmillen, C., Stoeter, S., et al. (2001). *Evaluation of the scout robot for urban search and rescue*. Paper presented at the AAAI 2001 Mobile Robot Competition and Exhibition Workshop, Seattle, WA.

Sahami, M., Dumais, S., Heckerman, D., & Horvitz, E. (1998). A bayesian approach to filtering junk e-mail. In *Proceedings of the AAAI Workshop on Learning for Text Categorization* (pp. 55-62).

Şahin, E., & Franks, N. R. (2002). Simulation of nest assessment behavior by ant scouts. In *Proceedings of the 3rd International Workshop on Ant Algorithms (ANTS'2)* (pp. 274-281). New York: Springer-Verlag.

Salomon, R. (1995). Reevaluating genetic algorithm performance under coordinate rotation of benchmark functions. *Bio Systems, 39*(3), 263–278. doi:10.1016/0303-2647(96)01621-8

Sandgren, E. (1990). Non linear integer and discrete programming in mechanical design optimization. *Journal of Mechanical Design, 112*, 223–229. doi:10.1115/1.2912596

Saravanan, M. S., Slochanal, M. R., Venkatesh, P., Stephen, J., & Abraham, P. (2007). Application of particle swarm optimization technique for optimal location of FACTS devices considering cost of installation and system loadability. *Electric Power Systems Research, 77*(3), 276–283. doi:10.1016/j.epsr.2006.03.006

Secker, A., Freitas, A. A., & Timmis, J. (2003). AISEC: An artificial immune system for email classification. In *Proceedings of the IEEE Congress on Evolutionary Computation (CEC'031)* (Vol. 1, pp. 131-139).

Seeley, T. D. (1989). The honeybee as a superorganism. *American Scientist, 77*, 546–553.

Seeley, T. D. (1995). *The Wisdom of the Hive*. Cambridge, MA: Harvard University Press.

Seeley, T. D. (2003). Consensus building during nest-site selection in honey bee swarms: the expiration of dissent. *Behavioral Ecology and Sociobiology, 53*, 417–424.

Seeley, T. D., & Buhrman, S. C. (1999). Group decision making in swarms of honey bees. *Behavioral Ecology and Sociobiology, 45*, 19–31. doi:10.1007/s002650050536

Seeley, T. D., & Buhrman, S. C. (2001). Nest-site selection in honey bees: how well do swarms implement the "best-of-n" decision rule? *Behavioral Ecology and Sociobiology, 49,* 416–427. doi:10.1007/s002650000299

Seeley, T. D., & Visscher, P. K. (2003). Choosing a home: how the scouts in a honey bee swarm perceive the completion of their group decision making. *Behavioral Ecology and Sociobiology, 54,* 511–520. doi:10.1007/s00265-003-0664-6

Seeley, T. D., & Visscher, P. K. (2004). Quorum sensing during nest-site selection by honeybee swarms. *Behavioral Ecology and Sociobiology, 56,* 594–601. doi:10.1007/s00265-004-0814-5

Seeley, T. D., & Visscher, P. K. (2004a). Quorum sensing during nest-site selection by honey bee swarms. *Behavioral Ecology and Sociobiology, 56,* 594–601. doi:10.1007/s00265-004-0814-5

Seeley, T. D., & Visscher, P. K. (2004b). Group decision making in nest-site selection by honey bees. *Apidologie, 35,* 1–16. doi:10.1051/apido:2004004

Seeley, T. D., Visscher, P. K., & Passino, K. M. (2006, May/June). Group decision making in honey bee swarms. *American Scientist, 94*(3), 220–229.

Segall, J. E., Block, S. M., & Berg, H. C. (1986). Temporal Comparisons in Bacterial Chemotaxis. *Proceedings of the National Academy of Sciences of the United States of America, 83,* 8987–8991. doi:10.1073/pnas.83.23.8987

Senjyu, T., Yamashiro, H., Uezato, K., & Funabashi, T. (2002). A Unit Commitment Problem by Genetic Algorithm based on Unit Characteristic Classification. In. *Proceedings of the Power Engineering Society Winter Meet, 1,* 58–63.

Sen, S., & Kothari, D. P. (1998). Optimal thermal generating unit commitment: a review. *Electrical Power & Energy Systems, 20*(7), 443–451. doi:10.1016/S0142-0615(98)00013-1

Settles, M., Nathan, P., & Soule, T. (2005, June). Breeding swarms: A new approach to recurrent neural network training. In *Proceedings of GECCO '05,* Washington, DC.

Shafir, S., Waite, T. A., & Smith, B. (2002). Context-dependent violations of rational choice in honeybees (apis mellifera) and gray jays (perisoreus canadensis). *Behavioral Ecology and Sociobiology, 51,* 180–187. doi:10.1007/s00265-001-0420-8

Shang, Y.-W., & Qiu, Y.-H. (2006). A note on the extended Rosenbrock function. *Evolutionary Computation, 14*(1), 119–126. doi:10.1162/evco.2006.14.1.119

Shapiro, J. A. (1997). Multicellularity: The Rule, Not the Exception. In J. A. Shapiro & M. Dworkin (Eds.), *Bacteria as Multicellular Organisms* (pp. 14-49). New York: Oxford University Press.

Sheble, G. B. (1990). Solution of the unit commitment problem by the method of unit periods. *IEEE Transactions on Power Systems, 5*(1), 257–260. doi:10.1109/59.49114

Sheble, G. B., & Fahd, G. N. (1994). Unit commitment literature synopsis. *IEEE Transactions on Power Systems, 9,* 128–135. doi:10.1109/59.317549

Shi, Y. H., & Eberhart, R. (1998). A modified particle swarm optimizer. In *Proceedings of the IEEE World Congress on Computational Intelligence* (pp. 69-73).

Shi, Y. H., & Eberhart, R. C. (1998, May 4-9). A Modified Particle Swarm Optimizer. In Proceedings of the *International Conference on Evolutionary Computation,* Anchorage, AK (pp. 69-73). Washington, DC: IEEE Computer Society.

Shi, Y., & Eberhart, R. (1998). A modified particle swarms optimizer. In *Proceedings of the IEEE Int. Conf. on Evolutionary Computation* (pp. 69-73).

Shi, Y., & Eberhart, R. (2008). Population diversity of particle swarms. In *Proceedings of the IEEE Congress on Evolutionary Computation* (pp. 1063-1067).

Shi, Y., & Eberhart, R. C. (1999). Empirical study of Particle Swarm Optimization. In *Proceedings of the 1999 Congress on Evolutionary Computation* (CEC 99).

Shi, Y., & Eberhart, R. C. (March 1998). *Parameter selection in particle swarm optimization.* Paper presented at the 7th Annual Conference on Evolutionary Programming, San Diego, CA.

Shi, Y., & Krohling, R. (2002). Co-evolutionary particle swarm optimization to solve min-max problems. In Proceedings of the Congress on Evolutionary Computation, Honolulu, HI (pp. 1682-1687).

Shimkets, L. J., & Dworkin, M. (1997). Myxobacterial Multicellularity. In J. A. Shapiro & M. Dworkin (Eds.), *Bacteria as Multicellular Organisms* (pp. 220-244). New York: Oxford University Press.

Shi, Y., & Eberhart, R. (2009). Monitoring of particle swarm optimization. *Frontiers of Computer Science in China, 3*(1), 31–37. doi:10.1007/s11704-009-0008-4

Sierra, M. R., & Coello Coello, C. A. (2005). Improving PSO-based multi-objective optimization using crowding, mutation and ε–dominance. In *Proceedings of Evolutionary Multi-Criterion Optimization Conference* (pp. 505-519).

Simon, S. P., Padhy, N. P., & Anand, R. S. (2006). An Ant Colony System Approach for Unit Commitment Problem. *Electrical Power and Energy Systems, 28*, 315–323. doi:10.1016/j.ijepes.2005.12.004

Simonson, I. (1989). Choice based on reasons: The case of attraction and compromise effects. *The Journal of Consumer Research, 16*, 158–174. doi:10.1086/209205

Simonson, I., & Tversky, A. (1992). Choice in context: Tradeoff contrast and extremeness aversion. *JMR, Journal of Marketing Research, 24*, 281–295. doi:10.2307/3172740

Singh, S. N., & Pachter, M. (2000). Adaptive feedback linearization nonlinear close formation control of UAVs. In *Proceedings of the American Control Conference*, Chicago (pp. 854-858).

Singh, H., Hao, S., & Papalexopoulos, A. (1998). Transmission congestion Management in Competitive electricity markets. *IEEE Transactions on Power Systems, 13*(2), 672–680. doi:10.1109/59.667399

Sinha, A. K., & Hazarika, D. (2001). A fast algorithm for line overload alleviation in Power System. *IE (I) JEL, 8*, 67-71.

Sirisanyalak, B., & Sornil, O. (2007). An artificial immune-based spam detection system. In *Proceedings of the IEEE Congress on Evolutionary Computation (CEC'07)*.

Skokos, C., Parsopoulos, K., Patsis, P., & Vrahatis, M. (2005). Particle swarm optimization: an efficient method for tracking periodic orbits in three-dimensional galactic potentials. *Monthly Notices of the Royal Astronomical Society, 359*(1), 251–260. doi:10.1111/j.1365-2966.2005.08892.x

Snyder, W. L. Jr, Powel, H. D. Jr, & Rayburn, J. C. (1987). Dynamic programming approach to unit commitment. *IEEE Transactions on Power Apparatus and Systems, 2*, 339–350.

Somasundaram, P., & Kuppusamy, K. (2005). Application of Evolutionary Programming to Security constrained economic dispatch. *Electrical Power and Energy systems, 27*, 343-351.

Song, Y. H., Chou, C. S., & Stonham, T. J. (1999). Combined heat and power economic dispatch by improved ant colony search algorithm. *Electric Power Systems Research, 52*(2), 115–121. doi:10.1016/S0378-7796(99)00011-5

Sood, Y. R., Pandhy, N. P., Gupta, H. O., Abdel Moamen, M. A., & Kumar, M. (2002). *A hybrid model for congestion management with real and reactive power transaction* (pp. 1366–1372). IEEE Proc.

Souad Larabi, M.-S., Ruiz-Gazen, A., & Berro, A. (2010). *Tribes: une méthode d'optimisation efficace pour révéler des optima locaux d'un indice de projection.* Paper presented at ROADEF, Toulouse, France.

Spall, J. C., Hill, S. D., & Stark, D. R. (2000). Some Theoretical Comparisons of Stochastic Optimization Approaches. In *Proceedings of the American Control Conference*, Chicago.

Spears, W. M., Spears, D. F., Heil, R., Kerr, W., & Hettiarachchi, S. (2005). An overview of physicomimetics. In E. Şahin & W. Spears (Eds.), *Swarm Robotics* (LNCS 3342, pp. 84-97).

Spears, W., & Gordon, D. (1999). Using artificial physics to control agents. In *Proceedings of the International Conference on Information Intelligence and Systems (ICIIS'99)* (pp. 281-288). Washington, DC: IEEE Computer Society.

Spears, W. M., Spears, D. F., Hamann, J. C., & Heil, R. (2004). Distributed, physics-based control of swarms of vehicles. *Autonomous Robots*, *17*(2-3), 137–162. doi:10.1023/B:AURO.0000033970.96785.f2

Spector, L., Klein, J., Perry, C., & Feinstein, M. (2003). Emergence of collective behavior in evolving populations of flying agents. In E. Cantu-Paz et al. (Eds.), *Proceedings of the Genetic and Evolutionary Computation Conference (GECCO)*, Berlin (pp. 61-73).

Srinivasa, R. V., Singh, S. P., & Raju, G. S. (2008, December). Active and Reactive Power Rescheduling for Congestion Management Using Descent Gradient Method. In *Proceedings of the Fifteenth National Power systems Conference (NPSC), IIT Bomba.*

Steiner, I. D. (1966). Models for inferring relationships between group size and potential group productivity. *Behavioral Science*, *11*, 273–283. doi:10.1002/bs.3830110404

Stewart, R., & Russell, R. (2006). A decentralized feedback mechanism to regulate wall construction by a robotic swarm. *Adaptive Behavior*, *14*(1), 21–51. doi:10.1177/105971230601400104

Stuart, I., Cha, S.-H., & Tappert, C. (2004). A neural network classifier for junk e-mail. In *Document Analysis Systems VI* (LNCS 3163, pp. 442-450).

Surmann, H. (2000, May). Learning a fuzzy rule based knowledge representation. In *Proceedings of the ICSC Symposium on Neural Computation, NC'2000*, Berlin (pp. 349-355).

Surowiecki, J. (2004). *The wisdom of crowds*. New York: Doubleday.

Taguchi, G., Chowdhury, S., & Taguchi, S. (2000). *Robust Engineering*. New York: McGraw-Hill.

Taher, S. A., & Besharat, H. (2008). Transmission congestion Management by determining optimal location of FACTS devices in deregulated power systems. *American Journal of Applied Sciences*, *5*(3), 242–247. doi:10.3844/ajassp.2008.242.247

Takagi, T., & Sugeno, M. (1983). Derivation of fuzzy control rules from human operator's control actions. In *Proceedings of the IFAC Symp. Fuzzy Inform., Knowledge Representation and Decision Analysis* (pp. 55-60).

Takahama, T., & Sakai, S. (2006). Constrained optimization by the ε constrained differential evolution with gradient-based mutation and feasible elites. In *Proceedings of IEEE Congress on Evolutionary Computation* (pp. 1-8).

Talukdar, B. K., Sinha, A. K., Mukhopadhyay, S., & Bose, A. (2005). A computationally simple method for cost-efficient generation rescheduling and load shedding for Congestion Management. *Electrical Power and Energy Systems*, *27*, 379–388. doi:10.1016/j.ijepes.2005.02.003

Tan, Y. (2006). Multiple-point bit mutation method of detector generation for snsd model. In *Advances in Neural Networks - ISNN 2006* (LNCS 3973, pp. 340-345).

Tan, Y., & Xiao, Z. M. (2007). Clonal particle swarm optimization and its applications. In *Proceedings of the IEEE Congress on Evolutionary Computation* (pp. 2303-2309).

Tan, Y., Deng, C., & Ruan, G. C. (2009). Concentration based feature construction approach for spam detection. In *Proceedings of the International Joint Conference of Neural Networks (IJCNN'09)* (pp. 3088-3093).

Tan, Y., & Wang, J. (2004). A support vector network with hybrid kernel and minimal vapnik-chervonenkis dimension. *IEEE Transactions on Knowledge and Data Engineering*, *26*, 385–395.

Taranto, G. N., Pinto, L. M. V. G., & Pereira, M. V. F. (1992). Representation of FACTS devices in power system economic dispatch. *IEEE Transactions on Power Systems*, *7*(2), 572–576. doi:10.1109/59.141761

Tatomir, B., & Rothkrantz, L. (2006). Ant based mechanism for crisis response coordination. In *Proceedings of the 5th International Conference on Ant Colony Optimization and Swarm Intelligence (ANTS'06)* (pp. 380-387). New York: Springer-Verlag.

Tessema, B., & Yen, G. G. (2006). A Self Adaptive Penalty Function Based Algorithm for Constrained Optimization. In *Proceedings of IEEE Congress on Evolutionary Computation* (pp. 246-253).

Tikanmäki, A., Haverinen, J., Kemppainen, A., & Röning, J. (2006). Remote-operated robot swarm for measuring an environment. In *Proceedings of the International Conference on Machine Automation (ICMA'06)*, Seinäjoki, Finland.

Tindle, S., Tindle, J., Fletcher, I., & Tann, P. (2002). *Particle Swarm Optimization with Restart*. IEEE Journal of Evolutionary Computation.

Ting, T. O., Rao, M. V. C., & Loo, C. K. (2006). A Novel Approach for Unit Commitment Problem via an Effective Hybrid Particle Swarm Optimization. *IEEE Transactions on Power Systems*, *21*(1), 411–418. doi:10.1109/TPWRS.2005.860907

Togelius, J., & Lucas, S. M. (2006). Arms races and car races. In *Parallel Problem Solving from Nature IX* (pp. 613-622). Heidelberg, Germany: Springer.

Treisman, A., & Gelade, G. (1980). A feature-integration theory of attention. *Cognitive Psychology*, *12*, 97–136. doi:10.1016/0010-0285(80)90005-5

Trelea, I. C. (2003). The Particle Swarm Optimization Algorithm: Convergence Analysis and Parameter Selection. *Information Processing Letters*, *85*, 317–325. doi:10.1016/S0020-0190(02)00447-7

Tripathy, M., Mishra, S., Lai, L. L., & Zhang, Q. P. (2006). Transmission Loss Reduction Based on FACTS and Bacteria Foraging Algorithm. In *Parallel Problem Solving from Nature - PPSN IX* (LNCS 4193, pp. 222-231).

Tripathy, M., & Mishra, S. (2007). Bacteria Foraging-Based Solution to Optimize Both Real Power Loss and Voltage Stability Limit. *IEEE Transactions on Power Systems*, *22*(1), 240–248. doi:10.1109/TPWRS.2006.887968

Tsai, J.-T., Liu, T.-K., & Chou, J.-H. (2004). Hybrid Taguchi-Genetic Algorithms for global numerical optimization. *IEEE Transactions on Evolutionary Computation*, *8*(4), 365–377. doi:10.1109/TEVC.2004.826895

Tse, G. T., & Tso, S. K. (1993). Refinement of Conventional PSS Design in Multi-machine System by Modal Analysis. *IEEE Trans. PWRS*, *8*(2), 598–605.

Tsung-Ying, L. (2007). Optimal Spinning Reserve for a Wind-Thermal Power System using EIPSO. *IEEE Transactions on Power Systems*, *22*(4).

Tversky, A. (1972). Elimination by aspects: A theory of choice. *Psychological Review*, *79*, 281–289. doi:10.1037/h0032955

van den Bergh, F. (2001). *An analysis of particle swarm optimizers*. Unpublished doctoral dissertation, University of Pretoria, Pretoria, South Africa.

Van den Bergh, F. (2002). *An Analysis of Particle Swarm Optimizers*. Unpublished doctoral dissertation, University of Pretoria, Pretoria, South Africa.

van den Bergh, F., & Engelbrecht, A. (2006). A study of particle swarm optimization particle trajectories. *Information Sciences*, *176*(8), 937–971. doi:10.1016/j.ins.2005.02.003

Vapnik, V. (1995). *The Nature of Statistical Learning Theory*. New York: Springer-Verlag.

Vasconcelos, J. A., Ramirez, J. A., Takahashi, R. H., & Saldanha, R. (2001). Improvements in Genetic Algorithms. *IEEE Transactions on Magnetics*, *37*(5), 3414–3417. doi:10.1109/20.952626

Vaz, A. F., & Fernandes, E. M. G. P. (2005). *Particle swarm algorithms for multi-local optimization*. Paper presented at the Congresso de Estatistica e Investigacao Operacional da Galiza e Norte de Portugal.

Venkatraman, S., & Yen, G. G. (2005). A generic framework for constrained optimization using genetic algorithms. *IEEE Transactions on Evolutionary Computation*, *9*(4), 424–435. doi:10.1109/TEVC.2005.846817

Wagner, I. A., Altshuler, Y., Yanovski, V., & Bruckstein, A. M. (2008). Cooperative cleaners: a study in ant robotics. *The International Journal of Robotics Research*, *27*(1), 127–151. doi:10.1177/0278364907085789

Wagner, I., Lindenbaum, M., & Bruckstein, A. (1999). Decentralized covering by ant-robots using evaporating traces. *IEEE Transactions on Robotics and Automation*, *15*(5), 918–933. doi:10.1109/70.795795

Waite, T. A. (2001). Background context and decision making in hoarding gray jays. *Behav Ecol*, *12*, 318–324. doi:10.1093/beheco/12.3.318

Waite, T. A. (2002). Interruptions improve choice performance in gray jays: prolonged information processing versus minimization of costly errors. *Animal Cognition*, *5*, 209–214.

Waite, T. A., & Field, K. L. (2000). Erroneous choice and foregone gains in hoarding gray jays. *Animal Cognition, 3*, 127–134. doi:10.1007/s100710000073

Wang, H. F., & Swift, F. J. (1996). Capability of the static VAR compensator in damping power system oscillations. In *Proceedings of the Gener. Trans. Distrib., 143*, 353-358.

Wang, L.-X. (1992). Fuzzy systems are universal approximators. In *Proceedings of the Fuzzy Systems, IEEE international conference* (pp. 1163-1170).

Wang, Y., Tan, Y., & Guo, G. (2002, May). Robust nonlinear coordinated excitation and TCSC control for power system. In *Proceedings of Gener. Trans. Distrib., 149*(3), 367-372.

Wang, C., & Shahidehpour, S. M. (1993). Effects of ramp rate limits on unit commitment and economic dispatch. *IEEE Transactions on Power Systems, 8*(3), 1341–1350. doi:10.1109/59.260859

Wang, L.-X., & Mendel, J. M. (1992). Fuzzy basis function, universal approximation, and orthogonal least squares learning. *IEEE Transactions on Neural Networks, 3*(5), 807–814. doi:10.1109/72.159070

Wang, Y., Cai, Z., Guo, G., & Zhou, Y. (2007). Multiobjective optimization and hybrid evolutionary algorithm to solve constrained optimization problems. *IEEE Transactions on Systems, Man, and Cybernetics. Part B, Cybernetics, 37*(3), 560–575. doi:10.1109/TSMCB.2006.886164

Wang, Y., Cai, Z., Zhou, Y., & Zeng, W. (2008). An adaptive trade-off model for constrained evolutionary optimization. *IEEE Transactions on Evolutionary Computation, 12*(1), 80–92. doi:10.1109/TEVC.2007.902851

Ward, C., Gobet, F., & Kendall, G. (2001). Evolving collective behavior in an artificial ecology. *Artificial Life, 7*(2), 191–209. doi:10.1162/106454601753139005

Weigel, T., Gutmann, J., Dietl, M., Kleiner, A., & Nebel, B. (2002). CS Freiburg: coordinating agents for successful soccer playing. *IEEE Transactions on Robotics and Automation, 18*(5), 685–699. doi:10.1109/TRA.2002.804041

Wei, S., & Vittal, V. (2005). Corrective switching algorithm for relieving overloads and voltage violations. *IEEE Transactions on Power Systems, 20*(4), 1877–1885. doi:10.1109/TPWRS.2005.857931

Werfel, J., & Nagpal, R. (2006). Extended stigmergy in collective construction. *IEEE Intelligent Systems, 21*(2), 20–28. doi:10.1109/MIS.2006.25

Wilke, D. (2005). *Analysis of the particle swarm optimization algorithm.* Unpublished master's thesis, University of Pretoria, Pretoria, South Africa.

Wilson, D. S. (2000). Animal movement as group-level adaptation. In Boinski, S., & Garber, P. A. (Eds.), *On the Move: How and Why Animals Travel in Groups* (pp. 238–258). Chicago: University of Chicago Press.

Wolpert, D. H., & Macready, W. G. (1997). No Free Lunch theorems for optimization. *IEEE Transactions on Evolutionary Computation, 1*(1), 67–82. doi:10.1109/4235.585893

Wong, K. P., & Yuryevich, J. (1998). Evolutionary Programming based algorithm for Environmentally constrained economic dispatch. *IEEE Transactions on Power Systems, 13*(2).

Wood, A. J., & Wollenberg, B. F. (1996). *Power Generation, Operation & Control* (2nd ed.). New York: Wiley.

Woodley, N. H., Morgan, L., & Sundaram, A. (1999). Experience with an inverter-based dynamic voltage restorer. *IEEE Transactions on Power Delivery, 14*(3), 1181–1186. doi:10.1109/61.772390

Woodward, D. E., Tyson, R., Myerscough, M. R., Murray, J. D., Budrene, E. O., & Berg, H. C. (1995). Spatio-temporal patterns generated by Salmonella typhimurium. *Biophysical Journal, 68*, 2181–2189. doi:10.1016/S0006-3495(95)80400-5

Wright, T., & Farmer, J. (2000). *A bibliography of selected statistical methods and development related to census 2000 (Statistical Research Rep. Series No. RR 2000/2).* Washington, DC: U.S. Census Bureau.

Wu, M.-W., Huang, Y., Lu, S.-K., Chen, I.-Y., & Kuo, S.-Y. (2005). A multi-faceted approach towards spam-resistible mail. In *Proceedings of the IEEE Pacific Rim International Symposium on Dependable Computing* (pp. 208-218).

Yamauchi, B. (1999). Decentralized coordination for multi-agent exploration. *Robotics and Autonomous Systems, 29*(1), 111–118. doi:10.1016/S0921-8890(99)00046-9

Yang, B., Chen, Y., Zhao, Z., & Han, Q. (2006). A master-slave particle swarm optimization algorithm for solving constrained optimization problems. In *Proceedings of the World Congress on Intelligent Control and Automation* (pp. 3208-3212).

Yao, X., Liu, Y., & Lin, G. (1999). Evolutionary programming made faster. *IEEE Trans Evolutionay Computation, 3*(2), 82–102. doi:10.1109/4235.771163

Yasuda, K., Ide, A., & Iwasaki, N. (2003). Adaptive particle swarm optimization. In *Proceedings of the IEEE International Conference on Systems, Man, and Cybernetics* (pp. 1554-1559).

Yi, T.-M., Huang, Y., Simon, M. I., & Doyle, J. C. (2000). Robust Perfect Adaptation in Bacterial Chemotaxis Through Integral Feedback Control. *Proceedings of the National Academy of Sciences of the United States of America, 97*(9), 4649–4653. doi:10.1073/pnas.97.9.4649

Yoshida, H., Kawata, K., & Fukuyama, Y. (2000). A particle swarm optimization for reactive Power and voltage control considering voltage security assessment. *IEEE Transactions on Power Systems, 15*, 1232–1239. doi:10.1109/59.898095

Yu, I.-K., Chou, C. S., & Song, Y. H. (1998). Applications of the ant colony search algorithm to short-term generation scheduling problem of thermal units. In *IEEE Proceedings.* doi0-7803-4754-4/98

Yu, Y. N. (1983). *Electric Power System Dynamics.* New York: Academic Press.

Zarzhitsky, D., Spears, D. F., Spears, W. M., & Thayer, D. R. (2004). A fluid dynamics approach to multi-robot chemical plume tracing. In *Proceedings of the 3rd International Joint Conference on Autonomous Agents and Multiagent Systems (AAMAS'04)* (pp. 1476-1477). Washington, DC: IEEE Computer Society.

Zarzhitsky, D., Spears, D., & Spears, W. (2005). Distributed robotics approach to chemical plume tracing. In *Proceedings of the IEEE/RSJ International Conference on Intelligent Robots and Systems (IROS'05)* (pp. 4034-4039). Piscataway, NJ: IEEE Press.

Zavala, A. M., Aguirre, A. H., & Diharce, E. V. (2007). Robust PSO-based constrained optimization by perturbing the particle's memory. In T. S. Chan & M. K. Tiwari (Eds.), *Swarm intelligence, focus on ant and particle swarm optimization* (pp. 57-76). Vienna, Austria: I-Tech Education and Publishing.

Zhang, J. Q., Liu, K., Tan, Y., & He, X. G. (2008). Random black hole particle swarm optimization and its application. In *Proceedings of the IEEE International Conference on Neural Networks for Signal Processing (ICNNSP 2008)* (pp. 359-365).

Zhang, J. Q., Xiao, Z. M., Tan, Y., & He, X. G. (2008). Hybrid particle swarm optimizer with advance and retreat strategy and clonal mechanism for global numerical optimization. In *Proceedings of the IEEE World Congress on Computational Intelligence (WCCI'2008—IEEE CEC'2008)* (pp. 2059-2066).

Zhang, X. Y., Duan, H. B., & Yu, Y. X. (2010). Receding horizon control for multi-UAVs close formation control based on differential evolution. *Science China Information Sciences, 53*(2), 223–235. doi:10.1007/s11432-010-0036-6

Zhijun, E., et al. (2009). Hybrid simulation of power systems with SVC dynamic phasor model. *International Journal of Electrical Power & Energy Systems, 31*, 175–180. doi:10.1016/j.ijepes.2009.01.002

Zhou, Y., & Tan, Y. (2009). GPU-based parallel particle swarm optimization. In *Proceedings of the 2009 IEEE Congress on Evolutionary Computation* (pp. 1493-1500).

Zhou, L. X., Zhang, X. H., & Li, W. (2007). Optimal design for PID controller based on differential evolution algorithm. *Machinery & Electronics, 12*, 54–56.

Zhuang, F., & Galiana, F. D. (1988). Toward a more rigorous and practical unit commitment by Lagrangian relaxation. *IEEE Transactions on Power Systems, 3*(2), 763–770. doi:10.1109/59.192933

Zhuang, F., & Galiana, F. D. (1990). Unit commitment by simulated annealing. *IEEE Transactions on Power Systems, 5*(1), 311–317. doi:10.1109/59.49122

Zielinski, K., & Laur, R. (2006). Constrained single-objective optimization using particle swarm optimization. In *Proceedings of IEEE Congress on Evolutionary Computation* (pp. 443-450).

Zimmerman, R. D., & Gan, D. (1997). *MATPOWER: A Mat lab Power System Package*. Retrieved from http://www.pserc.cornell.edu/Matpower

Zwillinger, D. (2002). *CRC standard mathematical tables and formulae* (31st ed.). Boca Raton, FL: Chapman & Hall/CRC. doi:10.1201/9781420035346

About the Contributors

Yuhui Shi is a Professor of Electrical and Electronic Engineering at Xi'an Jiaotong-Liverpool University (XJTLU), (Suzhou, China). He was the Director of the Research and Postgraduate Office at XJTLU. He is an adjunct professor at Indiana University Purdue University Indianapolis (Indiana, USA), Southeast University (Nanjing, China), and Jiangsu University (Zhenjiang, China), respectively. He has over eighteen years experience in algorithm design and implementation primarily using computational intelligence. He has extensively knowledge on innovation and creative problem-solving skills. Dr. Shi is an associate editor of the *IEEE Transactions on Evolutionary Computation* and the Chair of the IEEE CIS Task Force on Swarm Intelligence. He also serves as a member of the Editorial Review Board of the *Journal of Swarm Intelligence*. Dr. Shi has organized several international conferences since 2003, serving as the general chair or the program chair, etc.. He co-authored a book on swarm intelligence together with Dr. James Kennedy and Professor Russell Eberhart, and another book (*Computational Intelligence: Concept to Implementation*) together with Prof. Russell Eberhart. He has given tutorials and lectures in conferences and universities.

* * *

Richard Anderson-Sprecher is a professor in the Department of Statistics at the University of Wyoming, Laramie, Wyoming, USA. He received his BA in Mathematics from Carleton College, Northfield, MN, his MS in Mathematics from the University of Minnesota, Minneapolis, MN, and his PhD in Statistics from the University of Iowa, Iowa City, IA. His primary research interests are statistical applications and time series analysis.

Sujatha Balaraman is a Senior Lecturer in Electrical Engineering department, Government College of Engineering,Tirunelveli. She received the B.E. and M.E. degree in the Department of Electrical and Electronics Engineering from Thiagarajar College of Engineering, Madurai, in 1996 and 1997, respectively. She is currently doing the Ph.D. degree in Electrical Engineering from Anna University, Chennai. Her research interest includes power system operation and Control, Evolutionary Computation applications to power systems and Neural network. She published three papers in International Conferences.

Maurice Clerc received the M. S. degree in mathematics (algebra and complex functions) from the Université de Villeneuve-d'Ascq, France, and the Eng. degree in computer science from the Institut industriel du Nord, France, in 1972. He worked as R&D engineer for France Telecom. Now retired, he maintains his research activities as a consultant for optimisation projects.

Haibin Duan was born in August 1976. He received his Ph.D. degree from Nanjing University of Aeronautics and Astronautics in April 2005, and is currently an associate professor and Ph.D. advisor of Beijing University of Aeronautics and Astronautics. His current research interests are bio-inspired computing, advanced flight control, intelligent control and computer vision. His contacting email is: hbduan@buaa.edu.cn

Derek T. Green is working on his Ph.D. in computer science at the University of Arizona in Tucson. His primary research interests are in planning, learning, optimization and artificial intelligence. Currently his research focuses on intelligent tutoring systems and on the development of virtual students. While at the University of Wyoming he received a Graduate Student Symposium award. Currently he has six publications. Derek T. Green can be contacted at dtgreen@email.arizona.edu

Yaochu Jin received the B.Sc., M.Sc., and Ph.D. degrees from Zhejiang University, Hangzhou, China, in 1988, 1991, and 1996, respectively, and the Dr.-Ing. degree from Ruhr University Bochum, Germany, in 2001. He is currently a Professor (Chair) in Computational Intelligence, Department of Computing, University of Surrey, UK. Before joining Surrey, he was a Principal Scientist and Project Leader with the Honda Research Institute Europe in Germany. His research interests include computational approaches to understanding evolution, learning and development in biology, and biological approaches to solving complex engineering problems. He has (co)edited three books and three conference proceedings, authored a monograph, and (co)authored over 100 peer-reviewed journal and conference papers. Dr. Jin an Associate Editor of BioSystems, the IEEE Transactions on Neural Networks, the IEEE Transactions on Control Systems Technology, the IEEE Transactions on Systems, Man, and Cybernetics, Part C: Applications and Reviews, and the IEEE Computational Intelligence Magazine. He is also an editorial member of Soft Computing, Memetic Computing and Swarm Intelligence Research. He was the Tutorial Chair of CEC 2007 and CEC 2010, Program Co-Chair of IEEE MCDM'2007, 2009, 2011, and Program Chair of FSKD'2005. He also chairs Industry Liaison and Continuing Education sub-committees and the Task Force for "Evolutionary Computation in Dynamic and Uncertain Environments" of the IEEE Computational Intelligence Society. Dr. Jin is a Keynote Speaker on several international conferences and symposia. He is a Senior Member of IEEE.

N. Kamaraj is an Associate Professor & Head of the Department in Electrical Engineering department, Thiagarajar College of Engineering, Madurai. He received the B.E. and M.E. degree in the Department of Electrical and Electronics Engineering from Thiagarajar College of Engineering, Madurai, in 1988 and 1993, respectively. He did his Ph.D. degree in Electrical Engineering from Madurai Kamaraj University, in 2003. He published 18 International Journals, 25 National Journals and 45 International Conferences. He is a life member in IEEE, IE (I),KEMA. He has received a gold medal (IE-I) and Merit Award (IEEE). His research interest includes Power system Security assessment and its enhancement, Artificial Intelligence and its applications in electrical power engineering. Five research scholar completed Ph.D. degree under his supervisorship.

Leonard Kinnaird-Heether is a Ph.D. student in the Computer Science Department at Wayne State University, and a member of the Artificial Intelligence Lab there. He is currently a recipient of the University of Michigan-Wayne State NSF IGERT fellowship in connection with his participation in the similarly named UM-WSU IGERT program, focused on Incentive Centered Design. Leonard's current research interests are Cultural Algorithms, the application of auctions and other incentive-based mechanisms in Cultural Algorithms. He is interested in applying Cultural Algorithms to the simulation of virtual worlds including gaming. In 2008 he received an award for Outstanding Graduate Research Assistant in the Computer Science Department. His entry in IEEE 2008 World Congress Virtual Car Racing competition placed second.

Aleksey Kletsov is a Teaching Assistant Professor in the Department of Physics, East Carolina University, USA. He received his BSc in Physics from Saratov State University, Russia, PhD in Physics and Mathematical Sciences from Saratov State University, Russia, and PhD in Electrical Engineering from University of Wyoming, USA. His primary research interests are computational nanoscience and nonlinear dynamics of global processes.

T.S. Lee received his PhD from The University of Akron in 1998. He has published more than 25 technical papers in the areas of intelligent manufacturing and control, robotics, CAD/CAM and smart structure.

Wen Fung Leong received BS, MS and Ph.D. degrees all in electrical engineering from Oklahoma State University in 2000, 2002 and 2008, respectively. She is currently working as a PostDoc in the Boston University. Her research interest includes feature extraction, neural networks, and evolutionary computation.

Yan Meng received her Ph.D. in Electrical Engineering from Florida Atlantic University, Florida, USA in December 2000. She received her BSc and MS in Electrical Engineering from Xian Jiaotong University, China. She is currently a faculty member in the Department of Electrical and Computer Engineering, Stevens Institute of Technology, Hoboken, NJ 07030, USA. Her major research interests are self-organizing multi-agent systems, artificial life, computational intelligence, robot/computer vision, bio-inspired neural networks for machine learning and pattern recognition, and real-time embedded systems.

Kevin M. Passino received his Ph.D. in Electrical Engineering from the University of Notre Dame in 1989. He is currently a Professor of Electrical and Computer Engineering at The Ohio State University. He leads the education component of the IEEE/UN Humanitarian Technology Challenge. He has served as the Vice President of Technical Activities of the IEEE Control Systems Society (CSS); was an elected member of the IEEE Control Systems Society Board of Governors; was the Program Chair of the 2001 IEEE Conf. on Decision and Control; and is currently a Distinguished Lecturer for the IEEE Control Systems Society. He is co-editor (with P.J. Antsaklis) of the book "An Introduction to Intelligent and Autonomous Control," Kluwer Academic Press, 1993; co-author (with S. Yurkovich) of the book "Fuzzy Control," Addison Wesley Longman Pub., 1998; co-author (with K.L. Burgess) of the book "Stability Analysis of Discrete Event Systems," John Wiley and Sons, 1998; co-author (with V. Gazi, M.L. Moore, W. Shackleford, F. Proctor, and J.S. Albus) of the book "The RCS Handbook: Tools for Real Time Control Systems Software Development", John Wiley and Sons, NY, 2001; co-author (with J.T. Spooner, M. Maggiore, R. Ordonez) of the book "Stable Adaptive Control and Estimation for Nonlinear Systems: Neural and Fuzzy Approximator Techniques," John Wiley and Sons, NY, 2002; and author of "Biomimicry for Optimization, Control, and Automation," Springer-Verlag, London, UK, 2005. For more information, see: http://www.ece.osu.edu/~passino/

Antons Rebguns is working on his PhD in Computer Science at the University of Arizona in Tucson, AZ. He received his BSc in Electrical Engineering from Riga Technical University, and his MS degree in Computer Science from the University of Wyoming. This article is partially taken from his unpublished MS thesis, entitled "Using scouts to predict swarm success rate." His primary research interests are in multi-agent architectures, swarm robotics, planning, learning, cognitive science, cognitive architectures and artificial intelligence. Currently his research focuses on instructable computing with planning.

Robert G. Reynolds received his Ph.D. degree in Computer Science, specializing in Artificial Intelligence, in 1979 from the University of Michigan, Ann Arbor. He is currently a professor of Computer Science and director of the Artificial Intelligence Laboratory at Wayne State University. He is an Adjunct Associate Research Scientist with the Museum of Anthropology at the University of Michigan-Ann Arbor. He is also affiliated with the Complex Systems Group at the University of Michigan-Ann Arbor and is a participant in the UM-WSU IGERT program on Incentive-Based Design. His interests are in the development of computational models of cultural evolution for use in the simulation of complex organizations and in computer gaming applications. Dr. Reynolds produced a framework, Cultural Algorithms, in which to express and computationally test various theories of social evolution using multi-agent simulation models. He has applied these techniques to problems concerning the origins of the state in the Valley of Oaxaca, Mexico, the emergence of prehistoric urban centers, the origins of language and culture, and the disappearance of the Ancient Anazazi in Southwestern Colorado using game programming techniques. He has co-authored three books; *Flocks of the Wamani* (1989, Academic Press), with Joyce Marcus and Kent V. Flannery; *The Acquisition of Software Engineering Knowledge* (2003, Academic Press), with George Cowan; and *Excavations at San Jose Mogote 1: The Household Archaeology* with Kent Flannery and Joyce Marcus (2005, Museum of Anthropology-University of Michigan Press). He is currently an associate editor for the IEEE Transactions on Computational Intelligence in Games, IEEE Transactions on Evolutionary Computation, The International Journal of Swarm Intelligence Research, the International Journal of Artificial Intelligence Tools, International Journal of Computational and Mathematical Organization Theory, the International Journal of Software Engineering and Knowledge Engineering, and the Journal of Semantic Computing. He was also a program co-chair for the 2008 IEEE World Congress on Computational Intelligence, program co-chair for 2008 IEEE Swarm Intelligence Symposium, on the Advisory Board for the International Swarm Intelligence Symposium (2007, and current President of the Evolutionary Programming Society among other activities.

Shan Shao was born in October, 1972. He is currently senior engineer with the Department of Flight Control, Shenyang Aircraft Design and Research Institute. His current research interests include advanced flight control, intelligent control. His contacting email is: shaosh@gmail.com

Diana F. Spears received the Ph.D. degree in Computer Science from the University of Maryland in 1990. She is currently an owner and senior research scientist at Swarmotics, LLC, and an Adjunct Associate Professor at the University of Wyoming (UW). Previously, she worked at NASA Goddard Space Flight Center, the National Institute of Standards and Technology, and as an Associate Professor of Computer Science at UW. She is on the advisory board of the Journal of Artificial Intelligence Research. She is serving as an invited member on the AAAI Presidential Panel on the Future of Artificial Intelligence. She has over 80 publications, and is known internationally for her expertise on swarm robotics and multi-robot chemical plume tracing. Her other research interests include behaviorally assured adaptive and machine learning systems, and mathematical / graphical modeling and model reconstruction. Her web site is: http://www.swarmotics.com. Diana F. Spears can be contacted at: dspears@swarmotics.com

William M. Spears received a Ph.D. in Computer Science from George Mason University in 1998. He has an international reputation for his expertise in evolutionary computing and has a published book on the topic. He has co-edited books on swarm robotics and evolutionary computation. His current research includes distributed robotics, the epidemiology of virus spread, evolutionary algorithms, particle swarm optimization, complex adaptive systems, and learning and adaptation. He invented the field of physicomimetics and was co-founder of the University of Wyoming Distributed Robotics Laboratory. He has approximately 80 publications and is the CEO of Swarmotics, LLC. William M. Spears can be contacted at wspears@swarmotics.com

Ying Tan is a professor at the Key Laboratory of Machine Perception (MOE), Peking University, and Department of Machine Intelligence, School of Electronics Engineering and Computer Science, Peking University, China. He received his BSc in electronic engineering from Electronic Engineering Institute, China, MSc in electronic engineering from Xidian University, China, PhD in signal and information processing from Southeast University, China. His primary research interests are in computational intelligence, artificial immune system, swarm intelligence, intelligent information processing, machine learning algorithms and their applications in computer security.

H.C. Ting is a lecturer at the Division of Computer Science, Tunku Abdul Rahman College, Setapak, Malaysia. She received her BSc in Computer Science from University Putra Malaysia (UPM), Selangor, Malaysia, MSc from University Putra Malaysia (UPM), Selangor, Malaysia. Her primary research interests are in optimization and networking.

T. O. Ting is a lecturer at the Department of Information Technology, HKUSpace Global College, Suzhou, China. He received his BSc in Telecommunications Engineering from University Malaysia Sarawak (UNIMAS), Sarawak, Malaysia, MEng from Multimedia University (MMU), Malacca, Malaysia and PhD in Electrical Engineering from The Hong Kong Polytechnic University (PolyU), Hong Kong. His primary research interests are in optimization and power systems applications.

Yunhui Wang was born in October, 1972. He is currently senior engineer with the Department of Flight Control, Shenyang Aircraft Design and Research Institute. His current research interests include advanced flight control, intelligent control. His contacting email is: wyh6014b@sina.com

Gary G. Yen received the Ph.D. degree in electrical and computer engineering from the University of Notre Dame, Notre Dame, Indiana in 1992. He is currently a Professor in the School of Electrical and Computer Engineering, Oklahoma State University, Stillwater, Oklahoma. Before joined OSU in 1997, he was with the Structure Control Division, U.S. Air Force Research Laboratory in Albuquerque, New Mexico. His research is supported by the DoD, DoE, EPA, NASA, NSF, and Process Industry. His research interest includes intelligent control, computational intelligence, conditional health monitoring, signal processing and their industrial/defense applications. He is an IEEE Fellow.

Gomaa Zaki El-Far received his B. SC. and M. SC. degree in Engineering from Menoufia University, Menouf, EGYPT. He received his PhD. from Menoufia University. He is an Ass. Prof. Dr. in Faculty of Electronic Eng. (Menouf) since 1993. His current research interests are the design of control approaches based on Neural Networks, Fuzzy Logic Control, Particle Swarm Optimization, and Immune Genetic Algorithms. Also, he is interested in designing of robust control approaches for failure detection and isolation of faults.

Xiangyin Zhang was born in January 1986, he received the B.S. degree in Automation from School of Automation Science and Electrical Engineering, Beijing University of Aeronautics and Astronautics, Beijing, China, in 2009. He is currently a graduate with School of Automation Science and Electrical Engineering, Beijing University of Aeronautics and Astronautics, Beijing, China. His research interests include multi-UAVs cooperative control, swarm intelligence. His contacting email is: zhangxy@asee.buaa.edu.cn

Index